THE ENGLISH GARRISON OF TANGIER

Charles II's Colonial Venture in the Mediterranean, 1661–1684

Andrew Abram

'This is the Century of the Soldier', Fulvio Testi, Poet, 1641

Helion & Company

Helion & Company Limited
Unit 8 Amherst Business Centre
Budbrooke Road
Warwick
CV34 5WE
England
Tel. 01926 499 619
Email: info@helion.co.uk
Website: www.helion.co.uk
Twitter: @helionbooks
Visit our blog http://blog.helion.co.uk/

Published by Helion & Company 2022
Designed and typeset by Serena Jones
Cover designed by Paul Hewitt, Battlefield Design (www.battlefield-design.co.uk)

ISBN 978–1–915070–32–6

British Library Cataloguing-in-Publication Data.
A catalogue record for this book is available from the British Library.

For details of other military history titles published by Helion & Company
Limited, contact the above address, or visit our website: http://www.helion.co.uk

We always welcome receiving book proposals from prospective authors.

Contents

Acknowledgements

Work on this project got off to a proper start following a visit to Tangier at Easter in 2019, which provided the author with a sense of the historic city and its location, whilst serving as a fascinating eye-opener into Moroccan culture and architecture. In producing this book, I would like to thank the archivists and librarians of various institutions, especially The British Library, The National Archives, Bodleian Library, National Maritime Museum, University of Nottingham Library, Staffordshire Record Office. I am also indebted to Charles Singleton of Helion & Co. for advice and encouragement. My wife and fellow historian, Dr Kathryn Hurlock, continues to offer her endless encouragement, whilst putting up with my visits to archives and general conversations about the project. This book is dedicated, with love, to my parents.

Introduction

The following book represents a focused, and up-to-date assessment of the raising, equipping, composition and experience of the English military garrison at Tangier on the Mediterranean Coast of Morocco, between 1661 and 1684. When Charles II landed in Dover in 1660, he inherited two regular armies, both owing him allegiance – the Cromwellian (by then regular army) in England under General George Monck, and the English garrison of Dunkirk. Neither of the professional armies were in particularly rude health, being much in arrears of pay, and although the New Model regiments remained on paper an effective power, their morale was broken by the events leading to the Restoration. Additionally, Charles II's 'forgotten army' was a body of Irish, Scottish, and English soldiers in exile, fighting with the Spanish, and habituated to periods of hardship and privation. The military defeat of Charles's father, his own peripatetic experience in exile and the radical nature of the Cromwellian army convinced him of the desire for a standing army. Hence, the disbandment of Monck's regiments, with full payment of arrears, reduced the Establishment considerably. The political aspects of this aside, the financial cost of maintaining such a force (some £55,000 per month), as well as the war with the Spain and the upkeep of the Dunkirk garrison, had drained the Treasury. For the most part, the King remained unenthusiastic about the Restoration army, yet his concerns were tempered by the financial problems of his reign and his earnest belief that the military should be subordinate to the civil power. The security of the realm, however, remained paramount.

The marriage treaty of Charles II and the Portuguese Infanta Catharine of Braganza in 1660 brought with it a dowry of 2,000,000 Crowns or about £360,000, the acquisition of Tangier, Bombay, and free trade in the East Indies. Although the financial implications of the match played some part – the economic straits of the English Crown made it necessary to acquire money – the treaty represented an extensive renewal of the Anglo-Portuguese Alliance, opposed by Spain (currently at war with the Portuguese) and covertly supported by France. The King's chief minister, Edward Hyde, 1st Earl of Clarendon, swore to the Portuguese Ambassador that the principal inducement to the marriage was the 'piety, virtue and comeliness' of the Infanta, but then inadvertently asked for Tangier to be handed over 'quickly

Frederik Hendrik van Hoven, Charles II of England and Catherine of Braganza. (Rijksmuseum, Creative Commons Public Domain)

to reassure the English'.[1] During the Commonwealth and Restoration periods (1655 to 1661), English naval power grew exponentially, so as to protect the country's commercial shipping, which was also expanding.[2] The possession of Tangier marked a turning point in the development of England's expansionist policy. The Mediterranean remained indispensable to English commerce, although the State's aggressive approach against the Barbary States embroiled the Royal Navy in various operations designed to preserve it.

To a significant extent, the Portuguese marriage alliance initiated a new era of colonial and mercantile policies across the Atlantic and Indian Oceans, whilst in the southern part of the Mediterranean the occupation of

1 Edward Hyde, Earl of Clarendon, *The Life of Edward, earl of Clarendon, in which is included a continuation of his History of the Grand Rebellion* (Oxford: Clarendon, 1827), I, pp. 491–2.

2 This brief summary of these developments is based on Julian S. Corbett, *England in the Mediterranean: a study in the rise and influence of British power within the Straits, 1600–1703*, 2 vols (London: Longmans, 2nd edn, 1917); R. Davis, 'England in the Mediterranean, 1570–1670', F. J. Fisher (ed.), *Essays in the economic and social history of Tudor and Stuart England, in Honour of R. H. Tawney* (Cambridge: Cambridge University Press, 1961), pp. 117–37; Sari R. Hornstein, *The Restoration Navy and English foreign trade, 1674–1688: a study in the peacetime use of sea power* (Aldershot: Scolar Press, 1991); José Ignacio Martínez Ruiz, 'De Tanger a Gibraltar: el estrecho en la praxis commercial imperial Britanica (1661–1776)', *Hispania: Revista Espanola de Historia*, 65 (2005), pp. 1043–62.

Tangier was the first tangible sign of the expansionist policy adopted by the English Crown. After Charles II waived commercial duties on imports for five years, the Councils of New York and Barbados cited the precedent as a blueprint for reconstructing the English empire around the principle of free ports and vigorous trade. Even so, in conformity with the Navigation Act of 1660, the King's proclamation barred from Tangier all goods originating from English plantations, as well as other lands and territories. Before the seventeenth century England possessed no colonies in the Mediterranean, but Charles II wanted to establish commercial and trading links with the Levant, the Mediterranean States and elsewhere. The strategic location of Tangier, at the entrance to the Mediterranean and the Atlantic Ocean to its west, more than anything else, was an important factor in the acceptance of the royal marriage treaty, as well as the promotion of political and public interest in the colony. But even if it was 'physically at a remove from the rest of the Stuart's dominions', Tangier was far from peripheral to the English imperial imagination.[3]

In extolling the virtues of Tangier, in early 1662 the propagandist James Howell declared, 'what a glory it is for the King of Great Britain to have such a fort, and firm footing in the eyes of all the Levantine Southern world, so near the Pillars of Hercules, and the mouth of the Mediterranean, a place fit for great designs'.[4] Pepys confided in his diary that Tangier was 'likely to be the most considerable place the King of England has in the world'.[5] But such optimism was not universally shared, and the isolated location of, and the harsh local conditions encountered at, Tangier, quickly became apparent by the early months of the English occupation. This occurred during a period regarded today as one of the emergence of 'British colonialism' and trade, but also within the wider military, political and strategic context of expansionism and warfare in Europe and beyond. According to David Appleby, 'The deployment of military veterans overseas has attracted some attention, although relatively little has been published since the 1970s'.[6] Hence, this study of the English – or more accurately, English, Irish, Welsh and Scots – garrison of Tangier adds to an increasing body of work on later seventeenth-century soldiers and armies sent from the British Isles to fight overseas.[7]

---

3 Gabriel Glickman, 'Empire, "Popery", and the Fall of English Tangier, 1662–1684', *JMH*, 87 (2015), pp. 247–80 (p. 258).

4 TNA, SP 29/52, fols 263–4.

5 Pepys, *Diary*, 29 September 1663.

6 David J. Appleby, 'Veteran Politics in Restoration England, 1660–1670', *TSC*, 28 (2013), pp. 323–42 (p. 323).

7 P. H. Hardacre, 'The English Contingent in Portugal, 1662–1668', *JSAHA*, 38 (1960), pp. 112–125; John Childs, 'The British Brigade in France, 1672–1678', *History*, 69 (1984), pp. 384–97; *General Percy Kirke and the Later Stuart Army* (London: Bloomsbury, 2014); A. J. Smithers, *The Tangier Campaign* (Stroud: Tempus, 2003); Alistair Malcolm, 'Serving the King at Home and Abroad: The Tangier Garrison under Charles II, 1662–1684', McElligott, Anthony, et al. (eds), *Power in history: from the medieval to the post-modern world* (Dublin: Irish Academic Press, 2011), pp. 109–24; John Barratt, *'Better Begging than Fighting': The Royalist Army in Exile in the War against Cromwell 1656–1660* (Solihull: Helion & Co., 2016); Jonathon Riley, *The Last Ironsides: The English Expedition to Portugal 1662–1668* (Solihull: Helion & Co., 2014).

Among the early works on Tangier, John Davis' study offers a richly documented and engaging account of the English military experience in the colony, even though he used the collective pronoun 'our', as in 'our national history' or 'the gallant struggles made by our soldiers'.[8] Enid Routh's *Tangier, England's Lost Atlantic Outpost*, remains particularly relevant – none more so because of the depth and range of primary sources utilised.[9] The latter was once described as 'the standard work on the British occupation', whilst more recently Linda Colley declared that 'only one major book has been written about Tangier's rise and fall as seventeenth-century England's most elaborate and expensive extra-European colony'.[10] In contrast to Davis, Routh presented a romantic view of the colonial establishment and eschewed any evidence of the range of tribulations that confronted the garrison from the very beginning. Of England's Moroccan enemies, she wrote dismissively:

> The English Government had yet to learn that in a country such as Morocco 'peaceful penetration' was impossible, and that if trade was to follow the flag, the sword must go before it. The poorer people of the country were indeed willing enough to live on friendly terms with the English, who offered them a market for their goods and paid for what they bought, but the rulers of Morocco cared little for the well-being of the subjects whom they oppressed. They had nothing to gain from the friendship of a garrison which could do no more than defend its own walls; they had a deep-rooted contempt for all foreigners, and a strong belief in their own self-sufficiency; an effective demonstration of power was the only possible means of winning their respect.[11]

Routh claimed that most Britons in the 1660s would have known 'nothing at all of the Moors', and suggested an attitude among the officers of the Tangier garrison during the early stages of military operations, that because the Portuguese had been able to overcome the Moors during the preceding centuries of their occupation of Morocco, the defeat of what was regarded as an unsophisticated adversary was highly likely.[12] The same bigoted discourse is evident in a collection of essays entitled *The Lost Possessions of England: Essays in Imperial History*, by Walter Lord, a barrister and late civil servant in India. He lamented the few colonies that escaped English imperial rule, and attributed the loss of Tangier to a 'lack of experience' among its Commissioners in 'dealing with barbarians', it being 'impossible for Englishmen to settle peaceably in a country of barbarous or semi-barbarous people, our desire for peace they impute simply to timidity; and until they have been well-beaten, not only can we have no dealings with them, but

8 John Davis, *The History of the Second Queen's Royal Regiment: now The Queen's (Royal West Surrey) Regiment*, vol. I (London: Richard Bentley, 1887).

9 Enid Routh, *Tangier: England's Lost Atlantic Outpost 1661–1684* (London: John Murray, 1912).

10 Linda Colley, *Captives: Britain, Empire, and the World, 1600–1850* (New York: Anchor Books, 2004), p. 24.

11 Routh, *Tangier*, p. 114.

12 *Ibid.*, p. 22.

every load of food and forage had to be fought for'.[13] Such writers were part of a contemporary English narrative which echoed the country's imperial vision, and with it, a chauvinistic sense of superiority, an overriding sense nostalgia, and the innate 'patriotic zeal' of English subjects, who grappled manfully with unfamiliar and intimidating environments in the mold of the popular British heroes of the Victorian and Edwardian eras.

More modern scholars, from increasingly wide and diversified perspectives, have offered new insights into the complex economic, cultural, and political aspects of Mediterranean trade and diplomacy during the early modern period.[14] These have allowed more balanced and wider-reaching approaches of military and maritime contacts between Europeans, the Islamic East and further afield. Of particular note is the groundbreaking work of Nabil Matar on English representations of Moors and Turks, which explores the shifting balances of power in North Africa and the Mediterranean that affected western notions of barbarism in the region.[15] Similarly, Karim Bejjit's book *English Colonial Texts on Tangier, 1661–1684: Imperialism and the Politics of Resistance* explores 'the crucial role it played not only in influencing contemporary domestic politics in England, but also in shaping new imperial policies in the Mediterranean', from the perspective of literary texts and includes much relevant material on the English occupation of Tangier.[16]

The subject of Charles II's army and the history of the Tangier garrison is served by a range of manuscript sources – particularly the Colonial and War Office, and Admiralty Papers in The National Archives, and considerable quantities of documents in the British Library, Bodleian Library and other repositories. Of immense value also are MSS Add. and MSS Sloane in the British Library, as well as the MS Carte series in the Bodleian Library. Likewise, the manuscripts of George Legge, 1st Baron Dartmouth and last governor of Tangier, among the family and estate papers of the Earls of Dartmouth, held at the Staffordshire Record Office are especially important. These relate (among other things) to the Tangier expedition of 1683–84. Such material provides an important record of the lives of the inhabitants of the garrison and city of Tangier; the planning and carrying out of the evacuation; and the final destruction of the garrison. these documents provide a fascinating insight into the lives of the inhabitants of the garrison and the city of Tangier; the

13 Walter Frewen Lord, *The Lost Possessions of England: Essays in Imperial History* (London: Richard Bentley and Son, 1896), p. 61.

14 See for instance, Sir Godfrey Fisher, *Barbary Legend: War, Trade, and Piracy in North Africa, 1415–1830* (Oxford: Oxford University Press, 1957); Jamil M. Abun-Nasr, *A History of the Maghrib in the Islamic Period* (Cambridge: Cambridge University Press, 1987); Mohamed Hajji, *Al-Zawiyah al-Dilaiyah wa-dawruha al-dini wa-al-ilmi wa-siyasi* (Rabat: Matbat An-Najjah Al-Jadida, 1988); Johan de Bakker, *Slaves, Arms and Holy War: Moroccan Policy vis-à-vis the Dutch Republic during the Establishment of the 'Alawī Dynasty, 1660–1727* (Amsterdam: s.n. 1991); Amira K. Bennison, *Jihad and its Interpretations in Pre-Colonial Morocco: State-Society Relations during the French Conquest of Algeria* (London and New York: Routledge, 2002); Molly Greene, *A Shared World: Christians and Muslims in the Early Modern Mediterranean* (Princeton NJ: Princeton University Press, 2000).

15 Nabil Matar, *Britain and Barbary, 1589–1689* (Gainesville: University Press of Florida, 2005).

16 Karim Bejjit, *English Colonial Texts on Tangier, 1661–1684: Imperialism and the Politics of Resistance* (Farnham: Ashgate, 2015).

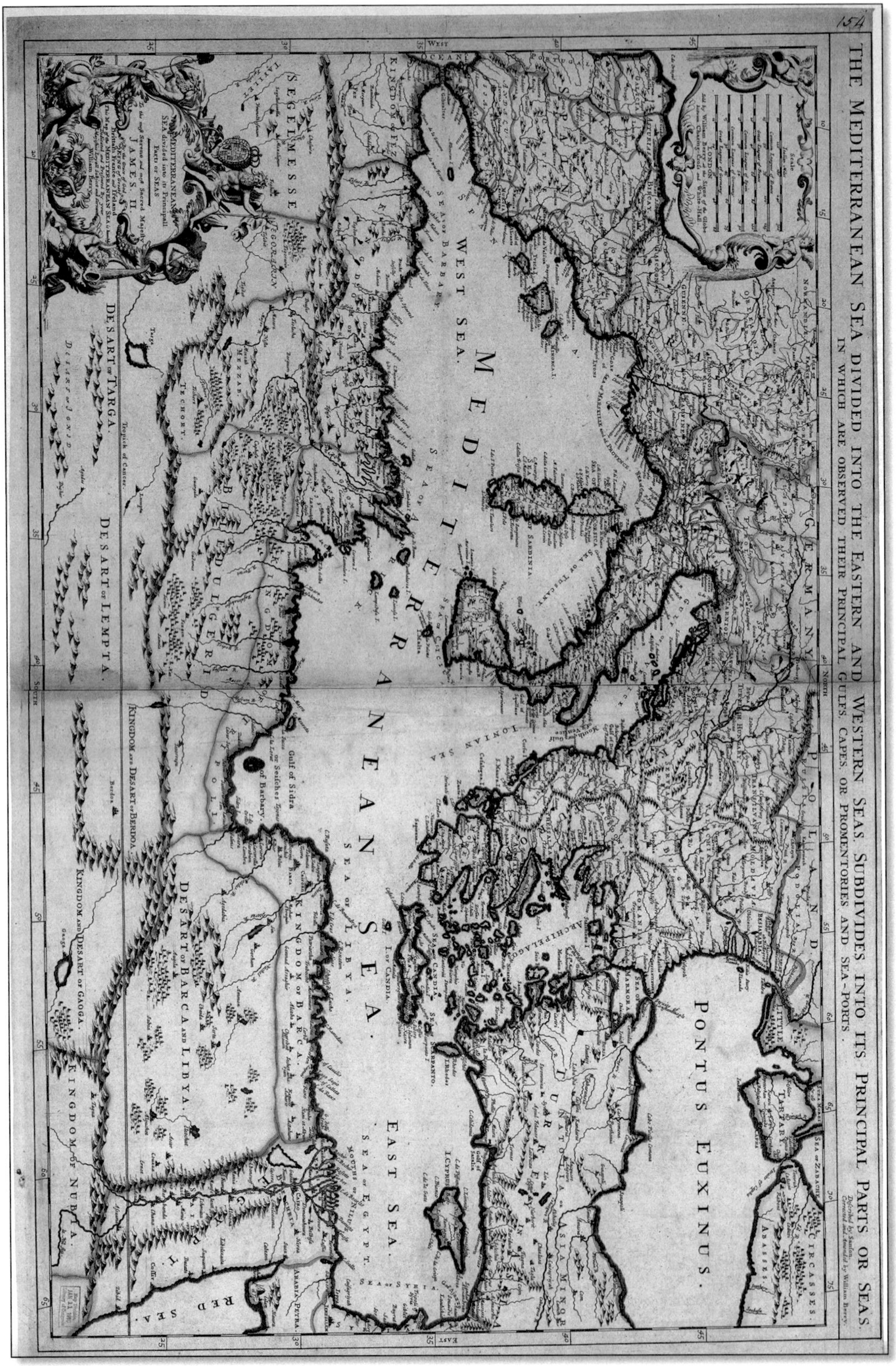

William Berry, *Mediterranean Sea divides into its Principall parts or seas* (1685). (Rijksmuseum, Creative Commons Public Domain)

planning and execution of the evacuation; and the destruction of the garrison in order to prevent its use as an enemy stronghold. Much of the wide-ranging primary sources remain to be tapped, interpreted, and published.

The English occupation of Tangier is also well-served by a large amount of published material, including journals, letters collections, and narrative accounts, mostly generated by English participants and government officials. Increasingly, however, Moroccan and Iberian sources, such as *Letters from Barbary, 1576–1774*, and *Cartas dos governadores do Algarve (1638–1663)* provide a much wider perspective on events. Hugely valuable too is the pictorial evidence of Charles II's forces, and the city and harbour of Tangier provided by the drawings of Wenceslaus Hollar and others. Though not in close detail, some of the Tangier illustrations provide rare contemporary depictions of officers, soldiers, and workmen of the garrison. Lastly, the story of the establishment of Tangier as an English colony and military garrison, as well as the close and sustained contact with the Moors, can be reconstructed by reading the abundant and often imaginative pamphlets published in England between 1661 and 1684. It must be remembered, however, that much of this material is propagandist in nature, conflates events in chronology and detail, and was produced for a home audience, often to justify the actions of particular governors and the viability of the colony.

Explanatory Notes

Although dates prior to 1752 are recorded with the year beginning 25 March, modern dating is used throughout, with the New Year being taken to start on 1 January. Spellings in contemporary manuscripts and printed sources (which varied considerably during the seventeenth century) have been modernised, while where appropriate, current forms of punctuation have been added to period accounts.

According to the imperial system, contemporary monetary values have been quoted throughout. Hence, 12 pennies (12d.) = 1 shilling (1s.); 20 shillings = one pound sterling (£1); £1 = 240d. Moreover, lengths and distances are given in inches, feet, yards, ells and miles; weights in pounds (lb), 112 lb = a hundredweight (cwt), 20 cwt = 1 ton.

Abbreviations

AP	*Archeologia Postmedievale*
AQDJ	*Army Quarterly and Defence Journal*
BL	The British Library
Bod. Lib.	Bodleian Library
BM	*Burlington Magazine*
CHJ	*Cambridge Historical Journal*
CJ	*Journals of the House of Commons*
CSPD	*Calendar of State Papers Domestic*
CSPI	*Calendar of the State Papers Relating to Ireland*
CSPV	*Calendar of State Papers Relating to English Affairs in the Archives of Venice*
EHR	*English Historical Review*
FM	*Fort Magazine*
HespT	*Hespéris-Tamuda*
HI	*History Ireland*
HJ	*Historical Journal*
HL	Huntington Library
HLQ	*Huntington Library Quarterly*
HMC	Historical Manuscripts Commission
HR	*Historical Research*
HREH	*Hispania: Revista Espanola de Historia*
HT	*History Today*
IJAHS	*International Journal of African Historical Studies*
IJMES	*International Journal of Middle Eastern Studies*
JAAS	*Journal of the Arms and Armour Society*
JBS	*Journal of British Studies*
JKSIAS	*Journal of the Kilkenny and South-East of Ireland Archaeological Society*
JMH	*Journal of Modern History*
JNAS	*Journal of North African Studies*
JSAHR	*Journal of the Society for Army Historical Research*
LH	Longleat House
LJ	*Journals of the House of Lords*
LRO	Lancashire Record Office
MHJ	*Melbourne Historical Journal*
MJSMS	*Morocco: Journal of the Society for Moroccan Studies*
MMM	*Military Modelling Magazine*

MrS	*Mediterranea, ricerche storiche*
MS	Manuscript
MSS	Manuscripts
N&Q	*Notes & Queries*
NMM	National Maritime Museum
NYRO	North Yorkshire Record Office
ODNB	*Oxford Dictionary of National Biography*
P&P	*Past and Present*
PS	*Portuguese Studies*
PSR	*PortugueseStudies Review*
RAC	Royal Armouries' Collection
RHM	*Revue d'Historie Maghrebene*
RCT	Royal Collection Trust
RSELC	*Restoration: Studies in English Literary Culture, 1660-1700*
SRO	Staffordshire Record Office
TNA	The National Archives
TRHS	*Transactions of the Royal Historical Society*
TSC	*The Seventeenth Century*
UNL	University of Nottingham Library
UYL	University of Yale Library
VMHB	*Virginia Magazine of History and Biography*
WAAS	Worcestershire Archive and Archaeology Service
WMQ	*William and Mary Quarterly*
WSHC	Wiltshire and Swindon History Centre, Chippenham

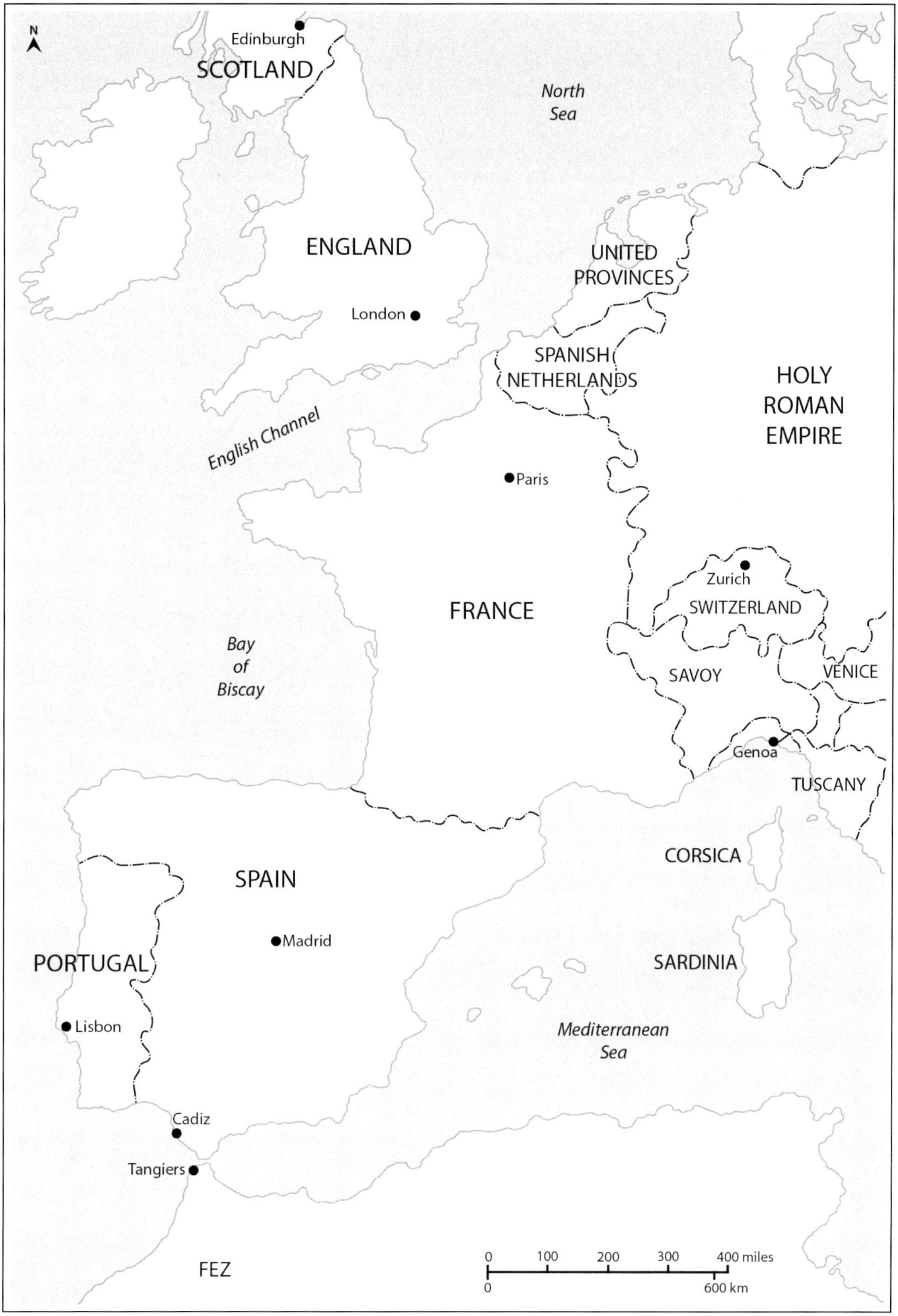

Western Europe and the Mediterranean

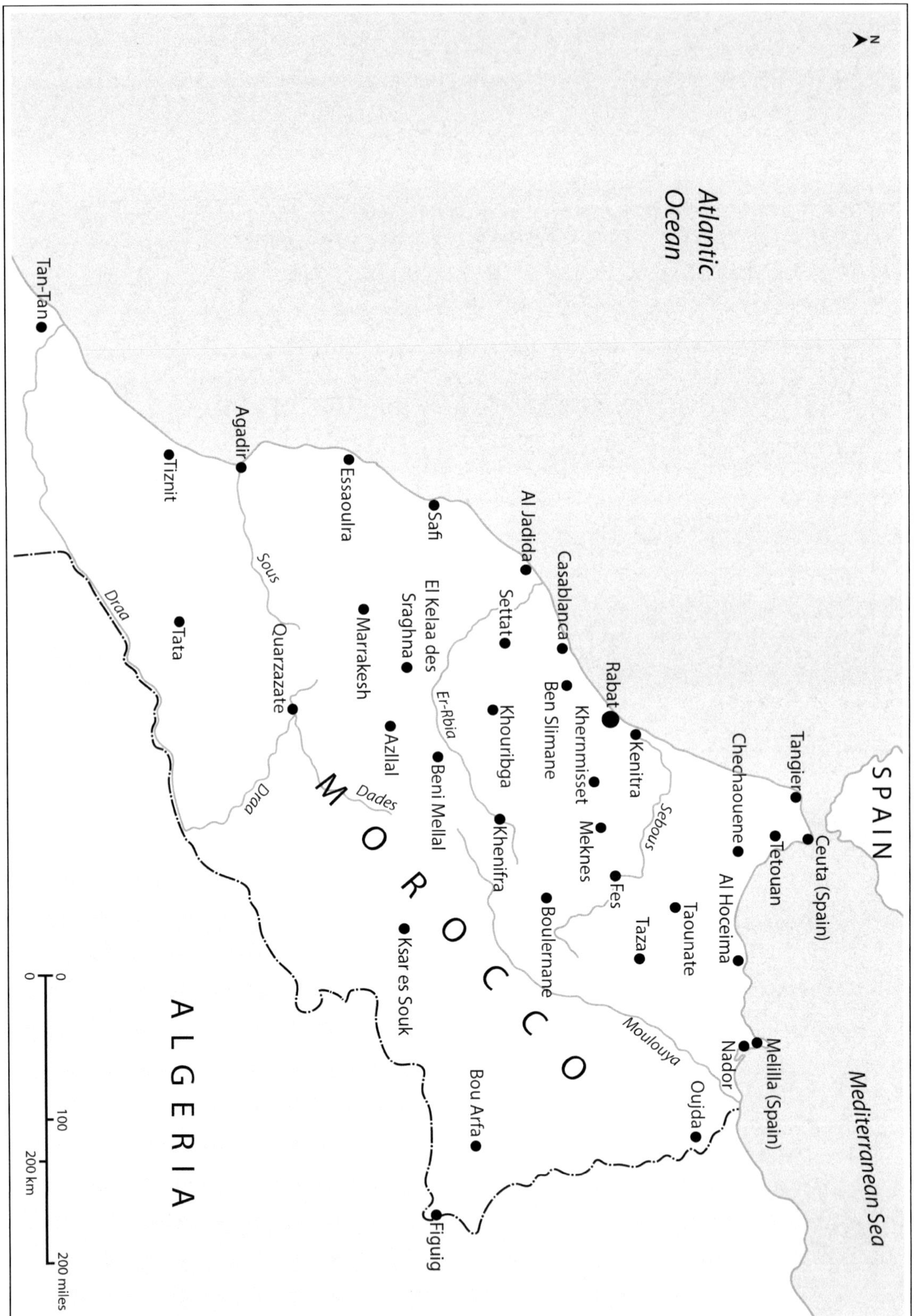

Tangier and Morocco

1

The Restoration Army

On 1 January 1660 General George Monck, commander of the military forces in Scotland, marched into England and headed for London. There he forced the Rump to vote for its own dissolution, thereby paving the way for the Convention Parliament, which assembled on 26 April. This had followed on from the Proclamation of Breda, in which Charles II promised a general pardon for crimes committed during the Civil War and Interregnum for those who recognised him as King. In gratitude for his assistance in bringing about the King's entry into England, on 7 July 1660 Monck was made Duke of Albemarle and rewarded with other titles. Charles II also appointed Monck Captain-General of the army for life on 3 August, with an annual pension of £7,000.[1] His immediate task was to dismantle his unique power base by a systematic programme for the disbandment of the New Model (or professional army). The strength of the army during the final year of the Commonwealth had been reduced to only 30,000 throughout the whole of the Three Kingdoms.[2] Monck's proposals for the creation of a small standing force of about 3,000 men to protect the Royal person and the security of the State were presented to the Commons on 30 August 1660, and embodied in law on 13 September 1660.[3]

Under the scheme, all officers and soldiers who were in pay on 25 April 1660, and had not deserted since that date, would receive their full arrears (plus an extra week's pay), while disabled soldiers were to be given 12 weeks' pay each. One incentive for accepting this on the part of the troops was the inclusion of a clause in the 'Act for the Speedy Provision of Money for Disbanding and Paying off the Forces of this Kingdom both by Land and Sea', which withheld the arrears from any man who attempted to jeopardise the operation. A second act, 'for the Speedy disbanding of the Army and Garrisons of this Kingdom', planned for the army to be dismantled three regiments at a time, the order of which was to be chosen by lots drawn by

1 Peter Reese, *The Life of General George Monck: For King and Cromwell* (Barnsley: Pen & Sword, 2008), pp. 150–1; Tim Harris, *Restoration: Charles II and his Kingdoms* (London: Penguin, 2006), pp. 278, 284.

2 *CJ*, VII, pp. 629–30.

3 *LJ*, VIII, pp. 153–67, 171.

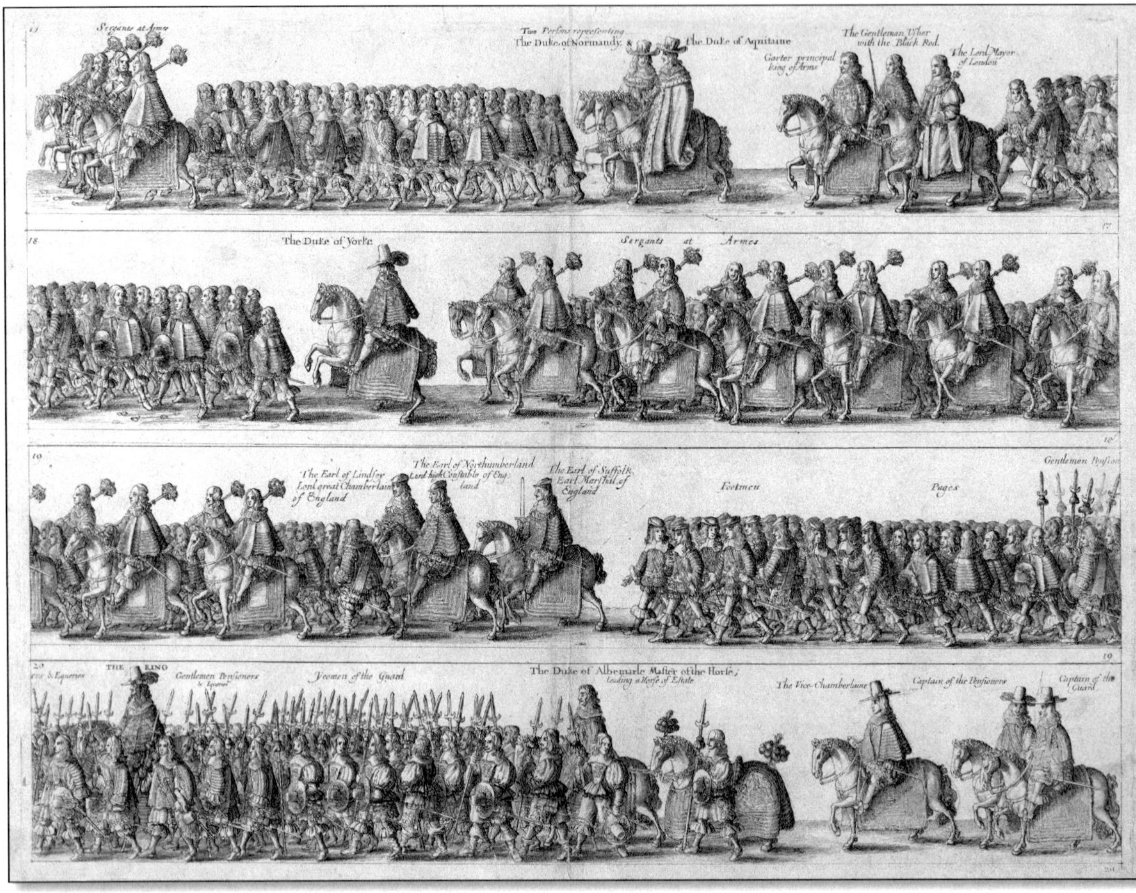

Wenceslaus Hollar, *Coronation Procession of Charles II through London* (1662). (New York, Metropolitan Museum, Creative Commons Public Domain)

the Privy Council. The army had so often intruded into politics during the Commonwealth period, yet if as many as 50,000 veteran soldiers had been permitted to remain under arms, they could have represented a continuous threat to the monarchy and its political establishment. The vast sum of £850,000 was required to achieve such payments, a quarter of which was to be raised through an unpopular poll tax, and the remainder taken from Parliament's assessments of around £70,000 per month. Upon disbandment, everything had to be done to assist the soldiers' assimilation into civilian life, although whether much occurred remains doubtful.[4] It was a graduated process, with Albemarle reducing regiments in stages.

In September 1660 the Orders in Council listed 16 regiments of horse and dragoons, and 20 regiments of foot for disbandment.[5] By 5 November 1660 15 regiments of foot, four of horse and 22 garrison companies had been dispersed, leaving three infantry regiments, nine cavalry regiments and 11 garrison units, predominately located in Scotland and Flanders. The process was completed in mid 1662 when the foot regiments of Colonels Morgan,

4 *CJ*, VIII, pp. 142–3, 176–7; John Childs, *The Army of Charles II* (London: Routledge & Kegan Paul, 1976), pp. 9–10; Henry Reece, *The Army in Cromwellian England 1649–1660* (Oxford: Oxford University Press, 2013), p. 224.

5 BL, MS Egerton 2542, fols 300–27; *CTB*, VII, App. III: Miscellaneous, 1660, pp. 1637–9.

Daniell and Mann, with Morgan's troop of horse, joined the English brigade in Portugal.[6] By Christmas 1660 the army in England had ceased to exist except for Monck's own regiments of horse and foot. The first official establishment for Charles II's army appeared on 26 January 1661, providing for the King's Own Regiment of Foot Guards (Grenadier Guards), the Lord Captain-General's Own Regiment of Foot Guards (the Coldstream Regiment), the Life Guards and the Royal Horse Guards (the Blues), at the overall charge of £122,407 15s. 10d. per annum.[7] It was meant to be a ceremonial, household force of royal guards, based on the model of the French army under Louis XIV. As Peter Reese asserts, 'By such means, at a time of anti-militarist sentiment the British army was born, just large enough to maintain internal order but small enough not to threaten the political establishment nor to fight foreign wars without further enlistments'.[8] Hence, the King's Guards were occasionally used to undertake basic policing functions. In 1663 the Royal Horse Guards were sent to disperse conventiclers in York, while in 1670 the Life Guards were employed in breaking up various nonconformist meetings in London in the aftermath of the passage of the second Conventicle Act.[9] These were years of unusual disorder in England, and large-scale riots and disturbances of the peace were frequent in London and the larger towns.

On 14 February 1661 Monck's regiments mustered on Tower Hill, where they were ordered to lay down their arms, only to immediately take them up again as the. As the newsbook *Mercurius Publicus* reported:

> Sir William Doyley, William Prynne, Esquire, Colonel Edward King, and Colonel John Birch (four of the commissioners), sent from Westminster in a coach to Tower Hill, about 10 of the Clock on Thursday the 14th of this Instant (being Valentine's Day) where the Lord General's Regiment of Foot and Lifeguard appearing with their arms before them, they ordered five companies of the foot to draw up in a ring about Mr Prynne, and the other five about Colonel Birch; who made two short speeches to them to this effect: 'That God had highly honoured them in the eyes and hearts of the king and kingdom; yea, and made them renowned throughout the world and to all posterity, in stirring them up to be eminently instrumental in the happy restoration of His Majesty to his royal throne, the Parliament to their privileges, and our whole three kingdoms to their ancient laws, liberties and government, without any battle or bloodshed. For which signal services His Majesty and the whole kingdom returned them not only their verbal but real thanks; the king having freely given them one week's pay by way of gratuity over and above their wages, and the Parliament and kingdom provided moneys for the payment of their just arrears stated in their respective accounts, which upon their disbanding should be forthwith paid for their use into their officers' hands. That this regiment, as it was the first of all the army

6 Charles Firth and Godfrey Davies, *The Regimental History of Cromwell's Army* (Oxford: Clarendon Press, 1991 edn), I, p. xxxiv; II, p. 497; Jonathon Riley, *The Last Ironsides: The English Expedition to Portugal 1662–1668* (Solihull: Helion & Co., 2014), pp. 47–8.

7 TNA, SP29/29, fols 45v.–7r.

8 Reese, *Monck*, p. 152.

9 *CSPD 1670*, pp. 233–4, 343.

> who promoted His Majesty's glorious restoration to his crowns, so it hath this signal badge of honour now put upon them to be the last regiment disbanded. And although they were ordered and declared to be disbanded in relation to the kingdom's pay, yet they were immediately to be advanced to His Majesty's service, as an extraordinary guard to his Royal Person, whom God long preserve in health and happiness.
>
> Which speeches being ended, they all cried out with reiterated shouts and acclamations, 'God save King Charles the Second', waving and throwing up their hats, displaying their ensigns, beating their drums, and discharging their muskets over and over, till commanded to draw off to their respective colours, when they were all called over and disbanded by Mr Prynne, Colonel King and Colonel Birch. Mr Prynne causing all those four companies he disbanded, to lay down their arms at his feet, in testimony of their disbanding, and then to take them up again as entertained by His Majesty in service.[10]

But this new expedient was not universally popular. Infuriated at the demise of the former fighting machine, Lieutenant-General Edmund Ludlow, a leading republican and opponent of the restoration of Charles II, wrote:

> The Army which had so long stood in the way of the Court, was now wholly disbanded, except only for Monck's Regiment of foot; and that was balanced by a regiment of horse under colour of being a guard to the king. This together with the payment of their arrears and a liberty of trading in corporations was the reward they received for their services, notwithstanding all the fair promises of Monck and the king. And thus these men who had accumulated treachery upon treachery, were dismissed with infamy.[11]

Perhaps more sanguine was the view of Gilbert Burnet, philosopher and historian, and Bishop of Salisbury, who observed:

> The army was to be disbanded, but in such a manner, with so much respect, and so exact an account of arrears, and such gratuities, that it looked rather to be dismissing them to the next opportunity, and a reserving them till there should be occasion for their service, than a breaking them. They were certainly the bravest, the best disciplined, and the soberest army that had been known in these latter ages: every soldier was able to do the functions of an officer.[12]

Whatever the political arguments for the disbandment, there seems little evidence of commotion among the ranks. In 1663, a Presbyterian friend remarked to Samuel Pepys, 'Of all the old army, you cannot see a man begging in the streets. You shall have this captain turned shoemaker, the lieutenant a baker, this a brewer, that a haberdasher, the common soldier a

---

10 *Mercurius Publicus*, 14–21 February 1661. Reprinted in Godfrey Davies, *The Early History of the Coldstream Guards* (Oxford: Clarendon Press, 1924), pp. 111–12.

11 C. H. Firth (ed.), *The Memoirs of Edmund Ludlow, Lieutenant-General of the Horse in the army of the Commonwealth of England, 1625–1672* (Oxford: Clarendon Press, 1894), II, pp. 325–6.

12 Gilbert Burnet, *History of His Own Time* (Oxford: Oxford University Press, 1823), I, pp. 280–1.

porter; and every man in his apron and frock as if they had never done anything else'.[13]

General George Monck, Duke of A lbermarle (1608–1670). (National Galleries Scotland, Creative Commons Public Domain)

On 26 January 1661, Charles II issued the royal warrant that created an English standing army, although Scotland and England maintained separate military establishments until the Acts of Union in 1707.[14] A third military establishment, the Irish Army also existed in the Kingdom of Ireland. But England's and Parliament's loathing and distrust of a permanent standing army resulted in a home-service force that had needed to be flexible and capable of expanding to react to any threats. The 1689 Declaration of Rights stipulated that 'the raising or keeping a standing army within the kingdom in time of peace, unless it be with consent of Parliament, is against law'.[15] The Life Guards and Foot Guards took precedence over the rest of Charles II's army, which also contained the garrisons of Tangier, Bombay, Dunkirk, Mardyke and Jamaica, and the garrison companies of the royal castles throughout England, Scotland, and Ireland. The King's land forces were supplemented by troops in foreign service, that could be recalled in time of emergency. These were a Scotch brigade in the service of Louis XIV of France; four regiments of the Anglo-Dutch Brigade; and the units of disbanded New Model Army veterans conveyed to Portugal as part of an alliance fighting for Portuguese independence from Spain. The English army reached its peak in 1678 with the threat of war against the French, when a force of 20,000 was raised within the Three Kingdoms, but later disbanded.

An 'Abstract of the Forces in the year 1680' lists the following:

> Three troops of [Life] Guards, 200 private men in each troop – 600
> Earl of Oxford's Regiment, 8 troops, 50 men in each troop – 400
> One Independent troop of dragoons, to duty near Berwick – 40
> First Regiment of Foot Guards, 24 companies, 60 in each company – 1,440
> Coldstream Regiment, 12 companies, 60 in each company – 720
> Duke of York's Regiment, 12 companies, 50 in each company, except the major's, who did duty in Sheerness Garrison and had 80 private soldiers in it – 630
> Holland Regiment, 12 companies, 50 in each company – 600

13 Pepys, *Diary*, 9 November 1663.

14 Childs, *Army of Charles II*, pp. 11–12; Allan Mallinson, *The Making of the British Army* (London: Bantam Press, 2009), p. 30.

15 *CJ*, X, p. 30; *LJ*, XV, p. 147.

24 Independent Companies, 50 private soldiers in each company, totalling 1,200 men:
1 at Berwick
1 at Carlisle
2 at Guernsey
1 at Gravesend
2 at Hull
2 at Jersey
1 at Pendennis
2 at Plymouth
2 at Portsmouth
1 at Tynemouth
3 at Tower of London
1 at Windsor Castle
2 at Isle of Wight
3 at York

1 company of 30 soldiers at Upnor Castle
1 company of 30 soldiers in Sandham Fort Isle of Wight

Total: 5,690 besides commissioned and non-commissioned officers

Forces in Tangier:
Troops of horse, 40 in each troop – 160
Captain Coy's
Captain Langston's
Captain Neatby's
Captain McKenney's

Royal [Dumbarton's] Regiment of Foot, 21 companies, 50 in each company – 1,050
Tangier Regiment, 12 companies, 50 in each – 600
Trelawny's, 16 companies, 75 men in each – 1,200
Total: 3,010
Total strength of the army: 8,700 besides commissioned and non-commissioned officers[16]

Clothing

The appearance of Charles II's troops at a London review was described by Count Cosmo of Tuscany in his travels through England in 1669:

16 University of Nottingham, Manuscripts and Special Collections, PwA/2028/14/C. For a similar list see BL, MS Add. 1023 (A Collection of Papers relative to the English Army, 1688).

His Highness … having heard mass at an early hour, went in his carriage to Hyde Park, the place appointed by his Majesty for the review of the soldiers, where, alighting from his carriage, he mounted his horse, and rode, with his attendants and Colonel Gascoyne, to the spot where the greatest concourse of people and carriages were assembled, awaiting the arrival of his majesty. The latter shortly after entered Hyde Park on horseback, accompanied by the duke of York and Prince Robert, and followed by many lords and gentlemen of the court. His highness, with his suite, pushed forward to meet his majesty, who with a numerous retinue was riding round the field. The duke of York, on seeing his highness, saluted him first. His Highness perceiving his Majesty, returned the compliment, and, joining him, rode after his majesty, who having taken a view of the soldiery that were arranged in the places assigned them on either side, commanded them to march by in files, retiring in the meantime with all his retinue to the shade of the trees, to protect himself from the sun, and to observe the march without interruption. The whole corps consisted of two regiments of infantry, and one of cavalry, and of three companies of the body guard, which was granted to the king by Parliament since his return, and formed of 600 horsemen, each armed with carabines and pistols, all well-mounted, and dressed in jackets which are uniform in everything but colour; they are now, however, reduced to three hundred, the King having the power of re-establishing them at pleasure.

The First, or King's own Regiment of infantry, having a white flag, with a red cross in the middle, commanded by Colonel Russel, was composed of twelve companies of 80 men each, who are increased to 300 in time of war, all dressed in red coats, turned up with light blue (which is the colour of the royal livery) except the pikemen, who are distinguished from the others by wearing a coat of a silver colour, turned up with light blue. The second regiment, that of General George Monck, duke of Albemarle, whose standard was green with six white balls and a red cross, commanded by Colonel Miller, was composed of fourteen companies, also of 80 men, who wore red jackets with green facings, the pikemen being in green faced with red. The third regiment (of cavalry) that of the Earl of Oxford, was formed from seven companies of 60 men each.

The first of the three companies of bodyguards, called the King's Company, composed of gentlemen and half-pay officers, dressed in red jackets faced with blue, and richly ornamented with gold lace, and wearing white feathers in their hats, was commanded by the duke of Monmouth. The second, called the Duke's, commanded by the Marquis of Blandford, nephew of Marshal Turenne, wore red jackets with blue facings without gold, and white feathers in their hats. The third, that of the General, whose place was supplied by Sir Philip Howard, of the family of the Earl of Carlisle, wore a dress similar to that of the Duke's, and instead of feathers a ribbon of a crimson colour. Each of these companies has its lieutenant, who are Sir Thomas Sandys, Sir Gilbert Gerard, Major-General Egerton, and Sir George Hamilton.

They marched by in files, in sight of His Majesty and their highnesses. The vanguard consisted of the company of the Duke of Monmouth, who marched at its head, in full dress. This was followed by the General's Company, and a troop of cavalry of the Earl of Oxford's Regiment. The infantry regiment of the king came next, with six pieces of cannon; that of General Monck following; which was succeeded by the regiment of cavalry of Oxford; the Duke of York's Company

> forming the rear-guard. When they had marched by, without firing either a volley or a salvo, his majesty dismounted from his horse, and entering his carriage, with the Duke and Prince Robert, returned to Whitehall; his Highness going home, and the soldiers being dismissed to their quarters.[17]

There was nothing akin to dress regulations during Charles II's reign. Colonels of regiments were responsible of the clothing of their soldiers, and undertook personal contracts with suppliers, consequently the substantial variations in uniforms between different units. In 1682 the governor of Tangier, Colonel Percy Kirke, recommended that regimental agents might be instructed to send to the outpost 'cloth, lining and buttons, not made up coats and hats', but that it be left to 'every captain to fit his own clothes'.[18] In 1677 the sum of £2 13s. was considered the proper cost of the annual clothing of the foot soldier. Regulations were issued periodically, indicating what items the soldier had a right to expect for the deduction of his pay.

On 10 January 1677, the Tangier Commissioners informed the Admiralty that a lunatic had been found among the recruits for the colony aboard the *James*. They recommend that he should 'be conveyed to Bedlam for care; as a little necessary charity to such a poor creature, he is to have his coat, two shirts, two cravats, a pair of stockings, shoes, that have been delivered him at the King's charge, not taken away, but left with him, wherein being assured of your good care'.[19] As per royal warrant, dated 1 February 1678, the supply consisted of baize-lined woollen coat, one pair of lined kersey breeches, two shirts, two cravats, one pair of shoes, one pair of yarn hose, one hat edged and with hat band, one sash, and also one sword and belt.[20] The said items were 'to be satisfied for out of the off-reckonings of their pay, over and above their weekly subsistence-money, from time to time. And in case the new-raised forces be disbanded before the off-reckonings reserved shall be sufficient to pay for the above clothing, what they fall short shall be paid out of Our treasure then remaining, or to come into providing that the particulars beforementioned do not exceed 53 shillings in the whole of each man'.

Expense of Equipping the Earl of Plymouth's Regiment in 1680[21]

Coat and breeches £1 16s. 00d.
Sergeant's coat and breeches £4 10s. 00d.
Hats 7s. 00d.
Sergeants' hats 15s. 00d.
Grenadier caps 9s. 06d.
Neckcloths 1s. 00d.

---

17 Magalotti, Count Lorenzo, *Travels of Cosmo the Third, Grand Duke of Tuscany, through England during the reign of King Charles the Second (1669)* (London: J. Mawman, 1821), pp. 304–7.

18 TNA, CO 279/30, fols 378–9.

19 TNA, ADM 106/322/462.

20 TNA, WO 26/4, fols 56–7; Clifford Walton, *History of the British Standing Army AD 1660 to 1700* (London: Harrison & Sons, 1894), App. IX.

21 Richard Cannon, *Historical Record of the Fourth, or the King's Own, Regiment of Foot Dragoons* (London: Longman, Orme & Co., 1839), pp. 4–5.

Sergeants' neckcloths 2s. 00d.
Shirts 3s. 06d.
Sergeants' shirts 6s. 00d.
Shoes per pair 4s. 06d.
Stockings per pair 2s. 00d.
Sergeant's stockings per pair 6s. 00d.
Sashes for pikemen 2s. 00d.
Waistbelts 4s. 06d.
Swords 4s. 06d.
Pikemen's swords 5s. 00d.
Grenadier hangers 6s. 00d.
Sergeants' swords 10s. 00d.
Collars of bandoliers 5s. 06d.
Cartridge boxes 2s. 06d.
Match boxes 1s. 00d.
Grenade bags 6s. 00d.
Knapsacks 1s. 06d.

Drawings made at Tangier by Wenceslaus Hollar in 1669 show that knee-length French style garments, hanging loosely and longer than those common in 1660, had already been introduced into the English army, although earlier they had been shorter in length. The coat has buttons all the way down to the hem, with turn-backs on the sleeves, and is worn beneath a bandolier and sword belt, both approximately four inches wide. Additionally, in Hollar's vivid watercolours of Tangier depict the common soldiers garbed in red coats, some with blue turn-backs, breeches (which were sometimes of a brownish hue, possibly representing canvas replacements) and stockings, and some with the same items in green. As the King's Battalion did not reach the colony until 1680, Hollar may have in the latter instance depicted soldiers from the Tangier Regiment, which by then incorporated Fitzgerald's and Farrell's Regiments. Hollar's *View from Peterborough Tower* depicts a group of red-coated musketeer sentries, with possibly two officers in the same hue, with green breeches and white hose, presumably of the Tangier Regiment. Pikemen and drummers, at least of the Foot Guards, appear to have worn coats of opposite colours to the musketeers, those of the Coldstreamers, being green coats with red turn-backs, red breeches, and stockings. Further information about the appearance of the garrison of Tangier comes from a set of paintings by the Dutch artist Dirk Stoop, who travelled to the colony in 1680.

One, *The Parade of the Army of Tangier*, shows the entire garrison mustered for a review held to honour the arrival of the Moroccan Ambassador, Mohamed ben Haddū Attār, in December 1681.[22] All the regiments are clothed in red coats, except one in grey (which might have been the city

22 Formerly in the Lord Dartmouth Collection in the National Maritime Museum (BHC 1942), following exhaustive enquiries to its current whereabouts by the author with the NMM, the painting was loaned to the National Army Museum in 1969. It appears, however, to have been returned since 2014, when it was reproduced in Jonathon Riley, *The Last Ironsides: The*

militia), and the stockings in many cases seem to be red, although Stoop might have chosen to simplify the painting. Though the individual figures are extremely small, every unit has cross belts of buff leather, while the pikemen are depicted wearing helmets and corselets. Both pikemen and drummers appear in red like the rest of the soldiers in their battalions. Additionally, one group seems to be a company of grenadiers, going by their red furred caps. The composite battalion of Guards (the King's Battalion) is distinguished by the standards of its individual companies. So too is the Governor's Regiment of Foot. During this period it was the custom of infantry regiments to carry a total of 10 colours – one each for the colonel, lieutenant colonel and major (who all commanded companies) and seven other company standards of the same design as that of the lieutenant colonel, but with a distinguishing numeral denoting the company.

The commissioned officers in Hollar's 1669 paintings of Tangier are illustrated wearing clothing and hats of a grey material. A long waistcoat, also grey, is fastened with a cord rather than a sash. Coat sleeves are short and decorated with coloured ribbons on the shoulders and cuffs, which may have corresponded with the colour schemes of individual regiments. Furthermore, these figures have baldrics, apparently made of a woven material, while the officers' gorget – by this period, his badge of rank – has been discarded, along with the capacious waist sash. The lace neck-cloth is also fastened by a small cord bow with tassels. The colours of these cords match those of the baldrics. As officers in Charles II's army habitually wore red or scarlet coats, this could have a special form of summer dress. In the Stoop painting, executed some 12 years after Hollar's illustrations, two officers are shown in detail. One wears a light coloured brimmed felt hat with a white ribbon and bow, a fringed white sash, blue cuffs edged in silver and blue breeches. The other is similarly attired, but wears a black silver-edged hat, blue stockings, buff waist belt, and holds a half pike. Questions concerning the accuracy of Stoop's details remain, as he never visited Tangier in person, and such details are difficult to corroborate.

Of the units in the Tangier garrison, the following clothing colours are known:

First Regiment of Foot Guards
Musketeers wore red coats, turned up with light blue; pikemen, a silver colour, turned up with light blue, with a white sash fringed blue.

Second Regiment or Coldstream Guards
Musketeers wore red coats with green turn-backs; pikemen in green faced with red, with white sash fringed green.

The Governor's or Tangier Regiment
Red coats all, green linings, green breeches, and white stockings.

English Expedition to Portugal 1662–1668 (Solihull: Helion & Co., 2014), to the owner's private collection.

Earl of Dumbarton's Regiment
Whilst in the French service on 29 October 1667, clothed in red coats, lined in white. Two years later their dress was described as 'red coats lined white, grey breeches and light grey stockings'. Pikemen wore white sashes with white fringes.

Earl of Plymouth's Regiment
Red coats, blue linings, blue breeches.

In 1676–7 a composite regiment of 630 regulars raised for the Virginia Expedition under the command of Colonel Herbert Jeffreys of the 1st Regiment of Foot Guards, was formed by taking companies from existing regiments: two companies from the 1st Foot Guards, and one each from the Coldstream Regiment of Foot Guards, the Duke of York's Regiment, and the Holland Regiment. To these were added 500 volunteers. Each man of the regiment was issued with a red cap, a large red coat lined with blue baize, a shirt, a cravat, breeches, stockings, and shoes. Going by their cartridge boxes, belts, and hatchets, these were grenadiers.[23]

Probably in 1683 Major Tiffin of Colonel Trelawny's Regiment, already in Tangier, took delivery of four casks of hats.[24] As Hollar's illustrations show, following the Restoration soldiers' hats were of black felt with a low crown, edged and with a hatband of ribbon. This was often white or yellow, depending on the regiment, or sometimes, as in the case of the Foot Guards and Horse, gold or silver galloon (braid).[25] Over coats or watch coats, the forerunner of the later surtout, were issued to foot soldiers in Charles II's army for sentry duty or during inclement weather, and there is no reason to believe that they were not used in Tangier. They were supplied and kept in repair at the expense of the Crown, and were first issued to the Foot Guards in 1675.[26] The Horse wore red or scarlet cloaks, which were often faced with the regimental colour. In November 1687, a deserter from Princess Anne of Denmark's Regiment of Horse was described wearing a 'coat red lined yellow', and 'cloak red faced red'.[27]

Rates of Pay for Charles II's Army

Throughout the period 1661 to 1685 the pay of both officers and soldiers remained constant, apart from a slight adjustment in the wages of a private foot soldier in 1672. The following amounts represent the full daily pay before any deductions were made. Off-reckonings were subtracted from this sum and the balance paid as subsistence money:

23 TNA, SP29/259, fols 40–1; *CSPD 1677–78*, p. 188.
24 HMC, *Eleventh Report, App. V*, p. 118.
25 Cecil C. P. Lawson, *A History of The Uniforms of The British Army* (London: Kaye & Ward, 1940), I, p. 20.
26 Clifford Walton, *History of the British Standing Army AD 1660 to 1700* (London: Harrison & Sons, 1894), p. 373; Lawson, *History of The Uniforms*, I, p. 17.
27 *London Gazette*, 24–29 November 1687.

The Horse
The Life Guards
Captain of the King's Troop £1 10s. 00d.
Captain of the Queen's Troop £1 00s. 00d.
Captain of the Duke of York's Troop £1 00s. 00d.
Lieutenant 15s. 00d.
Cornet of King's Troop 14s. 00d.
Cornet of the other two Troops 13s. 00d.
Quartermaster 9s. 00d.
Chaplain 6s. 8d.
Corporal of the King's Troop 7s. 00d.
Corporal of the other two Troops 6s. 00d.
Trumpeter 5s. 00d.
Gentleman Private 5s. 00d.
All other Regiments of Horse
Colonel (as Colonel) 12s. 00d. (+ 14s. 00d. as captain of a troop)
Lieutenant Colonel (as Lieutenant Colonel) 5s. 6d. (+ 14s. 00d. as captain of a troop)
Captain 14s. 00d. (10s. 00d. pay + 2 horses @ 2s. 00d. each)
Lieutenant 10s. 00d. (6s. 00d. pay + 2 horses @ 2s. 00d. each)
Cornet 9s. 00d. (6s. 00d. pay + 2 horses @ 2s. 00d. each)
Quartermaster 6s. 0d. (4s. 00d. pay + 2 horses @ 2s. 00d. each)
Corporal 3s. 00d.
Trumpeter 2s. 8d.
Private Trooper 2s. 6d.

The off-reckonings for the Horse amounted to 6d. per man per day, leaving 'Subsistence' of 3s. 6d. for the Life Guards and 2s. for all other troopers. From this money the soldier had to care for both himself and his horse.

Rates of Pay for the Dragoons
Colonel (as Colonel) 15s. 00d. (12s. 00d. pay + 3 horses @ 1s. 00d. each)
Lieutenant Colonel (as Lieutenant Colonel) 9s. 00d. (7s. 00d. pay + 2 horses @ 1s. 00d. each)
Major (as Major) 6s. 00d. (5s. 00d. pay + 1 horse @ 1s. 00d. each)
Captain 11s. 00d. (8s. 00d. pay + 3 horses @ 1s. 00d. each)
Lieutenant 6s. 00d. (4s. 00d. pay + 2 horses @ 1s. 00d. each)
Cornet 5s. 00d. (3s. 00d. pay + 2 horses @ 1s. 00d. each)
Sergeant 2s. 00d. (1s. 06d. pay + 1 horse @ 1s. 00d.)
Corporal 2s. 00d. (1s. 00d. pay + 1 horse @ 1s. 00d.)
Drummer 2s. 00d. (1s. 00d. pay + 1 horse @ 1s. 00d.)

The off-reckonings for the dragoons amounted to 2s. 6d. per week, or about 4½d. per day. Dragoons rode poorer-quality mounts, rated at half the value of the cavalry horses.

Rates of pay for the Foot
Colonel (as Colonel) 12s. 00d.

Lieutenant Colonel (as Lieutenant Colonel) 7s. 00d.
Major (as Major) 5s. 00d.
Captain 8s. 00d.
Lieutenant 4s. 00d.
Ensign 3s. 00d.
Chaplain 6s. 08d.
Adjutant 4s. 00d.
Surgeon 4s. 00d. (+2s. 06d. for a horse to carry his chest)
Quartermaster/Provost 4s. 00d. (performed by the same officer)
Sergeant 1s. 06d.
Corporal 1s. 00d.
Drummer 1s. 00d.
Private Soldier 10d (for all guardsmen not in garrison or stationed in London, and for all infantrymen up to 1672; 8d. for all soldiers or stationed outside London after 1672. All wartime levies were paid 8d. a day).

Whether on 8d. or 10d. the private foot soldier endured off-reckonings of 2d. per day. This left subsistence money of either 6d. or 8d. Deductions from full pay applied only to privates and non-commissioned officers. All commissioned ranks received their full pay.[28]

Along with the Articles of War, Charles II's army was governed by the *Regulations for Musters* of 5 May 1663:

> *Orders and Instructions to be observed by Our Commissary General of the Musters and his Deputy, and by the Officers and soldiers of Our respective Guards of Horse and Foot, and Our several garrisons in Our pay and entertainment.*
>
> I. None shall be allowed upon any muster, who by loss of limbs or otherwise is unable for Our service, but by order from us or Our General.
>
> II. No officer or soldier shall be allowed or passed the muster that deliberately attends not his duty, and is not present at the muster, except absent by permission of us or Our General, or the chief officer commanding the regiment, troop, or garrison to which he belongs, and none to be absent more than two months in a year, except such as are Members of Parliament, and them during their sitting in Parliament.
>
> III. All passes or licenses for being absent shall be presented to the Muster-master, who is required to enter the same in a book, newly written, to prevent collusion; and whoever exceeds the time limited by his pass for his absence shall be respited, and not to be allowed the muster without order of Our General.
>
> IV. None shall present himself or be presented to be mustered by a counterfeit name or surname, thereby to defraud Us of Our pay, or upon any other account;

28 Childs, *Army of Charles II*, pp. 257–9.

and that officer or soldier offending herein, upon complaint thereof to Our General shall be cashiered, and also lose his pay for such musters.

V. No housekeeper in the usual quarters of Our Guards of Horse or Foot, or Our other regiments, or in any other garrison, shall be received and entertained into Our service and pay, and mustered as a private soldier, without order of Our General; nor shall any officer demand or receive, directly or indirectly, any sum of money whatsoever, of or from any non-commissioned officer or private soldier for admitting and entertaining him into any of Our troops, companies, or garrisons under his command.

VI. All commissions granted by Us or Our General, to any officer in Our pay, shall be presented to the Muster-master, who is to enter the same in a book, fairly written; and no commissioned officer shall be allowed in musters who is not commissioned by Us or our General, or that refuses or neglects to enter the same with Our Commissary-General of the Musters, or his deputy.

VII. None shall be mustered but such as are completely armed, viz., every horseman to have for his defensive arms, back, breast, and pot, and for his offensive arms, a sword, a case of pistols the barrels whereof are not to be under fourteen inches in length, and each trooper of Our Guards to have a carbine besides the aforesaid arms. And the foot to have each soldier a sword; and each pikeman a pike of sixteen foot long and not under; and each musketeer a musket, with a collar of bandoliers, the barrel of which musket to be about four foot long, and to contain a bullet fourteen of which shall weigh a pound weight.

VIII. No soldier shall depart from his colours without license of his chief officer of the troop, company, or garrison to which he belongs, it being felony by the Statute of the 18th of Henry VI, Chap. 19.

Nor shall any non-commissioned officer or private soldier, after enrolment and being mustered, be dismissed or cashiered by any officer without order of Our General, or a regimental Court-Martial; and m case such non-commissioned officer or private soldier be of Our troop of Horse-Guards, by a court consisting of the then present commissioned officers of the three troops of Horse-Guards; nor out of any garrison, but by a Court-Martial as Our General shall direct, or by his order.

IX. The Muster-Master shall always give convenient notice to the officer in chief commanding the regiment, troop, or company, or garrison, before the muster-day of the time and place for the muster, that the officers and soldiers may have time to make ready for the muster, and that three muster-rolls may be prepared of their respective troops and companies; in which rolls the names of all the private soldiers are to be written alphabetically; one of which rolls is to be in parchment for the paymaster, and to be subscribed (with one also which the Muster-master is to keep) by two commissioned officers at least of their respective troops and companies, together with the Muster-master, and the other muster-roll to be subscribed only by the Muster-master, which the officer is to keep, and no roll to be received and allowed by the Muster-master and paymaster otherwise, and the said muster-rolls to be perfected forthwith after the muster.

X. No officer or soldier shall be mustered and paid in a double capacity, except a general officer or field officer in the same regiment whereof he is a field officer, or governor of a garrison having command of Horse and Foot for our service in the same, except by the special warrant or order of our General; which warrant or order shall be also registered with Our Commissary-General of Musters in a book.

All officers and soldiers, together with the Muster-masters, not duly observing these orders and instructions, or any of them respectively, shall be cashiered.[29]

29 *CSPD 1663–4*, p. 131; Walton, *History*, pp. 794–5.

2

The Tangier Garrison

The initial Establishment of the Tangier garrison, as of 10 October 1661, was 171 officers, 165 non-commissioned officers, 61 musicians, and 2,800 privates, in addition to 32 officers and gunners of the train of artillery, bringing the total to 3,239.[1] The garrison comprised: the Earl of Peterborough's Regiment of Foot, Sir Robert Harley's Regiment of Foot, Colonel John Fitzgerald's Regiment of Foot, Colonel Lewis Farrell's Regiment of Foot, and the Earl of Peterborough's Troop of Horse. It should be noted that establishments in seventeenth-century English armies, though their records provide valuable information on both the size and structure of individual regiments of horse, dragoons and foot, they represent theoretical maximum numbers, that sometimes bore little relation to the actual strength of military units. This was especially so for regiments in overseas stations, foreign service, and prolonged campaigns. Moreover, while the size of English regiments of foot became standardised in the later years of the 1600s at 12 companies of foot and one of grenadiers, this was not always the case. Both the number of companies and their strengths might contract or expand due to tactical and financial considerations, or changes in operational practices.

The first muster held at Tangier on 30 January 1662 recorded 2,723 foot, with 98 in the English troop of Horse, and 80 in the resident Portuguese troop (which was added to the garrison upon arrival), besides officers. Of the foot regiments, Peterborough's fielded 1,000; Colonel Harley's 947; Colonel Fitzgerald's 395; and Colonel Farrell's 381. By 23 October 1662, the infantry numbers had been reduced to 793 in Peterborough's; 559 in Harley's; 395 in Fitzgerald's; and 371 in Farrell's.[2] The initial garrison was established at an annual cost of £70,610 3s. 4d.

1 TNA, WO 24/1, fols 1–7.

2 TNA, CO 279/1, fol. 56; Davis, *History*, I, pp. 20–2; Wienand Drenth and Jonathon Riley, *The First Colonial Soldiers: A Survey of British Colonies and Their Garrisons, 1650–1714. Vol. 1: the British Isles, Europe, Asia and Africa* (Eindhoven: Drenth Publishing, 2014), pp. 108–10.

Table 1. Governors of Tangier, 1662–84

Term	Governor	Deputy/Acting
29 January 1662–9 May 1663	Henry Mordaunt, 2nd Earl of Peterborough	Colonel John Fitzgerald
10 May 1663–4 May 1664	Andrew Rutherford, 1st Earl of Teviot	Colonel John Fitzgerald
4 May 1664–7 June 1664		Sir Tobias Bridge
7 June 1664–January 1665	Colonel John Fitzgerald (temporary)	
January 1665–April 1666	John Belasyse, 1st Baron Belasyse	
21 February 1666–69	Colonel Henry Norwood	
1669–70	John Middleton, 1st Earl of Middleton	
1670–72		Sir Hugh Cholmeley
1672–74	John Middleton, 1st Earl of Middleton	Colonel Thomas Dungan
March 1675–80	William O'Brien, 2nd Earl of Inchiquin	Sir Palmes Fairborne
–27 October 1680	Sir PalmesFairborne	
–30 July 1680	Thomas Butler, 6th Earl of Ossory	
–17 October 1680	Charles Fitzcharles, 1st Earl of Plymouth	
October 1680–28 December 1681		Colonel Edward Sackville
28 December 1681–1683	Colonel Percy Kirke	
2 July 1683–6 February 1684	George Legge, 1st Baron Dartmouth	

Table 2. An Establishment for His Majesty's Service in the Kingdoms of Morocco, Sus, Féz, 10 October 1661

	Officers	NCOs	Musicians	Men	Total
His Majesty's Regiment of Foot Commanded by the Earl of Peterborough, consisting of 10 Companies of Foot (each of 100 men)	44	60	24	1,000	1,128
His Majesty's Regiment of Foot Commanded by Colonel Farrell, consisting of 12 Companies (each of 50 men)	41	36	12	600	689
His Majesty's Regiment of Foot Commanded by Colonel Fitzgerald, consisting of 12 Companies of Foot (each of 50 men)	41	36	12	600	689
His Majesty's Regiment of Foot Commanded by Sir Robert Harley, consisting of 12 Companies of Foot (each of 50 men)	37	30	10	500	577
Earl of Peterborough's Independent Troop of Horse	8	3	3	100	114
Staff belonging to the Train of Ordnance	11			21	32
Total	182	165	61	2,821	3,239

Table 3. An Establishment of the Force raised on the 10th day of October 1661 for His Majesty's service in the Kingdoms of Sus, Féz and Morocco, under the Command of his Excellency the Earl of Peterborough.

	£	s.	d.
Total charge of four regiments consisting of 3,100 soldiers besides NCOs and officers	59,531	10	00
Field and staff officers, and a troop of horse	6,080	05	10
General officers etc.	3,998	07	06
Contingencies	1,000	00	00
Annual cost of establishment	70,610	03	04

Added to this was: 'An Additional Establishment for a troop of Portugal Horse, consisting of eighty troopers, besides officers, making the 'Total of the whole Establishment' £73,388 12s. 6d.[3]

Specifically listed under the 1661 Establishment were:

Field Officers and Staff Officers of His Excellency's Own Regiment of Foot
Colonel as Colonel
Lieutenant Colonel as Lieutenant Colonel
Major as Major
Chaplain
Surgeon
Quartermaster
Marshall
Gunsmith

A Company of Foot
Captain
Lieutenant
Ensign
2 sergeants
3 corporals
2 drummers
100 soldiers
10 companies completing the regiment

One regiment more of the same number both officers and men:

Field and Staff Officers of an additional regiment of foot
Colonel as Colonel

3 TNA, SP71/13, fol. 100; WO 24/1, fols 4–5.

Lieutenant Colonel as Lieutenant Colonel
Major as Major
Quartermaster as Marshall

A Company of Foot
Captain
Lieutenant
Ensign
1 sergeant
2 corporals
1 drummer
50 soldiers
10 companies completing the regiment

One regiment more of the same number both officers and men:

Additional officers allowed for the two regiments [of 500 men each]
Chaplain
Surgeon
Surgeon's mate
Gunsmith

Field and Staff Officers of Horse
Colonel
Chaplain
Surgeon
Quartermaster
Gunsmith

A Troop of Horse
Captain
Lieutenant
Cornet
3 trumpeters
3 corporals
100 soldiers

General Officers with those of the Trayne
The Lord General
Judge Advocate
Secretary
2 Physicians
Apothecary
Engineer
Commissary of Musters
Commissary of Provisions
Commissary of Ammunition
Firemaster

Town Major [Mayor]
6 Gunners
6 Gunner's Mates
6 Matrosses

The annual cost of the 1668 Establishment was £31,999 10s. 0d. and remained relatively unaltered until 1679.[4] Endorsed 'the last intended establishment', that of 9 March 1678 (below) varies in a few details in terms of costings from that of 10 years before, although more information can be gleaned from the document about the composition of the garrison's regiments and rates of pay.[5] The total cost of maintaining the military garrison was £42,338 12s. 2d. per annum, being a reduction of £11,457 3s. 2d. from the previous figure.

Table 4. Revised Establishment, with daily and annual rates of pay, for the Tangier garrison, 16 March 1668 (TNA, SP44/30, fols 52–3).

	£ per diem			£ per annum		
1 Colonel at		12	00	219	00	00
1 Lieutenant colonel at		7	00	127	15	00
1 Major at		5	00	91	5	00
12 Captains each at		8	00	1,752	00	00
12 Lieutenants each at		4	00	876	00	00
12 Ensigns each at		3	00	675	00	00
36 Sergeants each at		1	6	985	10	00
36 Corporals each at		1	00	657	00	00
24 Drummers each at		1	00	438	00	00
1,440 Private soldiers each at			9	19,710	00	00
Total	2	3	3	25,513	10	00
30 horse each at		2	6	1,368	15	00
To an officer having lieutenant's pay		6	00	109	10	00
1 Corporal		3	00	48	13	04
1 Trumpeter		3	00	48	13	04
1 Farrier		2	6	45	12	06
Total		17	00	2,627	05	10

4 TNA, WO 24/3, unfol.; BL, MS Add. 38694, fol. 1.

5 TNA, AO 1/51/28 (Audit Office, Declared Accounts for the Army); HMC, *Eleventh Report, App. V*, pp. 28–9; Davis, *History*, I, pp. 108–10.

Since added by order of 15 January 1668:

A deputy-governor at per annum	300	00	00
A physician to be continued at per annum	182	10	00
An additional pay to the town major at 3s. per day	54	15	00
Total	537	5	00

	£ per diem			**£ per ann.**		
The governor				1,500	00	00
1 minister at		10	00	182	10	00
1 engineer at		6	00	109	10	00
1 judge-advocate at		5	00	91	5	00
1 surgeon at		4	00	73	00	00
1 surgeon's mate at		2	6	45	12	6
Quartermaster, provost-marshal and lieutenants		8	00	146	00	00
Commissary of the ammunition and provision for himself and assistants to the officers of the ordnance for ammunition at		6	00	109	10	00
Town mayor		10	00	182	10	00
Controller of the ordnance and firemaster to account to the office of the ordnance		5	00	91	5	00
Master-carpenter at		5	00	91	5	00
6 gunners each at		1	6	164	5	00
18 matrosses each at		1	00	328	10	00
Total	3	11	00	3,169	10	00

Further allowances to the garrison of which an extract account to be returned every six months:

	£ per diem			**£ per annum**		
For the hospital besides the soldiers' pay when sick, added to the hospital towards maintenance		10	00	547	10	00
For coal and candles at		10	00	547	10	00
For boats				145	00	00
For fortifications and all manner of stores and contingencies				2,210	00	00
Yearly impressed for the Mole				19,500	00	00

£25,513 10 00
1,627 05 00
3,169 14 06
22,950 00 00
£53,795 15 04

The State Papers for January 1668 contain a declared account of the same heading, which gives a total of £7,999 17s. 6d. per quarter (£31,999 10s. 0d. per annum), although this appears to be a preliminary draft as the 16 March order was enacted.[6] Daily rates of pay for the Tangier garrison were established by Order of Council on 25 October 1661.[7]

An Establishment with daily and annual rates of pay, for the Tangier garrison, dated 9 March 1678

Two Regiments of foot, each regiment consisting of sixteen companies, and each company consisting of a captain at 8s. a day, a lieutenant at 4s., an ensign at 3s., two sergeants at 1s. each besides victuals, three corporals and one drummer at 6d. each besides victuals, and 50 private footmen at 3d. each besides victuals, which for each company amounts to £574 17s. 0d. per annum, and for the said 32 companies to £18,396.

For the field and staff officers of the said two regiments, viz., two colonels at 12s. a day each, two lieutenant colonels at 7s. a day each, and two majors at 5s. a day each, making for each regiment £438 per annum, and for both £876.

Four troops of Horse, each to consist of a captain at 14s. a day, a lieutenant at 10s., a cornet at 9s., a quartermaster at 6s., two corporals at 3s. each, one trumpeter at 2s. 6d. besides victuals, a farrier at 2s. besides victuals, and 25 private horsemen at 2s. each besides victuals, making in all for each troop £1,809 15s. l0d., and for the said four troops £7,239 3s. 4d.

To the victuallers for victualling 1,916 men at 2s. 6d. per week each, viz., 1,600 foot soldiers, 64 sergeants, 96 corporals, 32 drummers, 100 troopers, 4 trumpeters, 4 farriers, and 16 gunners £12,454.

That the 3d. a day in money, made payable by this, our establishment to each foot soldier of our garrison at Tangier, shall be from time to time paid to the colonels of each regiment, out of which they are to furnish the said soldiers with clothes, shirts, shoes, stockings, and other necessaries, the same to be always bought in Ireland and nowhere else, and that at as easy rates as may be, and to pay the remainder (if any), in money to the said soldiers.

So that 8d. a day out of the 2s. a day made payable by this our establishment to each trooper of our garrison of Tangier shall be from time to time paid to such surveyor as we shall appoint, to be by him laid out for providing such sorts and quantities of horsemeat as are now allowed to each horseman there, and the remaining 16d. a day shall be from time to time paid to the respective captains of horse, out of which they are to furnish the said troopers with clothes, boots, belts, and other necessaries, the same to be always bought in Ireland and nowhere else, and that at as easy rates

6 TNA, CO 279/10, fols 197–8; WO 24/2, unfol.; BL, MS Sloane 3509, fols 230–1; Davis, *History*, I, pp. 91–3.

7 TNA, SP9/209/136, fols 1–2.

as may be, and to pay the remainder (if any), in money to the said troopers. And the lord lieutenant or other chief governor of Ireland to take care to appoint some fit persons to supervise the buying of the said clothes and necessaries for the soldiers so as the same may be effectually furnished good in kind, and at the cheapest rates.

Table 5. An Establishment with daily and annual rates of pay, for the Tangier garrison, dated 7 July 1680 (BL, MS Add. 28938, fols 28–42).

	Officers	NCOs	Musicians	Men	Total
Old Garrison Regiment				800	800
The Scotch Regiment when recruited with 680 from Scotland				680	680
The Battalion of Guards				600	600
Irish Regiment including 200 recruits				400	400
New Regiment to be raised Commanded by the Earl of Plymouth's Regiment of Foot, consisting of 16 companies	48			600	600
Total				3,080	3,080

Table 6. An Establishment with daily and annual rates of pay, for the Tangier garrison, 25 December 1682 (Bod. Lib., MS Carte 179, fols 1–14).

	£ per diem			£ per ann.		
The governor				1,500	00	00
The minister at		10	00	182	10	00
The physician at		15	00	273	15	00
The Town Mayor, without any manner of perquisites or other advantages, at		10	00	182	10	00
Judge Advocate at		8	00	146	00	00
Surgeon at		2	06	46	00	00
Surgeon's mate at		8	00	146	00	00
Quartermaster Provost Marshall and his servants at		6	00	91	5	00
Commissaries of the Musters at		10	00	109	10	00
Storekeeper for the garrison at		6	04	109	10	00
Engineer at		5	00	91	5	00
Storekeeper of the ammunition and stores, for himself and assistants at		6	08	121	13	04
Master Carpenter at		-	-	54	00	00

	£ per diem		£ per ann.		
Firemaster at	5	00	91	05	00
Master-gunner at	5	00	91	05	00
Gunsmith at	02	06	45	12	00
16 gunners, each besides victuals	01	00	292	00	00
Two regiments of foot, each consisting of 16 companies and each company of					
1 Captain at	08	00			
1 Lieutenant at	04	00			
1 Ensign at	03	00			
2 Sergeants, each besides victuals	01	00			
3 Corporals, each besides victuals	00	06			
1 Drummer, besides victuals	00	06			
50 Privates, each besides victuals	00	03			
Per company			574	17	06
Which is for 32 companies			18,396	00	00
For the field and staff officers of the said two regiments					
2 Colonels each at	12	00			
2 Lieutenant Colonels each at	07	00			
2 Majors each at	05	00			
For each regiment			438	00	00
Four Troops of Horse, each to consist of					
1 Captain at	14	00			
1 Lieutenant at	10	00			
1 Cornet at	09	00			
1 Quartermaster at	06	00			
2 Corporals each at	03	00			
1 Trumpeter each besides victuals	02	06			
1 Farrier, besides victuals	02	00			
25 Private horsemen each besides victuals	02	00			
Per troop			1,809	15	10
For 4 troops of Horse			7,239	03	04

	£ per diem			£ per ann.		
For the Hospital, besides the value of the sick soldiers' victuals added to the Hospital towards maintenance				700	00	00
For coals and candles				500	00	00
For boatmen, boats, intelligence, messages, presents and other contingencies at Tangier				400	00	00

The total of the above, viz. £31,544l. 17s. 4d., by paying 4s. 9d. with every 4s. 6d. will be defrayed by £29,884 12s. 2d.

To the victuallers for victualling 1,916 men at 2s. 6d. a week each viz. 1,600 foot, 64 serjeants, 96 corporals, 32 drummers, 100 troopers, four trumpeters, four farriers and 16 gunners £12,454 0s. 0d.

£42,338 12s. 2d.

That the 3d. a day in money made payable by this establishment to each foot soldier of the garrison of Tangier shall be from time to time paid to the colonels. of each regiment, out of which they are to furnish the said soldiers with clothes, shirts, shoes, stockings and other necessaries; the same to be always bought in Ireland and nowhere else, and that at as easy rates as may be; and [the colonels are] to pay the remainder, if any, in money to the said soldiers.

That 8d. a day out of the 2s. a day hereby payable to each trooper of said garrison shall from time to time be paid to such surveyor as the King shall appoint to be by him laid out for providing such stores and quantities of horsemeat as are now allowed to each horseman at Tangier; and the remaining 16d. a day shall be paid to the respective captains of horse out of which they are to furnish the said troopers with clothes, boots, belts and other necessaries to be bought in Ireland etc., as above.

The Lord Lieutenant of Ireland is to appoint some fit persons to supervise the buying of the said clothes and necessaries to see that they are good in kind and at the cheapest rates.

The establishment for March 1683 accounted for 1,700 men in two regiments of foot and four troops of horse, besides officers and NCOs. It was part of the Irish establishment, although it does not cover all the units sent to Tangier.[8]

8 TNA, WO 4/1/7, fols 128–9; *CTB*, VII, p. 750.

Tangier Garrison Musters

Table 7. The Earl of Peterborough's Regiment of Foot, 14 October 1661 (*Mercurius Publicus*, 24 October 1661; *Kingdomes Weekly Intelligencer*, 28 October 1661).

Colonel Henry, Earl of Peterborough	Captain Francis Annesley	John Neville, Quartermaster
Lieutenant Colonel Sir James Smith	Captain Humphrey Colls	James King, Gunsmith
Major Roger Johnson	Captain Stephen Bellatore	George Elliot, Surgeon
Captain Ambrose Blake	Captain Cuthbert Carr	Robert Spotswood, Surgeon's mate
Captain Palmes Fairborne	Captain John Clark	

Table 8. Sir Robert Harley's Regiment of Foot at Dunkirk, December 1661 (BL, MS Sloane 1956, fol. 22; *Kingdomes Weekly Intelligencer*, 23–30 December 1661).

Colonel Sir Robert Harley	Captain Lloyd
Lieutenant Colonel Kingwell, commanding the regiment	Captain James
Lieutenant Colonel Heywood	Captain Herbert
Major William Fiennes	Captain Wyerd
Captain Samuel Brooks	Captain Ballard
Captain Hargrave	Captain Summers

Table 9. Colonel John Fitzgerald's Regiment of Foot, November 1661 (Drenth and Riley, *First Colonial Soldiers*, I, p. 118).

Colonel John Fitzgerald	Captain-Lieutenant Mahon Mahony	Ensign Daniel Condon
Lt Colonel Edward Fitzgerald	Lieutenant James Fitzgerald	Ensign Redmond Burke
Major Blaggne	Lieutenant Erskine	Ensign John Harbord
Captain Wealy	Lieutenant Kennedy Brien	Ensign David Roche
Captain John Walsh	Lieutenant William Roche	Ensign Hugh Maghoo
Captain Thomas Fitzmorris	Lieutenant Walter Burke	Ensign Laughlin Hough

Captain Donough McNamara	Lieutenant Hugh McSwaine	Ensign Andrew Fitzgerald
Captain David Carey	Lieutenant Edmond Carey	Ensign Shohand
Captain James Fitzgerald	Lieutenant Dullond	Ensign Patrick Fitzmorris
Captain Phillip Burke	Lieutenant Morough Shoohy	Ensign Murragh Mahony

Table 10. Colonel Lewis Farrell's Regiment of Foot, November 1661 (Drenth and Riley, *First Colonial Soldiers*, I, p. 118).

Colonel Lewis Farrell	Captain-Lieutenant Brien Farrell	Ensign John Donovan
Lt Colonel Charles Molloy	Lieutenant Daniel Molloy	Ensign James Molloy
Major James Bolger	Lieutenant Holmes	Ensign Harry Leyes
Captain Henry Farrell	Lieutenant Thomas Burke	Ensign Connor Burke
Captain Hugh Farrell	Lieutenant Roger Farrell	Ensign Edward Farrell
Captain Thomas Fitzpatrick	Lieutenant Thadeus Farrell	Ensign Walter Reynolds
Captain James Farrell	Lieutenant Alexander Daron	Ensign Richard Dody
Captain John Molloy	Lieutenant William Farrell	Ensign James Farrell
Thomas Farrell	Lieutenant Edward Molloy	Ensign John Gilmour
	Lieutenant Hugh Granby	Ensign Harry Dermott
Richard Farrell, Quartermaster	Cornelius Broslan, Surgeon	Father Edward Nanglo, Chaplain

Table 11. Colonel John Fitzgerald's Regiment (Drenth and Riley, *First Colonial Soldiers*, I, pp. 118–19).

Captain John Walsh	Captain-Lieutenant Mahon Mahony	Ensign Hugh Maghoo
Captain Thomas Fitzmorris	Lieutenant William Roach	Ensign Laughlin Hough
Captain Donough McNamara	Lieutenant Walter Burke	Ensign Andrew Fitzgerald
Captain David Carey	Lieutenant Hugh McSwaine	Ensign Shohand
Captain James Fitzgerald	Lieutenant Edmond Carey	Ensign Patrick Fitzmorris

Captain Phillip Burke	Lieutenant Dullond	Ensign Murragh Mahony
	Lieutenant Murragh Shoohy	

A significant quantity of officers from 15 companies of Fitzgerald's and Farrell's regiments lost their commissions following the arrival of the Earl of Teviot and the subsequent reorganisation of the regiments on 25 May 1663. They petitioned the King for employment on 5 November 1663.[9] These officers were:

Table 12. Colonel Lewis Farrell's Regiment (Drenth and Riley, *First Colonial Soldiers*, I, p. 119).

Colonel Lewis Farrell	Captain- Lieutenant Brien Farrell	Ensign Connor Burke
Lt Colonel Daniell Molloy	Lieutenant Thomas Burke	Ensign Walter Reynolds
Captain Hugh Farrell	Lieutenant Thadeus Farrell	Ensign James Farrell
Captain Houghy Farrell	Lieutenant William Farrell	
Captain James Farrell	Lieutenant Hugh Granby	Ensign Edward Farrell
Captain Thomas Farrell	Lieutenant Roger Farrell	Ensign Richard Dody
Captain Charles Farrell	Lieutenant Alexander Daron	Ensign John Gilmour
Captain Thomas Fitzpatrick	Lieutenant Edward Molloy	Ensign Harry Dermott
Captain John Molloy		

Table 13. The Tangier, or Earl of Teviot's Regiment of Foot, 8 October 1663 (Dalton, *Army Lists*, I, p. 33; Davis, *History*, I, p. 49).

Captains, etc.	Lieutenants	Ensigns
Colonel Andrew, Earl of Teviot	Captain-Lieutenant John Giles	Ensign John Herbert
Lt Colonel Henry Norwood	Lieutenant Mansfield	Ensign Herbert Board
Major Edward Knightley	Lieutenant Stuart Scrope	Ensign Walter Reynolds
Captain Langton	Lieutenant Thomas Basset	Ensign Cornelius Kirke

9 TNA, SP29/83; *CSPD 1663–64*, p. 327.

Captains, etc.	Lieutenants	Ensigns
Captain Robert Needham	Lieutenant Benjamin Walsh	Ensign William Whittaker
Captain William Fiennes	Lieutenant Richard Heming	Ensign Colchester
Captain PalmesFairborne	Lieutenant Francis Jukes	Ensign Brookes
Captain John Morduant	Lieutenant John Michel	Ensign Carr
Captain John Chetham	Lieutenant Naismith	Ensign Piggott
Captain Benjamin Ridyard	Lieutenant Eubanke	
Captain Samuel Brooks	Lieutenant Dayley	
Captain Charles Daniel	Lieutenant Hinton	
Captain St Hill		
Captain Cuthbert Carr		
Thomas Morgan, Gentleman-at-Arms	George Elliott, Surgeon	

Table 14. Colonel John Fitzgerald's Regiment of Foot, 8 October 1663 (Dalton, *Army Lists*, I, p. 33; Davis, *History*, I, p. 49).

Colonel John Fitzgerald	Captain-Lieutenant James Fitzgerald	Ensign James Molloy
Lt Colonel Edward Fitzgerald	Lieutenant James Molloy	Ensign Holmes
Major Fitzgerald	Lieutenant Daniel Molloy	Ensign Roche
Captain Charles Molloy	Lieutenant Redmond Burke	Ensign John Harbord
Captain James Bolger	Lieutenant Daniel Condon	Ensign Harry Leyes
Captain Erskine		

Table 15. The Tangier, or Late Governor's Regiment of Foot, 26 May 1664 (TNA, CO 279/3, fols 76–88; Dalton, *Army Lists*, I, p. 38; Davis, *History*, I, pp. 67–70).

[Late Governor's Company]		
Captain-Lieutenant Brent Ely	Ensign Benjamin Walsh	John Neville, Quartermaster
George Elliott, Surgeon	Ronald Smallwood, Surgeon's mate	James King, Armourer
3 sergeants, 3 corporals, 3 lancepesades, 2 drummers, 72 men		

[Late Major Knightley's Company]		
Lieutenant John Giles	Ensign Herbert Board	Gent-at-Arms William Hadley
3 sergeants, 3 corporals, 3 lancepesades, 1 drummer, 75 men		
[Colonel Norwood's Company]		
Captain-Lieutenant Henry Norwood	Lieutenant William Moore	Ensign John Phillpot
Gent-at-Arms Obadiah Wadsworth		
3 sergeants, 3 corporals, 3 lancepesades, 1 drummer, 81 men		
Captain William Clinton	Lieutenant John Mitchell	Ensign Stephen Fabian
Gentleman-at-Arms John Shackleton		
3 sergeants, 3 corporals, 3 lancepesades, 1 drummer, 84 men		
Captain John Graham (coming at present)	Lieutenant William Whitaker	Gent-at-Arms Richard Bryan
3 sergeants, 3 corporals, 3lancepesades, 1 drummer, 66 men		
Captain Charles Daniel	Lieutenant George Leslie	Ensign Richard Hunter
Gent-at-Arms William Hodgson		
3 sergeants, 3 corporals, 3 lancepesados, 1 drummer, 75 men		
Captain PalmesFairborne	Lieutenant Richard Hemming	Ensign Richard Ward
Gent-at-Arms John Bateman		
3 sergeants, 3 corporals, 3 lancepesades, 1 drummer, 67 men		

Table 16. The Lieutenant-Governor's, or Colonel Fitzgerald's Regiment of Foot, 26 May 1664 (TNA, CO 279/3, fols 89–109; Dalton, *Army Lists*, I, p. 39).

Colonel John Fitzgerald	Captain-Lieutenant Kennedy Bryan	Ensign Redmond Burke
Gent-at-Arms William Corry		
3 sergeants, 3 corporals, 3 lancepesades, 1 drummer, 88 men		
Lt Colonel Edward Fitzgerald	Lieutenant James Fitzgerald	Ensign John Harbord
Gent-at-Arms Andrew Cotton		
3 sergeants, 3 corporals, 3 lancepesades, 1 drummer, 82 men		

Captain Charles Molloy	Lieutenant Daniel Molloy	Ensign James Molloy
Gent-at-Arms Daniel Hijrnan		
3 sergeants, 3 corporals, 3 lancepesades, 1 drummer, 72 men		
Captain James Bulger	Lieutenant Daniel Condon	Ensign Harry Leyes
Gentleman-at-Arms Charles Brady		
3 sergeants, 3 corporals, 3 lancepesades, 1 drummer, 67 men		
Captain Cuthbert Carr		Ensign John White
Gent-at-Arms David Hash		
3 sergeants, 3 corporals, 3 lancepesades, 1 drummer, 75 men		
[The late Captain Langton's Company]		
Vacancy	Lieutenant Evan Harris	Ensign Richard Chamberlain
Gent-at-Arms Evan Humphreys		
3 sergeants, 3 corporals, 3 lancepesades, 1 drummer, 65 men		
Captain John Mordaunt	Lieutenant James Pembridge	
Gent-at-Arms George Eastham		
3 sergeants, 3 corporals, 3 lancepesades, 1 drummer, 65 men		
Captain Robert Needham	Lieutenant Francis Jukes	Ensign Edward Pope
Gent-at-Arms David Atkins		
3 sergeants, 3 corporals, 1 drummer, 65 men		
Captain St Hill	Lieutenant Edward Emmes	Ensign Edward Blaney
Gent-at-Arms John Ironmonger		
3 sergeants, 3 corporals, 3 lancepesades, 1 drummer, 72 men		

Table 17. The Governor's, or Colonel Fitzgerald's Regiment of Foot, 11 August 1664 (TNA, CO 279/3, fols 110–12; Dalton, *Army Lists*, I, p. 40).

Colonel John Fitzgerald	Captain-Lieutenant John Giles	Ensign Francis Painter
Lt Colonel Edward Fitzgerald	Lieutenant James Fitzgerald	Ensign Francis Trelawny

Major Sir Arthur Bassett (absent)	Lieutenant Thomas Bassett	Ensign John Reskeymer
Captain Charles Molloy	Lieutenant Stuart Scrope	Ensign James Molloy
Captain John Chetham	Lieutenant Daniel Molloy	Ensign Edward Pope
Captain William Victor	Lieutenant John Brice	Ensign Richard Fitzgerald
Captain Charles Norwood	Lieutenant Evan Harris	Ensign Edward Blaney
Captain Brent Ely	Lieutenant Redmond Burke	Ensign Herbert Board
James Gorman, Quartermaster	Andrew Hickey, Surgeon	

Table 18. The Lieutenant-Governor's, or Colonel Norwood's Regiment of Foot, 11 August 1664 (TNA, CO 279/3, fols 113–14; Dalton, *Army Lists*, I, p. 41).

Colonel Henry Norwood	Captain-Lieutenant William Moore	Ensign John Philpott
Lieutenant Colonel Roger Alsop	Lieutenant Benjamin Walsh	Ensign John O'Neill
Major Palmes Fairborne	Lieutenant Richard Heming	Ensign Richard Chamberlain
Captain Charles Daniel	Lieutenant George Leslie	Ensign Richard Hunter
Captain John White	Lieutenant Erasmus Jukes	Ensign Henry Size
Captain Cuthbert Carr	Lieutenant David Condon	Ensign William Whitaker
Captain John Legge	Lieutenant Erasmus Izzard	Ensign George Clare
Captain Kennedy Brien	Lieutenant John Mitchell	Ensign Stephen Fabian

Table 19. The Tangier, or Colonel Middleton's Regiment of Foot, January 1668 (BL, MS Sloane 3509, fols 230–1; Davis, *History*, I, pp. 91–3).

Colonel John Middleton	Captain-Lieutenant John Giles	Ensign Stephen Fabian
Lieutenant Colonel Roger Alsop	Lieutenant Henry d'Arcy	Ensign Francis Trelawny
Major Palmes Fairborne	Lieutenant James Fitzgerald	Ensign Thomas Tesmon
Captain Marmaduke Boynton	Lieutenant John Graham	Ensign John Philpott

Captain Cuthbert Carr	Lieutenant Stuart Scrope	
Captain Charles Daniel		
Captain Brent Ely		
Captain John Legge		
Captain John Mordaunt		
Captain James Porter		
Captain John White		
Captain William Victor		
John Neville, Quartermaster		
George Elliott, Surgeon		

Table 20. The Tangier, or Earl of Inchiquin's Regiment of Foot, 23 August 1678 (Reconstructed from 'Commissions for Tangier, delivered to Sir Palmes Fairborne, 23 August 1678', TNA, SP44/104, fols 100–1).

Colonel William, Earl of Inchiquin	Captain-Lieutenant Teigh Mahon	Ensign Wingfield Wooton
Lt Colonel Palmes Fairborne	Lieutenant Henry Weston	Ensign James Adams
Major Charles Daniel	Lieutenant John Chapell	Ensign William Norwood
Captain Cuthbert Carr	Lieutenant Robert Ogi lby	Ensign George Westcombe
Captain Marmaduke Boynton	Lieutenant Nicholas Cusack	Ensign William Bound
Captain John Giles	Lieutenant William Fisher	Ensign Samuel Gardner
Captain Francis Trelawny	Lieutenant Henry Size	Ensign Richard Talbot
Captain Thomas St John	Lieutenant Thomas Fitzharris	Ensign Stafford Fairborne
Captain Brent Ely	Lieutenant Matthew Aylmer	Ensign Richard Roberts
Captain Sir James Leslie	Lieutenant Francis Chantrell	Ensign Richard Fitzgerald
Captain John White	Lieutenant Richard White	
Captain Stuart Scrope	Lieutenant James Guy	

All commissions are dated 1 August 1678. Colonel Thomas Dongan was also commissioned to be Lieutenant Colonel of a regiment at Tangier.[10]

10 TNA, SP44/104, fol. 104.

Table 21. The Second Tangier, or Earl of Plymouth's Regiment of Foot, 13 July 1680 (TNA, SP44/164, fol. 50; SP44/165, fol. 1; Davies, *Army Lists*, I, p. 269).

Colonel Charles, Earl of Plymouth	Captain-Lieutenant Heyman Rooke	Ensign Lassells
Lieutenant Colonel Percy Kirke	Lieutenant William Culliford	Ensign Berry
Major Charles Trelawny	Lieutenant Roche	Ensign Davies
Captain Roger Pope	Lieutenant Hedges	Ensign Pagett
Captain Henry Trelawny	Lieutenant John Miche lbourne	Ensign Dixon
Captain Edward Hastings	Lieutenant Edward Brett	Ensign Isaac La Brousel
Captain Walter Fitzgerald	Lieutenant Bradshaw	Ensign Coshen
Captain Edward Griffith	Lieutenant Johnson	Ensign Jeffreys
Captain John Grimes	Lieutenant Atkinson	Ensign Abercrombie
Captain Robert Annersley	Lieutenant Fitzgerald	Ensign Burke
Captain Fox	Lieutenant Coole	Ensign Hobson
Captain Arthur Cheffers	Lieutenant Williams	Ensign Pagett
Captain Thomas Southcott	Lieutenant Ramsey	Ensign Walham
Captain Edward Saville	Lieutenant Dungan	Ensign Hugh Meredith
Captain John Strode	Lieutenant Francis Nicholson	Ensign Caryll

Adjutant Davis	Quartermaster Marshall	Chaplain William Morgan	Surgeon Hubin

Table 22. The Tangier, or Governor Fairborne's Regiment of Foot, June 1680 to March 1682 (Reconstructed from commissions issued between these dates. TNA, SP44/29, fols 368, 390–2, 420; SP44/164, fols 57, 59).

Colonel Sir Palmes Fairborne	Captain-Lieutenant John Burgess	
Lt Colonel Marmaduke Boynton	Lieutenant George Westcombe	Ensign John Senhouse
Major Sir James Leslie	Lieutenant Henry Withers	Ensign John Pinkney
Captain George Talbot		Ensign James Hilton
Captain Richard White		

Captain Francis Chantrell	Lieutenant William Norwood	Ensign Bernard Tessine
Captain Zouch Tate	Lieutenant John Wilson	Ensign Patrick Farrell
Captain Cuthbert Carr		Ensign Vernon Parker
Captain John Giles	Lieutenant Jenkin Thomas	Ensign Joseph Bolland
Captain Brent Ely	Lieutenant John Wingfield	Ensign David Roche
Captain Mohun		Ensign Theobald Burke

Table 23. The Tangier, or Kirke's Regiment of Foot, 17 September 1683 (SRO, D742/0/4/10).

Colonel Percy Kirke	Captain-Lieutenant Berry	Ensign James Hilton
Lt Colonel Marmaduke Boynton	Lieutenant Westcombe	Ensign Atkins
Major Sir James Leslie	Lieutenant Withers	Ensign Elliot
Captain Giles	Lieutenant Thomas	Ensign Mortimer
Captain Thomas St John	Lieutenant Webster	Ensign Fairborne
Captain Ely	Lieutenant Wingfield	Ensign David Roach
Captain Rowe	Lieutenant Gerard	Ensign Penotier
Captain George Wingfield	Lieutenant Adams	Ensign Fitzgerald
Captain Barbour	Lieutenant Laws	Ensign Duff
Captain Matthews	Lieutenant Billing	Ensign Kirke
Captain Caulfield	Lieutenant Houghton	Ensign Barbour
Captain Talbot	Lieutenant Burke	Ensign Simons
Captain Francis Chantrell	Lieutenant Norwood	Ensign Teson
Captain Tate	Lieutenant Wilson (in slavery)	Ensign Patrick Farrell
Captain James Guy	Lieutenant Pinkney	Ensign Parker
Captain John Burgess	Lieutenant Maher	Ensign Lester

Table 24. The King's Battalion, 17 September 1683 (SRO, D742/0/4/7).

Lt Colonel Edward Sackville	Lieutenant Harris	
Captain George Bowes	Lieutenant Robinson	
Captain Thomas Tollemache	Lieutenant Collier	

Captain James Fortrey	Lieutenant Henn	
Captain Phillip Kirke	Lieutenant Robert Wilkins	
	Lieutenant John Hope	Ensign John Hill
	Lieutenant Henry Honet	Ensign Meols
		Andrew Harriott, Surgeon

Table 25. Colonel Trelawney's Regiment, 17 September 1683 (SRO, D742/0/4/8).

Colonel Trelawney	Lieutenant Roche	Ensign Bedford
Lt Colonel Churchill	Lieutenant Pring	Ensign Cornwell
Major Tiffin	Lieutenant Pagett	Ensign Tiffin
Captain Trelawney	Lieutenant Davies	Ensign Games
Captain Fox	Lieutenant Cole	Ensign Susey
Captain Hastings	Lieutenant Ramsey	Ensign La Bruce
Captain Flood	Lieutenant Nicholson	Ensign Dalhunty
Captain Saville	Lieutenant Dunscombe	Ensign Cousins
Captain Rooke	Lieutenant Lucy	Ensign Avery
Captain Culliford	Lieutenant Davies	
Captain Johnson	Lieutenant Martin	Ensign Mallam
Captain Collier	Lieutenant Atkinson	Ensign Fireby
Captain Rodney	Lieutenant Hobson	Ensign Culliford
Captain Webster		Ensign Aldus
Captain Pursell	Lieutenant Fitzgerald	Ensign Hobbs
Captain Jeffreys	Lieutenant Hedger	Ensign Kirke
		Adjutant Carrell
		Quartermaster Bush
		Surgeon Muston
		Halton and Middleton } mates

Table 26. The Earl of Dumbarton's Regiment, 17 September 1683 (SRO, D742/0/4/9).

Captain Douglas	Lieutenant Dury	Ensign Robson
Captain Monroe	Lieutenant McKenney	
Captain Lawder	Lieutenant Sterling	Ensign Bell
Captain Murray	Lieutenant Gordon	Ensign McTierney
Captain Moncrief	Lieutenant Scott	Ensign Chattum

Captain Hodges	Lieutenant Clark	Ensign McIntosh
Captain Urqhuart	Lieutenant Mowatt	Ensign Bannerman
Captain Carr	Lieutenant Stewart	Ensign Barclay
Captain White	Lieutenant George Murray	Ensign McCullock
Captain Colraine	Lieutenant Cunningham	
Captain Povey	Lieutenant Pierson	Ensign Farrell
Captain Charlton	Lieutenant Leviston	Ensign Salisbury
	Lieutenant Law	Ensign Ramsey
	Lieutenant Carr	
	Lieutenant John Murray	[Francis] Belloe, Surgeon
	Lieutenant Rutherford	
	Lieutenant Deanes	
	Lieutenant Small	
	Lieutenant Auckmutty	
	Lieutenant Robert Carr	
	Lieutenant White	
	Lieutenant Moultry	
	Lieutenant Maxwell	
	Lieutenant Widdrington	
	Lieutenant Latham	

Table 27. The Tangier Troop of Horse, 21 October 1661 (*Mercurius Publicus*, 24 October 1661; *Kingdomes Weekly Intelligencer*, 28 October 1661).

Earl of Peterborough	Captain-Lieutenant Robert Leech	Cornet James Mordaunt
1 quartermaster, 4 corporals, 1 trumpeter and 100 troopers		

Two further troops were added by late 1663, but the officers of the original unit appear to have gone by that time.

Table 28. The Tangier Horse, 11 August 1664 (TNA, CO 279/3, fol. 114; Dalton, *Army Lists*, I, p. 42).

Colonel Tobias Bridges	Capt-Lieutenant Thomas Stackhouse	Cornet Thomas Winfield	QM Jeffrey Symonds
Captain John Fitzgerald	Lt Alexander McKenzie	Cornet James Hackett	QM John Graham
Captain Edward Witham	Lt Robert Scarborough	Cornet James Leslie	QM Henry Ailward

Table 29. Troops of Horse raised for service in Tangier, 13 July 1680 (TNA, SP44/164, fol 49; Davies, *Army Lists*, I, p. 268).

Earl of Ossory	Capt.-Lieutenant Louis Billingsley	Cornet Slingsby
Captain Sir John Lanier	Lt Samuel English	Cornet Carpenter
Captain Robert Pultney	Lt Ward	Cornet Radney
Captain Charles Neatby	Lt Gamaliel Capell	Cornet Hugh Wyndham
Captain John Coy	Lt McCarthy	Cornet Williams
Captain Thomas Langston	Lt Francis Langston	Cornet Dunn

Table 30. Troops of Horse in Tangier, 17 September 1683 (SRO, D742/0/4/6).

<table>
<tr><td>Capt Alex. McKenzie</td><td>Lt Francis de La Rue</td><td>Cornet John Chappell</td><td>QM John Jenkins</td></tr>
<tr><td colspan="4">3 NCOs, 30 mounted men</td></tr>
<tr><td>Capt Charles Neatby</td><td>Lt Williams</td><td>Cornet Hugh Wyndham</td><td>QM Sotherland</td></tr>
<tr><td colspan="4">6 NCOs, 19 mounted men, 31 unmounted men</td></tr>
<tr><td>Capt John Coy</td><td>Lt Dunn</td><td>Cornet William Stamford</td><td>QM Kirke</td></tr>
<tr><td colspan="4">6 NCOs, 17 mounted men, 32 unmounted men</td></tr>
<tr><td>Capt Thomas Langston</td><td>Lt Langston</td><td>Cornet Thomas Pownall</td><td>QM Brereton</td></tr>
<tr><td colspan="4">5 NCOs, 13 mounted men, 37 unmounted men</td></tr>
<tr><td colspan="4">Henry Hawker, Adjutant</td></tr>
<tr><td colspan="4">20 women and 20 children</td></tr>
<tr><td colspan="4"></td></tr>
<tr><td colspan="4">Total: 16 officers, 20 NCOs, 79 mounted men, 100 unmounted men.</td></tr>
</table>

The establishment for each of the four troops in 1683 was:

> Captain, Lieutenant, Cornet, Quartermaster
> 2 sergeants, 3 corporals, 2 trumpeters and 50 men.[11]

11 SRO, D742/0/4/26.

Table 31. Commissioned and Staff Officers, 1 October 1683 (SRO, D742/0/4/11).

Colonel Trelawny's Regiment		
Captains, etc.	Lieutenants	Ensigns
Charles Trelawny, Colonel	Morris Roche	John Bedford
Charles Churchill, Lt Colonel	George Bing	Wolfran Cornwall
Henry Trelawny	Henry Pagett	Henry Tiffin
Charles Fox	Henry Davies	William Games
Edward Hastings	John Cole	Percy Kirke
John Strode	William Davies	Laurent La Bruce
Edward Saville	Francis Nicholson	Lancelot Dalhunty
Henry Rooke	Mark Duncan	John Cousins
Francis Russell	John Mickleburne	Lucy
William Culliford	Thomas Atkinson	John Culliford
Charles Johnson	Thomas Lucy	John Avery
Charles Collier	Alexander Ramsey	John Mallam
Robert Purcell	John Martin	Thomas Finch
William Webster	Michael Fitzgerald	Edward Hobbs
John Jeffreys	Stephen Hobson	Samuel Aldus
	John Hedges	Samuel Livesey
Troops of Horse		
Captains	Lieutenants	Cornets
Alexander McKenney	Francis La Rue	John Chapel
Charles Neatby	John Williams	Hugh Windham
John Coy	Samuel Dunn	William Standford
Thomas Langston	Francis Langston	Thomas Pownall
Other Officers		
Person's name	**Quality**	**To what regiment belonging**
Percy Kirke Esq.	Governor	
Thomas Hughes	Minister	
Thomas Lawrence	Physician	
John Hope	Town Mayor	
Frederick Baker	Judge-Advocate and storekeeper	
James Wiley	Surgeon	
William Poultney	Provost Marshall	

Person's Name	Quality	To What Regiment Belonging
Edward Hughes	Commissary of Musters	
Francis Povey	Storekeeper	
Edward Pipe	Firemaster	
Ernest Newland	Master carpenter	
James Hunter	Master gunner	
Richard Bassett	Captain of miners	
James Scott	Gunsmith	
Francis Belloe	Surgeon	Dumbarton's
Charles Carroll	Adjutant	Trelawny's
William Morgan	Chaplain	Trelawny's
Henry Mustoe	Surgeon	Trelawny's
James Bush	Quartermaster	
Hugh Davies	Drum-major	
James Scott	Gunsmith	
Henry Sheres	Surveyor-General of the Mole	
Balthazar St Michel	Adjutant-General for Naval Affairs	
John Earlisman	Comptroller	
Captain Thomas St John	Receiver of revenue	
Captain Charles Collier	Receiver of revenue	
Thomas Fowler	Minister	
William Smith	Mayor	
Henry Hordenell	Recorder	
William Morgan	Minister	
George Mercer	Schoolmaster	
John Eccles	Usher	} Officers relating to the civil government
George Talbot	Town Clerk	
Richard Stenhouse	Praticque Master	
William Coggs	Sergeant	
Nathaniel Johnson	Sergeant	
Thomas Paine	Clerk	
Edward Bourne	Sexton	

Abstract of Muster Rolls

Table 32. Tangier Garrison, 1 October 1681 (Davis, *Second Queen's*, I, pp. 38–9).

	NCOs	Ptes/Miners
5 companies of his Majesty's Battalion	60	431
The Governor's Regiment, 16 companies	128	831
The Earl of Dumbarton's Regiment, 16 companies and 4 independent companies	152	1,024
Colonel Percy Kirke's Regiment of Foot, 16 companies	112	686
4 troops of horse	19	Tprs m'ted 63
		Tprs unm'ted 112
Gunners, 33		
Company of miners (Captain Basset)	3	41
Total: 3,605		

Table 33. Tangier Garrison, 1 December 1682 (SRO, D742/0/4/4).

	Ptes		Ptes
The King's Battalion		**Colonel Percy Kirke's Regiment**	
Lt Col Sackville's Company	74	Colonel Kirke's Company	58
Captain George Bowes	82	Lt Col Trelawny	64
Captain Tho. Tollemache	88	Major Pope	33
Captain James Fortrey	65	Captain Tiffin Trelawny	36
Captain Phillip Kirke	70	Captain Fox	40
Total	379	Captain Griffith	42
		Captain Haston	53
Earl of Dumbarton's Rgt.		Captain Strode	28
Major Halkett's Company	48	Captain Saville	16
Captain Douglas	39	Captain Annesley	33
Captain Melville	44	Captain Rooke	35
Captain Robert Douglas	48	Captain Russell	31
Captain Monroe	45	Captain Culliford	41
Captain Landor	46	Captain Johnson	34
Captain Rollo	45	Captain Collier	30
Captain Murray	47	**Total**	564
Captain Lundy	48		
Captain Hume	49		

	Ptes		Ptes
Earl of Dumbarton's Regiment (cont.)		**4 troops of horse (mounted)**	
Captain Moncrief	43	Captain McKenzie	30
Captain Preston	46	Captain Neatby	19
Captain Barclay	44	Captain Coy	17
Captain Hodge	47	Captain Langston	13
Captain Urquhart	50	**Total**	79
Captain Forbes	40		
Captain Colraine	48	**4 troops of horse (unmounted)**	
Captain Povey	43	Captain McKenzie	0
Captain Caulfield	57	Captain Neatby	31
Captain Charlton	39	Captain Coy	32
Total	916	Captain Langston	37
		Total	100
		Combined Total	179
The Governor's Regiment		Captain Bassett's Co. of Miners	31
Governor's Company	47	**Gunners**	33
Lt Col Boynton	45		
Major Sir James Leslie	60	**Total soldiers, horse and foot, miners and gunners**	2,937
Captain Giles	59		
Captain St John	53		
Captain Ellis	47	**Non-commissioned officers**	475
Captain Rowes	40		
Captain Talbot	42	**Totals according to the muster rolls of 1 December 1682**	3,411
Captain Chantrell	45		
Captain Tate	45		
Captain Gage	43		
Captain Burgess	66		
Captain George Winford	36		
Captain Barber	49		
Captain Matthews	46		
Captain Charles Comfield	56		
Total	779		

Table 34. The Earl of Dumbarton's Regiment, 14 September 1683 (TNA, CO 279/32, fol. 100; SRO, D742/0/2/4).

Companies	Off's	NCOs	Ptes	Women		Children	
				married	unm.	male	female
Lt Colonel Halkett	2	8	41	1	0	0	0
Major Douglas	2	8	34	2	1	0	4
Captain Melville	3	8	29	1	0	0	0
Captain Robert Douglas	3	8	33	2	1	0	2
Captain Monroe	4	8	36	1	1	0	1
Captain Lauder	3	8	37	0	1	0	1
Captain Rollo	2	8	35	0	0	0	0
Captain Murray	2	8	37	1	1	0	1
Captain Lundy	2	8	33	4	1	3	4
Captain Hume	3	8	34	2	1	2	1
Capt Moncrieffe	3	8	34	2	0	0	0
Captain Barclay	3	8	33	0	0	0	0
Captain Hodges	1	8	34	3	0	0	1
Captain Urquhart	3	8	38	1	0	0	0
Captain Carr	3	8	27	3	1	1	0
Captain White	3	8	34	2	0	0	1
Captain Colgrave*	1	6	30	3	0	1	0
Captain Porree*	2	6	33	2	0	0	0
Captain Caulfield*	2	5	39	3	0	3	0
Captain Charlton*	3	6	27	3	2	4	2
Total	50	151	678	36	10	14	18

* List with four independent companies annexed.

Table 35. Tangier Garrison, 1 October 1683 (SRO, D742/0/4/23; TNA, WO 5/1, fols 19–22).

Colonel Kirke's Regiment		
Companies	**NCOs**	**Ptes**
Col Percy Kirke	8	61
Lt Col James Boynton	8	47
Major Sir James Leslie	8	60
Captain Giles	8	56
Captain St John	8	58
Captain Ely	8	46

Captain Rowe	8	47
Captain George Wingfield	8	40
Captain Barbour	8	51
Captain William Matthews	8	57
Captain Charles Wingfield	8	55
Captain Talbot	8	44
Captain Chauntrell	8	46
Captain Tate	8	45
Captain Gaye	8	42
Captain Burgess	8	65
Total	128	820
Earl of Dumbarton's Regiment		
Companies	**NCOs**	**Ptes**
Lt Col James Halkett	8	48
Major Archibald Douglas	8	40
Captain Patrick Melville	8	44
Captain Robert Douglas	8	49
Captain Andrew Monroe	8	45
Captain Robert Lauder	8	46
Captain Archibald Rollo	8	48
Captain James Murray	8	49
Captain Robert Lundy	8	43
Captain George Hume	8	44
Captain James Moncrieff	8	43
Captain Charles Barclay	8	44
Captain Robert Hodges	8	49
Captain Alexander Urquhart	8	50
Captain Cuthbert Carr	8	40
Captain John White	8	46
Captain George Colgrave	6	48
Captain Henry Poree	6	42
Captain Toby Caulfield	6	56
Captain Edward Charlton	6	37
Total	152	917
Colonel Trelawny's Regiment		
Companies	**NCOs**	**Ptes**
Col Charles Trelawny	7	64

Lt Col Charles Churchill	7	50
Major Zachariah Tiffin	7	46
Captain Henry Trelawny	7	60
Captain Charles Fox	7	45
Captain Edward Hastings	7	60
Captain John Strode	7	39
Captain Edward Saville	7	25
Captain Heyman Roche	7	36
Captain William Culliford	7	48
Captain Charles Johnson	7	41
Captain Charles Collier	7	51
Captain Alexander Rodney	7	39
Captain William Webster	7	42
Captain Robert Purcell	7	37
Captain John Jeffreys	7	40
Total	112	723
The King's Battalion		
Companies	**NCOs**	**Ptes**
Lt Col Edward Sackville	12	53
Captain George Bowe	12	68
Captain Thomas Tollemache	12	80
Captain James Fortrey	12	40
Captain Phillip Kirke	12	36
Total	60	277
Gunners		32

Company of Miners, Captain Richard Basset commanding	**NCOs**	**Miners**
	4	48
	Garrison Total	3,741

Table 36. Tangier Garrison, 4 November 1683 (SRO, D742/0/3/50)

Colonel Kirke's Regiment	
Companies	**Ptes**
Col Percy Kirke	43
Lt Col James Boynton	38
Major Sir James Leslie	45

Companies	Ptes
Captain Giles	48
Captain St John	56
Captain Ely	42
Captain Rowe	38
Captain George Wingfield	36
Captain Barbour	47
Captain William Matthews	50
Captain Charles Wingfield	36
Captain Talbot	34
Captain Chauntrell	41
Captain Tate	45
Captain Gaye	33
Captain Burgess	47
Total	679
Earl of Dumbarton's Regiment	
Companies	**Ptes**
Lt Col James Halkett	48
Major Archibald Douglas (Major Spott 12/11/83)	42
Captain Monroe	46
Captain Lauder	48
Captain Rollo	43
Captain Murray	46
Captain Lundy	39
Captain Hume	47
Captain Melville	37
Captain Robert Douglas	42
Captain Moncrieff	41
Captain White	37
Captain Barclay	46
Captain Hodges	37
Captain Carr	30
Captain Norcott	42
Captain Colgrave	33
Captain Poree	35
Captain Caulfield	44
Captain Charlton	33
Total	**816**

Colonel Trelawny's Regiment	
Companies	**Ptes**
Colonel Trelawny	53
Lt Colonel Churchill	34
Major Tiffin	30
Captain Trelawny	51
Captain Fox	29
Captain Hastings	52
Captain Strode	31
Captain Saville	17
Captain Roche	26
Captain Rodney	27
Captain Culliford	33
Captain Johnson	30
Captain Collier	34
Captain Purcell	31
Captain Webster	37
Captain Jeffreys	26
Total	**541**
The King's Battalion	
Companies	**Ptes**
Colonel Sackville	55
Captain Bowes	68
Captain Tollemache	71
Captain Fortrey	41
Captain Kirke	32
Total	267
The Horse	
Troops	**Troopers**
Captain McKenzie	11
Captain Neatby	29
Captain Coy	40
Captain Langston	36
Total	116
Colonel Kirke's Regiment	679
Earl of Dumbarton's Regiment	816

Colonel Trelawny's Regiment	541
Captain Bassett	41
Old gunners	29
New gunners	22
Smiths	4
Pratickmen	5
Total	101
The King's Battalion	267
The Horse	116
Captain Bassett	101
Garrison total	2,520

Table 37. Lord Dartmouth's orders to the Gunners, 19 September 1683 (SRO, D742/0/4/12A).

The Right Honourable the Lord Dartmouth's order for the gunners to attend daily in their turns, at the several posts hereafter mentioned:		
Mr Thomas Silver to command at my Lord's door	*The Mole*	*Hyde's Battery*
Henry Couden	Albin Howell	William Hart
John Dyson	John Milling	Thomas Nickson
Thomas Green	Thomas Sessions	
Robert Jacket	David Williams	*Irish Battery*
	Edward Ansell	Edward Coates
Peterborough Tower	Clement Dorrill	
Christopher Berry		
Henry Bishop		

Table 38. Names of soldiers (reinforcements) received on board the *Antelope*, 4 June 1680 (SRO, D742/0/4/1).

Gov. Legge's Company	Captain Churchill's men	Captain Mainwaring's men
Thomas Torrington	William Hardie	John Day
Edward Cassadice	Alexander Davison	Alphonso Bullmore
Nicholas Sanders	Nathaniel Grills	Edward Roe
Robert Scott	John Pringle	Christopher Frost
Charles Callaghan	Thomas Gaskell	Thomas Baggs
Thomas Woods	Robert Stace	John Moss
William Woolsey	Thomas Stroud	Hugh Lee
	William Calleck	John Barron
	Thomas Floyd	Abraham Thomas
	William Hodges	John Needham
Captain Nicholas' men	**Captain Fortrey's men**	**Captain Lee's men**
Richard Foster	John Dyer	Richard Motherwell
Edgar Bedford	Robert Poulton	William Conway
George Clarke	Richard Locke	Thomas Gilgreave
William Eglen	John Browne	Charles Drake
Peter Pierce	Robert Rice	William Fowler
Thomas Chilleys	Richard Richards	John Randall
Nicholas Ba lby	John Vance	Thomas Sadler
	John Greene	
	Richard Ballard	
	Phillip Harrison	
Captain Nicholas' men	**Captain Cornwell's men**	**Captain Stallsey's men**
Horace Mitchell	Osbert Dickson	John Watts
Alexander Roach	Thomas Rutter	Robert Burke
Angus MacLean	John Dodd	Thomas Christopher
John Cole	Matthew Kirby	John Frey
Scarlet Rose	Matthew Sweetman	John Naylor
Abraham Frank	Robert Hampson	Richard Hampton
John Balldock	James Hall	William Needles
Thomas Spicer	Lancelot Burton	John James
Henry Rugeley	Ferdinando Delpa	
Edward Shere		

Captain St Clare's men		Major Housden's men
James Mills		John Watkins
John Owen		Edward Redford
John Perry		James Bartlett
Thomas Clark		Edward Clemons
James Davison		Thomas Hughes
William Arnall		Isaac Thomas
Timothy Bryan		
Gilbert Constable		
Robert Harrison		
Richard Arlington		
	Total	97

Table 39. An Abstract of the four Independent English companies lately returned from Tangier, according to the first muster taken of them after their landing in April 1684 (HMC, *Ormonde*, II, p. 232).

	Sgts	Cpls	Dmrs	Ptes	Ptes wanting	Mustered
Captain George Colgrave: Lieutenant Thomas Power, Ensign George Colgrave	2	3	1	30	30	Kinsale
Captain Henry Poree: Lieutenant George Giles, Ensign Michael Farrell	2	3	1	32	28	Kinsale
Captain Toby Caulfield: Lieutenant Lewis Widdrington, Ensign Samuel Salisbury	2	3	1	37	23	Cork
Captain Edward Charlton: Lieutenant Peter Latham, Ensign Thomas Ramsay	2	3	1	25	35	Kinsale
Total	8	12	4	124	116	
13 women: 11 married, 2 unmarried, 10 children						

Table 40. Officers of the Tangier garrison regiments according to religion, 1667 (BL, MS Sloane 3509, fols 139–40).

Of the Protestant Faith	*Of the Romish Persuasion*
The Governor's Regiment	
John, Lord Belasyse [*sic*: Belasyse was a known Catholic]	
Captain-Lieutenant James Leslie	
Ensign John Graham	
	Lieutenant Colonel Edward Fitzgerald
	Lieutenant James Fitzgerald
	Ensign George Fielding
Major Sir Arthur Bassett	
Lieutenant John Reskeymer	
	Ensign Lawrence Fitzharris
Captain John Mordaunt	
Lieutenant James Pembridge	
	Ensign William Herbert
	Captain William Victor
	Lieutenant Richard Fitzgerald
	Ensign James Molloy
Captain Charles Norwood	
Lieutenant Evan Harris	
	Ensign Edward White
Captain Brent Ely	
	Lieutenant Redmond Burke
Ensign Herbert Board	
Captain Marmaduke Boynton	
	Lieutenant Daniel Molloy
Ensign Richard Symonds	
Captain John Giles	
	Lieutenant John Gi lby
	Ensign McHenrique
The Lieutenant Governor's Regiment	
Colonel Henry Norwood	
	Captain-Lieutenant William Moore
Ensign William Hoard	
Lieutenant Colonel Roger Alsop	
Lieutenant Richard Hemmings	

Of the Protestant Faith	*Of the Romish Persuasion*
	Ensign Henry Rumbold
Major Palmes Fairborne	
Lieutenant Robert Napier	
Ensign Edward Pope	
[Captain Gilby's Company]	
Lieutenant Francis Jukes	
	Ensign Henry Size
	Captain Charles Daniel
	Lieutenant John Philpott
Ensign Richard Hunter	
Captain Cuthbert Carr	
	Lieutenant Daniel Condon
Ensign William Whittaker	
	Captain John Legge
	Lieutenant Talbot
	Captain Kennedy O'Brien
Lieutenant John Mitchel	
Ensign Stephen Fabian	
	Captain Thomas Porter
Lieutenant Zouch Tate	
Ensign Nicholas Tomms	

Provisions for the Tangier Garrison and Naval Station

The most complete description of an English soldier's rations was given by the professional soldier, Sir James Turner. Drawing the connection between pay and provisions, he wrote, 'since money is generally scarce in the wars, in so much that soldiers cannot receive their wages duly, let us see what allowance of meat and drink (ordinarily called proviant) princes allow their soldiery'.[12] He described the soldier's ordinary rations thus:

> There are few princes who have not their particular establishment for their proviant both in field and garrison, as well as for money; the order whereof commonly is this, they allow so much bread, flesh, wine or beer to every trooper and foot soldier, which ordinarily is alike to both; then they allow to the officers according to their dignities and charges, double, triple and quadruple portions; as to an ensign four times more than to a common soldier, a colonel commonly having twelve portions allowed him. The ordinary allowance of a soldier in the

12 Turner, *Pallas Armata*, p. 201.

> field, is daily 2 pound of bread, one pound of flesh, or, in lieu of it, one pound of cheese, one pottle of wine, or in lieu of it, two pottles of beer. It is enough, cry the soldiers, we desire no more, and it is enough in conscience. But this allowance will not last very long, they must be content to march sometimes one whole week, and scarce get two pound of bread all the while, and their officers as little as they, who if they have no provisions of their own carried about with them, must be satisfied with commis-bread, and cold water as well as the common soldier, unless they have money to buy better entertainment from sutlers.

The procurement, organisation, accounting, and transportation of provisions (victuals and other foodstuffs) among seventeenth-century armies was essential to military operations, and to maintain the effectiveness and morale of the rank and file. Not only did soldiers need to be fed and provided with beverage, but horses and draft animals required large amounts of fodder. During the seventeenth century, Continental armies travelled with huge supply trains – both of ammunition and victuals – the latter controlled by the Commissary-General of the victuals, with assistant commissaries and clerks, as well as bakers, butchers and other victuallers. Even though troops in garrisons might fare better than those in marching armies, benefitting from a more varied and plentiful diet, much depended upon the resources of the locality, in addition to the attitude of the inhabitants who proffered them. There was a distinction between the types of food which were suitable for storage in garrisons or transportation with an army in the field, although the professional soldier, Francis Markham, who had been in the Dutch service, noted, 'if it be in marching or journeying, then he [the commissary] shall give them the victuals which is most easy for carriage, and the longest lasting, as biscuit, beef ready boiled, cheese and the like.'[13]

On 9 July 1658 the Governor of Dunkirk, Colonel William Lockhart, provided the following account of his measures for victualling the recently garrisoned port. It was cheaper, he thought, to buy provisions in Flanders that to have them sent from England:

> I shall go about the buying of wheat and rye, to make bread for the present subsistence of the forces, and shall keep the month's provision of biscuit in store, least at any time, either by siege or otherwise, we should be put to a pinch; and once in a year, the magazine of bread, I mean the month's biscuit for 4,000 men, must be renewed, and the old given out, and rebated of the soldiers pay; but before the old stock of biscuit so laid in be meddled with, the new stock to the same quantity must be first in store; and so this place will never want six week's provision of bread, which is the staff of man's life. If I find the butter and cheese may be kept without spoiling, I shall likewise save it; but I think, for provisions that are not to be made use of save once in a year, all cheese, or at least salt beef and bacon, or pork in lieu of the butter will be best.[14]

13 Francis Markham, *Five Decades of Epistles of Warre* (London: Augustine Matthew, 1622), p. 103.

14 Thomas Birch (ed.), *A Collection of State Papers of John Thurloe, Esq; Secretary to the Council of State* (London: 1742), VII, p. 216.

As was the case with Tangier, rations in garrisons were liable to be more varied when the town or city was not under threat, although preserved food was relied upon during siege conditions. Turner remarked that:

> garrisons and fortified places should be sufficiently provided with such meats and drinks as are most fit to preserve; these are corn, grain, and meat of several kinds, stock-fish, herrings, and all other salted-fishes, salted and hung-fleshes, especially beef and bacon, cheese, butter, almonds, chestnuts and hazelnuts, wine, beer, malt, honey, vinegar, oil, tobacco, wood and coal for firing, and as many living oxen, cows, sheep and swine, hens and turkeys as can be conveniently fed; for which purpose as also for horses, he is to provide straw, hay and oats.[15]

Like oatmeal, which might be boiled in the soldiers' quarters, grain (wheat) could be stored for baking bread in garrison conditions. Roger Boyle, Earl of Orrery, the contemporary professional soldier, who had served extensively in Ireland, warned of the importance for careful storage and the necessary regular inspection as 'the wheat in them [magazines] must be laid thin, and often turned, else it will heat, and be loathed by the soldiery, who when on most danger (as in the time of siege) ought not to have their staff of life nauseous unto them'.[16]

'Provisions in his Majesty's store at Tangier, 28 May 1664':

> 2,371 bushels of wheat; 2,352 lb of rice; 15,093½ lb of beef; 12,570 lb of pork; 91⅛ bushels of oatmeal; 5, 351 pints of oil in lieu of butter or cheese; 4,747 bushels of oats; 807¼ bushels of barley; and 794 bushels of beans.[17]

> Tangier, 15 September 1683
>
> In obedience for a demand for a state of stores of provisions do answer that not having had time to weigh and measure, have therefore made the highest computation, which according to the Abstract of Musters will serve 3,500 men (allowing pork for beef and peas for oatmeal) for the weeks underwritten:
>
> bread, 8 weeks; beef, 5 weeks; pork, 5 weeks; peas, 6 weeks; oatmeal, 6 weeks; butter, 36 weeks; cheese 12 weeks.[18]

'Provisions remaining in stores on 29 September 1683':

> 2,584 bags of biscuit; 285,169 lb of bread; 4,754 (4 lb) pieces of beef;

15 Sir James Turner, *Pallas Armata: Military essayes of the ancient Grecian, Roman, and modern art of war written in the years 1670 and 1671* (London: Richard Chiswell, 1683), p. 201.

16 Roger Boyle, Earl of Orrery, *A Treatise of the Art of War dedicated to the King's Most Excellent Majesty* (1677), p. 29.

17 SRO, D742/0/3/5.

18 SRO, D742/0/3/9.

> 9,609 (2 lb) pieces of pork; 1,366½ bushels of peas; 289⅓ bushels of oatmeal; 6,160 lb of butter; 22,107 lb of cheese.

'Sent to the navy':

> 2,584 bags of biscuit.

'Provisions for 3,500 men, waste excepted, allowing pork for beef and peas for oatmeal) for comestibles':

> biscuit, 0 weeks; bread, 11 weeks; beef, 3 weeks; pork, 3 weeks; peas, 3 weeks; oatmeal, 3 weeks; butter, 4 weeks; cheese, 12 weeks.

'But for 2,600 men, as the weekly issues do not exceed, will serve':

> biscuit, 0 weeks); bread, 15 weeks; beef, 4 weeks; pork, 4 weeks; peas, 4 weeks; oatmeal, 4 weeks; butter, 5 weeks; cheese, 16 weeks.

'Issued to 2,600 men, 4 weeks' provisions, pork in lieu of beef and peas for oatmeal':

> 101,024 lb of bread; 6,500 (4 lb) pieces of beef; 5,200 (2 lb) pieces of pork; 650 bushels of peas; 487 bushels of oatmeal; 3,900 lb of butter; 5,200 lb of cheese.

'Proportion of victuals for 4,000 men for 28 days, 24 October 1683':

> 112,000 lb of biscuit or bread; 3,654 gallons of beverage [this must be wine as beer is crossed out in the return. the quantity given would equate to ¼ pint per man per day; it is unclear from such documents how much beer was in store, and how it was accounted for]; 16,000 (4 lb) pieces of beef; 16,000 (2 lb) pieces of pork; 500 bushels of peas; 6,000 pieces of fish; 6,000 lb of butter; 12,000 lb of cheese.

'Provisions remaining in store, 29 October 1683':

> 184,145 lb of bread; 716 bushels of peas; 487 bushels of oatmeal; 2,260 lb of butter; 1,690 lb of cheese.

'The provisions in store will serve 2,600 men, cost excepted, money for beef and pork, and peas in lieu of oatmeal':

> bread, 9 weeks; peas, 2 weeks; oatmeal, 2 weeks; butter, 2 weeks; cheese, 11 weeks.

'That the first week the men had money given them instead of their beef and pork; the second week they had 48 head of cattle, which was bought off the Moors, and fish cooked in substitution for flesh; the third was given herrings, butter and cheese, bought off a ship; and the last, pilchards bought also out of victual, and given for of flesh'.[19]

One soldier's allowance for different types of provision for victualling Tangier, and to be deducted from his pay, was set on 29 October 1683 at:

> bread, @2d. per lb; beef, @1s. per 4 lb piece; pork, @6d. per 2 lb piece; peas, @6s. 08d. per bushel; oatmeal, @6s. 08d. per bushel; butter, @5d. per lb; cheese, @4d. per lb.

'One man's allowance for one week in money':

> bread, 1s. 02d.; beef and pork, 9d.; cheese, 2d.; butter, 2d.; oatmeal and peas, 10½d.; total, 1½d.

'One man's allowance for one week in provisions':

> 7 lb of bread or biscuit; 2½ lb of beef; 1 lb of pork; 4 pints of peas; 3 pints of oatmeal; 6 ounces of butter; 8 ounces of cheese.[20]

Allowance for one week's expense to each soldier in lieu of flesh, 8 November 1683:[21]

> 5 herrings each, at 16 barrels @ 8d. per herring £28 16 00d.; 1 lb of butter to each, @ 4d. per lb £43 4s. 00d.; ½ lb of cheese, @ 4d. per lb £21 12s. 00d.; total £93 12s. 00d.
>
> If no herring, then 1¼ lb of butter each more, and 1 lb of cheese:
>
> 1¼ lb of butter to each, @ 4d. per lb £54 00s. 00d.; 1 lb of cheese, @ 4d. per lb; total £97 04s. 00d.

'Notes upon the victualling of the garrison and fleet at Tangier, 29 September 1683':

> The victuallers of his Majesty's garrison are obliged by their contract to have a standing magazine always in store there of 8 months' victuals for 2,000 men. My Lord was told at his going away from England, that he would find [blank] weeks' victuals actually in store there, for the whole garrison, instead whereupon at his arrival on the 14 September 1683 he found only (as by the survey of the 29th appears) 11 week's bread; 3 weeks of flesh, peas and oatmeal; 4 of butter; and 12 of cheese for 3,500 men, which was then the muster of the garrison. From the said 29 September to 20 October the 3 week's flesh was expended, and the garrison fell under a want of victuals, and had it not been for the extraordinary and chargeable

19 Composite list from SRO, D742/0/3/25; SRO, D742/0/3/28; D742/0/3/30; D742/0/3/33.
20 SRO, D742/0/3/35.
21 SRO, D742/0/3/52.

> methods his Lordship was forced to take to get the fish [and] cattle from the Moors, and otherwise, must have suffered very much, for no supply arrived from England till 26 November, so there was near 40 days in which the whole garrison had not 1 ounce of flesh in it.
>
> The navy stores at my Lord's [Dartmouth's] arrival had not 7 day's victuals for 4,000 men, while at the same time the *Sapphire*, *Dragon* and other ships were then calling for supplies, having none on board, all which what other ships as they came down in convoys, were supplied by the extraordinary provisioning my Lord made in Spain and otherwise for them, for it was till 25 December before any recruiter for the navy came, so that for near 3 months, those ships that were immediately upon the station, and such others as should and did come to Tangier, from the westward and down the Straits to expect supplies, could have none thence, much less any of those who were of my Lord's own fleet, and came with, or followed him.

By the victualler's paper, which he says was delivered in July 1683, about the state of the garrison's stores, there should have been in store on 29 September:

> bread or biscuit, 15 weeks; beef, 8 weeks; pork, 11 weeks; peas, 11 weeks; oatmeal, 9 weeks; butter, 7 weeks; cheese, 27 weeks.

But there was found by the survey only:

> bread, 11 weeks; beef, 3 weeks; pork, 3 weeks; peas, 3 weeks; oatmeal, 3 weeks; butter, 4 weeks; cheese, 212 weeks.

So that by their own account, this falls short:

> bread, 3 weeks; beef, 5 weeks; pork, 8 weeks; peas, 10 weeks; oatmeal, 6 weeks; butter, 3 weeks; cheese, 15 weeks.[22]

On 30 November 1683, a survey of the food remaining in the Tangier garrison stores was undertaken and, when the results were compared with a list from London setting out the Admiralty Board's estimate of the remaining food stocks, considerable discrepancies were discovered in some items:

London estimates:

> beef, 7 weeks' worth; biscuit, 15 weeks; butter, 10 weeks; cheese, 13 weeks; oatmeal, 10 weeks; peas, 12 weeks; pork, 11 weeks.

Present in Tangier:

> beef, 3 weeks' worth; biscuit, 11 weeks; butter, 4 weeks; cheese, 12 weeks;

22 SRO, D742/0/3/54.

oatmeal, 10 weeks; peas, 11 weeks; pork, 11 weeks.[23]

These findings meant that in late 1683 the Tangier garrison was deficient of the equivalent of between one- and three-months' store of provisions, and, although the victualler's agent accounted for the discrepancies by claiming that the calculations made in England failed to identify provisions lent to the navy and others supplied for the for the use of the sick at the hospital, waste had been a considerable factor due to the climate and poor storage facilities.

Memorandum of Captain William Matthews to the Tangier Commissioners [mid 1679]

Several matters relating to the garrison, recommended by the solicitation of Captain Matthews.

Take care that no cloth be sent on account of either of the regiments or the troops of Horse but by their own agents, and that the said agents may send cloth, linen, buttons, silk and not coats made, that it may be left to every captain to fit his own cloth, that they may send no hats but an over-surplus of cloth for caps.

To solicit one company of grenadiers to each regiment, to consist of 100 soldiers each, one captain, two lieutenants, four sergeants, four corporals, and two drums. The captain of the company belonging to the Old [Tangier] Regiment to be Captain Matthews, and his lieutenants, Lieutenant Belling, Lieutenant Mahone; the officers to that belonging to Colonel Trelawny's Regiment to be Captain Trelawny, Lieutenant Davis and Lieutenant Carrol, all now upon the place. If this cannot be procured, such is the necessity of grenadiers, that rather than to want them, it may be then proposed that six men may be deducted out of each of the several companies of each regiment, reducing them to 50 soldiers in a company, and by these means make up the desired number of grenadiers, which will be of no additional expense to his Majesty besides that of the officers.

To press that some provision be made for supernumeraries and maimed men, and that there may be an order to send them home.

To know in what manner they intend to recruit us if one of the battalion of Guards and Dumbarton's Regiment which is certainly, most for his Majesty's service that orders be sent sergeants may be chosen, as well as private soldiers and that, the choice of them be committed to the governor, since if it be left to their officer, they will part with their unserviceable men only, and when the King thinks he has a good garrison, it will prove that they are so many eaters.

To procure out of the Guards in England as many soldiers as are willing to come over to be sergeants for you know the want we have of them here, and this must be pressed hard to the king, duke, etc.

To have a good drum-major, and as many drum beaters as can be procured sent over with them.

23 TNA, CO 279/32, fol. 364.

To press Colonel Legge for all manner of stores, especially those here mentioned, and that they may be sent with expedition.

To wait upon my Lord Hyde, Lord Halifax, Secretary Jenkins, etc., to confirm them in their good dispositions to the garrison, acquainting them, how unlucky it is, that the Moors shall maintain the peace with us, if they should happen to see the place neglected at home, and letting them know severally that we depend on each of them as our particular patrons.

To join our best endeavours with my brother and those that may be most instrumental for the removal of Mr Creed [John Creed, appointed secretary to the Commissioner of Tangier in 1662; friend of Pepys], and settling Mr Mountstevens in his place, this matter is so essential to the good of the garrison that it will be necessary all industry be used, and all proper engines set on work to affect the same.

To deliver our report upon the orders of the Lords of the Committee, about the examination of the Articles against Mr Mayor, Mr Recorder and their lordships at their first sitting with their own hands, and to desire it then opened, or else to make use of Mr Mountstevens' or my brother's directions for the delivery of it, as it may not pass through the hands of Mr Creed. Because it may sound harsh to the ears of the Committee, to make provision at home for our supernumeraries and maimed men, you may propose as an expedient that they me put into the companies that are recalled in the places as such as shall be drown out of them for recruits, and so be continued on the king's pay, until some other means may be found for their relief.

To procure a company for Adjutant Rock in Colonel Trelawny's Regiment, and another for Major Hope in the Old Regiment with leave to sell his position.

To take an opportunity of seeing Alderman Searle, making him my compliments, and commanding the goodness of the provisions herewith he furnishes the garrison, and if there be an occasion to acquaint the Lords of the Committee, how much satisfied you are here, with supplies he sends us, using the best arrangements, to prevail with them to continue with him in his service against any proposals that may be made of furnishing us of Irish provisions.

To acquaint the Lords, you shall wait upon particularly those of the Committee, that you was present at the review I made of the supernumerary men, and that we found 150 in the Old Regiment, 20 in Colonel Trelawny's and 50 in the Hospital, which will never be serviceable, and that we may very well change 150 more to make a good garrison.[24]

Memorandum of the Governor of Tangier to the Tangier Commissioners in London, 24 April 1683

Memorial for the Right honourable the Lords of the Committee for the Affairs of Tangier, humbly presented by command of the Governor thereof, by the agent for that garrison.

24 SRO, D742/0/4/25.

That your Lordships will please give directions for the clothing [of] the regiment commanded by Colonel Trelawny, according to the paper sometime delivered to, and now lying before your Lordships, it being about two years and a half since the last clothing [of] the said regiment, and the soldiers suffer great inconvenience in their health for want of clothes to cover them.

That your Lordships will please to give orders, that in the clothes sending over for the Horse, no cloaks may be sent, there being many spare ones in the hands of each captain, besides that the troopers are possessed of cloaks, the heat of the place making it seldom necessary to use them, so as one cloak does very well some four or five yards.

That it may please your Lordships also to direct a present supply of coal, the soldiers being reduced to great extremities, and the necessity of changing their meat, peas, etc., for bread or cheese, from the want of fuel to dress it. That whereas the great drought in Spain has made corn very scarce and excessive dear, if at all to be had, and there being not 20 days provisions of barley in the garrison for the Horse, your Lordships will think it fit to send a ship's load of barley hither, about 10,000 bushels being the quantity at the nearest estimate, to serve 128 Horse for one whole year, according as the governor has observed to your Lordships in his last letter. The governor of the said garrison prays your Lordships to consider of and give your directions to him about the disposal of Pole Fort, the timber of which is greatly decayed, and parts of it daily tumble down. And if it be your Lordships' pleasure it should be kept up and preserved, you will please to think of sending timber and other materials fit for doing it, otherwise that the governor may be directed rather then to take it down, and bring it in, than suffer it, as it now does, to fall in the sight of the Moors.

The said governor also prays your Lordships leave to remind you, of what he has some time since several times wrote, about Purbeck stone, for the building a fort, as the best and cheapest way of having a defence, if it be your pleasure any of that kind be made of that kind there. The miserable condition of the said garrison is also humbly laid before your Lordships, from the want of money, their arrears being now more than 20 months, and the inhabitants as well as the poor soldiers labour under the greatest difficulties and hardships there from several of the former having lately refused to trust the soldiers, and many of them every day running away to the Moors with complaints of this hardship. The whole stock of the merchants and townsmen being now exhausted, the one not being able to furnish us with commodities now the other to trust us further, the pitiful condition of the soldiers between these extremities, daily increases and becomes unstoppable without your Lordships' favourable regard, which the government and whole garrison in all humble manner earnestly commends to your Lordships.

By command of the Governor of his Majesty's garrison of Tangier

Samuel Atkins[25]

25 SRO, D742/0/3/16.

3

Vacant Possession: the Arrival of the English, 1662

Once the marriage treaty between England and Portugal had been signed on 23 June 1661, Charles II lost no time in claiming his prize. In August Sir Richard Fanshaw, a royalist officer during the Civil Wars, was dispatched to the Portuguese capital as envoy extraordinary to King Afonso VI to oversee the ratification of the agreement and the carrying out of its terms. By 24 September a naval squadron under the command of Admiral Edward Montagu, 1st Earl of Sandwich had been dispatched – via Lisbon – to secure Tangier until the arrival of a garrison, and a governor had been appointed.[1] Born at Barnwell, Northamptonshire in 1625, Montague raised a regiment of foot in the Parliamentarian Eastern Association, which morphed into the New Model Army in 1645. He served Oliver Cromwell loyally but played a large part in the Restoration of Charles II in 1660. Edward was created Earl of Sandwich and Admiral of the Narrow Seas, and in 1661 was appointed Ambassador Extraordinary to Portugal. He favoured the Portuguese marriage and later served as England's Ambassador to Spain. Montague was killed at the Battle of Solebay in 1672 and buried in Westminster Abbey.

Arriving in the Bay of Tangier on 10 October Sandwich was accompanied by 200 tons of stores and transports for the evacuation of the Portuguese garrison.[2] The admiral remained there for three months, while awaiting the additional fleet from England, bringing the new governor and troops. On 7 November 1661 Sandwich informed Fanshaw, 'this is only that no ship should come from hence but that you should have some advice of our station. I continue riding here for the same ends as before, but as yet we have not discovered over here any news of the fleet from England'.[3]

1 HMC, *Heathcote*, p. 22. Sandwich to Fanshaw, 22 September 1661, stating that his ships would be 'ready to sail on Tuesday next'. See also Corbett, *England in the Mediterranean*, II, pp. 306–7; Routh, *Tangier*, p. 9.

2 HMC, *Fifteenth Report, App. II*, pp. 160–1. John Creed to Pepys, 14 October 1661; R. C. Anderson (ed.), *The Journal of Edward Montague, First Earl of Sandwich Admiral and General at Sea 1659–1665* (London: Publications of the Navy Records Society, 1929), p. 112.

3 HMC, *Heathcote*, p. 22. Sandwich to Fanshaw, 7 November 1661.

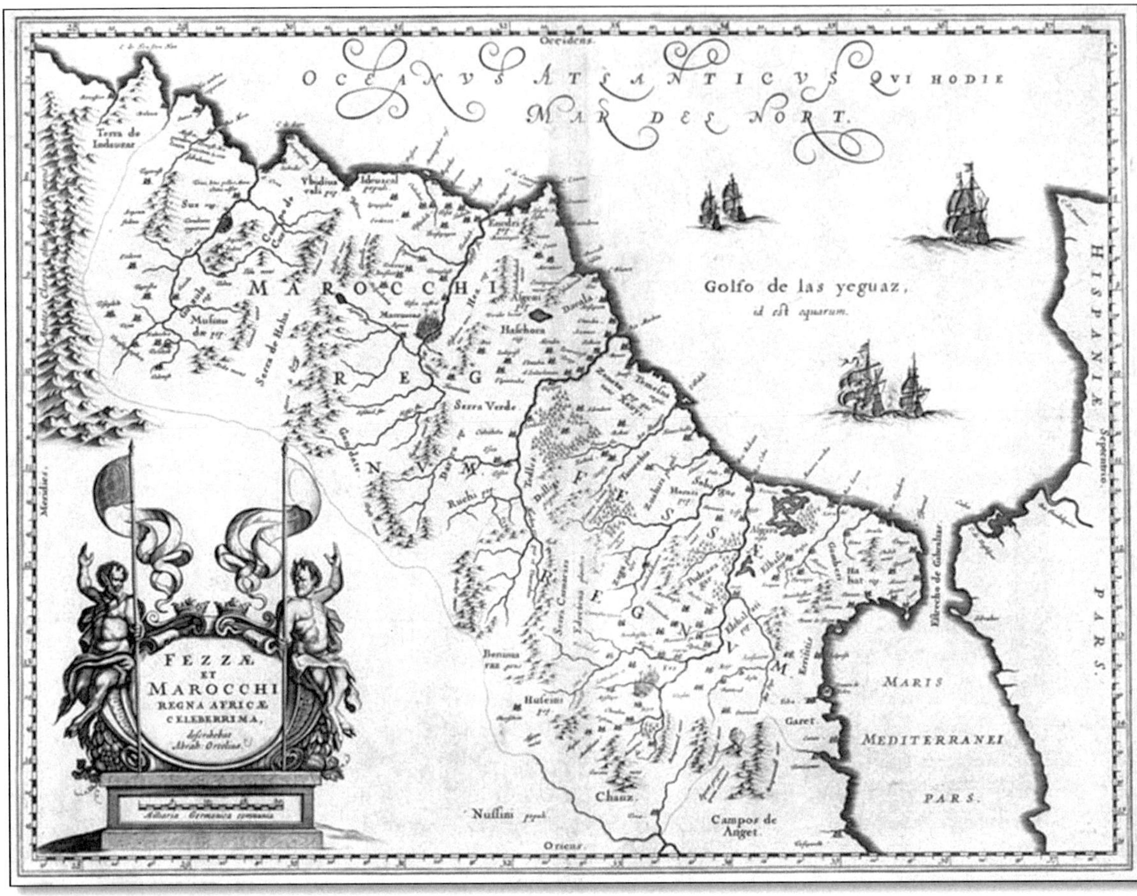

Abraham Ortelius, *Fezzae et Marocchi Regna Celeberrima* (1635). (Creative Commons Public Domain)

Even before the transferral of Tangier from Portuguese to English sovereignty, the Spanish government opposed Charles II's marriage alliance and tried to hinder the formation of an English colony. The possibility of provoking a war with Spain by providing military assistance to Portugal was a serious consideration, thus, Sandwich's immediate concern was the intervention of Spanish (as well as Dutch shipping) in the Strait of Gibraltar.[4] On 17 February 1662 Henry Rumbold, English consul at Cadiz, informed him that he had 'obtained a mandate from the King of Spain, forbidding Don Diego Vanegas from interfering either with myself or with other English subjects at Port St Mary, but it has had little effect. The English have had to protest against restrictions laid on their goods'.[5]

The advent of Vice-Admiral John Lawson in Tangier a few months later revealed the importance of the situation and the seriousness with which the English government treated such threats. During the years 1665 to 1667 Dutch warships imposed a severe embargo on Tangier, obstructing the existing transportation of provisions from English ports, and intercepted Spanish

4 R. A. Stradling, 'Spanish Conspiracy in England, 1661–1663', *EHR*, 87 (1972), pp. 269–86 (p. 271); Clyde L. Grose, 'The Anglo-Portuguese Marriage of 1662', *HAHR*, 10 (1930), pp. 313–52.

5 Bod. Lib., MS Carte 75, fol. 17. Rumbold to Sandwich, 17 February 1662.

Edward Montagu, 1st Earl of Sandwich (1625–1672). (Courtesy of the Royal Academy of Arts, London)

merchant ships which broke the ban on trade with Tangier.[6] When Admiral Sandwich arrived off Tangier in October 1661 his immediate task was to prepare for the arrival of the English garrison by reconnoitring a beachhead for the landing of troops and stores. He also opened communications with Abū'l-'Abbās Ahmad al-Khadir Ghaïlān, who had recently arrived on the Moroccan political scene after achieving a crushing military defeat over the zawiya of Dilā'. Ghaïlān belonged to a line of holy warriors (*mujāhidūn*), who fought to rid the coasts of the Maghrib of Christian occupation. However, 'the activities of these defenders of the faith often took on a political dimension in situations of crisis such as that in which Morocco was embroiled'.[7] Ghaïlān enhanced his reputation by waging war against the former Portuguese garrison of Tangier and was able to rally numerous supporters under his banner.

Sandwich and he had met before, in 1657, when watering the fleet during the Englishman's voyage with General-at-Sea Robert Blake in the Mediterranean. Four years later Sandwich was instructed to conclude peace treaties with the governments of the Barbary States – Algiers, Tunis and Tripoli – on such terms as prevented the search of English shipping or the confiscation of cargoes and enslavement of crews, under the pretext that on board they bore goods which belonged to enemy states. Sandwich was further directed to bombard these ports and seize hostile vessels if such conditions were not accepted.[8]

To all appearances Ghaïlān was not rigidly hostile towards Admiral Sandwich upon his arrival off Tangier, and he furnished a certain amount of forage and fresh meat for the English sailors. On 13 November 1661 Sandwich wrote in his journal:

> Some sixteen or eighteen Moors (one of them being the Governor under Gayland of this Province) came to the old Watch Tower to the east of old Tangier, and made a fire and sign to speak with us. Whereupon two boats were sent manned with musketeers, who had conference with them, and were very civilly treated, the

6 R. Davis, 'England in the Mediterranean, 1570–1670', F. J. Fisher (ed.), *Essays in the economic and social history of Tudor and Stuart England, in Honour of R. H. Tawney* (Cambridge: Cambridge University Press, 1961), pp. 117–37.

7 B. A. Mojuetan, 'Legitimacy in a Power State: Moroccan Politics in the Seventeenth Century', *IJMES*, 13 (1981), pp. 347–57 (p. 352). See also Mohamed Hajji, *Al-Zawiyah al-Dilaiyah wa-dawruha al-dini wa-al-ilmi wa-siyasi* (Rabat: Matbat An-Najjah Al-Jadida, 1988), pp. 217–8.

8 Sir Godfrey Fisher, *Barbary Legend: War, Trade, and Piracy in North Africa, 1415–1830* (Oxford: Oxford University Press, 1957), pp. 230–1.

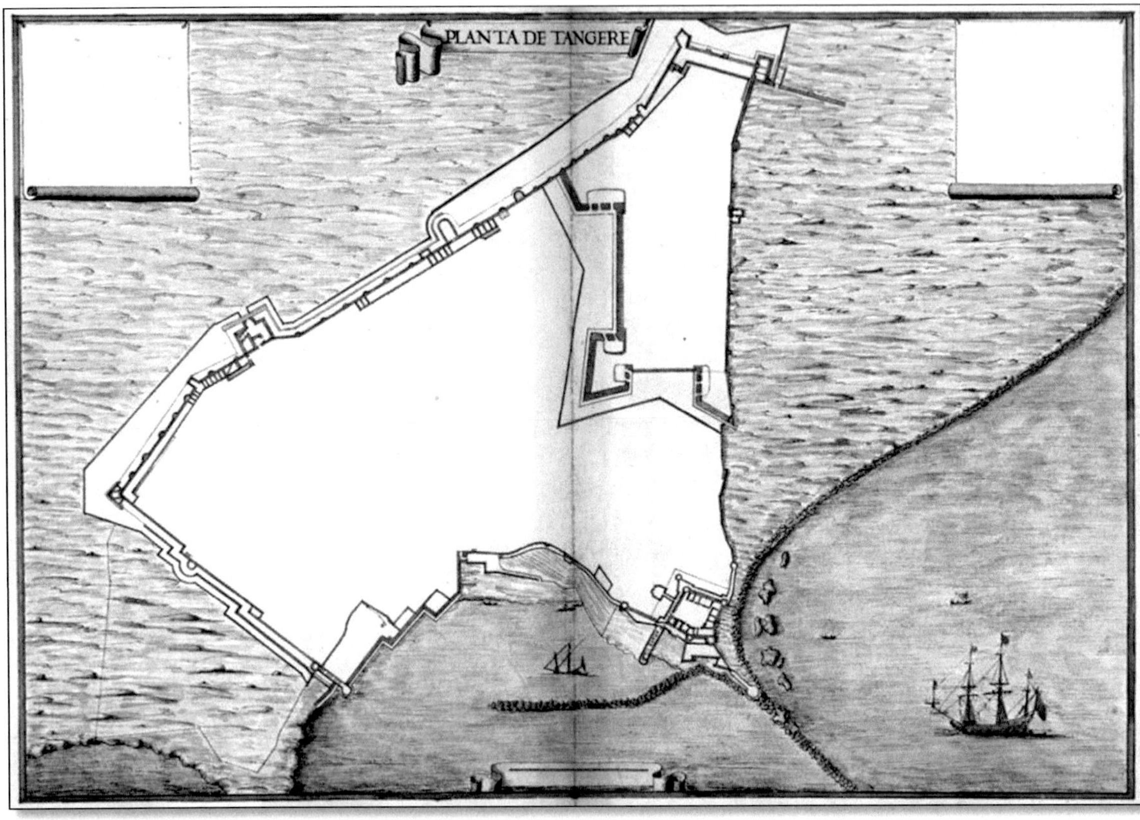

Leonardo de Farrari, *Planta de Tanger* (*c.* 1655), showing the extent of the Portuguese defences. (Creative Commons Public Domain).

> Moors expressing a desire to have trade and commerce with us, but could not do it without leave first from Gayland, to whom they said they would send for licence.[9]

Following an approach from a local tribal chief 'expressing a desire to have trade and commerce with us', Sandwich conversed freely with Ghaïlān, the admiral commenting on the respectful treatment of his men by the Moroccans, and even entertaining their leader's chief negotiator aboard his flagship for several nights.[10] Between 14 January and 18 February (the latter being the date when Sandwich sailed for Lisbon) he obtained details of the city of Tangier and its fortifications, and most importantly, identified a location for the construction of a breakwater or 'Mole', for the protection to shipping. The Swedish mercenary, Major Martin Beckman, was employed by the English Crown as military engineer and hydrographer. He was with Sandwich's fleet at Algiers and Tangier, and produced the plan later seen and esteemed by Samuel Pepys. Between 1662 and 1679 Pepys served on the Committee for Tangier, and as Treasurer from 1665. In 1683 he was a member of the mission sent by the King to dissolve the colony. Samuel possessed a

9 R. C. Anderson (ed.), *The Journal of the 1st Earl of Sandwich, 1659–1665* (Navy Records Society, 64, 1928), p. 106.

10 Lubbock (ed.), *Journal*, pp. 91–4, 96–7, 107, 109–111, 115, 119. Entries for 29 July–5 August, 25 August, 13 and 28 November, 2 and 10–13 December 1661, 19 January 1662, and 8 February 1662; Bod. Lib., MS Carte 73, fol. 633. Ghaïlān's letter to Sandwich, n.d.

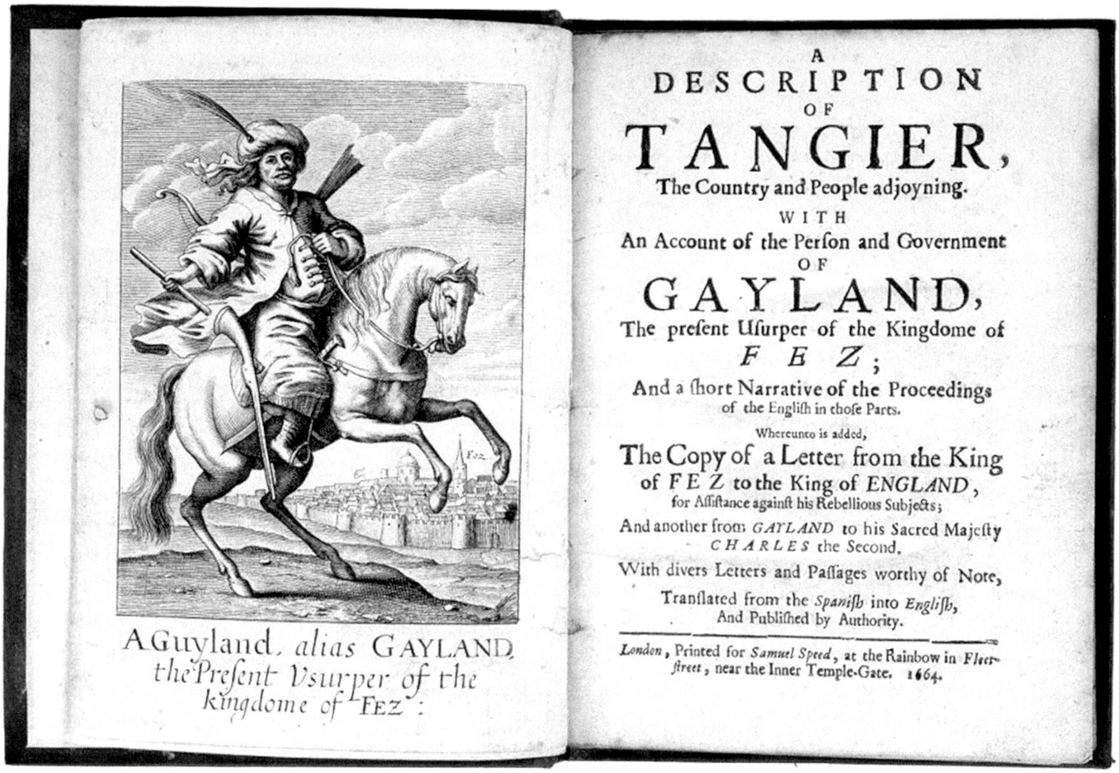

Abū'l-'Abbās Ahmad al-Khadir Ghaïlān, from *A Description of Tangier* (1664). (Creative Commons Public Domain)

keen interest in the Barbary Coast and the Levant due to his concern for the safety of English ships, and their crews both naval and mercantile. Writing to Pepys on 20 January 1662 Sandwich, his patron, told him, 'You will also receive a long box which is a map of Tangier, which you must be sure nobody opens or sees, but with your own hand deliver it to his Royal Highness'.[11]

Pepys presented to the Duke of York from Sandwich 'a fine map of Tangier, done by one Captain Martin Beckman, a Swede, that is with my lord. We stayed looking over it a great while with the duke'.[12] As Martín Elbl contends, this plan corresponds with British Library plans K.Top 117.78, catalogued under the title 'A Plan of the town of Tangier'.[13] Beckman and Sandwich appear to have had access to a now lost Portuguese plan before 29 January, with enough time for the engineer to make an enhanced copy annotated in English. This schema – Beckman's 'first masterplan' – gave the key positions of artillery batteries, the houses in the city and in the *Castel Velho* (Upper Castle), as well as one location, described as 'nice stables that my Lord Earl of Sandwich has made for our English horses that is daily expected hither'. This may refer to the Tangier Horse which came under the command of Peterborough, the English colony's

11 HMC, *Fifteenth Report, App. II*, p. 157.
12 Pepys, *Diary*, 28 February 1662.
13 M. M. Elbl, *Portuguese Tangier (1471–1662): Colonial Urban Fabric as Cross-Cultural Skeleton* (Peterborough, Ontario: Baywolf Press, 2013), pp. 105–8.

Ferdinando de Meneses, Conde Ericeira (1614–1699). (Creative Commons Public Domain)

first governor.[14] Beckman probably rendered such plans covertly, and could have gone ashore posing as a servant with the first naval parties, and 'having a compass under his cloak as a Spaniard', as he had done at Ceuta, Tétuan and most significantly the Spanish port of Cadiz. Beckman was appointed military engineer for Tangier on 26 August 1662. He possessed much knowledge of the fortifications and garrison, and assisted in the design, construction, and repair of the outlying redoubts.

On 12 January, with the English navy at anchor, the Portuguese governor, Fernando de Menezes, Count of Ericeira, marched out of *Castelo Novo* with his main force, leaving behind 140 mounted soldiers – the city's entire contingent of Horse. These troops undertook a foraging expedition deep into the hostile countryside beyond the network of trenches and forts, which divided the Portuguese from the Moors. But these were attacked and scattered by Ghaïlān's vigilant soldiers, who drove the survivors back the safety of Tangier's walls. Menezes hastily requested Sandwich to land 400 seamen to protect the city until the arrival of the English soldiers.[15] The admiral's journal contains an informative account of the incident:

> This morning, the Portuguese, 140 horse in Tangier made a sally into the country for booty, whereof they had possessed about 400 cattle, 30 camels and some horses, and 35 women and girls, and being 6 miles distant from Tangier were intercepted by 100 Moors with harquebuses, who in the first charge killed the Aidill [military commander] with a shot in the head, whereupon the rest of the Portuguese ran, and in the pursuit 51 were slain, whereof were 11 of the knights beside the Aidill. The horses of the 51 were also taken by the Moors and all the booty relieved.[16]

Whether this debacle was a miscalculation by Menezes or a deception so that he might be allowed to deliver up the place without opposition is unclear, but it had the desired effect. Pepys reported, 'Now the Spaniards'

14 Paul E. Beckmann, 'Martin Beckman and the English Occupation of Tangier 1662–1684. Part 1', *Fort Magazine*, 41 (2013), pp. 146–56 (p. 147).

15 Greenwich, National Maritime Museum, JOD/4 (Journal of Edward Barlow, 1659–1703); Basil Lubbock (ed.), *Barlow's Journal of His Life at Sea in King's Ships, East and West Indiamen and other Merchantmen from 1659 to 1703*, 2 vols (London: Hurst & Blackett, 1934), I, p. 70.

16 Anderson (ed.), *Journal of Edward Montague*, pp. 114–5.

designs of hindering our getting the place are frustrated'.[17] Sandwich, taking *de facto* possession of Tangier, ordered naval parties, armed with muskets, bandoliers, halfpikes and swords, ashore under the command of Vice Admiral Sir Richard Stayner, to man the fortifications. About 4:00 p.m. on 16 January the first party of some 80 men took possession of the Castle (later renamed York Castle after the Duke of York), while another 120 seamen and some officers directly under Stayner occupied the city. The next day provided the first possible opportunity to observe the fortifications in daylight. A further party of 100 men disembarked a week later. Occasionally, when they observed Moors in the fields, they fired a volley or two of musket shot, 'to put them in fear and let them know that the town was well manned'. By 23 January the admiral was able to note the presence of 'between 300 and 400 men in the city and castles, and the command of all the strengths and magazines'.[18] The significance of this was not lost on Routh, who asserted:

> This move was a masterstroke of diplomacy and good fortune, for, though Queen Luisa of Portugal was glad enough to be honourably rid of a possession which was too costly to be maintained by her hard-pressed treasury, some of her subjects inn Tangier bitterly resented the cession to English heretics of this, almost the last remnant of their country's once considerable dominions in Morocco, which she had held for nearly 200 years. Had they had the power they would have resisted the incoming of the English, as their compatriots did in Bombay.[19]

The main fleet of 27 ships under Henry Mordaunt, 2nd earl of Peterborough, arrived in Tangier Bay during the foggy morning of 29 January 1662. Prior to embarkation Charles II had written to him, 'I desire to let those honest men know who are along with you, that they shall always be in my particular care and protection as persons that venture themselves in my service'.[20] Peterborough's commissions as Colonel of a regiment of foot and Captain of a troops of horse, both specifically recruited for service in Tangier, had been issued on 6 September 1661.[21] He marched into the citadel at the head of his regiment on 30 January 1662 and took formal possession of the colony in the name of Charles II of England.[22] The author of *A Description of Tangier* claimed, 'the Portuguese were very civil to the English, and made great expressions of their welcome', yet Fernando de Menezes was reluctant to hand over the colony, and had to be replaced by Don Luis de Almeida, who performed the transfer. Thus, Peterborough received the insignia of the

17 Pepys, *Diary*, 20 February 1662.

18 *Ibid.*, p. 116.

19 Routh, *Tangier*, p. 10.

20 BL, MS Harley 6844, fol. 95. Charles II to Peterborough, 21 December 1661; Richard Cannon, *Historical Record of the First, or the Royal Regiment of Dragoons* (London: Longman, Orme & Co., 1840), p. 3.

21 BL, MS Harley 1595, fols 1–9. Warrant of Charles II for the following commission to Henry Mordaunt, Earl of Peterborough, 6 September 1661.

22 TNA, CO 279/1, fols 29, 98; BL, MS Harley 1595, fols 10–14; MS Sloane 1956, fols 68–9. Commission of Charles II constituting the said Henry Mordaunt, Earl of Portsmouth, Governor of Tangier and Captain-General of his forces there, and in those parts, 6 September 1661.

governor's office, and the keys of the city, with a horse, saddle and bridle, silver spurs, a scimitar and a lance.[23]

The importance of the office of the governor, as the direct representative of royal authority and foreign policy in the region, was key to the whole enterprise. Writing in the 1670s the engineer, Sir Hugh Cholmeley recommended:

> The greatest good or evil that can happen to Tangier will constantly depend upon the choice and qualifications of the governor that is sent, who ought to be a man of honour and known generosity, such as may render him above either open exactions or underhand contrivance to enrich himself, by ways and means that will always be set afoot by men either desiring to share in the booty, or to ingratiate themselves with the governor, which sorts of profit will be one way or other to the public prejudice of the place. And that the governor have less temptation in this kind, it would be very convenient his salary was made sufficient for the honourable and expensive post he has; and that, in the same cause, the pay both to the officer and the soldier might be such, and so regular, as to answer the exigences of the place, and their reasonable occasions; and then that they be held to a strict and severe discipline, so that they may do violence to no man, and learn to be content with their wages.[24]

With the newly appointed Governor and Captain-General of all the forces in Tangier went with a sizeable garrison to occupy the colony. The Earl of Peterborough's Regiment of Foot was raised from among the disbanded officers and men of the Cromwellian army. It mustered on Putney Heath on 14 October 1661. Another regiment, that commanded by Colonel Robert Harley, travelled from Flanders to Tangier, as did two smaller regiments under Colonel John Fitzgerald and Colonel Lewis Farrell. A single troop of Horse, commanded by Peterborough, accompanied them with a train of artillery and the requisite staff officers. Harley's Regiment, previously commanded by Colonel Henry Lillingstone, had been raised for service in Flanders in 1657. The regiment participated in the siege of Dunkirk in May 1658, while during the Battle of the Dunes against the Spanish cavalry, with Lockhart's soldiers 'had the hardest pull where there are thirty or forty killed'.[25] After the surrender of Dunkirk, Lillingstone's was one of the four regiments of Cromwellian foot that undertook that field service with the Viscount of Turenne's army during the rest of the campaign. It is doubtful if any of the regiment's officers who survived Parliament's revision of August 1659 went to Tangier, however.[26]

---

23 *A Description of Tangier, The Country and People Adjoyning* (1664), p. 15; TNA, CO 279/33, fol. 136.

24 Sir Hugh Cholmeley, *An Account of Tangier with some Account of Himself and his Journey through France and Spain to that Place, where he was engaged in building the Mole in the Time of King Charles the Second; and a Journal of the Work carrying on* (London: 1787), p. 96.

25 *Clarke Papers*, III, p. 154.

26 *CSPD 1659–60*, p. 152.

Wenceslaus Hollar, *The Southeast corner of Tangier* (c. 1669). (New York, Metropolitan Museum, Creative Commons Public Domain)

In April 1661 Lillingstone's Regiment was still at Dunkirk, but was now under the command of Colonel Robert Harley, a former New Model Army officer, Colonel of a regiment of horse and 'a person whose abilities are not unknown as a member of Parliament, or of the army'.[27] The Lieutenant-Colonel who was given command of the unit (Harley did not go to Tangier) was Maurice Kingwell. He had held the same rank in Colonel Alsop's Regiment in the Dunkirk garrison in 1659.[28] In January 1662 Harley's Regiment sailed with the Earl of Peterborough to Tangier. One newsbook enthusiastically observed, 'None did ever go to sea upon any foreign design with greater willingness and courage than that regiment of English (from Dunkirk) so that in this one regiment there are 1,244 veteran soldiers besides officers'.[29] Following its arrival in Tangier the new governor, Peterborough, wrote to Sir Robert Harley, 'You have here come under my inspection, a regiment of the most estimable I have known, and that is governed by sober, able and discreet officers'. However, Kingswell delivered a bad report to his colonel about the condition of the regiment, and his wife later scolded Harley for 'the wretched neglect' of it.[30] The regiment bore the brunt of the fighting during the following year – it mustered 947 men in February 1662, and was reduced to 559 by the following October when it was incorporated into the Tangier Regiment.[31]

The regiment of foot raised by Lord Peterborough in 1661 was the first regiment after the Foot Guards to be placed on the Establishment of Charles II's army. Peterborough's original orders were to raise a regiment of 1,500 men, however, the first Establishment, dated 10 October 1661 was for 44 commissioned officers, 60 non-commissioned officers, 24 drummers and 1,000 soldiers.[32] Known as 'Lord Peterborough's' or the 'Governor's' Regiment', the unit was formed into 10 companies. Succeeding governors of Tangier were appointed to its command, as a matter of course, and the regiment was known by the name of its colonel until 1680, when, after the death of Colonel Sir Palmes Fairborne, it was commonly termed the 'Old Regiment' or 'First Tangier Regiment'. The initial Establishment of the garrison was 171 officers, 165 non-commissioned officers, 61 musicians, and 2,800 soldiers, in addition to 32 officers and gunners of the train of artillery, bringing the total to 3,239.[33] The first muster held at Tangier on 30 January 1662 recorded 2,723 foot, with 98 in the English troop of horse and 80 in the Portuguese besides officers. Of the foot regiments, Peterborough's fielded 1,000; Colonel Harley's 947; Colonel Fitzgerald's 395; Colonel Farrell's 381. By the muster of

27 HMC, *Fifteenth Report, App. III*, pp. 224–7, 250; *Mercurius Publicus*, 19–26 July 1660.

28 Dalton, *Army Lists*, I, p. 9.

29 *Mercurius Publicus*, 9 December 1661.

30 HMC, *Fourteenth Report, App. II*, pp. 258–61.

31 Davis, *History*, I, pp. 27, 31, 33, 41, 49.

32 TNA, CO 279/1, fol. 36. Order to Sir George Carteret, Treasurer of the Navy, to pay Lord Peterborough £3,800 for his own payment, and for raising 100 horse and 1,500 foot, 13 September 1661; BL, MS Harley 1595, fols 1–9; TNA, WO24/1, fols 1–7.

33 TNA, WO 24/1, fols 1–7.

23 October 1662, the infantry numbers were somewhat diminished to 793 in the Governor's; 559 in Harley's; 395 in Fitzgerald's; and 371 in Farrell's.[34]

In December 1661, the Navy Commissioners had reckoned for 3,500 men's victuals for 6 months and the cost of transportation from England at £21,940, with an additional £6,125 for beer. On 16 December a warrant for the payment of £10,351 14s. was also issued for the charge of conveying soldiers and provisions, although it is difficult to know whether this was as part of the overall sum or a separate amount.[35] The total number of soldiers was estimated by one contemporary at just over 2,700, with almost 100 mounted troops – accompanied by the families of 200–300 of the soldiers.[36] Moreover, Sir William Morrice, Lord Treasurer, recorded on 29 March 1662, 'We have taken possession of Tangier in Barbary, where we have carried 3,000 men under the conduct of the earl of Peterborough'.[37] At the time, this was the largest garrison outside the British Isles prior to the acquisition of Gibraltar and Minorca during the War of the Spanish Succession (1701–14), and represented 30 per cent of Charles II's standing army. This was also the first time that the wives of non-commissioned officers and private sentinels were permitted, officially, to accompany an English army on an overseas posting. These wives and families were accounted for later in regimental muster rolls.[38]

The Portuguese Horse was added to the Establishment of the English garrison at an annual cost of £4,778 9s. 2d. Mustering in Tangier on 10 February 1662, it consisted of four officers, three corporals, two trumpeters, a surgeon, a gunsmith and 80 troopers.[39] However, after three months, when the Portuguese soldiers refused to remain in English service the unit was discontinued, and left Tangier. Their horses were confiscated by Peterborough, who mounted some of his infantrymen and others on them to form a second troop.[40] Although Thomas Povey, Treasurer for Tangier garrison, asserted in a petition to the Privy Council that 92 Portuguese officers and men were taken into Charles II's service, these soldiers no longer formed part of the garrison after 1662.[41] Within a few days of his arrival in Tangier, Peterborough pledged, as governor, that the colony would remain free from military 'intermeddling' and extended hospitality to 'such as come hither to trade or traffic', to safeguard 'the good and wholesome laws by this nation already established'.[42] Such assurances heightened the reputation of Tangier across the wider reaches of the King's territories, and attracted a stream of settlers from the American colonies and the Caribbean.

34 TNA, CO 279/1, fol. 56.

35 TNA, SP44/3, fol. 71; BL, MS Harley 6844, fols 75–6.

36 Lubbock (ed.), *Journal*, I, p. 117.

37 HMC, *Finch*, I, pp. 188–9.

38 SRO, D742/O/7/1–28.

39 TNA, SP71/13, fol. 100; CO 279/33, fol. 134; WO 24/1, fols 4–5.

40 TNA, CO 279/33, fols 134–5; BL, MS Harley 6844, fol. 113.

41 TNA, CO 279/1, fol. 106; SP44/1, fol. 428; SP44/2, fol. 573.

42 Bod. Lib., MS Rawlinson D491, fol. 2. Peterborough to all his Majesty's subjects in the aforesaid dominions, 5 February 1662; same to the subjects of Tangier, 22 February 1662.

Wenceslaus Hollar, *Prospect of the North Side of Tangier regarding the main sea from the hill as you come from Whitby or the West, toward the town* (c. 1669).
(Rijksmuseum, Creative Commons Public Domain)

Tangier's first mayor, John Bland, was a native of Virginia and easily the most prosperous merchant in the Mediterranean colony.

The Portuguese inhabitants of the city were hardly pleased by the presence of a new garrison, whom they saw as Protestant heretics – although a large proportion of the troops were Catholics. Strains between the two communities were intensified by claims of theft and damage caused by the soldiers, and concerns among the Portuguese about their conduct towards their wives and daughters. Despite efforts by the governor to address such issues, most of the residents volunteered for repatriation and accepted his offer of conveyance back to Portugal. According to Peterborough, they took with them everything they could carry, including 'all other materials of economic and household subsistence, to the very floors, the windows and the doors'.[43] All that remained of the Portuguese population of Tangier was a small group of settlers, six Catholic priests, and a number of Jewish families – 'a kind of retailing dealers', who in the infancy of the settlement had proven useful, given the soldiers of the garrison 'were altogether ignorant and helpless as to furnish themselves with any of those accommodations necessary to human life'.[44]

Writing in 1672 the then chief-engineer, Sir Hugh Cholmeley claimed the Portuguese:

> chose rather to quit their dwelling than to live in ways so far different from the customs of southern countries. The free conversation, which in the north is used between men and women … was intolerable in a people that make jealousy their dishonor, and therefore could not submit to those public liberties which soldiers would take with their wives and daughters, though in this, perhaps more in innocency than might be at many other times, where the scandal seemed less open and apparent.[45]

These of course were rather one-sided English accounts. Portuguese sources record that the former residents were repatriated to the Algarve region of Portugal, where the Governor of Lagos had requisitioned nearly 300 houses for them. In February and March 1662, they were transported in seven or eight English frigates to the ports of Lagos, Faro and Tavira. Many of the passengers were widows who requested conveyance by Portuguese vessels, as they feared being abused by the English sailors. A list, dated 2 May 1662, presented to King Afonso VI records that 497 couples, 1,667 single persons, 140 cavalrymen and 282 soldiers had been relocated to the Algarve.[46] The officers of the Horse were given commissions in prestigious regiments, while the rest were incorporated into the Portuguese forces.

43 TNA, CO 279/1, fol. 97. Peterborough to the Lords of the Council, 17 February 1662.

44 TNA, CO 279/1, fol. 112. Report of the Council of Officers, 12 February 1662; CO 279/33, fols 134–7, 142. A survey of Tangier and its prospects, n.d.

45 Sir Hugh Cholmeley, *An Account of Tangier with some Account of Himself and his Journey through France and Spain to that Place, where he was engaged in building the Mole in the Time of King Charles the Second; and a Journal of the Work carrying on* (London: 1787), p. 17.

46 Alberto Iria, *Cartas dos governadores do Algarve (1638–1663)* (Lisboa: Academia Portuguesa de História, 1978), pp. 464–67.

Detail of British soldiers relaxing, from *Prospect of Tangier from the Land, it being the South-West side* (*c.* 1669). (Rijksmuseum, Creative Commons Public Domain)

Situated on the northern coast of Morocco (Barbary Coast), Tangier is separated from Iberia by the Strait of Gibraltar. Critically, the anchorage required protection from the elements and the construction of a Mole, which though expensive, would be a necessary engineering project. Tangier, however, was ideal as a base for naval patrols engaged in convoy work or punitive raids against the Barbary Corsairs. In particular, the Salé Rovers preyed on smaller merchantmen and fishing vessels off the Atlantic Coast, while Algerian pirates remained a serious problem to English interests in the region. In November 1661, shortly before the arrival of the English garrison, the Moroccan governors of Tétuan had appealed to the Portuguese Captain-General at Tangier to open traffic between their port and his garrison, whilst a passport and protection for a negotiator between them was also issued, thus strongly emphasising the importance of mutual trade.[47] Cholmeley described Tangier as sitting 'in the midst of the trading world, upon an inlet into a sea that goes near three thousand miles in length, and washes the most noble and most polished countries of Europe, Asia and Africa', and yet at such a distance from England that it afforded the only port for English ships passing into the Mediterranean that was not 'precarious, and depending on the will of foreign princes'.[48] Sir Henry Sheres, who succeeded him as surveyor-general of the Mole in 1676, and a fervent advocate of the worth of the colony in the wider context of the English struggle with other European powers, and against the Corsairs, reported:

> Tangier is, as I have observed, so advantageously situated, that it surveys the greatest thoroughfare of commerce in the world; having in one view having almost the whole sea comprehended between the four capes of Trafalgar, Gibraltar, Spartel and Ceuta; those on the European, these on the African shore: so that no ship or vessel can pass in or out of the Mediterranean, unobserved from thence. It comes therefore to pass, by means of this narrow gap or inlet that men of war,

47 Bod. Lib., MS Carte 73, fols 625, 627.

48 BL, MS Lansdowne 192, fols 85–6. Hugh Cholmeley, 'Several discourses concerning the interest of Tangier', n.d.

pirates and corsairs of all nations, covet to ply and cruise in and about that station, where they are sure to speak with all ships that pass.[49]

The local climate, which would have a significant affect upon the English garrison, was described by one of its members as 'very temperate and less obnoxious to incommodious heats than either Spain or Portugal'.[50] Moreover, in 1676 Thomas Philips stated:

> The air is temperate, and cooled with the annual breeze in the summer, called Etesian Winds [strong, dry winds blowing from the north over the Mediterranean, especially from mid-May to mid-September]; and often purged from the distempers, which otherwise might rain there, from the easterly and westerly winds. By this means it happens that it is neither very hot in the summer, nor excessive cold in the winter, but temperate, and agreeable with the disposition of our human bodies.[51]

For the newly installed garrison the beginning was hardly encouraging. Near the waterside stood the fortified structure of York Castle, which was utilised as a magazine. In 1676 Thomas Philips described the Castle (slightly fancifully) as:

> situated most securely and most delightfully upon a very high hill, overlooking the town, country and harbor; fortified beside its foundation, on inaccessible rocks, by four of the most regular, high, and well-built bastions that can anywhere be seen; several excellent and inexhaustible wells within it; and is, in a word, to all appearance, a place impregnable; all the storehouses of ammunition and provision, many houses, streets and gardens contained within it, and very near the third part of as much ground as is in the whole city, being divided from it by a wall that reaches to the sea.[52]

Close to its landward gate was the spacious Parade Ground, where 2,000 foot could be drawn up in open order.[53] At the top of the steeply rising hill, behind this, stood the Upper Castle, 'situated securely and delightfully', 200 feet above sea level, and covering a considerable area. The Castle was strongly fortified with four colossal bastions, previously constructed by the Portuguese. Inside its outer walls were storehouses and gardens, whilst towards the southeast lay the Governor's House, which Lord Middleton later made 'very noble, large and commodious' at a cost of £800. The entire complex, consisting of the westward ramparts of the Upper Castle, with

---

49 Sir Henry Sheres, *A Discourse Touching Tangier in a letter to a person of quality* (London: 1680), p. 5; William Oldys and John Malham (eds.), *The Harleian Miscellany: A Collection of Scarce, Curious, and Entertaining Pamphlets and Tracts* (London, 1810), pp. 391–405.

50 TNA, CO 279/33, fols 134–7, 142–4.

51 *The Present Interest of Tangier* (London: 1679), p. 1.

52 *Present Interest*, p. 8.

53 Bod. Lib., MS Rawlinson D916, fols 67–8.

Detail of British officers, from Wenceslaus Hollar's *Part of Tangier from above, without the Watergate* (*c.* 1669). (University of Toronto, The Wenceslaus Hollar Collection, Creative Commons Public Domain)

Peterborough Tower and Gate, overlooked more open terrain (the Marshān Plain, rising to 260 feet above sea level).

The houses and other buildings of Tangier were in a reasonable condition, and the fortifications adequate – though crumbling – but the available accommodation was completely insufficient for the number of English troops. Although Governor Peterborough was unconvinced that he could secure the city with the forces at his disposal, Cholmeley attributed the situation and some of the other early problems in the city to what he believed was an excessively large garrison, which he blamed on the intriguing of the Portuguese ambassador, whom he suspected had hoped that a large body of English troops across the Strait of Gibraltar would distract the Spanish.[54] The former Portuguese garrison of Tangier, consisting mainly of a city Militia and some Horse, had been pushed back inside the walls, but given that Portugal had been hopeful of disposing of the colony in the face of war with Spain at home, and the problem of raising a substantial dowry for the marriage of Catherine of Braganza to Charles II, some level of material neglect of the city was inevitable. Those structures abandoned by the Portuguese were to be valued and purchased, although English officers with money bought pleasant houses with gardens, the bulk of the garrison did not fare so well.

54 Cholmeley, *Account of Tangier*, pp. 17–18.

Peterborough reported to Parliament, 'The place left very little better than a ruin of walls and full of spoil, scarcity and want as to all such materials and utensils as could have given assistance to English soldiers'. Even the artillery, which the Portuguese had agreed to leave behind was almost unserviceable, 'the guns being the greatest part dismounted and the rest with carriages unfit for service on any occasion'.[55]

The precariousness of the situation in which the English garrison found itself in the first few months of 1662 soon became apparent. A warrant had been issued on 10 October 1661 in the name of Charles II for £7,346 to William Legge, Lieutenant of the Ordnance Office, for arms, ammunition, and other provisions of war to be sent to Tangier. Four days later a further warrant ordered the payment of £9,007 to the Earl of Peterborough 'for providing a magazine for men and horses' in the colony.[56] Within a short space of time after their arrival in Morocco, some of the garrison's soldiers were famished, partly due to a dearth of quality foodstuffs there. Initially their diet consisted mainly of salt beef, but the harshness of the local conditions made its preparation especially difficult. As Cholmeley noted:

> Many houses were destroyed to make fire for the pot and yet the soldiers had so little care or conveniences for the dressing of their victuals that, from want of watering [soaking] their salt meats or ordering their provisions as they ought to have done, appeared the bad effects of an ill diet in the great mortality which presently followed, the noise of which sufferings the poor soldiers endured.[57]

But the men – largely English, Scots, Welsh, and Irish Catholic veterans – were hard put to it, particularly due to a shortage of cooking equipment and the most basic facilities. Orrery, writing in the 1670s from his experiences during the British Civil Wars and later service in Ireland, observed:

> Biscuit, butter, cheese, and oatmeal, if carefully looked unto, would be better relished, and keep longer than most flesh or fish salted, and are commonly in sieges better liked by the soldiery; for they carry their bread, butter and cheese with them to their guards, those being dressed to their hands without their labour to cook it, or to get fire to do it; and make them less thirsty by much, than powdered, or dried flesh, or fish. The oatmeal also boiled in their quarters, is a great refreshment to them, and very grateful, whether they be sick or well.[58]

Similarly, in April 1683 the governor made the Tangier Commissioners aware that the extremities suffered by the garrison's soldiers were exacerbated by 'the necessity of changing their meat, peas etc., for bread and cheese, from the want to fuel to dress it'.[59] Besides, as Eric Gruber von Arni puts it, 'it

55 TNA, CO 279/1, fols 90, 92. Peterborough to the Lords of the Council, 12 and 17 February 1662.

56 TNA, SP44/14, fol. 255; SP44/7, fol. 3; *CTB*, I, pp. 293–4.

57 Cholmeley, *Account of Tangier*, p. 18.

58 Roger Boyle, Earl of Orrery, *A Treatise of the Art of War dedicated to the King's Most Excellent Majesty* (1677), p. 49.

59 SRO, D742/0/3/16. Memoranda to the Tangier Commissioners, 24 April 1683.

was unsafe to venture outside the walls of the town, there were only limited supplies of fresh meat within and the little that was available was bad, and sold at highly exorbitant prices'.[60] Such privations were not uncommon among troops in foreign service. Suffering from lack of pay, Dumbarton's Regiment was accused of looting after the attack on the Medway, during the Second Anglo-Dutch War in 1667, and ordered back to France, but while awaiting transport, over 700 of the 1,500 men deserted. When in 1672 the British Brigade arrived in France in the service of Louis XIV, they discovered that their French allies had failed to provide satisfactory provisions or quarters. As the Royal English Regiment only carried three days' victuals, over 400 men succumbed to starvation and exposure before they reached the front, and eight of its 16 companies were broken up. Moreover, three further regiments arrived in Dieppe the following year as 'fine troops … although in rags and ill-armed'. By 1674 every unit in France was debilitated by hunger, disease, battlefield casualties and desertion.[61]

In contrast to their officers, non-commissioned officers and privates were habituated to a diet of biscuit, salt beef or pork, dried peas, cheese, butter and oatmeal, with the infrequent variety of fresh bread and dried fish.[62] In 1675 private soldiers were paid 9d. per day, but only 3d. of this was handed over in 'dry money', the remainder being composed of an equivalent value of provisions. The weekly allowance of victuals (seven days) purchased by commissaries with the 6d. comprised: 5 lb of biscuit, 2 lb of wheat, 2 lb of salt beef, 2 lb of salt pork, 4 pints of dried peas, 3 pints of oatmeal, 4 oz of oil and ½ lb of butter.[63] Between September 1678 and February 1684 two victuallers of Tangier were authorised to issue provisions to the garrison at the rate of 3s. 2¼d. per man per week, whilst sea provisions were delivered on board several ships for victualling 240 troopers 'that came from Spain for the assistance of Tangier, viz. for five days at 8d. per man per day (which was the rate allowed to the victuallers of the navy for sea victuals)'.[64]

During periods of open conflict with the Moors provisions were mostly sent by contractors, who bought their rights from the Lords Commissioners for Tangier. But even if the correct quantities were shipped there was no guarantee that the stores would reach their destination. Victualling ships could be wrecked during the three-week voyage through the turbulent Bay of Biscay, or captured by Corsairs, as happened to the *Phoenix* in 1677.[65] Besides, Sir Dennis Gauden, the contractor for victuals during most of the colony's occupation, was unaccustomed to dispatching generous quantities. In May 1662 he provided food stuffs to the value of £1,000 to Tangier, although 11 years later the then governor, John Middleton, protested that although a

60 Eric Gruber von Arni, *Hospital Care and the British Standing Army, 1660–1714* (London: Routledge, 2017), p. 10.

61 John Childs, 'The British Brigade in France, 1672–1678', *History*, 69 (1984), pp. 384–97; Matthew Glozier, *Scottish Soldiers in France in the Reign of the Sun King* (Leiden: Brill, 2004), pp. 50–2.

62 BL, MS Sloane 1956, fol. 9.

63 TNA, CO 279/3, fol. 225.

64 TNA, SP71/13, fol. 109; BL, MS Sloane 3509, fols 230–1.

65 Adrian Tinniswood, *Pirates of Barbary: Corsairs, Conquests and Captivity in the 17th-Century Mediterranean* (London: Vintage, 2010), p. 238.

Detail of British musketeers relaxing and smoking, from Wenceslaus Hollar, *The Southeast corner of Tangier* (*c.* 1669). (New York, Metropolitan Museum, Creative Commons Public Domain)

consignment had just arrived, it was utterly insufficient for the needs of the garrison.[66] Furthermore, Tangier operated as a naval station for squadrons patrolling the western Mediterranean, meaning that whenever vessels put into the place they were meant to be victualled from the already depleted garrison stores.

Paradoxically, the soldiers would have been in even greater straits during the early stages of the English occupation of Tangier in 1662 had it not been for the valuable support given by Sandwich and his sailors, who supplied the garrison with fuel and other necessaries, and were busy for a fortnight landing stores, and provisions – a difficult task, given that the ships were blown from their moorings – and taking off some of the Portuguese with their belongings. Peterborough admitted, 'Had not his lordship continued his care, I know not to what extremity we should have come'. The council of war summoned for 12 February (composed of the Governor, Colonel Farrell and Major Bolger of Farrell's Regiment, Lieutenant Colonel Maurice Kingwell and Major Blague of Harley's, Lieutenant Colonel Fiennes and Major Johnson of the First Tangier Regiment, Lieutenant Colonel Edward Fitzgerald and Major Rudyard of Fitzgerald's, along with Nathaniel Luke as Secretary) issued a report, which embodied a list of necessities to be dispatched the same day to the Ordnance Office in London. Among a range of items, it recognised the shortage of mortar ammunition, hand grenades, saltpetre, sulphur, pitch, cooking oil, tallow, beeswax, canvas, twine, thread, needles, copper kettles, iron cauldrons, powder-horns, nails, lead for bullets, 2,000 beds, 1,500 cauldrons of coal, brandy and lanterns.

66 TNA, CO 279/1, fols 106, 116; CO 279/16, fol. 287.

It was agreed also that payments for the garrison, which were meant to be disbursed every three months, should be expended in the form of more nutritious rations as follows:

> Some trusty person in England to provide peas and oatmeal for 3,218 men three months, after the rate of four pints of peas and three pints of oatmeal a week to each man. The remainder of the three months' pay to purchase 5 lb of wheat and 10oz of oil for each man per week, the 'small over-plus of money to be sent to the soldier.[67]

Such items were to be procured in Cadiz and immediately dispatched to Tangier. If the food supply at Tangier was largely irregular, sparse and unsuitable for troops operating in a hot climate, the water supply to the garrison needed to be piped in from the hinterland via a system of underground Roman watercourses. As a result, supplies were limited and continually subject to the threat of local tribesmen. In November 1682 the governor, Colonel Percy Kirke, reported the 'damage done to the town wall … by the late rains', and concluded:

> There is scarce anything of more consequence to the preservation of the garrison than water, which, however, hath been much neglected, many wells having been filled up and springs lost, that I am now endeavouring to retrieve. I have opened about fifty wells and by the help of some ancient Portuguese have found an excellent watercourse which had been unknown for many years. They tell me of a book left with my Lord Peterborough that retains an account of the watercourses and many other necessary secrets, which if it were possible to recover would prove of great use to us.[68]

Moreover, Pepys, who participated in the final evacuation of the colony, related a tale about the local water supply, which if true, suggests that the Portuguese were not so obstructive when relinquishing Tangier to the English in 1662 as has been generally assumed:

> Speaking with Kirke about want of water … he added that at my Lord Peterborough's receiving the place from the King of Portugal, there was given him a book (with other customary things) which used among the Portuguese people to be always given from one governor to another, never to be looked into by any other, that did give a secret account of all the conduit heads and heads of watercourses in and about the town, of which this place was the fullest in the World, every house in the town having a particular well or two, which are now lost and dry, by losing the knowledge whither to go to the conduit head to remedy it. My lord Peterborough having taken away the book with him, and upon being asked for it, has always answered that he has mislaid it and cannot

67 TNA, CO 279/1, fol. 92.

68 HMC, *Eleventh Report, App. V*, p. 78.

> recover it, which is another pretty instance of the fate this place has always, and in everything, met with.[69]

The staple beverages among the Tangier garrison were beer, cider, and wine. These were cheap and at times plentiful, and drunkenness became the scourge of the colony as it significantly contributed to ill-health, penury and ill-discipline among the soldiery. In 1680 two victuallers, James Bush and Paul Harris, were appointed by Governor Kirke to supply soldiers working on the fortifications with wine, to the value of £861 2s. In settlement, money was stopped from the soldiers' pay.[70] During the frequent periods of inactivity experienced by the garrison, the men had little else to do during their off-duty hours other than to drink and frequent the numerous brothels. There were at least 14 licensed taverns in the city in 1681. When the private secretary to the ambassador in Portugal viewed the place in September 1663, he reported that although the city had plentiful provisions, it was 'the drunkest place that ever I came into in my life'.[71] Twenty years later, Pepys was alarmed at the spread of drinking and prostitution, combined with an absence of discipline, that had damaged the reputation of the garrison.[72] Nevertheless, three years later his friend, Sir John Wyborne, who had recently been appointed Governor of Bombay, called the Indian colony 'a cursed place', and commented, 'for swearing, lying, backbiting, and all manner of villainy, it very much outdoes Tangier'.[73]

Of immediate concern for the redcoats was the fact that Tangier was on all sides – bar the sea – overlooked by hills that appeared unoccupied, although they were controlled by hostile forces. Probably worst affected by the situation were the regiments of Colonel John Fitzgerald and Colonel Lewis Farrell. Both units of Dunkirk veterans had served among the exiled royalists in Flanders, but although strongly monarchist they were mostly Irish, except for two companies of Scots which had joined them at Dunkirk, all that remained of the regiment of the Earl of Newburgh.[74] These soldiers knew how to make the best of hardships, but without most of the basic items of equipment, such as beds and cooking vessels, both veterans and new men found themselves seriously up against it. Dunkirk had been acquired by England in 1658 and remained under English control until November 1662, when Charles II ordered the evacuate the garrison and the handing over the city to the French, in return for the sum of £200,000. Although most of the officers who had served in Flanders remained with Fitzgerald's and Farrell's commands, both regiments

69 Chapel, Edwin (trans. & ed.), *The Tangier Papers of Samuel Pepys* (Navy Records Society, 73, 1935), p. 91.

70 TNA, SP44/18, fol. 141; *CTB*, VII, p. 1426; SRO, D742/O/3/14–15. Accounts of wine issued to soldiers, etc. employed in demolishing the works of the garrison and the Mole at Tangier, October 1683.

71 HMC, *Finch*, I, p. 280.

72 *Tangier Papers*, p. 89.

73 J. Smith, *The Life, Journals, and Correspondence of Samuel Pepys ... including a narrative of his voyage to Tangier* (London: R. Bentley, 1841), II, pp. 99–100.

74 C. H. Firth, 'Royalist and Cromwellian Armies in Flanders, 1657–1662', *TRHS*, New Sers, 17 (1903), pp. 67–119 (p. 105); Stephen Collins, 'Longford Musketeers: The Farrells of Annaly and the Sieges of St Ghislain and Tangier', *HI*, 11 (2003), pp. 17–21 (p. 20).

Detail of British foot marching and cavalry pickets outside the walls of Tangier, from Wenceslaus Hollar, *Prospect of the lower part of Tangier, from the hills west of Whitehall* (*c.* 1669). (University of Toronto, The Wenceslaus Hollar Collection, Creative Commons Public Domain)

were significantly below strength when they reached Tangier. The numbers of these hardy soldiers fell steadily throughout 1662. Peterborough, an old royalist, believed that such misfortunes were due to the idleness of the men, but more likely the unprepared condition of the expedition and the fighting during the subsequent months took a significant toll.[75]

While the poor diet caused malnutrition and illness among the soldiers, while most of the commissioned officers – largely indifferent to the needs of their men – spent much of their time squabbling and neglecting their duty. Childs suggests that during much of the English occupation, 'Duty in Tangier was most unpopular with the officers. It was far from England, leave difficult to obtain, death never far distant, and for the political animals the service was disastrous, removing them from England for long periods'.[76] Francesco Giavarina, the Venetian Resident in England informed the Doge and Senate on 14 October 1661, that when the first expeditionary force under Peterborough was forming, the drums were beating all over London, though very few recruits enlisted as they would rather stay at home than to be sent to so different a climate.[77] On their march to Portsmouth for embarkation there were sizeable desertions, the men taking their bounty before departing from their colours. Sir Hugh Cholmeley considered that the poor diet endured in Tangier and the general sufferings of the soldiers 'have so bad an impression of the place among the Commons of England, that they heard nothing with more detestation than being sent to Tangier, which they usually esteemed no better than an ill prison, from which they could only hope to be freed by the grave'.[78]

The regimental officers did little to rectify the situation. Being stationed in the midst of hostile territory on the Atlantic coast of Morocco, they proved too restive to endure the monotony of garrison life and a restricted diet without a modicum of sport and adventure. However, when they ventured outside the city walls to hunt, they were attacked by the Moors. When the Earl of Teviot arrived to replace Peterborough as governor in 1663, he found that the common soldiers were disheartened and unwilling

75 TNA, WO 24/1, fols 9–19; CO 279/1, fol. 156.
76 Childs, *Army of Charles II*, p. 121.
77 *CSPV*, p. 54.
78 Cholmeley, *Account of Tangier*, p. 18.

to venture beyond the fortifications of the city. Incensed by the habitual and casual dereliction of their duty, as well as the mercenary attitude of some of his officers, Peterborough reported on his return from leave in England in October 1662:

> I have been of late forced to use some severity to the officers of the place ... [they] began to breed disobedience and neglect of duty, but it has, falling in the regiment of Harley and among men so bred in the principle of faction and rebellion as the wonder will not be great. Kingwell, his lieutenant-colonel, I have sent home, a man so seditious and insolent a native as rendered him incompatible with all government where he may not rule.[79]

On 27 October Mordaunt complained to Admiral Sandwich of the conduct of Lieutenant Colonel Kingwell, 'who, during my own absence from his government, had done nothing that was not prejudicial to the service'.[80] Kingwell's dissatisfaction reportedly began when he refused the profitable continuance of 'an old duty of brokerage', which went against the principles of the King's policy of a free port at Tangier, but he was also a strong republican, and thus increasingly out of place in Charles II's army. Such complaints about the conduct of commissioned officers of the garrison was echoed by a contemporary, who observed:

> the ill-usages of Popish officers, who to my knowledge have valued more 10s. or 20s. at payday than the lives of their soldiers, and have not treated them like men, much less like Christians. I have saved the lives of a great many of my neighbours, when they have wanted necessaries: for which good deed I have been reproved by some Irish officers, who expected their pay between their death and the following muster. The meanest soldier must be encouraged, and not suffered to want when fallen into sickness, though most times through his own intemperance, I dare affirm, and will offer to prove, that the unmercifulness of the officers, and the neglect of physicians and apothecaries, who though paid for that purpose by his Majesty, have killed three parts of those that are dead in Tangier. I have sometimes buried three or four in a day, dead for of that which his Majesty hath provided for them in case of sickness.[81]

The system of 'dead pays' referred to here, was a form of false musters, which were highly prevalent in Charles II's army, although they dated from the Elizabethan period and banned during the Cromwellian period. When a soldier died, his name was retained on the muster roll indefinitely, and many captains drew pay for men who were long dead. Such money went towards increasing the officer's own pay, and the rest disbursed by him to any gentleman volunteers attached to his company. But the practice had been encouraged by the King since his inspection of the Life Guard at Blackheath in 1663, and he was compelled to grant officially 10 dead pays in each company.

79 TNA, CO 279/1, fol. 156.
80 Bod. Lib., MS Carte 75, fols 15–16, 79. Peterborough to Sandwich, 27 October 1662.
81 *Present Interest of Tangier*, pp. 3–4.

Thus, English officers regarded the usage as normal and acceptable.[82] Charles II, Pepys reported, found 'so many absent men, or dead pays' among the Guards, and 'complaints of false musters, and ships being refitted with victuals and stores at Plymouth, after they come fitted from other ports'. He also reported in October 1683 the presence at Tangier of 900 false musters in 2,700 men.[83] Issues relating to foreign service were similarly not confined to Tangier. From the outset, service in Portugal was disliked. The soldiers of the English Brigade – most of them New Model Army veterans – felt that they were being exiled, and as early as 1662 Sir Thomas Morgan, a former Parliamentarian officer, reported that many of the officers preferred to return home.[84] In 1672–3 many of the army's recruits were obtained by coercion, and 'the forces designed for France are preparing for their embarkation, though, to say truth, general unwillingness as well in the soldiers and officers to go into the French service'.[85] When Lockhart's Scottish regiment of foot embarked for France, 'many of them are ran away, and those that are gone having mutinied before they could be got on board; on which occasion an ensign of one of the companies being somewhat brisk and drawing his sword to frighten them into better order, the poor gentleman was immediately knocked on the head by them and left dead on the place'.[86]

Despite concerns expressed about the condition of the city of Tangier, and the shortage of basic equipment and commodities of the soldiery, initial perceptions among the new occupants were not all bad. Peterborough himself reported, 'this city of Tangier will be if sustained at first, so considerable as to pay back all, in the meantime it must be nourished'.[87] Enlistment for soldiers in Charles II's army was essentially for life or during the King's pleasure. The earliest existence of limited terms of service can be found in the recruitment of troops for Tangier in 1679, upon the 'assurance to all as such as shall list themselves, that they shall be relieved the third year, and come for England, and be well-paid in the meanwhile'.[88] This was probably in imitation of the East India Company, which during the 1660s enlisted troops to protect its factories, and as part of its charter of 1698 was empowered to 'raise, train, and muster such military forces as shall be necessary for the defence of the said forts, places, and plantations'.[89]

While the governor was generally optimistic about the future of Tangier, in October 1662 he reported on the adverse effects of poor conditions and the variation of climate on the garrison, observing that there had been many

---

82 Charles G. Cruickshank, 'Dead-Pays in the Elizabethan Army', *EHR*, 53 (1938), pp. 93–97; Childs, *Army of Charles II*, p. 106.

83 Pepys, *Diary*, 13 October 1663, 3 December 1667; *Tangier Papers*, p. 96.

84 Jonathon Riley, *The Last Ironsides: The English Expedition to Portugal 1662–1668* (Solihull: Helion & Co., 2014), pp. 64–5.

85 W. D. Christie (ed.), *Letters addressed from London to Sir Joseph Williamson* (London: Camden Society, 1874), II, p. 32. Robert Yard to Williamson, 3 October 1673.

86 *Ibid.*, p. 81. Yard to Williamson, 21 November 1673.

87 Bodl. Lib., MS Carte 75, fol. 80. Peterborough to Sandwich, 27 October 1662.

88 *London Gazette*, 21–24 July 1679.

89 Huw V. Bowen, 'The East India Company and Military Recruitment in Britain, 1763–71', *HR*, 59 (1986), pp. 78–90 (p. 78).

Detail of British garrison civilians outside the walls of Tangier, from Wenceslaus Hollar, *Prospect of the North Side of Tangier regarding the main sea from the hill as you come from Whitby or the West, toward the town* (*c.* 1669). (Rijksmuseum, Creative Commons Public Domain)

deaths and desertions. Before leaving for Lisbon on 18 February to escort Queen Catherine to England, Admiral Sandwich, with the professional guidance of Beckman, had surveyed Tangier Bay, and taken soundings around the ledge of rocks running out from the shore on the north side. They had particularly understood the need to construct a stone pier or breakwater, which would help facilitate a more secure anchorage for naval and merchant vessels – this would become the Little Mole. As Peterborough and his officers assessed the broader situation, the governor may have felt some misgivings as to his ability to carry out the task entrusted to his 'honour, courage, wisdom and fidelity' by the King's commission of 16 September 1661, which had given him in overall command. As Routh observes though, '[Peterborough's] commission is a remarkable document; it sketches in clear outlines a bold and ambitious policy which contained the elements of success, but which was destined to be confused and spoiled through the inability of the government of Charles II to carry out the well-designed plan of commercial and colonial expansion.'[90]

Although the English garrison had only recently settled in its quarters at Tangier, it would soon encounter the realities of colonial life. The outpost was a place of conflict, its sheltering ramparts concealing a vast and hostile landscape that for the next two decades would see numerous ferocious encounters between the defending troops and the Moroccan forces. Although the Earl of Peterborough's instructions under the terms of his commission were to enlist and train native volunteers, merely a portion of the former Portuguese garrison was retained. There was, however, some employment of

90 Routh, *Tangier*, p. 16.

'Arabian spies' to gather intelligence, and a few Moors entered English service in 1662. On 14 January 1667 Peter the Moor petitioned Charles II that he be 'mounted and listed in the Life Guard, or to have some employment in the navy'.[91] He had served five years in Tangier, bringing in horses, cattle and other goods for the garrison, whilst his brother and 12 other natives had been killed in the service. In addition to these, various military officers of the garrison acted as envoys and intelligencers. Moreover, as we have seen, Beckman, 'a man motivated by the financial possibilities of espionage', undertook secret work in Morocco and Spain. He temporarily lost his position in mid 1663, partly due to the influence of Colonel Fitzgerald, the lieutenant-governor, 'a quarrelsome man who disliked Beckman'.[92] Suspicious of the engineer's incentives and unreliability, Fitzgerald reported to the Earl of Arlington, 'Beckman the intelligencer is to be feared', though he admitted, 'I conceive what he gives us [is] so far not neglected'.[93]

During the early weeks of the English occupation, the Moroccan leader was fighting with his army at the port of Salé against his rival, Mohammed al-Hajj ibn Abu Bakr al-Dila'i, but although he was unable to deploy all his troops against Tangier, he spared enough to harass the garrison with various minor, if ferocious encounters.[94] Probably the most pressing issue for the garrison, however, was its relationship with Ghaïlān. With the dubious condition of the city and its fortifications adding urgency to the matter, there was a growing realization that the success of the colony (if not its very survival) depended on establishing a mutually advantageous connection with the local population. During skirmishes with the Moors, as many as 30 members of the garrison had already been killed during the first few weeks.[95] But the prospects for peace seemed encouraging. From inside Tangier's fortifications Peterborough had written to Ghaïlān several times but had only received 'dilatory answers'. Then, on 24 March 1662 two messengers arrived under a flag of truce, conveying news that their master was ready to meet, while the governor acknowledged his desire to conclude a treaty that would provide 'security unto both parties'.

The Moorish commander further sent into the city 'three great personages' whom he authorised to parley, with the proposal that when Peterborough and he met, they had 'only to shake hands and embrace, and have no further occasion of dispute'. When a few days later the two sides met with the intention of concluding a peace treaty, the English were favourably impressed with what they saw of the enemy horsemen, with Peterborough writing, 'Their army which appeared here were about 5,000 horse, able, dexterous, sober, valiant, incomparably well-armed and clothed, and horsed to very much

91 *Description of Tangier*, pp. 27–8; *CSPD 1666–67*, p. 453.

92 Marshall, *Intelligence and Espionage*, p. 178.

93 TNA, CO 279/2, fols 122–3.

94 Lancelot Addison, *The Moores Baffled being a discourse concerning Tangier, especially when it was under the Earl of Teviot* (London: William Crooke, 1681), p. 3. Common contemporary renderings of Mohammed's name by Britons included: Ben Bowcar, Ben Barka and Benboukir, although he was also referred to as the 'Saint' of Salé owing to his intense religious faith.

95 BL, MS Sloane 3509, fol. 16.

use, if they were not the fairest that I ever saw'.[96] However, the negotiations broke down over the issue of access to firewood as Ghaïlān's envoys refused to allow the redcoats to collect it within nine miles of the city. Not only was this highly inconvenient for the garrison, but any attempts at gathering fuel would expose them to the risk of attack. Of this experience Peterborough reported, 'We thought fit to conclude a peace for six months were it but to begin the way of trade, and to show the Moors by practice with us that we were men of such manners, and dealing might procure a love and confidence at last'.[97] When all was agreed, and the governor had sent out officers to 'view and mark bounds' (of the area to which the English were entitled, so that disputes might be avoided), Ghaïlān refused to sign the treaty. Instead he handed the English commissioners a list of further demands, which were returned into the city that evening.

Among other things, 50 barrels of powder were to be handed over (this would need to be furnished from London as they could not be spared from garrison's magazine); the use of English ships whenever he required them; an embargo on trade and communications between Tangier and the city of Tétuan – the second major port in Morocco, located about 40 miles to the southeast, which was an enemy of Ghaïlān's, although it provided an important source of beef for the garrison. Such terms were clearly intolerable to the Tangier garrison, and however necessary a peace treaty was, Peterborough wisely rejected them. The Moorish leader subsequently withdrew with his army, offering no response to the governor before he left. But the full motivations of the Moors remain unclear. The governor later reflected, 'But for themselves it must be a great fear, or an exceeding interest, that brings them to be kind to any stranger, especially to a Christian'.[98] Peterborough also suspected that Ghaïlān had designs other than peace, because intelligence reports suggested that he was colluding with the Spanish.[99]

Skirmishing occurred frequently during May 1662 as Ghaïlān's troops came audaciously close to the walls of Tangier and clashed with the minor patrols of its garrison in an increasingly hostile environment.[100] Cholmeley noted that the English soldiers 'continued the foresaid skirmishing war, without any more considerable loss at any one time than what befell one Baker, who was cut off with about five or six others, that ventured with him to a little hill, which was then too far from relief though within the present lines, and now commonly called Baker's Folly'.[101] Although musketry might prove decisive at medium and longer ranges, the fighting performance of the English soldiers was profoundly tested during close-quarter action by the ferocious nature of their opponents. The Moors' reliance on the scimitar or *saif* had an impact on men who were used to more familiar methods of

96 TNA, CO 279/1, fols 108, 127. Peterborough's reports, April 1662.

97 TNA, CO 279/1, fols 127–9. Peterborough's letter, April 1662, with 'Guylan's demands and my answers thereunto', attached.

98 *Ibid.*, fol. 128.

99 *Ibid.*, fol. 130.

100 Addison, *Moores Baffled*, pp. 3–4; Routh, *Tangier*, pp. 25–6.

101 Cholmeley, *Account*, p. 39.

Detail of British cavalry troopers, from Wenceslaus Hollar, *Prospect of the lower part of Tangier, from the hills west of Whitehall* (*c.* 1669). (University of Toronto, The Wenceslaus Hollar Collection, Creative Commons Public Domain)

fighting. Scimitars were mainly used in mounted warfare because of their relatively lightweight and their curved design, ideal for slashing opponents from horseback.[102] But though Peterborough's soldiers were habitually disadvantaged by sickness and inadequate supplies, he steadily developed the colony by seizing land around Tangier and then safeguarding it with fortifications. To the Moroccan leader, Ghaïlān, this was unacceptable, so early April 1662 he led a large part of his army to Tangier to attempt to draw the troops of the garrison into the open.

On 3 May Peterborough yielded and ordered Major Nathaniel Fiennes, an officer of his own regiment, with 500 men to drive off a party of Moorish cavalry from beneath the city walls. Sparse though the evidence is, it is likely that rather than being a chance encounter, the Moors' movements represented a feigned retreat – a well-executed plan of a kind regularly employed by Arab armies for centuries, designed to lead European troops into ambushes, or to initiate a fake retreat to exhaust the enemy. The garrison's troops, with no prior intelligence of either the strength nor dispositions of their enemy, sallied out and pursued the retreating Moorish horsemen. Fiennes eagerly pursued them, 'thinking to fall in upon the enemy with the butt-end of the musket', but it quickly became clear that his soldiers and he had stumbled

102 A. Rahman Zaky, 'Introduction to the Study of Islamic Arms and Armour', *Gladius*, I (1961), pp. 17–29.

into a disastrous situation, having been led into a trap.[103] Surrounded on three sides by warriors who had emerged from behind sand hills, the English troops were set upon and routed. Perhaps two-thirds of the force was killed or disappeared into captivity, while the rest performed a fighting retreat to the safety of Tangier's walls.[104] According to rumour, some prisoners were either tortured to death or walled up alive, although commonly throughout the occupation, those captured by the Moors were mutilated and beheaded, or at best sold into slavery.

Although the city itself was in little danger, this painful introduction to irregular warfare momentarily sapped the morale of Peterborough and the soldiers under his command. The encounter also gave Ghaïlān's troops the advantage of dominating the terrain, as they established a series of deadly ambushes that drove the garrison to a defensive strategy. Thus, for the time being, no further patrols were sent out of the city and the gates were permanently closed. Moreover, sentries were ordered to stand aside as the Moors stole cattle from under the walls they were defending. On 21 May 1662, Colonel John Fitzgerald notified the captains of English warships in the Mediterranean of 'the great need of the presence of his Majesty's ships at Tangier, advice having been received of the assembling of a large Spanish force at Ceuta who are to join with the Moors in an attack upon the settlement'.[105] He also urged any officer in receipt of his letter to communicate the intelligence to Vice-Admiral Lawson. Similarly, the following month Captain William Staines, English consul at Tétuan, alerted the vice-admiral that 'intelligence has reached me, mainly by means of the governor of Tétuan, of plans concerted between the Moors and the Spaniards for a joint attack upon the English at Tangier'.[106] Although Routh's suggestion that Ghaïlān used the negotiations with Peterborough as a means of discovering the strength of the English garrison is realistic, the latter's suspicions reveal that to some extent there was a misunderstanding of the Moroccan political landscape, as well as the Islamic leader's rationale and aspirations.[107]

European writers have observed that during the early 1660s at least, Ghaïlān possessed his own agenda, one designed to consolidate his rule across north-western Morocco. In achieving this, he imitated what other pretenders had done for over 150 years – a political and military alignment between himself and the various European powers. Thus, Ghaïlān, who had made his reputation by attacking the Portuguese garrison of Tangier, sought both to evade hostilities with them, and, more importantly, acquire military supplies and other aid to prosecute his campaigns against his domestic rivals.[108] The Moorish leader later reversed this policy, however, and allied with

103 Cholmeley, *Account of Tangier*, p. 39.

104 Bodl. Lib., MS Rawlinson D916, fol. 78; Davis, *History of the Second Queen's*, I, p. 33.

105 Bod. Lib., MS Carte 75, fol. 38. Fitzgerald to captains of his Majesty's vessels, 21 May 1662.

106 *Ibid.*, fol. 50. Staines to Lawson, 26 June 1662.

107 Routh, *Tangier*, p. 25.

108 Jerome Bookin-Weiner, 'Anglo-Moroccan Relations in the First Decade of the Occupation of Tangier (1662–1672)', *Hespéris-Tamuda*, 18 (1978–79), pp. 63–75 (pp. 65–6); P. Collyer, 'The British Occupation of Tangier, 1662–1674', *Morocco: Journal of the Society for Moroccan Studies*, 1 (1996), pp. 52–61.

Spain, attacking English-held ports as part of a *jihād* designed to enhance his legitimacy.[109] Throughout his career Ghaïlān played a 'double-game' between the two powers.[110] One Moroccan historian has accused the Barbary leader of collaborating with the infidel, namely the Spanish government and the Tangier garrison, in his conflicts against his domestic opponents, the Dilāites.[111] The characteristics and tactics of the Barbary forces encountered in 1662 by the Tangier garrison made a significant impact upon soldiers schooled in western forms of warfare, established largely by the major European conflicts of the mid-seventeenth century, as well as the conventional doctrines of the period. Charles II's establishment of the outpost coincided with the beginning of an effective Moroccan dynasty which asserted itself in the later 1600s.

Ghaïlān and his commanders led forces that fought as a relatively uncoordinated body, their irregular methods being so different to anything which Charles II's troops had encountered before, and they were a formidable enemy. Significantly for the Tangier garrison, whenever the Moors brought their considerable weight to bear on the city's defences, they were incapable of sustaining pressure for long, while they were also unable to attack it by sea, thus rendering a serious siege impossible. Through high levels of discipline, at times resourceful leadership, and the ability for adaptation, the English were gradually able to resist (sometimes desperately) their numerically superior foe. But during the spring and summer of 1662 this doubtless appeared a long way off. Tangier had failed to thrive as a trading outpost during the two centuries of Portuguese occupation, largely because although the city lay in a coastal depression, and thus encircled by dominating high ground. Crucially, this allowed the Moors to observe any movements made by the garrison, both inside and outside of the fortifications. Armed with such intelligence, they utilised their greatest skill, that of surprise assaults and ambuscades. Ghaïlān brought his troops to such a level of efficiency that 2–3,000 soldiers could conceal themselves barely a quarter of a mile from Tangier's walls, to take by surprise enemy patrols. They could also maintain strict silence for long periods, and their predominant use of bladed weapons made their ambushes doubly effective. The Moors were greatly assisted by the broken terrain outside the city, with its hollows and hillocks, which were covered in thick scrub.

This state of 'low-intensity warfare' represented a nuisance to the English regiments and were alien to their doctrine. Although their superior organisation, discipline, and firepower usually matched the Moors in open combat. Although a lack of effective scouting, mediocre intelligence gathering or carelessness on the part of officers on occasion, placed units in positions of unnecessary danger, any early reversals suffered by the garrison

109 For the relationship between the ideology of Holy War and state formation in Morocco, see Johan de Bakker, *Slaves, Arms and Holy War: Moroccan Policy vis-à-vis the Dutch Republic during the Establishment of the 'Alawī Dynasty, 1660–1727* (Amsterdam: s.n. 1991); Amira K. Bennison, *Jihad and its Interpretations in Pre-Colonial Morocco: State-Society Relations during the French Conquest of Algeria* (London and New York: Routledge, 2002), pp. 15–33.

110 Jamil M. Abun-Nasr, *A History of the Maghrib in the Islamic Period* (Cambridge: Cambridge University Press, 1987), p. 226; Bejjit, *English Colonial Texts*, pp. 13, 33.

111 Mohamed Hajji, *Al-Zawiyah al-Dilaiyah wa-dawruha al-dini wa-al-ilmi wa-siyasi* (Rabat: Matbat An-Najjah Al-Jadida, 1988), pp. 217–19.

were caused by surprise attacks, which made it difficult for the soldiers to deploy from marching column into line of battle. Such tactical limitations were equally indicative of a shortage of cavalry among the Tangier garrison. It was difficult and expensive to obtain suitably acclimatised mounts, while the hilly, broken ground was deemed unsuitable for mounted action. Yet contrary to official reasoning, horsemen were invaluable for scouting and reconnaissance, uncovering ambushes, foraging, skirmishing, patrolling, and providing support to infantry operations. It was a steep learning curve for the English garrison, but Peterborough's foot deserved the approbation of their countrymen for the tenacity with which they held their own against so skilful an enemy. The rank and file of the Tangier garrison rapidly came to understand the hardships they had to endure at the hands of their enemies, and further skirmishes followed the engagement of 3 May.

The garrison's muster rolls reveal that during the nine-month period of between January and October 1662, 605 soldiers – more than a fifth of its initial establishment – were killed or missing, although the number of wounded who avoided capture is unreported. Of these the Governor's Regiment of Foot suffered nearly 200 casualties, and that of Colonel Harley's a little under 400.[112] As the two, smaller regiments maintained a consistent strength it is reasonable to assume that these were battlefield losses and not the result of some epidemic. Reliable estimates of the Moors' casualties cannot be gleaned from English sources of the period, although Ghaïlān's army was said to have suffered more than 500 men, the leader's brother being among the dead. Approximations of the strength of the Moorish army at Tangier are notoriously unreliable, but accounts from 1664 and 1666 put the number of soldiers at between 10,700 (excluding irregular levies) and 17,500, although Ghaïlān could not sustain a campaign beyond three months due to logistical constraints.[113] Some of the fighters were Berbers – light cavalry mounted on small hill-ponies as hardy and determined as their riders, who could be mobilised with extreme rapidity. One observer gave the figure for these troops as '2,700 horse, 2,000 harquebusiers and 6,000 royal squadron of gentlemen', the latter mounted on excellent horses 'with furniture and arms for variety of colours most beautiful, and for riches of armament beyond measure estimable, for everything about them shineth with gold, silver, pearls, jewels, and whatsoever else may please the eye'.[114]

Governor Peterborough was aware that a forced armistice with Ghaïlān had not been the only option available to him. In late April, the governor had contacted Sultan Muhammad al-Hajj Abū Bakr, the son of the Dilā' leader, Sidi Abdalah, although his reasons for doing so are uncertain. Peterborough may have been attempting to draw Ghaïlān into a more favourable peace, although a genuine attempt by the governor to investigate the option of a

112 TNA, CO 279/1, fols 55–8; Routh, *Tangier*, p. 27.

113 Bod. Lib., MS Rawlinson D916, fols 106–8; Lancelot Addison, *West Barbary, or, A short narrative of the revolutions of the kingdoms of Fez and Morocco with an account of the present customs, sacred, civil, and domestick* (Oxford: John Wilmot, 1671), pp. 40–2.

114 *Description of Tangier*, pp. 17–18. Routh incorrectly cites the 2,700 horse as 27,000 (*Tangier*, p. 26).

coalition with the Dilā' (who were just as threatened by Ghaïlān) is another possibility.[115] Muhammad had entered into a pact with the English as recently as 1657, whilst his father responded to Peterborough's appeal by professing his desire for peace and friendship. He also criticised their mutual foe and requested that the English hold 'no commerce with our enemies either of Asilah or Salé', claiming that both were 'lost and undone'.[116] What Ghaïlān came to realise was that an accord with the English was of particular value to him, and thus he made renewed proposals of peace.[117] Peterborough returned home at the end of May 1662 for three months, to report on the condition of Tangier. Negotiations continued in his absence between Colonel John Fitzgerald, the deputy-governor, Captain James Wilson, and the Moorish envoys. Ghaïlān hoped additionally to obtain English naval assistance against Salé, but this could not be agreed to.

On 21 June 1662 Fitzgerald wrote that Ghaïlān was hoping to secure for himself the sultanate of Fès and citadel at Salé, 'which he has in his imagination swallowed already, but dare not adventure to take possession of until he has secured himself by a peace with us'.[118] In a separate letter the Colonel reported the progress of efforts by the garrison to strengthen the fortifications and city, thinking it his duty 'since the unhappy loss of Lieutenant Colonel Fiennes and his party', not to hazard any more men abroad. He further mentioned receiving news from Tétuan, 'which town Ghaïlān has lately forced to composition'.[119] But Colonel Fitzgerald remained suspicious of his adversary's motives. On 30 June, after confirming a previous report on Spanish movements off the coast of Tangier from Sir John Lawson to Admiral Sandwich, he added, 'Ghaïlān is, at this instant, drawing with his army towards this place. He gives out it is to make a *court de guard*, in the fields of Tangier, within a quarter of a league of the town'.[120] The cessation of hostilities between the Tangier garrison and Ghaïlān improved the situation of the soldiers as the Moors brought in cattle and other goods for sale, while at the same time Spanish vessels began to trade regularly with the colony, despite more general embargoes on the practice.

Captain Wilson informed Peterborough (who was by now in England), 'our condition is better ... we want not refreshment, beef excepted'.[121] The only thing they required was more men for the depleted garrison. In a report to Charles II following his return to Tangier in late September 1662, Peterborough was more cautious about the situation. Whilst observing that the state of the garrison had improved, he assured the King that Tangier 'will be a great place if your Majesty's designs proceed'. This appraisal, however, would be dependent

115 Matar, *Britain and Barbary*, p. 136.

116 BL, MS Harley 6844, fols 91–4. Cidi Abdalah to Peterborough, 12 May 1662.

117 Bod. Lib., MS Carte 75, fols 48–9. Propositions, or Additional Articles, adduced on behalf of Ghaïlān, the Moor, upon a Treaty for a truce between himself, and the Governor of Tétuan (endorsed: 'Guylan's Propositions; with my [the governor's] Answers'), n.d. 1662.

118 *Ibid.*, fol. 44. Fitzgerald to Sandwich, 21 June 1662.

119 *Ibid.*, fols 44–5. Fitzgerald to Sandwich, 21 June 1662, enclosing 'An Account of all that I have done towards the security and strengthening of this City, since his Excellency [Lord Peterborough]'s departure', n.d. 1662.

120 Bod. Lib., MS Carte 75, fol. 56.

121 Cited in Routh, *Tangier*, p. 27.

on the 'constant attendance of ships' in the anchorage, which, he noted, was threatened by the Spanish embargo and their attempts to avert the Moorish leader from concluding a peace.[122] But the advantage gained so ambitiously and energetically by the English in securing their presence in Morocco had also given cause for anxiety to the French. The colossal expenditure of money and manpower put into Tangier by the Crown testified to the importance of the Mediterranean for England's commercial and maritime expansion. Hence, the cost of the military establishment in the American colonies in 1679 was £12,816, about 20 percent of the nominal annual expense of Tangier, which was initially set at £70,000 and then reduced to £55,000 in 1668.[123]

In the 1660s, during its peace with Spain, France enjoyed no significant maritime presence in the Mediterranean and East Indies, and the English possession of Tangier and Bombay posed no apparent threat. But intent on establishing his own foothold in North Africa, despite his original support of the Portuguese alliance, Louis XIV was anxious that English sovereignty in the Strait of Gibraltar would be exerted by English squadrons operating from Tangier. The Venetian Ambassador in England reported on 7 September 1668 that 'England would reap not only the advantage of the duties, but being rendered arbiter of the trade of the Mediterranean she would combine her reputation with the advantage and little by little would bring into her own hands the control of all the most profitable navigation'.[124] But although they had declared war on all the Barbary States, the French struggled to emulate the success of the English in establishing a firm presence in the region. The purpose of the expedition to Jijel in north-eastern Algeria in July 1664 – involving Louis XIV's navy, commanded by François de Vendôme, duc de Beaufort, and army forces commanded by Lieutenant General Charles-Félix de Galéan, duc de Gadagne – was to establish a naval base from which forays could be made against the Corsairs of the Mediterranean. However, after three months, lacking food and supplies, suffering from various illnesses, combined with poor organisation, and quarrelling between the commanders, the French abandoned the port and fortress.

Charles II's proclamation of Tangier as a free port in November 1662 represented a necessary step to encourage trade from all nations and break the embargo imposed on the city by the governor of Adalusia, the Duke of Medina-Celi, who was consistently hostile to the English.[125] The instructions issued to the Earl of Peterborough as the first Governor-General of Tangier emphasised that the transformation of the city into a trading hub and free port lay at the centre of the Crown's wider aspirations for its new possession. Charles II ordered Peterborough to announce that 'no duties, customs or other taxes whatever' would be levied on goods imported or exported from Tangier, the city remaining a free port for five years. he was further directed

122 BL, MS Harley 6844, fol. 105. Peterborough to Charles II, Tangier, 27 September 1662.

123 Routh, *Tangier*, pp. 115–16; Colley, *Captives*, pp. 25–30.

124 *CSPV*, p. 264.

125 TNA, CO 279/1, fol. 29; *By the King A Proclamation Declaring His Majesty's Pleasure to Settle and Establish a Free Port at His City of Tangier in Africa* (London: John Bill and Christopher Barker, 1662).

to contemplate what means would most effectively induce 'our subjects and strangers to reside and trade' there. The Crown intended Tangier to be an open city that would entice foreign merchants and their business. Tangier was in a strategic location, overlooking the entrance to the Mediterranean, the globe's greatest area for commerce. The colony also provided a base from which the English could monitor the rival fleets of France and Spain, while it offered a stop-off for merchant shipping trading to the East Indies and the Levant. In 1661 the ambassador to Portugal had commended that if Tangier and Bombay were to fall into the King's hands, 'such a door will be opened to all trade as will make England again to be numbered amongst the most nourishing kingdoms of Christendom'.[126]

Yet implicit even in this self-consciously maritime adventure was the application of military force. At issue was how it was to be employed and with whom lay the authority to exert it. Tangier's governors frequently emphasised their efforts to encourage the Moors towards peaceful outcomes by establishing mutually beneficial trading relationships, whilst affirming that their territorial aspirations extended no further than the fields surrounding the city, that would provide sustenance for the garrison, as well as space for outworks for its protection.[127] The English Crown was likewise convinced that only naval power and frigates patrolling off Barbary ports would restrain Muslim Corsairs and tempt Moroccans to come to Tangier to trade.[128] During the summer of 1661, Peterborough's request for a large body of horse was denied by Whitehall, on the basis that they intended 'not to make a war with the Moors' but to forge a peace with them through commerce. Although the governors and their officials wished to expand the colony, they largely sought only to control enough terrain to make Tangier self-sufficient, rather than aiming for wider territorial conquests.[129] By November 1662 England's foothold on the shores of the Mediterranean seemed secure. Charles II inaugurated a 'Committee for the Affairs of Tangier', based in London and composed of leading men to maintain its purpose, including the Duke of York, Prince Rupert, General Monck, Admiral Sandwich, the Earl of Peterborough, Samuel Pepys (Clerk of the Acts of the Navy) and Thomas Povey (Treasurer for Tangier).[130]

126 HMC, *Finch*, I, p. 99.

127 TNA CO 279/1, fol. 108. Earl of Peterborough, Tangier, 2 April 1662; Longleat House, CO/70, fol. 52. Earl of Middleton to Lord Arlington, 12 October 1673.

128 BL, MS Sloane 3509, fol. 104. Lord Belasyse to the Lords Commissioners for Tangier, n.d.; Bod. Lib., MS Rawlinson 342, fol. 379. Henry Sheres to Colonel Palmes Fairborne, 5 December 1678.

129 TNA CO 279/19, fol. 205. John Bland to Joseph Williamson, 20 July 1676; BL, MS Lansdowne 192, fols 86, 96. Cholmeley, 'Several discourses concerning the interest of Tangier'.

130 TNA CO 279/1, fol. 83; *CTB*, I, p. 523.

4

The Mole and Harbour of Tangier

As was mentioned in the previous chapter, in 1662 Charles II established the Tangier Committee, an organisation exclusively devoted to the colony's affairs. Tangier's relative nearness to England, and the strategic value of its port and military outpost could be made beneficial to English interests if suitable investment of resources and skills were instituted. When the Committee met on 1 December, it judged, despite a general level of under-investment, that Tangier would ultimately prosper and reduce the cost of its maintenance when its port was made navigable by sizable vessels and the city itself transmuted into a free market. The need for a breakwater to protect Tangier's harbour from westerly, Atlantic gales was acknowledged from the beginning – without it the greater English ships could not safely anchor. Such craft were needed both to supply the garrison and more profitably, to target other shipping venturing through the Straits of Gibraltar. Before the Portuguese marriage treaty was signed the King had learned, on good authority, that the harbour was capable of improvement, whilst in early 1662 Admiral Sandwich made a survey of the bay, in order to find the best position for a Mole. Consequently, during the early months of 1663 the Commissioners considered the project of building the structure, which had been presented by Sir Hugh Cholmeley, the Earl of Teviot (then governor of Tangier) and Sir John Lawson, commander of the Mediterranean Squadron. Cholmeley, who had supervised the building of Whitby Pier, on his Yorkshire estates, planned to progress by erecting a solid structure of stone, extending far enough into the sea to interrupt the ferocious tidal waters, and therefore secure the harbour shipping.

Four months after the creation of the Tangier Committee it awarded a contract, the price agreed upon being 13s. per cubic yard.[1] The agreement was for 'A Mole or Pier of Stone', beginning from a rocky ledge just below York Castle, extending out 400 yards in an east-north-east direction and thence

1 TNA, CO 279/2, fols 16–21; Bod. Lib., MS Rawlinson A341, fol. 95. Contract for the Tangier Mole, 30 March 1663.

200 yards east-south-east; 30 yards broad in foundation; 20,000 cubic yards to be completed before 30 June 1664, and annually at least 30,000 cubic yards, until completed. There would also be a lesser section 'from the east end of the city to the great Mole', with mooring posts and rings. The Commissioners agreed to advance £2,000 for tools and materials, to be deducted from future payments; 13s. per cubic yard was be paid quarterly: £3,250 in April next, £3,250 in October next, and £3,250 in January next. The breakwater was to be kept in repair for five years after completion, at £6,000 per annum. However, the contract would be cancelled if stone could not obtained within three miles of Tangier in safety, thus reducing the cost of the enterprise. The foundations for the Mole were begun in August 1663, under the immediate supervision of Cholmeley, who acted as resident-engineer from 1663 to 1674, and surveyor-general of the Mole from 1669 to 1676. His first challenge was to find skilled artisans and workers willing to risk their lives in a city reputed to be under constant siege. He arrived in Tangier in June 1663 with 'about 40 masons, miners, and other proper artists and workmen', whom he had with difficulty persuaded to come to 'a place where, in the beginning, so many men had died'.[2]

The main construction work on the Mole (described by Routh as 'the greatest engineering work till then attempted by Englishmen') was eventually undertaken by soldiers of the garrison, although Moorish slaves augmented the labour force from the 1670s onwards. During the siege of Tangier in 1680 the Engineer-General specifically requested 'Derbyshire men for mining'. Thus, an independent company of miners was specially raised and sent out under the command of Captain Richard Bassett. The unit constituted one sergeant, two corporals, and 47 miners from Cornwall.[3] The foundations were begun in August 1663, but the engineers soon found that the cost of the work had been considerably under-estimated, while progress was hindered by the want of materials. In February 1664 Cholmeley was called to England by the death of his elder brother and did not return until 18 January 1665. Upon his return, Sir Hugh discovered that more delay had been caused by his workmen 'being forced to the duty of soldiers', and after Teviot's death in May 1664, strong winds and violent sea conditions further restricted the enterprise. A survey made immediately after his return shows that 10,558 cubic yards had been cast into the sea to form the base of the Mole.[4] Finding it impossible to carry on the undertaking at the original contracted price, Cholmeley and Lawson, the two remaining contractors, presented their difficulties to the Commissioners, and on 31 March 1665 this was increased to 17s. per cubic yard.

Rapid progress was made on the breakwater, and soon there were 200 soldiers labouring under Cholmeley's supervision. But given the arduous nature of the work and the effects of the frequently severe weather conditions,

---

2 Much of the details for the construction of the Mole are set out in two narratives written by Cholmeley: *A Short Account of the Mole at Tangier, from the First Beginning of that Work* (London: 1679), and *An Account of Tangier with some Account of Himself and his Journey through France and Spain to that Place, where he was engaged in building the Mole in the Time of King Charles the Second; and a Journal of the Work carrying on* (London: 1787).

3 TNA, WO 93/1082, fol. 151. Beckman to Legge, 12 July 1680; WO 5/1, fol. 22; SRO, D742/0/4/21–22; Routh, *Tangier*, p. 343.

4 TNA, CO 279/4, fol. 15. Colonel Fitzgerald to Commissioners, 25 January 1665.

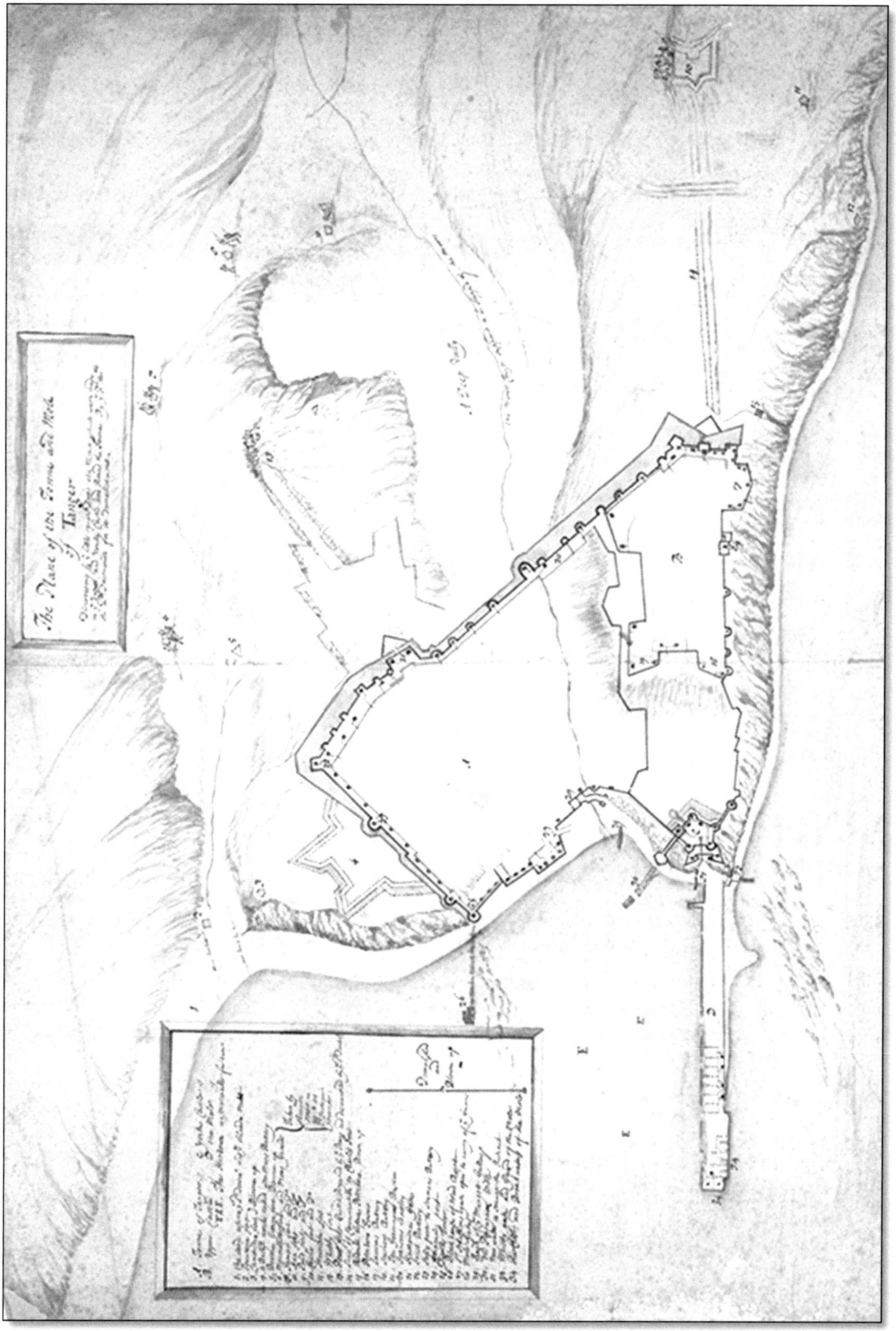

Thomas Phillips, *The Plane and the Town and Mole of Tanger* (1684?). (University of Toronto, The Wenceslaus Hollar Collection, Creative Commons Public Domain)

it was a dangerous undertaking. On 21 October 1670 one man was mortally injured by a stone that fell on his back, 'and by the force struck an iron crow into his body, so that his lungs appeared'. Similarly, in the following June, as 'the Levant wind continued very raging', a number of men were 'sorely wounded, with broken arms and legs' as they were pitching great stones into the Mole's foundations.[5] Sir Hugh employed another qualified surveyor, and began the construction of a Little Mole 'for the safeguard of the boats'. He requested that the Committee provide 'a supply of horses' for the use of pulling carts from the quarry to the construction sites.[6] The winter of 1664–65 was particularly bad, and the engineers found it hard to keep the men to their work, as they were soaked to the skin both by sea and rain on a daily basis. Fortuitously, plenty of stone was found at nearby quarries – named 'Whitby' by Yorkshire miners – close to the shore immediately west of Tangier city. The rock was first transported to the Mole by boat, but stormy weather made this so trying that carts were built to carry it. In 1678 both methods were in usage. According to one report, there were 44 horses for drawing carts full of stone, in addition to numerous 'lighters, sloops and other imbarcations which float great stones to the head of the work'.[7] Cholmeley also assembled 'a little town' (probably timber huts) at Whitby Quarry, with quarters for the workmen and their families, stabling for 90 horses and storehouses for provisions and materials of all kinds.

The type of structure at the Mole varied from section to section. Leonardo de Ferrari's plan of the Portuguese fortifications at Tangier, dated *c.* 1655, shows a low rocky breakwater projecting from the north-western tip of the harbour, as well as a smaller inner structure.[8] Sir Hugh Cholmeley clearly incorporated this into a foundation layer of loose rock on the sea bottom. Placed upon this deposit were layers of large stone, cemented with *tarras* (a form of cement, described by Cholmeley as 'a certain sand made into mortar which hardens in the water'), and stapled together with lead and iron bars.[9] This mass was reinforced on the north or seaward side by three rows of piles, supported by pillars 10 or 12 feet square, built of huge cemented rock, weighing 60 to 100 tons, set obliquely to the direction of the tide. The Mole was so far advanced in 1665 that a battery of cannon was placed on it. This formed a valuable defence against Dutch and Barbary shipping at a time when Tangier would otherwise have been open to attack from the sea. Although Cholmeley was in overall charge, much of the day-to-day work was supervised by the engineer Henry Sheres. Yet frequent friction between the professionals and the military authorities at Tangier caused various difficulties. Colonel Fitzgerald, when Lieutenant-Governor, refused to make allowance in his survey of the Mole for anything that he could not observe, while Cholmeley requested payment for the foundations which had sunk in the sand. Moreover, he asked that the cubic yards be measured by the quantity of materials transported to the Mole, as

5 Cholmeley, *Account*, pp. 151, 194.
6 *Ibid.*, pp. 247–8.
7 TNA, CO 279/22, fol. 146. R. Bolland to Commissioners, 12 April 1678.
8 Stockholm, Arquivo Militar de Estocolmo, Krigsarkivet, *Atlas de Leonardo de Ferrari* (1655).
9 Cholmeley, *Account*, p. 249; *Short Account*, pp. 5–6.

it was difficult to calculate the quantity of already sunken masonry. In 1666, Colonel Henry Norwood attempted to inflict his own ideas on the engineers, who did not progress as rapidly as he thought they should do. But his letters to the Tangier Commissioners also emphasised the continual impairment of the Mole by storms and the futility of the measures taken to rectify the situation:

> I had much ado to persuade Major Taylor (Sir Hugh Cholmeley's chief agent in this work) to forbear filling up a great unnecessary piece joining to the Castle and to employ all his force to lengthen his work into the sea, he pretended Sir Hugh's especial commands to finish the first 200 yards before he went on, but I hope the liberty to hinder him by force, and after prevailed upon him to begin another 50 yards forwards, which will be done by Christmas to the great advantage of our harbour, wherein we every year lost all our boats, which by this means will be preserved and all small vessels of trade secured. Perhaps Sir Hugh will complain at my straining a point of my authority by intermeddling in the work of the Mole but I hope his Majesty will be pleased to justify me herein, I had not patience to see them work backwards at so great expense to his Exchequer, since that piece (if it be needful) may as well be made seven years hence as now, and now can be of no more use to the Mole then the making a causeway at Edinburgh.[10]

In August 1668, the Earl of Sandwich was charged with making an exact survey of the Mole during his stay in Tangier. He was assisted by Sheres, and it was shown that 380 yards of the breakwater had been completed. Under the scheme or 'model' designed by Cholmeley the following year, the principal officers of the Mole – the deputy-surveyor, the comptroller, and the clerk examiner – were to personally oversee the placing of the stones, work in the quarries, and the loading and dispatch of the carts and boats.[11] Additionally, the deputy-surveyor was to act in the absence of the surveyor-general, the comptroller examined all the construction materials and passed them fit, whereas the clerk examiner was responsible for all the works and materials ordered. Among the minor officials, the storekeeper kept account of all the stores received, while the muster-master would muster the artisans and labourers four times per day, and take their names.

Sir Hugh Cholmeley returned to Tangier in April 1670, but the Mole had sustained considerable damage from the storms of the two past winters. There erupted a sharp controversy as to the most advantageous method of building to be employed. Sheres, who after visiting Genoa was drawn to the foundation of the Mole there, which was constructed by sinking huge wooden chests or caissons filled with rocks and bound with iron straps. With dimensions of 40 feet or more in length and 20,000 cubic feet, these chests were for the young engineer the solution. The Governor, Lord Middleton was impressed with the system and ordered its trial, but they proved most difficult to set into place, and few of them were ever incorporated into the whole structure.[12] On 18 September 1670 the first chest was placed, though

10 TNA, CO 279/6, fols 88–9. Norwood to Arlington, 31 August 1666; Cholmeley, *Account*, p. 246.
11 TNA, CO 279/12, fols 97–100.
12 TNA, CO 279/13, fol. 56. Profile of a design for the Mole at Tangier, 10 March 1670.

not without great difficulty, the work being hindered by fierce gales. Henry, after working through the night and sustaining an injury from a fall, appealed to Cholmeley for help, following the failure of the seventh attempt to place a caisson. Sir Hugh succeeded in locating the chest placed, though not very firmly, and the wrong side out. Reports sent to the Tangier Commissioners in July and August 1670, and February 1671 conveyed significant progress. Sheres would replace Cholmeley as surveyor-general of the Mole in 1676, and held this post until 1683 when he was commanded to demolish the complete structure as part of the greater operation of abandoning the colony.

In February 1672, Sir Hugh Cholmeley returned home again, leaving instructions for the continuation of the breakwater. On 14 February 1673, it was reported that 437 yards had been completed, and two weeks later, 440 yards, with 'the whole walk curiously flagged so that it is supposed the like walk is not upon the Exchange of London.'[13] Sheres began his work as Surveyor-General on 24 June 1676, and was initially successful. One great chest was placed September – despite strong winds and tempestuous seas, and a second was added in October. In mid 1677, more caissons were sunk and various repairs to the Mole were completed. Since the project had come under Sheres' leadership, 11 chests were sunk, which, with other works accomplished, computed to 116,306 cubic feet in stone and tarras. A survey of the breakwater, dated 22 October 1677, reported, 'the largest [chest] is 83 feet x 30 x 20. The work has been repaired and secured, and advanced 15 feet since the last survey of 1 October 1676. Quarters, granaries, storehouses and stables have been erected.'[14] In November, the length of the Mole was given as 457 yards.[15] The same year, the author of *The Present State of Tangier* was able to write:

> The Mole is in its design the greatest and most noble undertaking in the world (all other Moles, as at Genoa, Malaga, Algiers, etc., not deserving more than the name of a quay, in comparison of it), it is a very pleasant thing to look on; and if it may be finished according to his Majesty's purpose, who hath spared no cost upon it, it will not only secure the bay and ships in it, but in time render Tangier very considerable and advantageous to his Majesty and his Kingdoms. It is now near 470 yards long, and 30 yards broad, several pretty houses upon it and many families; on the inner side 24 arched cellars, and before them a curious walk, with pillars for the mooring of ships. Upon the Mole are a vast number of great guns, which are almost continually kept warm during fair weather, in giving and paying salutes to ships which come in and out.[16]

After the conclusion of peace with the Moors in 1680, it was hoped that work might be resumed on the Mole, but the question of abandoning Tangier

13 TNA, CO 279/16, fol. 285. Bolland to Cholmeley, 28 February 1673.

14 TNA, CO 279/21, fols 228–9. Survey of the Mole, 22 October 1677.

15 TNA, CO 279/21, fol. 287. Drafts of the Mole, 22 November 1677, showing position of the line of chests: Charles, York, Peterborough, Anglesey, Coventry, Old Chest, Craven (in a breach of the slope work), two breaches needing repair and a small chest placed since the last survey.

16 [George Phillips], *The Present State of Tangier*, p. 17.

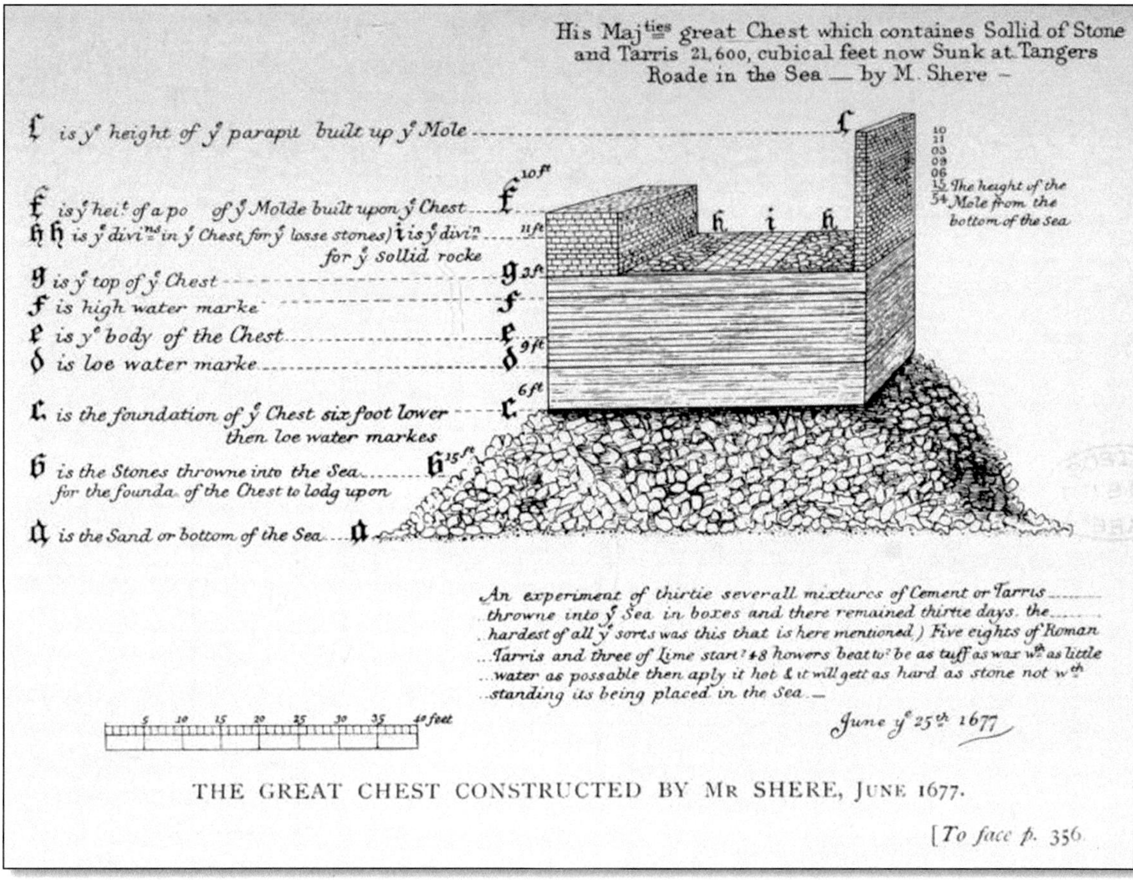

The Great Chest Constructed by Mr Shere, June 1677. (Creative Commons Public Domain)

being already under discussion, nothing more was done. On 14 February 1681 Sir Leoline Jenkins wrote to Sheres:

> I knew you would be sorry to see the Mole at a stand, but it must be so for some time, so exhausted are we here at home. We expect to see what the new Parliament will do … the last Parliament was not all kind to Tangier and some of our leading men did declare with much vehemence that Tangier was not nor ever would be worth the keeping, therefore wished it blown up in the air.[17]

In 1682, when its destruction necessitated 2,000 men working for months, it was 1,436 feet long, with a mean width of 110 feet, and mean height from high to low water of 18 feet. Yet ultimately, when a final report was compiled by officials commissioned by Lord Dartmouth in October 1683 concerning the demolition the structure, it concluded that the Tangier Mole was 'altogether unuseful to his Majesty for the receiving, careening or preserving his Majesty's ships, so in our opinions grounded on the foregoing considerations, it is not a place to be rendered so to answer in any degree the time and expense of doing it, if it can be done'.[18] In all, the sum of £340,000 had been spent on the construction and maintenance of the structure, which was intentionally demolished by a combination of explosives and months of hard physical effort.

Table 41. Account of the expenses attending the construction of the Mole of Tangier, 11 August 1669.[19]

	£.	s.	d.
For vessels, boats, floats, and other engines, with cordage, sails, pitch, tar, and necessaries thereunto belonging	4,400	00	00
For iron and brass work, lead, etc. about	2,600	00	00
For plank and other timber, with bolts, and timber utensils of all sorts, to about	4,300	00	00
To lime, tarras, coals, brick, and gunpowder, to about	1,900	00	00
To horses brought, with provisions and tackle for them, about	6,100	00	00
To freight of materials of all sorts, and transportation of horses and workmen, to about	10,700	00	00
To pay of artificers and workmen and labourers, with wages and allowances at Tangier, to about	41,100	00	00
To rewards and payments for services and assistance in the management of the affair, to about	2,600	00	00
For other disbursements of sundry natures, not well deducible to any head, to about	4,100	00	00
	84,800	00	00
And appears by this account, that, including salaries and money advanced to Lord Teviot and Sir John Lawson, there had been on the whole issued to that period, upon account of Tangier Mole, £103,965			
Amount of the expenses under the management of Sir Hugh Cholmley, Surveyor-General, from the end of the foregoing account to the last of June 1676, when the work finished was	139,932	05	4½
	103,965	00	00
Total expenditure for Tangier Mole	243,897	05	4½

19 Cholmeley, *Account*, pp. 295–6.

5

Know Your Enemy: the Army of Khadir Ghaïlān and Moroccan Warfare

The establishment of the English garrison at Tangier in 1662 coincided with the beginning of the effective rule of Morocco by the Alaouite dynasty, which asserted itself in the later seventeenth century. Ghaïlān and his commanders led forces that fought like a feudal mass, their tactics being so different to anything which Charles II's troops had experienced before, and they were a formidable enemy. Significantly for the garrison, whenever the Moors brought their considerable numerical weight to bear against it, they were incapable of sustaining their pressure for long. Similarly, Barbary Corsairs were unable to blockade Tangier by sea, thus rendering a serious siege of the city and port impossible. Although there are scant references to the military exploits of Ghaïlān in Moroccan sources, descriptions of his person and the military threat posed by his troops to the new outpost do appear in English texts. However, there is less information about the men who followed him, while speculation about their strength, potency and arms varied from one source to another, although their fierceness and ingenuity on the battlefield would gradually supersede all other notions of their qualities.

In his journal, Edward Barlow, an English sailor who served under Sandwich during his Mediterranean voyage of 1661–2, provided a first-hand description of Ghaïlān's troops in Tangier, barely days before the colony was formally handed over. Barlow was among those instructed to watch the movements of the Moors from behind the walls of Tangier. From his vantage point he closely observed them when, following an agreement with the Moorish leader, he accompanied other seamen to cut wood around Tangier – a concession not afforded to the Portuguese. This was not the first time that the English had been allowed to go ashore to obtain supplies of water and timber. They had been doing so since December the previous year.[1] Barlow's vivid testimony recounts local people coming to observe his naval

1 Anderson (ed.), *Journal of Edward Montague*, pp. 110–11.

Códice De Trajes, *North African Cavalryman* (1547). (Biblio de Espãna, Creative Commons Public Domain)

party, offering to sell livestock and local produce. Accordingly, he described the appearance and horsemanship of Ghaïlān's fighters, as being:

> very well mounted on Barbary horses, which are the best in the world for swiftness. The men going in habit in thin woollen cloth of a whitish colour made in loose bodied coats and long breeches; many of them wearing a kind of mantle of the same colour, with a light blue or green silk sash about their middle, with a 'turbite' or little knit cap upon their heads, which are the finest knit caps of that sort in all the world, and are dyed into a fine scarlet dye as thick as any cloth: and upon their feet a coarse kind of shoe, and spurs of three inches long, and their weapons are a lance, and a large kind of cutlass or hanger; but with the lance they will ride at full speed and heave it forward as they ride, and catch it in their hands again before it can fall to the ground, they ride with such speed and swiftness.[2]

While the military skill of the Moors and frequent presence near to the English fortifications about Tangier forced an immediate recognition of their threat, these very factors prevented any substantial contact beyond the lines

2 NMM, JOD/4; Lubbock (ed.), *Journal*, I, p. 67.

of confrontation. But whatever their warlike ambitions, according to one pamphleteer:

> they fight in disorder, without ranks or files, the horse by themselves, and the foot by themselves … They fight in the same manner as the Roman authors have represented the Ancient Mauri; neither are they better skilled in marshalling an army or fighting. Let any man that knows the art of war compare them with us, and judge whether we may not be able to encounter them. If they have had successes against us, it is through our weakness and unpreparedness.[3]

The dividing line, as far as this source was concerned, was predominantly one of military skill and discipline. In another narrative, victory over the natives is not attributed to mere superiority in military skill. There was a far more important moral and ethical dimension to the English triumph:

> Though much is due to the conduct and bravery of Colonel Sackville, Vice-Admiral Herbert, and all the officers, as well as to the undaunted courage of the soldiers … yet must wholly be ascribed to the Divine Assistance and Protection, without which it would have been impossible for such a handful of men to have performed what they did.[4]

Contemporary notions of the impenetrability of Moroccan religion, culture, identity, and geographical hinterland were articulated by the first-hand accounts of some travellers and members of the Tangier garrison, but these were often recycled narratives in the form of pamphlets. Even so, one modern historian notes, 'Charles II may not have been prepared to entertain advice which questioned the value of Tangier, but he was not oblivious to the state of affairs in Morocco; in fact, the English were reasonably well-informed about current developments while preparing for the expedition'.[5] Admiral Sandwich had spent his time awaiting the arrival of Peterborough's contingent in January 1662 by acquiring intelligence, and furnished regular reports about 'the state of Barbary, of the government, present wars, of the nature of the people, and condition of the soil'. Shortly before the occupation, he prepared a further report which considered diplomatic relations and trade, and clearly presaged subsequent English strategy in Morocco.[6] Hence, in a general sense, 'as contact with Morocco and knowledge about it increased during the course of the seventeenth century, perceptions concerning its peoples advanced from simple, predominantly bigoted, stereotypes to increasingly more ambivalent,

3 *The Present Interest of Tangier* (London: 1680), p. 3.

4 *A Particular Narrative of a Great Engagement between the Garrison of Tangier and the Moors* (London: Thomas Newcomb, 1680), p. 3.

5 Rickie Lette, 'Confronting Barbary: Reappraising the Responses of Britons to Engagement with Moroccans, and their Influence on Anglo-Moroccan Relations, 1625–1684', PhD thesis (University of Tasmania, 2018), p. 197.

6 BL, MS Sloane 3509, fols 25–7. A copy of a discourse of Barbary sent his Royal Highness by my Lord Sandwich, 1662.

A Moor or Berber (c. 1580). (Bayerische Staatsbibliotheck-BSB, Cod. 361, Creative Commons Public Domain)

nuanced, and even openly positive understandings which existed alongside the old ones'.[7]

Analysis shows that actual relations between the Muslim world and England were complex. Lancelot Addison, who spent seven years in Tangier as chaplain to the governor, and acquired a profound understanding not only of the colony's domestic concerns (but also of the history, customs and socio-religious rituals of Moroccans), reminded his readers, 'those who acknowledge Humanity in all its habits, may in perusing the remarks made upon these Barbarians, meet with something that may civilise the title, and induce them to think, that what is commonly called Barbarous, is but a different mode of civility'.[8] Such understandings of the political and cultural nature of Tangier have been scrutinised by an increasing number of literary scholars. In compiling published accounts on the English occupation of 1661–84, each based on 'close and sustained contact with the local population both in times of peace and war', Bejjit concludes that they were overwhelmingly filtered through the wants and ambitions of the garrison's community.[9] Nat Cutter contends that narratives based partially on interviews with Moroccans, were beginning to become popular in England during this period. Still, 'none of these texts enjoyed a large circulation, and aimed to distinguish and describe North Africa and its people. Therefore, what accurate information they offered was often lost among a confusion of fiction, polemic and fear'.[10]

Although during the early military encounters in Tangier with the Moors quickly developed an admiration for their foe, the devastating nature of the defeat of 3 May 1662 had a strong psychological impact on the English and Irish soldiers, one that gave shape to enduring images of the indestructibility and menacing disposition of their enemy. One contemporary provided a description of the tactics and military strength of the Moors from an English viewpoint, which fostered the notion of them as resourceful and disciplined fighters:

> He [Ghaïlān] has not any fortress of great importance, but only upon the seacoast, for as Cabo de Guer, Larache and Tetuan. For as the Turks and Persians do, so

7 Lette, 'Confronting Barbary', p. 90.
8 Addison, *West Barbary*, pp. 7–8.
9 Bejjit, *English Colonial Texts*, p. 43.
10 Nat Cutter, 'Turks, Moors, Deys and Kingdoms: North African Diversity in English News before 1700', *MHJ*, 46 (2018), pp. 61–84 (p. 63).

he for his cause he stands not much upon his artillery; although he has very great store (which his predecessors took from the Portugals, and others) in Fèz, Morocco, Tarudant, and in the aforesaid ports; causing also more to be cast when need requires; for he wants not masters of Europe in this science. He has a house of munition in Morocco, where they make ordinarily six and forty quintals of powder every month; as likewise calivers and steel bows. His forces are first, of 2,700 horse and 2,000 harquebusiers.

The second is, of a royal squadron of 6,000 gentlemen, being all of noble parentage, and of great account. These men are mounted upon excellent horses, with furniture and arms; for variety of colours, most beautiful; and for riches and ornament, beyond measure estimable; for everything about them shines with gold, silver, pearls, jewels, and whatsoever else may please the eye, or satisfy the curiosity of beholders. These men, besides all sorts of provision for their family, receive further in wages, from seventy to one hundred ounces of silver a man.

The third sort of forces which he has consists of his *Timarioth*. For he granted to all his sons and brothers, and other persons of accounts and authority, among his people of Africa, or to the princes of the Arabians, the benefit of great lordships and tenures for sustentation of his cavalry; and the *Archiades* [Qā'ids] themselves till the fields, and afterwards reap rice, oil, barley, butter, sheep, hens and money, and distribute the same monthly to the soldiers, according to the several quantities of their persons. They also give them cloth, linen, and silk to apparel themselves. Arms of offence and defence, and horses, with which they serve in the wars, and if they die, or be killed, they allow them other. Every one of these leaders contends to bring his people into the field well-ordered. Besides this, they have between four and twenty, and thirty ounces of silver wages every year.

His fourth military forces are the Arabians, who live continually in their *Avari* (for so they call their habitations, each one of them consisting of a hundred or two hundred pavilions) governed by divers *Alchiades*, to the end they may be ready in time of need. These serve on horseback; but they are rather to be counted thieves than true soldiers.

His fifth kind of forces military, are somewhat like unto the trained soldiers of Christian Princes; and among these, the inhabitants of cities and villages of the kingdom, and of the mountains are enrolled, whom the King makes very little account of, and very seldom puts arms into their hands, for fear of insurrections and rebellions, except in wars against the Christians, for then he cannot conveniently forbid them. For it being written in their law, that if a Moor kill a Christian, or is slain by him, he goeth directly into Paradise. Men, women, and those of every age and degree, run to the wars hand afore head, that at least may there be slain, any by this means gain Heaven.

200,000 men he brought against Tetuan [in] 1659. Yet he cannot long continue at war; yea, not above three months, because his forces living on that provision which he hath daily coming in, as well for sustenance, as for apparel; and not being and not being able to have all this conducted thither, where the war requires, it follows of necessity, that in short time they must return home for their maintenance. We want nothing but men, and those men nothing but the apprehension of that infinite treasure we might have in Manginda, Ethiopia, Congo, Anglola, Pratua, Toroa, Monomotapa, etc., if we could but bring this man to terms. His men march not all in company, but the respective commanders set

> forth two hours one after another, everyone having an ambuscado and stratagem, not in any strict order of rank and file. Yet though their discipline is not exact, their order is so without confusion and violence. All the commanders have their wives and boys attending them well-guarded. Their hoarse drums serve to deafen the ears, and to confound the senses to any other clamour, with some brass dishes, and wind instruments, to noise the Varnes, carried by fellows on horseback, a little before every company; whose horses are very swift, it being a shame there to lose a drum. His weapon is bow and arrow, an iron pole, a shrene, a petronel, a harquebus, scimitar; all over armed like a porcupine.
>
> They eat and lie in one blanket, tying their horses' bridle to their arms while they graze. When they come towards an enemy, they march very exactly and silently, not a man, upon pain of death, daring to break the order. When they are near an engagement, the horse encompass their foot in the rear, in form of a half-moon or crescent; those horse have order not to meddle with the enemy, but only to drive and necessitate the foot upon them, till they have pierced through their battalia, if possible; and if they chance to recoil, to hold then to the slaughter, till they have wearied and dulled the enemy's swords; and then the reserve and they together fall in with fresh fury and vigour; and this serves for all advantages of military policy, to quicken the multitudes through despair to high and gallant services. He [Ghaïlān] chooses rather to tire out a town, than storm it; then as soon as he has raised his battery, and made a kind of breastwork, with some mounts in it, to overlook the place, he makes his approaches in spite of the bullet, and fills up the trenches with bodies, if he cannot do it with any other matters; and when once a breach is made, it is either a soldier's death in honour, or a dog's in the camp, for any to retreat; their patience and resolution making up their defect of skill and art.
>
> He trains up the Moors to such discipline that they shall march 20,000 together, with that order and silence, for forty mile that they cannot be discovered; yea, there is not a word spoken in the camo for two days together sometimes, except in his own tent. And what is more remarkable, 2,000 or 3,000 of them shall lodge themselves in the ferns, and among their rising grounds, so that you may ride through those very grounds and not discover a man, nay, bear up your belief a little longer, while I tell you that 10,000 of them shall hide themselves in the sand so that you may go over to them, and not discover them.[11]

The Moors possessed two specific kinds of troops. The light cavalry, mainly recruited from Berbers or Amazigh – the ancient peoples who had occupied North Africa since the beginning of recorded history and until the Islamic conquests of the eighth century – were mounted on tough, agile hill-ponies, exceedingly suited to Moroccan warfare. These soldiers were equipped primarily with sword (*casara*), scimitar (*shamshir*), lance, and infrequently, the *adarga* or heart-shaped leather shield, which had a greater surface area that offered better protection. These shields were employed together with lances, affording users maximum mobility on the battlefield and the capability to quickly respond to enemy attacks. Western observers from earlier periods offer some idea of the appearance of these troops. Between 1496 and 1499 the German knight Arnold

11 *Description of Tangier*, p. 16; TNA, CO 279/33, fol. 138.

von Harff undertook a pilgrimage through various countries, including Arabia, Palestine, Turkey, France and Spain. One manuscript version of his travels, illustrated in the 1550s, shows a mounted Moor dressed in a light robe, and armed with lance and scimitar.[12] Similarly, a North African cavalryman from the Spanish *Códice De Trajes* (1547) is depicted wearing a substantial looking coat, with scimitar, *adarga* and lance.[13] Little is known of the armour of Moroccan and Saharan Africa before the late nineteenth century, when qualities of weapons and dress were brought back to Europe as souvenirs of colonial wars (including the Omdurman Campaign of 1898). The Moorish cavalryman of the seventeenth century may have been garbed in a quilted fabric coat (*jibbah*), decorated with coloured panels, and with split skirts for riding. These could be worn on their own, or with shirts of rivetted mail. A set of Sudanese armour in the Royal Armouries' collection, dating from the late 1800s, comprises a padded coat and a helmet with a mail aventail.[14]

The Moorish infantryman was variously armed with a musket or *moukalla* (either matchlock or more rarely, snaphance), bow, spear and scimitar. One late sixteenth-century image of 'A Moor or Berber' depicts a figure wearing a traditional *lithan* or cloth turban, with a coloured *burnous* (long sleeveless cloak of coarse woollen fabric with a large hood). In Morocco the closure at the front of the cloak could be thrown over the shoulder to free the wearer's arms. The infantryman is also portrayed gripping a scimitar with his left hand.[15] Invariably the two types of troops were deployed together, the preferred Moorish tactic was to overtly place troops as close as possible to their opponents, often under cover of darkness, and conceal them in any slight depressions in the ground. At a decisive point during an ensuing battle, the concealed troops would appear, often 'rising out of the ground', and fall on their adversaries. The late-eighteenth-century English military surgeon and traveller, William Lemprière, described that in Morocco:

> The dress of the men consists of a short linen shirt, with large and loose sleeves hanging half-way down to the ground. A pair of loose linen drawers, reaching almost to the ankle, over which they wear another loose pair, made of wollen cloth. Over the shirt they wear two or three woollen cloth waistcoats of different colours ... over these waistcoats they throw a velvet cord, which crosses the right shoulder, and suspends on the left side a curved dagger or knife, sheathed in a brass case.[16]

Similarly, James Riley, Captain of the United States merchant ship *Commerce*, shipwrecked off the coast of Western Sahara in 1815, described the Moroccan Arab captors of himself and his crew:

12 Bod. Lib., MS Bodl. 972, fol. 1. Costumes and arms of the Arabs.

13 Madrid, Biblioteca Nacional de España, Res/285.

14 Leeds, Royal Armouries' Collection, XXVIA.137. See also XXVIA.104 and XXVIA.170 for further examples. See also David Nicolle, *The Moors: The Islamic West 7th–15th Centuries AD* (Oxford: Osprey, 2001), pp. 12–14.

15 Munich, Bayerische Staatsbibliothek, BSB Cod.icon. 361, fol. 20.

16 William Lemprière, *A Tour from Gi lbralta to Tangier, Salle, Mogodore, Santa Cruz, Talrudant, and thence over Mt Atlas to Morocco* (London: J. Walter, 1793), p. 6.

Johannes Lewenklau, *Pictures of Turkish rulers, soldiers, courtiers, cities etc.: African firing a rifle from a sitting position* (undated). (Osterreichisches Staatarchiv., Cod. 8615, fol. 160r., Creative Commons Public Domain)

These natives were of a different race of men from any we had hitherto seen; they wear a *haik* or piece of woollen cloth wrapped about their bodies, which covering them, falls down below their knees; or else a cloak called *gzlabbia*, made in a similar manner, cut with short sleeves, and one fold of the *haik* generally covered the head; but those who had not their heads covered with their *haik* or *gzlabbia*, or *sulam*, wore a kind of turban; the cloak or *sulam*, is made of coarse black cloth, very shaggy, and much in the form of the European cloak, with a hood or headpiece to it; it is, however, sewed together part of the way down in front, so that to get it on, they slip it over their heads, and it covers their arms. They are generally stout men, of five feet eight or 10 inches in height, and well-set; their complexion a light olive – they wear their beards as long as they will grow, and consider a man without a beard an effeminate being, and hold him in great contempt. Their saddles are well-made and very high, at least eight or 10 inches, fitted before and behind so as almost impossible for the horse to throw his rider; their bridles are of the most powerful Arabian kind; their stirrups are made of broad sheets of iron that cover almost the whole foot – many are plated with silver. All the men wore slippers and spurs, and had their stirrups tied up very short.[17]

Forming the bulk of the standing army of the Sultan of Morocco, Sultan Malawy Ismăïl, was the renowned Black Guard or *'Abīd al-Bukhārī* ('slaves of al-Bukhari'), a corps of Black-African slaves and *Haratin* (free Blacks) soldiers. These descended from captives, transported to Morocco from sub-Saharan Africa, who were settled with their families, and considered more loyal than Arab or Berber warriors because of their lack of tribal affiliation. By the time of Malawy's death in 1727 these soldiers numbered 150,000.[18] At Tangier the Moors had grown bolder because they were better equipped than their opponents for small-scale encounters. Moreover, the garrison's limited knowledge of their enemies had nurtured an inveterate notion that the Moors were formidable troops when, according to the author of a contemporary pamphlet, their military strategy was primitive and could not measure up to the skill and order of the English troops. Thus, the writer

17 James Riley, *An Authentic Narrative of the Loss of the American Brig Commerce* (Hartford, Conn.: privately published, 1817), p. 160.

18 Daniel Pipes, *Slave Soldiers and Islam: The Genesis of a Military System* (New Haven: Yale University Press, 1981), pp. 140–1; Allan R. Meyers, 'Class, Ethnicity, and Slavery: The Origins of the Moroccan 'Abid', *The International Journal of African Historical Studies*, 10 (1977), pp. 427–42 (p. 427).

proposed concrete remedies for overcoming the considerable military threat posed by the Moroccan warriors:

> They fight in the same manner of the Roman authors have represented the ancient *Mauri*; neither are they better skilled at marshalling an army or fighting. Let any man who knows the Art of War compare them with us, and judge whether we may not be able to encounter them. If they have had the successes against us, it is through our weakness and unpreparedness. We have marched against them with only muskets and swords, and they have come against us with horse and lance: before our men had time to discharge their muskets, the horse and lance had disordered our men, broken our ranks, and cut them all to pieces on a sudden. Had we had a wall of pikes to oppose against them, lined with muskets, all the horse of Barbary could do us no mischief, and we may march safely through the country.[19]

19 *The Present Interest of Tangier.*

6

The Governorship of Andrew Rutherford, 1st Earl of Teviot, 1663–64

A change of leadership at Tangier was required. Lord Peterborough had returned home in May 1662, leaving the command of the garrison in the hands of his deputy, Colonel John Fitzgerald, and claiming to have left everything in good order. Fitzgerald was an experienced officer who had commanded an Irish Regiment in the service of Charles II in exile in the Low Countries. He conducted the evacuation of the Dunkirk garrison and had gained a formidable reputation for his leadership during the fighting with the Moors in recent operations, and so the Tangier Committee preferred him as Peterborough's successor. But following the latter's return to the colony in September, he was replaced as governor by Andrew Rutherford, a Scottish Catholic, and professional soldier, who was created Earl of Teviot 'to hearten him' for the service.[1] Although Peterborough's performance as commander of the Tangier garrison was largely ineffective, he at least attempted to improve the military situation. In October 1662 Captain Charles Horbord, commanding the naval squadron at Tangier, reported the 'great merits of Lord Peterborough, than whom he never saw a man more zealous for the King's service and the good of the town entrusted to him'. On 9 May 1663, he added, 'Lord Peterborough will leave Tangier with all manner of love and satisfaction from the garrison'.[2]

The reason for the specific appointment of Teviot was never made public, but Pepys, who had recently been appointed to the Tangier Committee – thanks to his patron, the Earl of Sandwich – wrote, 'this day [Rutherford] made governor of Tangier, for I know not what reasons; and my Lord of Peterborough to be called home; which, though it is said it is done with

1 BL, MS Harley 6844, fols 89–90. Commission to the Earl of Teviot, to be Captain-General at Tangier, 13 April 1663; Matthew Glozier, *Scottish Soldiers in France in the Reign of the Sun King* (Leiden: Brill, 2004), pp. 64–5.

2 Bodl. Lib., MS Carte 75, fols 75–6, 114–15. Horbord to Sandwich, 14 October 1662 and 9 May 1663.

kindness, yet all the world may see it is done otherwise, and I am sorry to see a Catholic governor sent to command there, where all the rest of the officers almost are such already'. On 26 January 1663 Samuel confided, 'Thence by coach to Whitehall, and met upon the Tangier Commission, our greatest business the discoursing of getting things ready for my Lord Rutherford to go about the middle of March next, and a proposal of Sir John Lawson's and Mr Chomley's concerning undertaking the Mole, which is referred to another time'. Tellingly also, on 29 April he added:

> Talking of the business of Tangier, he [William Coventry, Secretary to the Admiralty] tells me that my Lord Teviot is gone away without the least respect paid to him, nor indeed to any man, but without his commission; and (if it be true what he says) having laid out seven or eight thousand pounds in commodities for the place; and besides having not only disobliged all the Commissioners for Tangier, but also Sir Charles Berkeley the other day, who, speaking in behalf of Colonel Fitzgerald, that having been deputy-governor there already, he ought to have expected and had the governorship upon the death or removal of the former governor. And whereas it is said that he and his men are Irish, which is indeed the main thing that hath moved the King and Council to put in Teviot to prevent the Irish having too great and the whole command there under Fitzgerald.[3]

Rutherford's acceptance of the governorship might had been something to do with the considerable enticements offered to him to accept the post. One of these was his appointment as Sheriff-Principal of Roxburgh, the other was his elevation in the Scottish Peerage. Both occurred in April 1663.[4] Although Pepys thought him 'a most careful, thoughtful, and cunning man', Teviot, like his predecessor, aimed to make a profit from supplying the Tangier garrison.[5] Pepys' employment on the Committee also allowed him to associate with various influential men, including successive governors of Tangier and their clerks, who were frequently in London.[6] Though he dismissed accusations that he made money on the side, Pepys considered the colony 'one of the best flowers in my garden', and his personal accounts were sometimes mixed up with those of Tangier.[7] Nonetheless, he recorded that, in the Tangier business, nothing was done 'with true integrity', and officials posted there lined their own pockets. Rutherford was instructed to reduce the cost of the garrison (which was to number only 2,000 men). The sum of £50,000 a year, minus Peterborough's pension of £1,000, was allocated for 'the entertainment of the civil and military power', the remaining £20,00 per annum being anticipated for the construction of the fortifications and the improvement of the harbour.[8]

---

3 Pepys, *Diary*, 15 December 1662, 27 January 1663, 29 April 1663.
4 BL, MS Add. 23119, fol. 5.
5 Pepys, *Diary*, 8 December 1663.
6 Margarette Lincoln, 'Samuel Pepys and Tangier, 1662–1684', *HLQ*, 77 (2014), pp. 417–34 (p. 419).
7 Pepys, *Diary*, 26 September 1664; 29 December 1667.
8 TNA, CO 279/2, fols 169–70. Instructions for Andrew Rutherford, the Earl of Teviot as Governor of Tangier, 2 December 1663; BL, MS Harley, 6844, fol. 90.

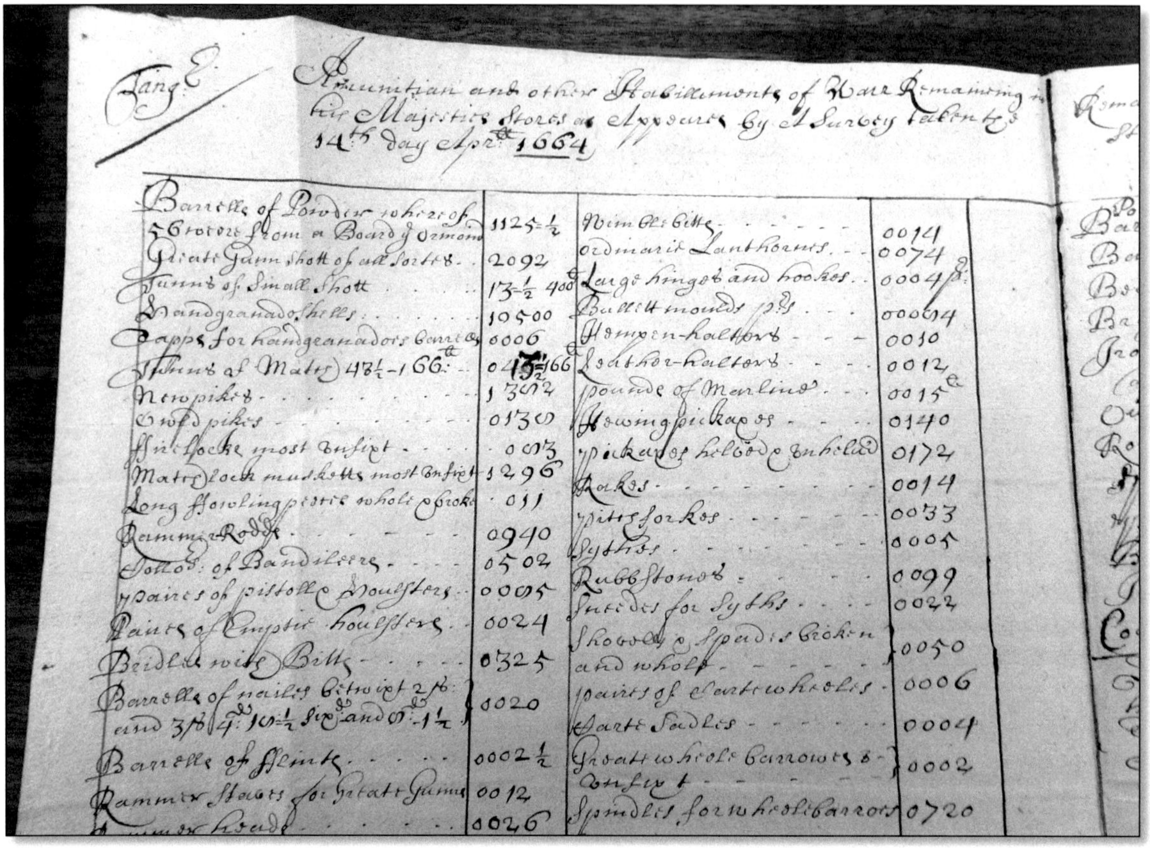

Ammunition and other habilliaments of war remaining in his Majesty's stores, 14 April 1664 (SRO, D742/0/3/4). (Courtesy of Staffordshire Archives)

On 30 March 1663, a contract for building the Mole was signed by Teviot, Lawson and Cholmeley. Pepys observed that the Tangier Committee voted on funds without a grasp of how to cost the enterprise and sanctioned the governor's accounts, knowing them to be fraudulently excessive.[9] The work on the Mole commenced soon afterwards, but at first made little progress.[10]

In April Teviot was directed to combine the garrison's four regiments of foot into two, one English and one Irish, each of 10 companies of 100 men. Teviot commanded one unit and Fitzgerald the other.[11] However, in October it was deemed that the first regiment should have 15 companies and the second five.[12] The new governor arrived in Tangier on 11 May 1663 and took immediate action. He stipulated that the soldiers sent as reinforcements should be Englishmen, rather than Scots, 'so as it may not appear a diminution of the [English] assistance his Majesty intended for the Crown of Portugal'.[13] Unlike his predecessor, Teviot pursued a bold strategy of expansion and confrontation with the Moors. He realised that the key to a successful defence was the construction of a series of fortifications which

9 Pepys, *Diary*, 26 January 1663; 16 February 1663; 10 August 1663.

10 TNA, CO 279/2, fols 16–21; Chomley, *Account of Tangier*, pp. 39–40.

11 TNA, CO 279/2, fol. 66. Teviot's instructions sent by Mr Luke, 27 April 1663.

12 TNA, CO 279/2, fol. 112.

13 Bod. Lib., MS Tanner 47, fol. 35. Teviot to Fanshaw, 8 July 1663.

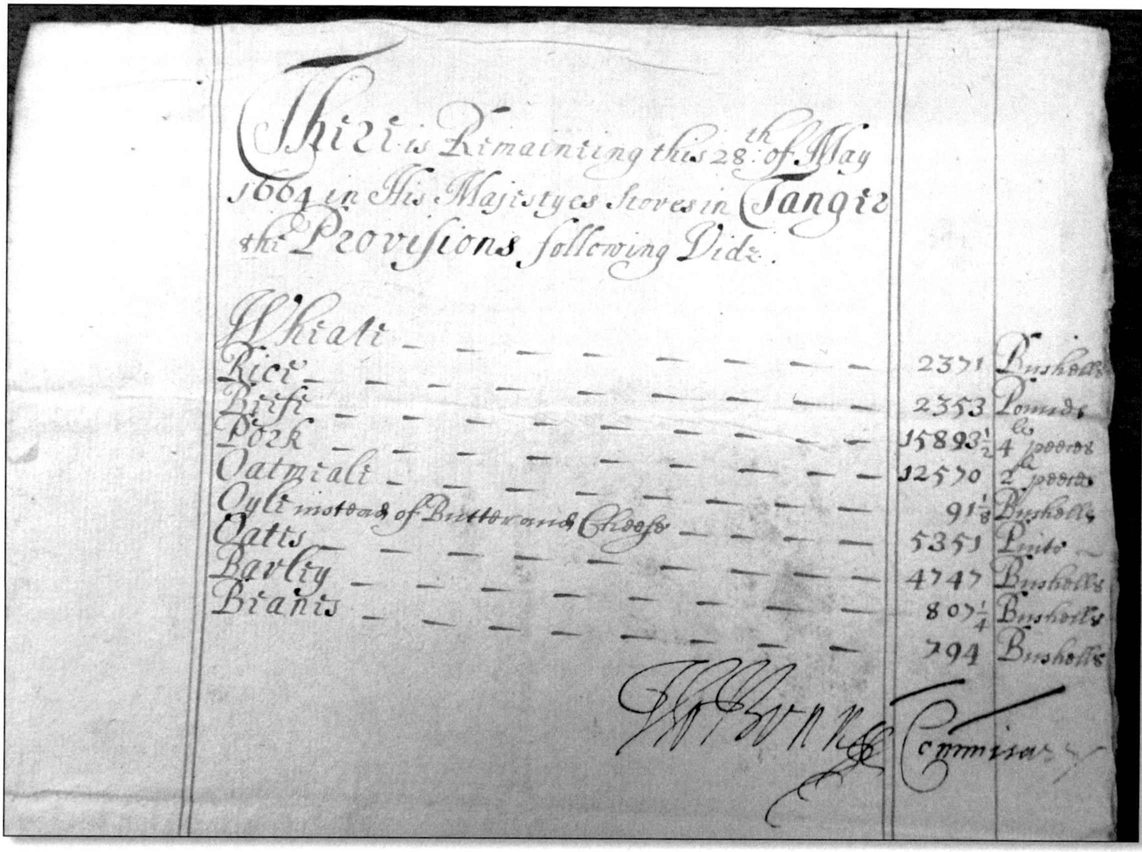

Theire is Remaining this 28th of May 1664 in His Majestyes Stores in Tangiere the Provisions following Vidz.

Wheate	2371	Bushells
Rice	2353	Pounds
Beefe	15893½	4 lb peeces
Pork	12570	2 lb peeces
Oatmeale	91⅛	Bushells
Oyle instead of Butter and Cheese	5351	Pints
Oatts	4747	Bushells
Barley	807¼	Bushells
Beanes	794	Bushells

[illegible] Commissary

Provisions remaining in stores, 28 May 1664 (SRO, D742/0/3/5). (Courtesy of Staffordshire Archives)

would allow the garrison, rather than its adversaries, to dominate the high ground overlooking the city. The brief period of Teviot's governorship (May 1663 to April 1664) saw a flurry of construction as it coincided with the first of Sir Bernard de Gomme's two voyages to Tangier.

He and Major Beckman were instructed to draw up proposals for the defence of the city, as well as directing the construction of earthworks and small redoubts. Sir Bernard first arrived in Tangier in mid January 1664, and when he returned to England on 30 May 1664, he left behind various unfinished additions to a system of forward outworks, which partly followed the lines of previous Portuguese structures. His 'exact platt' (plan) is probably the map in the National Maritime Museum, signed and dated 1664.[14] This delineates the extent of the fortified city and Mole. It also incorporates plans of Charles Fort and other outworks. Other plans, unsigned and undated, but in de Gomme's hand, represent working drawings of details of the Tangier fortifications.[15] The final map in the series embodies a scheme for making the Tangier defences more compatible with current European conventions. Much attention was given to a continuous counterscarp, built to protect the outer

14 NMM, P43, fol. 2.

15 NMM, P43, fol. 3; TNA, MPH 1, fol. 43; Andrew Saunders, *Fortress Builder: Bernard de Gomme, Charles II's Military Engineer* (Liverpool: Liverpool University Press, 2004), pp. 94, 342; Elbl, *Portuguese Tangier*, pp. 94–5.

Wenceslaus Hollar, *Prospect of Tangier from the Land, it being from the South-West side* (*c.* 1669). (Rijksmuseum, Creative Commons Public Domain)

ring of redoubts from Moorish attack.[16] A final drawing shows the profile and measurements of the old Portuguese curtain walls, such as those by the *Porta do campo*, improved during the administration of Lourenço Pires de Távora in 1564–6 (otherwise known to the English as Catherina Gate).[17] Some work commenced on this feature, and was completed on 9 June 1663. In February 1665 de Gomme set out again for Tangier. This time he brought with him instructions for the development of the defences both in the immediate and long-terms, and provided a system extending over four years, establishing the nature of the works intended and their proposed costs. Five forts were erected to form an outer line of defence beyond the walls. Moreover, 800 acres of land was annexed and protected with palisades, to provide pasture for the horses and cattle, and to allow the garrison to become more self-sufficient.

But the Moorish leader, Ghaïlān, who was with the main part of his army besieging Salé, was soon provoked into action. That night (9 June 1663) 500

16 TNA, MPH 1, fol. 21.

17 TNA, MPH 1, fol. 20.

Moors attacked Catherina Fort, but the soldiers commanded by Captain William Fiennes beat them off after two hours' hard fighting.[18] Three of Hollar's drawings, executed in late 1669, depict the fort as a substantial defensive structure consisting of an inverted earthen bank, with single embrasures – openings in a wall or parapet which is bevelled or splayed out on the inside – positioned at either flank of the forward angle. An inverted line of palisades is shown roughly 30 yards in advance of this.[19] One of Hollar's carefully rendered illustrations ('Prospect of Tangier from the Land, it being the South-West side'), showing Catherina Fort, was probably copied for Charles II by the Dutch landscape painter Hendrick Dankerts, as *A View of Tangier* (signed and dated 1669) because it is remarkably

18 Lancelot Addison, *The Moores Baffled being a discourse concerning Tangier, especially when it was under the Earl of Teviot* (London: William Crooke, 1681), pp. 7–8.

19 'Prospect of Tangier from the Land, it being the South-West side', 1669; 'Prospect of the lower part of Tangier, from the hill west of Whitehall', 1669; 'A Prospect of the Lands and Forts wherein the line of Communication before Tangier, now in possession of the English, drawn from Peterborough Tower', September 1669. See also Hendrick Danckerts' painting, 'A View of Tangier', signed and dated 1669 (RCT, RCIN 402578).

similar.[20] During the foggy night of 14–15 June 1663, and with four other bastions under construction, Beckman began working on Pole Fort, located some 300 yards to the south-west of Catherina. He later reported:

> Then I waited for a while until a thick fog set in and I took as many bricklayers as I would need and 600 men who carried stone and chalk [lime?]. I then began to construct a redoubt under command of […] and after much hard work the redoubt reached 4 feet in height by the evening. That night I alone with three musketeers defended the redoubt by putting out three double Spanish [*chevaux-de-frise*?] around it and throwing out 6,000 caltrops as well as placing 2,000 port fires [musketeers' matches] upon it. I also had a large number of hand-grenades which confused the enemy, and did not know what it meant.[21]

Work on the fortifications was undertaken with much difficulty, the builders being 'daily interrupted by the Moors, who, meeting in parties, gave continual alarms'.[22] Due to tensions with Spain, building materials shipped from Cadiz were increasingly hard to come by. Sir Richard Fanshaw, the ambassador to Lisbon attempted to obtain labour and materials in Portugal with little success, but reported of Teviot's efforts, 'in a fortnight space he hooked in a little piece of country by two new erected forts and a circular trench to the city, and I verily believe that in process of time he will add many skins to it, one without another, as there are in an onion'.[23] The governor himself reported on 15 June 1663, 'It [Pole Fort] gives such jealousy and inquietitude to Guyland that this three days by passed, by the intelligence we receive from his fugitives, we have been under arms all night, he having 4,000 horse and 2,000 foot to attack our new little fort, at this instant I expect his falling on us'.[24] For 10 days the fortifications outside Tangier's walls were manned by the entire garrison, being some 1,200 effectives of the foot, divided into three bodies, with 90 garrison Horse in support.

According to an anonymous report, published in *Mercurius Publicus* on 23 July 1663, and utilised by the compiler of *A Description of Tangier* – a confusing mélange of events, names and dates, and drawn from numerous sources – Colonel Fitzgerald with his regiment covered the sector adjacent to Tangier Bay; Colonel Henry Norwood, with half of the Governor's Regiment was in the centre, near to Pole Fort; Lieutenant Colonel Knightley, commanding the other half of the regiment covered the redoubts to their right; while Colonel Tobias Bridges remained with the horse, 'to give succour as need should require, and repel the enemy if they entered our works'. An outer line of positions, established as a screen for the protection of the men working on the fortifications, consisted of three posts: one commanded by a lieutenant and 30 men; another by an ensign and 18 soldiers; and a third (the

20 RCT, RCIN 402578.

21 Stockholm, Riksarkivet, Biographica B60. Beckman to Charles XI of Sweden, 11 December 1664 – quoted in Beckman, 'Martin Beckman', pp. 153–4.

22 Addison, *Moores Baffled*, p. 8.

23 HMC, *Heathcote*, pp. 119–20. Fanshaw to Sir Henry Bennet, Secretary of State, 19 June 1663.

24 CO 279/2, fol. 92. Teviot to Bennet, 15 June 1663.

most advanced) by a sergeant and 12 men. A 6-pounder cannon was placed at the latter, so 'the garrison should be in readiness, and at the shooting of the said gun, should take arms'.[25] At midday on Sunday 14 June, when the garrison officers were at dinner, three Moorish regiments, one carrying red and white colours, another black, and a third 'a sort of violet colour', launched a determined assault on the newly completed Pole Fort (later renamed 'Norwood Fort'), situated in an elevated position overlooking the city. They were seconded by a large body of cavalry. Defending the fortification was Major Rudyard of Fitzgerald's Regiment (who wrote a report of the action), with Beckman and 40 redcoats.[26]

To their aid came Captain Giles of the Governor's Regiment and several reformado officers. Ghaïlān himself, leading one of the detachments, reportedly acted 'with onset brave and brisk', and 'struck his colours between it and the town'. In preparation for such an attack Teviot had placed 36,000 caltrops on the rapidly sloping ground to impede the advance of cavalry, together with sow-guards with some landmines constructed by the garrison's fire-workers, 'loaden above with stones, granadoes and Swedes feathers were put into those farther posts'.[27] Swedish feathers, known sometimes as Swine Feathers, were fundamentally a musket rest, but with a pike head on the business end. As an early attempt to introduce a greater degree of flexibility and self-defence to the musketeer, without the need to be supported by slower moving divisions of pike, they could be used to form a defensive palisade of spear points if placed in the ground. Theoretically musketeers might retreat behind them and fire at their enemy in safety. Swedish feathers were used extensively on the Continent during the early seventeenth century, but although some troops were issued with them during the British Civil Wars there is little evidence of their usage. Turner, in 1670–71, described the device thus:

> I think I may reckon in this place the Swedish feather, among the defensive arms, though it does participate in both defense and offence. It is a stake five or six-foot-long, and about four fingers thick, with a piece of sharp iron nailed to each end of it. By the one end it is made fast in the ground in such a manner that the other may lay out so it may meet the breast of a horse, whereby a body of musketeers is defended as with a palisade, against the rude charge of a squadron of horse, which in the meantime they gall and disorder with their shot. I have seen them made use of in Germany, and before I left that war saw them drop out of use. When the infantry of several regiments or brigades are drawn up in battle, and the pikes and those stakes are fixed in the ground, they make a delightful show representing a wood. The pikes resembling the tall trees and the stakes the shrubs.[28]

25 *Mercurius Publicus* on 23 July 1663; *A Description of Tangier, the Country and People Adjoining with An Account of the Person and Government of Gayland the present Usurper of the Kingdom of Fez; And a short Narrative of the Proceedings of the English in those Parts* (London: Samuel Speed, 1664), p. 8.

26 TNA, CO 279/2, fols 96–104. Mr Rudyard's account of the late action at Tangier, 16 June 1663. Another narrative of this action is given in a letter from John Luke (CO 279/2, fol. 94).

27 *Mercurius Publicus* on 23 July 1663; *Description of Tangier*, p. 9.

28 Turner, *Pallas Armata*, p. 216.

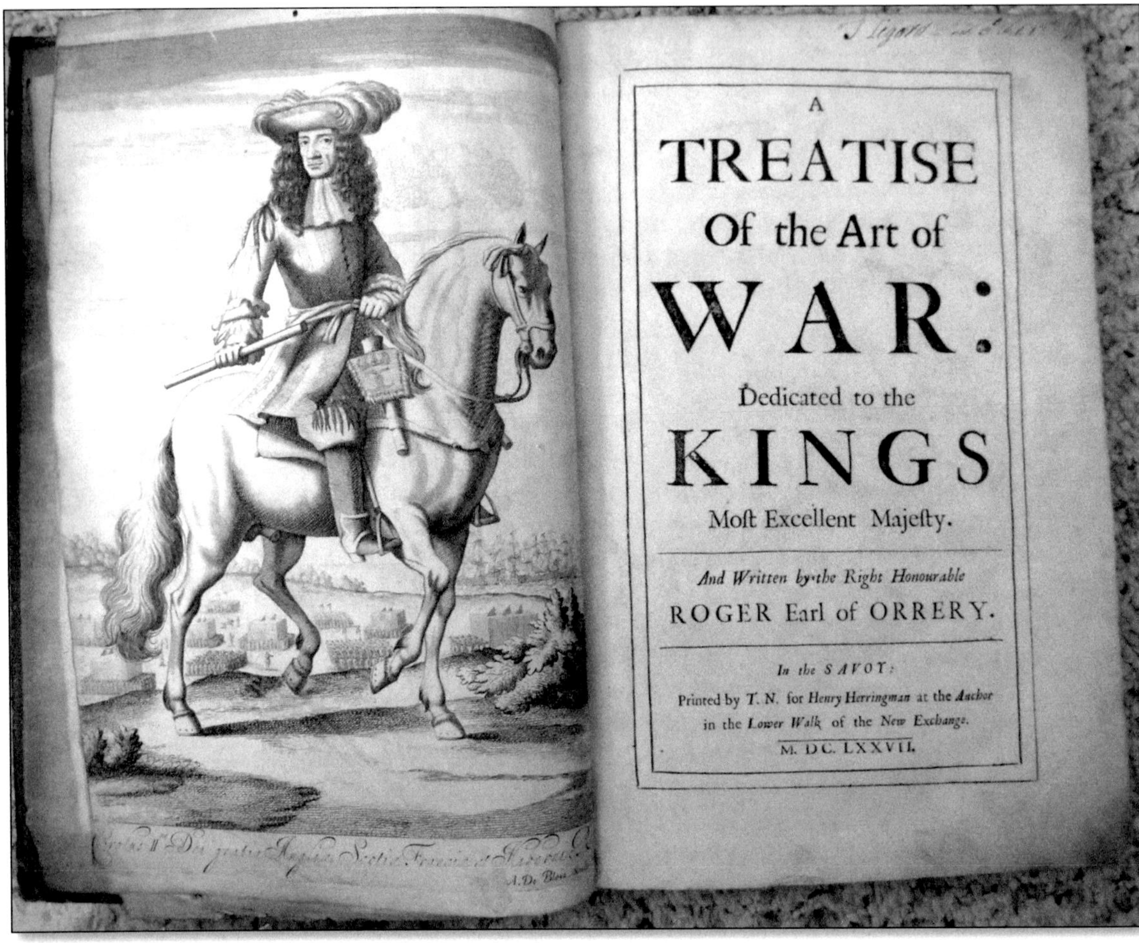

Roger Boyle, Earl of Orrery, *A Treatise of the Art of War* (1677). (Creative Commons Public Domain)

The value of these items to the defence of Tangier is further suggested by the presence of 1,000 of them among the garrison's stores on 14 April 1664 and 353 on 20 August 1679.[29]

Even though the English troops in Pole Fort were well prepared, when it came, the attack caught them momentarily by surprise.[30] The redoubt was 10 feet high and the Moors, having no ladders, attempted to climb on each other's backs and the backs of their horses. But during the 30-minute battle the garrison's soldiers maintained a firm defence until a supporting party of Horse under Colonel Bridges – which had been formed in close order within Catherina Port – marched out of one or both embrasures and fell upon the enemy. Though the Moors were accomplished light horsemen the weight and shock of the charge by the heavier English cavalry was something they were unused to. The arms and equipment carried by the garrison Horse were also more suited to this type of combat. Writing in 1644 the cavalry officer John Vernon recommended:

29 *Mercurius Publicus*, 23 July 1663; SRO, D742/0/3/4; D742/0/3/6.
30 Addison, *Moores Baffled*, pp. 9–10.

> The harquebuses and carbines arming is chiefly offensive, his defensive arms, as only an open cask or headpiece, a back and breast with buff coat under his arms; his offensive arms are a good harquebus, a carbine hanging on his right side in a belt by a swivel, a flask and cartridge case … and good fire-lock pistols in holsters. At his saddle a good stiff sword sharp pointed.[31]

According to Roger Boyle, Earl of Orrery:

> I acknowledge I would have every private trooper have his sword, or long tuck, his case of pistols, and carbine; and for defence, his back, breast and pot; at least, I would have the front and flanks of every troop in such armour. For besides the terror it gives to an enemy in his doublet, to fight with men of iron, and the encouragement it gives our own men; none knows what proof the armour is of. And it is most certain, that in combat, as well as pursuit, the sword does most execution; and no armour is less than sword proof … for defence, his back, breast and pot; at least, I would have the front and flanks of every troop in such armour. For besides the terror it gives to an enemy in his doublet, to fight with men of iron, and the encouragement it gives our own men; none knows what proof the armour is of. And it is most certain, that in combat, as well as pursuit, the sword does most execution, and no armour is less than sword proof. I therefore earnestly wish that the officers, the troopers, and the pikemen were bound under severe penalties, to fight in armour, and constantly to march in armour, which piece of discipline, if it were revived by strict commands, and if broken punished exemplarily, I am confident the advantages would be considerable.[32]

Present at Charles II's Coronation in 1661, the Horse Guards were described by Sir Edward Walker, as being 'all well-mounted, having buff coats, with white armour, their horses furnished with hoses (being a short foot cloth) with red scarves, and plumes of red and white feathers … the Guards of His Royal Highness the Duke of York … all having black armour, red, white and black feathers, and red scarves, with belts of His Highness's livery'.[33] Within the Tangier garrison serviceable arms and equipment were at a premium for the Horse. An undated list of 'arms wanting for the four troops of horse' includes 100 saddles with furniture, 100 back and breast with headpieces, 100 carbines with belts, and 100 pair of pistols and holsters.[34] Likewise, some of the armour issued to the Tangier Horse was unsuitable, however, and reflected an earlier form of design. Probably in 1680 one of the officers made recommendations to the Tangier Committee as to the composition and arming of the proposed new troops to be sent out, reporting, 'most of the armour previously sent, being in the late war lost and made unserviceable, there being a great part of them made too short'.

31 John Vernon, *The Young Horseman, or, The honest plain-dealing cavalier* (London, 1644), p. 8.

32 Roger Boyle, earl of Orrery, *A Treatise of the Art of War dedicated to the King's Most Excellent Majesty* (1677), pp. 32–3.

33 Sir Edward Walker, *A Circumstantial Account of the Preparations for the Coronation of His Highness, Charles the Second* (London: Baker, 1820), pp. 67–8.

34 SRO, D742/0/4/27.

He further requested for the new contingents, '112 saddles, holsters, carbine belts, suits of armour, back and breast, and pots larger than them last sent'.[35]

It was also desirable among the Horse during the Civil Wars and Restoration to wear thick leather coats known as 'buff coats' as protection against sword cuts. Made of ox or bull hide, these were mostly purchased by officers and troopers themselves, although a good-quality officer's coat cost was considerably expensive. Writing in early 1642 the earl of Bedford had recommended that troopers 'be handsomely furnished [in] comely apparel with coat of buff with long skirts [and a] coat of cloth to keep both himself and furniture from the violence of the weather'.[36] The latter, known as riding coats, were common, although there is evidence that the English cavalry at Tangier were issued with cloaks. In 1662 the Earl of Orrery's Regiment in Ireland were described wearing 'all buff coats and caps', whilst four years later the Gloucestershire mounted militia were 'all in buff coats'.[37]

The numbers of casualties given for the fighting around Catherina Fort on 14 June 1663 vary, depending on the source. Ghaïlān's men carried away 50 or 60 dead and wounded, one of whom appeared to be a chief, 'attired in crimson velvet', and left about 20 others where they fell. About two-thirds of the protectors of Pole Fort were killed or wounded. The Moors attacked the redoubts again on 3 July but were repulsed with the loss of 100 men.[38] It was 13 days later that the decisive action occurred. At 2:00 a.m. on 16 July Teviot's guard dogs, chained at the outposts, alerted the British soldiers to a party of Moorish cavalry waiting in ambush. Upon finding themselves discovered, however, the Moors set fire to the grass between themselves and the city, hoping that the smoke would obscure them from the view of the English gunners. Concentrating the troop of Tangier Horse, Teviot charged the Moors, but before they could make contact, the troopers fell back in the face of an approaching body of enemy foot.

The five recently constructed forts around the hinterland of Tangier were hastily manned, and stocked with ammunition and provisions. Making use of the smokescreen, the Moors advanced to within musket range of the forts, but the wind changed direction, blowing the smoke back over them. Ghaïlān, now in a hopeless situation, dispatched a herald to request a truce. After the fighting the two commanders exchanged a series of letters, written in Spanish:

> *The Governor of Tangier to the Most Excellent Cidi Hamet El Chader Ebn Ali Ghaïlān, Governor of Arzilla, Alcazar, Tetuan, etc. whom God preserve.*
>
> The King of England, my Master, having honoured me with the government of this place, I hoped for no less courtesy from your Excellency than you used to my predecessor. But instead of giving me the welcome, you have disturbed my hour of eating, which according to your own customs, ought to be secured from visits. Yet notwithstanding what is past, if your Excellency decline to a

35 SRO, D742/0/3/79.
36 TNA, SP16/492, fol. 49.
37 *Mercurius Publicus*, 13 July–7 August 1662; *London Gazette*, 23–26 July 1666.
38 TNA, SP89/6, fol. 85. Fanshaw to Bennet, 18 July 1663.

better correspondence, either by peace or war, you shall find me no less inclined. Valuing myself upon the laws of a soldier, I will take care to bury those of yours that you left dead in the field. Or if your Excellency please to bury them in your own manner, you have leave to fetch them off.

God preserve your Excellency the many years I desire.
Tangier, 14 June 1663.

Ghaïlān to the Governor of Tangier.

I received your Excellency's letter of the 14th current, wherein you complain I have not given you the welcome. But I knew not you were come into these parts. For persons of your quality and character, use first to give notice of their coming, and not to dispose of anything in another's lands, as your Excellency has done in mine. I gave order to my vassals, that, occasion offering, they should give quarter to all belonging to your Excellency, as they did to the soldier they took the other day, whom I charged should be well treated. As to your correspondence, I much esteem it; and as to what has formerly passed, it was the fault of the former governor, as you may inform yourself. I expected no less humanity from your Excellency that you showed toward the slain, for which I highly thank you.

If your Excellency wishes to send ambassadors to me, you are at liberty to do so, my servant, the bearer of this, carries a safe-conduct.

God preserve your Excellency the many years I desire.
15 June 1663.

Teviot to Ghaïlān.

Yesterday I received your Excellency's letter of the 15th instant in the afternoon of the same day, by the hand of your servant, who brings back this. And if there has been any fault on my part, in not observing the rights of your country, it was a sin of ignorance, for which your Excellency has sufficiently chastised me. I much esteemed the good quarter which your Excellency commanded to be given my soldier. If my fortune gives me the like occasion, I will repay it with interest. As to a peace and good correspondence between the King my Master and your Excellency, there wants nothing but a disposition on your Excellency's part to have it effected. And if your Excellency desire, I will send you the persons fit to treat about it.

God preserve your Excellency many and happy years.
Tangier, 16 June 1663.[39]

39 TNA, CO 279/2, fols 90–2.

As Addison related the story, Ghaïlān and Teviot initially engaged in a civil form of warfare in which quarter was given and the corpses of fallen soldiers were treated with respect.[40] Negotiations between the commanders soon brought hostilities to a halt and a six-month truce was concluded. This provided the Tangier garrison with a distinct advantage because it needed as much time as possible to complete its system of fortifications. Addison reported, 'Accordingly, a tent being pitched without the lines, and furnished with rich chairs and carpets, Gayland drew up his army about it, and the Earl, attended with twenty of his guards in rich coats, rode thither to meet him'.[41] The negotiations were followed by a banquet, and the treaty was eventually concluded on 21 July 1663. Teviot, pleased with his triumph, hurried his departure to England to report in person on the situation in Tangier. Ghaïlān, in an expression of his appreciation of his adversary's qualities and his own desire to uphold the peace treaty, wrote to Charles II:

> His Excellency the Earl of Teviot having advised me of his approaching voyage to these parts, I was moved to write this present because of the peace and good friendship we have established in your Majesty's name; and because I found his Excellency so valiant and high-minded a gentleman, I could but make him a fitting response to show my good-will in all matters pertaining to your Majesty's service, which if I formerly omitted doing, was because there was no one competent to meet the case. I now hope by God's will this will continue, and very considerable benefit ensue to your Majesty's service and great rewards to his Excellency for his successful endeavours. I beseech your Majesty to despatch him hither in all speed, for the great love and good-will I bear him, and if in any of my dominions there is opportunity of serving you, let your Majesty advise me thereof, you will be conferring on me the greatest possible favour.[42]

However, as Bejjit asserts, 'If Charles put any faith in these courteous professions, he was bound to be disappointed. Ghaïlān could not be brought to allow increased fortifications in the area surrounding the city as Teviot's new instructions demanded'.[43] Though he had only recently arrived in Tangier, in September 1663 Teviot returned for a period of leave in his native Scotland, leaving the lieutenant-governor, Fitzgerald, in charge. During his stay Teviot organised the regular supply of ammunition and provisions for the city and garrison of Tangier, and for the initiation of work on the new Mole, which he was appointed to command. The garrison's chief engineer, Beckman, had completed his work of providing a preliminary series of forts some days prior to Ghaïlān's latest foray. He prepared his draught of the proposed works, hastily completing them so that Teviot could take the plans back to Westminster to secure the finance necessary to complete the

40 Addison, *Moors Baffled*, p. 10.

41 *Ibid.*, p. 12.

42 TNA, CO 279/2, fol. 108. A Letter from Ghaïlān to His Sacred Majesty Charles the Second, King of Great Britain, 10 September 1663.

43 Bejjit, *English Colonial Texts*, p. 16.

scheme.[44] In his absence, Colonel Fitzgerald continued to construct the lines of defence around Tangier. The forts and redoubts were positioned up to 900 yards from the city walls, so that cannons on the Upper Castle of Tangier and the guns along the main fortifications could provide supporting fire.

The forts were equipped with light artillery (sakers and 3-pounders), as well as stocks of rations and ammunition. According to 'an account of the stores and ammunition to be kept at the alarm posts', dated 27 January 1684, at Catherina Fort there was stored ready for use 750 hand grenades, 1½ cwt of powder, ½ cwt of match and 1 cwt of musket shot.[45] Although the new fortifications differed greatly in size – some of the smaller positions, such as Cambridge Fort were simple breastworks – they covered Tangier in a great curve between the sea on both sides, and occupied the inner range of knolls outside the city. These were linked together by an internal scheme of passageways, known as 'the Lines'. They have been referred to as 'trenches' or 'covered trenches', yet various contemporary illustrations show the main ones to have been akin to roadways, upwards of 20 feet wide, protected by waist- or shoulder-high earthen banks or 'mud walls'. As later events would show, however, these defensive positions were often overlooked by more elevated territory, and vulnerable to surprise attacks, undermining and infiltration along the system of trenches and passageways by the Moors. For a short while after Teviot's parting, trade occurred energetically between the garrison and the Moors, fresh foodstuffs were abundant and to an extent, sociable interaction became possible.

But the professed friendship of Ghaïlān had little substance, and his alliance with Spain, though nothing new, had the potential to seriously threaten the future existence of the Tangier garrison. English relations with the Spaniards had impeded the prosperity of the colony from the outset, with a jealousy that was part of a greater struggle for dominance of the Mediterranean and beyond. Even before Teviot's arrival Fitzgerald had reported the arrival of a Spanish delegation bearing a gift 'worth more than forty thousand pieces of eight', and various spies were rumoured to be in the city. A nominal peace remained, but the activities of Spanish shipping and merchants continued to be monitored by the Tangier garrison. Intelligence of a possible Spanish–Moorish alliance reached the English government, when on October 1663 Beckman delivered to Martin Westcombe, the vigilant Consul at Cadiz, evidence of a plot by the Spanish and the Moors to grab Tangier. The Moors were to besiege the city, while the Spanish undertook a seaborne invasion.[46] Westcombe alerted Secretary Bennet to 'the countenance of it amounting to the discovery of a combination which the Spaniards and Ghaïlān, the

44 TNA, MPH 1/1/1. Design and draft of fortifying Tangier *per* Mr Beckman, 1662, inscribed: 'The ship is just now going I have not time to make it as it should be yet the proportion is done'. BL, MS Add. 16370, fol. 27. Similar plan, annotated: 'This is made in hast because the ship stays for it, yet true proportion'.

45 SRO, D742/0/3/13.

46 TNA, CO 279/2, fols 130–3; SP94/45, fol. 115.

Moors' general, have complotted against his Majesty's city of Tangier to be in December next'.[47]

Acting on such intelligence Whitehall decided on a diplomatic warning. Fanshaw was appointed ambassador to Madrid, while his instructions made it clear how he was to use the knowledge that had come into English hands. Consequently, 'The regime attempted to convey in diplomatic language the warning of possible retribution if Philip IV and his chief minister, Ramiro Núñez de Guzmán, Duke de Medina las Torres, continued their schemes. It also revealed to the Spanish that the design had been uncovered and that the Tangier garrison as well as the English intelligence system were on their guard'.[48] In the meantime, Colonel Fitzgerald, the deputy-governor, articulated his disquiet about the state of the fortifications of Tangier. He informed the Committee that, in his opinion, the principal hope of security lay in:

> the difficulties that may arise between the Spaniard and the Moor, in the management of this attempt, of which could they once agree it is probable the rest would not stay to be effected, for it is certain we neither are nor suddenly can be secure against a Christian enemy … I wish we could make ourselves secure of the Castle, in case there be no further supplies, I humbly conceive it is better to deduct it out of the found of the mould (fund of the mole) than by continued neglect to endanger the whole.[49]

On 26 September 1663 Paul Rycaut arrived at Tangier with orders to survey the colony. He worked in Constantinople as Lord Winchilsea's private secretary (from 1661), then as English Consul at Smyrna from 1667–78, and was the author of *The History of the Present State of the Ottoman Empire* (1666). Rycaut left a detailed report of the subsequent military operations and their strategic consequences for the Tangier garrison:

> The next day, being the 27th, I went ashore and found the town in a good and plentiful condition. In the time of my Lord Peterborough (whose reputation in this garrison is as much diminished as my Lord Teviot's is extolled and adored) none durst so much as open the gates or look over the walls. But as soon as my Lord Teviot arrived, at the same instant before he entered into any house he opened the gates and in person went about half a mile from the walls, where he designed his line and five redoubts which he with an extraordinary diligence and admirable resolution applied himself to, that in three or four days' time working day and night he had raised them so high as they became very defensible, all which time my Lord entered not so much as into a house nor reposed in any other place then at the outmost guard of the gate with his cloak about him and an ammunition pillow under his head. The Moors espying unawares strange kind

47 TNA, CO 279/3, fols 134–36. Westcombe to Bennet, 27 October 1663; *Fanshaw Letters*, pp. 41–4. See also Westombe's report to Fitzgerald of the same date (CO 279/2, fol. 130).

48 Alan Marshall, *Intelligence and Espionage in the Reign of Charles II, 1660–1685* (Cambridge: Cambridge University Press, 1994), p. 183.

49 TNA, CO 279/2, fol. 122. Fitzgerald to Bennet, 24 October 1663.

of buildings to appear, and fearing that it might be something very prejudicial, speedily attacked the forts with about 12,000 or 14,000 men led on by Guiland, but received a very great repulse with a signal slaughter of them and their horse by the crow's feet which my Lord Teviot had caused to be scattered in the grass, which they being then unacquainted with and finding them in their feet and sitting down to pull them out felt a worse wound behind.

And yet these Moors were so courageous that they ventured to the very walls of the redoubts and there one upon the other's back shot in at the loopholes; but the service was too hot for them, that with a very great loss they were forced to retire. Some days after with a fresh courage and more bold resolution they designed to make a second assault, but then the English soldiery being well in heart with the former success met them in their outward trenches with all the force of the town, leaving the walls to be defended by the seamen of the fleet, who with the great guns made several admirable shot to the great discouragement of the enemy, who that day could never pass the line, but in the evening were forced to retreat with the loss of 300 or 400 men. At the later end of the day and of the fight, Guiland sent a white flag to desire a treaty, which my lord granted and appointed for the next day. The place agreed on was my lord's tent, which he had pitched a little without his works. There he met Guiland in person and agreed upon a truce for six months. A copy of the articles I would have procured for your lordship, but could not obtain them from the deputy-governor. My Lord Teviot, having thus built several forts, opened the gates, foiled the Moors in two fights and made a peace with them, and all in the space of two months, is returned into England to give his Majesty an account of all that hath passed, to receive new orders as to the establishment of the garrison, the building the Mole, and the ascertaining the right and propriety of the houses of the town. The Mole proceeds forward very vigorously, 300 men being employed in it every day, and have brought it a good way out into the sea. The breadth of it is 30 yards. The draught of it Sir John Lawson hath showed me; when finished will be the best Mole and rarest fabric of the world. The work is undertaken by the Duke of York, the Duke of A lbermarle, Sir John Lawson and Mr Cholmeley.

The town is now plentiful of all provisions, and is the drunkest place that ever I came into in my life. It hath a great trade with Tétuan, especially in hides, and great caravans come in thither every day. The garrison consists of about 1,500 soldiers; the other inhabitants maybe 1,000 more of Portuguese, Jews and merchants. I have seriously viewed the redoubts, one of which is a large fort very strong; the others are three square and are situated to that advantage that the Moors cannot lurk now in ambush to kill our men from the walls as formerly they have done. I have also ridden about the bounds allotted us by the capitulations, out of which if a man be taken, he is lawful prize, unless he carries the pass of the governor, and then he may travel all over the country. The English butchers go every day almost to the market at Arsila. The bounds assigned the English are about 10 miles in compass, in which our officers go often to hunt the wild hog, and when they exceed their bounds with the company of the out-guards of the Moors they have liberty to go where they please. There are not above 50 horse in the town, amongst which there are not above 20 serviceable. My Lord Teviot hath gained so much reputation here that after the peace was made the chief men of

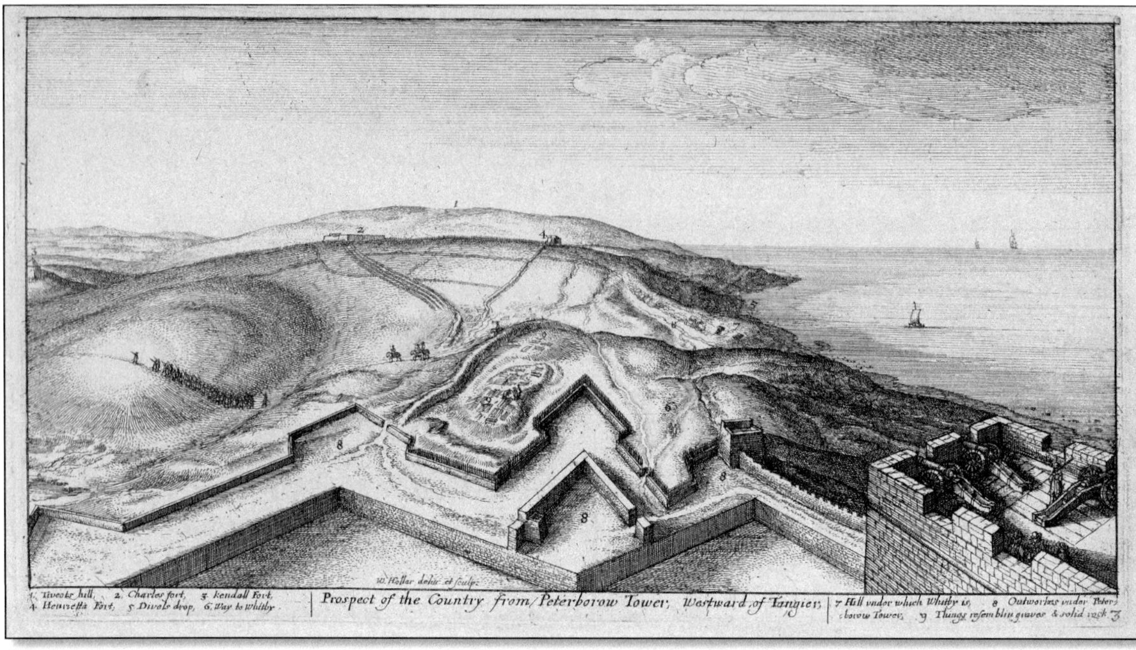

Wenceslaus Hollar, *Prospect of the country from Peterborough Tower* (*c.* 1669). (University of Toronto, The Wenceslaus Hollar Collection, Creative Commons Public Domain)

> the Moors came from all places to kiss his hand, having him in a very great esteem and admiration.
>
> And indeed, I conceive much of the happiness of this town depends upon my Lord's return, and the annexation of it to the Crown of England. For most of the garrison here coming from Dunkirk are afraid it should run the same fortune of that place, which discourages all people from furnishing or repairing their houses, not knowing how long they may enjoy them. And indeed, the great men in this fleet cry out how much they fear that Tangier will be a morsel for the hungry courtiers. But I hope better things, for I cannot imagine the king should so little understand his interest as to release so fair a jewel from his crown, which all the neighbouring people begin to fear and is their only discourse.[50]

To all intents and purposes then, the garrison of Tangier appeared in rude health. But Colonel Fitzgerald knew that it also remained in considerable strategic danger. On 24 October he again emphasised the need to increase the garrison and to concentrate funding on improving the fortifications, in view of a possible attack.[51] Moreover, a system of spies and informers was supplying intelligence of an impending Hispano-Moorish threat to the colony. On 28 October Consul Westcombe advised Fitzgerald from Cadiz, 'my life lies now in your breast by the letter I now write you, which if the Spaniards should know of or hear of what I know of their plot against Tangier they would by all the private ways they could let them do their worst for he that will serve his king'.[52] He also requested the colonel not to leak

50 HMC, *Finch*, I, pp. 279–81. Rycaut to Winchilsea, aboard the *Bonadventure*, Cadiz Road, under sail for England, 3 October 1663.

51 TNA, CO 279/2, fol. 122. Fitzgerald to Bennett, 24 October 1663.

52 TNA, CO 279/2, fol. 138. Westcombe to Fitzgerald, 28 October 1663.

such information to the garrison soldiers, for fear that some of the Spanish boats that routinely visited Tangier might reveal it in their home port, thus compromising English networks in Spain, which were headed by the engineer and intelligence agent, Beckman. The latter's increasingly accurate reports disclosed that 30 or 40 Spanish ships, including galleons recently returned from the West Indies, and 14 galleys, were ready to embark at the end of December from Cadiz and the port of Santa Maria with a landing force of roughly 1,800 men, in conjunction a major ground offensive conducted by the Moors.[53] This was confirmed in late November 1664, when a Jewish informant told Fitzgerald that the King of Spain had increased negotiations with Ghaïlān, conveying to him with great splendour a treasured gift, whose value exceeded 40,000 pieces of eight.[54]

The early months of 1664 were marked by the conclusion of the treaty brokered between the Tangier garrison and the Moors, continuing work on the fortifications and the renewal of warfare. Returning from leave on 14 January – eight days before the expiration of the Peace – Governor Teviot had with him instructions from Charles II, to proceed with further fortifications, although this was at odds with the terms of Colonel Fitzgerald's truce, which had been extended for two more months.[55] January was the best time of year for digging as the winter rains softened the soil, thus providing an ideal opportunity for extending the garrison's outer defences – especially the construction of a new earthwork before Peterborough Tower, 'which will give us the enjoyment of a great deal of ground'. Ghaïlān dispatched emissaries, who informed Teviot that 'Muhammadan Law forbad them to suffer the Christian to erect fortifications in their country; and that if the Earl would not desist from that work, he was not to expect any longer continuance of the Peace'. The Governor reportedly made no other reply, 'but that the sword should decide whether Muhammad's Law or his Master's orders were more powerful', and declared that he would neither take nor give quarter.[56] Addison makes it clear that civil diplomacy rapidly degenerated into a more aggressive form, and that Teviot was guilty of violating the treaty and escalating hostilities. Such a rupture to the 'amicable hostility' would not only in due course cost the Earl his life, but it ensured that the dead bodies of his soldiers would be left unclaimed and unburied where they fell.

Quickly, the Moors began a series of raids on the English positions and laid various ambushes, although these were repulsed by the garrison. In response, 'the Earl set upon building of Fort Charles, on the hill next the Upper Castle; whose situation was advantageous, not only to secure a considerable quantity of ground for the garrison, but also to discover the enemy at a great distance'.[57] Addison specifically described the new structure as 'a great new fort … upon a base that consists of two half bastions and a

53 Marshall, *Intelligence*, p. 175; Matteo Barbano, 'Una guerra discreta: la minaccia ispano-moresca a Tangeri del 1663', *Mediterranea, ricerche storiche*, 32 (2014), pp. 511–24 (pp. 516–17).

54 TNA, CO 279/2, fol. 152.

55 TNA, CO 279/2, fol. 169; Davis, *History*, I, p. 53.

56 Addison, *Moors Baffled*, pp. 22–3; Cholmeley, *Account*, pp. 65–6.

57 Addison, *Moors Baffled*, p. 23.

curtain, cannon-proof on all sides, with a vast trench about it, made to lodge a company of 100 foot'.[58] On 29 February there was a sharp engagement during which the Tangier Horse, led by Captain Witham, charged out and seized Ghaïlān's personal standard, killing the standard bearer and a leader of some distinction, 'the general of the Algarnes Horse'. Such a psychological blow to the Moors led them to desert the field, pleading that it was time of Ramadan. Teviot's cavalry again proved its value a few days later, putting the enemy to flight, in spite of the rocky ground over which the fighting took place. The morale of the garrison was especially high, whilst the somewhat mercurial governor, who often lived in the field with his soldiers, developed a reputation among the Moors for invincibility.[59] Addison, keen to portray a positive image of Teviot as an exemplary commander, who was revered by the Moors for his diligence and resolve, reported, 'The Moors call his Excellency 'Devil', they report that he never sleeps but leaning against some part of the works, that he has made flying ships (meaning, I suppose, the tents that are in the camp), that his great guns run of themselves ... that he is a man of success and cannot be beaten. And they have good reason to admire his performances'.[60]

Something of the buoyant mood among the Tangier garrison may be gleaned from Teviot's enthusiastic letter of 25 April 1664:

> It is wonderful the progress we have made in fortifying our retrenchments be the indefatigable pains and labour of our soldiers and extraordinary diligence of our officers, all striving to surpass one another for his Majesty's service ... if his Excellency Guyland whom we have expected these five days do not attack us with all his forces tomorrow or Monday, I dare answer to his Majesty to put a pair of spectacles on Guyland's nose that will trouble him so as to oblige him at last to a peace, and make this place very comfortable to the garrison and inhabitants. Nay, which is more, that for attacking I dare almost promise good success, for I never saw officers and soldiers more eager and ready to fight. I know not if it be a motive of Christianity against infidels that cause it ... we have good lines before us to defend us. I hope my next shall afford better news, whereof I shall give your honour the detail.[61]

Another eyewitness wrote, 'Our other lines and trenches were in a few days brought to that perfection that the enemy durst not attack us. It is a great comfort to see how cheerfully, from the highest to the lowest every man here puts his hands to the work'. He continued:

> Next day, was the foundation laid of the horn-work strong in the walls, being cannon-proof, strong in the situation, being on the Castle Hill, every way advantageous and important because it covers the Castle, fenced above 600 acres of ground, discovered the enemy at a great distance and makes the place

58 TNA, CO 279/3, fol. 33. Addison to Williamson, 14 March 1664.
59 TNA, CO 279/3, fol. 41. Teviot to Fanshaw, 4 March 1664.
60 TNA, CO 279/3, fols 33–4. Addison to Williamson, 14 March 1664.
61 TNA, CO 279/3, fol. 43. Teviot to Westcombe, 25 April 1664.

> comfortable. Securing the whole hill for our walk and use (being 600 yards from the Castle). Our lines and trenches in a few days were brought that perfection, that the enemy durst not attack us. The great advantage hereof we have experienced in several disputes with the Moors, who on the last of February, betwixt 11 and 12, appeared their whole army, and took up their posts. The greatest forces coming from the west part towards the sea, where they continued pelting for some hours till they were forces off, and considerable loss, and not one of our men killed or wounded.[62]

Towards the end of April 1664 an ominous silence prevailed in the Moorish camp, and for five or six days not a sign of Ghaïlān's troops was detected. Lord Teviot, suspicious of the apparent quietness, ordered wide-ranging scouting, and led a mounted patrol more than three miles to the westward, crossing the Jews' River and traversing a thick wood without so much as sighting the enemy. Although work on the garrison's fortifications was well-advanced, the governor was faced with some significant difficulties, none more so than the procurement of building materials (especially stone and lime) for the completion of Charles Fort in particular. As opponents of the English occupation, the Spanish refused to assist in obtaining supplies from Cadiz, while voyages to and from Portugal ran the risk of both poor weather and being taken by Barbary Corsairs. Instead, Teviot adopted to look inland, where quantities of building materials were to be had a mile or two in front of the lines. Whatever his motives, on 4 May 1664 Teviot led some Horse and a composite force of 500 foot towards Jews Hill and Tangier's hinterland. According to Colonel Roger Alsop, an experienced officer who had commanded a regiment of foot at Dunkirk in 1661, the cutting down or burning of brushwood on the far side of the Jews' River, which had provided effective cover for the concentration of Moorish troops, was a particular imperative.[63]

Precisely two years previously, Major Fiennes had marched forth with his battalion, but had been surrounded and cut to pieces, so it is possible that there was a desire for revenge. Pepys recorded:

> It seems my Lord Teviot's design was to go a mile and half out of the town, to cut down a wood, in which the enemy did use to lie in ambush. He had sent several spies, but all brought word that the way was clear, and so might be for any body's discovery of an enemy before you are upon them. There they were all snapped, he and all his officers, and about 200 men, as they say; there being left now in the garrison but four captains. This happened the 3 May [*sic*: 4] last, being not before that day twelvemonth of his entering into his government there: but at his going out in the morning he said to some of his officers, 'Gentlemen, let us look to ourselves, for it was this day three years that so many brave Englishmen were knocked on the head by the Moors, when Fiennes made his sally out'.[64]

62 *A Brief Relation of the Present State of Tangier and of the Advantages with which his Excellency the Earl of Teviot has Obtained against Gayland* (London: T. Mabb, 1664), p. 1.

63 HMC, *Heathcote*, pp. 156–7. Colonel Roger Alsop to Fanshaw, 13 June 1664.

64 Pepys, *Diary*, 2 June 1664.

Wenceslaus Hollar, *Prospect of the grounds about Henrietta Fort* (*c.* 1669). (University of Toronto, The Wenceslaus Hollar Collection, Creative Commons Public Domain)

This foray may have indeed been a calculated risk on Teviot's part. Westcombe, the well-informed Consul at Cadiz, was sure that the governor was aware of a Moorish force in the vicinity of Jews Hill, and it must have occurred to Teviot that his manoeuvre would have been observed by Ghaïlān's scouts before he reached the river.[65] Encountering no resistance Teviot's party crossed Jews River, but suddenly ran into a body of 3,000 Moorish Horse, which they drove off. Teviot pressed on, but the first contact had been a feint, intended to entice the English into a wooded area, were a much larger force lay in wait. As enemy infantry closed in around them, Moorish cavalry cut off their escape routes. A servant of Teviot, one of the nine survivors of the detachment led by the governor himself, described that having been forced to retreat to Jews Hill, and with little expectation of relief, but without a thought of surrender, Teviot rallied his soldiers in the face of the enemy. The Moors were momentarily checked by musket fire, but eventually the remaining redcoats, their ammunition spent, succumbed to the overwhelming rush of the enemy. Most (including the governor) were killed, although 74 privates were known to have been captured. Barely a handful of soldiers escaped, and it seems unlikely that Teviot and his men could have been rescued. The officers left in command of Tangier hardly understood the scale of the disaster until all was over, but the extended line of fortifications was so thinly manned that there was little chance of dispatching an effective relief force.

Captain Mordaunt of the Tangier Regiment tried to get some boats up the Jews' River, but they were driven back by a strong east wind. Besides, Ghaïlān's troops subsequently advanced towards the outworks, and the remaining

65 TNA, CO 279/3, fol. 63.

garrison was fully occupied in holding the lines. According to Fanshaw's letter to Secretary Bennet, 500 men died in the field.[66] Similarly, Alsop recounted on 13 June, 'The officers slain in the conflict were his Excellency the Earl of Teviot, Major Knightley, Major Fitzgerald, Captain Langton, Captain Rudyard, Captain Brookes, Captain Bolger, with five lieutenants, seven ensigns and sixteen gentlemen and reformadoes'.[67] Moorish losses were probably in excess of 1,000. A more comprehensive report, sent to the King by Sir Tobias Bridges, in the absence of Fitzgerald, the lieutenant-governor, related that the Moors' recent lack of aggressive activity:

> gave encouragement to my lord to march over the Jews River up into a thick bushy wood, opposite to the hill on the westward sea, and went there with a party of foot over three miles without any resistance made, where they found only one house built with stone and lime, the which was by them quit upon my Lord's approach ... Upon the 3rd of this instant, my Lord, having made early in the morning a further discovery with his horse than ever he had done at any time before to the southeast, and having placed sentinels and guards, judging the country for a great distance at least to be clear of any enemy, ordained all the horse to forage there, directing some of the foot to lie near them for making good the retreat if anything should happen; and he himself took a resolution to go into the wood with some foot to cut wood, and immediately went over the valley to the west hill towards Fort Charles and took with him seven battalions of foot, all firelocks, the best and choicest of our men, and the principle and chief officers of the garrison to command them; he himself being accompanied with several gentlemen volunteers and reformed officers, marched over the Jews River into the wood and went up three several ways, they being all appointed to meet at some particular place some distance above the hill. But it was not withstanding his far discovery before made by the horse, which I fear produced more than ordinary confidence; before they came up to the middle party of the hill in the wood, several ambushes of foot discovered themselves with which our men skirmished and drove to a retreat, but presently on all hands they rose up and appeared in such great numbers that they had immediately surrounded our men, at the same time the horse started up round about in the valley and on the hills to the southeast, not less than 2,000 and came pouring down not only upon our horse, but took the advantage in a moment to fall between the wood, where our foot were, and the hill, that although it was evident that our men fought as resolutely and gave a good fire as men could do, they being surrounded with their army of horse and foot. Our worthy general, the officers and gentlemen with him, and all the whole party of the soldiers, were cut off, not thirty of them, as I can find, that ever came off. There is lost in this action his Excellency the Earl of Teviot, our general, with nineteen commissioned officers, and fifteen gentlemen and volunteers, the doctor, together with 396 non-commissioned and private soldiers, the particular of which and other things is sent to Mr Secretary.[68]

66 TNA, CO 279/3, fol. 36. Fanshaw to Bennet, 4 May 1664.

67 HMC, *Heathcote*, p. 157.

68 TNA, CO 279/3, fols 53–5. Bridges to Charles II, 5 May 1664; *Fanshaw Letters*, p. 99. Bridges to Fanshaw, 8 May 1664.

The reaction from Whitehall, which disparaged Teviot's leadership abilities and judgement, was condemned by Routh. With her late-imperial bias, she stated, 'surely ungenerous criticism of one who was a gallant, if too daring, soldier, and a pioneer of the Empire, who, in the early days of the British standing army, helped to establish a tradition of devoted service which succeeding generations have not been slow to uphold'.[69] For Routh, who regarded Teviot as an heroic martyr, the battle was an exemplar of bravery, gallantry, and noble action, that inspired the 'succeeding generations' of troops fighting with 'swarms' of fanatical natives throughout the British Empire. More recently, Matthew Glozier soberly concluded, 'The nobleman's death was a catastrophe, which greatly retarded the defence of the garrison in the name of Charles II. It also deprived the King of a highly skilled professional and a loyal, honest and effective governor'.[70]

Ghaïlān's triumph was short-lived, however. He withdrew his army to deal with internal disputes to confront his increasingly powerful enemies in the region. Even so, the loss of Teviot and a considerable number of his men was an undoubted blow to Charles II's ambitions in Tangier. Before obtaining the colony, the English leadership had underestimated the effectiveness of the local military forces. As Childs contends, 'The Moors of Barbary were a resourceful enemy. Although they had no organised standing army they fought as a feudal mass, their tactics were so different to anything which the British had encountered before that they were a formidable foe'.[71] Similarly, Colley observes that the place faced significant 'pressure from powerful Moroccan armies, equipped with weapons fully comparable to those of Tangier's English garrison'.[72] Yet the events of 4 May 1664 illustrated that even a pronounced setback could not weaken the resolve of the garrison to allow the enemy further advantage, even though later governors restricted their ambitions in the colony to holding fast to the fortifications. 'This sad misfortune and great breach have filled us all with sorrow and distraction', wrote Bridges, 'yet are all willing to contribute our utmost for the safety of this place and, if possible, to preserve those forts which already have cost so much care and charges'.[73]

Colonel Alsop considered that all measures of defence enabling them to defy the Moors had been taken, and 'notwithstanding our great watching, working, and poverty, we are knit together, so as I may be bold to say it must be a more knowing enemy than Guyland, through the providence of God, can break us'.[74] But despite such dogged declarations, one writer admitted dolefully, 'We have never sent away to understand their [the Moor's] country, to search into their strength and dependencies, to examine their interest'.[75] Starved of manpower, its garrison's pay continuously in

69 Routh, *Tangier*, p. 70.
70 Glozier, *Scottish Soldiers*, p. 68.
71 Childs, *Army of Charles II*, p. 135.
72 Colley, *Captives*, p. 36.
73 TNA, CO 279/3, fol. 58.
74 HMC, *Heathcote*, p. 157.
75 BL, MS Lansdown 192, fols 123–9; *A Discourse Touching Tangier [sic] to which is added The Interest of Tangier, by Another Hand* (London: 1680), p. 37.

arrears, and blockaded on both sides, Tangier became a hotbed of festering internal tensions. Several of the soldiers had fought in the Civil Wars for Parliament, and in the cause of a godly Cromwellian Republic, and some of them questioned why they should risk their lives for the sake of Charles II. One corporal protested in 1663, 'I was paid like a man, but now I serve I do not know whom, I am paid like a turd'. Another soldier grumbled that the King was 'no Englishman, but a Scotchman or a Frenchman'. Both were shot for uttering words tending to sedition or mutiny.[76] On 25 June 1664 one of the garrison's women, Margaret Summerton, was convicted of sedition and attempted mutiny. These were grave offences, but rather than execution she received 50 lashes on her bare back, 10 each at five different stations, and to be deported from the colony on the first available ship, being whipped also from the prison to the quayside.[77]

Like other garrisons Tangier was governed by the 'Articles of War'. At Carrickfergus in May 1666 the garrison's foot companies mutinied because of pay, whereby 10 soldiers were sentenced to death and others to transportation.[78] Similarly, on 23 July 1678 James Ponte, a sergeant in the forces at Nieuport in Flanders, was convicted of speaking mutinous words, was condemned to sit for one hour astride a wooden horse with two muskets tied to each leg, and afterwards to be sent back to prison until a fit opportunity to transport him beyond the seas occurred. Two privates in the same regiment were sentenced to be shot for similar offences, and another in Sir John Fenwick's Regiment to ride the wooden horse for three days, one hour per day.[79] In the absence of a lieutenant-governor in Tangier, the post fell to Colonel Alsop, but due to ill-health he resigned soon afterwards. A council of war fixed on Bridges as his successor. Bridges immediately appraised the garrison's two regiments of foot, and found 'but four captains, the one of namely Captain Mordaunt is very sick and unserviceable at present, very few lieutenants and ensigns, and these not of the best, some companies not any commissioned officers left, which has necessitated me, in order to the discharge of our duty, to elect such persons amongst ourselves as were judged the most sufficient to act as officers for the present until your Majesty's further order'.[80]

According to muster rolls of 26 May 1664 there was present (excepting officers) 1,415 foot and 140 horse, 29 of the latter being unmounted.[81] To add to the garrison's troubles, the following month sickness broke out among the soldiers. Stores were also low, fresh victuals were meagre and expensive, the grass outside the city walls was burnt so there was insufficient hay for the horses, and no pay had been received since the previous November. Colonel Alsop wrote, 'In truth, we are as poor as may be, for excepting the provisions in the King's stores we have scarce an officer in the garrison that is able to

76 Bod. Lib., MS Rawlinson C423, fols 1, 127.

77 BL, MS Sloane 1957, fols 45–6. Minutes of Court-Marshal at Tangier, 1663–67.

78 *London Gazette*, 4–7 June 1666.

79 HMC, *Eleventh Report, App. V*, pp. 27–8.

80 TNA, CO 279/3, fol. 55.

81 TNA, CO 279/3, fols 65–8. Bridges to Bennet, 26 May 1664. For the muster rolls see CO 279/3, fols 76–109.

buy himself a good dinner, but courage and fidelity is ever most known and set forth in the greatest want'.[82] The quantities of provisions remaining in 'his Majesty's stores in Tangier' on 28 May 1664 (amounting to five weeks' supply) were: 2,371 bushels (each equal to 8 dry gallons) of wheat; 2,352 lb of rice; 15,093½ lb of beef; 12,570 lb of pork; 91⅛ bushels of oatmeal; 5,351 pints of oil instead of butter or cheese; 4,747 bushels of oats; 807¼ bushels of barley; and 794 of beans.[83]

In addition to the general state of ill-health, and the scarce and insufficiently nutritious diet, conditions such as scurvy were common. Tangier's climate was frequently detrimental to the health of new arrivals, who were 'troubled with a flux', and 'welcomed constantly with strange blisters and pimples like to the smallpox, which is generally attributed to the biting of mosquitoes (which are just the gnats in some parts of England, but a little more pert)'.[84] Another view was that the problem stemmed from 'an ebullition of the blood, upon change of the air'.[85] The sickness which distressed the garrison, during both the hot conditions and the rains, was thus often attributed to the climate. There were, however, more precise causes for serious levels of sickness, which included the 'flux and scurvy which made men die apace'.[86] Much illness might have been avoided if the Tangier garrison could – like the Portuguese – have lived mainly on fish, fruit, bread and herbs, with moderate quantities of meat, either purchased or seized from the Moors. But want of money hampered trade and local agriculture, and the soldiers depended largely on provisions – for the most part, biscuit, salt beef and pork, oatmeal, peas, cheese, and butter – supplied by contract by victuallers in England and Ireland, those from the latter being considered to be better, lower-priced, and more transportable. One merchant vessel loaded with corn from Ireland departed for Tangier in December 1666.[87]

The quantity and condition of soldiers' provisions was further disadvantaged by the accounting methods employed by commissaries at Tangier. Although victuallers received 2s. 6d. per man per day to supply rations, the usual practice of the period was to issue them at 14 ounces to the pound, instead of 16 ounces. On 29 January 1671 Luke reported, 'Mr Wollaston [a garrison official] and I had a great deal of discourse concerning the victualling, which comes to at least about £13,000 per annum, out of which there may be gained at least £3,000 per annum, viz. by the 2 ounces in the pound, by what provisions are bought by the officers, and what might be gained all though neither of these two were allowed'.[88] The allowances to officers – who were supplied with food from the stores in return for payment – were greater than those of the soldiers and varied in proportion to their rank, an ensign usually obtaining those of four privates and a colonel 12. In

82 HMC, *Heathcote*, pp. 157–8.
83 SRO, D742/0/3/5.
84 *Present State of Tangier*, p. 4.
85 *Description of Tangier*, p. 2.
86 BL, MS Add. 17021, fol. 38. Fairborne to Commissioners, 5 December 1677.
87 TNA, CO 279/1, p. 116; *CSPD 1666–7*, p. 335.
88 Luke, *Tangier at High Tide*, p. 55.

1671 Sir Hugh Cholmeley questioned the wisdom of a system that supplied expensive, unsuitable, and decayed provisions to the garrison, when a little ready money in circulation would have ensured a thriving trade with Morocco and Spain:

> The late fleet has well recruited our public stores, which were before (as it often happens) very bare of provisions, yet there can be no want of meat when there is not of money, the markets being supplied with good mutton and beef at about 4d. the pound, and excellent French claret bought under 3d. the quart, this with the advantage the gardens do now afford is conceived what may occasion the present good health of the place, which makes me wish the soldiers had money instead of the provisions allowed, because they would find a better food at as easy rates, and the town upon this expectation would never be without large quantities of eatable stores, whereas the present contract with the victualler, by disappointing the market, hinders the endeavour of the trader, and does besides depend itself on so many chances, as subject the garrison very frequently to the danger of being starved.[89]

Although periodic attempts were made to procure local fruit and vegetables for the garrison, the frequent outbreaks of scurvy are particularly traceable the over-reliance on salted meat, which constituted a major component in the garrison's diet. One author reported on the health of the garrison during the 1670s, 'the soldiers' diet being salt meat, disposes them in two or three years to inveterate all habits of body, instructions, scurvies, fluxes, etc. Whereof by reason of returning to the same diet again, when a little mended by the care of the physician, they relapse, and nothing but removing them to a better can recover them'.[90] The supply of fresh meat was irregular, and consignments of salted meat often arrived in Tangier in a sub-standard condition. In 1669 Captain Charles O'Brien of the *Leopard*, whilst inspecting the King's stores at the Italian port of Livorno, uncovered 127 casks of beef and pork which had been kept for three years, the contents of which were just eatable'.[91] These he sent to Tangier 'to prevent waste', but even the garrison refused to accept an allowance of meat of which 4 lb raw boiled down to 1 lb, and the governor insisted on returning it. O'Brien subsequently issued it to his sailors, but discontinued after a week, as it triggered 'great grumbling and almost a mutiny'.

In similar fashion, in October 1682, Governor Kirke objected to the provision of Irish meat, which was not preserved to last six months, and if cured as much as English beef became too dry and hard. As much as 23,972 lb of beef and pork in the navy stores at Tangier was so bad that it had to be thrown into the sea, 'so extremely corrupted', that it was both unserviceable and 'of a noisome smell'.[92] Problems with the supply and condition of provisions continued. On 25 September 1683 Sir John Berry

89 TNA, CO 279/14, fol. 120. Cholmeley to Williamson, 14 August 1671.

90 *Discourse touching Tangier*, p. 22.

91 *CSPD 1668–9*, pp. 264, 431. O'Brien to the Navy Commissioners, 4 April and 29 July 1669.

92 Routh, *Tangier*, p. 128; Cowper, *King's Own*, p. 17.

reported to Dartmouth in Tangier that the commanders of the colony's naval station 'complain much of want of water, and our victualling expends very fast. In the *Henrietta* I have thrown away 30 butts of stinking beer and 10 more defective, with a quantity of stinking cheese. If your lordship thinks fit to send your orders to Sir James Leslie, provisions of all sorts may be had at Cadiz, although at a dearer rate than the king's price – Irish beef, Spanish pork (and rusk if timely bespoke) may be had at any time, and Newfoundland fish very cheap as soon as the fleet arrives'.[93]

On the same day, Leslie wrote from Cadiz, 'I have made all diligent enquiry, but can find neither beef, pork, peas, nor fish at present here, but they are daily expected from Ireland and other parts. Have bought a small quantity of bread, rice, butter and flour, which is all that offers, and am endeavouring to get rusk made here'. Moreover, during the severe winter of 1683 to 1684 various supply fleets found themselves in ice-covered ports. On 28 January 1684, officials of the Victualling Office in London informed Dartmouth:

> It is not possible (by reason of the severe frost) to send any provision from hence towards you. Wherefore what bills you shall draw on us for victualling shall be punctually complied with. We have freighted a ship of 400 tons to load with 700 men's victuals for eight months to be at Lisbon, but she is and hath been frozen up these five weeks, the frost continuing very severe, as hath been known in the memory of man.[94]

But the combination of poor food, excessive alcohol, and filthy conditions severely affected the health of many of the soldiers in Tangier, as well as the local civilian population. The maintenance of public health was problematic, even during the period of military government. In 1666 widespread and random butchering of animals for meat, with the concomitant hazards to health, forced Lord Belasyse to bar the slaughter of animals except at the public abattoir, although this was later ignored.[95] Piles of waste were left to rot in the closely packed streets, and little attention was paid to the cleanliness of the water supply. In 1669 the Corporation was charged with the care of the streets and market, public buildings, sewage, and water, but few lasting improvements were made.[96]

The poor health of the garrison was intensified by the lack of appropriate medical care. As Gruber von Arni contends, 'From the earliest days, the hospital's reputation was so bad that men would suffer anything rather than admit to being ill for fear of being sent there. Shortage or misappropriation of funds combined with lack of genuine concern or commitment to healthcare provision resulted in a varying quality of service to say the least'.[97] This is corroborated by one contemporary account, which urged with some bitterness:

93 HMC, *Eleventh Report, App. V*, I, p. 109.

94 *Ibid.*, p. 107.

95 Bod. Lib., MS Rawlinson C423, fols 84, 89; TNA, CO 279/19, fols 180, 328.

96 TNA, CO 279/12, fols 163–5. Instructions for the Corporation, 30 June 1669; CO 279/13, fol. 140.

97 Eric Gruber von Arni, *Hospital Care*, p. 12.

> The meanest soldier must be encouraged, and not suffered to want when fallen into sickness. I dare affirm, and will offer to prove, that the unmercifulness of the officers, and the neglect of physicians and apothecaries, who though paid for that purpose by his Majesty, have killed the three parts of those that are dead in Tangier. I have sometimes buried three or four in a day, dead for want of which his Majesty hath provided for them in case of sickness.[98]

The garrison hospital was a converted house, where the small windows and thick walls helped to maintain lower internal temperatures. However, they provided poor lighting and ventilation. In 1667, Colonel Norwood, the lieutenant-governor, proposed a purpose-built structure, but this was rejected. Less than a year later, when a new bout of sickness broke out among the troops, he wrote to Lord Arlington, the chairman of the Tangier Committee, 'Had your Lordship thought fit to have gone thereon with the proposition I made sure to erect a hospital, it would have turned to good account unto his Majesty I am sure, besides the charity … of the easing the sick'.[99] As late as March 1683 Henry Sheres reported the place to be 'much too streight, so it is very incommodiously situated, being built against an old battery where the damp and cold in winter season annoy the sick people'.[100] Yet like everything else in Tangier, the hospital was perpetually short of money and the patients suffered accordingly. Never far away was the spectre of plague. There were outbreaks in Algiers and Tétuan (situated 40 miles southeast of Tangier) in late 1662, while for a time in 1681 reports of the disease in various Moroccan cities induced Governor Kirke to forbid the entrance of Moorish traders into Tangier. They were ordered to leave their goods at the bounds, 'if not of a dangerous nature', to be fetched in and sold for them by the resident Barbary Jews, and those commodities liable to infection, such as animal hides, were to be left at the Mole to be shipped away without passing through the city.[101] At the same moment, plague touched Cadiz through inadequate precautions, and Tangier again was besieged on all sides from the most virulent of enemies.

Listed among military stores wanting in July 1664 were 800 collars of bandoliers, and for the cavalry, 100 lanceheads, 150 ash lance staves and 100 long carbines. Also required were '500 snaphaunce muskets of the best sort, there being so many lost on 3 May last'.[102] These must be offset, however, by the recent arrival in Tangier of 23 barrels of powder, 25½ barrels of small shot, 216 sets of bandoliers, 131 bundles of match and 600 ready-cut musket flints.[103] Moreover, on 15 July 1664 a warrant was issued to the governor of the Tower of London, to deliver 50 firelocks and 50 matchlocks, with ammunition for service at Tangier.[104] Another inventory records 292 firelocks

98 *Present Interest of Tangier*, p. 8.

99 TNA, CO 279/6, fol. 59; CO 279/8, fol. 72.

100 SRO, D742/0/2/29.

101 *Letters from the Governors of the Algarve*, p. 501; TNA, CO 279/28, fol. 108. Kirke to Omar ben Haddū, 12 July 1681.

102 SRO, D742/0/3/1–2.

103 SRO, D742/0/3/4.

104 TNA, SP71/16, fol. 177; *CSPD* 1663–4, p. 660.

in good condition, with an additional 156 requiring repair.[105] Wanting in stores at Tangier two weeks later were six barrels of flints for snaphances; 3,000 fuses of the smallest size for hand grenades; 50 powder horns for the artillery; and 20 reams of paper royal for making gun cartridges.[106] Further supplies were landed from the merchant vessel *Nathanial Peter* on 27 January 1667, including another 600 matchlocks and 400 snaphances.[107] Furthermore, on 29 March 1666, a consignment of 200 matchlocks and 200 snaphaunce muskets reached the garrison. There were also 400 bandoliers, with 400 swords and belts – this indicates a half-and-half division between soldiers issued with matchlocks and snaphaunces.[108]

All necessaries of equipment and weapons, as well as food and clothing for the garrison, were sent to Tangier customs free. In January 1675 the frigate *Chichley* transported Ordnance stores 'for his Majesty's service at Tangier', including 20 demi-culverin (iron); 1,000 round shot for culverins; 3,000 for demi-culverins; 1,500 for sakers, 2,000 for falcons; 3,000 for 12-pounders; 2,000 for 3-pounders; 1,500 snaphance muskets packed in mats; 60,00 flints, ready cut; 800 barrels of corn powder (fine blackpowder); 6 tons of match; 50 tons of musket shot; 30 bags for powder; four dozen drumheads of vellum; 24 drums, furnished; 50 pair of pistols with holsters; and 600 long pikes.[109] Such stocks are confirmed by a survey of the arms of the garrison in June 1680, which recorded 1,834 matchlock muskets, 1,856 snaphance muskets, 3,336 collars of bandoliers, 14,133 cwt 11 lb of match, 40,000 flints for muskets and pistos, in addition to 1,756 long pikes.[110] The number of pikes suggests a ratio of one pikeman to two musketeers among regiments the sent to Tangier, a common feature in the New Model Army and some provincial forces during the Civil Wars. A warrant issued to the Ordnance Commissioners for the delivery of arms and other equipment to the Earl of Plymouth's Regiment prior to embarkation in 1680, bears this out by mentioning, 'the proportion of arms for each company to be one partizan, two halberds, and one drum, with muskets and pikes for 60 soldiers and 3 corporals, of which two-thirds are to be muskets and the other third pikes'.[111]

According to Orrery:

> Our foot soldiers generally are two thirds shot, and one third pikes, which I have often lamented; for methinks the pikes should be at least half, especially in his Majesty's dominions in which are few strong places, and consequently battles, and fightings in the field, are more common than sieges; and, without dispute, the pike is the usefullest weapon for the foot: and a good stand of them, assisted by shot if the angles be well guarded, are not easily broken by horse and shot united … And therefore I must again say, I wish our companies consisted of fewer shot,

105 BL, MS Sloane 3509, fols 180–81. Account of stores at Tangier, 29 July 1666.
106 SRO, D742/0/3/3.
107 BL, MS Sloane 3509, fol. 237.
108 SRO, D742/0/3/1; BL, MS Sloane 3509, fol. 119. Arrival of stores on the Hoy, 29 March 1666.
109 TNA, SP44/5, fols 275–6; *CTB*, IV, p. 693.
110 SRO, D742/0/3/6.
111 TNA, SP44/65, fols 14–15.

> and of more pikes; for besides the excellency of that weapon, it is not only always in a readiness for service, but needs no ammunition to make it do execution; both which cannot be said of the musket, which is often unfixed, requires always powder, bullet, and match, and in windy or wet weather, often disappoints the service, especially if it be the matchlock, and then to firelock muskets.[112]

Although pikes were traditionally employed in a defensive role, especially against enemy cavalry, the formidable offensive capacity of the weapon was witnessed by Sir John Meldrum in October 1643, when leading a sally from the besieged Parliamentarian garrison of Hull. He wrote, 'The violence of our soldiers was abated by 100 pikes of the enemy, who charged the van of our foot, scattered and in disorder did drive us backward again … and enforced us all to a shameful retreat'.[113] The 'push of pike' technique was described by Sir John Smythe in 1595:

> [When the pikes are] ready to encounter with another … letting fall the points of their pikes and carry them close breast high with both hands steadily and firmly, the points full in the face of their enemies. And the second rank likewise straightening and closing themselves by rank and front, and joining themselves to the back of the first rank, and following them step with step carrying their pikes above hand over the shoulders of the first rank, the points of their pikes likewise towards the face of the enemy's.[114]

Monck, writing in 1645–6 regarded the helmet and corselet as a necessary part of a pikeman's armour, although Glenn Foard postulates that the lack of purchases of back and breast plates, and helmets to the fledgling New Model in April 1645 'supports the argument that armour was no longer issued to pikemen by this time in the war, although some soldiers may have brought such equipment from old armies'.[115] But the defensive worth of this equipment is alluded to by a request from Colonel William Lockhart to Secretary John Thurloe in 1658, that 'if his Highness [Cromwell] could spare 12 [or] 1,500 corselets for our pikemen, I would accustom them to wear them, when they mount their guards, and at all other reviews. A stand of 500 pikes well-armed, with headpiece and corselet, will be a very terrible thing to see in these countries'.[116]

The other weapon prevalent to the Tangier garrison was the bayonet. On 14 March 1662 it was ordered that 'the French pikes and the short swords or bayonets that lately were received from Dunkirk be surveyed and an account presented to the [Ordnance] Office of their defects to the end a contract

112 Orrery, *Treatise*, p. 25.

113 *A True and Exact Relation of the Great Victories Obtained by the Earl of Manchester and the Lord Fairfax Against the Earl of Newcastle's Army in the North* (London: 1643).

114 Sir John Smythe, *Instructions, Observations and Orders Mylitare* (London: 1595), pp. 25–6.

115 Glenn Foard, *Naseby: The Decisive Campaign* (Barnsley: Pen & Sword, 2004 edn), p. 61.

116 Thomas Birch (ed.), *A Collection of State Papers of John Thurloe, Esq; Secretary to the Council of State* (London: 1742), VII, p. 215.

may be made for the speedy repair'.[117] Such bayonets were of the plug variety with tapering handles and could be fitted to the muzzles of muskets. Though it was conceivable to employ the bayonet with the matchlock musket, the firelock was better suited to the combination.[118] Turner, writing in the early 1670s, endorsed the use of the bayonet, commenting, 'when musketeers have spent their powder, and come to blows, the butt-end of a musket may do an enemy more hurt than these despicable swords, which most musketeers wear at their sides. In such medleys knives whose blades are one foot long made for cutting and thrusting (the haft being made to fill the bore of the musket), will do more execution than the sword or butt of musket'.[119]

As Shearwood suggests, 'the evidence suggests that bayonets were considered suitable for units that were not issued with pikes to protect them against horse – dragoons, grenadiers and marine units until 1689, but these were in addition to pike and not its replacement'.[120] The Board of Ordnance ordered 10,000 plug bayonets in 1678, but there is evidence that bayonets had been issued to soldiers of the Tangier garrison much earlier, and brought by the regiments from Flanders in 1662. The courts martial records pertaining to Tangier show that on 15 August 1663 a private in Captain Fairborne's Company of the Governor's Regiment was punished for 'drawing his short dagger when in anger', while on 24 March 1664 another soldier was indicted 'for striking a fellow soldier with a dagger which he took from Corporal Wilkie's side'.[121] An abstract of stores found at Tangier, undated but endorsed by Governor Kirke, lists 2,000 bayonets.[122] In mid 1664 Captain Witham was sent from Tangier to England with despatches from Colonel Bridges, beseeching the Committee to convey recruits, lime and workmen's tools – shovels, spades, pick-axes, hand-barrows and wheel-barrows – to enable them to complete the fortifications; he also requested supplies of provisions, and, above all, money, for several months' pay owing to the entire garrison. Colonel John Fitzgerald, a forthright, competent, and likeable Irishman, who had been on leave, was ordered to return to Tangier immediately.

117 Cecil C. P. Lawson, *A History of The Uniforms of The British Army* (London: Kaye & Ward, 1940), I, p. 36.

118 Mark W. Shearwood, *The Perfection of Military Discipline: The Introduction of the Bayonet 1660–1705* (Solihull: Helion & Co., 2020), p. 17; J. Black, *A Military Revolution? Military Change and European Society, 1550–1800* (Basingstoke: Palgrave, 1991), p. 20.)

119 Turner, *Pallas Armata*, p. 175.

120 Shearwood, *Perfection of Military Discipline*, p. 152.

121 BL, MS Sloane 1957, fols 9, 29.

122 SRO, D742/0/3/82.

7

The Governorships of Fitzgerald, Belasyse, Norwood and Middleton, 1664–74

When Colonel John Fitzgerald arrived in Tangier on 10 June 1664, he was appointed lieutenant-governor and colonel of the First Tangier Regiment. The King's instructions to Fitzgerald were comprehensive and far-reaching.[1] Moreover, having served during the Civil Wars as a colonel of Royalist Horse, Bullen Reymes was a Commissioner for Tangier and special agent to Charles II. His subsequent report on conditions there greatly impressed both the King and Pepys. On 9 July 1664 Reymes received his instructions from to inspect both 'the civil and military part of our city'; to 'view the progress made in the building of the Mole and the works and fortifications without the town'; and to examine all of Teviot's records and inform himself 'of the disposition of Gayland ... toward a further peace or Truce'.[2] His observations, which provide important evidence for the condition of the garrison during this period, were largely complementary of the military activities and improvements to the fortifications. They also reveal, however, the often lax management of the garrison's affairs, and his increasing frustration with the often incompetent and dishonest administrators and merchants in Tangier.[3] Besides, Colonel John Fitzgerald (with whom Bullen forged a close friendship) had endured many differences of opinion with the former governor. Reymes advised Pepys back in London:

> how it is clear that, if my Lord Teviot had lived, he would have quite undone Tangier, or designed himself to be the master of it. He did put the King upon most

1 TNA, SP71/174B, fol. 34; *CSPD: Charles II, Addenda 1660–1685*, pp. 103–7. Instructions for Colonel John Fitzgerald, going to Tangier as lieutenant-governor, 7 June 1664.

2 TNA, SP71/174B, fols 32–2; Helen A. Kaufman, *Conscientious Cavalier* (London: Jonathan Cape, 1962), pp. 191.

3 WSHC, 865/8/1/434. Bullen Reymes' Journal of his voyage from England to Tangier, 12 June–11 August 1664. His accompanying letter to Colonel Fitzgerald (865/8/1/435) possesses few details of his experiences, but includes much gossip about London society upon his return.

> great, chargeable, and unnecessary works there, and took the course industriously to deter all other merchants but himself to deal there, and to make both King and all others pay what he pleased for all that was brought thither.[4]

Having arrived aboard the frigate *Swallow* in company with Fitzgerald and others on Sunday 10 July 1664, Reymes quickly went about his task. The garrison was mustered, and a letter was prepared and translated into Spanish to be sent to Ghaïlān forthwith. On 12 July Reymes inspected the stores of victuals held in three storehouses in the Parade, as well as the garrison's mills – nine hand-mills and one horse-mill – and the bakehouse, which 'had two ovens, that would bake 8cwt of meal at a batch, and bake twice a day, each loaf weighing 3½ lb and two of them is each soldier's proportion a week, all provisions are delivered to the sergeants of each company'. That day, Captain Charles Norwood and 100 soldiers, who had also sailed in the *Swallow*, came ashore and were provided with quarters. A further draft of 100 foot, 50 from the Plymouth garrison, and 50 from Pendennis 'shouted their joy to serve the King, which much satisfied the spectators' as they were put aboard transports for Tangier.[5]

On 13 July, the Tangier foot regiments were 'new modelled' into two of roughly equal size. Reymes described how 'the several officers made ready their new muster rolls, nominated sergeants, corporals, drummers, gentlemen of the arms [and privates]'. This reorganisation was done for three reasons: first to spread the veterans of good fighting ability around and stiffen the rest; to mix together men of national differences; and to eliminate a dangerous degree of republicanism present among the soldiery of the Tangier Regiment, who to a greater extent had previously served in the Cromwellian army. During the next few days Reymes, accompanied by the governor, inspected the fortifications and Mole, while on 16 July the garrison mustered, and commissions were distributed to every officer. But reorganisation involved a loss of places for some officers. The 'late disbanded officers of Colonel Farrell's and Colonel Fitzgerald's Regiments at Tangier', having 'served faithfully in France, Flanders, and Tangier, seven or eight years', petitioned the King, 'for provision, as the rest of their fellow officers, payment of arrears, recommendation to some foreign prince, and money to bear their charges thither'. They claimed to have been dismissed on 25 May, with arrears unpaid.[6]

Reymes also reported problems with the accounting for pay and victuals. 'The governor', he wrote, 'came into Council here, where order was given to Captain Baron to make up his accounts of victuals according to the charge I gave him and that the muster roll of the present effects be paid'. Two days later, Captain St Clare was summoned to make up his accounts for the musters of the previous six months, 'that so we may go to payment'. On 23 July, much to the annoyance of Reymes and Colonel Fitzgerald, the same officer 'could not find the muster rolls for January and February'. The problem of delayed

4 Pepys, *Diary*, 19 September 1664.
5 *CSPD 1664–5*, p. 261.
6 *CSPD 1663–4*, p. 630; *1664–5*, p. 128.

accounts was common practice in the garrison. During the 1670s Thomas St John, the treasurer's agent and paymaster to the garrison, and later captain of foot, aroused the antagonism of John Luke, the secretary of Governor John Middleton.[7] St John was evasive about having his accounts checked, whilst wider difficulties were complicated by the custom of officials reaping an advantage by acquiring certain percentages of the formal transactions of administration. On 21 July 1664, following a dawn alarm, Colonel Reymes was tasked by the governor to 'make all the officers and soldiers to know the posts in case a same alarm should happen', but later visited the garrison hospital, which he found to be in sound condition.

The 'dog rounders' brought intelligence on 26 July 1664 of enemy activity at the far end of Jews Hill (renamed Teviot's Hill after the May battle), while two messengers appeared from Ghaïlān to treat with Fitzgerald and Norwood. The garrison began to be paid on 3 August, almost a month after the commissioner's arrival, whilst on Tuesday 16 August Reymes departed for Cadiz. His contribution to the improvement of the garrison was enormous. Fitzgerald commended his industry, ability, and grasp of the situation in Tangier.[8] By 24 July Sir John Lawson could tell Fanshaw, 'Tangier is now in a good condition, Colonel Fitzgerald, deputy-governor, having arrived, and most of the recruits'.[9] The garrison muster rolls of 11 August 1664 show a distinct amount of reorganisation, especially among the officers, some of whom received promotions or were transferred to other commands. Each of the foot regiments possessed eight companies, while there remained three troops of Horse, commanded by Colonel Tobias Bridges, Captain John Fitzgerald and Captain Edward Witham respectively.[10] Under the instruction of Bridges and Fitzgerald, a series of 11 forts was now erected or commenced at strategic points about the city. A new redoubt, known as Kendal Fort, faced south towards the sandhills as a defence against Moorish movements, whilst Fort Anne (located further to the south) stood 26 feet high and was built of stone. Fort Charles, the largest of all the fortifications (whose ground plan indicates that it possessed four bastions), was elevated and strengthened, and another new structure, Whitby Fort, was constructed by the sea, to protect the labourers transporting stone from the quarries to the Mole.

Two further works – Henrietta Redoubt and Giles Fort (otherwise known as 'Devil's Drop', originally the name of the steep precipice extending westward along the coast from Whitby redoubt, although the term 'drop' was a familiar term among engineers for a small detached fort or blockhouse) protected the workings at Whitby. Such fortifications and 'lines' (connecting trenches) were primarily laid out by Major Beckman and Sir Bernard de Gomme, 'the King's Engineer-General', who was responsible for the fortifications at Dunkirk and elsewhere – and were employed by the Commissioners to fortify Tangier. The cost of the work was estimated at £800 a year for four years.[11] However,

7 Luke, *Tangier at High Tide*, pp. 28, 40.
8 TNA, CO 279/3, fol. 90.
9 HMC, *Heathcote*, p. 160. Lawson to Fanshaw, 24 July 1664.
10 TNA, CO 279/3, fols 100–14.
11 TNA, CO 279/3, fol. 282. Estimate of fortifications, 1665–8.

John Belasyse, 1st Baron Belasyse (1614–1689). (Creative Commons Public Domain)

their efforts were extremely hampered by the urgent requirement of building materials. Beckman appealed that 'his Majesty would make haste with relief for Tangier', while de Gomme composed a list of absolute necessaries, including tools, tar, pitch, and other items. Carpenters, masons and labourers, with ordnance stores and supplies of all types were sent from England during the summer of 1664, but the needs of Tangier were never more than half supplied.[12] The rest of the summer was relatively quiet, although the weather was extremely hot, and by October, Fountain Fort, which contained a well that was one of the most vital water supplies to the garrison, was completed. 500 palisades – fences made up of wooden stakes – were secured around the fort, as well as Devil's Drop.

The Catholic peer, John, Lord Belasyse, was appointed governor of Tangier and commander-in-chief of the King's forces in Africa in January 1665. He arrived there on 12 April of that year. A man of considerable military experience, he had been a royalist during the Civil Wars, and was an energetic and efficient officer. Although Pepys claimed that Belasyse only accepted the position for the profit it brought, he took a notable interest in the welfare of the garrison, seeing that the soldiers were paid regularly, and ensuring that the barracks and quarters were well-maintained. He was also responsible for the construction of the redoubt and counterscarp on the west flank of Peterborough Tower, and the instillation of a 10-gun battery on the Mole.[13] On 5 March, prior to Belasyse's arrival, the consul at Cadiz had appraised Ambassador Fanshaw of the situation in Tangier:

> A soldier from Tangier reports that two Moors of importance, well-clad in outward vests of scarlet and attended by several servants, have been at Tangier with letters from Guyland to Colonel Fitzgerald. stating that the two Englishmen detained at Arzila are well, and shall one day be at liberty, and that the Moors will not hearken to a peace with Tangier until they have a brush first against it. Guyland has had above 20,000 Moors above Tangier all this cold and wet weather, which must have killed many of them. They still remain about the garrison, dispersed and hid in the bushes, according to their custom, but, thank God, Tangier is in a good condition and quite ready for them. My belief is that they will make no attempt until 3 May, a day which these barbarous people build upon for success to their

12 TNA, CO 279/3, fols 71, 244; HMC, *Heathcote*, p. 159.
13 Pepys, *Diary*, 9 January 1665; Cholmeley, *Account*, p. 71.

> enterprises, which indeed by sad remembrance those villains have had twice, in my Lord Peterborough's time, and the most noble Lord Teviot then lost his life.[14]

With the new governor came a batch of reinforcements, comprising 200 officers and soldiers, half of whom were from the Plymouth garrison. On 4 May 1665 Belasyse informed Fanshaw:

> We are in a more secure and prosperous condition than ever, I having already succeeded in rectifying several disorders, dissipating of factions, putting the civil government into a way of settlement and the martial into better discipline. We did yesterday – being the Moors' superstitious and our formerly unfortunate day – draw our garrison into arms, but Guyland did not appear. I hear that Benbuker is advancing towards him considerable strength. Sir Bernard de Gomme will tell you more of our affairs. His merit and prudence in settling our fortifications has contributed much to his Majesty's service and our security.[15]

But the size and effectiveness of the garrison was once again of serious concern. Six months after Colonel Fitzgerald's return to Tangier, he reported that following the remodelling of the two regiments, there was barely 1,450 foot, although he estimated that 4,000 were required. This included 400 men to work on the fortifications according to the King's wishes, 400 to mount guard, and 400 continually engaged on the Mole. Additionally, there were around 200 soldiers sick and 100 officers' servants without employment.[16] The Tangier Committee lowered the estimate of men needed to 2,000, but there were not enough funds to maintain even these. A renewed Commission for Tangier of 17 August 1664 had allocated £70,500 for the wants of the garrison, but the sum was not forthcoming.[17]

On his arrival in April 1665 Governor Belasyse learned that most of the garrison's funds were exhausted, while the soldiers were nine months in arrears of pay and their provisions wholly consumed. He wrote that 400 troops were daily working on the fortifications and Mole, 'but as we labour and toil like horses to promote these great works, so I beseech your Lordships to let two new companies be added to make up the establishment to 2,000 foot as in My Lord Teviot's time … our duty is so hard as it is impossible to perform it under a less number'.[18] Emboldened by their previous successes, the Moors continued to appear outside of Tangier's walls, causing the garrison to remain vigilant. Moreover, reports sent by Fitzgerald and Westcombe emphasised the state of emergency affecting the garrison by the continued Spanish embargo on trade, which outlawed the sale of food and other supplies to the English. Any negotiations for a truce with Ghaïlān were undermined by renewed Spanish machinations threatening the security of the colony.[19]

14 HMC, *Heathcote*, pp. 181–2. Westcombe to Fanshaw, 5 March 1665.
15 *Ibid.*, p. 190.
16 TNA, CO 279/4, fols 4–5. Fitzgerald to Lords Commissioners, 12 January 1665.
17 TNA, CO 279/3, fol. 240. Commission for Tangier, 17 August 1664.
18 TNA, CO 279/4, fols 69, 71, 76. Reports from Belasyse, 12, 13 and 29 April 1665.
19 HMC, *Heathcote*, p. 162.

The situation in Tangier was made more hazardous by the Second Anglo-Dutch War (1665–67). In 1664 a report from the colony informed the Earl of Clarendon that 'the Dutch war is much talked of and desired in these parts', as an opportunity for Tangier to prove its mettle in securing a naval base that would 'bring terror to all the princes of Christendom'.[20] Unofficially aided by Spain, the Dutch squadron under Jacob van Meeuwen received its provisions in Cadiz and prizes could be disposed of in all Spanish ports.

The Duke of Medina Celi, the governor of Cadiz, considered Tangier to be blockaded by the Dutch Republic, and thus according to the Law of Nations, no trade was permitted with the colony. Thus, the Dutch could continue to jeopardise English military, economic and maritime interests in the Mediterranean.[21] Yet the Navy Board lacked the funds to dispatch warships to protect trade, meaning that English ships would be forced to sail in groups to prevent capture, or remain in local harbours. On 4 May 1665 John Bland, the mayor of Tangier, informed Pepys that he had:

> passed over to Spain, to engage his old acquaintances, upon the present opportunity offered by the Dutch war, to establish Tangier convoys, and lay the foundation of a sound trade for time to come; requests that good passage and freight may be given to all victuallers and ammunition ships for Spain, by way of Tangiers, thus making it the deposit of all commodities between Spain and England. Nothing can be of greater service to the King than to make Tangier famous, which can be done by making it cheaper for ships to land and re-ship from thence than go direct to Spain.

A few days later Captain Nixon of the *Elizabeth* reported to the Board from Plymouth Sound, having 'hastened from Tangier without stop, except to exchange two or three broadsides with two Dutch men-of-war met with off Scilly; not much injury was done on either side, being stopped by night. At break of day, [we] found the Hollanders at a considerable distance, and being bound by his instructions, dared not venture to pursue them'.[22]

In mid 1665, a squadron of 18 Dutch warships entered Tangier Bay, where some Royal Navy vessels and merchantmen lay at anchor, intending to blockade the English port into surrender. But reluctant to take on the powerful battery at the end of the Mole, the Dutchmen remained out of range, before contrary winds forced them to withdraw. Threats from Dutch shipping lurking about the Straits continued, however. On 1 August Barbary Corsairs pursued a Spanish ship, *Margareta*, which they had intercepted on her voyage from the Caribbean, into the bay. They were followed by a Dutch squadron. The English gunners at the Mole batteries opened fire on the North African vessels, causing most of their crews to throw themselves into the sea and swim for safety. But a violent artillery duel ensued with the Dutch, who fired 'several broadsides and shot furiously all the guns of their fleet at our

20 Bod. Lib., MS Clarendon 81, fols 284–5.

21 Gijs Rommelse, *The Second Anglo-Dutch War (1665–1667): raison d'état, mercantilism and maritime strife* (Hilversum: Uitgeverij Verloren, 2006), pp. 139–40.

22 *CSPD 1664–65*, pp. 347, 350.

battery and city walls from whence ours returned again so their damage far more than ours'.[23] Governor Belasyse quickly ordered that the *Margareta* be anchored under the English batteries, to prevent any other initiative from the now retreating Dutch. Major Palmes Fairborne and Lieutenant John Philpott from the governor's own regiment were ordered to board her, 'with upwards of 30 soldiers, with muskets, pikes and hand grenades, and other necessaries, but for that purpose giving [Fairborne] strict orders to take care that no injury should be done either to the ship goods or men'.[24]

The major deployed his men to guard the vessel overnight, while next morning, some English privateer officers went ashore to discuss with the governor what should be done with the ship and its cargo. Belasyse duly reported:

> I easily resolved myself, Algiers being at this time one of his Majesty's allies, I was obliged in his Majesty's port to give the ship protection, although the pursuer had been a friend likewise; and much more concerned to afford them all relief and succours when they were distressed, by one, who is an enemy to his Majesty no less the to them. But this notwithstanding I met with another inclination in almost all in place, who having no great kindness for the Turks, who would have persuaded themselves and me that as it was reasonable the ship should be defended against the Dutch. So it was no less justiced that she should be declared a wreck, whereby she would have been exposed to plunder.[25]

The consequence of designating of *Margareta* as a wreck (and thus abandoned) was not lost on the governor. Throughout 6 August 1665, assisted by warm conditions and a low swell, several boats shuttled between the Spanish vessel and the beach, unloading commodities such as sugar, cocoa, tobacco and granadillo. These were listed and stored in the garrison warehouses. The following day, around 10:00 a.m., while salvage operations continued, a strong easterly breeze suddenly rose, causing *Margareta* to flounder on nearby rocks and damage to her hull. The remaining crew attempted to seize whatever goods they could, but alerted by Fairborne that the situation was rapidly deteriorating, the governor ordered the soldiers to recover the remaining goods before they were lost to the sea.

Before they could do so, however, 'encouraged thereto by some disorderly people in the city for their own advantages', the sailors sold much of the booty to the citizens, causing considerable harm to the merchant community residing in Tangier. Belasyse hurriedly ordered that several houses and private storehouses be searched, and confiscated most of the merchandise, reporting, 'Thus this affair standing, I expect hourly the Turks from Algiers to take order about their sheltered ship, and goods secure, having used all the diligence imaginable to give them all reasonable satisfaction'.[26] News of the encounter quickly reached Fanshawe, the English ambassador to the Spanish

23 TNA, CO 279/4, fols 13–14.

24 TNA, SP 72/1, fols 10–11. Deposition of Major Fairborne, 30 September 1665.

25 TNA, CO 279/4, fol. 22; HMC, *Heathcote*, pp. 201–2. Belasyse to Fanshaw, 9 August 1665.

26 TNA, SP 72/1, fols 10–11; CO 279/4, fol. 25.

King Louis XIV of France (1638–1715). (Creative Commons Public Domain)

Court, making him tremble with rage. Since the outbreak of hostilities between England and the Dutch Republic, he had worked tirelessly to convince the Spaniards to forbid the sale, by the Dutch, of captured vessels to the English in Iberian ports, without first being judged as a prize by a regular Admiralty Court. The ambassador communicated his discontentment to Belasyse, who somewhat prudently wrote on 31 August, 'My Lord Ambassador from Madrid gives me to understand, it is against his opinion I should allow the Turks to sell off their goods in this port.[27]

The following month, the Admiralty – despite the other demands of the war – assembled a convoy of 20 ships to transport provisions to Tangier, but on 12 October 1665 these were intercepted off Cape Spartel at the entrance to the Strait of Gibraltar. Two English merchantmen and the biggest of the victuallers were captured, and another two sunk, but under covering fire from the Mole battery, some vessels got through with enough stores to keep the garrison supplied for a further two months.[28] Even so, the loss of most of the long-awaited provision fleet was an acute setback for the garrison. The governor complained of the neglect of his affairs in England, and the ships, he said, were dispatched poorly manned, the convoy defective and the stores that did arrive were in bad condition. Fortunately, supplies procured in Spain and Portugal aided the garrison through winter of 1665–6. The political and military situation altered on 26 January 1667, when, in accordance with his obligations to the Dutch, King Louis XIV of France declared war on England, his ally in the war with Portugal. French maritime operations in the Mediterranean subsequently strove to drive away English shipping from the region. But except for the actions surrounding the recovery of *Margareta*, the fortunes of the Crown colony were not greatly retarded by the Second Anglo-Dutch War, despite the paucity of English men-of-war in the neighbouring seas.

One reason for this was the successful actions of a flotilla of 'private men-of-war' (privateers) – vessels well-armed and fitted for the sea – whose captains had been provided with letters of reprisal against the Dutch on 23 December 1664. For over two years, they patrolled the Barbary Coast, making prize of any Dutch or French craft they could apprehend, and taking them to be sold at Tangier. The English captains were bound 'not to attack the ships of any subject, especially those of Jersey and Guernsey; to bring their prizes into a British port or into Tangier; and not to meddle with such

27 TNA, CO 279/4, fol. 28. Belasyse to Bennett, 31 August 1665.

28 HMC, *Heathcote*, pp. 210–11. Belasyse to Fanshaw, 12 October 1665.

ships or goods till adjudged lawful prizes by the Admiralty Court'.[29] The cargoes of vessels condemned as prize by a Court of Admiralty were sold in the open market under the direction of officers selected for the purpose. Charles II sued for peace and signed the Treaty of Breda on 24 August 1667. This was a compromise by which New York and New Jersey, with Cape Coast Castle in Africa, were ceded to England; France retained Acadia and French Guiana; while the Dutch held onto Dutch Guiana, their monopoly of the spice trade in the east, and remained as fearsome as ever at sea. Pepys wrote, 'The war ended in disgrace. A peace was made only to preserve the King for a time in his lusts and ease, and to sacrifice trade and his kingdoms only to his own pleasures'.[30]

Before the formal establishment of a Court Merchant in 1668, the governor of Tangier was empowered 'to appoint, constitute and keep a Court of Admiralty, and appoint judges and officers for the same for the hearing and determining all maritime causes'.[31] All 'confiscations, prizes, goods and merchandises' condemned by this court were to be recorded, and the proceeds thereof used for the supply of stores and munitions for the garrison. As one officer remarked, privateering was highly beneficial, as 'it busies troublesome heads, and by it we have (I believe) above 4,000 bushels of wheat now in Tangier'. Another writer noted, 'This opens an honest way of livelihood to those Englishmen, whose necessities have debauched them to unable and shifting ways of living'.[32] In 1666 Belasyse was authorised to 'have the care and management of prizes brought into Tangier, to receive prize money and nominate officers necessary to that affair'. He nominated Colonel Henry Norwood and two garrison officials as Commissioners of Prizes, with salaries of £250 per annum each, to be disbursed by the treasurer by warrant from the governor out of the prize money. In November 1666, the sum of £1,800 from the proceeds of prizes was allowed for earnings for army officers of the garrison.[33]

Tangier was greatly advantaged by the creation of a weekly post to Spain. In August 1664 Colonel Fitzgerald arranged for a packet-boat to sail once a week to and from Cadiz, so that correspondence could be sent to England, enclosed with that of the consul there. The arrangement was suspended early in the Dutch war, but in June 1665 Westcombe reported that in accordance with Belasyse's order, he had re-established it, adding, 'The boat comes to Tarrifa, which confronts Tangier, and from thence the letters reach me on Saturday or Monday, and go on by this day's post to Madrid and England.'[34] As the Moorish leader Elkhadir Ghaïlān's power waned, he tried to build a closer rapport with the English. In May 1665 he began negotiations for a truce, even though his ability to honour it was rapidly diminishing. During the latter part of the year more provisions and recruits were dispatched to

29 *CSPD 1664–65*, pp. 180, 250.

30 Pepys, *Diary*, 27 July 1667.

31 TNA, CO 279/1, fol. 29; BL, MS Harley 1595, fol. 10.

32 *Description of Tangier*.

33 *CSPD 1666–67*, p. 240.

34 HMC, *Heathcote*, p. 195. Westcombe to Fanshaw, 11 June 1665.

the garrison. On 15 December, Treasurer Povey, preparing to return from a spell in England, reported having observed provision ships under sail, and 'all the Tangiers ships are ordered by Sir Jeremiah Smith to ride at anchor at Plymouth, till the convoy calls them out. All is ready on board the frigate for the men marching from Somersetshire. Ninety brave young fellows from Pendennis were shipped aboard the victuallers'.[35] Westcombe informed Fanshaw on 25 March 1666, 'All well in Tangier, praised be God, and believed that Gayland will suddenly court a peace with that garrison, now that he hath totally lost his credit with the grandees of this nation'.[36] A week later the Moorish commander concluded a peace treaty with Lord Belasyse on terms he had long refused to grant to his predecessors.[37]

Characteristically, in his letters to the governor and other officers of the garrison, Ghaïlān verbosely claimed that he had never broken peace with the English, who were responsible for the return of hostilities. He also demanded the demolition of all fortifications since the beginning of 1664 on the grounds that Teviot had reneged on promises by Fitzgerald to limit their extent.[38] Yet the conclusion of the agreement in April 1666 represented a watershed in the history of the English settlement in Tangier. For the past four years Ghaïlān's conduct towards the garrison had been marked by open hostility and warfare, punctuated by intervals of ceasefire. However, in early 1666 he faced serious challenges from his chief antagonists, the head of the zawiya of Dilā', Abdallah ben Abu Bakr, and the Prince of Tafileta, Mulai al-Rashid. Ghaïlān's failed assault on the Spanish coastal station of Larache in February 1666 demonstrated his treachery and cost him his alliance with Spain.[39] Thus, completely isolated, the Moorish leader was compelled to turn to the English for supplies of arms and ammunition to ensure his very survival. The Tangier garrison itself was emerging from a difficult period marked by a dearth of supplies sent from England, pay in arrears of many months, the conditions of the blockade inflicted by Dutch naval operations, and the prohibition on commerce enforced by the governor of Andalusia.

The first major concession Ghaïlān granted Lord Belasyse as part of the peace treaty was the acknowledgment of the legality of Charles II's settlement in Tangier. In accepting the 'true and firm peace' to be made forever – rather than the habitual six months – he surrendered the right to oppose the infidel's usurpation of Muslim land, which had the focus of his *jihad*. The second important compromise was allowing the garrison 'all that field that doth begin from the Jews' River, running as the line is marked out, unto the River Ticeros of Old Tangier; in which line they may sow what they please'. Crucially, this would reduce the garrison's reliance on the local

35 *CSPD 1665–66*, p. 102. Povey to Williamson, 15 December 1665.

36 HMC, *Heathcote*, p. 245.

37 TNA, CO 279/6, fols 27–30; Bod. Lib., MS Carte 75, fols 428–29. 'Articles of Peace Concluded and Agreed between His Excellency, Governor of His City and Garrison of Tangier in Africa, etc., and Cidi Hamet el Hader Ben Ali Gayland (2 April 1666)'. Printed in Bejjit, *English Colonial Texts*, pp. 103–8.

38 BL, MS Sloane 1955, fols 29, 33, 35, 37–8, 40, 44–5, 54, 57–8, 62, 64, 66, 68–9, 73, 77, 80, 86, 91–4, 96, 98.

39 HMC, *Heathcote*, pp, 202, 241; Mojuetan, 'Legitimacy in a Power State', p. 354.

population for foodstuffs. In return, the Moorish leader obtained an annual supply of 200 barrels of black powder, and a promise of aid by sea if required. There is little doubt that Belasyse benefited the most from such conditions. Even with the supply of powder, Ghaïlān was unable to compete with his more powerful rival, the Sultan of Morocco. Ghaïlān suffered a catastrophic defeat in battle near Alcazar in July 1666, which had a disastrous effect on the morale of the Moorish cavalry, and the Berber tribesmen, who deserted him. After a brief, yet bitter fight, in which he was five times wounded, twice in the face, Ghaïlān was forced to escape to Asilah with a handful of followers.[40] Even though he would appear before Tangier briefly a few years later, the garrison had small reason to fear his power again.

On 1 December 1665, Major Palmes Fairborne, who was recruiting in the West Country with Colonel Henry Norwood, reported that raising men for Tangier was delayed by want of money, but Norwood and Mr Povey had procured some on credit in Plymouth, until the deputy lieutenants of Somerset paid what they had been ordered. Fairborne added that he was hoping to procure recruits at Taunton, while Norwood remained at Plymouth to receive 100 men from Pendennis, whom 'a Tangier captain with the fleet will take into his care the recruits, and an ensign whom Lord Belasyse ordered him to make'.[41] Nine days later Norwood, having returned from Cornwall, arranged with Lord Arundel, the governor of Pendennis, for the 100 soldiers to be transported to Plymouth, testifying that he had purchased large hammocks and clothing for them out of his own pocket. More recruits for Tangier had been anticipated by these enterprising officers, but as Fairborne declared, he 'would have got 400 men; but being anxious to reach Plymouth before the fleet sails, is setting forward with 120 choice men, hoping to make them 200 on the road. The distance and the encouragement needful for the men make it very expensive'.[42]

Back in Tangier, in January 1666 Governor Belasyse wrote to Lord Arlington (formerly Secretary Bennet) that he had been engaged in constructing 'new redoubts and breastworks to secure the city against both Dutch and French, and expressing the desire to come home'.[43] The Commissioners did not object, and within days of the April agreement Belasyse left for England, boasting that he had achieved what his predecessors had been unable to obtain. He also attempted to sell his title as governor, preferring a place at Charles II's Court. Pepys, who generally possessed a low opinion of Lord Belasyse, referred to him as 'a man of no worth in the world but compliment'.[44] The obvious choice among the Tangier garrison of a successor was Colonel John Fitzgerald, who had long experience of the place, and had been in command during Teviot's six-month absence from the colony in 1663, as well as the period between his death in May 1664 and the arrival of Belasyse as governor in April 1665. However, Fitzgerald, an

40 TNA, CO 279/6, fols 65, 76. Ghaïlān to Norwood, 29 June and 3 July 1666.

41 *CSPD 1665–6*, p. 81.

42 *Ibid.*, p. 93.

43 BL, MS Sloane 1955, fols 20–1.

44 Pepys, *Diary*, 6, 17 March 1667.

Irish Catholic, was not only overlooked, but had his commission as deputy-governor rescinded. The large number of Catholic commissioned officers in Charles II's army reflected its heterogeneous nature.

Claims that Tangier was a nest of Papist sedition are adequately documented.[45] As Routh asserted, 'Not only was Tangier an admirable military training ground, a depot for troops of undoubted loyalty to the King, but it was known to contain many Irish Catholics'.[46] Among the original four regiments sent to the colony – two English and two Irish – 61 officers can be identified as Catholics, but any Protestant dominance was broken by the high rate of casualties sustained in the fighting of May 1664.[47] A list, breaking down the garrison's officers by religion, reveals 23 'of the Romish Persuasion' and 29 Protestants, although 10 identifiable Catholics remained. Moreover, Lord Belasyse was also a known Catholic, but was erroneously listed as 'of the Protestant Faith'.[48] Although the Test Act – a statute that excluded from public office (both military and civil) all those who refused to take the oaths of allegiance and supremacy, who refused to receive the communion according to the rites of the Church of England, or who refused to renounce belief in the Roman Catholic doctrine – was passed in 1673, it did not apply in Tangier and other overseas stations, and it remains doubtful whether soldiers serving there were required to take the oaths, although some did take them, probably voluntarily. In 1681 Governor Kirke and 56 officers took the oaths of supremacy and allegiance.[49]

However, Popery was no obstruction towards promotion within the garrison, although the religious toleration practised at Tangier was regarded with profound misgivings at home. Charles II's call for the increase in the strength of garrison in the late 1670s renewed such suspicions. Even so, some Catholic officers were barred from service. In 1682 Maurice Flynn, adjutant to Captain White, the city mayor, and an officer of 'great diligence and ability', lost his place 'by reason of his refusing to take the oaths of allegiance and supremacy'.[50] In addition to this, there were religious tensions within the civilian population. One merchant claimed in 1667 that Catholic office holders in the courts of justice had proved 'factious in deciding causes in favour of their religion'. Thirteen year later the mayor declared that three of the six aldermen were 'professed Papists' and his successor 'more Popish than Protestant', whereas the composition of the garrison was dangerously and disproportionately Irish'.[51]

On 21 February 1666 Colonel Henry Norwood was commissioned lieutenant-governor of Tangier and commander-in-chief, 'in the absence of a governor'. He held the post until October 1669, when the new governor,

45 John Miller, 'Catholic Officers in the Later Stuart Army', *EHR*, 88 (1973), pp. 35–53 (pp. 44–5).

46 Routh, *Tangier*, p. 239.

47 Wienand Drenth and Jonathon Riley, *The First Colonial Soldiers: A Survey of British Colonies and Their Garrisons, 1650–1714. Vol. 1: the British Isles, Europe, Asia and Africa* (Eindhoven: Drenth Publishing, 2014), p. 108.

48 BL, MS Sloane 3509, fols 139–40.

49 TNA, CO 279/28, fols 240–7.

50 TNA, WO 25/11, fol. 247; *CTB*, VIII, p. 659.

51 BL, MSS Sloane 3509, fol. 208; 3512, fol. 283.

John Middleton, 1st Earl of Middleton arrived. Norwood had returned to England the previous autumn and was quickly employed in work on the accounts of Tangier. He, with the assistance of Major Fairborne, was also occupied in the West Country with raising recruits for the colony. On 14 December 1665 it was reported that '90 brave young fellows from Pendennis' were shipped aboard victualling vessels, while more men were marching from Somerset. A further 300 enlisted from the Plymouth area, although the country tradesmen were reluctant to serve. Norwood informed Lord Arlington from Taunton that the local deputy lieutenants, though eager to please the King, were much averse to raising men for Plymouth garrison, but afterwards transporting them to Morocco.[52] Norwood departed for Tangier once again in March in 1666. According to his report, dated 10 June, the condition of the garrison had improved after the late truce with Ghaïlān. With the safety of a protected peace, the Anglo-Irish garrison began another round of construction on the landward defences, although the treaty had specifically forbidden the building of any new works. Between 1665 and 1668 £32,230 was spent on Tangier's fortifications.

John Middleton, 1st Earl of Middleton (*c.* 1608–1674). (National Trust, Creative Commons Public Domain)

The city walls received some repairs, and were strengthened with ravelins (outworks of fortifications, with two faces forming a salient angle) and supplementary ditches. A crownwork (a full bastion with the walls on either side ending in half bastions, from which longer flank walls run back towards the main fortress) was hastily constructed at the north-west front of the Upper Castle. Moreover, Catherina Port benefited from the placing of a more general line of palisades which enveloped the entire landward side of the city.[53] However, as Childs asserts, 'Whether all these works were ever completed is open to serious doubt, for the government never spared much money for Tangier and the state of the fortifications in 1678 was bad enough to suggest that no repairs had been carried out on them for years'.[54] More recently, Elbl suggests that 'it would be naïve' to extrapolate from English descriptions and illustrations of Catherina Port in particular, that the proposed improvements were all completed. He credits the former Portuguese garrison with the construction of its protective bastion between 1647 and 1657.[55]

By 1666 the King was growing considerably short of money, and wider financial constraints were placed upon his military forces. The charge of the

52 *CSPD 1665–66*, pp. 59, 61, 67, 69–70, 102.

53 TNA, CO 279/3, fols 323–4. Memorandum of the method of the new fortifications as they are to be made in his Majesty's City and Castle of Tangier.

54 Childs, *Army of Charles II*, p. 141.

55 Elbl, *Portuguese Tangier*, pp. 186, 200–2.

navy was reduced to £200,000 per year, whilst the annual cost of maintaining Tangier, set at £75,388 12s. 6d., would have to be substantially cut.[56] Accordingly, Colonel Norwood recommended a reduction in the extent of the garrison:

> which is now kept up to this proportion merely for the cause of the Mole, may be safely reduced to one regiment of 1,200 foot, and when the town is better fortified, the charge might again be reduced by half, and might moreover in part be raised upon the place by perquisites that I can chalk out, and as for the horse, they are already a needles burthen and may be abolished, for every officer and citizen will keep a horse if given a load of hay yearly and a little land to raise corn.[57]

But Norwood's proposal to shrink the garrison to an all-time low of 1,200 men was disparaged by his subordinate, Major Fairborne, who believed it would limit Tangier's defence 'to less than third nights' duty, and the guards but weakly manned'. The notion of establishing a 'citizen militia' was based on the method of defence maintained by the former Portuguese inhabitants of Tangier, 1,300 of whom (1,000 foot and 300 horse) were in royal pay, the foot for guarding the walls, the horse used only for offensive warfare. A 'militia of freemen' was later established, and at first placed under the control of the civil government. In 1677 it was decreed that officers of the militia must be members of the Corporation, selected by the mayor and commissioned by the commander-in-chief. Musters were held by order or agreement of the commander-in-chief and with the knowledge of the city mayor.[58] Though Norwood's scheme was rejected by the Tangier Committee, one formulated by Belasyse – now back in London – was accepted. In October 1666 it was agreed that the two regiments of foot, each with a nominal strength of 1,000 men, would be reformed into one of 1,600 (designated the Old Tangier Regiment). Additionally, the remaining single troop of horse would be reduced by half, while the officers' pay was to be reallocated and the garrison staff reduced to a minimum level. This would bring about savings of £10,000 per annum.[59]

The new Establishment for Tangier, which came into force on 16 March 1668, diminished the annual charge to £53,797 15s. 4d.[60] A total of £7,999 17s. 6d. per quarter (£31,999 10s. 0d. per annum) represented pay for the military garrison.[61] As with earlier reorganisations, those of 1666 forced several officers and soldiers to be sent home for reasons of economy. From the numbers provided in abstracts of musters, the strength of the garrison remained static at 1,550 between 1670 and 1672.[62] Nevertheless, a survey taken at Tangier on 30 December 1676 shows that due to the rigours of service and disease,

56 TNA, SP71/13, fol. 109; WO 24/1, fols 4–5.

57 TNA, CO 279/6, fols 59–60. Norwood to Arlington, 10 June 1666.

58 TNA, CO 279/17, fols 1–2. Commissioners to Corporation of Tangier, 26 November 1675; CO 279/21, fol. 320. Order of 8 December 1677.

59 TNA, CO 279/6, fol. 121.

60 TNA, SP44/30, fols 52–3; SP44/72, fol. 135; *CTB*, II, pp. 482, 484, 488; *CSPD 1667–68*, p. 290.

61 TNA, CO 279/10, fols 197–8; WO 24/2, unfol.; BL, MS Sloane 3509, fols 230–1.

62 BL, MS Sloane 1952, fols 42–7.

numbers had fallen considerably to 96 non-commissioned officers, 1,085 privates and 34 troopers.[63] On 10 July 1676 one soldier, William Harrison, was found to be 'maimed, decrepit and indigent, like the other poor soldiers returned from Tangier'. His captain, John Giles, issued him a certificate of service, which stated that Harrison 'had been two years a soldier in the Earl of Middleton's Regiment and received several wounds in said service. Giles certified his good behaviour and confirmed that he was dismissed by the governor's order, the soldier receiving a pension from the royal bounty.[64]

By early 1669 the garrison was in its weakest state since the colony had passed to Charles II. The reappearance of Moroccan troops was serious enough to prompt Colonel Fairborne – never a man to exaggerate the hardships of military life – to report, 'Tangier was never in worse condition than at present. I hope some care is taken to remedy this or else the Lord have mercy upon us'.[65] Demands for reinforcements for Tangier were constant. The peace with Spain eased tensions and made it possible to redeploy 400 veterans from the English Brigade in Portugal. These 'very brave men', commanded by Colonel John Rumsey, but accompanied by no officers, arrived from Lisbon on 12 September 1668.[66] Half were intended to increase the effective fighting strength of the garrison, and half to replace the 130 men said to be troublesome. Although the soldiers of the brigade had received full arrears of pay 'to their great satisfaction', on 5 September they received an unenthusiastic welcome from Colonel Norwood. He subsequently wrote to Arlington:

> It is a sad paradox to tell your Lordship that I am sorry men are come here at this juncture, but I must tell your Lordship that much I have often repeated to the Lord Commander by their office (viz, the victuals sent in April last) is wholly spent and that since the middle of this instant September there had been no flesh in the stores but what I have borrowed of Sir Thomas Allen or procured upon my proper credit, much bad meat has been rejected of that which should have served the six months, in so much that if the weakness of the garrison had not retarded our necessity we had been truly put ere this; but now that more months fall upon us as then the Establishment, and no supply from England to help us out, our case is deplorable and a very great allay to the arrival of these great men. I will use all importunity to persuade Sir William Jennings to take our old desperate men, which if I please it will some ease for us besides this want of victuals and stores, to repair the walls and quarters, the arrears due unto the garrison is almost insupportable the 9th of September next, a complete year the account thereafter will make God send his Majesty's exchequer to [succour] us.[67]

Lord Belasyse's proposals of 1666 further asserted that the garrison should be provided with fresh provisions purchased from local traders, that the

63 TNA, CO 279/19, fol. 371.

64 TNA, SP44/7, fol. 234; *CTB*, VII, p. 949.

65 TNA, CO 279/12, fols 158–9.

66 TNA, SP28/89/9, fols 108–9. Sir Robert Southwell to Arlington, 17 September 1668.

67 TNA, CO 279/10, fol. 1. Norwood to Arlington, 24 September 1668.

soldiers should not be compelled to remain at Tangier more than 5 years, and that they should receive pay on a regular basis. Such reforms, though, were criticised by Norwood as 'small retrenchments, useless and harmful'. On 13 October Pepys wrote, 'He [the Duke of York] and my Lord Chancellor, and Duke of Albemarle, and Prince Rupert, Lord Belasyse, Sir Hugh Cholmeley, Povey and myself met at a Committee for Tangier. My Lord Belasyse's propositions were read and discoursed of about reducing the garrison to less charge; and indeed I am mad in love with my Lord Chancellor for he do comprehend and speak out well … Most things moved were referred to Committees, and so we broke up'.[68] The general plan of reform devised by the Commissioners included the creation of a corporation and civil government for Tangier. It was anticipated that the substitution of municipal for military regulation in some departments would enable a tighter control of local expenditure, and that the establishment of courts of justice and the mechanism of civil administration would encourage merchants to operate in the port and undertake business in the city. Charles II declared Tangier a free city with all its corporate privileges and powers on 4 June 1668.[69]

The Earl of Sandwich arrived in Tangier Bay on an official mission to the colony on 14 August. After two years of diplomatic activity in Madrid, he had negotiated the terms of a peace treaty between England and Spain, and mediated between the Spanish and Portuguese to bring about the Treaty of Lisbon, and with it an end to the Portuguese Restoration War.[70] Sandwich's visit to Tangier was directed by the Commissioners during a period of their consolidation of the colonial establishment. He recorded in his journal that he was met by the lieutenant-governor, and 'towards evening we went ashore together, when he saluted me with all the guns of the town, and all the soldiers and townsmen drawn out, and fireworks at night; and lodged me at his own house, and provided all sort of good entertainment for me'.[71] A week later Sandwich surveyed the defences of the city and harbour, and made an estimate to the condition and progress of the Mole. He held a muster of all men in Tangier, 'fit for service of any kind', and noted 1,424 soldiers, 159 Mole workers, 100 militiamen, and 63 'strangers' (supernumeraries). Sandwich also enquired into the practices of baking, brewing, and fishing, the construction of mills, and scrutinised the licensing of taphouses and victualling stores. Other considerations were the building of a hospital, the health of the inhabitants of the colony, and the state of relations between the garrison and the Moors.

From the engineer, Henry Sheres, the Earl soon acquired much information about the Mole, the first work of the kind undertaken by the English, and of which he possessed a keen interest. Headway was particularly slow, however, not for lack of effort, but because both project and contract

68 Pepys, *Diary*, 13 October 1666.

69 Cholmeley, *Account of Tangier*, pp. 73–4.

70 Henry B. Arlington, *The Right Honourable the Earl of Arlington's Letters* (London: Thomas Bennet, 1701), II, pp. 236–54.

71 TNA, CO 279/10, fols 179–80; Frank R. Harris, *The Life of Edward Montagu, First Earl of Sandwich, 1625–1672* (London: J. Murray, 1912), II, pp. 154–8.

had been conceived in an experimental fashion, with vague notions of cost. Moreover, a combination of enemy activity, absence of skilled workmen, the dislodgements caused by violent sea storms, and alterations to the methods of construction, significantly impeded progress.[72] Within a decade of its possession, Tangier had gained a reputation as something of a moral desert that would blight it for many years. One of the inhabitants declared, 'The number of our soldiers is few, but of fighting men much less, many being superannuated, but more disabled by debauchery'.[73] Arriving in the colony in 1683 Pepys – no prude – observed, 'Nothing but vice in the whole place of all sorts, for swearing, cursing, drinking and whoring … runs to corruption here'.[74] Behind many such reports lay the frictions between the military garrison and civilian authorities. There were also constant accusations from merchants that officers assumed unconstrained levels of power, eroding the 'rules, orders and institutions' designed to safeguard commercial activity.

One contemporary pamphlet, circulated in England, observed, 'the difference and variance between traders and soldiers, encouraged by the rulers' covetousness, and the citizens' poverty and wants; and the unreasonableness of both, unwilling to comply with one another: for this discourages all wealthy persons from inhabiting there, because they are not countenanced, nor have those liberties which it hath pleased his Majesty to grant them'.[75] Colonel Norwood lamented, 'nothing has more retarded the improvement of Tangier than military grandees 'arriving with their own creatures, who assume an arbitrary power over every man's possession, [which] do greatly discourage the inhabitants to do anything tending to a settlement of their families on the place'.[76] The official inauguration of the city corporation occurred on 21 August 1668. Sandwich, Norwood, various military officers, and other persons of quality congratulated the newly appointed representatives, and a loyal address was sent to the King to acknowledge the charter, while the new Constitution came into force.

On 9 November the *Providence* fireship, having been ordered from Algiers by Sir Thomas Allen with a party of released English prisoners, was forced ashore in Tangier Bay, where the captain, 'despairing to get her off, and to prevent her from falling into the hands of the Moors, was forced to set fire to her, himself, with the men, escaping in their boat'.[77] This event was a timely reminder of the precariousness of the wider strategic and maritime fortunes of the garrison. The lieutenant-governor and the mayor of Tangier, John Bland, remained at odds throughout this period, especially after a disagreement arose between them over the unlicensed sale of wine, which Norwood opposed, and the management of revenues generated by services such as careenage and portage offered in Tangier's port. It was a

72 [Sir Hugh Cholmeley], *A Short Account of the Mole at Tangier, from the First Beginning of that Work* (London: 1679), p. 5.

73 *Exact Journal*, p. 13.

74 *Tangier Papers*, p. 89.

75 *Present Interest of Tangier*, p. 6.

76 Bod. Lib., MS Clarendon 85, fols 291–3. Norwood to Clarendon, 29 May 1667.

77 *London Gazette*, 3–7 December 1668.

bleak period. Towards the end of the year the Treasury dispatched £10,000 to the garrison, which, according to the deputy-governor 'cheered our hearts'. On 10 November Norwood explained to his friend Colonel Legge:

> I am gotten out of the frying pan into the fire; no sooner escaped the fury of the Turks but I sum by the ears with the mayor of Tangier. I know I must be tender of corporations, they have been much blessed birds unto the Crown … I thought within this month that Satan himself in person could not have put me into any manner of disorder with this man, nor could I have been brought to be in earnest with him unless his malice had been such as you will see on much ill consequence to the garrison.[78]

John Middleton, 1st Earl of Middleton arrived in Tangier to take up the post of governor on 9 October 1669. Yet although he was an experienced ex-royalist soldier who had been appointed commander-in-chief in Scotland after the Restoration, he was known for his drunkenness and dissolute lifestyle, and was sacked from his command in Scotland in 1663 for unscrupulous conduct. For some weeks in June 1669 the Tangier garrison had been alarmed by the appearance of great numbers of Moroccan troops, both horse and foot. These hardly hid their observance of the defences. As Ghaïlān's influence had declined, the English at Tangier gradually understood that they would have to contend with an even more formidable enemy in Mawlay el Rachid, who, as Major Fairborne noted, 'is grown exceeding great and proud, being now sole Emperor of Salé, Fès and Morocco'. Rumours were brought by Jewish traders of his determination to drive the English and Spanish garrisons in Morocco into the sea, and as a result, affairs between Tangier with Spain became more affable in face of the common menace. Norwood duly reported, 'God be thanked we are both able and willing to receive him, and when so ever he dares attack us your Lordship may depend upon such an issue as our master may justly expect from good subjects and honest men who live like brothers together'.[79]

In the emerging light of dawn on 27 June sentries at Cambridge Fort observed Moorish soldiers waiting in ambush for the relief party due to arrive that afternoon. The guns in the fort opened fire, and supported by enfilading fire from other batteries, the enemy was repelled. Four days later another incursion near Anne's Lane, the covered way leading from Catherina Fort and Anne Fort, was scattered by artillery fire, although every shot diminished the garrison's small stock of powder and ammunition. A third attempt, this time at Western Cove, where a circular block-house had been constructed to overlook the terrain and to shield the stone quarries, was warned off by three guard dogs, placed at the position for that very purpose. But such probing attacks by the Moors continued. At first light on 2 July 1669 further attempts were made along the western flank, specifically to intercept soldiers passing towards Devil's Drop, and Henrietta and Charles

78 HMC, *Eleventh Report*, *App. V*, p. 16. Norwood to Legge, 10 November 1668.

79 TNA, CO 279/12, fols 158–9. Fairborne to Williamson, 3 July 1669.

Forts. Hollar's *Prospects of the grounds about Henrietta Fort*, drawn in 1669, shows Henrietta as a rectangular block, with a small observation tower and possibly a penthouse on its flat roof, with a with a ladder providing access to a side doorway located halfway up the fort. It is also protected by palisades and earthen banks. Immediately overlooked by the structure is Devil's Drop, seemingly a single-story wooden building, surrounded by palisades, and positioned very close to the sea shore.

Several skirmishes occurred after this, during which the defenders drove off the Moors with musketry and grenades, but the garrison's commanders soon became wise to their enemy's strategy. The forts were armed and victualled for a fortnight, while the soldiers defending them were instructed to remain alert. At 9: pm on the same day, Mawlay's troops positioned themselves in force between Monmouth and James Forts, intent on rushing Catherina Port and Fort, the main western entrance into the city – some 600 yards away. However, Major Fairborne, continuously at the forefront of the action throughout his service in Tangier, led with immense gallantry 150 men under Lieutenant James Fitzgerald and Ensign John Philpott of the Governor's Regiment, to confront them. With their flanks covered by cannon and musket fire, they counter-attacked with the disciplined use of pikes, muskets, and grenades, inflicting large numbers of casualties on the startled tribesmen. As Norwood, observing from the city's defences later put it, 'after a hot dispute for an hour the enemy was forced to retire with considerable loss, and we consider some great man slain by hearing three salvoes of shot fired by the enemy, we think for the funeral'. Such a feat of arms against a much larger number of skilful and ferocious warriors was both remarkable and timely. Barely two weeks later, Fairborne and his troops repeated their exploits on the same ground. This time a mass of Moorish infantry 'drew to the sandhills between James and Monmouth Forts, whereupon the lieutenant-governor commanded Major Fairborne with a good party of musketeers to the line, where began a warm dispute for over an hour after, whereupon the enemy with considerable loss retired; the garrison receiving no hurt, but only the death of one corporal'.[80]

During this period, the all-important hay crop beyond the lines was brought in, but only with some difficulty, while forays were made by the Moors on the corn sown close to the city walls, some of which was burnt. On 31 May 1670 Sir Hugh Cholmeley, the Surveyor-General of the Mole, wrote:

> This day my Lord [Middleton], in discovering the ground which he did design to mow out the lines, exposed his person to some dangers, by riding a little to call back some of the horse scouts that had placed themselves farther than my Lord had ordered; when a party of the enemy's horse, by the advantage of the bottoms, got between the scouts and my Lord, killed two of the scouts, and took a third prisoner; my Lord, with 14 more, making a stand, so that the enemy durst not attempt him. And we did bring off the dead bodies, and found a horse of the

80 *London Gazette*, 24 July 1669.

> enemy's killed with an *alhague*, and much blood, which made us conclude that they had an equal loss.[81]

The defence of Tangier against a major assault would have been no easy feat. The garrison was reduced to around 1,000 fit for service, making it difficult to maintain an effective guard along all the lines. The new Establishment of January 1668 had reduced the foot to one regiment of 12 companies, while on 6 March 1672 Luke, noted in his journal, 'A muster in the fields, where the regiment made a very handsome appearance, being present in the fields at least 190 files. My Lady Middleton walked out to see them, stayed at Charles Fort till all was done, then went down to Whitby where Mr Sheres treated her'.[82] At six men per file, this would equate to about 650 men, besides officers.

The infiltration of the outer defensive works by the Moors, and their ability to pass through them and withdraw largely unmolested, suggests that the lines were in a somewhat porous state. To the unwary, danger abounded, even for more senior members of the garrison. On 13 December 1670 Luke recorded a typical encounter:

> when I came to Sandhill Fort about eight of the clock I heard some firing from James and Anne Forts. Just underneath the hill to the former, two horsemen of the enemy discovered themselves. The firing at the other was at two footmen who rose out of an ambuscade at Anne Lane end. I viewed round, see much ground ploughed without any vacancies, and two or three walking sentinels [of the Moors] all up and down the fields, and on the westward great green hill two parties of about forty Horse in the whole, which had made near a hundred, as the sergeant at Kendall Fort told me. When I was gone two others discovered themselves, as they tell me, on the approach of four of our horsemen almost within pistol shot.[83]

Sandhill Fort was, it seems, a temporary structure, which appears in none of the numerous drawings of the Tangier defences. It is alluded to in a report by the garrison's ordnance officers, dated 20 March 1683, while Lord Dartmouth's commission for surveying the fortification in later in the year recognised the need to fortify the 'Sandhills' to the south-west of the existing line of forts.[84] Anne Lane, leading to the outer works, was certainly a danger spot. On 12 March 1671 the engineer, Henry Sheres, evaded being caught in an ambush there whilst 'riding too near Anne Lane end', having been forewarned by an alert sentry at Anne Fort, who 'shot a musket to call him off'.[85]

In February 1672 it was reported that half of the palisades before Teviot Hill 'were blown down, being as rotten as dirt itself', and it was discovered

81 Cholmeley, *Account of Tangier*, p. 131.
82 H. A. Kaufman and P. Kaufman (eds), *Tangier at High Tide: The Journal of John Luke, 1670–1673* (Geneva: Librairie E. Droz, 1958), p. 106.
83 *Ibid.*, p. 25.
84 SRO, D(W)1778/I/i/765; D(W)1778/V/1397, fols 61–2.
85 Luke, *Tangier at High Tide*, p. 75.

that during one night the Moors had dug up a turnstile leading to Catherina Fort.[86] Colonel Norwood requested '12 culverin or demi-culverin', and reported, 'the guns now sent are not fortified, almost all of them twelve-pounders only fit for flanking on the wall which already is furnished of that sort in good proportion'.[87] He was concerned to strengthen the outer forts, but his ideas would have cost money that had hardly been forthcoming in the past. However, Charles II, who was conversant with the persistent difficulties of the garrison, preferred to turn to diplomacy, rather than attempt to contain the Moorish threat by expensive and unproductive military methods. In August 1669 Henry Howard, 6th Duke of Norfolk, arrived from England on a special embassy to the Sultan's Court in Fès, with instructions to arrange, if possible, a treaty of peace and commerce, which would safeguard for Tangier free trade and communication with the interior of Morocco. Two days before Howard's arrival, Norwood advised the governor of Tétuan of his coming, and requested him to send word to the Sultan, so that a pass or safe-conduct could be arranged for the ambassador.

Howard duly came with a 'great train', including the secretary to the embassy, Thomas Warren, merchant of London, who brought a considerable trade in saltpetre, copper and beeswax from Santa Cruz, and gunpowder from Salé. The transaction was sanctioned by the English Crown, while £4,000 was spent on presents from the King, which included 40 cases of pistols and 10 cannon.[88] Even so, after a period of three months had lapsed Howard had failed to make proper contact with Mawlay, and the disastrous mission – characterised by poor local intelligence, missed opportunities and innumerable excuses for delay – and described by Bejjit as 'a complete fiasco', was abandoned.[89] The ambassador would eventually leave Tangier on 7 July 1670 with two brigantines to protect him from pirates on the way to Cadiz. One of the members of Howard's party was Wenceslaus Hollar – 'his Majesty's scenographer or designer of prospects' – who had petitioned Charles II to travel to Tangier. Hollar sketched a series of views of the city and its surrounding arrangement of forts, that were designed to be majestic and reassuring representations of the colony. Hence, they form an indispensable source of visual documentation of the English presence in Tangier.[90] Upon his return to England he executed several etchings, allowing a more sympathetic rendering of the panoramas of the city and its defences.

To Colley, these 'suggest something of the scale of the English investment in Tangier, and their confidence at this stage in its permanence'. Further, she noted that Hollar 'makes Tangier appear familiar and even domestic, and thus participates in a larger ideological endeavour to represent it as a clean, orderly, and benign settlement where daily life was little different than in

86 *Ibid.*, p. 61.

87 TNA, CO 279/10, fol. 113. Norwood to Williamson, 22 September 1668.

88 *CSPD, 1668–69*, pp. 238, 441; BL, MS Add. 19872, fol. 2. My Lord Ambassador's instructions to Henry Sheres, going to Genoa, 27 August 1669.

89 Bejjit, *English Colonial Texts*, p. 31.

90 F. C. Springell, 'Unpublished Drawings of Tangier by Wenceslaus Hollar', *The Burlington Magazine*, 106 (1964), pp. 68–74 (pp. 70–3); Richard T. Godfrey, *Wenceslaus Hollar: A Bohemian Artist in England* (New Haven: Yale University Press, 1994).

Europe.[91] Of the artist's depiction of the sentries manning the fortifications, Godfrey suggested that, 'Their purpose is topographic, but the platoons of soldiers marching dejectedly or lounging by their cannon also give Hollar an unacknowledged status as Britain's first war artist. Both the drawings and the set of prints he made on his return to England suggest the sheer ennui and boredom of garrison life in a remote country'.[92] During the summer of 1671, some 6,000 men of the Sultan's army positioned themselves about the hills above Tangier in bodies of between 500 and 800, continuing their practice of intercepting stragglers and parties of men cutting hay. Such harassing activity again proved burdensome for the garrison. Cholmeley identified the root of the problem:

> [The Moors] lodge their ambushes within our very lines, they sometimes killed our men as they passed to discover, which they continually do without any other danger than hazarding a few shots, whilst they leap over the lines and run into the fields of their own country. This insecurity makes all men more shy in passing about the fields, and cannot be prevented but my walling the lines about. I am sure that half the money that is said to have been spent here in making several insignificant forts, would, if some had been well husbanded, have surrounded our whole lines according to the best way of modern fortifications.[93]

In Tangier the situation remained much the same until the following year. The bulk of Mulai el-Rachid's troops had been fighting rebellious tribesmen in southern Morocco, and after the Sultan's death following a riding accident, his brother Mulai Ismā'īl faced even more fierce resistance. Yet Tangier, now under its new governor, Lord Middleton, was fully absorbed in its domestic problems. Luke's journal provides an intimate portrait of the colonial community during this period. His account of daily activity is interspersed with official business, social gatherings amongst senior officers and the civil elites, and the comings and goings of commerce, but it also discloses a scene of dire misery and privation suffered by the soldiery. Pay was two years in arrears, and although rumours abounded in mid 1672 that 'there was money come to pay off the garrison to this August', nothing came of it. Recent blockades of the port, occasioned to a great extent by the Dutch Wars, added to the not inconsiderable supply problems. The guards at the Mole under Ensign Whittaker were allowed each man three pints of wine, 1 lb of beef and ½ lb of pork per day. On New Year's Day 1672 a soldier of Captain Carr's Company was discovered to have 'had gotten drunk, stumbled, so stunned himself that he could not rise, and so with much drink and cold died, for the surgeon examined his head, found a bruise but the skin not broken'.[94]

The scarcity of provisions became characteristic of the administration of Lord Middleton. Victuallers continued to reach Tangier, but not in substantial numbers. In December 1670 Luke recorded a dogger boat (twin-

91 Colley, *Captives*, pp. 27–8.

92 Godfrey, *Wenceslaus Hollar*, p. 27.

93 TNA, CO 279/14, fol. 121. Cholmeley to Williamson, 14 August 1671.

94 Luke, *Tangier at High Tide*, p. 40.

masted fishing vessel) from England landing provision of 40 tons of beef, pork, butter and cheese, yet on 4 February 1672, the arrival of 'an Irish vessel laden with beef, mutton, and fish', was, in Luke's words, 'very seasonable, we being at the last pinch'.[95]

On 23 March he wrote:

> In the morning his Excellency having been informed overnight that the soldiers grew mutinous about receiving their provision, viz., what was owing them for short allowance, caused all the soldiers to be drawn to their arms at their several posts and called all the officers together, when he told them what he had heard; and then said that he wondered to have the business of two ounces in the pound started now, for he found the provisions was delivered now at the same rates as they had always been from the beginning. For his part he was sure he had not one penny advantage and had done what he could to get everything to their own advantage. However, he did desire them if they thought fit to pitch upon an officer of their own, whom they might sent to England to make known all their grievances.[96]

On 4 June 1672 there remained in the garrison stores biscuit for three weeks, beef for 16, oatmeal and peas none, butter for two weeks and no cheese.[97] There was no cause to expect better things in the foreseeable future. In 1675 the ebullient George Phillips reported the presence of a range of available local produce in Tangier, including Calabash (a bottle, or white-flowered gourd), beans and cucumbers, though he opined that they were incomparable to cabbage and turnips. The fields about Tangier city had been full of fruit trees, but 'sometimes since, there being no timely provision made for firing, the soldiers were necessitated to cut them down, and burn them, for want of other fuel'.[98]

The military threat to the garrison remained during this period of undeclared war. In January 1672, 'The Moors tempted our people to fall into their ambuscadoes by placing some cattle near the lines betwixt Charles Fort and Kent Fort. One cow was brought in without any loss or danger, so the ambuscadoes rose as they had lain down to no purpose'.[99] The final part of Luke's journal turned towards the activities of the garrison's old adversary, Ghaïlān, and his relationship with the governor. After three years of fighting the Moorish leader reappeared in northern Morocco with an army equipped with English weapons obtained by the treaty of 1666, and a new determination to defeat his enemies. But the garrison of Tangier was once again drawn into England's broader strategic and military orbit as Charles II, was obligated to assist Louis XIV against the Dutch Republic. The declaration of the Third Anglo-Dutch War (1672–74) was reported by Luke on 21 May 1672:

95 *Ibid.*, pp. 150, 33, 59.

96 *Ibid.*, p. 111.

97 TNA, CO 279/10, fol. 100.

98 *Present State of Tangier*, pp. 12, 15.

99 Luke, *Tangier at High Tide*, p. 89.

> Early in the morning arrived an express from Consul Colson of Malaga advising of six Dutch ships, very rich, bound from thence to Cadiz, together with two Hamburghers and one Leghornese. Upon this his Excellency resolved to send out Captains Leggat and Lyddell with as many of the merchantmen as could get ready. Orders were given accordingly; and in the meantime, in pursuance of his Majesty's order, the war was proclaimed against the Dutch, the solemnity this: the Mayor and Aldermen came up on horseback with Lieutenant Colonel Alsop, Major Fitzgerald, Majors White and Fairborne, and Mr Bacher (one of the judges of the Admiralty). They had before them a kettledrum and three trumpets in my Lord's livery. In the first place it was proclaimed in Stayner's Battery, read in a very audible voice by Mr Bacher and repeated by Peast. It was the King's own proclamation which was read. From thence they went and did the like at Catherina Port, the marketplace, and Sandwich Port, and so on the Mole, where his Excellency entertained everybody with an excellent dinner of cold meat.[100]

Two weeks later, on 7 June, the naval battle of Solebay off the east coast of England was fought to a tactical stalemate, although the Dutch (commanded by Lieutenant-Admirals Michiel de Ruyter, Adriaen Banckert and Willem Joseph van Ghent), claimed a strategic victory because the English-French plan to blockade their fleet was abandoned. Admiral Sandwich, aboard his stricken flagship, refused to jump into the sea and subsequently drowned. In Tangier, in December 1672 the Moorish leader Ghaïlān despatched envoys to the governor with presents of food and livestock, in return for weapons and ammunition. Middleton, bound by the former agreement, and in urgent need of provisions for the garrison, exhibited a great willingness to collaborate. Ghaïlān's letter to him is somewhat revealing:

> I received your Excellency's letter of 6 January 1673. I received the 50 barrels of powder as agreed upon, I also received the 200 guns, 200 lances and 6 barrels of ball, for which I am most grateful to your Excellency. I instructed my secretary to approach your Excellency respecting a sum of money … I am in very great need of a sum of 30,000 dollars. I beg your Excellency in the name of friendship to assist me as much as possible … I must take this opportunity of troubling your Excellency for arms, begging you to supply me with 500 hundred guns and some pistols, even though you are compelled to take some of those belonging to the soldiers of that fortress, because many men have joined me and I have no arms wherewith to supply them. In this need I am compelled to apply to a friend such as your Excellency. I also require a good gun and a pair of pistols for myself, even though they be your Excellency's own, you are so good a friend that I trouble you for everything.[101]

Nonetheless, the Moorish commander's days were numbered. In mid 1673 he was defeated and killed by Mulai Ismāʾīl's troops near Alcázar. Ghaïlān fought with his habitual boldness, although was shot, and his head impaled

100 *Ibid.*, p. 128.

101 TNA, CO 279/16, fol. 300. Ghaïlān to Middleton, Alcazar, 12th of Sual, 1083.

on a lance by Mulai's men and carried before their master, as a warning to all who dared to resist the new Sultan. The following year was one of protracted skirmishing among the 'insignificant forts' of Tangier, during which neither side gained any positive advantage. On 3 July 1674 Governor Middleton reportedly fell down some steps after a bout of drinking and died of his injuries, although Phillips, who was unusually well-informed, claimed that he fell ill of a flux and 'stumbled over his servant, who lay across his threshold fast asleep, and with the fall broke his arm short at the shoulder, and within a few days died'.[102] It was also rumoured that Middleton died after falling from his horse. Although no official report of Middleton's death survives, a letter from Colonel Alsop to the Tangier Commissioners, dated 10 August 1674, alludes to it as a recent event.[103] In any case, Middleton's soldiers loved him as a commander, and his officers had great trust in his abilities.

102 Edward M. Furgol, 'Middleton, John, first Earl of Middleton (c. 1608–1674)', *ODNB* (2004); *Present State of Tangier*, p. 30.

103 TNA, CO 279/16, fol. 58. Alsop to Commissioners, 10 August 1674.

8

Hardship, Resilience, and Close-Quarter Action, 1675–78

Lord Middleton was succeeded as governor and colonel of the Tangier Regiment by William O'Brien, 2nd Earl of Inchiquin in March 1675. Lieutenant Colonel Alsop and Major Fairborne were jointly commissioned as deputy-governors in May 1676, but the post fell solely to the latter following Alsop's death five months later. Inchiquin spent most of his early life on campaign overseas, with his father, Murrough O'Brien.

In 1660, during an expedition to Portugal to fight against the Spanish, both were captured by Algerian pirates. William was held hostage for nearly a year before a ransom of 7,500 dollars was paid by the English government. It was under his governorship that the Tangier garrison suffered its third serious defeat. In September 1675 intelligence revealed that the besieging Moors had been withdrawn to the Sultan's main army in Féz. Moreover, as George Philips wrote, being 'induced to it by the encouragement of James Hamet, a renegade Moor, recommended to the governor as a fit person to be a spy', Governor Inchiquin learned of a large herd of cattle within five miles of Tangier.[1] To an officer of his experience this information ought to have appeared highly dubious, but he possessed little knowledge of local conditions. Hamet, a Moroccan, who was said to have escaped to the garrison, travelled to England and became a member of the Duke of York's household. But having returned to Tangier he defected and proved to be behind the ruse.[2]

On the evening of 19 September, the Lieutenant-Governor, Fairborne was placed in command of 500 men, with orders to seize the reported cattle. This experienced officer separated his force into a forlorn hope consisting of 80 musketeers, 20 horse and 20 volunteers; 300 men under his own command; and a 100-strong reserve under Captain Marmaduke Boynton. At 9:00 p.m., an hour or so after dark, the force marched out of Catherina Port towards a hill west of Anne Fort. Here Fairborne positioned himself with the main

1 *Present State of Tangier*, pp. 131–32.
2 Routh, *Tangier*, pp. 168–9.

party, having ordered the forlorn to move ahead. This immediately ran into a well-laid ambush. Hearing firing, Fairborne hurriedly formed the 300 soldiers under his immediate command into a square formation and withdrew towards Boynton, who was waiting with the reserve. However, they were fiercely attacked on all sides by large numbers of the enemy. Preserving the difficult formation, Fairborne and his soldiers successfully gained Anne's Lane, but of Boynton there was no sign. According to reports of the action, he had made his way back inside the city, where he reported to the governor that Fairborne and his men were lost. Inchiquin subsequently ordered Boynton to fall back within the lines. In the meantime, Sir Palmes had regrouped and advanced up the hill, expecting to encounter any survivors from the forlorn hope.

William O'Brien, 2nd Earl of Inchiquin (1640–1692). (Creative Commons Public Domain)

Here he remained for 15 minutes but was compelled to withdraw in the face of 1,500 Moors. One observer reported that Fairborne 'made his retreat with his party without any considerable loss, only with the assistance of a stand of pikes, which kept off the Moors' horse, whilst his foot fired upon them'.[3] Nevertheless, the English suffered 10 killed and several wounded, while the forlorn of 120 men was completely lost.[4] A detailed description of the formation and operation of a square in battle by an infantry battalion was provided by Brigadier-General Richard Kane, in *A New System of Military Discipline for Foot on Action*, published in 1745, after his death. Kane, an Irish Protestant, and professional soldier, served in William III's campaigns in Ireland, and under the Duke of Marlborough during the Spanish War of Succession. The colonel was, with the major and adjutant, to remain outside of the formation, 'and to keep the grenadiers by him, to oppose any small body that may be for making attempts, or feints, to retard our march'. He added that if an enemy's Horse were to approach, such officers and grenadiers would get inside the formation. If this was attacked on all sides, the colonel was to appoint 'the eldest officer of each face of the square to fight his own division, who are to advance two paces before the centre intervals, and are to fire by ranks, the rear rank first'.[5]

This combination of concentrated firepower and the positioning of grenadiers 'to such part as be in most danger of being attacked', was

3 *Present Interest of Tangier*, p. 12.

4 TNA, CO 279/17, fol. 112. A True Narration of Sir Palmes Fairborne's, Major, deportment against the Moors on the 19th of September 1675, at nine of the clock at night, to three the next morning. The English casualties may have been higher, see *CSPD 1675–76*, pp. 368, 394.

5 Richard Kane, *Campaigns of King William and Queen Anne, from 1689 to 1712. Also, A New System of Military Discipline for Foot on Action* (London: J. Millan, 1745), p. 123–6.

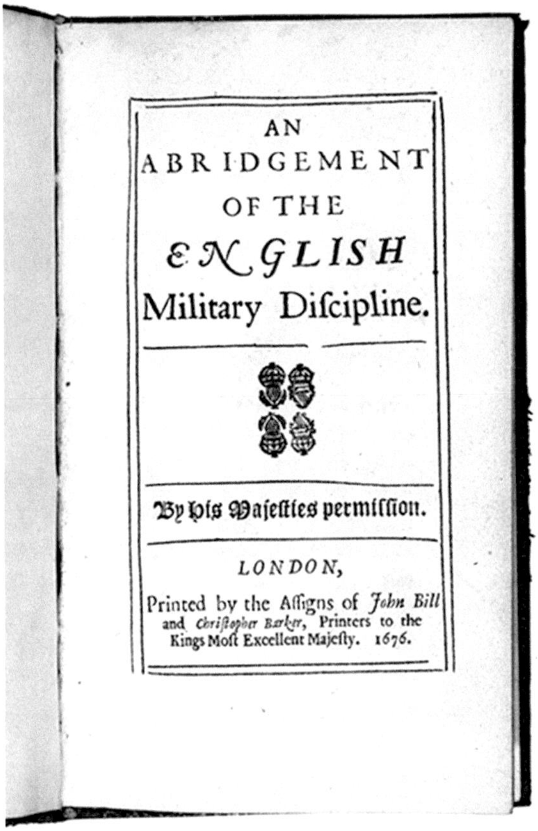
AN
ABRIDGEMENT
OF THE
ENGLISH
Military Diſcipline.

By his Majeſties permiſſion.

LONDON,
Printed by the Aſſigns of *John Bill* and *Christopher Barker*, Printers to the Kings Moſt Excellent Majeſty. 1676.

An Abridgement of the English Military Discipline (1676). (Creative Commons Public Domain)

highly effective during the fighting at Tangier, both within the above context, as well as during other defensive and offensive operations against the Moors. Alongside dragoons, grenadiers were regarded as shock troops, and were usually the biggest and most experienced men in each battalion. According to the 1678 edition of the drill manual *An Abridgement of the English Military Discipline*, 'the grenadiers (when there are any) are to be drawn up on the right of the battalion, and to augment it, without intermixing with it, or troubling the order of it, they being a separate number of men that are to be always ready for whatever shall be commanded them'.[6] Later in the century, grenadier companies were divided into two or three sections, positioned on the right and left flanks of the battalion (the third section, where employed, was placed before the centre companies of the battalion).[7] In 1677 Charles II planned the enlargement of the English army to a comparable size with other European states. There were to be 26 regiments of foot, consisting of 10 companies of 100 men each; four regiments of horse at 600 per regiment; two regiments of dragoons of 800 men, together with 700 grenadiers to attend the foot and 200 grenadiers to attend the horse. For the grenadiers attached to the foot, each man would be issued with a long carbine, bayonet, hatchet and six hand grenades. All soldiers were to be issued with 100 rounds of ammunition.[8]

Similarly, on 26 January 1684 the Duke of Albemarle, Captain of the Horse Guards, was ordered to equip each of the three troops of grenadiers added to the Horse Guards with 50 hand grenades and 100 fuses for them, and to deliver yearly to each troop four barrels of powder, 121 lb of match and 'such a quantity of shot as he shall from time to time direct'.[9] As their name implies, grenadiers were trained to throw hand grenades – small iron or ceramic spheres filled with gunpowder fused with a length of slow-match, roughly the size of a cricket ball. Hence, in foot regiments grenadiers played an important role with their companies and battalions during field engagements with the enemy, while both the drill books and descriptions of the fighting at Tangier confirm that they operated against troop formations and defensive fortifications. The 1678 edition of *Abridgement* provided exercises for the use of grenades:[10]

6 *An Abridgement of the English Military Discipline* (London: John Bill and Christopher Barker, 1678), pp. 218–9.
7 Shearwood, *Perfection*, pp. 58–9.
8 SRO, D(W)1778/V/1380, fols 1–20. Correspondence between the King and the Board of Ordnance, 27 December 1677, proposing the expansion of the army to 30,000 men.
9 TNA, SP44/69, fol. 88; *CSPD 1683–4*, p. 250.
10 *Ibid.*, pp. 148–9.

Open your pouch
Stepping forward with your right leg, with your left hand at the bottom of your pouch
Take out your grenade
Uncase your fuse

Facing to your proper front,
Blow your match
Stepping back with your right leg,
Sling your fusée
Expecting the word of command to deliver,
Deliver your grenado
Lay your right hand on your fusée
Poise
Rest
Cock
Present

Methods for the application of musket fire and the use of bayonets in the context of battalion drill are not included, but the 1684 version adds:

> Those grenadiers on the right and left of the battalion, are to fire as the musketeers fire, that is the last two ranks, to fire with the musketeers, and as soon as fired are to put their daggers [bayonets] into their firelocks.
>
> The front rank of the grenadiers, having their grenados ready, are to kneel when the first rank of the musketeers kneels, and after the last two ranks have fired,
>
> They are to stand up, and when the first rank of musketeers fire, they are to deliver their grenados, and immediately to fix their daggers into their firelocks.
>
> When the musketeers club muskets and fall on, they are to charge with their daggers aforesaid.

On 29 June 1678 John Evelyn described the appearance of English grenadiers drilling on Hounslow Heath, where we saw the newly raised army encamped, designed against France:

> His Majesty and a world of company were in the field, and the whole army in *battalia*; a very glorious sight. Now were brought into service a new sort of soldiers, called grenadiers, who were dexterous in flinging hand grenadoes, everyone having a pouch full; they had furred caps with coped crowns like Janizaries, which made them look very fierce, and some had long hoods hanging down behind, as we picture fools. Their clothing being likewise piebald, yellow and red.[11]

11 William Bray (ed.), Evelyn, John, *The Diary of John Evelyn* (London: Dunne, 1901), II, pp. 122–3.

Whilst this provides a broad description of such troops, a memorandum of 'several matters relating to the garrison, recommended by the solicitation of Captain Matthews' in Tangier, dated to mid 1679, recommended that:

> no cloth be sent on account of either of the regiments or the troops of Horse but by their own agents, and that the said agents may send cloth, linen, buttons, silk and not coats made, that it may be left to every captain to fit his own cloth, that they may send no hats but an over-surplus of cloth for caps. To solicit one company of grenadiers to each regiment, to consist of 100 soldiers each, one captain, two lieutenants, four sergeants, four corporals, and two drums. The captain of the company belonging to the Old [Tangier] Regiment to be Captain Matthews, and his lieutenants, Lieutenant Belling, Lieutenant Mahone; the officers to that belonging to Colonel Trelawny's Regiment to be Captain Trelawny, Lieutenant Davis and Lieutenant Carrol, all now upon the place. If this cannot be procured, such is the necessity of grenadiers, that rather than to want them, it may be then proposed that six men may be deducted out of each of the several companies of each regiment, reducing them to 50 soldiers in a company, and by these means make up the desired number of grenadiers, which will be of no additional expense to his Majesty besides that of the officers.[12]

Moreover, among the items indented for the Tangier stores during the governorship of Colonel Kirke (1680–83) were 500 grenade pouches of seal skin; and 500 cartridge boxes, made of tin and covered with leather to contain 20 cartridges.[13]

Though surviving examples are comparatively rare, in 1983, a hoard of several hundred ceramic grenades was discovered next to the New Castle at Ingolstadt, Germany, during construction work for an underground car park.[14] Based upon the history of the site, a date before 1723 is suggested. These explosives are heterogeneous spherical vessels, weighing between 1,275 g and 4,474 g, whilst their outer diameters are a mean average of 132 mm, with wall thicknesses from 30 mm to 65 mm. The volumes of the powder chambers of the examined pieces averaged 102 cc, which corresponds to an average charge of about 137 g of black powder. Fuses were made of conical-shaped wooden plugs with a length of 60 mm to 70 mm drilled in the longitudinal axis, and filled with a slow-burning charge of gunpowder. Accordingly, 'The Ingolstadt ceramic grenades complex is by far the most important and substantial find of early-modern pottery grenades in Europe, if not world-wide, since it surpasses comparative finds in quantity as well as variety of shapes, sizes, processing qualities and workshop marks'.[15]

12 SRO, D742/0/4/25.

13 SRO, D742/0/3/82.

14 Andreas Franzkowiak and Chris Wenzel, 'Keramikgranaten aus dem 17. Jahrhundert', *Bund Deutscher Feuerwerker und Wehrtechniker: Mitteilungen*, 2 (March/April 2019) pp. 10–14.

15 Andreas Franzkowiak and Chris Wenzel, 'Explosives aus der Tiefgarage – Ein außergewöhnlicher Keramikgranatenfund aus Ingolstadt', *SammElblatt des historischen Vereins Ingolstadt*, 125 (2016), pp. 95–110 (p. 96).

The disastrous operation and subsequent fighting retreat undertaken by the English troops on 19 September 1675 cost the Tangier garrison – already gravely below strength – 150 casualties. Fairborne complained to the Commissioners that his superior officer had acted on deficient and untrustworthy intelligence, and that he himself had drawn the governor's attention to the 'hazard he was run to by exposing so many men upon the faith of a Moor'.[16] On 8 November the Commissioners informed Inchiquin:

> We wholly disapprove of the affair, both for the design and conduct, the pretence of want of victuals we have already shown to be groundless … the sending the forlorn hope so far beyond the main body and the too early withdrawing of Captain Boynton's party, and the not making sure that Praytor Hamet in all events, are parts of conduct we cannot reconcile with the usage of soldiers in such cases.[17]

The governor continued in his attempts to allay such concerns, and to deflect any blame for the defeat away from himself. He wrote the following letter to Edward Mellish, former merchant in Porto, on 21 September 1675:

> Lest by misinformation both yourself and others might receive a fake impression of an action lately passed here, I have thought fit to give you this particular and true account of it by this first opportunity, our provisions growing very scant and this greater part of those few we had left being very bad, I thought it was time for me to see by what means I might afford some relief to these threatening events, moreover where unto I sent some spies into the country to bring me an account of what flocks of cattle were in our neighbourhood and how it was manned, this brought me an account of several flocks, and there were very few people, the king having exhausted these parts both of men and arms. On Saturday evening, being the 18th instant, I summoned the commanders of all the companies here to a council-of-war, where when I had told them the condition we were reduced to by the state of our provisions and made them acquainted with the intelligence I have received, unanimously resolved some attempt should be made for our relief, which the following night was done in this manner: at 9 of the clock 500 men marched out of this town, under the command of Sir Palmes Fairborne, Captain Boynton, Captain Lely [and] Captain McKenzie, Sir Palmes commanding the whole. Captain Boynton with 100 of the said men, I ordered to stay at the end of Anne Lane to be a reserve for the rest in case of a retreat, which he accordingly did. Sir Palmes Fairborne to march with the two battalions such as I know was hardly possible for all the foot in those parts to break, to a hill that was an advantageous post about two miles from the place, and a mile and a half short of the place, where we expected the body to secure the retreat of our forlorn hope, which consisted of 80 musketeers, 20 horse and 20 volunteers, who when they arrived at the place they were once all sudden fallen upon by the Moorish horse and foot, that most of that party was in a short time cut off, the enemy then came up in pursuit of those few that were left of them, so the main body where they were

16 TNA, CO 279/17, fol. 102.
17 *Ibid.*, Commissioners to Inchiquin, 8 November 1675.

> warmly received and met with a different success, not being able to break any of our battalions of 160 men each, and there being so many as could be judged 1,000 horse. Thus in battalia our body made their retreat to the end of the Anne Lane, where the enemy gave them over, when having some shot behind them they imagined some of our forlorn hope were yet in a posture of defence and to receive them, they faced about and marched through those of the enemy who were in their way under their formed fort, where hearing nothing of their commands, they a second time retreated towards this place. By this time the enemy was grown more numerous so that during all this last retreat were all the way charged in front, flank and rear, but were never broken and so perfected their retreat as much to their honour as if they had gained a victory, and with the loss of six men killed and seven or eight wounded. In the forlorn hope there was lost Lieutenant Napper, Lieutenant Bourke, Ensign Molloy, 70 of our foot soldiers, nine horse and all the officers, amongst whom was Captain Primes, my cousin William St Leger, Mr Thomas Fitzgerald, Mr Mayor White's nephew, two of my gentlemen, my butler, my cook, two footmen and groom, so do attribute this miscarrying of the forlorn to the treachery of their conductor, one James Hamet, who for many years served his Royal Highness, and had at this time so good employment that I took upon him to be as happy as any other servant in Barbary. But my opinion is that it proceeded merely from the hands of fate, there always of these parts being just at that time as I find by a letter of one of themselves that came thither to gather the king's corn and our men unhappily fell into their mouths, and yet the wise have no reason to brag, this loss being far greater than ours, I confess their men may be better spared, they were the next morning employed until one of the clock, them carrying their dead bodies which lay very thick so far as we could see, and we believe more thicker in other places. The heat of action being out of our fight, Captain McKenzie, who was with the forlorn hope is taken prisoner, there are now those wanting in his place who are amenable to make the worst of everything and especially if it may be a means to draw reflection upon the governor's government. I do therefore give you this tedious account of it, which I hope you will be so kind to me as to give credit to and to give the same of it since I do assure you upon the word of a man of some honour, I write you the whole truth and nothing but the truth.[18]

But for all his abilities and experience as a soldier and adventurer, William O'Brien was incapable of exercising effective military command in Tangier. In April 1676 he was permitted to return to England and spent most of the next two years on leave. Operational control fell to Fairborne as lieutenant-governor of the Tangier garrison, but throughout this period Inchiquin sought to turn the officers and soldiers against him, and to shift the blame for any mutinies onto his shoulders.[19] Sir Palmes was a professional soldier, who encountered the difficulties of his position with energy and thoroughness. He had come to Tangier in 1662 as a company commander in Peterborough's Regiment and became its commanding officer, although he

18 NUL, Me C 10/4. The document is unsigned from Tangier, but its content and tone point directly to Inchiquin.

19 TNA, CO 279/18, fols 363–4. Fairborne to Commissioners, 31 May 1676.

Wenceslaus Hollar, *Part of Tangier from above, without the Watergate* (*c.* 1669). (University of Toronto, The Wenceslaus Hollar Collection, Creative Commons Public Domain)

had already gained distinction in fighting against the Turks at Candia, and enhanced his reputation in his dealings with the Moors. Fairborne's constant arrears of pay frequently pushed him to the verge of poverty, while anxiety on behalf of his wife and seven children led him to employ every means to augment his income. He was more than once accused of misappropriating the soldiers' wages, and of taking bribes from the victuallers. Sir Palmes denied these charges, declaring he had received nothing 'excepting 4 sheep, 2 dozen of neats tongues and 10 cwt of white biscuit'.[20] According to Routh, 'his administration was honest according to the standard of the times and far more conscientious than that of his predecessors. He gave eighteen years of his life to the service of Tangier and never spared himself in its defence, which he put into as good a state of organisation as his resources permitted'.[21]

In Charles II's army corporal punishment, including the physical correction of soldiers by commissioned and non-commissioned officers, was common practice, and the garrison of Tangier was no different. It was known for an ensign to strike a sergeant on the head with the flat of his sword. Likewise, sergeants were permitted to use their halberds, though Turner insisted that corporals 'must only beat with a musket rest'.[22] The Articles of War deemed that no man should resist 'any officer correcting him for his offence, upon pain of death'.[23] On 11 February 1669 a sergeant was tried for excessive correction of a soldier, but acquitted, he having only beaten him with a hollow bamboo cane. Similarly, on 20 September, a sergeant and corporal were fined one month's pay for grievously beating soldiers under their command.[24] During Charles II's reign, martial law – the power of the monarch during time of war or national emergency to suspend the workings of the common law and replace it with a written code of regulations enforced by the military – was never present in England. In foreign service stations, such as Tangier, Portugal and Flanders, martial law was imposed as the only possible method of ruling a garrison far from home.[25] At Tangier, military applied to both soldiers and civilians alike, until a Court of Record was established to treat civilian offenders. Under martial law the arbitrary code was administered by a court martial, a panel of military officers guided by no jury and with little provision for legal representation.

In 1668 the Governor, Colonel Henry Norwood, appointed Francis Juke as Provost Marshal, and made recommendations as to the trying of military cases. Similarly, on 10 February 1675 Lord Middleton, the governor Tangier,

20 TNA, CO 279/19, fol. 428. Fairborne to Commissioners, 26 June 1676; CO 279/20, fol. 22. Fairborne to Commissioners, 23 May 1677.

21 Routh, *Tangier*, p. 159.

22 Turner, *Pallas Armata*, p. 349.

23 TNA, CO/279/1, fol. 100; Davis, *History*, I. p. 285.

24 BL, MS Sloane 3512, fols 166, 201.

25 SRO, D(W) 1778/I/i/253. Regulations laid down by the Duke of A lbermarle for the holding of courts martial, 11 April 1668; HMC, *Eleventh Report, App. V*, p. 27. Orders signed by Colonel George Legge [Governor of Nieuport] for the better regulation and government of the English soldiers there under his command, against drunkenness, taking goods without paying for them, affronting the religious, going into churches or convents, going without the gates of the city, being out of quarters after the tattoo was beaten, and fighting duels, July 1678.

received a warrant for summoning a court martial.[26] The garrison's court martial records for the period 1662 to 1674 survive.[27] These record the military crimes and punishments as governed by the Laws and Ordinances of War, and prevalent before the Munity Act of 1689, which provided the army with a full legal code of practice.[28] Martial laws and military courts provided prompt sentences that were intended as both punishment and deterrent. Corporal punishment was preferable to lengthy prison sentences, as insubordination, which might lead to the more serious offence of mutiny, was treated with great severity. Each commissioned officer possessed a printed copy of the Articles of War, and at every muster the Commissary was supposed to read it out at the head of every regiment. At a court martial at Tangier on 8 September 1663, two of the accused were deemed not guilty on the plea that the Articles relating to their offence had not been read to their company since they had enlisted.[29]

Childs shows that between 1662 and 1674, '531 cases came before the courts martial, the vast majority ending in proof of guilt. Over one fifth dealt with petty larceny and theft (117 cases), and 71 involved the abuse of brink if one form or another'.[30] More serious offences, such as cowardice before the enemy, desertion, murder, neglect of sentry duty, insubordination, and rape were punishable by death (either by shooting or hanging). In the Articles of Peace agreed between Lord Belasyse and the Moorish leader, Ghaïlān, on 2 April 1666, a distinct clause stated that each side should return the deserters of the other.[31] Some soldiers deserted to evade the harsh sentences of court martials. A later governor described this type of desertion as 'too frequent', adding that many men absconded directly after committing an offence for fear of harsh punishment.[32] For a military execution by shooting, the regiment or garrison assembled in a semi-circle, while the prisoner, his arms pinioned, and with a guard and chaplain in attendance, was paraded along the line of men to the blank side of the formation, where the grave had already been dug. Here the prisoner stood or knelt against a stake, to which he was bound and his eyes blindfolded. Either he or the provost marshal gave the signal to fire. The troops filed past the corpse before returning to their

26 BL, MS Sloane 3299, fols 61–2, 73.

27 BL, MS Sloane 1957. Minute book of court martials at Tangier, 1663 to 1664; MS Sloane 1960. Minute book of court martials at Tangier, 1664 to 1665; MS Sloane 1959. Minute book of court martials at Tangier, 1665 to 1669; MS Sloane 1961. Evidence book begun in Tangier, 28 January 1672 to October 1673; MS Sloane 3498. Proceeds of the Judge Advocate in civil and criminal affairs at Tangier, from 5 February 1662 for several years; MS Sloane 3509–12. General papers relating to Tangier, 1660 to 1680.

28 TNA, CO/279/1, fols 99–110. Laws and Ordinances of War Established for the Better Governing of His Majesties Forces in the Kingdoms of Sus, Fès and Morocco, under the Command of his Excellency the Earl of Peterborough, 1661.

29 BL, MS Sloane 1957, fol. 45; Walton, *History*, p. 541.

30 Childs, *Army of Charles II*, p. 128.

31 TNA, CO 279/6, fols 27–30; Bod. Lib., MS Carte 75, fols 428–29. Articles of Peace Concluded and Agreed between His Excellency, Governor of His City and Garrison of Tangier in Africa, etc., and Cidi Hamet el Hader Ben Ali Gayland (2 April 1666). Printed in Bejjit, *English Colonial Texts*, pp. 103–8.

32 TNA, CO 279/31, fol. 308. Kirke to Jenkins, 17 May 1683.

quarters, or sometimes the body was carried three times around the parade. But hanging for crimes such as desertion was also carried out.

On 14 May 1664 one soldier was sentenced for this crime 'to be hanged and then continue hanging until he rot off'.[33] When there were too many offenders, an example was sometimes made by the selection of every tenth man to suffer, the remaining nine-tenths being either punished in a different fashion or pardoned. Men might also decide their lot by the throw of a dice. On 18 August 1665 Thomas Shaw and Peter Craggs had to throw dice 'upon a drumhead in the face of the parade', while the one that threw least had the sentence inflicted upon him. Likewise, on 4 August 1668 an order was issued to Bartholomew Hudson, provost-marshal, that 'several soldiers to throw dice for their lives'.[34] The punishment of whipping or scourging by the provost was varied. On 12 October 1663 Thomas Finlay, of Lieutenant Colonel Churchill's Company, was sentenced 'to be whipped by the executioner forward and backward through the parade drawn in two ranks, his lashes to be soundly laid on, for being asleep on the sentinel's post'. However, other soldiers were tied, stripped to the waist, to a post and thrashed with stout switches or birch rods. Sometimes, more serious offenders were flogged, standing beneath the gallows with a rope around their necks, or tied upon their tiptoes by the neck to the gallows.

A variant was awarded in Tangier on 17 May 1665, when one man was 'at the time of the parade to have his back stripped and to run the gauntlet of his regiment paraded with open ranks, each man furnished with a stout switch to strike the prisoner's back, breast or arms or where his cudgel should light as he marched down the lanes'. Another man, found drunk at his post, was sentenced 'to be tied neck and heels', an especially brutal punishment in which the offender sat for half an hour with one musket placed behind his knees, and another over his neck, which were forcibly brought closer together by means of two cartridge box straps. Such measures often resulted the gushing of blood from the nose, mouth and ears, and cause ruptures of a fatal nature.[35] The recurrence of offences and the severity with which they were punished points to a deepening crisis within the garrison, as soldiers, faced with arrears of pay, poor victuals and living conditions, were prone to take desperate action, such as mutiny, desertion, theft and insubordination. Moreover, drunkenness, violence and other minor infractions were often indicative of the plight in which many men found themselves in. The journal of John Luke, Judge-Advocate to the garrison and secretary to Lord Middleton between 1670 and 1673, contains numerous references to courts martial and the punishments awarded to wrongdoers. On 8 February 1672 Gabriel Goedown was condemned to be hanged and remain on a gibbet at the brow of the hill next to Charles Fort 'for running away to the Moors six years and a half since'.

However, a week later his sentence was altered, for Luke reported, 'in the afternoon Gabriel Goedown was executed in the great Parade, where he

33 BL, MS Sloane 1960, fols 36–7.
34 BL, MS Sloane 1959, fols 44, 60.
35 BL, MS Sloane 1957, fol. 30.

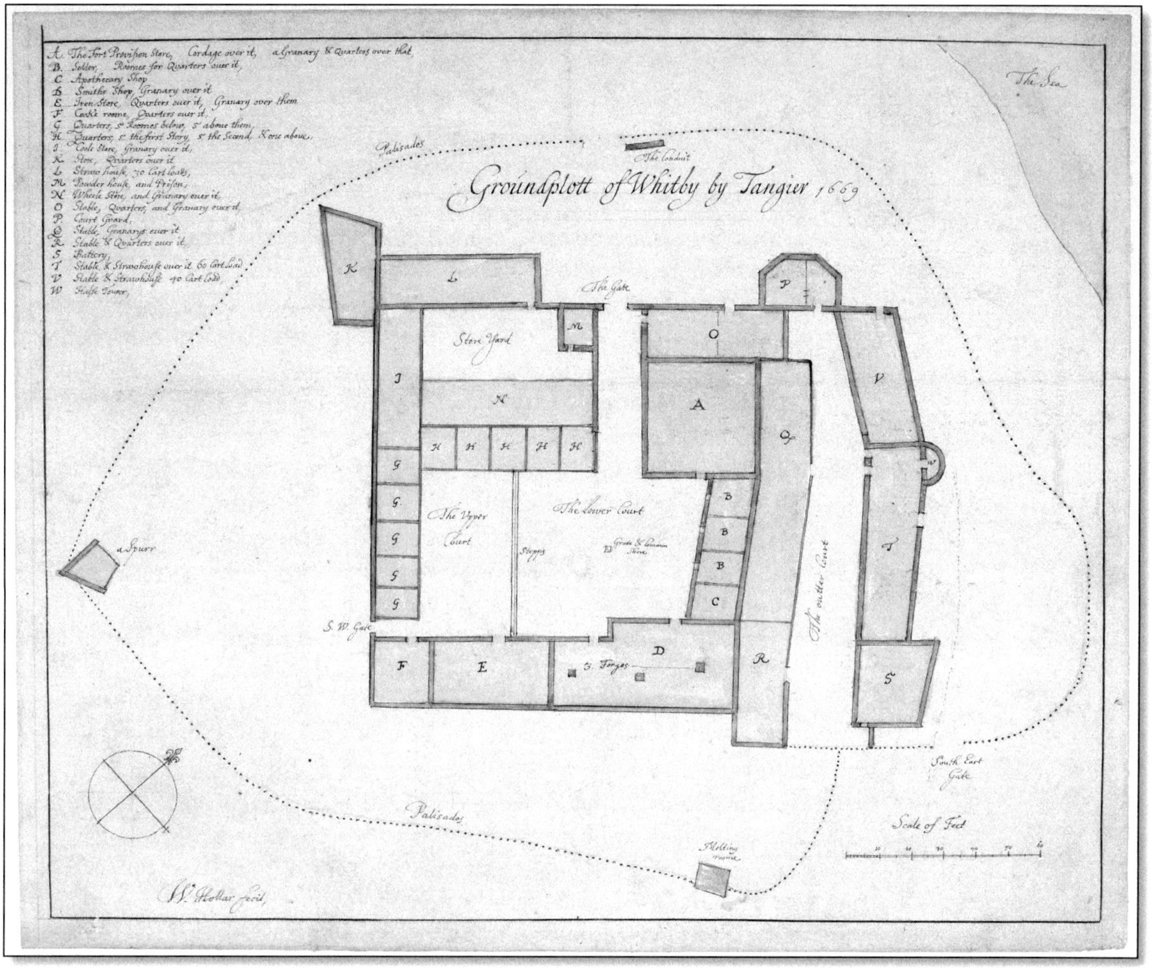

hung until after sunset and then buried under the gallows. He died without any due sense of his crimes, never enduring to leave Mr Turner speak of our Saviour to him neither at the time of execution nor before'. During the same month, Abraham Dacres of Lieutenant Colonel Alsop's company was sentenced riding the wooden horse for three days for quarrelling with a sergeant. Similarly, Corporal Purdy was ordered to ask forgiveness from Ensign Fitzharris for some unrecorded infraction. Clearly, both soldiers were provoked – Luke noted, 'I must not omit here to remark that Lieutenant Colonel Alsop was passionate in the cause of Sergeant Hodges, who in all probability was very much to blame in giving the soldier exceeding ill-language; the lieutenant colonel was as partial against Fitzharris in the case of Purdy, and the whole court inclined to favour the corporal, he having always approved himself a good [non-commissioned] officer in his quality and the ensign being none of the discreetest in his behaviour'.[36] Severe punishments continued to be inflicted upon soldiers of the garrison. On 10 March 1671,

Wenceslaus Hollar, *Ground Plot of Whitby Fort* (*c*. 1669). (University of Toronto, The Wenceslaus Hollar Collection, Creative Commons Public Domain)

36 Luke, *Tangier at High Tide*, pp. 61, 64.

Robert Moody, one of Captain Cuthbert Carr's men, was charged with using 'gross and abusive language' against Mrs Swinford (presumably an officer's wife). 'Only Jack Phillpot, and Lieutenants Pembridge and Napier [wrote Luke] were justly sensible of the greatness of the misdemeanour. But at last he was sentenced to ride the horse three days and ask her forgiveness the last day. When the sentence was read he said in open court he would not ask her forgiveness, upon he had a second trial for insolent behaviour before the court and ordered him to be whipped, and in case he should refuse to ask forgiveness to be whipped every day 39 lashes till he did ask forgiveness'.

Another private was accused by the same woman of abusing her with foul language and assault, for which he was condemned 'to remain with his hands tied to the horse and a gag in his mouth for three parade days together, and to receive 10 lashes each day of the first days and eleven the third'.[37] The wooden horse – used almost exclusively in the infantry – was the most common of the punishments among seventeenth-century armies for minor offences, with the length of ride and the weighting the legs of the rider with items (up to four muskets) tied to his feet, meant to be proportionate to the crime. But the device was especially made a means of disgrace to public exposure. Consequently, among the sentences of courts martial at Tangier between 1663 and 1670, we find soldiers, for crimes committed whilst drunk, ordered to ride the wooden horse 'at the time of the parade with pots and cups about their necks'.[38] Artillerymen were not exposed to the horse, but instead were sentenced to 'riding the gun'. On 25 June 1664, a gunner of the Tangier garrison, convicted of insubordination, was 'in the face of the parade for the space of an hour to ride the gun with a 12- lb ball at each heel'.[39]

The long-continued neglect suffered by the soldiers (pay was from two to two and a half years in arrears during 1676 and 1677), combined with the general level of intoxication and boredom with garrison life, significantly affected levels of morale and indiscipline. On 27 August 1672 Ralph Thompson and John Chandler of Captain Giles' company were found not guilty of mutiny, though later one of them was punished for disobedience towards the officer. Two days later, a soldier under Captain Daniel, was 'condemned to die for mutinous words while he was upon the guard at Port Catherina'.[40] Minor cases of individual mutinies, insubordination and similar breaches in discipline continued, but Fairborne dealt with these with a firm hand. If men were not required for sentry duty, patrolling and ration parties, they were employed daily in working at the fortifications or Mole. On 30 May 1676, the soldiers refused to work, but Sir Palmes compelled them to march to the fortifications, which they were repairing. However, 'when they came to the Lines, little or none would they do'. This mutinous act occurred because of widespread drunkenness, that day being Charles II's birthday,

37 *Ibid.*, pp. 73–4.

38 BL, MS Sloane 1957, fol. 59; MS Sloane 1959, fols 10–11, 40.

39 BL, MS Sloane 1957, fol. 8.

40 Luke, *Tangier at High Tide*, pp. 152–3.

and his health had been taken in 'Malaga wine'.[41] In another incident fatigue parties could only be made to march out after various arrests, and even then, the more voluble among them protested that life was 'all work and no pay'.[42]

When in December there was a general refusal to obey commands. The underlying mutiny was halted by the lieutenant-governor, who ordered two of the ringleaders to be marched out of the ranks and shot 'in the face of the parade'.[43] Fairborne reported to the Commissioners the following day:

> I had them [the soldiers] in the market place by five o'clock in the morning, drawn up in order to their marching forth, but of a sudden I was saluted by a cry from them of *home, home,* upon which I commanded silence and was obeyed, then turning myself to some officers by me, again they cried *home, home,* meaning they would not work, whereupon observing three among the rest I commanded them forth of the body, sent them to the martials, and marched them out to their work, where I kept them four hours according to my usual custom, being the heat was troublesome to work them longer … and then dismissed them after a small harangue.[44]

A short time after this, it was discovered that an insurrection was arranged for 20 June. The mutineers, believing that Sir Palmes was withholding 12 months' pay, planned to secure him and Captain Bowles, the treasurer, and seize Charles Fort. However, the conspiracy was divulged by an officer's servant, and the ringleaders were duly arrested. Five men were condemned by court martial to be shot, and eight others were severely punished. Fairborne's resolve and the opportune arrival of two months' wages restored the peace for a while. In December 1677 mutiny flared up again, but was rapidly squashed by the Lieutenant-Governor, who with his own hand shot down a corporal for insubordination. Subsequently, discipline was well-maintained, nonetheless discontent was kept alive by 'several maimed, aged, troublesome, and debauched rascals', whom Fairborne declared he 'would fain rid the garrison of'.[45]

But as Childs points out, the officers were often as poorly behaved as the soldiers, although they enjoyed more freedom than their men and only their most serious offences resulted in a reprimand.[46] Journals and reports from this period contain various references to the drunkenness, bickering and degenerate conduct of some commissioned officers of the Tangier garrison. Luke, who was indifferent to the brutalities meted out to the common soldiers, reported that in May 1672 Ensign Tate used 'very ill language' against one of his men, but was admonished upon Major Wickham's petition to the governor.[47] A quartermaster was found not guilty of wounding a corporal,

41 BL, MS Sloane 3512, fols 238–41; TNA, CO 279/18, fol. 363. Fairborne to Commissioners, 30 May 1676.

42 TNA, CO 279/20, fol. 252. Fairborne to Commissioners, 18 April 1677.

43 TNA, CO 279/21, fol. 364. Fairborne to Commissioners, 24 December 1677.

44 TNA, CO 279/18, fols 363–4. Fairborne to Commissioners, 31 May 1676.

45 TNA, CO 279/18, fol. 361. Fairborne to Williamson, 10 June 1676.

46 Childs, *Army of Charles II*, p. 130.

47 Luke, *Tangier at High Tide*, pp. 126–7.

and after killing a fellow officer a lieutenant was tried by the court of the Corporation of Tangier rather than by a court-marshal. Excessive drinking and dereliction of duty was just as prevalent among officers than among their men. In 1683 the newly arrived Pepys was informed by Governor Kirke:

> the soldiers did generally sell their flesh, that was delivered them on Mondays, to the townspeople for some money, that they might have it in drink. And many of them would drink it all away in three days, and then directly fast the rest of the week, by which they grew sick and many died, insomuch that he swore he believed that more men had been killed in this place by brandy than by the Moors. And upon this ground, the townspeople, knowing their love of drink, would tempt them (a little before they heard money was coming over) with selling them anything the most ridiculous, even to women's hoods and bodices, at great rates upon the score of their pay, only to have where with to raise a little money by selling those things again to buy present drink with.

Moreover, during an inspection of the Mole by Lord Dartmouth, Pepys reported finding 'one officer of the guard drunk below the church and another asleep upon his bed below that'.[48] The Laws and Ordinances of War expressly stated, 'if any officer shall be found drunk by the day of his guard, he shall be cashiered for it; and if any soldier be found drunk when he is upon duty, he shall receive such corporal punishment as a court martial shall think fit; nor shall any officer or soldier be allowed to excuse himself for any fault committed by him upon pretence of his being drunk at any time whatsoever'.[49] Undoubtedly, the officers set a bad example to the soldiers under their command, although much of their disorderliness stemmed from intoxication, religious and political differences, and social privilege.

But during the reign of Charles II entering the army as a commissioned officer hardly required military knowledge and physical fitness. On 26 June 1673, Henry Ball, one of Sir Joseph Williamson's intelligencers, wrote, 'But all men fear our officers of this army are not well picked out, for the most of them debauched profane persons and public atheists which they say openly they learn of the Duke of Buckingham, one yesterday publicly in company I am told saying he believed neither Heaven nor Hell'.[50] As Childs notes, after the days of disciplined military forces during the Commonwealth and Protectorate, such officers did much to harm the standing of the army.[51] A report on some of the garrison's officers was compiled by Fairborne in 1677. Captain Cuthbert Carr was described as not having performed 'three months' duty in a year, and that always at such times when no action appears, and then is still disturbing the peace and quiet of the place, besides his continual endeavours to defraud poor men of their rights'. Captain John Giles was held

48 *Tangier Papers*, pp. 97, 99–100.

49 TNA, CO/279/1, fols 99–110. Laws and Ordinances of War Established for the Better Governing of His Majesties Forces in the Kingdoms of Sus, Fès and Morocco, under the Command of his Excellency the Earl of Peterborough, 1661, chap. 6.

50 Christie (ed.), *Letters of Sir Joseph Williamson*, I, p. 67.

51 Childs, *Army of Charles II*, p. 43.

to be 'so ill-affected to the monarchy as having served all along against the King in the late civil wars and a person of so ill-principled that he always cunningly underhand formenting and broaching stories to disturb and incite a discontent in the private soldiers'. Similarly, Captain Brent Ely, a known republican, was 'so given to laziness that [he] cannot endure the soldiers should do any manner of work lest he should be involved in its himself'. Lieutenants, Harris and Hemmings were so old that they should have been returned to England and a pension, while Ensign Hughes was enduringly drunk.[52] Luke's journal is peppered with references to commissioned officers who had 'quarrelled and gone to cuffs', as well as others acting violently and drunkenly whilst commanding guard posts. But there were other infractions too. On 31 November 1672 Mr Crabb, the fire-master and master-gunner of the garrison was court-marshalled:

> for selling the powder committed to his charge, found guilty, condemned to be cashiered, and ordered to remain prisoner till his Excellency should order the contrary. He behaved himself very insolently and after the sentence was passed he thanked the court for removing him, declaring that his salary was so low for his part he could not live on it.[53]

Significantly, Tangier by this period 'was officered by a mixture of old royalists, ex-Cromwellians, Scots, Irish, English, drunkards, and men too old or lazy to do their duty. That such men were able to retain their commands was largely due to the unpopularity of Tangier in England'.[54] In 1678 Fairborne recommended that ensigns of foot companies should be abolished, because not enough men were available to fill all the ranks, and several men in the garrison wholly lacked the qualities expected of regular officers.[55]

Although officers were commissioned by the King, they were typically required to purchase them, the cost depending on their new rank and regiment.[56] Commissions in the Horse Guards and Foot Guards were particularly expensive, although those of cavalry regiments were dearer than those of the foot. In 1668 Charles II persuaded Lord Gerrard to surrender his troop of Life Guards to the Duke of Monmouth for £12,000, whilst in 1681 the Duke of Grafton spent £5,100 on the colonelcy of the 1st Foot Guards, even though he was without military training or experience.[57] When an officer was promoted, he would sell his old commission, which would then part-fund his promotion. However, the purchase system did not apply in foreign service stations such as Tangier, where – unlike among the standing army in England – there was a shortage of commissioned officers. Nevertheless, patronage in high places remained important for obtaining

52 TNA, CO 279/21, fol. 44. Fairborne to Williamson, 28 July 1677.

53 Luke, *Tangier at High Tide*, pp. 36–7, 165–8.

54 Childs, *Army of Charles II*, p. 122.

55 TNA, CO 279/22, fol. 110. Fairborne to Williamson, 1 March 1678.

56 A. P. C. Bruce, *The Purchase System in the British Army, 1660–1871* (London: Royal Historical Society, 1980), pp. 9–10; R. E. Scouller, 'Purchase of Commissions and Promotions', *JSAHR*, 62 (1984), pp. 217–226 (p. 218).

57 Childs, *Army of Charles II*, p. 45.

positions and securing further promotion. Tangier also attracted some of the more adventurous men or professional soldiers, such as Percy Kirke, Charles Trelawny and Lewis Farrell.[58] At company level, William Victor was commissioned Captain in the Tangier Regiment on 16 June 1664:

> Charles by the grace of God, King of England, Scotland, France and Ireland, Defender of the faith, etc. To Our trusty and well-beloved William Victor, Esquire. Greeting. We reposing especial trust and confidence in your fidelity, courage and good conduct do by these presents constitute and appoint you to be Captain of the Company of Foot in the Regiment raised or to be raised in Our Garrison of Tangier, whereof Colonel John Fitzgerald is Colonel, you are therefore carefully to discharge the duty of a Captain by exercising the said Company in arms, both officers and soldiers, and keep them in good order and discipline. And We hereby command them to obey you as their Captain. And you are to observe such order and commands as you shall receive from time to time from your said Colonel, or other your superior officer according to the discipline of War in pursuance of the trust We repose in you.[59]

Similarly, Thomas Lucy of Charlecote Park, Warwickshire, was commissioned captain in the Duke of Monmouth's Regiment of Foot on 1 November 1678; he went to Tangier as an ensign in the Earl of Plymouth's Regiment; on 1 April 1683 Lucy was appointment lieutenant to Captain Edward Hastings' company in Colonel Trelawny's Regiment by Governor Kirke, whilst his commission was confirmed by Lord Dartmouth on 1 October 1683.[60] Another career officer was Captain Thomas St John, who petitioned the Crown on 29 November 1684 for his arrears of pay. He declared that he 'served the King 30 years, whereof 20 in Tangier [as a company commander in the Governor's Regiment], and that in extremity, being undrawn, I went to Charles Fort and there suffered seven weeks' siege and at the blowing up of the fort received a musket shot through my body'. He was later appointed Comptroller of the Ordnance, in which he received 22 wounds 'by the splitting of a gun' and endured 15 months without any consideration or remuneration.[61] Unlike their men, some commissioned offers were granted extended leave in England, where they were supposed to recruit, with the result that the garrison regiments became exceedingly short of officers. They drew their pay regularly while their comrades in Morocco were constantly in arrears, although many officers owed substantial sums to landlords and merchants in the colony for unpaid bills by the time of the garrison's departure in 1684. This may have been partially alleviated in November 1683 by the loan of £800 to Colonel Trelawny and his officers to

58 *Ibid.*, pp. 42–3, 120–1; Mark W. Shearwood, *The Perfection of Military Discipline: The Introduction of the Bayonet 1660–1705* (Solihull: Helion & Co., 2020), p. 83.

59 Dominic Winter Book Auctions, sold by lot (lot 31) on 31 January 2007, <www.the-saleroom.com/en-gb/auction-catalogues/dominic-winter-book-auctions/catalogue-id-2703300/lot-3909475>

60 WA, L6/1625–5, 28–9.

61 SRO, D742/O/3/75; TNA, SP44/18, fol. 141; *CTB*, VII, p. 1417.

Wenceslaus Hollar, *Prospect of the lower part of Tangier, from the hills west of Whitehall* (c. 1669). (University of Toronto, The Wenceslaus Hollar Collection, Creative Commons Public Domain)

cover outstanding pay and expenses.[62] Governor Kirke's constant complaints about the lack of officers in Tangier had some effect, however, and most of the absentees returned on 2 March 1680.[63]

Officers and wives of the garrison led a social and sporting life. The hinterland outside the city provided opportunities for hunting, shooting wildfowl, horse riding, and boating trips around the Mole. Plays, put on by Spanish actors and comedians, were performed at York Castle, but in the main, garrison officers socialised at White Hall Fort, 'a place where the ladies, the officers, and the better sort of people do refresh and divert themselves with wine, fruits, and a very pretty bowling base'.[64] Cholmeley noted that the troupe arrived on 13 December 1670, at the site time as a 'good plenty of fresh meat, very seasonably to the poor soldier'.[65] According to Luke, during the 15-week tour, 25 performances were given, including *The Earl of Essex*. Significantly, Major Fairborne loaned each of the soldiers of his company two Spanish dollars (equivalent to two pieces of eight, or 9s. 6d.) for entertainment, but although the officer did not think that they would spend it on plays, this deed indicates how prominent this theatrical opportunity was in the consciousness of the garrison.[66] Some of the soldiers were keen, not only to watch but to produce the plays, and one document from the mid 1670s records a space being cleared in the military storehouse of York Castle for dramatic performances, even firearms being moved out to make room for the stage.[67] Various observers reported excellent dinners of fresh beef, chicken and fowl, and expensive wines being relished by officers, their wives and garrison officials in their quarters, or aboard ships in the harbour.

Violent quarrelling among commissioned officers, often heightened by excessive alcoholic consumption, at times led to dualling (which was strictly forbidden). Two officers of the King's Battalion fought when the garrison was under attack in 1680. The survivor was convicted of manslaughter and sentenced to have his hand branded by burning. Governor Kirke cashiered several officers for drunkenness and disobedience, while others, a few in chains, were sent to work at the quarry or Mole. In late 1676 Fairborne had employed his diplomatic skills in bringing about the conclusion of a two-year truce with the corsairs of Salé, and he strove (unsuccessfully) to agree a treaty with the commander of the army in northern Morocco.[68] On 17 January 1677 new commissions were issued to some officers of the Governor's Regiment 'in the King's service in the garrison of Tangier'. Sir Palmes himself was promoted to lieutenant colonel; Charles Daniel was to be major; Stuart Scroope was commissioned captain of Colonel Roger Alsop's late company in the same regiment; Stephen Tabram was promoted to lieutenant to Captain John Giles' company; while Matthew Aylmer was commissioned ensign

62 SRO, D742/0/5/3.

63 UY, MS 2572, fols 66–8, 86–7, 94–8, 125–30, 162–9.

64 Luke, *Tangier at High Tide*, p. 36.

65 Cholmeley, *Account of Tangier*, p. 164.

66 Luke, *Tangier at High Tide*, pp. 72–3.

67 TNA, WO 93/1786, fol. 148.

68 TNA, SP44/29, fol. 121; SP71/14, fol. 149; *CSPD 1676–77*, pp. 401, 442.

to the same company.[69] During the late 1670s Fairborne strove to alleviate the condition of the Tangier garrison. He forwarded regular reports to the Commissioners, in which he demanded supplies of food, ammunition, pay and recruits. Although their response was hardly adequate, a small batch of much needed men for the garrison arrived from England aboard the *Woolwich* on 30 August 1677.[70]

English naval activity continued to maintain the colony throughout this key period. Sir Robert Robinson, aboard the *Assurance*, riding off Tangier Bay, reported to the Lords of the Admiralty on 28 July that having sighted various Turkish men of war, his squadron complained even more about their short allowance money and want of wine. Whilst cruising with the *Portsmouth*, *Charles* and *James*, the *Dragon* had remained to attend the garrison.[71] At the end of January 1676, Charles II ordered a survey of Tangier and its garrison, which was soaking up an average of £75,000 per year, more that the King spent on all his other overseas outposts, or all his home garrisons combined.[72] The appraisal showed that the total inhabitants numbered 2,225, of whom 50 were army officers, 1,231 other ranks, with 302 military wives and children. There were also 130 foreigners, 156 Mole workers, 200 wives and offspring of citizens, 70 widows and single women, and various priests and servants. Amid the buildings was a hospital and a military school. Among the foreign inhabitants of Tangier were Carlo Antonio Soltrani, a Genoese merchant, who together with his brother Nicola Andrea had moved to the colony during the early years of English occupation. Matteo Barbano shows that Carlo was fluent in Spanish, probably had several interests in the Iberian Peninsula, and 'in all probability he exploited the colony's dependence on Spain to make a fortune, until he was able to rise to the highest ranks of Tangerine society'.[73] Although he was dismissed as an alderman, on 13 January 1675 Soltrani became master of pratick (harbour customs) at the port of Tangier, with the job of inspecting incoming vessels before granting them access to the town.[74]

Sir Palmes Fairborne's foremost responsibility was the military effectiveness and security of the garrison. He re-established regular musters, which had been allowed to lapse by the previous governor, and despite orders from the Tangier Committee to expend no moneys without express permission, he undertook the repair of the soldiers' quarters and town walls, as well as an overhaul and extension of the remaining forts around the defensive perimeter. He increased measures to protect the outlying positions against Moorish ambushes and sniping activity. The walls by the Old Parade were improved, although Fairborne reported, 'there is not 6d. to do it, I hope your Lordships will not be offended if I put it forward, advancing my own

69 TNA, SP44/29, fol. 196; *CSPD 1676–77*, p. 501.

70 TNA, ADM 106/323/508.

71 TNA, ADM 106/327/400.

72 TNA, CO 279/19, fol. 30; Bod. Lib., MS Rawlinson A185, fols 37–8.

73 Barbano, Matteo, '"Most thought the City in no security but under Lock and Key": Tangeri, gli inglesi e la frontiera nordafricana (1662–1684)', Gallia, A., Pinzarrone, L., Scaglione, G. (eds) *Isole e frontiere nel Mediterraneo moderno e contemporaneo* (Palermo, 2017), pp. 35–47 (p. 42).

74 TNA, CO 279/3, fol. 18.

until your Lordship's further pleasure be known'.[75] In 1677 two of the timber forts were reconstructed with bricks from Spain, and most of the 29 great guns previously without carriages, were mounted in defensive batteries. Improvements were also made to Monmouth and James Forts, 'to about 8 foot from the superfrise of the graft with stone … and a handsome foot bank within, with a parapet 4 foot high, at no charge except a little brandy to encourage the men'.

In January 1677, an area between James and Anne Forts, measuring 300 yards by 300 yards, was protected by earthen banks and palisades. This reportedly 'served Ann Lane and discovered a bottom where generally the Moors build their ambushes', and although there was 'pretty store of Moors about', the work was completed without a single casualty. Within this sector was erected a prefabricated wooden fort, 24 feet square at the base and 24 feet high, while another timber building was placed between Cambridge and Monmouth Forts, in order to clear the sandhills and secure the watercourse of the town. However, the Moors strongly objected to this, and any palisades erected during the daytime were taken down by them at night. The English soldiers were somewhat hampered by the small number of loopholes along Cambridge Fort, which flanked the position, so a further redoubt was built to guard the zone. While work was progressing, Fairborne had flares attached to the top of the palisades to illuminate the area and to deter the enemy from approaching. Mines (packed with gunpowder and stones) were placed along the forward earthworks. A few skirmishes occurred here, but only one of the defenders was wounded in a two-hour exchange of fire.[76]

It was during this period that the garrison's surgeons treated wounded sailors from naval vessels protecting merchant shipping to and from the colony. On 3 November 1677 they attended men from the *Charles*, the *James* and the *Sapphire* on shore at Tangier, while in April 1678 Robert Spottswood and James Tarres healed 60 wounded seamen from the frigates *Charles*, *James* and *Sapphire* that were put ashore by order of Admiral Sir John Narborough.[77] The Admiralty records also contain examples of the difficulties encountered by ships' officers in obtaining victuals and other commodities from the overburdened garrison and naval station, whose own supplies were particularly meagre. Captain Thomas Hamilton, commander of the *St Margaret*, who was responsible for the transportation of slaves to and from Tangier, reported on 16 July 1676:

> The galley is discharged and as the ketch will not take all the men, he has hired a ship, the *Anne*, Captain Kell master, to transport the rest for which he has drawn a bill signed by Captain Beverley, the purser and himself. He wants care how the slaves are disposed, there are no provisions except what the governor of the garrison will let him have. Sir Thomas Clutterbuck has told Mr Gascoyne not to supply the galley any further, but to take a survey of the remains which was done yesterday. The officers in charge of the slaves are discharged and he has no orders

75 TNA, CO 279/18, fol. 360. Fairborne to Commissioners, 30 May 1676.

76 BL, MS Add. 17021, fol. 32; TNA, CO 279, 21, fol. 45.

77 TNA, ADM 106/333/421–3.

> about them, so has hired four men to look after them. Captain Curlo has accepted the King's bounty and gone home. As soon as Mr Burdett, the galley's purser, has settled his business with Mr Gascoyne he will return home. The rent has not been paid for the houses where the officers, mariners and soldiers were lodged.[78]

Writing on 28 February 1678 Henry Sheres, the Chief-Engineer and Commissioner for Tangier, drew specific attention to the difficulties of procuring provisions:

> The ship with navy stores has arrived under convoy of Captain Wilshaw and will be unloaded in five or six days. They rely on the garrison for assistance, but they are hard pressed. They lack storerooms but I have obtained warehouses at the water side. I have furthermore ordered Mr Bowles to prepare for a survey of naval stores, and humbly ask whether I should inspect his past accounts. In the meantime, I have made repairs to the public stores, and have often told Secretary Pepys that it would be beneficial to have a hulk which could ride in all weathers. The Mole is in good condition and ships may safely be careened there this summer.[79]

By 1678 the rulers of the Alaouite dynasty in Morocco had begun to re-establish their power base, suppressing regional challenges, and driving the Spanish out of their remaining Barbary outposts. Pepys warned that the Moors were 'No more the ignorant and unskilful neighbours they were to the Portuguese' and had developed 'a great deal of knowledge in the business of war'.[80] Moreover, Sir Hugh Cholmeley, with his engineer's eye, wrote:

> the people are so barbarous in themselves, and so poor, and so continually embroiled in civil wars, that no near prospect can be imagined to make them apprehend, because of their improvement in martial discipline, according to the methods of Europe, so the country being so exceedingly hilly about Tangier, makes all sorts of carriages, and preparations for a siege, not only difficult, but almost impossible to be brought, though endeavoured, by a people of the most polished industry and pains.[81]

Yet it was not merely the strength of the enemy that alarmed commentators reporting on the state of Tangier. Moneys and victuals frequently failed to arrive, the existing building supplies for the Mole and other barriers proved inadequate against the storms that struck the Straits, and medical resources were insufficient to deal with the diseases that affected the population of the settlement.[82] With the construction of the harbour and fortifications

78 TNA, ADM 106/318/16.

79 TNA, ADM 106/333/284.

80 *Tangier Papers*, p. 78; Bod. Lib., MS Rawlinson A342, fols 223–4. Pepys to Sheres, 10 October 1677.

81 Cholmeley, *An Account of Tangier*, p. 86.

82 TNA, ADM 106/326/339–40. Sir John Narborough to the Admiralty, 31 August 1677; Bod. Lib. MS Rawlinson A342, fols 4–9. Sheres, 'Reflections upon the Affairs of the Mole at Tangier in a Letter to a Friend', n.d.

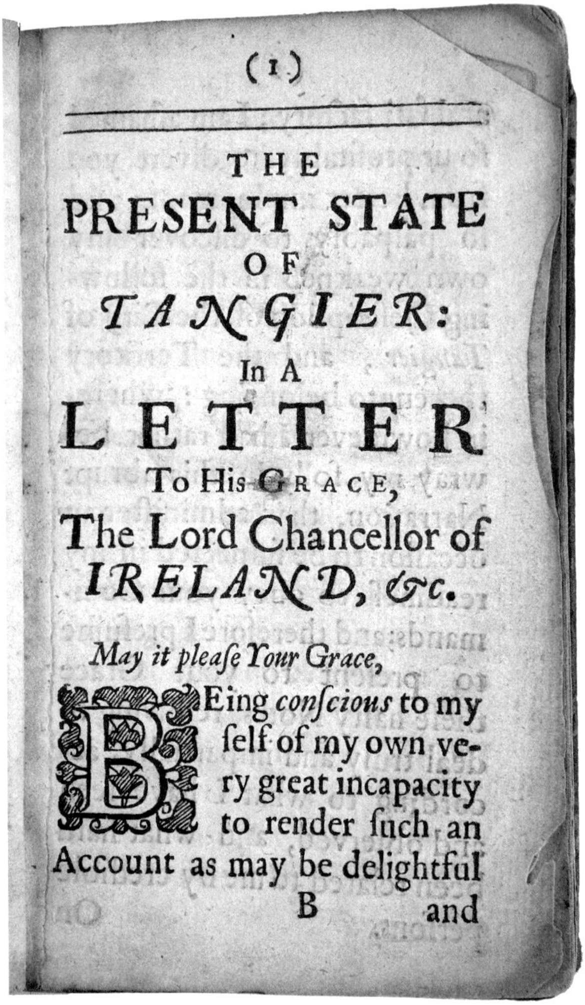

(1)

THE
PRESENT STATE
OF
TANGIER:
In A
LETTER
To His GRACE,
The Lord Chancellor of
IRELAND, &c.

May it pleaſe Your Grace,

BEing *conſcious* to my ſelf of my own very great incapacity to render ſuch an Account as may be delightful

B and

George Phillips, *The Present State of Tangier* (1675). (Creative Commons Public Domain)

threatening to flounder, Cholmeley was forced to invest privately drawn sums from city bankers, plunging himself 'into great debts to procure moneys for so vast a charge'.[83]

Despite the vigorous efforts of the garrison to repair and bolster the forts and city walls over the previous year or so, their condition remained inadequate. During one of the periodic surveys of their condition, great flaws were discovered in the fortifications, while the insufficient amount of funds available for correcting the faults was highlighted. The defences were in poor condition, the town walls were cracked and partially tumbling down, while the towers and the raised earthwork platforms were crumbling.[84] Likewise, the crownwork before the Upper Castle, delineated by Hollar, was greatly reduced by 1678.[85] After the death of Ghaïlān in 1673, Qā'id Omar ben Haddū Hamāmi was appointed commander of the Sultan's forces in northern Morocco. At the head of an army of 7,000 men, he waged war against the English and would conclude a truce with them two years later. In restricting the activities of the *infadel* Qā'id Omar's troops were deployed to destroy the fortifications constructed about Tangier and reduce the garrison to its former state in the early 1660s.

At 9:00 p.m. on 6 January 1678 heavy firing erupted from Charles, Henrietta, Kendall, Pond and Anne Forts, along the south-western flank of Tangier, and it became immediately evident that the Moors were attacking these positions in considerable force. Fairborne, watching from the town walls, knew from long experience that the enemy would be concealed between the system of trenches and the forts in overwhelming numbers, ready to ambush any relieving English force. Within 30 minutes of the commencement of first assault, as the lieutenant-governor looked anxiously into the darkness from the Upper Castle, he noted, 'Kendall Fort blown up and soon after afire, and the enemy still very hot against Charles and Henrietta; on a sudden I perceived … the door open and a great light in Henrietta by which I concluded it lost, which proved accordingly, so after

83 NYRO, ZCG 5/1/1/2, fol. 5. Cholmeley to Norwood, 24 December 1666; ZCG 5/1/1/2, fol. 31. Cholmeley to Lord Treasurer Thomas Clifford, 24 April 1670.

84 BL, MS Sloane 1952, fols 20–1.

85 Hollar, 'Prospect of the Country from Peterborough Tower, Westward of Tangier'; Elbl, *Portuguese Tangier*, pp. 70–1; Saunders, *Fortress Builder*, pp. 92–7.

about three hours conflict the enemy withdrew out of shot'.[86] Charles Fort was strongly defended by Captain Trelawny, and the officers and soldiers manning the other fortifications also held out, but only with great difficulty. When dawn arrived a patrol under Captain James Leslie cautiously advanced from the town to assess the situation on the ground.

As his soldiers approached Henrietta, located on a hillock close to the sea, to the north-west of the city, no enemy was in evidence, but the small building was in ruins and the garrison unaccounted for. The bodies of two soldiers lay among the wreckage and the remaining eight men had apparently been taken prisoner. The picket continued onwards – even more cautiously this time – but Leslie's men suddenly encountered around 500 Moorish horse lying in wait for them, but by the disciplined use of musketry they drove them off. At Kendall Fort, which had been held by 10 men under a sergeant, the situation was no less desperate. According to Fairborne, the fortification was 'found all in a ruin, the men burnt to ashes'. He further observed with a professional interest the Moorish methods of attack, including their employment of incendiary weapons, that had been so effective against the two British forts in releasing clouds of suffocating smoke and setting fire to everything inside them (somewhat akin to modern flares or white phosphorus munitions). Sir Palmes reported to the Secretary of State, Sir Joseph Williamson:

> They have found a way of stink pots which upon its breaking makes a sudden flame and from them proceeds such a stink that men are suffocated with it. This fort was tiled and about 20 foot high, so to room for their pots to get in they had long forks, and as we suppose, stood upon one another to get the tiles off, which done with great force, they broke the door and entered.[87]

Retrieving two of these devices, Fairborne and Sheres 'made trial of their operation', discerning that they were 'made as big as a large hand grenade, match to be lighted at both ends, which breaking upon its fall kindles the combustion matter with in it'. Similar contraptions were commonly used by Barbary pirates and captains of English fireships. In 1621 Admiral Mansell wreaked havoc on Corsair shipping in the harbour of Algiers by the use of containers of 'wildfire' – fashioned from brimstone, black powder and petroleum oil – as well as incendiary grenades, and fire-pikes which stuck bags of explosives to the timbers of ships. The mainly wooden forts recently constructed at Tangier could hardly stand against such implements, and the scaling ladders brought up by the Moors, on which four men could stand abreast, expedited their use. The sentries at every point were doubled to 'welcome the Moors', but they could do little else for the present, even though owing to the fighting and damage from heavy rain, their outer lines of palisades and ditches were in need of repair.

Inclement weather prevented the Moors from exploiting their success, and the English spent the next few months in rebuilding the ruined forts

86 TNA, CO 279/22, fol. 6. Fairborne to Williamson, 7 January 1678.
87 *Ibid.*

to render them as far as possible, impervious to further assaults of this kind. The ingenuity of the Tangier soldiers was limitless as they went about their task, assisted proficiently by the garrison's engineers, but the nature of the recent attacks had created a state of emergency in the colony and compelled Inchiquin to return to Tangier to recover his command. Three weeks after the loss of Henrietta and Kendall Forts, Fairborne received instructions from Charles II – dispatched before the news reached England – to conclude a treaty with the enemy on the terms they had offered; but, until he could re-possess the forts, he 'could not conceive it for his Majesty's honour to make any overtures to them therein'.[88] In January 1678 the Lieutenant-Governor had informed Williamson that men should be obtained from standing regiments at home, rather than newly raised inexperienced troops, and 'for the sending of such recruits as has come hitherto just throw the king's money away … being for the most part young boys and old men'. On 1 March he wrote further:

> Again I humbly lay down before his most Sacred Majesty that it is of absolute necessity that a reinforce[ment] be made to the garrison or at least that the establishment be completed with good men drawn of the standing regiments, for hitherto we have had nothing but the very worst of our nation sent us; I mean since I have had the honour to command.[89]

As spring 1678 approached, the remaining fortifications outside Tangier itself remained in the possession of the garrison, despite the need for men and warlike stores of every kind. On 28 February Sheres reported to the admiralty, 'The ship with navy stores has arrived under convoy of Captain Wilshaw and will be unloaded in five or six days. They rely on the garrison for assistance, but they are hard pressed [and] lack storerooms, but I have obtained warehouses at the waterside … I have often told Secretary Pepys that it would be beneficial to have a hulk which could ride in all weathers. The Mole is in good condition and ships may safely be careened there this summer'.[90]

Of the repairs to the outlying redoubts Sir Palmes Fairborne was able to report of Fort Kendal on 1 March, 'I have made both that and Henrietta the two best forts about the lines and will by degrees strengthen all the forts … the £1,000 allotted in June last is now near expended, so that I shall be at a loss, nevertheless rather than stand still I will borrow and employ all my own until I can hear his Majesty's pleasure'.[91] The arrival in Tangier harbour of the *Foresight* in the same month, with a consignment of stores, ammunition and six months' pay, and promises of further reinforcements, rekindled hope in the garrison, though recruits were still badly needed.

A few weeks later, Governor Inchiquin returned after a long period of absence, and Fairborne went home on leave. In his stead, Colonel Thomas

88 HMC, *Eleventh Report*, *App. V*, I, p. 347.
89 TNA, CO 279/22, fols 20, 110. Fairborne to Williamson, 10 January and 1 March 1678.
90 TNA, ADM 106/333/284.
91 BL, MS Sloane 1952, fols 19–33.

Dongan – an Irish Catholic veteran of the French Wars, and later Colonial Governor of New York – received commissions as lieutenant-governor of the garrison and lieutenant colonel of the Governor's Regiment.[92] Moreover, on 1 August 1678 commissions were issued for 12 lieutenants and 10 ensigns in the same regiment.[93] In May 1678, English sentries and patrols had clashed with the Moors, who were becoming more 'insolent and adventurous'. A party of soldiers sent to cut grass for fodder was set up outside Charles Fort, the attackers using the cover of the abundant summer growth to crawl up to them. Two sentries were killed, but the rest scrambled back to the safety of the earthworks. A fortnight later, 200 horsemen lay in ambush between the quarry and the eastern tower of Tangier's main fortifications in the hope of intercepting the working parties at the Mole. This time their intelligence failed them, for the Molemen were busy placing a finished casement into position and the only casualty was an unfortunate fisherman. The watchful sentinels saw what was occurring and informed the garrison gunners, who tore into the Moors with grapeshot. The survivors fled and there were no more attacks from that quarter for the rest of the year. Tangier thereafter was subject to sporadic alarms, and an undeclared war of 'posts and ambuscades' continued until January 1679, when it intensified into a closer blockade.

The supply of the garrison and naval station remained problematic, prompting Admiral Sir John Narborough, aboard the *Plymouth* in the bay of Alicante to report to the Admiralty Board on 5 November 1678, 'There are no stores or provisions in Tangier and those that came with the *Royal Oak* to Tangier and Cadiz will not last six weeks'.[94] He added that the victuals which came to the colonel with the *Bristol* will soon be spent, the garrison was owed meat that had been borrowed from elsewhere, whilst 'Governor Lord Inchiquin has spared pork from his stores. Vice-Admiral Herbert sailed five days ago has been ordered to cruise and victual at Tangier and take in provisions at Cadiz'. Various consignments of provisions, ammunition and clothing to Tangier fell foul of the harsh winter sea conditions, as well as the unsatisfactory lack of storage space in the Citadel itself. On 2 February 1679 Phineas Bowles, the storekeeper of the Tangier garrison, reported to the Admiralty Board:

> The storehouse on the Old Parade which I made use of, some part is now filled with the garrison's stores and I humbly request an order to prevent it. Mr Shere has been furnished with tackle blocks and barge oars for the use of the Mole, and I desire directions how to govern himself in future. On the 30th January the *Adventure* with Vice-Admiral Herbert on board, also the *Charles* and *Marigold* frigates came in. The *Marigold* was run on shore and lost in a great storm with the loss of 66 men, also seven merchant ships went on shore, but the *Woolwich* sloop escaped. I have assisted distressed merchant ships with stores. On the 30th Captain Dunbar came ashore about supplies of victuals and stores but could not get back on board due to the weather. Lieutenant Aylmer from the *Adventure* also

92 TNA, SP44/29, fols 104–5; *CSPD 1678*, pp. 406, 444.
93 TNA, SP44/29, fols 100–1; SP44/41, fol. 235; *CSPD 1678*, pp. 121, 337.
94 TNA, ADM 106/337/2/176.

> tried to get back on board, but it is feared he is lost. Vice-Admiral Herbert and the *Castle* fireship slipped at midnight and the *Charles* Galley rode out the storm.[95]

In February 1679, a batch of 40 reinforcements, drawn from Captain Wharton's company of Lord Morpeth's Regiment, quartered at Dover, were shipped to Tangier under the command of a sergeant. Each soldier was paid a 10s. bounty, while the NCO returned to England in the same vessel that carried them thither.[96] On 26 July a warrant was issued to Captain Thomas Barbour 'or the officers of the company therein mentioned', to raise 100 volunteers by beat of the drum, to serve under his command in a company to be sent to the garrison of Tangier. If he felt it necessary to recruit within the city of London, he was first to show his warrant to the Lord Mayor, and, 'as he shall list any of the said men, he is to bring them to the commissary of the musters or his deputy to be mustered and from the first mustering of 20 men the officers of the said company are to be entertained in pay'. Barbour was further commanded that once he had enlisted 'any competent number', he was 'to send them on board the vessels appointed to receive them in the Thames, in order to their transportation to Tangier'. A warrant of the same date, sent to the commissioners of the Ordnance Office, instructed them to deliver to Captain George Wingfield 200 quilts and covertures, and 400 pairs of sheets for the use of four companies going under his command to the garrison of Tangier.[97]

Even so, the author of a letter of July 1679 presented a pitiful image of the colony as the two-month truce was reaching its end, with the garrison hardly able to defend the settlement and the expected reinforcements looking far from forthcoming. As the author of *The Present Danger of Tangier* wrote:

> I have nothing to send you, but the like tidings of more disasters and that is, of the great danger the town and garrison of Tangier seems to be in at this time; being, 'tis credibly reported here, under a blockade, and in some distress, for there are many thousand Moors lie against it, some say fifteen thousand, others more; for indeed, they can bring down what multitudes they list, at an hours warning upon them; but hitherto there have not passed many acts of hostility between them; for they are now upon a treaty of sixty days; which is said to be politically proposed and held on foot by the town, in hopes that they may in that time receive some supplies of provision, ammunition, etc., from England; for they complain lamentably, that they are very ill-furnished in case of a siege.[98]

Captain Matthews of the Governor's or Tangier Regiment reported to the Committee that some of its members should be made aware, 'how unlucky it is, that the Moors should maintain the peace with us, if they should happen

95 TNA, ADM 106/341/642.

96 TNA, SP44/48, fol. 97; *CSPD 1679–80*, p. 91.

97 TNA SP44/58, fols 41–2, 245; *CSPD 1679–80*, pp. 207, 215.

98 E. M., *The Present Danger of Tangier or An Account of its being Attempted By a great Army of the Moors by Land, and under some Apprehensions of the French at Sea In a Letter from Cadiz, dated 29th of July 1679 (old style) To a Friend in England* (London? 1680?), pp. 1–3.

to see the place to be neglected at home'.[99] There were rumours in Tangier that English merchants had placed their personal interests over national honour and the safety of their fellow countrymen by landing 1,500 barrels of gunpowder and selling it at a profit to the Moors. At home anti-Catholic reports suggested that it was the French who had supplied powder and ammunition to Qā'id Omar's men.[100] The substance of these rumours was echoed in a letter sent from Sir Palmes Fairborne in June 1678, in which he complained to Secretary Jenkins about English vessels carrying ammunition to the enemy at a time when the garrison needed supplies very urgently.[101]

Foreign service remained unpopular at home, and often the only effective way of obtaining recruits was impressment. One such recruit was James Arnold of Upton upon Severn, who petitioned at the Worcestershire Quarter Sessions of Midsummer 1675 for relief, testifying that he was pressed at Upton and served almost eight years in the garrison at Tangier.[102] Some of the difficulties encountered in finding men for service in Tangier are outlined in a letter from the Duke of Monmouth to the Commissioners of the colony, dated 12 April 1679:

> In answer to yours of the 10th, I must acquaint you that in obedience to the king's command I gave orders for 300 men to be drawn out of the companies in Kent and to be shipped in the Downs for recruits for Tangier. But 200 of them drawn out of the Duchess' regiment then quartered at Canterbury mutinied in a body and all deserted, and his Majesty, being informed by Colonel Villiers, that part of them offered to go, if they might be commanded by officers of their own regiment and the service requiring dispatch, thought fit that another company be added to the establishment of Tangier to be commanded by Captain Jeyne, who acquainted your secretary with the king's pleasure, who promised to receive your directions thereon. Besides these 100, 100 more were drawn out of Lord Morpeth's and Colonel Salisbury's Regiments, some of which likewise deserted; the rest were put on board the *Edgar* in the Downs, where they now are, as many as remain, amounting in all with Captain Jeyne's men to 150. Mr Pepys has taken care for their transportation to Tangier as, I suppose, you will for their establishment and subsistence.[103]

Sir Hugh Cholmeley thought that the bad diet which had to be tolerated in Tangier and the general hardships of the soldiers 'gave so bad an impression among the Commons of England, that they heard nothing with more detestation than being sent to Tangier, which they usually esteemed no better than any ill prison, from which they could only hope to be freed by the grave'.[104]

---

99 SRO, D742/0/4/25.

100 *Domestick Intelligence, or, News Both from City and Country* (London: B. Harris, 1679–80), 30 December 1679.

101 TNA, CO 279/25, fols 253–4.

102 WAAS, 1/1/123/29.

103 TNA, SP44/41, fol. 235; *CSPD 1679–80*, p. 121. Captain Jeyne's Company left Portsmouth for Tangier on 7 June 1679 (SP44/58, fol. 29; *CSPD 1679–80*, p. 167).

104 Cholmeley, *Account of Tangier*, p. 18.

During the next few months, more drafts of troops were prepared and sent to Tangier. Monmouth informed Captain Wingfield that 'there may be an equal distribution of the soldiers ordered for Tangier betwixt the four companies under your command on your arrival at Tangier, you are to give orders that the respective captains divide their men by lot and that they draw their lots according to seniority'. The infantry companies in question were those of Wingfield himself, and Captains Barbour, William Matthews and Charles Wingfield – these officers were to receive a bounty of £20 each 'out of the moneys for the garrison'.[105] In addition to this, in September four companies of Monmouth's own regiment, 'very good men', were shipped to Tangier, but so many soldiers were reduced by illness due to the neglect of sound dietary provision, that barely 200 serviceable men remained among them. Moreover, 150 pairs of pistols were supplied to the three cavalry troops embarking from Portsmouth.[106] In an attempt to bolster the effectiveness of the existing garrison, on 28 April 1679 a royal warrant ordered that 'twelve lieutenants be added to the regiment of foot in Tangier, so that each company should have two lieutenants'.[107]

During the latter part of the year the Moorish pressure on Tangier increased considerably, making it even more obvious that a substantial garrison was essential for the survival of the colony, regardless of the additional cost. Fairborne had repeatedly demanded reinforcements since 1676, especially urging that any troops sent over should be drawn from the standing regiments in England, as the men who usually appeared as replacements were either youths or old men, 'the one never immuned to hardship and the other past helping himself'.[108] In December 1679, 200 veterans of the Earl of Dumbarton's regiment were ordered from Ireland, their pay to be maintained out of the Irish establishment.[109] The Moors encamped about Tangier again in March 1679, under the command of Qā'id Omar. Of major significance for the security and future of the English garrison was that the fighting methods of his army were unlike the intermittent attacks of Ghaïlān's undisciplined warriors during the first years of occupation. By 1679–80 Malawy Ismā'īd, the Sultan of Morocco, had sought military assistance from the Turks, who were in a class of their own in terms of siege-craft. The art had not altered much since the fall of Constantinople to the invading Ottoman army in 1453, and during the sixteenth century both Malta and Vienna had come close to being stormed. In 1669 the Turks had honed their knowledge of modern warfare and new scientific inventions at the siege of Candia in Crete, where they successfully undermined the stronghold, thus bringing the Cretan War (1645–69) to a conclusion.[110]

105 TNA SP44/41, fols 245–6; SP44/65, fol. 24; *CSPD 1679–80*, pp. 207, 215.

106 BL, MS Sloane 1952, fol. 26. Inchiquin's report, n.d.

107 BL, MS Add. 27277, fol. 1.

108 TNA, CO 279/22, fol. 20. Fairborne to Williamson, 10 January 1678.

109 TNA, WO 26/5, fol. 338; H. M. McCance (ed.), Halkett, Sir James, 'Tangier–1680: The Diary of Sir James Halkett', *JSAHR*, 1, Special No. (1922), pp. 1–24 (p. 4).

110 Christopher Duffy, *Siege Warfare: The Fortress in the Early Modern World 1494–1660* (London & New York: Routledge, 1997), pp. 210–11; Molly Greene, *A Shared World: Christians and Muslims in the Early Modern Mediterranean* (Princeton NJ: Princeton University Press, 2000), p. 78.

Although some historians have suggested that in northern Morocco the Moors possessed no artillery and little knowledge of siege warfare, by the 1670s their proficiency in undermining and isolation of the fortifications at Tangier, and usage of pyrotechnics had advanced enormously. In April 1679 Moorish attacks on the Tangier fortifications were renewed, and some of these techniques were put into practice. During the hasty improvements made to the garrison's defences in 1663, Whitby Fort had been established to guard the men transporting stone from the nearby quarry (which it overlooked) to the Mole. A view of Whitby from the southeast by Hollar, with a corresponding detailed ground-plan, both executed in 1669, depict a two-storied gated complex measuring approximately 170 feet by 150 feet, complete with courtyards, barrack and storerooms, smithy, stables, gun battery and a half tower. The building was protected by a screen of surrounding palisades.[111] How intact and unassailable the fort was 10 years later, is open to debate, however, but on the night of 3 April 1679 the entire western side of the Lines came under enemy attack. A general assault by about 5,000 infantry and 600 cavalry was made on all the outlying positions, although the Moors' chief force was concentrated before Whitby Fort and its adjoining redoubt, being the most forward (and exposed) of the English positions.

The house and tower were defended by a platoon-sized formation, comprising a sergeant and 28 men. They held out until 50 or 60 Moors were assisted onto the roof by their comrades, but the soldiers demolished the main building, and with it the enemy soldiers, with explosives. The English troops retreated to the tower, which they maintained for over an hour, until a corner of a wall collapsed under the sheer weight of the pressing Moors. The now exhausted soldiers had stubbornly defended the fortification for some time, and when the enemy eventually broke in they encountered the non-commissioned officer and seven men, who 'resolved to take no quarter, for death was preferable to slavery, and they made a rush for their lives. One or two escaped, but the gallant sergeant did not live to tell the tale of his own doings'.[112] The timber-built redoubt near Whitby was guarded by a sergeant and 12 men, who, with their ammunition expended and the Moors pressing in on all sides, held the enemy at bay with swords and half-pikes, until most of them were either killed or wounded. Having ordered the survivors to retreat, the sergeant bravely set fire to his store of powder and blew up the redoubt, killing himself and 40 of the enemy. No account of this action appears in the official Tangier correspondence, but according to the *London Gazette* the Moors lost over 250 men in the assaults, while the English casualties were put at 20 dead and 15 missing.[113]

Though heavily outnumbered during these desperate actions and unsupported from their own side, the fighting spirit, tenacity, and leadership displayed by the English troops was noteworthy. Thus, a payment of £60 was later awarded to the sergeant's widow, Mary Heathley, 'whose husband

111 'Prospect of Whitby at Tangier where the stone for the Mole and workmen do quarter, drawn from the southeast', 1669; 'Ground plot of Whitby by Tangier', 1669.

112 Walton, *History*, p. 28.

113 *London Gazette*, 24–28 April 1679.

blew up Whitby Fort [*sic*: redoubt] at Tangier, and lost his life there', while £15 10s. was granted 'for one and thirty decrepit soldiers from Tangier, as of his Majesty's bounty'.[114] Some of the latter may have been wounded in the fight at Whitby and managed to make their way to safety. A two-month truce reached with the Moors in June 1679 fell apart as Omar, the Barbary commander, learned that the Sultan would not consent to it because of reports of a supposed French landing on the Moroccan coast. On 25 July the Moors attempted a further attack on the English positions under cover of darkness, but the soldiers, perhaps reminded of the performance of the redcoats at Whitby Fort and redoubt, could not be induced by their commanders into making a sustained attack. Although warfare continued, little fighting occurred during the following autumn and winter.

114 John Ackerman (ed.), *Moneys Received and Paid for Secret Services of Charles II and James II* (London: Camden Society, 1851), pp. 11, 22.

9

The Great Siege of Tangier, 1680

The year 1680 witnessed the greatest crisis of the English occupation of Tangier, 'the time of greatest danger to the garrison, and the most conspicuous success of the Moors, when it seemed that the Sultan was within measurable distance of fulfilling his wish to 'drive the Christians into the sea".[1] On 10 February 1680 Francis Gwyn MP informed Ormond, 'On Sunday in the evening came an express from Tangier which brought the news of their apprehension there of another attack from the Moors, whereupon Sir Palmes Fairborne is sent over to be Lieutenant-Governor in the room of Colonel Dungan, who is recalled, and leave given to the Lord Inchiquin to return home upon the arrival of Sir Palmes Fairborne there'.[2] Upon his return to Tangier in April Fairborne inspected the military defences, which he found closely besieged by the Moors, and already in desperate straits.[3] Unfortunately for the garrison, Inchiquin's governorship had been largely characterised by uncertainty, drunkenness, terrible carelessness, and long periods of leave in England. Tangier has been referred to as 'a good training school', yet despite the sporadic fighting, there had been few opportunities to hone the skills of many of the soldiers because of the frequent periods of inactivity and inclement weather. Even so, the enemy attacks of January 1678 and April 1679 gave the Tangier garrison warning of the grave danger posed by the Moors after years of relative peace.

As recent English military operations in Flanders had shown, foreign service stations devoured soldiers, although in a general sense, Tangier's affairs received little support in Parliament – which was preoccupied by other pressing and tumultuous affairs of state – the increasingly concerted attacks by Moroccan forces made it imperative to comply with Fairborne's requests for seasoned veterans. In April and May 1680 Sir Palmes sent numerous letters to Jenkins (who succeeded Williamson as Secretary) in which he

1 Routh, *Tangier*, p. 167.

2 HMC, *Ormond, V*, I, p. 273.

3 For Fairborne's commissions from Charles II, dated 9 February 1680, see TNA, SP44/29, fol. 349; *CSPD 1679–80*, p. 388.

urged the sending of reinforcements for the coming fight and the release of the soldiers' pay, which was 18 months in arrears. Fairborne informed the King unequivocally, that unless 500 horse and 4,000 foot were immediately despatched, the outpost could not be held and may as well be relinquished.[4] On 4 April 1680, a few days before Fairborne's return, four companies belonging to the Earl of Dumbarton's (Scotch) regiment, 'all old soldiers', arrived on the *James* and the *Swan*, whilst in late May, 147 aged and maimed soldiers were returned home.[5] Whereas the walls of Tangier remained in a poor state of repair and their defence had become problematic, it was (as in previous periods) the outlying forts that were in the greatest danger from enemy attack. Both Charles and Henrietta Forts were furnished with 'ammunitions of war and provisions requisite for five months' siege', while the garrison of Charles was reinforced by a company of 70 men and three officers, and had established a 'sally-port and line of communication, between themselves and the Upper Castle, but this line was soon cut by the Moors.[6]

However courageously these fortifications were defended, the tactical reasoning behind their sighting has been questioned by some modern writers. Elbl, for instance, asserts:

> By holding fast the entire crest of the high ground from the modern Stade de Municipal through the *Kasba* made the Marshān [Plain] into a partially fortified backbone from which the valley of the Oued Aherdane could conceivably be controlled, while it was barred by 'lines' between Charles Fort and Anne Fort. This was essentially a mistake. The crest positions would have required much more extensive fortifications and much larger forces to hold. The only thing Teviot created was an irresistible and relatively weak target. Instead of a key log holding the northwest front, Charles Fort became a trap.[7]

Governor Inchiquin, who had allowed his own regiment to fall into poor habits, had also been struck by increasing inertia. No sorties from the city were attempted to divert the enemy from their siege-works, no counter-attacks were launched to regain contact with the isolated fort, and even the artillery was ineffective, although the range was less than a mile. On 13 April Fairborne wrote in dismay:

> I must confess I never saw a place more ruinous than this, nothing being in a condition fit for defence, and what is worse not one spare arm in the stores excepting a few blunderbusses that is come at this time with me. I beseech you to dispatch with all speed at least 1,200, the Scotch companies being very ill-armed and if we come to a brisk action we shall be in great distress.[8]

4 TNA, CO 279/25, fols 209–10, 253–4, 269–70, 286–7; CO 279/26, fols 11–12, 43–8.

5 TNA, CO 279/25, fol. 224, Fairborne to Jenkins, 3 June 1680; *London Gazette*, 17 May 1680.

6 *An Exact Journal of the Siege of Tangier, from the First Sitting Down of the Moors before it on March 25th, 1680, to the late truce, May 19th, following* (London: Joseph Hindmarsh, 1680); Bejjit, *English Colonial Texts*, pp. 178–9.

7 Elbl, *Portuguese Tangier*, p. 758.

8 TNA, CO 279/25, fol. 183, Fairborne to Jenkins, 13 April 1680.

His cynicism was by no means unfounded. The garrison, although lately reinforced, was still short of troops. These remained unpaid, under-equipped, exhausted from frequent nights of sentry duty, and faced with little prospect of relief. They would be hard-pressed by the fighting of March–May 1680, events that would represent a significant diminishment of the colonial adventure in the Mediterranean.

On 25 March 1680 Qā'id Omar Ben Haddū was commanded by the Sultan of Morocco, Mawaly Ismā'īl (reigned 1672–1727) to reduce the size of the English hinterland to that which had been formerly held by the Portuguese. At the head of 7,000–8,000 men he began the 'Great Siege' of Tangier, which lasted until 19 May. During this period the Moorish forces, who had developed into 'a formidable enemy, being improved in all the arts of war, as mining, sapping, scaling, and battering', busily dug trenches of such length and depth as to isolate Charles, Henrietta and Giles Forts, located to the south-west of the city, and cause a breach in the 'lines' – a system of trenches and breastworks, often with palisades added along vulnerable sectors. The improved performance of the Moors during 1680 resulted from their being advised in siege warfare by the Turks and a number of English deserters, one of whom was 'Hansett', a Moor who had been present at the siege of Maestricht in 1673, where French engineers under the direction of Vauban had perfected the art of investing fortified towns.[9] From all quarters came reports that the Moors had assembled in large numbers. A refugee from their camp reported that they had mobilised 'all that ever the country could afford, besides several thousands of the King's army of blacks'.[10] Ismā'īl's standing army of hereditary troops was drawn into great camps from all parts of his dominions and imported in large numbers from the Sudan. These soldiers were inured from boyhood to warfare and taught to look to the Sultan alone for advancement. They formed the nucleus of the Moorish forces, and, supplemented by tribal levies, made the army a formidable and highly mobile organisation.

From his headquarters on Jews Hill, on 25 March 1680 Qā'id Omar commenced his attack. The following day he opened his trenches for a formal siege and assault on Henrietta, Charles, and Giles Forts, to isolate them from the city and clear the south-west arc of outer works. This plan revealed a serious flaw in Tangier's fortifications. Although contemporary engineering practice, refined during the Thirty Years' War and the United Provinces of the Netherlands during the reign of Louis XIV, advocated systems of interlocking bastions and communication trenches, there were no such structures at Tangier. Hence, there was little sense of depth within the English defences and those troops stationed in the various redoubts were commonly isolated from the main garrison, from which they relied upon for succour. Once the first line was destroyed the entire scheme was in danger of becoming unsustainable. As Childs remarks:

9 TNA, CO 279/25, fol. 209. Fairborne to Jenkins, 11 May 1680; Childs, *Army of Charles II*, p. 147.

10 Budgett Meakin, *The Moorish Empire* (London: Swan Sonnenschein & Co., 1899), pp. 155–6.

> We must not assume that these fortifications were anything wonderful. Images of angled the masterpieces of Vauban and Coehoorn in Flanders and Germany must be dismissed from the mind. The tangier forts were no more than primitive blockhouses defended by wooden fences and ditches. Only Fort Charles and Fort Anne had flanking bastions, whilst the rest of the forts were mere gun-platforms.[11]

Much of the information about the siege operations against the colony between 25 March and 19 May 1680 is provided by a pamphlet entitled *An Exact Journal of the Siege of Tangier*.[12] Composed of three letters, they were written in the form of journals by eyewitnesses describing events as they happened. As the first part of the document, penned from the perspective of a besieged soldier in Charles Fort relates, despite the rain and English musket-fire from the forts, the Moors, who were closely observed from behind the walls, advanced steadily to with a short distance from their objective, aided by their shields and mobile palisades.[13]

Qā'id Omar's men excavated their trenches with great rapidity and a skill which surprised the defenders, while the works were of such depth that crossing them in the final escape proved to be extremely difficult for the English troops. The main trench dividing Charles Fort from the walls of Tangier, for instance, was nine feet broad and six feet deep, with a profusion of narrow saps and cross-works. Entrenching themselves between Forts Charles and Henrietta, and between Kendal and Pond Forts, with lines towards Teviot Hill, the Charles garrison, under Captain John Trelawny attempted by constant firing to stop the enemy's efforts, yet little impression was made on the Moors. By 29 March, the besiegers had cut across the rear of Fort Henrietta, thus isolating it from the city. The English forts or bastions were timber, brick, and stone blockhouses, some with the addition of upper storeys; conditions inside must have been cramped and desperate. Trelawny's men at Fort Charles, located some 550 yards to the south of Tangier's main defences, were in the thick of it from the start. On the same night that Henrietta was cut off (29 March), Trelawny's soldiers got their enemy's range so effectively that they were forced to leave the works for a time, to clear the dead. The next day a *cavalier* (a small tower, used as an observation platform or for mounting cannon) was erected on the left-hand battery of the fort, 30 feet above the ground, from which eight or nine men could fire into the depths of the trenches.

The task confronting Captain Trelawny's vastly outnumbered force was formidable. To avoid being defeated in detail his officers were forced to keep their soldiers in a tight formation or division to maximise their firepower, and to prevent stragglers from being detached and captured. Their situation was exacerbated by shortages of ammunition and wine, and the discomfort of torrential rain. On 31 March 1680, the Moors:

---

11 Childs, *Army of Charles II*, p. 138.

12 *An Exact Journal of the Siege of Tangier: from the first sitting down of the Moors before it on March 25, 1680 to the Late Truce, May following In Three Letters, written by Three Eye-Witnesses on the whole Transaction* (London: Joseph Hindmarsh, 1680).

13 *Ibid.*, pp. 1–2.

> continued their work very hard all day, and about three of the clock pitched eight of their colours in their lines, *viz.* one all red under Kendal [redoubt], four with yellow stripes within pistol shot betwixt us and Henrietta fort, as also one all green, and two all red. Captain Trelawney, out then governor, planting his guns towards them, very happily shot down one of their colours, the green, and tore another of them, so that they were forced to remove them. They continued working 'till six or seven of the clock, but did not work one stroke all night. This morning [Thursday, 1 April] we espied their army marching over the hill in great bodies, both horse and foot, colours flying, but to what intent we knew not. About three of the clock in the afternoon they all returned, and pitched up their colours in some of the former places, and towards sunset fell to their work again, so that the trenches on that side nearest Pond fort, before sunrising, were advanced within sight of our lines of communication; and on the other side, entered our line betwixt between us and Henrietta.[14]

By 9 April, the Moors had severed all normal lines of communication and surrounded the forts. During his reconnaissance that day Sir Palmes Fairborne had discovered the Moors, 'entrenched between Charles and Henrietta Forts and the town, and with a treble trench deep and broad as we guess at least twenty foot, with several places of arms within their trenches entrenched, and avenues from each to succour one another upon any sally we should make against them, so formidable and so regular that no Christian enemy ever proceeded better nor more resolute'.[15] Charles, Henrietta and Giles Forts (Devil's Drop) were manned by less than 300 soldiers in total. Each evening the officers communicated with the Castle by various means, including speaking trumpets, reporting the movements of the enemy and their own position to the commander-in-chief. Notably, this was done in Irish Gaelic, lest English deserters among the Moors should understand and translate their conversation to the enemy. The initial assault on Henrietta Fort – now isolated from both the Tangier walls and Charles Fort – began on Easter Sunday, 11 April 1680. An account of the state of the garrison, penned the following day, told that the 8,000 men of Qā'id Omar's army continued their attack on Charles and Henrietta. The former was manned by 160 volunteers under Captains Trelawny and St John, while the latter had 32 men commanded by Lieutenant John Wilson. Moreover, 13 soldiers led by a sergeant clung onto Giles Fort. The author confirmed the so-far unsuccessful assaults on Henrietta Fort, adding, 'they [the English] relieve the redoubt every day but can only communicate using flags during the day and lights at night'.

In a broader context, he also mentioned 'the *Charles* and *Swan* frigates are in the road of several merchant ships bringing stores, which are difficult to receive because of the very deep trenches being dug by the Moors near the Charles Fort.[16] The wheeled engines (known variously by the English as 'truckles', 'cats' or 'tortoises') that had puzzled many in the Tangier garrison

14 *Ibid.*, p. 2.

15 TNA, CO 279/25, fol. 181, Fairborne to Jenkins, 9 April 1680.

16 TNA, ADM 106/351/157.

turned out to galleries, which were trundled under the walls of Henrietta Fort to facilitate the hurling of incendiary bombs, known as stinkpots – devices the size of hand grenades, with a match lit at both ends, which on breaking open kindled the combustible material inside – but Lieutenant Wilson's soldiers fought tenaciously with muskets, bayonets, half-pikes and a plentiful supply of hand grenades. Used throughout the wars of the seventeenth century these grenades were hollow iron or ceramic balls filled with gunpowder. They were ignited by a slow burning fuse rolled in dampened powder and dried. In his diary entry for 4 February 1664, Evelyn recorded that he 'had discourse with the King about an invention of glass grenades, and several other subjects'.[17] Although not especially reliable, a well-thrown bomb was highly effective among tightly packed troops and in enclosed spaces. Their use in both a defensive and offensive sense would come to the fore in later engagements at Tangier. Henrietta Fort's assailants fled, and some of the defenders climbed down and burnt the machines to ashes. Against another section of the fort an attempt was made to mine the wall by erecting long booms, covering them with faggots (bundles of brushwood), and using them for shelter as the labourers toiled. Again, the Moors who were busy placing them were cut down by musket fire, while some of the enterprising English soldiers slid down ropes to put the booms to the torch. As the enemy retreated, Lieutenant Wilson defiantly adorned his fort with two Moors' heads on a pole.

Though it was a morale-boosting success, the defensive action suggested worse things to come. Sir Palmes Fairborne described the ferocious close quarter fighting that had occurred, in some detail:

> they made an attack upon Henrietta, and continued from eight o'clock till near three, with great resolution on both sides, and if you had seen the hand grenades that were thrown down at that time you would conclude that 50,000 hand grenades is no great store for this garrison, the nature of the stores being such as will require much of them for good defence thereof … The enemy came close to the forts with their galleries in hopes to have met with a very thin wall, and so to have wrought a hole in to throw the stink pots, but the fort in my time was filled 10 feet with earth besides the wall about four feet thick, so that by the valour of the defenders the enemy was forced to quit their attack, leaving some of their lathers behind them, and their galleries which those of the fort fired with fire-brills thrown down from the fort upon it. We expect they will be at it again tonight, and if our men doth but preserve our hand grenades I hope they may make the enemy weary of attempting much more against them, he that commands is a brave lieutenant called Wilson, and an excellent sergeant with him and thirty soldiers, select men, which is the strength of the fort.[18]

The defenders of Henrietta, like those of nearby Charles and Clive Forts resolutely continued – the prospect before them was deeply unattractive, but they had to endure it in the hope of some sort of relief from the garrison. In

17 Bray (ed.), *Diary of John Evelyn*, I, p. 372.

18 TNA, CO 279/25, fol. 183, Fairborne to Jenkins, 13 April 1680.

the meantime, Fairborne was keen show a determined front to the Moors. He continued his patrols as far as Pole Fort and Norwood redoubt, constructing a covered way between them. Before Peterborough Tower, part of the south-western ramparts of the defences, Fairborne constructed palisades, while men in the city were put to 'making fireworks and fitting hand grenades'.[19] The small garrison of Giles Fort on the beach west of Whitby, had to be temporarily abandoned as it was now untenable, being surrounded by enemy trenches on all sides but the sea. Against such determined pressure, and in the absence of relief from troops inside the city walls, it was only a matter of time before Henrietta's defenders would be overwhelmed. Three mines had now been set beneath the fort's ramparts, while a breach was made in the walls by a light cannon they had captured from Anne Fort the previous day, and having been seen hauling it up a nearby hill in readiness for a bombardment.

On Friday 16 April, the attackers' drumbeat 'like a cooper upon a tub, and pipe playing for the most part of the time. Last night Captain St John, speaking to our governor of the town in the speaking trumpet, the Moors fell a hallowing and shouting all along their lines'. The following day:

> They continued their work in making their trenches deeper; they proceeded little or no farther to any purpose this day. We made use of our hand-granadoes out of a small mortar-piece, which threw some of them into their trenches amongst their colours. This night they made a blind of stones upon their trenches, about a man's height, whether for their own, or colours' shelter, we could not certainly tell, but supposed both.[20]

By now, the situation was completely desperate. At some point Qā'id Omar demanded the immediate surrender of the forts, but the garrison's commanders rebuffed him.[21] On 9 May Lieutenant Wilson called to Charles Fort that the walls of Henrietta were disintegrating, and he could not hold for another 24 hours. His message was relayed to the Upper Castle, where Lord Inchiquin convened a council of war to consider the possibility of mounting a sortie to rescue Wilson and his men. The council felt, however, that the risk was too great and declined the opportunity.

The next day, under a flag of truce, the Anglo-Irish commanders offered to surrender the outpost if Qā'id Omar would permit the garrison to withdraw into Tangier unmolested, but the Moors replied that they did not place any value in stones, but instead wanted slaves. Francis Povey, Ordnance Officer of the Tangier garrison, stated in his account of the affair that Inchiquin promised the soldiers holding Henrietta Fort to 'do his endeavour to relieve them by sally within a day or two'.[22] However, this is not confirmed in the official report of Sir Palmes Fairborne, who was at the meeting. At the final hour Fairborne managed to scrape together the makings of a relief column

19 HL, 8471. Fairborne to Lord Bridgewater, 24 April 1680.
20 *Exact Journal*, p. 3.
21 HL, 8473. Copy of letter of Moorish commander and reply, 5 May 1680.
22 HMC, *Eleventh Report, App. I*, p. 50.

following the arrival of 100 sailors from Captain Arthur Herbert's naval station, who took over the defence of the Mole in order to make available 450 of the best and fittest soldiers for the task. But ultimately little more could be done, and so during the evening of 13 May 1680 the defenders of Harriet Fort surrendered.[23] The captives were observed being whipped as they were taken away by a reported 1,000 Barbary warriors. At dawn the following day, a detonation carried away most of the building – probably the work of the Moors who had detonated a final mine set by the English soldiers before their capitulation.[24]

The fortunes of the soldiers at the larger Charles Fort, located approximately 300 yards to the east, remained equally perilous. In 1676 the author of *The Present State of Tangier*, had described the way leading from the city to the structure as 'an even, plain and very pleasant walk', and Charles Fort itself as 'the great terror to the Moors, and which they dare not come near, [being] the greatest delight of the inhabitants of Tangier, and continually visited like Spring-Garden'.[25] From the city walls and Pole Fort the Moors had been spotted assembling under Teviot Hill at first light on 29 April 1680, while a large party was busy preparing a mine beneath Charles Fort. Their commanders rode about to encourage their men, who spent two hours bringing up stones and timber to the opening of the mine, which was located out of sight of the fort. After placing 200 Berber troops into the adjoining trenches, the Moorish commander summoned its garrison, declaring that he intended to detonate the mine underneath the walls, and invited Captain Trelawny and his second-in-command, Captain St John, to inspect it. Unless they surrendered at once, all to be slaves, Qā'id Omar would blow them up within an hour. Having inspected the device, Trelawny and St John declared boldly that 'they would stand it out to the last' and 'he might do his worst, they were there to maintain the fort and not to yield it'.[26]

They confirmed their response by firing a volley of shot and hoisting their colours over the fortifications. At 8:00 a.m. Fairborne, from the roof of the Pole Tower, felt the place rocked as the Moors exploded the mine, but it was 30 yards short and as the smoke cleared, he 'saw the fort safe and sound to my no small satisfaction was saluted with three hollows from the fort as a sign that all was well'. But the worst was yet to come. On 13 May, some seven weeks or so after the commencement of the fighting, Captain Trelawny informed the governor, Inchiquin, that his position was no longer defensible, 'the Moors having several mines, and that his men mutinied, so that they designed to quit Charles Fort next morning at eight of the clock, and endeavour their escape to the city'.[27] Events, however, would soon engulf

23 TNA, CO 279/25, fols 211–12. Fairborne to Jenkins, 17 April 1680; *An Exact Journal of the Siege of Tangier*.

24 HL, 8471. Fairborne to Bridgewater, 24 April 1680.

25 George Philips, *The Present State of Tangier in a Letter to His Grace the Lord Chancellor of Ireland and one of the Lords Justices there: to which is added the present state of Algiers* (London: Henry Herringman, 1676), p. 32.

26 TNA, CO 279/25, fol. 202. Fairborne to Jenkins, 29 April 1680; HL, 8472. Fairborne to Bridgewater, 29 April 1680.

27 *Exact Journal*, p. 6.

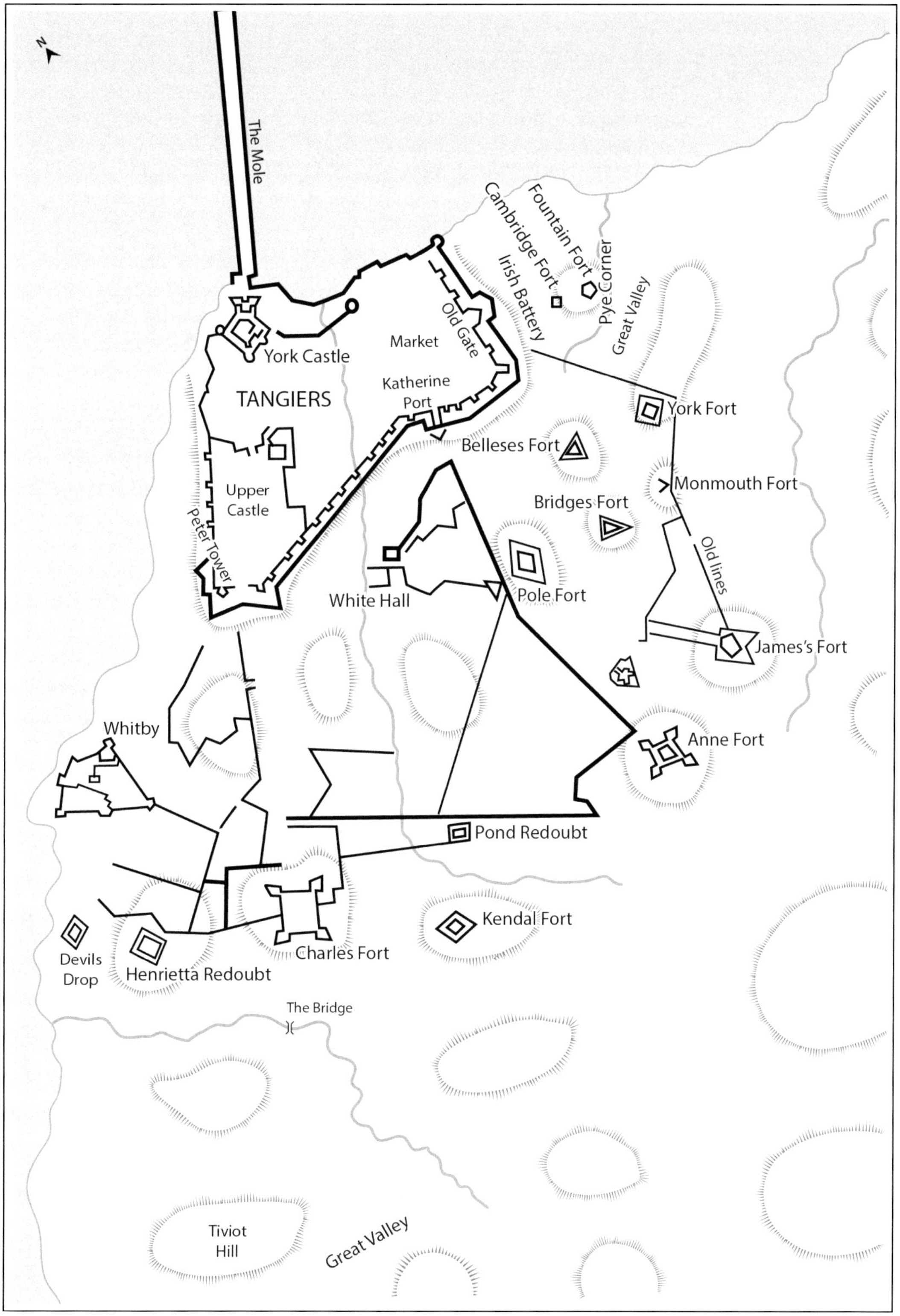

The Ground and Forts around Tangier, 1680. (Routh, *Tangier*, p. 194)

Trelawny and his command. The next morning Ismāʿīl's troops detonated a mine against the south angle of the fort, which Captains Trelawny and St John – 'both men of valour and conduct' – had attempted to frustrate with countermines, doing their utmost to hold their post until relief should come. Yet Inchiquin decided not to risk a sortie, and only to support the forts by means of mortar fire on the enemy's trenches. Predictably, encouraged by such inaction on the part of the garrison, the Moors intensified their efforts against the redoubts.

When Trelawny shouted through his trumpet that Charles Fort had also become impossible to possess any longer, the damaged inflicted by the blast of the mine must have been far greater than had been previously reported, as the walls of the fortification were irreparable. The remaining 176 men, with 'Captain Trelawny's little boy', left the guns 'double-shotted, spiked and wedged with steel, as also one little mortar piece', and placed their remaining ammunition into a mine, before fleeing to the city. St John, the youngest captain, would lead the vanguard, while Trelawney brought up the rear. The breakout from Charles Fort was planned to coincide with the emergence of a covering force from the main garrison, intended to suppress any attacks and to bring Trelawny's soldiers across three lines of enemy trenches to the safety of the Upper Castle some 700 yards away. At 7:00 a.m. on 14 May, barely hours after the destruction of Henrietta Fort, five divisions of English soldiers under the command of Major Marmaduke Boynton – Lord Inchiquin having refused to allow Fairborne to participate in the venture – advanced out of the city defences to their aid.

The *Exact Journal* and other reports narrate how the leading forlorn-hope, commanded by Captain George Hume, consisted of two lieutenants, four sergeants and 80 men of the recently arrived Earl of Dumbarton's regiment; the main body, positioned 150 yards in their rear and led by Boynton, had eight officers, eight sergeants and 128 soldiers; the reserve, formed six deep and some 100 yards behind the main body, was commanded by Captain James Moncrieff, and comprised four officers, four sergeants and 100 soldiers; a flank guard 40 yards away 'on the right of the rear towards the Burying Place', covering the seaward side above the now deserted Whitby, were two officers, three sergeants and 66 soldiers under the command of Captain Leslie; lastly, Captain Rowe's company of two officers, four sergeants and 66 men were positioned in the outer-works of Peterborough Tower.[28] At 8:00 a.m., as Captain Trelawny's men left the fort and closed-up into one division, Ensign Richard Roberts, a 'nimble, stout young man', lit the two-inch fuse leading to the last of the powder placed as a counter-mine. This blew up the southeast bastion, though other charges failed to ignite.[29] The grenadiers under Captain St John immediately rushed for the first trench, which they carried, while the remaining soldiers tumbled into the second, feverishly hacking and stabbing their enemy with swords, half-pikes and musket butts. The third depression, however, was a much more difficult proposition, 'being the deepest, was at

28 *Ibid.*, p. 7.

29 TNA, CO 279/25, fols 211, 217.

least fourteen foot with water and dirt in the bottom, by reason of the late rains, the first that came into it, some got over by the help of the other, and escaped meeting with places not so difficult'.[30]

Here many of the soldiers lost momentum and became disorganised as they tried to scale the sides of the trench. Coming to their assistance, Captain Hume's Scotsmen cleared the positions with grenades, but the Barbary troops were quickly upon them. It was later reported by a participant:

> Our forlorn did bravely under the command of Captain Hume, a Scotch officer; we killed several Moorish horsemen, an Alcaide of great note called Garboose, who endeavoured to cut off our men that escaped the trenches. When the Forlorn retreated, one brave Moor charged them all, but his horse riding over Captain Hume, stumbled at him and threw him down, our men clubbed their muskets and presently despatched him. In the forlorn three or four were killed, several wounded, a captain shot in the leg, and a lieutenant shot in the body.[31]

Captain Trelawny was shot dead as he scrambled up the bank to attempt to save his son. The boy and 14 wounded soldiers were captured, with only St John, two brother officers (Lieutenant Clause and Ensign Roberts), and 36 men managing to fight their way clear. It was only the outstanding steadiness of Hume in leading his men in such a desperate action – having been further disabled by a musket wound to the leg – that kept the last party together, and enabled Captain Thomas St John to take overall command.

The main body and reserve of the relief column, finding themselves too exposed, were broken by the sheer weight of numbers of the Moors, who had stormed in behind the forlorn-hope and put them to flight. Amongst those who escaped the onslaught were the wounded Captain Moncrieff. The following day Fairborne reported that upon enquiry it appeared that the formation kept its ground until the forlorn extricated itself, and that Ensign Adams advanced from the main force and rendered Captain Hume good service.[32] However, a less reliable account is provided by Povey, who, though an eyewitness to the conflict, wrote 'All this while, those brave men of the forlorn killed the Moors but the [main] body ran away and not above five officers stood, he [an unnamed officer nicknamed 'Wheel-about'] that should failed as formerly'.[33] Povey also claimed, somewhat unjustly, 'We have too many cowardly officers, instead of doing their country service they run it and run like sheep, I cannot speak bad enough of them'.[34]

Now at the third trench, the Fort Charles soldiers faced about, and exhausted as they were, fought off the masses of enemy for long enough to see the heavily depleted party of their comrades over the last ditch and into the Upper Castle. At the last, Captain St John was wounded by a bullet (reportedly

30 *Exact Journal*, pp. 7–8.

31 *Ibid.*, p. 8.

32 TNA, CO 279/25, fol. 212.

33 HMC, *Eleventh Report, App. I*, pp. 50–1, Povey to Colonel George Legge, governor of Portsmouth, 18 May 1680.

34 TNA, WO 93/1082, fol. 143, Povey to the officers of the Ordnance Department, 3 June 1680.

'through the shoulder under the plate-bone'), although he managed to make his way to safety.[35] He subsequently recovered, but an altogether different fate befell most of his men. Of the 176 defenders of the Charles garrison who entered the trenches that morning, 124 lost their lives, while a smaller number were taken prisoner under the pressing force of their assailants.[36] Povey reported graphically, 'Captain Trelawny with 117 men was killed and all their heads cut off, and I think every man had a thousand wounds. I never saw such a barbarous sight … if affairs had been well-managed we need not have lost 10 men'.[37] Such losses not only give testament to the importance of Charles Fort – which exceeded any of the other defences – but the skill at arms, resilience, fierce determination and resourcefulness of the officers and men of its meagre garrison, and against an irrepressible and numerically stronger foe at such cost to themselves.

A further, small encounter occurred at Devil's Drop (Giles Fort) later in the day. The outwork was held by a party of 12 men, but the entrenchments around Charles Fort had disconnected them from the city sometime earlier. In an attempt to alleviate the situation, and in another episode of joint-operations, Admiral Herbert sent some boats belonging to the *Adventure* to operate inshore to rescue the small garrison of Devil's Drop, but 22 seamen were killed by enemy fire before they could reach them, and thus late in the afternoon the tiny redoubt surrendered. It ended a day of disaster for the Tangier garrison, the worst since the reverses of 1664 under Teviot. According to Fairborne's official account, casualties sustained by the garrison during the surrender of Henrietta Fort, the fatal evacuation of Charles and the loss of Devil's Drop numbered 160 killed and 53 captured for Forts Charles and Henrietta; 15 dead and 'several' wounded for Boynton's relief force; and 11 prisoners taken at Giles. Separately Fairborne described the death of 15 soldiers from the forlorn hope, although these may have been the same number previously reckoned for the whole of Boynton's troops.[38] By comparison, the author of the *Exact Journal* accounted for losses during the breakout from Charles Fort alone as 140 dead, 14 taken prisoner and 'only forty-seven escaped', adding 'in the forlorn three or four were killed, several wounded'.[39] A list of the 57 prisoners taken during the action was later sent to the governor of Tangier, although their fate is unknown.[40]

After the action, by leave of Qā'id Omar, the mutilated bodies of the English dead were brought into the city for burial; their heads were sent by the Barbary commander during the afternoon. Among them, Captain Trelawny, who was 'much beloved by all this city', was interred in the Protestant church in Tangier beside a volunteer named Wray, who was killed during the naval operation to rescue the defenders of Fort Giles. Estimates of losses

35 In his later petition and pay accounts St John described himself as having been 'shot through my body' during this action (TNA, SP44/18, fol. 141; SRO, D742/O/3/75).

36 TNA, CO 279/25, fols 211–12.

37 HMC, *Eleventh Report, App. V*, I, p. 51.

38 TNA, CO 279/25, fols 209, 211–12.

39 *Exact Journal*, p. 8.

40 TNA, CO 279/25, fol. 12.

sustained by the Moors during this period are impossible to compute, but they must have been significant. The want of cavalry belonging to the Tangier garrison was much felt during the battle – especially as large numbers of Berber soldiers, mounted on small hill ponies, as hardy and untiring as their riders – operated around Fort Charles and elsewhere. Any English Horse might have aided their comrades-in-arms in the beleaguered foot. Following the fighting of 18 May 1680, Povey wrote, 'In this engagement we played our ordnance and destroyed their horse much, I likewise played the mortar piece upon Charles Fort and destroyed them like flies. Here is no person that knew how to use it if I had not undertook it'.[41] Such a claim, in the face of ineffectual Moorish gunnery, has some credence. More accurate artillery fire from English cannon and mortars in the earlier stages of the attacks on the outlying forts could have hindered the construction of the entrenchments by Qā'id Omar's men close to the city, which made the retreat from Charles Fort so devastating for the soldiers attempting to escape from it, and rescue attempts by the main garrison.

Qā'id's letter to the governor, dispatched the day after the fighting, declared, 'If his Lordship had a mind to be eased of this troublesome war he should quit all the forts and be content to keep the place as the Portugals had it, otherwise he (the Alcaid) would not stir from hence till he had reduced them all'. Sir Palmes thus recommended to the governor that 'If his Excellency does not accept these terms, the next business will be the town, for since the enemy are both skilful in mining and great guns, we cannot hold out long if they proceed after the rate they have done'. Nevertheless, in response to the Moorish commander, Inchiquin himself thanked him for his civility, but added, 'as to quitting the forts, it did not consist with honour of his Majesty nor his own, and though he knew them not to be impregnable, yet would sell them as dear as he could'.[42] Such defiance, however, was greeted by a continuation of hostilities against the Tangier garrison. Although 13 cannon and a mortar piece in Charles Fort had fallen into enemy hands, 'notwithstanding they were spiked the Moors drove out the spikes to admiration'.

The Moors further discovered in the fort a large store of hand grenades and some mortar bombs which had failed to explode in the English countermine. These with seven guns taken from other captured positions, and a quantity of musket bullets, collected and stored by Qā'id Omar's troops during the siege, gave the Moors a good supply of artillery and ordnance. The Moors lugged their heavy guns up Teviot Hill and trained them on Forts Pole and Norwood, in addition to urban Tangier. Francis Povey, whose knowledge of gunnery gained him a commission as 'Comptroller of Ordnance', later stated smugly, 'I think I sent some of them to Mahomet with the mortar-piece to the view of all the garrison'.[43] Ever the practical-minded and optimistic soldier, Fairborne remarked on 17 May 1680, 'We have secured Pole Fort about 10 foot high

41 HMC, *Eleventh Report, App. I*, p. 52.

42 TNA, CO 279/25, fols 211–12.

43 *Ibid.*, fol. 211. Povey later published *The Sea-Gunners Companion* (London: Richard Mount, 1702).

with great rum butts filled with earth, which will preserve her some time from being battered down, but the enemy have now brought a twelve-pounder and demiculverin, and are making another battery near James'.[44]

The English quickly set about excavating new trenches and lines of communication, 'so they leave nothing undone that may gain advantage upon us'. Nevertheless, the governor was faced with an acute shortage of men and a dispirited garrison. This was alleviated to a small extent by the arrival aboard the *Antelope* in mid June of a draft of 96 soldiers distributed among the companies commanded by the Governor Inchiquin, Major Housden, and Captains Nicholas, Littleton, St Clare, Churchill, Fortrey, Cornwell, Mannering, Lee and Stallsey.[45] It is conceivable that these men were the volunteers that Captain Barbour had been authorised to recruit in London the previous July.[46] On 21 May 1680 renewed proposals of peace were brought in by a Jewish messenger from Qā'id Omar, and the governor convened a council of war to consider them. The meeting concluded bitterly that the rest of the outer fortifications were unlikely to hold for three more days, while for want of cavalry no effectual sortie could be made to save Pole Fort, although its capture would mean the loss of its garrison of three officers and 100 soldiers. Significantly too, as Pole commanded the city, Inchiquin feared that from it the Moors would be able to both undermine and fire into the Upper Castle, and even set ablaze the houses crowded in narrow streets around the marketplace. The tactical option was to consent to dismantle Pole rather than to allow the enemy to gain the position intact.

Thus, the only option for the senior officers of the Tangier garrison was to negotiate a truce. Three envoys – Captain Leslie, Lieutenant Fitzgerald and Mr Luddington (an English merchant) – were sent to make terms. During the talks Leslie and Fitzgerald were able to observe the saps and galleries by which the enemy had approached Henrietta redoubt. As Fairborne reported, 'They affirm that the mine is as ingeniously carried out as ever they saw, at least 25 yards in whole rock with holes drilled to the top for air and to know when they were under the fort, besides several galleries made to sap under the wall. It seems when they blew it up, it was from the sapping and not from the mine as I formerly advised'.[47] In consenting to a four-month ceasefire the commander of the garrison of Tangier agreed to demolish Pole and Norwood redoubts, leaving only Cambridge, Fountain and Bridges Forts in the hands of the garrison. This agreement was made, however, on condition that the Moors removed their guns and threw down the batteries that threatened the walled city.[48] In the space of two months' fighting, the Moorish leader had to all intents and purposes achieved his objective of clearing the English defensive positions across the Marshān Plateau. According to a detailed manuscript plan of Tangier drawn by the surveyor Thomas Phillips, who accompanied Lord Dartmouth's expedition to the colony in 1683, listed under 'Taken by

44 HL, 8476. Fairborne to Bridgewater, 21 May 1680.

45 SRO, D742/0/4/1.

46 TNA SP44/58, fols 41–2.

47 TNA, CO 279/25, fol. 212.

48 *Ibid.*, fols 217–18.

Alcayde Omer in '79 and '80, Lord Inchiquin governor', were: Monmouth, James, Anne, Pond, Charles, [and] Henrietta Forts; Pole Fort is recorded as 'quitted, regained by peace and dismantled by Lord Dartmouth'.[49]

Despite the gloomy outlook of the garrison's officers, Captain Gerard – who arrived in England from Tangier soon afterwards – reported to the Council of State that Inchiquin 'had agreed with the Moors for a truce for four months, they being induced on account of their harvest and quieting some divisions in their own countries'.[50] This factor, it seems, was an imperative one, especially as the Moorish commander was to feed his troops and horses, and thus keep his army in the field, not only during the remaining summer, but for any forthcoming military operations in the autumn. In terms of the English defence of Tangier, the system of fortifications to the south and south-west of the city had proved ineffective when subjected to serious attack, despite the skill, tenacity and sacrifice of the English troops defending them. As Childs illustrates, 'There was no was no link between the town and forts; to contact the outer works, troops had to march for half a mile over open country under observation from the higher ground. One of the main features of the works of Vauban and the Dutch engineers, was that each work within a system was mutually supported, but this sophistication was not found in Tangier'.[51]

The fragile truce had undoubtedly placed the Tangier garrison in a perilous situation. On 25 June 1680 Major White of Dumbarton's Regiment reported:

> [the commanders] have neither men nor money to put the town in a posture to resist their powerful enemies, their forts being taken. Though there is a cessation for four months, the enemy have their guards of horse and foot within a carbine's shot of the town walls, and set their sentries upon the hills about so that they can see men walking in the streets. All the advantages are on the enemy's side [and] unless a great supply of men is sent before the end of the truce it will be a hard pull with them. I call God to witness that I would rather die in defending the King's interest than dispute with death in his bed. We cannot have less than 1,000 horse and 4,000 foot to beat them in the field, otherwise an ambassador should be sent to treat for peace, and to give them such sum of money in powder and arms for a considerable space of ground to feed cattle, and where stones can be dug to fortify the town, and make an end of the Mole … it may be communicated to his royal Highness, so that a speedy remedy may be ordered against the great storm the Moors are preparing.[52]

---

49 'The Plane of the Town and Mole of Tanger Discovering by ye little square Dotts the Mines which were made in ye Upper and Yorke Castle and Round the Towne By Ye Rt. Honble. the Lrd. Dartmouth for its demolishment [1683–4]'. Ombersley Court, Worcestershire – sold by the trustees of the Sandys Trust at Sotheby's London, 14 May 2019, lot 61 (with other unrelated maps) <www.raremaps.com/gallery/detail/61976/the-plane-of-the-town-and-mole-of-tanger-discovering-by-ye-l-phillips>.

50 TNA, SP44/41, fol. 159; *CSPD 1679–80*, p. 520.

51 Childs, *Army of Charles II*, p. 148.

52 HMC, *Eleventh Report, App. I*, p. 51.

In the meantime, Sir Palmes Fairborne informed the Tangier Commissioners that a 'council of captains' had assessed the immediate needs of the garrison and concluded that 8,000 foot and 600 horse were necessary for the defence of Tangier.[53] On 17 July 1680 he informed Lord Bridgewater, one of the commissioners, that the soldiers were five quarters in arrears of pay, while on 7 August he added, 'the garrison is eighteen months in arrears. The men of the reinforcements [who had arrived six days earlier] are paid up, which is a source of discontent'.[54] Similar issues were observed by other officers of the garrison, including Povey, who stated:

> Major Beckman is very well but cannot employ himself as yet by reason our cessation obliges us not to fortify within or without. The Alcade is bringing down a considerable army, and it is generally believed that he will break the cessation. The horse that were intended for this place are very much wished for, and I do assure your honour if they do not come our foot will signify nothing. I could wish your honour would send a master-gunner for this that is here is a most ignorant sot, and two-thirds of the gunners are not fit, neither have they warrants for their places Sir Palmes Fairborne was pleased to give me a commission to be Captain-Controller of the Train and Ordnance of this garrison.[55]

Artillery and ordnance, in the form of cannon and mortars, were an increasingly important (and mobile) form of warfare during the seventeenth century. Though their effects were firepower and destruction, ordnance logistics (the production, supply and storage of gunpowder, shot, grenadoes, petards, fuses and match, not to mention carriages, wagons and large numbers of draught animals) taxed most armies.[56] There were a great many sizes of cannon, the heavier types being regarded as 'siege or battering pieces'; those of smaller bore being more readily transportable, and regarded as 'field pieces'.

An important omission from the above is the drake, which fired a ball of about 3 lb and operated as light artillery. By the outbreak of Civil War in the British Isles in 1642, these had become the standard infantry support weapon among most armies.[57]

A particularly valuable resource in siege-warfare, however, was the mortar, a weapon designed to fire projectiles (hollow spheres filled with black-powder, known as granadoes or shells) at a high trajectory yet low velocity. Commonly operated by engineers or 'firemasters', mortars were ideal for lobbing explosive projectiles over the top of fortifications. For those on the receiving end the effects of mortar bombardments were often highly

53 HL, 8483–4. Fairborne to Bridgewater, 3 July 1680.

54 *Ibid.*, 8486, 8494. Fairborne to Bridgewater, 17 July and 7 August 1680.

55 HMC, *Ormond*, V, p. 52. Povey to William Legge, Major General of the Ordnance in the Tower, 19 July 1680.

56 Stephen Bull, '*The Furie of the Ordnance*': *Artillery in the English Civil War* (Woodbridge: Boydell, 2008), chap. 3.

57 *Ibid.*, p. 141; Simon Marsh, 'A Case of Drakes – James Wemyss and Artillery Innovation in the Civil War', Serena Jones (ed.), *A New Way of Fighting: Professionalism in the English Civil War*, Proceedings of the 2016 Helion and Company 'Century of the Soldier' Conference (Solihull: & Co., 2017), pp. 91–107.

Table 42. Principal types of ordnance, from William Eldred, *The Gunner's Glasse* (1646).

Artillery Piece	Calibre in inches	Weight of gun (lb)	Length of piece (feet)	Shot weight (lb)
Cannon Royal	8	8,000	8	63
Cannon	7	7,000	10	47
Demi Cannon	6	6,000	12	27
Culverin	5	4,000	11	15
Demi Culverin	4.5	3,600	10	9
Saker	3.5	2,500	9.5	5.25
Minion	3	1,500	8	4
Falcon	2.75	700	6	2.25
Falconet	2	210	4	1.25
Robinet	1.25	120	3	0.75

destructive and terrifying, especially 'fire balls' or incendiaries, which were designed to burn and obliterate buildings. However, their ammunition was expensive and intermittently supplied, while the method of ignition (by lighting the mortar using two matches – one to ignite the fuse of the shell, the other to set off the propelling charge) could be especially hazardous to their users, hence they were habitually sighted in specially dug pits. In Charles II's reign the artillery and all warlike stores (weapons, accoutrements and ammunition) were controlled by the Office of Ordnance, at whose head was the Master-General of the Ordnance. He received his orders direct from the Privy Council. An unfavourable report of the affairs of the Ordnance department at Tangier was drawn up by Povey, who wrote:

> The troublesome and tedious survey of the stores of war belonging to this office here I finished the 10th day of May excepting the guns, which were constantly employed against the Moors … here is good storehouses but no care has been used to preserve the stores, I could not tell when first I came whither there was any serviceable stores, all being covered with unusable stores and dust … I have been at an extraordinary charge more than I could have thought, I never came in any place soe exacting as this.[58]

Carelessness was responsible for a huge amount of waste at Tangier. In one instance, 6,000 shot fell into the sea through the breaking of the barrier against which they were stacked, while powder and other ammunition were left out in bad weather.[59] Moreover, the practice of keeping the garrison and navy stores in the same storehouse in York Castle caused confusion,

58 TNA, WO 55/1082, fol. 143. Povey to Ordnance Officers, 3 June 1680.
59 *Ibid.*, fol. 144.

although Fairborne attempted to keep some order by requesting Povey to issue no stores to the navy without his say-so. The efficiency of the gunners was also an issue. In June 1680 there were only eight of them in the garrison. On 16 June, the *Adventure*, arriving with stores and ammunition, brought five gunners, but according to Povey they were hardly competent. One, he said, he was blind, another 'cried and blubbered and told Sir Palmes he knew nothing but was forced to come, and the third though small was very willing to do anything, but Sir Palmes does not like him'. He added, 'If they are discharged, I am sure I can find seamen that would be glad to embrace the employment and will think themselves princes'.[60] Things had hardly improved by the following year, when Colonel Kirke complained that seven of the gunners of the garrison were incompetent and the fire-master lacked knowledge of his trade.

Fairborne continued to press for reinforcements in late July 1680, and repeated to Lord Bridgewater his opinion that 'the Moors have no intention of continuing the cessation'.[61] Moreover, this man who had done so much to hold the garrison together in the face of overwhelming numerical odds and inhibited by a lack of military resources, petitioned the Crown in August 1680 that 'the small pittance of £500 per annum allowed me as commander-in-chief might not be taken away, nor yet my pension, as things at Tangier are three times as dear as in England, and I have not received a farthing of pay'.[62] Political unrest in England over the succession issue and the consequences of the contrived Popish Plot gripped England and Scotland in anti-Catholic hysteria between 1678 and 1681. As soon as reports of the Great Siege of Tangier began to circulate in England, Charles II utilised the opportunity to relieve political pressure by licensing the publication of numerous official and privately printed pamphlets celebrating the bravery of the garrison, and emphasising the national advantages to be gained from the retention of the colony. But he realised, that if Tangier was to endure, it was advisable not only to strengthen the garrison, but to replace the governor-general with someone of more proven ability. This fell to Thomas Butler, Earl of Ossory, a close associate of Charles II, who had served commendably as Lieutenant-General of the army in Ireland and Vice-Admiral.[63] However, he contracted typhus and died on 30 July 1680 before he could take up the post.

This news did not reach Sir Palmes Fairborne – who had exercised sole command between 1676 and 1678, and remained in Tangier as deputy-governor – until a month later. The fortifications fell into disrepair, and sickness laid low the latest draft of recruits, 'very sad creatures, some old men and two of them women in men's clothes'.[64] With no other appointment made, Fairborne was confirmed as governor and commander-in-chief of the colony. He continued to promote a cessation of hostilities with the Moors. Sir Palmes reported, 'The Alcade seems very inclinable to a peace and possible

60 *Ibid.*, fols 145–6.

61 HL, 8487–9, 8493. Fairborne to Bridgewater, 24, 29 and 31 July 1680.

62 Davis, *History*, I, pp. 158–60.

63 HMC, *Ormonde*, V, pp. 332–3, 342, 345–7.

64 Davis, *History*, I, p. 130.

may really intend it, but at the same time I am informed he is in the field with 8,000 men'.[65] On 26 August 1680 he outlined his proposals for peace to the Tangier commissioners, and suggested that:

> some presents should be made fit for the emperor [*sic*: Sultan] of curious arms, viz.: pistols, fusils, fine watches, clocks, fine cambrics, fine Holland, fine broadcloth, scarlet, green and violet, and two fine tables and stands, all which is to be remitted by the first ship to be ready upon the closure of peace to make present to the emperor'.[66] Yet Sir Palmes' other correspondence reveals that the pragmatist officer also anticipated war, regarding an increase in the size of the garrison's cavalry and artillery as 'absolutely necessary.[67]

Such details are confirmed by the diary of Major James Halkett of Dumbarton's Regiment, who arrived with reinforcements from Ireland on 1 August 1680:

> we continued with the expectation of the arrival of my Lord of Ossory with a considerable body of horse and foot, till we got the news of his sickness and soon after his death; during the rest of the time of the cessation of arms, Sir Palmes was much employed in causing make conveniences for the troops he expected from England and the troops in exercising, but I believe the great expense and charge of that design of fortification with the misfortunate death of my Lord Ossory made the king resolve to endeavour to have peace on reasonable terms … Sir Palmes assembled a council-of-war [in] August of the field officers and all the captains to have their opinion whether they thought it convenient or fitting to undertake anything without the town immediately after the expiring of the cessation, or wait for the horse from England or the horse that was promised from Spain.[68]

65 HL, 8495. Fairborne to Bridgewater, 26 August 1680.
66 TNA, CO 279/26, fol. 43. Fairborne to Jenkins, 26 August 1680.
67 HL, 8496–8. Fairborne to Bridgewater, 28 August and 6 September 1680.
68 McCance, H. M. (ed.), Halkett, Sir James, 'A Short and True Account of the most remarkable things that passed during the late Wars with the Moors at Tangier in the year 1680 etc.', *JSAHR*, 1, Special No. (1922), pp. 1–24 (pp. 5–6).

10

Reinforcements and Later Battles, 1680–81

During the winter of 1677–78 the English nation had clamoured for an Anglo-Dutch alliance against the French. Charles II realised that he could raise a standing army of 20,000 men, which included the English regiments in the service of France brought home in the spring of 1678. In March 1680, the Lord Lieutenant of Ireland, James Butler, 1st Duke of Ormond, arranged the embarkation of four companies belonging to the Royal English Regiment from the port of Kinsale. Having recently returned from France they were commanded by Captains George Wingfield, Thomas Barber, William Matthews and Charles Wingfield.[1] This detachment reached Tangier on 4 April 1680 in time to participate in the latter stages of the fighting in defence of the redoubts.

Twelve of the 21 Catholic companies of the Earl of Dumbarton's Regiment (later Royal Scots), under Major James Halkett, were ordered to assemble in Munster within four days' march of Cork. Halkett reported, 'As soon as I got my orders at Dublin to cause our twelve companies that was ordered with me for Tangier to move from their several garrisons to Cork', his officers found it difficult to get the soldiers to march because they had not received pay for 12 months.[2] He was also authorised 'to take what men that was good of those five companies of ours that did remain in Ireland' and mustered a total of 740 men. Having reached the port, however, the Major was notified that there was no longer any need for promptness since a six-month truce had been settled at Tangier. Halkett's veterans now received their pay arrears, plus an advance of three months, which led to a considerable reduction in the rate of desertion.

These companies sailed aboard the *Ruby*, *Phoenix*, *Garland* and *Guernsey* on 15 or 16 July, and made a quick passage to Tangier, arriving on 1 August 1680. Among them was a grenadier company, which had been established in 1678 under Captain Robert Hodges. According to the regiment's historian,

1 Dalton, *Army Lists*, I, p. 255.

2 Halkett, 'Account', p. 4.

'Dumbarton's came to Tangier with a great reputation, and when they left it, that reputation was greatly enhanced.'[3] On 5 September Captain Charles Barclay 'of the Scots regiment at Tangier', was ordered forthwith to march a further 200 recruits to the Downs and board the *Prudent Mary*, which was ready to sail to the Mediterranean colony. Once they were underway, the five sergeants who had accompanied them took 'the first opportunity for returning to their former employments in Ireland'.[4] On 30 November the sum of £530 was spent on clothing these recruits, who were by now stationed in Tangier.[5] With Major Halkett also came the erroneous news that Ossory was coming to take command. The four English companies that had already arrived from Kinsale were added to the 12 from Dumbarton's Regiment, forming a composite unit of 16 companies, divided into two battalions. A warrant of 10 August 1680 ordered the Ordnance Commissioners to dispatch 130 muskets (in the usual proportion of matchlock and snaphance muskets), 'with the like number of collars of bandoliers and 70 pikes to the Downs under the charge of some fit person, who is to deliver them on board the vessel or vessels bringing 200 foot soldiers sent from Scotland for service at Tangier'.[6]

The following day the same officials were issued a warrant:

> for providing and issuing all the stores now demanded, specified in the annexed particular, and for shipping the same for the garrison of Tangier and further for stopping all the train and stores directed to be sent thither by the warrant of 14 July and for discharging all the officers and ministers appertaining to that train, excepting only the 47 miners and 20 of the gunners, which, as also the coals and lime directed in the said warrant, they are to cause to be sent to Tangier as soon as possible.[7]

During the Second Anglo-Dutch War (1664–67) Dumbarton's Regiment was stationed at Chatham Dockyard. Pepys encountered its Colonel in Rochester and noted, 'Here in the streets, I did hear the Scotch march beat by the drums before the soldiers, which is very odd'.[8] In 1667 the regiment was accused of looting and ordered back to France, but while awaiting transport over 700 of the 1,500 soldiers deserted.[9] Even so, this experienced regiment had an enviable record. During the Third Anglo-Dutch War it was part of English Brigade that fought with the French, while in 1675 it became the Régiment de Dumbarton after its colonel, George Douglas was made Earl of Dumbarton.[10]

Following the departure of the unit from France it was quartered in East Anglia before relocating to Ireland in April 1679, where it consisted of 21 companies. Major Halkett of Pitferrane, Fife, had already served in Tangier as a

3 Richard Cannon, *Historical Record of the First, or Royal Regiment of Foot* (London: Parker, Furnivall & Parker, 1847; reprint Outlook Verlag, 2018), p. 61.
4 TNA, SP44/65, fol. 40; *CSPD 1680–81*, p. 7.
5 TNA, SP31/10, fol. 166; *CTB*, VIII, pp. 307–8.
6 TNA, SP44/65, fol. 23.
7 *Ibid*., fols 32–3.
8 Pepys, *Diary*, 30 June 1667.
9 Childs, 'British Brigade', p. 20.
10 Glozier, *Scottish Soldiers*, p. 2; Childs, 'British Brigade', pp. 20–1.

Charles Fitzcharles, 1st Earl of Plymouth (1657–1680). (Creative Commons Public Domain)

cornet in Captain John Fitzgerald's troop of horse during the governorship of the Earl of Teviot in 1663 and 1664. By August 1666 he had returned to Scotland and was commissioned cornet in General Thomas Dalyell's troop in Lieutenant General William Drummond's newly raised cavalry regiment. Resigning in 1667, Halkett entered Dumbarton's in France, where he served for 12 years, rising to captain, then major by 1679. He was a courageous, highly experienced and intrepid officer, who was well-respected by his men.[11] The next addition to the Tangier forces – authorised by royal warrant, dated 27 May 1680 – was the 'King's Battalion', composed of 600 regulars drawn from Charles II's standing army, and led by acting Lieutenant Colonel Edward Sackville (a captain in the 1st Regiment of Foot Guards and another veteran of service in France in the 1670s). Having departed from Portsmouth, the unit landed at Tangier on 2 July.[12]

The King's Battalion comprised two companies (240 men) from the 1st Foot (Grenadier) Guards, led by Sackville and Captain George Bowes; one company (120 men) from the 2nd Foot (Coldstream) Guards under Captain Thomas Tollmache, who was Major of the battalion; 120 men from the Duke of York's Regiment of Foot commanded by Captain James Fortrey; and 120 men from the Earl of Mulgrave's (the Holland) Regiment of Foot under Captain Philip Kirke, the younger brother of Lieutenant Colonel Percy Kirke. On 29 April 1664, a bill was raised to pay Colonel William Legge, Lieutenant of Ordnance, £247 4s. for drums, bandoliers, and other items for Colonel John Russell's Regiment of Foot Guards. Additionally, a warrant was issued to the Master of the Great Wardrobe in April 1669, to provide 12 colours for the King's Regiment of Guards under the Duke of Albemarle (Coldstreamers), 'according to the pattern sent, the same as those of Colonel John Russell's Regiment, the colours for the captains to be distinguished by such figures as John Miller, Major of the regiment, shall direct'.[13]

A vivid description of the arrival of the King's Battalion from England and Ireland is provided by John Ross, 'gentleman, a sentinel in the Foot Guards', whose *Tangers Rescue* appeared in 1681:

> When the glad news came of the arrival of His Majesty's frigates, the *Rupert*, the *Sapphire* and others with six hundred of his Majesty's Guards from England, under the command of Colonel Edward Sackville, a man of most estimable gifts and parts, with many brave volunteer gentlemen, encouraged to undertake

11 Halkett, 'Account', pp. 3–4; Glozier, *Scottish Soldiers*, pp. 181–91.

12 SRO, D(W)1778/I/i/562–3.

13 TNA, SP44/29, fol. 32; *CSPD 1663–4*, p. 573.

> this noble enterprise in the service of their king and country, by that hopeful young youth the earl of Plymouth (whose mature fruit did anticipate his years, and anti-date his age). This gallant recruit changed the effeminate designs and stupid procedures of the burghers to a more propitious and generous resolution and did animate the old soldiers to a more qualified gallantry, and courage and so confirmed the resolutions of all, they that thought themselves in a sufficient posture of defence. These volunteers landed at Tangier 2 July 1680, with 240 of the King's Own Regiment under the command of Colonel Edward Sackville, and one Mr Bowes; 120 of the Earl of Craven's Regiment, under the command of Colonel Tollemach (a gentleman gifted with the acuteness and flourish of wit); 120 of the Duke of York's Regiment, under the command of a modest young gentleman, Captain Fawtry; 120 of the Earl of Mulgrave's Regiment, under the command of Captain Kirke, a youth of admirable endowments, according to the politeness of Court. All those with the volunteers and drafts of the Independent Companies were regimented under the command of Colonel Edward Sackville as their colonel, and were called the King's Battalion. After this landed the valorous Halkett, major to that renowned regiment of the earl of Dumbarton, all of them men of approved valour, whose fame echoed the sound of their glorious achievements in France and other nations, leaving behind them a report of their glorious victories, wherever they came, both home and abroad, every place witnessing and giving a large testimony of their renown. So that the arrival of this illustrious regiment more and more increased the resolutions and the united courage of the inhabitants and added confidence to their valour.[14]

Authorisation for the raising a new regiment of foot, especially for service in Tangier was given on 13 July 1680. This new formation was to be commanded by Charles Fitzcharles, Earl of Plymouth and illegitimate son of Charles II, and sent in place of 600 men previously ordered from Ireland.[15] The unit (the Earl of Plymouth's) was also known as the 2nd Tangier Regiment, and later the 4th (King's Own Royal Lancaster Regiment). Although Plymouth had obtained some military experience in the Dutch army during 1677 and 1678, executive command of the formation fell to Percy Kirke (who had served in the Royal Horse Guards on the Continent, and was promoted to Lieutenant Colonel), and the regimental Major, Charles Trelawney. But neither Plymouth nor Kirke played any part in organising the unit because, anxious not to miss the action, they went to Tangier with Sackville's battalion, in the company of several gentlemen volunteers.[16] Plymouth's Regiment consisted of 16 companies each of 65 soldiers, besides officers, and was half recruited in London and half from the West Country, close to the embarkation ports of Plymouth and Falmouth.

14 John Ross, *Tangers Rescue, or a Relation of the Late Memorable Passages at Tanger … and Particularly of that Bloody Engagement* (London: Henry Hills, 1681).

15 TNA, SP44/164, fol. 50; *CSPD 1679–80*, p. 563. Commission to the Earl of Plymouth to be Colonel of a Foot Regiment to be forthwith raised and sent to Tangier.

16 BL, MS Carte 222, fol. 226; John Childs, *General Percy Kirke and the Later Stuart Army* (London: Bloomsbury, 2014), p. 34.

Warrants issued by the Crown to various officials and army officers in England, dated 17 July 1680, illustrate the methods employed in the recruitment, supplying and transportation of Plymouth's Regiment to Tangier:

> Warrant to Henry Howard, Commissary-General of the Musters, when the captains or other officers of the 16 companies of the Earl of Plymouth's regiment shall produce 20 privates besides officers to be mustered, for taking the first muster of them respectively, from which time the said soldiers and also the officers of the said company are to enter into pay and, when 20 more privates shall be produced to muster, for mustering them accordingly, and, as soon as the said companies respectively shall be completed, for mustering them so completed.
>
> The King to Lieutenant Colonel Kirke or other the officer commanding the Earl of Plymouth's regiment. Ordering him to signify to the captains appointed to raise the 16 companies of the above regiment that they send notice to the Commissary-General of the Musters when and where they will produce 20 privates of such their companies respectively to be mustered, and in like manner when and where they will have 40 privates and that they send like notice to him when their companies respectively shall be completed.
>
> The King to Henry Howard, Commissary-General of the Musters. Notwithstanding the former orders, signifying his pleasure that after the first muster of 20 soldiers in each company of the Earl of Plymouth's regiment he muster the rest of the soldiers of the respective companies by 10 or more in each company as they shall be produced till the said companies be completed.
>
> The King to Lieutenant Colonel Kirke. Informing him of the last order and directing him to signify the same to the captains or other officers in chief of the said companies.
>
> Warrant to the Ordnance Commissioners for the delivery of arms, beds and bedding for the 16 companies of the Earl of Plymouth's Regiment, one moiety thereof to be delivered out of the Tower to Lieutenant Colonel Kirke for the use of eight of the said companies that will be raised about London and the other moiety to be delivered to Major Trelawney at the Citadel of Plymouth for the use of the other 8 companies, the proportion of arms for each company to be one partizan, two halberds, and one drum, with muskets and pikes for 60 soldiers and 3 corporals, of which two-thirds are to be muskets and the other third pikes.
>
> The King to the Governors of Clerkenwell Workhouse. Informing them that he had ordered Lieutenant Colonel Percy Kirke to order the captains now raising about the city of London 8 companies of the Earl of Plymouth's regiment that, as they shall raise their soldiers, they bring them to Clerkenwell Workhouse to be lodged, trained and exercised thereabouts, till they may conveniently be sent on shipboard, and that the officers had been ordered to contract for the diet of the said soldiers at not exceeding the rate of 6d. a day for each, and signifying his pleasure that they clear the said workhouse and the places belonging to it of any

persons or lumber, so that there may be convenient room for the bedding and accommodation of the said companies accordingly.

The King to Major Charles Trelawney or other the officer in chief commanding the 8 companies of the Earl of Plymouth's regiment therein mentioned. Directing him to give orders to the captains now raising in the western parts of the kingdom the said 8 companies that, as soon as they shall raise their soldiers, they march with them to the Citadel of Plymouth, to be lodged, trained and exercised there, till they may conveniently be sent on shipboard, and the officers are to be very careful that their soldiers behave orderly and pay for their diet and lodging on their march to Plymouth, where they are to contract for their diet so as not to exceed the rate of 6d. a day per man, and to preserve the bedding ordered for them that the same may be entirely shipped with the men.

The King to Lieutenant Colonel Percy Kirke. Similar letter to the last, for ordering the captains of the 8 companies now raising about London to bring the soldiers as raised to Clerkenwell Workhouse and to keep them there.

The King to the Earl of Bath, Governor of Plymouth, or in his absence to the Lieutenant Governor. Informing him of the order for bringing the 8 companies of the Earl of Plymouth's regiment to the Citadel of Plymouth and for keeping them there, and signifying his pleasure that he give order for admitting the officers of the said companies to bring in, train, exercise and lodge their men within the said citadel accordingly, and for affording what accommodation is necessary for their officers.

Warrant to Henry Howard, Commissary-General of the Musters, for allowing and passing on the musters during his absence Sir Samuel Clarke, lieutenant colonel of Colonel John Russell's regiment of Foot Guards, who has been sent to be major-general of the foot at Tangier.

Warrant to Lieutenant Colonel Percy Kirke for ordering the captains of the Earl of Plymouth's regiment to raise five soldiers more in each of their companies over and above the 60 soldiers ordered to be raised, so that each company shall consist of 65 soldiers.

Warrant to Henry Howard, Commissary-General of the Musters, after reciting the last warrant, for, on the completing of the said companies to 65 soldiers in each, allowing and passing them on the musters.

Warrant to Major Charles Trelawney for ordering the captains of the six companies of the Earl of Plymouth's Regiment to be raised in the western parts to raise their companies to 65 soldiers in each.

Warrant to the Ordnance Commissioners for delivering arms and bedding for the additional 80 soldiers to be raised in the Earl of Plymouth's regiment.

Warrant to Captain Edward Hastings for raising by beat of drum 65 volunteers, to serve as private soldiers in his company in the Earl of Plymouth's Regiment, but, in case he beats his drums within the City of London or the liberties thereof, he is first to show this warrant to the Lord Mayor.

Warrant to Henry Howard, Commissary-General of the Musters, for allowing and passing on the musters the staff officers of the Earl of Plymouth's regiment from the time when one half of the established number of the private soldiers of the said regiment were raised.

Order to Captain Saville with his company of the Earl of Plymouth's Regiment forthwith to march to Scarborough Castle, where he is to join with Captain Graham's company of the said regiment, to the intent that they may be both embarked together for service at Tangier.

The King to Sir Thomas Slingsby, Governor of Scarborough Castle. Ordering him to receive Captain Saville's company into the said castle and accommodate them as well as he can, and the officers of the said company will take care to provide diet for the soldiers or give them subsistence money.[17]

The King informed Kirke on 7 August 1680:

Having thought it needful that 400 privates of the Earl of Plymouth's Regiment be with all possible speed embarked with their arms at Blackwall with two captains, two lieutenants, two ensigns, four sergeants and eight corporals, which officers you are to appoint, you are therefore to give order to the respective captains to hasten the completing their proportions of the said number, and you are to apply yourself or send an officer to the Commissioners of the Admiralty and the Navy to know when shipping will be ready with victuals on board for the said officers and soldiers, on which you are to give order and take care that as many of the said soldiers as are mustered or in readiness be forthwith embarked in these ships with their arms, and the said officers or so many of them as you shall think fit be then embarked with them, and, as the rest of the soldiers shall be raised, you are to cause them to be shipped with their arms in like manner with the residue of the said officers; you are to give order to the eldest captain going with them to take care of getting together and securing their arms on shipboard under the custody of the commanders of the respective ships, who are to deliver them at Tangier as the lieutenant-governor shall direct. You are also to give order to the said officers and soldiers to pass over in the said ships to Tangier, where the officers are to dispose of the soldiers according to the lieutenant-governor's orders, whose certificate or receipt they are to desire for the numbers of men so disposed of, wherewith the said officers are then to return back hither, and you are to send notice to the Commissary-General of the Musters when the said

17 TNA, SP44/65, fols 2–6, 9, 11, 14–15, 19–22, 48.

> officers and soldiers shall embark in order to their being mustered according to the orders given in that behalf.[18]

On 15 September the advance party of Plymouth's Regiment, consisting of six companies under Major Trelawny, was ordered to quit the citadel of Plymouth, and embark immediately aboard the merchant ship *Seratt*, waiting in the harbour to take them on board and transport them to Tangier. During the voyage Trelawny was to follow the commands of the ship's Captain and to deploy his troops as directed by the deputy-governor upon arrival. The other 10 companies, currently quartered in London, were to be loaded onto ships in the Thames and subsequently transported in such vessels as the Commissioners of the Admiralty should appoint to receive them.[19]

Meanwhile, having arrived in Tangier, Lieutenant Colonel Sackville maintained daily training and rigid discipline within the King's Battalion, which encouraged the remaining officers and soldiers of the garrison. Such was the martial enthusiasm that the chief-engineer, Sheres, left his Mole and enlisted as a volunteer in the Tangier Horse. In their letter of instructions of 13 August to Sir Palmes Fairborne, the Lords of the Council at Whitehall informed him:

> by the particular brought by Captain Leslie that there were at Tangier, 10 July, forces amounting in the whole to 2,432, and 640 more from Ireland being on the sea, if not yet arrived, and three troops of 180 horse being already sailed as far as St Helens, where they wait for the first fair wind, and 200 recruits of foot sent for from Scotland, [which] may be speedily expected with you, these forces his Majesty accounts sufficient to defend the place till the beginning of spring, when the season and condition of the ground will permit entering on fortifying, and then he intends to send out such addition of forces as shall be judged convenient. Nevertheless, he, being mindful of his resolution of not suffering the soldiers to be overlong continued at Tangier, has ordered 400 foot more of the men newly raised to be speedily shipped as recruits for Tangier to be disposed of for recruiting the Old Regiment as you shall find best and on the arrival of these 400 it is left to you to discharge and send back two or three hundred as you think best of the men that have been longest at Tangier and are most desirous to be discharged and the Admiralty have order about bringing them for England.[20]

It was ordered on 23 August 1680 that the sum of £395 9s. 0d., being part of the £2,766 9s. 0d. intended to be paid to the victuallers of Tangier by the end of the month, was disbursed to Colonel Kirke for subsistence money for the Earl of Plymouth's Regiment, which was in the process of being recruited. Three weeks later, the same unit received £2,826 15s. 1d. out of the £4,989 18s. 8d. intended towards the pay of the officers and soldiers of the Tangier garrison upon the Old Establishment.[21] Likewise, in response

18 *Ibid.*, fols 25–6.

19 TNA, SP44/65, fols 46, 49–50; *CSPD 1680–1*, pp. 9–10.

20 TNA, SP44/65, fol. 29; *CSPD 1679–80*, p. 603.

21 TNA, WO 4/1, fol. 77; *CTB*, VI, pp. 679, 693.

to a petition from Sackville, on 15 December 1680 'the non-commissioned officers and soldiers of the five companies that were drawn out of the Guards for the service of Tangier' had their four pay for the previous July, August, September and October adjusted, in that, after deduction of victuals and adding 1d. per day to Captain Fortrey's and Captain Kirke's Companies who are allowed but 8d. a day, they received the sum of £1,041 1s. 8d. However, the net sum paid for the said four months (after deduction of £2,007 19s. 6d. for victuals and £154 17s. 10d. for poundage) came to £934 14s. 6d., thus leaving a balance of £106 7s. 2d. still to be supplied for pay according to the muster rolls. According to a report by Treasurer William Hewer and his assistant, Charles Fox, the discrepancy arose because:

> the private soldiers and some few of the non-commission officers were drawn out of the several companies of the Guards [in London] and that Mr Johnson [paymaster in Tangier] in adjusting their pay accounts for no more non-commission officers than were actually so drawn, but the said number not being near sufficient for the well governing of the said companies, Colonel Sackville made such officers of the private soldiers as were wanting and has accordingly paid them after the usual rates of officers of that quality. This item of difference arises from this source and from the different musters made here and at Tangier.[22]

There had been desertions among Dumbarton's Regiment whilst awaiting transportation to France in 1667, and it was reported on 27 July 1680 that several men listed in London under the Earl of Plymouth's Regiment fled from their colours. Some of them were apprehended and sent to Bridewell. Moreover, at Portsmouth, a fortnight later, 'This week the soldiers raised for Tangier were guarded on shipboard in order to their transportation, 16 of whom leaped overboard to escape, where they were taken up half drowned and secured again'.[23] The reinforcements meant for the colony also included 180 horse, 200 foot from Scotland and 500 sailors under the command of Admiral Herbert. Among the numerous demands for extra cavalry for the garrison, one request sent to 'Lord Dartmouth, Master-General of his Majesty's Ordnance', that four new troops, each of 25 soldiers, two corporals and one trumpeter, to be raised and sent. This contains a detailed list of arms, armour, and horse tack, including saddles (112 of each) to accompany them.[24]

The government eventually ordered that six independent troops, including one corporal and 20 privates from three troops of the Horse Guards, should muster and assemble at Portsmouth. But reports of peace in Tangier reached England before the latter could leave and their transportation was cancelled. These units were disbanded on 9 September 1680, but not before £9 9s. was spent on a new standard for Sir Francis Compton's Troop.[25] In the meantime, troops commanded by Captains Charles Neatby, John Coy and Thomas Langston, drawn from the Duke of Monmouth's late Regiment of Horse, and

22 TNA, SP44/8, fol. 10; *CTB*, VII, p. 1451.

23 *CSPD 1679–80*, pp. 559, 596.

24 SRO, D742/0/3/79, n.d. but *c.* 1680.

25 TNA, SP44/65, fol. 16; SP44/164, fol. 49; *CSPD 1679–80*, p. 570.

raised for service in Tangier, were to be mustered complete with 50 troopers in each, besides officers. These were highly experienced soldiers who had fought in France and Scotland before the regiment's disbandment in late 1679. Initially it was decided that horses for Neatby's, Coy's and Langston's troops would to be provided 'in foreign parts', and hence the units were to muster without them. Yet following their seabound passage from Greenwich to their embarkation point at Portsmouth, they were hastily equipped with mounts and arms left by the Horse Guards, who had been come ashore and returned to London. It was ordered that the mounts, with saddles, bridles, holsters, collars, backs, breasts, helmets and carbines belonging to the troopers:

> be delivered on shipboard proportionably to the captains commanding the said three troops, who are to receive them for the use of the said three troops, and further signifying his pleasure that the said horses with their furniture and the said arms shall not be delivered to the soldiers till their arrival at Tangier, it having been directed that the horses with their furniture and the arms which will be wanting for the complete mounting and arming of the said three troops shall be provided and sent to Tangier after.[26]

Similarly, on 4 August 1680 Treasurer Hewer was instructed to pay £1,196 5s. 0d. 'for clothing three troops of Horse marched for Portsmouth in order, to their embarkation for Tangier', with £808 for the remainder of the pay of their pay for 47 days from 16 July, after deductions for clothing and horse meat for the soldiers. A further £300 was be expended as pay for the three troops raised for the service of Tangier that were ordered back to London.

At the end of the month, the mounts and tack, recently transferred from the Horse Guards, were purchased by the State for £2,371. The sum of £200 was expended on 65 horses and their furniture, whilst the remaining 63 horses went for £17 each. On 8 September it was reported that among the armour left on board ship at Portsmouth – that belonging to the King's own troop – 'was better than any in the Tower and bought by the King's order in Lord Gerard's time and cost £3 10s. per suit. The King has been pleased to promise that so many shall be made by the same man which amounts to £70'.[27] On 21 July 1680 the merchant Robert Gargrave received £50 from the Treasury 'for providing ships and conveniences to transport horses to Tangier', and another £397 10s. for 150 loads of hay for them.[28] The three new cavalry troops reached the outpost in late September, where they and the resident garrison Horse were augmented by a Spanish auxiliary component, numbering 200 troopers, that had been placed at the disposal of the governor. In addition to the various reinforcements, a company of miners under the command of Captain Richard Bassett was raised and sent to Tangier.[29]

26 TNA, SP44/65, fols 31, 39.

27 TNA, WO 4/1, fols. 79, 86; *CTB*, VI, pp. 660, 681, 687.

28 John Ackerman (ed.), *Moneys Received and Paid for Secret Services of Charles II and James II* (London: Camden Society, 1851), p. 16; *CTB*, VI, p. 644.

29 TNA, SP44/164, fol. 51; SRO, D742/0/4/4.

Something of the anxiety felt by Sir Palmes Fairborne in his efforts to obtain mounted forces for the garrison, as well as the urgency of the moment, can be gleaned from the following letter from Secretary Jenkins to Sidney Godolphin, member of the Privy Council, dated 20 September 1680:

> You will see and, I doubt not, represent to his Majesty in what anguish Sir Palmes Fairborne is, finding the war to begin anew upon him and himself disappointed of the Horse he has all this while relied on and that were once intended for him. I can, without being anything of a soldier, guess what inconvenience and danger too having and using the Spanish Horse offered his Majesty may prove to the garrison of Tangier, yet I do not know but that that place may come to those extremities, in which such an offer is not to be refused. I hope therefore I may move you to lay before his Majesty whether he will not leave it to the governor and council-of-war to call in or not those troops, that are within call on the Spanish coast, for the service of the garrison and that his pleasure in this be signified to the Committee that first meets to give their instructions to the governor.[30]

The same issue later taxed Governor Kirke, who lamented the lack of cavalry. English horses performed poorly in Tangier and many died, although Kirke noted that most were aged when they arrived. By July 1681, there were only 80 cavalry mounts in the garrison, and the governor recommended purchasing Spanish remounts, which were cheaper and better adapted to local conditions.[31] For both officers and men the loss of their horses, either in battle or by misfortune, was a serious matter. By order of a court martial at Tangier on 14 August 1665, a private was sentenced to have his horse sold for the benefit of the orphans of his opponent in a duel.[32] Likewise, on 10 April 1666, Captain Arthur Campbell petitioned the King for money to purchase another mount in lieu of his own, which had died, 'as he must else lose his place in his Majesty's Guards'.[33] The type of cavalry horses used in Charles II's army is suggested by an advertisement placed by a corporal in the Horse Guards, dated 23 March 1685, for the sale of 'a tawny mare with short bushy hair, very well-shaped, in grey livery lined with yellow, about 17 or 18 years of age'.[34]

The Establishment of the Tangier garrison had been revised on 7 July 1680 to 3,080 effectives.[35] On 4 August a warrant was issued for the payment of £2,766 9s. 0d. 'to William Hewer, as impressed for the present expedition designed for Tangier and in part of the £50,000 as by the Privy Seal of July 21 last, viz., £1,701 17s. 6d. thereof to be paid over to the victuallers of Tangier by the latter end of this month in part of a greater sum for the victualling of 2,100 men; £397 18s. 2d. thereof to be paid over to them in part of a quarter sum for hay, oats and beans; and £666 13s. 4d. thereof to be paid

30 TNA/44/62, fol. 77; *CSPD 1680–81*, p. 29.
31 UY, MS 2572, fols 5, 7–18.
32 BL, MS Sloane 1957, fol. 31.
33 *CSPD 1665–6*, p. 345.
34 *London Gazette*, 23 March 1685.
35 BL, MS Add. 28938, fols 28–42.

to them towards the provisions for 1,320 men'.[36] The military forces sent to reinforce the garrison during the summer and autumn of 1680 brought the total number of troops, once all in theatre, to over 3,000 men. On 30 July the governor wrote, 'It rejoices me to see so many brave men come over, I make no doubt but their Lordships are preparing stores of provisions suitable to the forces intended besides arms of all kinds'.[37] He had expended all his reserve funds on reconstructing the soldiers' quarters, and on 'timber, nails, tools, pots, and charcoal', and bidden that timber from England, 'with all sorts of nails … be forthwith sent before the horse comes and the rest of the recruits, that there may be quarters prepared for them in order to preserve them in health when they are come over, for winter will be coming on, and if they be too much exposed to the violence of the rains at first it will destroy all the men'.

The four-month truce with the Moors expired on 15 September 1680, the respite having been granted on condition that any act of fortification of the outer strongholds left under English authority would cease.[38] Fairborne had already begun to make preparations for regaining the lost territory and the sites of the demolished forts. On 6 September he related:

> I am now a preparing everything in order to my going abroad at the end of the cessation but do conclude I cannot march so far nor take in the ground intended without the horse I have been made to hope for. The 8th instant I intend a council of war and in the meantime have ordered Mr Sheres to fit me several *chevaux-de-frise* to secure our flanks at our first marching out, and under the protection of several bags of straw lodged within the *chevaux-de-frise* I hope to secure our men pretty well from the enemy's shot. I am also removing guns from the batteries at the waterside to the castle, the better to annoy the enemy, and am also raising from Johnson's Battery to Catherina Port where we shall place a battery of seventeen great guns in ship carriages, and the next work in the town shall be to fit the wall for more great guns between Catherina Port and Irish Battery, but we are in want of great guns for the service.[39]

On 15 September the governor notified the Tangier Committee of the renewal of hostilities, as Qā'id Omar had 'acquainted us that war was proclaimed against us, and accordingly fired upon us'.[40] Moreover, at about 7:00 a.m., the Moors, having removed the markers laid out for grazing land during the truce, took shots at the sentries around York Fort, 'upon which we replied with our cannon from the castle, but they laying close (as their manner is) gave us little or no occasion of firing'. Fairborne possessed two immediate imperatives: to regain territory towards the vulnerable south-west

36 *CTB*, VI, p. 660.

37 TNA, CO 279/25, fol. 298. Fairborne to Jenkins, 30 July 1680.

38 TNA, CO 279/26, fols 78–9. Account by Henry Shere of what passed at Tangier from the 15th to the 23rd September 1680.

39 HL, 8498. Fairborne to Bridgewater, 6 September 1680.

40 *A Particular Relation of the Late Success of His Majesty's Forces at Tangier against the Moors* (London: Published by Authority, 1680); TNA, CO 279/26, fols 88–9. Fairborne to Jenkins, 15 September 1680.

side of the city, particularly by recapturing Pole Fort and its surrounding entrenchments; and to launch offensive operations, which would bolster the morale of the garrison and provide more leverage in any future negations. He only awaited the arrival of the much-needed cavalry troopers to make a dash for the fort.

Finally, the vessel carrying the Horse anchored in the bay, although there were 135 men, rather than the promised 400 or 500. The governor reported their arrival:

> Although I had put all things in a very good readiness against the day to have sallied out yet upon the arrival of the horse and the several stores, I judged it rational to get all the horse ashore and stores to have the horse new shod, having lost all their shoes aboard, as also that they might feel their legs, so deferred my sallying out to possess myself of the ground where Pole Fort stood until the 20th instant.[41]

In determining the direction of military strategy, Fairborne encountered difficulties with some of his senior officers. Lieutenant Colonel Edward Sackville and Major Thomas Tollemache still hoped for peace, although Major Halkett and others advocated that no operations should be attempted outside the city's walls until the arrival of further reinforcements.[42] A council of war, convened in the Upper Castle, debated the strategic problem of whether the garrison should await a new phase of enemy assaults – as had been disastrous in the past – or utilise the strength of its growing reinforcements to attack the Moors in their prepared positions. The governor decided upon the latter.

In the early hours of 20 September 1680 Sir Palmes Fairborne assembled almost the entire garrison on the Parade Ground of York Castle. The regiments marched the short distance to Catherina Port, where the gates were opened, and before dawn they silently formed up in pre-planned positions outside the fortifications. Kirke, Henry Sheres and various gentlemen volunteers led the way with the newly reinforced Tangier Horse, which galloped past the empty trenches towards Pole Fort (across the lower slopes towards the left centre of the city). To their immediate rear was an advance-guard from the King's Battalion under Major Tollemache of the Coldstream Guards, who advanced at the double across 400 yards of ground to close-up with the cavalry. Forming the first line of the main force was Dumbarton's sizable regiment of Scots veterans, plus the remainder of the King's Battalion and Herbert's battalion of seamen (led by Major Charles Barclay of Dumbarton's, and armed with muskets, half-pikes and cutlasses), divided into five companies. The 1st Tangier Regiment brought up the rear. Lieutenant Colonel Sackville, in command of the King's Battalion, at this point rode up to his men and spoke to them some inspiring words. Addressing them as 'My good fellows', he told them that as guardsmen much was expected of them; that they were to be courageous like the King of England's Guards, in a manner worthy of

41 TNA, CO 279/26, fol. 78.

42 Halkett, 'Account', pp. 6–7.

themselves, and that they must show to the world that they were worthy of their status.

He warned them against advancing out of the ranks, however tempted they might be by the enemy to do so. He recommended them to maintain cohesiveness, and to strictly obey the orders of their officers. Sackville had no doubt that 'they would overcome the rude and undisciplined ranks of the enemy, gain for themselves the favour of the King and the love of their country, as well as secure for themselves a glorious and everlasting fame and the good repute of all persons'.[43] Major Halkett expressed similar words of encouragement to the soldiers of Dumbarton's Regiment. Taken by surprise by the rapid and aggressive English attack, the Moors offered little opposition, and Pole Fort and its adjacent trenches were hurriedly reoccupied without any loss.[44] Halkett took up the narrative:

> we marched out with the whole force of the garrison, leaving only the ordinary guards within, the four troops of horse first, then the detachment of 300 men designed to be our advanced men commanded by Lieutenant Colonel Tollemache, that honour was put upon him I believe upon the account of his quality and being a man of interest at court in prejudice of Captain Bowes that was the older captain, and his tour the troops was embattled as it was designed all in one line. Our right hand being covered by the old line of communication betwixt the town and Pole Fort, and our left by Norwood Redoubt, which was still in being then, the discoveries [reconnaissance] being made as far out as was judged necessary, and … in the most fitting places, some little firing being made at our discoveries, be some few scattering Moors, not yet any body of men appearing nor any guard upon that hand. Then Lieutenant Colonel Tollemache with his 300 men was commanded to post himself about the mines of Pole Fort, then an engineer went about the viewing of the ground about Pole Fort after he resolved upon the design of the work, it was resolved to cause work a battalion at time so many hours. The battalion of seamen being posted on the east of the town, the rest standing to their arms and it being necessary to advance fire men [musketeers] upon all hands of Pole Fort to keep the enemy off and in skirmish in favour of our workmen; the detachments being made was posted at three several places, some shelter being made in haste for the men, the Moors about this time appeared with several colours from the bottom near Mes River [Jews River] where they camped, I judge about the number of 6 or 700 men, all foot very few horse … that they came very scatteredly, fearing our cannon and posted themselves at the ruins of James Fort and at Anne Fort, and upon the old lane betwixt the two forts. The advanced men that kept our advanced posts in skirmish all the day over, where we had some few men killed and wounded. I am very confident at this time the Moors could not make a thousand men before the town. We continued all that day till 7 o'clock at night in working about Pole Fort and in relieving our workmen and the advanced

43 Quoted in Sir Frederick William Hamilton, *The Origin and History of the First or Grenadier Guards* (London: John Murray, 1874), I, p. 242.

44 *A Particular Relation of the Late Success of His Majesty's Forces at Tangier against the Moors* (London: Thomas Newcomb, 1680), p. 4; *A Particular Narrative of a Great Engagement between the Garrison of Tangier and the Moors* (London: Thomas Newcomb,1680), p. 1.

> posts from time to time, till that palisade about the ruins of the fort was done, and a breastwork within the palisade, and the place put as the best posture of defence. For the night following Lieutenant Colonel Sackville, with the battalion of guards took possession of the place to make guard that night, there being a detachment of 300 men of reserve left in the place of arms before Catherina Gate; we then retired our advanced and work men, and marched into town, we having that day's work much easier than we imagined.[45]

A Particular Relation, penned by an eyewitness, details the garrison's deployment:

> Lieutenant Colonel Sackville, with the battalion of Guards, was posted on the right, upon the skirt of the said hill, on the left of whom was a battalion of the Old Regiment of the garrison, commanded by Captain Giles; the other two battalions, drawn out of the Scotch Regiment, were on the left of them, commanded by Major Halkett and Captain Spott, with a company of grenadiers commanded by Captain Hodges. In the spur within the stockades, before Catherina Port, was posted another battalion of the Old Garrison, commanded by Major Boynton. Vice-Admiral Herbert, with 500 seamen, marched out at the sally-port, on the southeast of the town, and possessed the ground between that and Cambridge Fort, where they entrenched themselves. The parties being thus disposed, a competent number of men, appointed for the works, advanced in order to their entrenching on the ground of Pole Fort, where Major Beckmann the engineer assigned them their work.[46]

During the next few hours, the Moors – who had been stunned by the English attack – moved about in large numbers, harrying the soldiers 'very warmly with their small shot', but not venturing too close. In order to clear the old defences running from James to Monmouth Forts, fighting patrols from 'were drawn out of the several battalions, who advancing to the very line where the enemy was lodged, forced them thence; in which service a party of grenadiers, commanded by Captain Hodges, behaved themselves bravely'.[47]

Ross further described how the fighting continued 'for the space of seven or eight hours desperately, and continually firing on both sides from right to left, that it was nothing for a musketeer to empty three or four bandoliers notwithstanding of their reliefs every two hours'. During another stage in the battle, he recorded, 'The Scots grenadiers once forgot their powder and ball in the enemy's trench. Their lieutenant, called McCracken, endeavoured to recover and regain it, but in vain, which perceiving; he threw three or four grenades with his own hand to set it afire before it should fall in the enemy's hands, to the great danger of his life.[48] The expenditure of ammunition was considerable. As the garrison's Laws and Ordinances of War made it a capital offence for any musketeer to 'fling away his powder out of his bandoliers

45 Halkett, 'Account', pp. 7–8.

46 *Particular Relation*, pp. 1–2.

47 Ross, *Tangers Rescue*, p. 9.

48 *Ibid.*, pp. 10, 14.

that he may the sooner come off', or 'complain he wants powder or bullet without acquainting his officer privately with it', there must have existed an established procedure for distributing fresh (pre-loaded) bandoliers on the battlefield. David Blackmore suggests that to prevent the ignition of powder barrels, 'it would seem that it was the normal practice to carry into battle a supply of lose powder and musket balls. It would have to be lose powder in order to be able to refill individual charges on a bandolier'.[49]

It might be supposed that any replenishment was via leather powder bags or small barrels. Issues of musket ammunition were collected by sergeants and corporals, who apportioned them out as required. Besides, as Orrery notes, links of match were given out by corporals to individual soldiers.[50] Perhaps the supply destroyed by Lieutenant McCracken (of Captain Monroe's Company, from Dumbarton's Regiment) was such source of resupply. Ross mentions 'Gentlemen of the pouch, a most useful officer in an army, and it is requisite he be stout also, they may want powder, and ball when they have most to do'.[51] Various surveys of ammunition and 'other habiliments' either wanting or present in the garrison's stores reveal substantial numbers of bandoliers, although whether these were included in those issued to musketeers directly (or those to be pre-loaded among companies) is uncertain. One survey taken on 14 April 1664 accounted for 502 collars (also referred to as 'pairs') in store, with a further 216 recently delivered, while among items wanting by Commissary James Brough in July 1664 were 800 bandoliers. Similarly, 'An account of the remaining state of the stores of war at Tangier' records the presence of 568 bandoliers on 20 August 1679; a further 2,768 were 'received since', bringing the total in store to 3,336.[52] The latter survey also lists 42 tanned calf leather powder bags. Moreover, an 'abstract of stores to be sent' to Tangier, undated but signed by Governor Percy Kirke, includes 100 powder bags.[53]

By 1680 the English army's development of firing methods was influenced by principles laid down in Richard Elton's *The Complete Body of the Art Military* (1668 edition), and *An Abridgement of the English Military Discipline* (1676), the first official drill book for Charles II's forces and published 'By His Majesties permission'.[54] As Blackmore observes, 'During the English Civil War a particularly aggressive way of fighting based upon the close-range delivery of overwhelming firepower followed by an immediate advance to hand-to-hand combat was developed in England Scotland and used by all protagonists. This was not something found in drill book and although it

49 David Blackmore, *Destructive and Formidable: British Infantry Firepower, 1642–1765* (Frontline Books: London, 2014), p. 34.

50 Orrery, *Treatise*, p. 31.

51 Ross, *Tangers Rescue*, pp. 26–7.

52 SRO, D742/0/3/4; D742/0/3/1/1; D742/0/3/6.

53 SRO, D742/0/3/82.

54 Richard Elton, *The Complete Body of the Art Military* (London: W. L., 3rd edn, 1668); Anon., *An Abridgement of the English Military Discipline* (London: John Bill and Christopher Barker, 1676). A later edition, titled *An Abridgement of the Military Discipline*, was published in Edinburgh in 1680 for the use of the Scots army (Anon., *An Abridgement of the Military Discipline Appointed by His Majesty to be used by all His Forces in His Ancient Kingdom of Scotland* (Edinburgh: 1680).

was similar to the Swedish *salvee* developed by Gustavus Adolphus there were important differences, primarily in the manner of its application'.[55] At the Battle of the Dunes on 14 June 1658 the Commonwealth contingent, drawn up in advance of the Anglo-French army, 'on hands and knees crept up the hill, and gave the enemy's foot two good volleys, and with our pikes forced them to retreat'.[56] Similarly, Colonel Thomas Morgan, commanding the English foot (numbering 4,000–5,000), described, 'Immediately the enemy were clear shocked off their ground, and the English colours flying over their heads, the strongest officers and soldiers clubbing them down'.[57] The performance of these veterans was attested to by James, Duke of York, who commanded the exiled royalist army for the Spanish in Flanders:

> The English came on with great eagerness and courage. But their heat was such, that they outmarched the French, so that had the opportunity been taken, they might have paid dear for their rash bravery ... While they were thus preparing themselves, their commanded men opening to the right and left, to give way for their main body which was to mount the height, were continuingly firing at Boniface, and as soon as the body were in a condition to climb, they began their ascent with a great shout, which was general from all their foot.[58]

The future James II also led a frontal cavalry charge against Colonel Lockhart's Regiment – which had led the attack – but was repulsed with substantial losses. Soon afterwards he led a flank attack which broke the unit. In describing the action, the Duke of York paid attention to the fighting spirit and resilience of Lockhart's men:

> It is very observable that when we had broken into this battalion, and were got amongst them, not so much as one single man of them asked quarter or threw down his arms; but everyone defended himself to the last: so that we ran as great danger by the butt end of their muskets, as by the volley which they had given us. And one of them had infallibly knocked me off my horse, if I had not prevented him when he was just ready to have discharged his blow, by a stroke I gave him with my sword over the face, which laid him along upon the ground.[59]

The regiment's Lieutenant Colonel, Roger Fenwick, and two of its captains died, and most of the remaining officers were wounded, as well as 40 to 50 other ranks killed in battle. Colonel Lillingston's Regiment, fighting alongside Lockhart's soldiers 'had the hardest pull where there are thirty or forty killed'.[60] Reformed as Harley's Regiment, Lillingston's would form part

55 Blackmore, *Destructive and Formidable*, p. 35.

56 *Clarke Papers*, III, p. 158.

57 Sir Thomas Morgan, *A True and Just Relation of Maj. Gen. Sir Thomas Morgan's Progress in France and Flanders* (London: J. Nutt, 1699), p. 9.

58 A. Lytton Sells (ed.), *The Memoirs of James II: his campaigns as Duke of York, 1652–1660* (Bloomington: Indiana University Press, 1962), pp. 264–5.

59 *Ibid.*, p. 266.

60 *Clarke Papers*, III, p. 154.

of the Tangier garrison in 1661–62 and contain some of the veterans of the campaign in Flanders.

The brigade of Cromwellian veterans sent by Charles II to Portugal exhibited similar methods and fighting qualities at the Battle of Ameixial in 1663. The foot regiments drew up in the Dutch formation, that is, in six ranks, with their pikes in the centre to provide protection against cavalry and to form the offensive element in the advance. During the action the English infantry traversed a slope to within 220 yards of the Spanish main positions, wherein they 'marched on shouting as if victorious, but discharged no shot till they came within push of pike of the enemy, and then they poured in their shot so thick upon them that made them quit their ground and fly towards the left wing, leaving their cannon behind them, which were afterwards turned upon them, much to their prejudice'.[61] Their discipline was such that they redressed their lines and withstood a counter-attack by the Spanish Horse, 'but having their fire ready at all hands, they quickly quitted themselves of those troops.

As during the British Civil Wars of the 1640s and 1650s, musketeers on both sides were commonly issued with smoothbore, muzzle-loading matchlock muskets, bandoliers, and swords, although increasingly, firelock units and dragoons were armed with snaphances. Instructions issued in 1636 for arming the English and Welsh militia declared that matchlock muskets were to be of one standard bore (12 bullets to the pound) and that each musketeer 'shall be furnished with a sufficient whole musket, the barrel thereof shall be four feet in length and no more', the total length of the weapon being five feet two inches.[62] Moreover, 'every such person appointed to serve with a full musket shall be further furnished and armed with a good bandolier, and with fifteen good and serviceable charges of turned wood, covered with leather and fastened there unto. Also with a good primer, worm and scourer, and a bullet bag annexed unto it, with a mould to cast such bullets as aforesaid'. In 1645 matchlocks costing 10s., 11s. and 11s. 6d. were obtained for the New Model Army, while in 1646 Parliament contracted for *English* matchlock muskets and bandoliers, at 14*s. apiece* for its forces in Ireland.[63] As Orrery related:

> As to the musket, and what is useful to it, I find many things in my poor judgment worthy consideration and redress. As first, that all our muskets be of one bore, or at most of two sorts of certain bores; the bigger for the stronger, the lesser for the weaker bodies. For want of this, I have seen much hazard undergone; for generally our musket shot is of one certain size, and the bores of muskets are of various sizes, whereby having been once engaged in a fight, which by reason of the many enclosures in which we fought, the musketeers were to be supplied with

61 HMC, *Heathcote*, p. 104. See also Riley, *Last Ironsides*, pp. 103–6.

62 W. Wrye (ed.), *State Papers Relating to Musters, Beacons, Ship-money, &c. in Norfolk from 1626 chiefly to the beginning of the Civil War* (Norwich, 1907), p. 89; David R. Lawrence, *The Complete Soldier: Military Books and Military Culture in Early Stuart England, 1603–1645* (Brill: Leiden, 2008), p. 189.

63 Mungeam, 'Contracts', pp. 106, 112, 114; *CJ*, IV, p. 698.

> more shot than they carried in their pouches, and barrels of musket bullets being opened, few of the shot in them would fit the muskets, but were a size too large, whereby we had like to have been worsted; for the soldiers were forced to gnaw off much of the lead, others to cut their bullets; in which much time was lost, the bullets flew a less way, and more uncertainly; and, which was worse, so many pauses, animated the enemy, by making him think our courages cooled. If there be two sizes of muskets, and shot, on both ends of the barrels, which hold the shot, should be written lesser, and bigger, that in the hurry of a fight there might be no mistake, but that bullets be distributed according to the bores of the muskets.[64]

At the Dunes in 1658 Morgan had 400 men armed with firelocks.[65] Two hundred of them were in the stores at Tangier in 1662, whilst in January 1684 the 12 companies of the Coldstream Guards were resupplied with 43 snaphance muskets, 20 pikes, two halberds and two drums, the old arms being returned into the stores.[66] According to Orrery, firelock muskets were preferable to matchlocks for several reasons:

> First, it is exceedingly more ready; for with the firelock you have only to cock, and you are prepared to shoot; but with your matchlock, you have several motions, the least of which is as long a performing, as but that one of the other, and oftentimes much more hazardous; besides, if you fire not the matchlock musket as soon as you have blown your match (which often, especially in hedge fights, and in sieges, you cannot do) you must a second time blow your match, or the ashes it gathers, hinders it from firing.
>
> Secondly, the match is very dangerous, either where bandoliers are used, or where soldiers run hastily in fight to the budge-barrel, to refill their bandoliers; I have often seen sad instances thereof.
>
> Thirdly, marching in the nights, to avoid an enemy, or to surprize one, or to assault a fortress, the matches often discover you, and informs the enemy where you are; whereby you suffer much, and he obtains much.
>
> Fourthly, in wet weather, the pan of the musket being made wide open for a while, the rain often deads the powder, and the match too; and in windy weather, blows away the powder, ere the match can touch the pan: nay, often in very high winds, I have seen the sparks blown from the match, fire the musket ere the soldier meant it; and either thereby lose his shot, or wound or kill someone before him. Whereas in the firelock the motion is so sudden, that what makes the cock fall on the hammer, strikes the fire, and opens the pan at once.
>
> Lastly, to omit many other reasons, the quantity of match used in an army, does much add to the baggage; and being of a very dry quality, naturally draws the moisture of the air, which makes it relax, and consequently less fit, though carried in close wagons. But if you march without wagons, the match is the more exposed; and without being dried again in ovens, is but of half the use which

64 Orrery, *Treatise*, pp. 29–30.

65 Sir Thomas Morgan, *A True and Just Relation of Maj. Gen. Sir Thomas Morgan's Progress in France and Flanders* (London: J. Nutt, 1699), p. 8.

66 BL, MS Sloane 3509, fol. 119; TNA, SP44/69, fol. 87; *CSPD 1683–4*, p. 250; Daniel MacKinnon, *Origin and Services of the Coldstream Guards* (London, 1833), p. 167.

> otherwise it would be of. And which is full as bad, the skeans you give the corporals, and the links you give the private Soldiers (of which near an enemy, or on the ordinary guard duty, they must never be unfurnished) if they lodge in huts or tents, or if they keep guard in the open field (as most often it happens) all the match for instant service is too often rendered uncertain, or useless; nothing of all which can be said of the Flint, but much of it to the contrary. And then the soldiers generally wearing their links of match near the bottom of the belt on which their bandoliers are fastened, in wet weather, generally spoil the match they have; and if they are to fight on a sudden, and in the rain, you lose the use of your small shot, which is sometimes of irreparable prejudice.[67]

But although such weapons possessed certain advantages over matchlocks, they were more expensive. In April 1645 Parliament contracted with two London gunsmiths for 200 'snaphance muskets English full bore and proof', at 15s. 6d. each, while in October 1646 the sum of 17s. was paid for them.[68]

Continuing the desperate fight to protect Tangier's outer fortifications, detachments from the King's Battalion and the Governor's Regiment were commanded to the shattered Anne and Kendall Forts. The soldiers were rotated every two hours with their reliefs. Although somewhat exposed, these English troops suppressed the attacking Moors with musket fire. Ross mentioned that Admiral Herbert 'increased addition of terror and multiplied horror to the Moors by putting ashore 600 seamen, excelling in strength and courage, nothing inferior to the Moors (the most agile people in the world) in agility and activity of body'.[69] Moreover, his naval contingent, 'exercised by an expert old soldier, Captain Barclay', showed resilience by driving back its tenacious foe, trench by trench. Thus protected, Beckman's working parties were able to bring up quantities of timber and stone, and make the immediate repairs to the Pole fortifications and trench system. After seven or eight hours' combat the enemy finally fell back, leaving the work of entrenchments to continue until nightfall. Fairborne now extracted his main force to the safety of the garrison, leaving Tollemache's volunteers from the King's Battalion to guard the heavily damaged Pole Fort. These tired, yet resilient soldiers did so throughout a particularly rainy, cold night. English casualties were reported as 'five men killed, twelve wounded, of the Horse several were shot in their arms'.[70] It was a commendable feat of arms that would be repeated throughout the coming days and weeks, as the Tangier garrison sought to exploit its territorial influence over the Moors.

On 21 September 1680, troops from the garrison again marched out early, with Major Boynton leading a battalion of foot in the field and Captain Giles 'in the place of arms before Catherina Port'. The fighting continued throughout the day, during which some of the Moors' outposts were carried, while blinds and parapets were constructed to screen Pole Fort from enemy

67 Orrery, *A Treatise*, pp. 30–1.

68 Mungeam, 'Contracts', p. 107; *CJ*, IV, p. 698.

69 *Tangers Rescue*, pp. 15–16. This is the only contemporary source to mention the figure of *600* for the sailors, and hence 500 seems more likely.

70 *Particular Relation*, p. 2.

fire. Losses among Boynton's men amounted to seven killed and 18 wounded, while the Horse sustained 'various' wounded, with two mounts killed and two others injured.[71] This achievement was repeated the following day when Lieutenant Edward Fitzpatrick led parties from the King's Battalion and the 1st Tangier Regiment in extending the territory under control. The Moors made strenuous efforts to dislodge the English troops and there was 'very hot service' on both sides. A company of grenadiers attached to the naval battalion was positioned at Monmouth Fort, and the remaining sailors, in conjunction with elements of Dumbarton's Regiment, were heavily involved in bombing the Moors from their trenches. Some men desperately attempted to seize the Moorish standards, and faced with such resolute action, the enemy eventually 'lost heart and turned and ran', leaving their dead behind.

The grenadiers, later described by Sheres as 'very active and daring men', lobbed their bombs with great skill and effect, although in their eagerness some soldiers 'advanced to the sandhills a little too far, where, mixing with the enemy, they were cut in pieces, and others advancing to fetch off the dead were much hurt in the attempt'.[72] It was further reported, 'The 22nd we sallied out again and advanced to the outlines, where the Scotch grenadiers behaved themselves bravely and beat the Moors out, and all the day maintained the ground. The Moors were very brave but were paid off and lost abundance of men. Our loss was not above eleven men, some few wounded'.[73] This defensive position, maintained with much endeavour and not inconsiderable casualties, was nevertheless somewhat exposed and at a considerable distance from the rest of the English fortifications. Halkett, in overall command of the position, duly recounted:

> when the time drew near that we usually retired to town, I told Sir Palmes that I believed that they designed to undertake something against us upon our retiring our advanced post, they having continued strong about James Fort since the skirmish in the morning, he told me he had the same thoughts, I said that there was at the advanced post and on the line betwixt the post and Monmouth Fort above 300 men, what of ours and other detachments, that was made to sustain our advanced post, and that our captain that commanded our advance was a young man that never before had seen action, Captain Forbes, and prayed him to give me leave to undertake the management of the retreat, he was pleased I made the offer, and ordered me to go about the doing it and to take what men of ours I judged necessary for the doing it, there was 200 firemen of our second battalion, commanded be Captain Lundy and Captain Moncrieffe, that had been on the guard with me the night before at Pole Fort, that had continued within the palisades all the day without skirmishing or working. I made choice of them for the business and marched them up to a convenient place near Monmouth Fort, where they could not be seen be the enemy, and ordered them to continue there in readiness, without showing themselves, till the rear of our advanced men came their length, and if the Moors followed, I would be with them in time to do with them as I judged

71 HMC, *Ormond*, V, p. 52. Povey to Legge, 23 September 1680.

72 TNA, CO 279/26, fols 78–9. Sheres' account, 23 September 1680.

73 HMC, *Ormond*, V, p. 52.

> convenient. I then went up to our advanced post (where I caused to retrieve some of the ammunition) that was there, I then endeavoured to make our men retire a file or two at a time so that the Moors might not perceive, but they very well observed our motions, perceived we intended to retire, they advanced with their colours from the mines of James Fort and from all the places on that hand. I put our best men on our rear and retired homewards, the Moors was very soon with us on our rear, I judge the number of 500 men within and without that old line that runs from James Fort to Monmouth Fort, then they began to bestow their fire amongst us and kept close on our rear till we came the length of our 200 men commanded be Captains Lundy and Moncrieffe, so soon as our rear past them, I ran and caused them [to] advance and made a fresh discharge on those Moors that were on the inside of the line, they not expecting to find fresh men so near them, they passed all of them very precipitately to the outside of the line, I made our men to the right hand about, and marched down the hill till we was quite out of sight of the enemy; upon this all the Moors believed we were running, came precipitately after us, our men having be that time charged again, I made our men face about again, being very near one and other, where we continued in skirmish a long half hour against all that had followed us, we having some advantage of the ground be some old lines and places that gave us some covert against their fire, we having them still exposed with full body to our fire, where certainly we killed many of their men. The Moors having spent their ammunition, they continued for some time in throwing of great stones amongst us, but they, finding our fire too sharp for them, they found it convenient to retire, so we ended that day's work very well and retired in town with the troops.[74]

It was reported, albeit biasedly, that the officers 'behaved themselves like brave and gallant men', while 'the soldiers in general that were in the actions have likewise approved themselves men of courage'.[75] Singled out for individual note were Lieutenant Colonels Sackville and Tollemache, Major Halkett, Captains Philip Kirke and Fortrey, and Lieutenants Fitzpatrick and Bridgeman. Governor Fairborne also praised his officers, especially commending to the King's favour the actions of Beckman ('a stout and able man in his profession'), the Earl of Plymouth and others. He also noted the personal courage of Admiral Herbert – who had been slightly wounded – praising his judicious advice and willingness to assist the garrison on all occasions. But Fairborne also took the opportunity to report that muskets remained in short supply among his men, stating, 'the Office of Ordnance has sent an account of 100 firelocks and 1,000 matchlocks to have come with this supply, not one has yet appeared and the commissary of the stores assures me not one is come, which is a great disappointment, for there is never a day that 50 or 60 arms are not spoiled, so that unless a speedy supply be sent both of them and iron pots I must give over fighting and eating, for without the one and the other, nothing can be done'.[76] For more than a week the Tangier garrison marched out in the morning, and after a day's hard toil on

74 Halkett, 'Account', pp. 10–11.

75 *Particular Relation*, p. 4.

76 TNA, CO 279/26, fols 87–8. Ross' account is the only contemporary source to mention the figure of 600 for the sailors, and hence 500 seems more possible (*Tangers Rescue*, pp. 15–16).

the forts and lines, and fierce fighting at the outposts, retreated into the city at nightfall. Overall, the English operations were successful and continued until mid October 1680.

Since earlier in the year Charles II had been eager to form a purely defensive alliance between England and Spain in the interests of the security of Tangier. The treaty was signed at Windsor on 10 June 1680.[77] In respect of the urgent need of cavalry at Tangier, and the difficulty of transportation from England, the King of Spain ordered 200 Catalan Horse to be placed at the garrison's disposal, and it was also arranged that horses might be purchased in Spain for the use of the Tangier troopers. On 6 October Spanish Horse arrived from Barbate in the province of Cádiz, and soon showed their mettle against the mounted squadrons of the Moors. By comparison, though the English troopers that had also recently embarked at Tangier had performed well during the three days of fighting, they were mounted on old horses purchased from the Life Guards, and as Fairborne reported, so poorly equipped that they appeared 'more like ruinated troopers than men fit for service'. Even so, he estimated that 'their officers are very good men'.[78] The new cannon, in addition to much of the garrison's artillery pieces, were in a sub-standard condition too. On 7 October Major Beckman dolefully reported from Pole Fort, where he was supervising the rebuilding of the fortifications:

> I hope to have finished this work about the beginning of the next month, the upper rampart is now almost cannon proof round, I hope to have some cannon mounted this week. I began to sink a countermine yesterday morning. The enemy's battery doth very much incommode the Mole, but the other two batteries have had but small effect on my work. I have no time to make a draught of this siege or attack. We have not above six cannons about town to fire, three are broken, no gunners worth bread, no garrison so neglected. Materials begin to grow rare. We have had about 145 killed and wounded.[79]

The threat from the Moorish guns had 'at last been taken seriously and at least one fort was extensively remodelled to carry artillery'.[80] During the ensuing exchange of cannon shot another piece, sited near Charles Fort, was disabled by fire from Peterborough Tower, but the Moors relocated one of their great guns to the south of Charles Fort. From here they fired on the governor's residence, with some rounds reportedly passing through the walls and 'frightening the ladies'. A battery of three guns was also placed on the sandhills overlooking the harbour, in order to disrupt the landing of men and stores, but these 'proved to no effect save a poor cook's broth on the Mole they battered off the fire'.[81] On 9 October 1680 one of the garrison's cannons

77 TNA, SP44/187, fol. 21; HMC, *Ormond, V*, III, p. 334. Jenkins to Ormond, Whitehall, 12 June 1680.

78 TNA, CO 279/26, fol. 88.

79 HMC, *Ormond, V*, I, pp. 52–3. Beckman to Legge, 7 October 1680.

80 Paul E. Beckmann, 'Martin Beckman and the English Occupation of Tangier 1662–1684. Part 2', *Fort Magazine*, 42 (2014), pp. 182–90 (p. 186).

81 Ross, *Tangers Rescue*, p. 16.

burst whilst firing, seriously injuring Captain Thomas St John, wounding Henry Sheres, and narrowly missing the governor and Admiral Herbert who were standing nearby. St John, who had served in Tangier as an infantry officer since 1662, had suffered seven weeks' siege in Charles Fort and was wounded during the garrison's evacuation, had recently been appointed Comptroller of the Ordnance. He received 22 wounds from the splitting gun and was incapacitated for 15 months 'without any consideration or salary'.[82]

The early part of October 1680 presented a period of consolidation of the military gains made in the September clashes, and notwithstanding the discernible weaknesses in the garrison's supply and condition, there was a distinct optimism among the soldiery. However, on 24 October, as the Moors were busy siting new batteries and digging mines in readiness for further assaults against Pole Fort, Fairborne decided to reconnoitre their positions in person. As lieutenant-governor and governor he had conducted the defence of Tangier with boundless energy and was always to be found at the point of danger, leading forays and riding about the lines frequently under fire to encourage the men. But during that evening Sir Palmes ventured too close to Charles Fort and was 'unfortunately shot in the body as he was giving directions for breaking of ground upon a little eminence to the left of the spur under Peterborough Tower, by which work he designed to amuse the enemy'.[83] This momentarily emboldened the Moorish troops, but they were observed by an officer in charge of 50 Catalan Horse, who 'bravely charged them, and forced them back into their trenches, pursuing them to their very line'. Although the unnamed officer and some of his troopers were killed, the unit was quickly reinforced by a troop of English cavalry and some foot, who dissuaded the Moors from continuing the action. During this somewhat sharp encounter the Spaniards sustained eight or 10 casualties and as many horses, whilst in Dumbarton's Regiment seven or eight privates were wounded.

However, Captain Francis Forbes – a young officer, who had four days previously led 300 infantrymen in the spirited advance to Monmouth Fort and been commended by Major Halkett for his service – received a desperate wound, from which he later died.[84] Sir Palmes Fairborne himself was brought back, mortally wounded, and would expire a few days later. He was succeeded as governor of the garrison of Tangier by Lieutenant Colonel Sackville. At a council of war held the following day, Sackville insisted that immediate action was necessary to raise the siege. By 3:00 a.m. on 27 October the garrison was under arms and drawn up in silence. The plan was to repeat, on a larger scale, the sortie of 20 September. This would involve the entire garrison, which had been reduced by battlefield casualties, sickness and fever (exacerbated to exposure in the trenches during the rains) to just over half, to 1,500 effectives in six infantry battalions, seven cavalry troops amounting to about 300 men, plus the naval contingent and other specially assembled units. According to

82 TNA, SP44/18, fol. 141; SRO, D742/O/3/75.

83 *A Particular Narrative of a Great Engagement between the Garrison of Tangier and the Moors* (London: Thomas Newcomb,1680), p. 1.

84 TNA, CO 279/26, fols 93–100. Shere's account, 24 October 1680.

Ross, Sackville spoke in stirring terms to his Guardsmen, while the dying Fairborne, carried out in a litter, intreated Dumbarton's Regiment thus:

> Countrymen and fellow-soldiers, let not your approved valour and fame in foreign nations be derogated at this time, neither degenerate from your ancient and former glory abroad; and as you are looked upon here to be brave and experienced soldiers, constant and successive victories having attended your conquering swords hitherto, do not come short of the great hopes we have in you, and the propitious procedures we expect from you at this time. For the glory of your nation, if you cannot surpass, you may imitate the bravest, and be emulous of their praises and renown.[85]

The Tangier garrison quietly departed the city and formed up beyond the walls. But unlike the previous occasion, the sailors and various auxiliaries were tasked with creating a diversion. While the garrison Horse and various Molemen, issued with muskets, drums, improvised colours and carts – 'to amuse and divert the enemy', marched to Peterborough Tower, making as much noise as possible. On the other side of the bay, where the Moors possessed a battery of seven or eight guns, Admiral Herbert ordered out all the boats of the fleet 'with waste clothes and colours' to make a simulated attack. As anticipated, the Moors responded by weakening their centre, so to bolster their flanks. Into the fray Sackville's main force moved forward. The English Horse advanced from Catherina Port, and formed up in the stockade, and then the foot, marching so noiselessly and with commendable discipline that their enemy did not take alarm until they were virtually all were drawn up. This force consisted of the King's Battalion (including the Guards companies) on the right, and Dumbarton's Regiment and the Old Tangier Regiment in the centre and left flank respectively. At a prearranged signal, the 150-strong garrison of Pole Fort deployed as a forlorn hope and immediately attacked the enemy positions before it.[86] Sheres, in his account of the battle, which was penned at the request of Sackville, reported:

> The attack proved a very hot and bloody piece of service, as well by reason of the enemy having a greater guard there than ordinary as through the slow march of the parties that were appointed for their reserve. The two Captains (Lundy and Hume) which commanded [companies from Dumbarton's] were immediately carried off ill-wounded, as were most of the other officers, amongst which Lieutenant Robinson, a very brave young man, and had not the reserve come timely to their relief that party had run great hazard of being all cut off.[87]

Beckman's engineers, covered by the musket fire of the infantry, now filled in the captured trenches to make a passage through them easier and to deny them to the enemy. The main body of the garrison's foot now attacked the Moors, with devastating results, 'the enemy very stubbornly disputing every

85 Ross, *Tangers Rescue*, p. 17.
86 Halkett, 'Account', p. 12; *Particular Narrative*, pp. 3–4.
87 TNA, CO 279/26, fols 98–9.

line and trench wherein we attacked them, coming to push of pike and handy blows in several places'.[88] Dumbarton's Regiment was the first in, with Ross writing, 'This day the Scots and their grenadiers charged first, if there was any time at all between their charging: for, like fire and lightning, all went on at once', while on the right the Guards 'charged and drove back the Moors from the ground whereupon they had planted their guns.[89] The grenadiers, with Captain Hodges (who had led his men with effectively on 23 September) carrying a firelock and bag of grenades charging at their head, oversaw the bombing of the trenches from traverse to traverse, and when they ran short of explosives, his soldiers laid about the Moors with their hatchets.

The sheer persistence, resourcefulness and fighting performance of both officers and other ranks during this assault was further attested to by the commanding officer of Dumbarton's Regiment (since the death of the Earl of Plymouth on 17 October), Major Halkett. He wrote:

> Our detachments in platoons being ordered to fall on to attack the several places that was designed, Captain Fortrey, that commanded the detachment of Guards with the half of the company of grenadiers of Dumbarton's Regiment commanded by Lieutenant McKraken having bravely advanced near to the place of arms where they had the piece of cannon, the enemy being strong in guard there, made great fire so that they killed several of the grenadiers and of Fortrey's detachment, so that the men did shrink and retire towards the fort, the 150 men that sallied out of Pole Fort commanded by Captains Lundy and Hume that was ordered to attack their advanced trench, finding likewise great resistance there, and both the captains being wounded very soon in the beginning, and carried off, upon this the detachment retired towards the fort, our right hand being put in this condition merely be[ing] the fault of the battalion of the Guards that did not move at a fit distance with Fortrey's detachment to keep their men in countenance, I, who had charge and management of the attack on the left hand their place of arms, at Monmouth Fort, with our two battalions and the battalion of seamen, I commanded Captain Melville with his detachment and the other half of our company of grenadiers to fall on and attack the place of arms, I moving at a just distance to him with our battalions beside, I prayed Captain Coy, that was upon the left hand of all with his troop, to advance towards the place of arms at a soft gallop. This encouraged our detachment so that they immediately fell into the place of arms with the Moors, and the Moors seeing our battalions so near with Coy's troop of horse they ran, so we were masters of it, with little loss. Captain Lockhart, who commanded the detachment of our first battalion, seeing Captain Fortrey's men in disorder and likewise the 150 men that sallied out of Pole Fort, he very opportunely fell in upon their trench on the left hand of their piece of cannon in the place of arms, where they continued disputing the business hotly till Lieutenant McCracken who had kept his grenadiers together and seeing all things going well on the left hand at Monmouth Fort, he advanced again to the place of arms so near as to bestow his grenades amongst them which he did liberally, and being followed with Captain Fortrey and them that sallied out

88 *Ibid.*

89 Ross, *Tangers Rescue.*

> of the fort advanced again, then the battalion of guards began to move. Lieutenant McCracken seeing the disorder he had put amongst them with his grenades fell in amongst them, and being followed by Captain Fortrey, the Moors ran and left our men masters of the place of arms.[90]

Having carried the position, the entire Anglo-Scots formation advanced beyond the Moor's new trenches and into the old ones, along a line adjacent to the demolished James and Monmouth Forts. Barely conscious, Sir Palmes Fairborne was carried in a chair to the ramparts of the Upper Castle to witness the final phase of the battle. He died soon after receiving news of victory. Paradoxically, he was appointed governor and colonel of the Tangier Regiment on 10 November 1680, 14 days after his death. Major Boynton and Sir James Leslie were commissioned Lieutenant Colonel and Major of the same regiment.[91] Henry Sheres, who knew Fairborne well, described him as 'a worthy, brave and able officer, who had made it his special study to qualify himself for his Majesty's service here where he had been an officer for near eighteen years, and I am obliged in justice to his memory to aver that (I believe at least) his Majesty had not a subject in his three kingdoms of more proper qualification for this post'.[92] Moreover, Ross attributed to Sir Palmes an elaborately composed farewell speech, although the accurateness of this remains doubtful.[93] Of the closing stages of the desperate encounter on 27 October 1680, Sheres recorded:

> The particularities of every action that occurred is hard to set down, but after we had beaten them from their new trenches and were advanced to the old line whereon our forts formerly stood (which was attained with great loss on our side) one of the battalions of my Lord Inchiquin's Regiment [Old Tangier] having not above 50 men left upon the spot, at length by levelling the trenches we made a passage for our horse (without whose assistance nothing memorable would have been performed) through which Captain Neatby with his troop advanced upon the enemy, as did likewise Don Salvador de Monforte and Don Manrique de Moronia with theirs, who found a passage a little more to the right, upon which the enemy turned their backs and betook themselves to flight from all quarters, being pursued by both horse and foot who made very great slaughter amongst them. Many of their horse performed very daringly for the rescue of their foot, amongst which several of their principal men likewise fell. We pursued them, scattered like sheep on the mountains at least a mile into the country, killing several of them in their very camp among their tents.[94]

By mid afternoon, the fighting was all but over, and the remaining soldiers of the Tangier garrison retired unmolested into the city in good order. But

90 Halkett, 'Account', pp. 15–16.

91 TNA, SP44/164, fol. 54; *CSPD 1680–81*, p. 84

92 TNA, CO 279/26, fol. 98.

93 Ross, *Tangers Rescue*, pp. 19–20.

94 TNA, CO 279/26, fols 98–9. See also *Particular Narrative*, pp. 3–4, which repeats the same text almost exactly.

although this operation – alongside that of the previous month – can be seen as a tremendous achievement, the recovery of the vitally important Pole Fort and the carrying of all the forward positions of the enemy were 'the only significant successes gained by the Tangier garrison since Teviot's time and demonstrated that British discipline and firepower were usually decisive in the open field. For too long they had allowed their opponents to dictate tactics'.[95] After the battle, Lieutenant Colonel Sackville ordered that any enemy dead not been buried in the levelled trenches should be conveyed to the palisade at Catherina Port. The remains of about 40 were brought, and the governor wrote to the Qā'id Omar, inviting him to carry them away, and expressed regret for 'their heads being all cut off, wherein no order whatsoever could restrain the soldiers, many of their comrades having been formerly treated with the like barbarity'. The apology was received by the Moorish leader without mention, but he reciprocated by sending the bodies of three or four of the English dead to the garrison.[96]

Prior to the action, the Moors had numbered approximately 3,000 troops, and were estimated to have lost between 500–600 and 2,000 men, although Sackville afterwards thought their casualties were perhaps about 1,000, 'besides *Mounteniers* [Berbers] which they do not reckon'.[97] Garrison losses were no less substantial. Between 20 September and 27 October 1680, the garrison sustained between 600 and 700 killed and wounded in the fighting. The battlefield performance of the Tangier garrison during this and previous actions is best summarised by Childs:

> Little more could have been asked of the fighting troops. They acquitted themselves bravely and kept good discipline on the battlefield, even if their behaviour when off duty left much to be desired. The same was true of the junior officers. When in action they accomplished all that was demanded of them, and during the actions of 1675 and 1680 they commanded with a diligence and a professionalism that was a credit to the army. Blame for the repeated military failures at Tangier must be laid at the feet of the senior officers.[98]

The most detailed casualty list from the 'day of the great sally' was published in the pamphlet *Particular Narrative*:

List of the Killed and Wounded

The King's Battalion
Lieutenant Robinson shot through the arm and body; seven private soldiers killed and 51 wounded.

Dumbarton's Regiment
Captain Forbes killed three days before this action.

95 John Childs, *General Percy Kirke and the Later Stuart Army* (London: Bloomsbury, 2014), p. 36.
96 Halkett, 'Account', pp. 18–19.
97 TNA, CO 279/26, fol. 100.
98 Childs, *Army of Charles II*, p. 150.

Wounded
Captain Julius Lockhart
Captain Robert Lundy
Captain George Hume
Captain Robert Douglas
Captain James Fortrey
Lieutenant Scott killed

Wounded
Lieutenant William Guscott
Lieutenant George Murray
Lieutenant Alexander Ennis
Lieutenant Charles Corson
Lieutenant George Bainesman
Lieutenant James MacRoben
Lieutenant James Stuart
Lieutenant John Aukmooty
Lieutenant Gilbert Butler

Killed
Ensign Daniel Farrell
Ensign Archibald Murray

Wounded
Ensign John Mowatt

Reformed Officers Killed
Lieutenant Alexander St Leger
Ensign John Bell
Ensign Henry Rue

Six sergeants killed and mortally wounded; 30 private soldiers killed, 100 wounded.

The Tangier Regiment
Wounded
Captain Philpott dangerously wounded in the knee
Lieutenant Guy
Lieutenant Tate
Ensign Roberts dangerously wounded in the thigh
Ensign Thomas
Ensign Fitzpatrick
Ensign Webster
Ensign Norwood
Ensign Beckford
Ensign Elliot

Killed
Ensign Watson
Ensign Trant

34 private soldiers killed, 124 wounded

Vice-Admiral Herbert's Battalion
Killed
Captain Dungeon
Lieutenant White

10 private soldiers killed; 2 sergeants and 22 private soldiers wounded.

The Spanish Horse
In the troop of Don Salvador de Monforte, his cornet and two others killed; three reformed officers and 17 private soldiers wounded; twelve horses killed, and as many wounded.

Don Antonio Penatelo's Troop
Two private soldiers killed, and three wounded; three horses killed, and three wounded.

The Two Troops of Don Manrique de Moronia
The lieutenant, cornet and a reformed officer wounded; 9 10 private soldiers killed and 10 killed; eight horses killed, and eight wounded.

English Horse
In Captain Neatby's Troops, Lieutenant Capel wounded in the right arm; Cornet Windham shot in the right arm, which is cut off; 5 private soldiers wounded; nine horses wounded, and five killed.

In all, seven commissioned officers killed.

Wounded, whereof many mortally, 24.

Non-commissioned officers and private soldiers, 90 killed.

Wounded, whereof a third part mortally, 348.

Horses killed 41, wounded 54.

Following the expiration of the truce with the Moors in September 1680, and in anticipation of renewed hostilities, measures were taken to send further reinforcements to Tangier, and to furnish supplies. Hence, following various delays, the Earl of Plymouth's Regiment, led in person by the veteran, Major Charles Trelawney, left from Plymouth aboard the *Newcastle*, and arrived at Tangier on 28 December 1680. Their month-long voyage had been a terrible one, and pounded by strong gales and mountainous seas, one officer and 50 men died of sickness or accident.[99] The regiment did not learn of its colonel's recent death from dysentery until it arrived. Nevertheless, these new troops were led by officers of proven ability and combat experience (including several officers and a few veterans of the Duke of Monmouth's 'Holland Regiment'), who brought with them proficiency, motivation, and a renewed fighting spirit. Regiments such as Plymouth's had been partially or fully equipped for war before embarking. Warrants issued to the Ordnance Commissioners, ordering them to supply arms from the Tower Stores to regiments that had previously sent drafts of soldiers to Tangier, provide a clue to how those troops were equipped. One dated 30 November 1680, recites:

> that, since the late order for delivering arms for the 600 recruits lately ordered to be raised, the King has been given to understand that it is necessary that arms should be delivered for 24 soldiers more for Colonel John Russell's Regiment of Foot Guards, and for seven more of the Coldstream Regiment, for the complete arming of these two regiments in regard of private soldiers advanced to be sergeants and corporals to go with the drafts to Tangier, for causing arms to be delivered for 24 and seven soldiers more accordingly in the usual proportions of snaphance and matchlock muskets and pikes with collars of bandoliers to the firearms.

Similarly, on 10 December 49 pikes, 40 snaphance muskets and 38 matchlock muskets, with 78 collars of bandoliers 'instead of the foot arms for 127 soldiers lately ordered to be delivered in the usual proportions' were delivered to Major Thomas Mansfield of the Coldstream Regiment, 'it appearing by his certificate that such were the arms wanting for the 127 soldiers recruited in lieu of those sent to Tangier'. Three days later, the Commissioners were ordered to issue to Thomas Jones, Quartermaster of Colonel John Russell's Foot Guards, 132 snaphance muskets, 44 matchlocks, 176 collars of bandoliers, 88 pikes and three drums 'instead of the arms formerly directed to be delivered in lieu of those sent to Tangier'. The original document is endorsed by the Major of the regiment, who noted that such were the arms that had been sent to Tangier with the King's Battalion in July 1680.[100] On 30 December 1680 a warrant was issued by the Treasury in London for the transportation of 1,000 pair of shoes and 1,000 pair of stockings for the supply of Colonel Kirke's Regiment.[101]

---

99 SRO, D(W) 1778/I/i/562–3.
100 TNA, SP44/59, fols 77, 79, 82.
101 TNA, SP44/69, fol. 66; *CTB*, VI, p. 784.

11

Final Days and Diplomacy, 1681–83

Given the scepticism with which the affairs of Tangier were seen in Parliament, and despite some exaggerated accounts of the recent fighting (intended to foster political and popular support for the venture), the plight of the garrison was an increasingly desperate one. On 1 March 1681, the Duke of Ormond wrote to Secretary Jenkins:

> I knew no way so likely to recruit the remaining companies of the Scotch Regiment [Dumbarton's], having no advance money to give the officers, than to allow them full pay, though their effective men were few, on which encouragement the lieutenant colonel has been long in Scotland to raise men, and I doubt the fear of being sent to Tangier is the cause that men come not in to this service, which in all other respects is as good, at least to common men, as most in Christendom, and I fear it may also obstruct the recruits his Majesty designs out of England for his army here, whereof a more particular account shall be shortly given.[1]

A few days later, it was reported from Tangier, 'there has been much sickness since the engagement amongst the soldiers, near 500 being dead, the garrison otherwise in good plight'.[2] Between December 1682 and December 1683, the number of men in Tangier decreased by one-third from 3,411 to 2,299.[3] Moreover, estimates made by Beckman indicated that the cost of refortifying the garrison would be between £2,000,000 and £3,000,000, and would necessitate a garrison of 8,000–10,000 men.[4] In September 1680, Charles II sent a letter to Qā'id Omar ben Haddū Al-Hamāmi, who had led the fighting against the garrison of Tangier, expressing his wish for a peace treaty and intention to despatch an ambassador for that purpose. In reply, the Moorish commander stated:

1 *CSPD 1680–1*, p. 198.
2 *Ibid.*, p. 200.
3 UY, MS 2572, fols 296–9; Davis, *Second Queen's Regiment*, I, p. 261.
4 TNA, CO 279/26, fol. 183. Beckman to Sunderland, 29 October 1680.

> I received the letter of your royal Majesty of the 14th of September, which I am much pleased with and do greatly esteem it, I am in the Court of Meknès with the King my Master, whom God preserve, and your Majesty advising me that you have great friendship for me … as soon as I received your Majesty's letter, I went from the Court to the camp of Tangier, and being arrived, quitted the war between the Moors and your Majesty's subjects of Tangier, in consideration of your Majesty's letter, and they of Tangier desiring me to give them peace for six months in consideration of the said letter I complied with all they desired, and have given it to them under my hand, and will fulfil all that I have said to your Majesty and to those of Tangier. For the war between the Moors and those of Tangier, I was not present, but those of Tangier went out and would build on the ground of the Moors, and this was the cause of making the war.[5]

A six-month truce was concluded by Lieutenant Colonel Edward Sackville on 25 November 1680.[6] But although he was an experienced officer, who had arrived at Tangier in charge of the King's Battalion, Sackville made the mistake of apprising the Moors of the considerable English losses in the recent fighting. Thus, he was severely criticised by Major Halkett, commanding officer of Dumbarton's Regiment, in particular. This caused the garrison's officers to fragment into 'peace' and 'war' factions at a time when considerable unity was essential.[7] Sackville was further reproached by Sir James Leslie, the ambassador-designate to Fés, who had arrived in Tangier who had arrived in the convoy with Plymouth's Regiment. Leslie had been a surprising choice, because he had at one time served as a private in the Tangier Horse. Within days of his arrival Sir James was demanding that Lieutenant Colonel Sackville provide written reasons for agreeing to a treaty, which he 'would never have condescended to'. But Sackville strongly believed that the garrison was too weak to participate in another series of encounters, and that to expect additional reinforcements was naïve. In January 1681, in a letter addressed to the Committee for the Affairs of Tangier, he wrote:

> I know not whether it has been the interest or error, or both, in my predecessors, who have charmed the ministers at home into so low an opinion of these people, that we make no account of them. But my Lords I think I may modestly say I have practised them both in war and peace, since I have had the honour to command in chief, more than any who have gone before me – and I must ingeniously avere, that I think this belief hath been of great prejudice to his Majesty's service. To speak of them as enemies, I never saw men bolder in the field when they find it reasonable to fight, nor more prudent to avoid it, when it was wisdom to decline it; nor is there I believe in the whole race of mankind a more vigilant, hardy, patient and laborious people, all qualities necessary to a soldier – inasmuch as had they the discipline of Europe, there would not be a more formidable enemy in the world.

5 *Ibid.*, fols 236–8. Qā'id Omar ben Haddū Al-Hamāmi to Charles II, 29 November 1680.
6 *Ibid.*, fols 252–5; BL, MS Add. 17021, fol. 49.
7 Halkett, 'Account', pp. 21–2; Ross, *Tangers Rescue*, p. 31.

> In their treaties they discourse, and debate matters calmly and judiciously, and therefore I see not where the reason of this contempt of them lies.[8]

The acting governor's appeal for a prudent, critical evaluation of the somewhat biased information about the Moors conveyed in both official correspondence and contemporary pamphlets is important, because it reveals a particular disparity between the first-hand assessments of soldiers who were experiencing regular battlefield encounters with them, and corresponding images in print, largely produced for the home market.

Wenceslaus Hollar, Mawaly Ismāʿīl, Sultan of Morocco (c. 1669). (University of Toronto, The Wenceslaus Hollar Collection, Creative Commons Public Domain)

Peace with the Moors seemed the only logical course of action. As Childs asserts, 'In his first independent command, Sackville had emerged as an effective and pragmatic leader, and his approach probably influenced Kirke's subsequent governorship. He showed self-assurance, and the strength of character to risk unpopularity by discounting the opinions of the majority of his colleagues, and acted promptly and decisively'.[9] The new peace treaty stipulated that fortification outside the walls of Tangier was to be suspended. In return for an annual supply of ammunition to the Moors, the garrison was allowed freedom of commerce and admittance to grazing land outside the walls. By 10 March 1681 Mawaly Ismāʿīl, the Sultan of Morocco, was preparing to take the field against his nephew, Mawaly Hamet, governor of the southern province of Sous, as part of his consolidation of the region. However, he undertook talks with Colonel Percy Kirke and Leslie although Ismāʿīl would assent to no further concessions, he reluctantly offered a four-year cease-fire based on the conditions of the truce. This was signed on 29 March.[10]

At this juncture, Charles II appealed to the House of Commons for further assistance, but though the Parliament of 1679 had professed inordinate anxiety on behalf of Tangier, even then there had been very little, if any, concern for the maintenance of the colony for its own sake. The only aim of the House had been to prevent its loss to the French. The remark by the republican MP, Sir Thomas Player, 'Hang Tangier!', indicated the opinion of the majority.[11] The latest agreement with the Moors was followed by a frustrating succession

8 Quoted in P. G. Rogers, *A History of Anglo-Moroccan Relations to 1900* (London: Foreign and Commonwealth Office, 1977), p. 54.

9 Childs, 'Percy Kirke', p. 37.

10 TNA, CO 279/27, fols 207–11. Peace concluded between Sir James Leslie and the Alcaid Omar Benhadu el hamany, on behalf of King Charles II and the Emperor Mawaly Ismāʿīl, 29 March 1681; *CSPD 1680–81*, p. 33.

11 *CSPD 1680–81*, p. 178.

of disputes on every point of its terms, while the maintenance of peace with the Moroccan government was made more difficult by the capitulation of the Spanish citadel of La Mamora to a considerable Moorish army early in May 1681. Following a gallant defence, the governor was received by Governor Kirke at Tangier on his journey to Cadiz. Boosted by his success, Ismā'īl bragged that he could seize Tangier in one night if he wished. This encouraged his troops, who increased their harassment of the garrison. On 4 June Colonel Percy Kirke reported:

> They are very high upon the taking of Mamora, and the guards were too saucy and strict to their Articles, I was forced to complain to the Alcayde, who has given better order and more liberty, we forage every day some three miles from the town, and the Moors cut us grass and bring it into the town where we make hay of it. I hope the wants of the garrison are well supplied from home, for though the Moors have made a peace for four years, and may keep their words, yet they are Moors and not to be trusted too far, and the better condition our garrison is in, the better their peace will be kept.[12]

Colonel Boynton, of the Old Tangier regiment, wrote at the same time, 'I must confess, ere jealousy our subtle Alcayde Omar hopes to lull us into false security that his Majesty may withdraw or lessen his troops here, when he will take any slight occasion of breaking with us, for there is no credit or trust to be given to his honour where there is the prospect of so vast an advantage that would accrue to him by the surprisal of this place'.[13]

Soon afterwards, a Moorish prince or *Sharif*, who, having quarrelled with the Sultan, took refuge at Tangier, where he was accommodated for a time by Kirke. The latter observed drolly, 'In all his behaviour and discourse he appears extravagant even to a degree of madness, which is a true character of a prince of the Morocco family and one of the best arguments that he is of the royal blood'.[14] Potentially, however, this presented an advantageous opportunity to the Tangier garrison. The government in England believed that such a hostage might be utilised, and Kirke was directed 'to demand all such fugitives as have deserted his Majesty's service and are fled from the said garrison into the Emperor's dominions', but a few days before receiving the order, in fear of inciting war, he surrendered the prince, who expressed his wish to return to the Moorish Court.[15] In early May 1681 Sackville and Leslie returned to England, the former in poor health. Kirke succeeded Sackville as acting governor and was transferred from the colonelcy of the 2nd Tangier Regiment to the Old Tangier Regiment on 19 April 1681. Four days later, Kirke's friend, Charles Trelawney, was promoted to colonel of the 2nd Regiment, whilst Kirke was confirmed as governor on 26 January the following year. Despite Mawaly Ismā'īl's abhorrence of foreigners, during

12 TNA, CO 279/28, fols 8–10. Kirke to Jenkins, 4 June 1681.
13 *Ibid.*, fol. 7. Boynton to Jenkins, 3 June 1681.
14 *Ibid.*, fols 191–2. Kirke to Jenkins, 8 September 1681.
15 *Ibid.*, fol. 272. Order in Council, 14 October 1681.

the negotiations he took a liking for Kirke, and swore 'there never would be bullet shot against Tangier, as long as Kirke was in it'.[16]

To most contemporary Christians, the Sultan was a 'vicious, blood-thirsty, tyrannical, capricious thug and slave-master, whose rule relied upon murder, terror and sadistic violence'.[17] One member of the Colonel's delegation to Meknès and Fès remarked, 'He excels all mankind in barbarous and bloody actions, massacre and murder being his royal game and divertisement, which, that it may not cloy his Majesty in one kind, he invents every day a new pastime of cruelty'.[18] But, although extremely potent, Ismāʿīl was little different to other rulers in North Africa during this period, Nonetheless, he and Colonel Kirke exchanged gifts in the form of Barbary horses and cattle, in return for some Irish greyhounds. But in the negotiations for the release of prisoners from his *bagnio* in Meknès, which was reputed to hold at least 30,000 slaves, including 2,500 Christians and 70 English soldiers, prisoners of war from the garrison of Tangier – many from Dumbarton's Regiment, who were eagerly waiting in hope of redemption. But only a few could ever be redeemed from their terrible fate.[19] Though Mawaly Ismāʿīl demanded too high a price for their ransom, after 1680 all captives seized by Moroccan Corsairs had become the Sultan's property, and European States were no longer permitted to redeem nationals on an individual or group basis. Instead, they had to pay for their entire captives detained in Morocco at any given time.

Besides, England's treaty with Algiers in 1682 stipulated that its inhabitants were not liable 'against their wills, to set any [slaves] at liberty', and that the English State was under no obligation to ransom its subjects. Such terms help to explain why England had a reputation in Barbary for being less forthcoming than other states in its response to its captives. In 1674, the governor of Algiers protested to Charles II that an earlier arrangement to redeem the city's English captives had still not been honoured.[20] Most of Ismāʿīl's European slaves were employed on building projects – gruelling work, quarrying or stone-breaking, with hardly a moment's breather in which to rest or eat their scanty allowance of barley bread. This often so black and sour that even dogs would not touch it. At night they were lodged under a strong guard in the most wretched conditions imaginable, while the chances of escaping were extremely slim.[21] But the English in Tangier hardly behaved well toward Muslim captives, whom they put to work before transporting them away. While in Tangier, Pepys heard about how poorly they were treated by Admiral Herbert, who starved 100 'Turks and Moors', even though he had

16 HMC, *Tenth Report, App. IV*, p. 175.

17 Childs, 'Percy Kirke', p. 38.

18 *The Last Account from Fez, in a letter from one of the Embassy*, p. 2, in Bejjit, *English Colonial Texts*, pp. 201–6.

19 TNA, CO 279/29, fols 88–9. Kirke's report, 23 February 1682; *CSPD 1680–81*, p. 277.

20 Colley, *Captives*, pp. 45–6; G. E. Aylmer, 'Slavery under Charles II: The Mediterranean and Tangier', *EHR*, 114 (1999), pp. 378–88 (p. 380).

21 Thomas Phelps, *A True Account of the Captivity of Thomas Phelps at Machaness in Barbary* (London: Joseph Hindmarsh, 1685), p. 503.

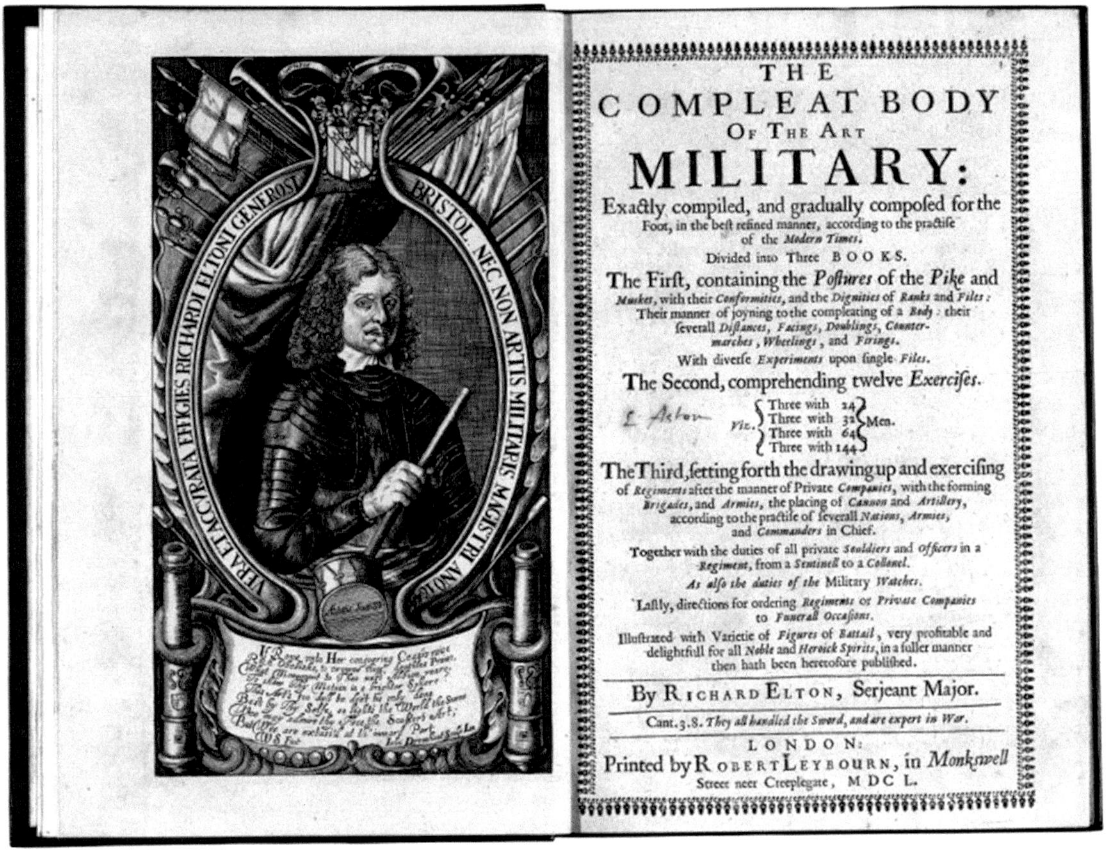

THE
COMPLEAT BODY
OF THE ART
MILITARY:
Exactly compiled, and gradually composed for the Foot, in the best refined manner, according to the practise of the *Modern Times*.
Divided into Three BOOKS.
The First, containing the *Postures* of the *Pike* and *Musket*, with their *Conformities*, and the *Dignities* of *Ranks* and *Files*: Their manner of joyning to the compleating of a *Body*: their severall *Distances*, *Facings*, *Doublings*, *Counter-marches*, *Wheelings*, and *Firings*.
With diverse *Experiments* upon single *Files*.
The Second, comprehending twelve *Exercises*.
Viz. Three with 24, Three with 32, Three with 64, Three with 144 Men.
The Third, setting forth the drawing up and exercising of *Regiments* after the manner of Private *Companies*, with the forming *Brigades*, and *Armies*, the placing of *Cannon* and *Artillery*, according to the practise of severall *Nations*, *Armies*, and *Commanders* in Chief.
Together with the duties of all private *Souldiers* and *Officers* in a *Regiment*, from a *Sentinell* to a *Collonel*.
As also the duties of the Military *Watches*.
Lastly, directions for ordering *Regiments* or *Private Companies* to *Funerall Occasions*.
Illustrated with Varietie of *Figures* of *Battail*, very profitable and delightfull for all *Noble* and *Heroick Spirits*, in a fuller manner then hath been heretofore published.
By RICHARD ELTON, Serjeant Major.
Cant. 3. 8. *They all handled the Sword, and are expert in War.*
LONDON:
Printed by ROBERT LEYBOURN, in *Monkswell* Street neer Creeplegate, M DC L.

Richard Elton, *The Complete Body of the Art Military* (1668). (Creative Commons Public Domain)

hung up 'for the Turks to see' the allowance of victuals they were permitted. Another 500 slaves had reportedly succumbed to famine.[22]

Despite Mawaly Ismā'īl's vows of eternal comradeship, Colonel Kirke, who was to be one of the most effective governors of Tangier, did not trust him, and held the garrison in a state of constant military readiness. Out of a total of some 1,200 to 1,400 men, 400 would be on guard each night, and no soldier was ever allowed more than three nights' sleep, 'lest he should fall into idle ways'. The Castle, built on rock some 200 feet above sea level, was strongly fortified and in good repair, but only three of the numerous forts built upon the surrounding sandhills remained in English hands. York Castle housed the ammunition stores, carried by garrison troops from the Water Gate, where the provisions were unloaded from the supply vessels. Kirke, who built upon the measures imposed by Fairborne, issued detailed standing orders, which significantly improved the discipline and effectiveness of the garrison. At 6:00 a.m. or 6:30 a.m. (depending on the season) the drummers of the governor's own company beat the reveille, before the drums of the others took up the call to sound the 'Assembly'. Each regiment mustered at the Old Parade adjacent to York Castle, where an ensign or lieutenant would exercise them for an hour. Three days a week (Tuesdays, Wednesdays, and

22 *Tangier Papers*, pp. 209, 225.

Fridays), the adjutant of the Governor's Regiment came down to the Parade, and detailed soldiers for guard duties and working parties.

On the other three days (Sunday being a rest day), after regimental prayers, a formal garrison parade was held in the marketplace. Soldiers were exercised by two captains – drill movements, including marching, countermarching, and doubling of ranks and files, together with the specific postures required by divisions of pike and shot, as well as the grenadiers. Regiments 'stood to' at dawn and dusk, and at intervals the field officer of the day checked all sentry posts and patrols, which moved around the boundaries every two hours, and made sure the password of the day was universally known. There were also two-hourly patrols for the Horse around the perimeter of the outer defences.[23] Moreover, a system of special flag, bell, or drum signals was instituted for different contingencies. The sentry on Peterborough Tower was to raise a blue flag if a party of 10 or more of the enemy on foot was spotted; for similar parties of horse a red one; and if 'he perceive them to increase numerous', he was to hoist 'the great flag, not taking in the other two'. For shipping he was to run up three balls, depending on their numbers, and the 'great flag' signalled that they were proceeding towards the city. The alarm was to be given by the great bell in the tower, taken up by the drums of every foot company. In case of surprise anyone could fire three shots in succession, on hearing which, all members of the garrison were to respond as if the bell had pealed. Distinctive signals existed for calling individual military units: 10 bell rings for the King's Battalion; 20 for Dumbarton's Regiment; 30 for the Tangier Regiment, 40 for Trelawney's; and a separate bell for gunners. This scheme was practiced regularly, to avoid confusion.[24]

In similar fashion, Kirk appointed the garrison and the town militia to their alarm posts, which were at Peterborough Tower, Lawson's Battery, Johnson's Battery, the Irish Battery, Catherina Port, the Old Parade, and the Spur without the Castle. The ready ammunition placed at these key positions was, at Peterborough Tower: 2 barrels of powder, 450 hand grenades, 1½ cwt of match, and 3 cwt of musket shot; at Lawson's Battery: ½ cwt of match and 1 cwt of musket shot; at Johnson's Battery: 950 grenades; at the Irish Battery: ½ barrel of powder and ½ cwt of match; at Catherina Port: 750 grenades, 1½ cwt of powder, ½ cwt of match and 1 cwt of musket shot; the Old Parade: 200 grenades, ½ cwt of match, 2 cwt of musket shot and ½ cwt of powder; and at the Spur: 150 grenades, ½ cwt of match and 1½ cwt of powder.[25] Additionally, In September 1683 Pepys described being shown 'some hand grenades shot off and flung about 300 yards off with an instrument lately invented for that use'. [26] In 1682 the garrison's soldiers were gathered from billets dispersed across the city into new barracks created within the Upper

23 SRO, D(W) 1778/I/i/958. Orders to the Tangier Garrison from Governor Kirke, n.d.

24 HMC, *Eleventh Report, App. V*, I, p. 79. Methods observed in his Majesty's garrison of Tangier whilst under the command of his Excellency Colonel Percy Kirke [1682?].

25 SRO, D742/0/3/13. Account of stores and ammunition to be shipped and to remain at alarm posts, 1683.

26 *Tangier Papers*, p. 28.

Castle, complaining of 'the decayed state of their quarters'.[27] Moreover, on 19 October it was reported, 'Here is a most miserable complaint for want of beds, the soldiers lying merely on the boards; as for the Lord Dumbarton's they have none because the first they had here [were] made of straw, and the rest of the regiments are spoiled by having so many sick men'.[28]

During the early months of the English occupation there was a deficiency of 2,000 beds, although later, beds and bedding were sent to Tangier in various quantities. In January 1675 350 flock-beds (canvas mattresses filled with flocks or locks of coarse wool, or pieces of cloth cut up fine), quilts, rugs and blankets, with 500 pairs of sheets arrived on the *Chichley*. By order in council of 6 April 1677, the Lord Treasurer was ordered to permit the transportation to Tangier of 500 loads of oak and 500 flock beds for the use of the Mole there.[29] On 22 June 1680, 221 flock-beds, 830 quilts, 320 bolsters, 669 rugs, 442 blankets and 860 pillows were accounted for in the garrison stores, and when Plymouth's Regiment was sent from England in late 1680 it brought with it beds and bedding for its 16 companies.[30] During this period it was usual to allot two soldiers to a bed. In December 1688 the Mayor of Portsmouth reported that there were 150 beds in the barracks, and that he had requested Colonel Reresby to send 300 men to quarter in the said beds, although the officer replied that it was inconvenient to put any soldiers into the barracks until they were finished. Moreover, in the same year, the Surgeon-General of navy and land forces, James Pearse, reported that two London hospitals contained beds for 90 patients to lie single, 'but they being pretty large, as men grow into a state of recovery, they may lie two on a bed so that hospitals will always receive above 100 persons'.[31]

No special provision was made aboard ships for the soldiers and civilians brought back from Tangier. On 15 November 1683 the Customs Commissioners at Gravesend were instructed to pass customs free 'the bedding, clothes and other goods of the soldiers or the inhabitants come from Tangier on the *Unity*', although this may have been an exception as this was a hospital ship.[32] Hammocks had to be improvised in some vessels by the cutting up of sailcloth. On 10 December 1665 Colonel Norwood had bought 100 of them for soldiers sent to the colony. Daniel Furzer, Bristol sailmaker, contracted with the Navy Commissioners in March 1666 to provide hammocks of 'good English sailcloth, 6 foot long, at 3s. each'. Similarly, such items were purchased for between 1s, 2d. and 2s. 4d., while John Harris provided 1,500 hammocks for the fleet at 1s. 8d. each.[33] Between October 1683 and January 1684, in preparation for the evacuation of Tangier, the storekeeper, William Smith, was ordered by Colonel Kirke to issue a total of 12,052 biscuit bags, to be utilised as hammocks – 5,072 for the foot

27 SRO, D742/O/3/8. Estimate of materials required for repair of quarters, 1682; HMC, *Eleventh Report, App. V*, I, p. 77. Kirke to Legge, 5 October 1682.
28 HMC, *Eleventh Report, App. V*, I, p. 77. Povey to Ordnance Office, 19 October 1682.
29 TNA, SP44/5, fols 275–6; WO 4/1, fol. 57; *CTB*, IV, p. 693; VI, p. 101.
30 SRO, D742/0/3/6; TNA, SP44/65, fols 19–20.
31 HMC, *Eleventh Report, App. V*, I, p. 244; III, p. 145.
32 TNA, SP44/7, fols 337–8; *CTB*, VII, p. 952.
33 *CSPD 1665–6*, pp. 132–3; *1666*, p. 286.

Colonel Percy Kirke (*c.* 1646–1691). (Creative Commons Public Domain)

(including a single issue of 465 bags to Kirke's own regiment), and 6,980 for the Mole workers. Another, unspecified quantity of biscuit bags was supplied to the Horse for carrying straw.[34]

Governor Kirke, with the consent of the Tangier Committee, also addressed the more immediate consequences of the garrison's pay arrears by requisitioning money from local agents for pay to his troops, and to alleviate the lack of money in the city. He also endeavoured to increase the health of the soldiers by allotting a cook to each company, and attempted to unearth additional resource for the hospital and veterans returning to England, advising that they be allocated to garrison companies.[35] As Childs observes, 'Kirke demonstrated a degree of care and consideration for the common

34 SRO, D742/0/3/37–47.

35 UY, MS 2572, fols 254–7, 266–7, 277–8.

soldier rare among his contemporaries'.[36] Even so, he was probably the most colourful and controversial governor of Tangier. While an energetic, capable, and highly experienced officer, who was enormously popular with his men, Kirke flouted the law and profited from all transactions in the colony through tariffs, which rendered it useless as a trading centre. This caused many civilians to leave, while soldiers absconded and joined the Moorish army.

After reaching Tangier in 1683, Pepys heard from naval officers that English seamen in the station had grown unruly for lack of pay, and 'if a master do not humour them, they will ordinarily turn papists, thereby to make the master by the Church to be forced to pay them their wages, and it may be in two or three months become a protestant again when they come to another port'.[37] Soldiers and sailors were also known to have 'turned Turks' (converted to Islam), following their desertion. Pepys, who held Kirke in contempt, was infuriated that he had also banished Jews from Tangier, writing:

> Du Pas tells me of Kirke's having banished the Jews without, or rather contrary to, express orders from England, only because of their denying him, or standing in the way of, private profits. He made a poor Jew and his wife, that came out of Spain to avoid the Inquisition, be carried back, swearing they should be burned; and they were carried to the Inquisition and burned ... Everything runs to corruption here.

Pepys also regarded Kirke to be the most foul-mouthed man he had ever met, and condemned the drunken and dissolute way of life which the governor both tolerated and practised in Tangier, as well as 'his exactions on poor merchants, letting nothing be sold till he had the refusal'.

When in March 1681 the English embassy to Mawaly Ismā'īl resulted in a peace treaty – although Kirke and Leslie raised objections to its terms – a promise was obtained from the Sultan that he would dispatch an ambassador to London, with plenary powers to amend any of its conditions. As a way of confirming the peace treaty and introducing the Moroccan ambassador, Ismā'īl wrote the following letter to King Charles:

> From the servant of the high God, Governor over all people, Ismā'īl Keriffe, overflowing with good deeds, he, though high, demands of the Most High God and the Angels, but of none other, he that hath millions of horse at his command. Sends peace unto you that follow the truth. We have understood by the way of Tangier, that we are in perfect friendship and that peace is concluded over all our countries, and, therefore, the letter we send is to confirm this peace and the treaty we have made with you, for we have a desire to trade with you, but let us not make the same terms that we had in the beginning of the war, wherein so many dyed by the sword when we were enemies, but let our enemies dye. We, therefore, have slain such as have run away from you to us, but you have not done the same, for the second act, that if any renegado shall run from us to Tangier you shall be obliged to send them

36 Childs, 'Percy Kirke', p. 45.

37 *Tangier Papers*, pp. 16, 30, 97, 100–2.

> back again. And for your security in this treaty, we send you our servant, Hada, for the management of it. And our will is that it shall be like the things that begin to grow. And I, who am the tree itself, have sent you one of my servants (being a branch of myself) which I recommend to you as if it were the tree itself. And we have strictly charged him what he shall say unto you. Look upon him as you would do upon myself. That which he shall do shall be well done and you shall value it as a gem from heaven. We heartily desire you to write to us, for neither our habits nor our customs are like yours, but if you will build anything upon our ground we will pull it down and we shall do ourselves right. Also, we have amongst us some Christians, who understand themselves and are more esteemed than our own servants. They have eagle's eyes, but hate us and our belief, and thereupon are a scandal to us. He that values our honour, honours God. And because it is our desire you should receive something from us, we send you 30 ostriches out of the deserts, and we expect that you should furnish us with 6,000 pieces of eight yearly. As for Tangier we stand in no manner of fear of it. And after the ratification of the peace, all hostility shall cease. Ismā'īl son of the beloved Keriffe, descended from God.[38]

But the Sultan prevaricated, and the ambassador to England, Mohamed ben Haddū Attār, was delayed on one pretext after another all through the summer of 1681. On 23 September Leslie wrote, 'The Emperor hath given no answer to our letters about the ambassador, and I believe will not till this dispute be over, but Jonas, an English renegade who brought the Emperor's letters … tells me that Alcaide Hammett, Alcaide Omar's brother, is nominated and that as soon as the Ram-Dam is over which is this month, he may set out'.[39] However, it was not until the end of November that ben Haddū approached Tangier, and 2 December 1681 before he reached the city itself. He was initially met by the four troops of English Horse, and as he drew near, Governor Kirke rode out past Fountain Fort to greet him. Kirke himself was flanked by 20 gentlemen well-mounted, and on either side of them paraded six of the tallest men of the garrison, armed with muskets. According to the governor's later report of the Ambassador's reception:

> It having been agreed that the ambassador from the King of Fes, who had now continued several days in the fields, should come into the town on Monday the 28th past, Colonel Kirke, our commander-in-chief, went out to meet him between eleven and twelve. Four troops of Horse marched first; after that, 50 chosen grenadiers of the Earl of Dumbarton's Regiment, and then 30 gunners with their linstocks, in their new livery coats and caps, followed by 30 negroes clothed in painted coats, with their brown bills, and after these (surrounded with about 20 gentlemen well-mounted) rid Colonel Kirke, having six men of the tallest stature, with long fusils, on each side of his horse. In which order, having proceeded a good distance beyond Fountain Fort, the main body of the Moors (which were about 200 Horse with their lances) being now within musket shot of us made a halt, and the Ambassador, with about 30 persons in his company, advanced towards Colonel Kirke, whom he

38 LRO, DDKE/HMC/426.

39 TNA, CO 279/28, fol. 214. Leslie to Jenkins, 23 September 1681.

received with those compliments that were suitable to the occasion; and those first ceremonies over, Colonel Kirke went to make his make his salutations to the Alcaid and Bemoucala, Viceroy of their country, who remained in the head of the other Moorish party; which being heard the Alcaid and the Ambassador, with each of their parties, began a skirmish, it being their manner of rejoicing and expressing their satisfaction; where having shown their horsemanship and skill in managing their lances and fusils, they at length parted, the Alcaid going off with his men, and the Ambassador with his train proceeding, in Colonel Kirke's company, towards the town. In their way, passing by Bridge Fort (at a sign made) he was saluted from Pole Fort with 10 charges, the great gun and a volley of small shot. By the time that was ended, he was arrived at the Spur of the Catherina Gate, and then the guns began to fire from Peterborough Tower, as far as Devil's Tower. Immediately on his entrance into the gate the mayor, with the whole corporation in all their formalities, met him, Mr Recorder welcoming him with a speech. From thence they proceeded towards the Water Gate, the streets being lined on both sides with musketeers of the Scotch Regiment, all the officers saluting the Ambassador as he passed. At Hyde's Battery he was saluted by the officers of the Second Battalion of Colonel Kirke's Regiment, which was drawn up there, and by all the guns from that battery and the Mole. In the Little Parade the Ambassador rode through a lane of the town militia, who appeared very well in arms; and thence to the Old Parade, through the governor's whole regiment drawn up in two battalions. On a new place of arms, fronting the Castle Gate, he saw the first battalion of Colonel Kirke's Regiment, which was drawn up there; thence he entered the castle, both sides of the bridge, and the way into the castle, being lined with grenadiers, with their muskets rested, and their bayonets in the muzzles of their muskets.

Immediately on his entrance into the castle, the guns began to fire from Stainer's Battery along the curtain to Peterborough Tower, the main guard of the castle being drawn up in Stainer's Battery, and four troops of Horse flanked by the King's Battalion of Guards that were drawn up before the house; the officers saluting him as he passed to the Court Gate, from which gate to the foot of the was a line of gunners on the left hand with their linstocks; and unmounted troopers with their carbines on the right; here the Ambassador lighted, and Colonel Kirke led him up the stairs, on which were likewise placed 20 unmounted troopers, through the Great Hall to his apartment, where after their stay, Colonel Kirke conducted to a large open gallery on the west side of the house, from whence he had a good prospect of the Bay, Mole, and the whole of the town, and then being saluted with three volleys of every division of each regiment, Colonel Kirke again brought him into the Great Hall, where the officers of each regiment paid respect to him in their several bodies; which ended, Colonel Kirke reconducted him to his apartment, where he left him until the evening, when Colonel Kirke returned to the castle, and finished the honours of the day with an entertainment of fireworks.[40]

40 TNA, 279/28, fols 339–41. Kirke's report to Commissioners, 2 December 1681; *London Gazette*, 5–9 January 1682.

On 9 December 1681, the Moorish ambassador, accompanied by Sir James Leslie, sailed for England. The courtier John Evelyn described Mohamed ben Haddū as 'a handsome person, well-featured, of a wise look, subtle and extremely civil'.[41] Charles II hoped that improved commercial relations might be established between Morocco and England, and to that end he received the ambassador and his presents of two lions and 20 or 30 ostriches with great courtesy. A treaty – hardly more than a confirmation of that concluded in 1681 – was ratified on 23 March 1682. Mohamed ben Haddū negotiated the return of captured ammunition, guns, and Muslim slaves in the English colony of Tangier without ransom. The civilian population of Tangier in 1680 had been estimated at 600; the two regiments composing the garrison numbered about 1,400, and there were 300 slaves in 'his Majesty's *bagnio*' or compound. Although the wider subject of slavery and captives in the Mediterranean and North Africa is beyond the scope of this book, they are an important part of the history of the colony.[42] The slaves who had been on the English-owned galley were transferred to work on the fortifications and Mole at Tangier. By 1678 the Mole's construction was coordinated by Henry Sheres, who had succeeded Sir Hugh Chomley as the project surveyor. He also took possession of the slaves that had previously been under the authority of the acting governor, Sir Palmes Fairborne, who had probably employed them on the fortifications around the city. Sheres was fervent about this labour source, writing to Pepys, 'I have yet received no account touching the slaves, which you tell me shall be turned over to the Mole service, the expediting of which resolution will be of great use to us'.[43]

Whether these former galley slaves were the 'labouring people' for whom in March Sheres requested the despatch of 5–600 pairs of shoes from Northampton, and corresponding numbers of stockings and shirts, is unclear.[44] From 1676 onwards, slaves and 'bonavolioes' were issued with a suit of clothes approved by Captain Thomas Hamilton, master of the *St Margaret* galley, and the officer directly responsible for their activities and welfare.[45] In April 1678 there were reckoned to be 248 workmen (Irish, Dutchmen, Italians, seamen and soldiers) engaged on the Mole, 'besides slaves'. Two years earlier the same source had referred to more than 300 galley slaves in English hands, before their transfer to the Mole.[46] Another list of slaves prepared for Sheres in 1677 shows that 69 possessed North African or Turkish names and places of origin, but ten, however, were described as 'Indians' and had just Christian first names.[47] As Gerald Aylmer suggests, 'Contrary to what we might suppose, they were not Asian Indians but native (North) Americans,

41 Evelyn, *Diary*, II, p. 432.

42 See, for instance, Colley, *Captives*; G. E. Aylmer, 'Slavery under Charles II: The Mediterranean and Tangier', *EHR*, 114 (1999), pp. 378–88; Meyer, Alan R., 'Class, Ethnicity, and Slavery: The Origins of the Moroccan 'Abid', *IJAHS*, 10 (1977), pp. 427–42.

43 Bod. Lib., MS Rawlinson A323, fols 119–20. Sheres to Pepys, 10 January 1677.

44 *Ibid.*, fols 140, 152–3.

45 TNA, ADM 106/318/8; ADM 106/318/16.

46 Bod. Lib., MS Rawlinson A323, fol. 24; TNA, CO 279/22, fols 146–7. Captain Richard Bolland to Commissioners, 12 April 1678.

47 Bod. Lib., MS Rawlinson A341, fol. 210.

the unhappy victims of 'King Philip's War', so called after the name given to the Wampanoag chief Metacom, who led the uprising. This conflict had been raging in distant Massachusetts and Rhode Island during 1675–6'.[48]

The treaty of 23 March 1682 had 'nothing in it of sea, the ambassador professing complete ignorance of sea affairs', although Mohamed ben Haddū had been invited to England for the specific purpose of discussing them.[49] He would merely consent to a maritime truce for four months, subject to the approval of the Sultan. When the Moroccan ambassador returned from England in August 1682, he brought with him the so-called Whitehall Treaty. It was heavily criticised by Governor Kirke, who protested strongly that all Moorish prisoners – the bulk of his workforce for repairing the Mole and the fortifications – were to be released without any Christians being given in exchange. Furthermore, 30 free Moors were to remain in Tangier, where they would be able to discern the resources of the English, 'who are naturally credulous and without any reserve … we are but too apt to think ourselves secure'. He also discovered, against his advice, that the Moors had obtained permission to purchase unlimited contraband from the English. They would, as Kirke observed, able to store it for use against the Tangier garrison, 'our powder being near expended, at the same time we have liberally furnished the Moors with it'.[50]

King Charles' agreement to release Moroccan slaves in Tangier, caused discontent in the colony. Mawaly Ismā'īl, though professing gratitude, claimed there were still 400 held back by the garrison, and made the confinement of these inflated numbers an excuse for contravening his guarantee to set at liberty his English slaves. The Moorish captives, numbering only 79, were employed either by contractors as porters on the quayside, or were owned by private individuals (including a few army officers), who were compensated by 100 pieces of eight for each slave. The governor had difficulties in satisfy the claims of owner's claims, as they were unwilling to accept credit notes, and Kirke himself lacked the necessary funds.[51] While the Sultan had assured his ambassador that he would possess full power during his embassy to London, to act on his behalf, Ismā'īl suddenly disassociated himself from the Whitehall Treaty. Kirke, ever suspicious of the motives of the Moors, felt that they were making excuses for prolonged talks. To the Tangier Committee he reported:

> Our presents bring so pleasing a taste with them … which they think they cannot better or more cheaply procure than by the coming and going of ambassadors. If we gratify them our easiness as it will be interpreted by them to be an effect of our fears, will but draw on us harder exactions for the future. If we do not comply with their desires, we must then put ourselves in a position here of asserting his Majesties honour, and letting them see we are not a people to be sported with, and

48 Aylmer, 'Slavery under Charles II', p. 384.

49 BL, MS Add. 19872, fol. 83. Jenkins to Sheres, 27 March 1682.

50 TNA, CO 279/30, fol. 220. Kirke to Commissioners, 16 November 1682.

51 TNA, CO 279/30, fols 75, 328, 367; SRO, D742/O/6/60. Account of cash paid for redemption of English slaves, February 1684.

indeed the Moors (if I can judge of them) will never value us, or be the more our friends, for what we give them, but for what we are able to refuse them.[52]

On 4 November 1682 Kirke wrote to George Legge, the Captain-General of Portsmouth, Master-General of Ordnance, and later, Lord Dartmouth:

When you consider this state of our affairs and the nature of the people we are to deal withal, you will not admire if I urge with all earnestness the speedy sending all sort of ammunition supplies, since there is no means to prevent my master's reputation or interest from suffering by the capriciousness of these people, but the putting ourselves into a posture of being re-doubted by them, and of receiving no affronts. It would be very seasonable, if, upon this emergency and conjuncture, the Moors might see that we are not abandoned or neglected at home, and his Majesty would be the better able to take his measures on this unexpected reverse of affairs, did our neighbours observe we are preparing ourselves for the worst of events'.[53]

Communications between Charles II and 'the Captain of Tangier, Kirke the English the governor of Tangier', and the Sultan and his chief advisers during this period show the futility of negotiating with the Moroccan government.[54] In actuality, Ismāʿīl had few reasons to fear the military resources of the King, of whom he spoke as 'an old woman, a slave to his Parliament'. But his assessment of English power was based solely on the garrison of Tangier, which he learnt from his own scouts, was left ill-provided with troops and ammunition. The Moorish defeats in 1680 had been described to him by his military commanders, and Ismāʿīl knew himself that his enemies had followed up their victory only by a clear willingness to enter into peace agreements. Thus, the rumour of the coming of a fleet from England in 1683 was enough to force a change in Moorish strategy. On 12 January 1683 Kirke remarked, 'It is not credible how much they have abated of their former pride, when they believed that provision was to be made for Tangier'.[55] The same day he wrote:

I am extremely sorry the Lords of the Committee did not think fit to recruit our Horse, for upon my word it is of the greatest consequence. As for a dependence on Spanish succours, it is certain that our misfortunes may be too sudden to give us time to expect them from thence; nor indeed can we well rely on a nation which loses its own places out of neglect to relieve them. However, I do not think we are in so ill a condition that we should fear anything of that kind, though I could wish we were better, and as long as we have so good a garrison we question not to be able to defend ourselves till we hear from England. I hope we shall have occasion of neither, for since the Moors perceive his Majesty and the lords of his Council take care of us, they speak no longer in the high strain they were wont, and the Alcade alarmed with the news that stores, officers, men, ammunition, and

52 TNA, CO 279/30, fol. 220.
53 HMC, *Eleventh Report, App. V*, p. 78. Kirke to Legge, 4 November 1682.
54 TNA, CO 279/29, fol. 97; CO 279/30, fols 340, 353, 581–2; CO 279/31, fols 113–4, 169–70.
55 TNA, CO 279/31, fol. 59. Kirke to Jenkins, 25 January 1683.

money are coming from England, expresses now an extraordinary complacency and kindness, to that degree as I almost persuade myself we shall at length see our Whitehall treaties ratified. I am sure I have applied my greatest study and endeavours for that end, though, I hear, malicious people do surmise that I consider a war, as my interest, and that consequently I promote it; wherein, I am sure, you will believe they are unjust to me, nor indeed ought I to be suspected of so great a weakness of judgment as to have a war in my aim, wherein I can propose no advantage to myself, but must enter upon it (considering our unprovided state) with a certain prospect of disgrace As for Mr Sheres' proposals some of them are very necessary, and to that degree, that above two months since I have set men to work on the batteries of Peterborough Tower, and have finished those batteries whereof I gave your Lordship an account.[56]

56 HMC, *Eleventh Report, App. V*, I, p. 79. Kirke to Legge, 25 January 1683.

12

No Part of England: the Evacuation of Tangier, 1683–84

Despite the improvements made by Colonel Percy Kirke, the situation at Tangier remained perilous. Since the 1670s the viability of the colony had been questioned, whilst in December 1680, Parliament refused to grant further supplies to the King. As the reports of the engineers, Beckman and Sheres indicated, there was little chance that the outworks could be repaired and improved, whilst the appearance of working parties outside the walls were liable to prompt further Moorish attacks that could overpower Kirke's soldiers. If Font (Fountain) Fort – the triangular structure built by Beckman – was lost, the garrison's water supply could be lost with it. All the earlier accounts of the occupation concur that the supply was both plentiful and reliable. In 1682, Kirke improved the inadequate situation by opening around 50 wells and, with the assistance of some 'ancient Portuguese', located an excellent watercourse which had been unknown for many years.[1] According to him, it was Lord Peterborough who was chiefly to blame for the situation. Pepys later confided, 'Speaking with Kirke [on 19 November 1683] about want of water, he owned that, this dry year, if it had not been for Fountain Fort, where our only supply of water is (of which if the Moors knew they might prevent us) the place could not have subsisted'.[2] The dependability of the water became a significant issue during the latter part of the occupation. Almost 400 soldiers were sick in hospital from drinking impure water. Though 1683 was an exceptionally dry year, this fact alone was not sufficient to account for the poor condition of the supply.

The Moors were tampering with the old aqueducts, and this was the cause of a great deal of sickness which unexpectedly broke out in the garrison in September. The soldiers asserted that 'they never had any ill effects from the water till the last siege by the Moors, nor any since that time till now'.[3] Hence, following his arrival in Tangier, Lord Dartmouth was compelled to procure fresh water from the Spanish coast, for both the garrison and the fleet. For

1 *Ibid*., p. 78. Kirke to Legge, 16 November 1682.

2 *Tangier Papers*, p. 16.

3 TNA, CO 279/32, fols 138–9. Dartmouth's Report, 16 September 1683.

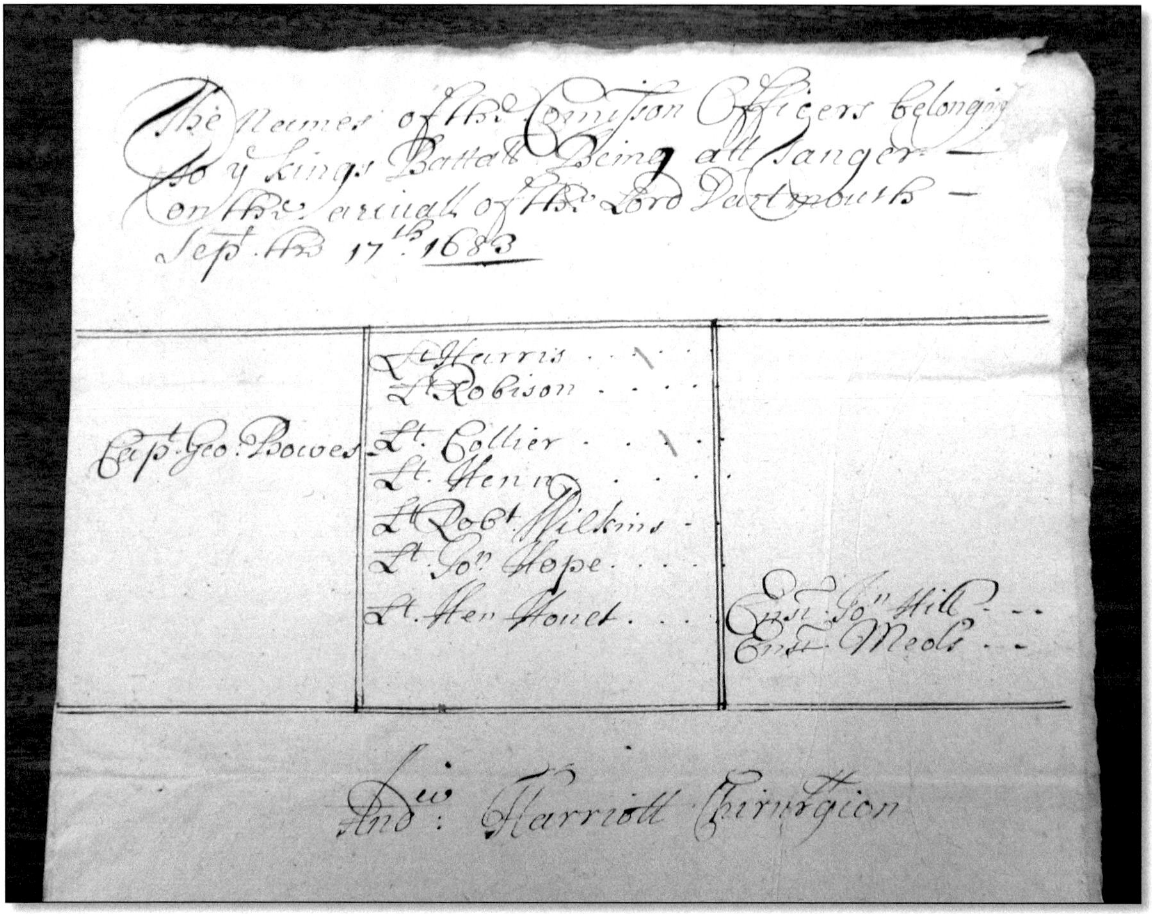

The Names of the Comission Officers belonging to ye Kings Battall Being att Tanger on the arrivall of the Lord Dartmouth — Sept the 17th 1683

Capt Geo: Bowes	Lt Harris Lt Robison Lt Collier Lt Henry Lt Robt Wilkins Lt Jon Hope Lt Hen Honet	Ens Jon Hill Ens Meols

And: Harriott Chirurgion

Names of the commissioned officers belonging to the King's Battalion, 17 September 1683 (SRO, D742/0/4/7). (Courtesy of Staffordshire Archives)

example, on 22 September, as shore parties were being sent to assist the demolition work at the Mole, the *Centurion* and *Delight* flyboat, sailed to Cadiz for water for the naval fleet.[4] In the days before the final evacuation of the garrison in February 1684, amid stormy weather (which caused much damage among the assembled ships), much activity went into the transportation of water casks from the shore.[5] Nevertheless, once the fleet had embarked, further shortages occurred, causing Dartmouth to later report:

> After the blowing tip of the town, and our retreat aboard, finding a great want of water cask and water in the fleet, to supply so many persons as were to be transported home in it, which all the endeavours we used could not procure at Tangier … I sent immediately the Henrietta, Montague, and another ship or two, which most wanted water to Cadiz with directions to water themselves and procure 200 tuns of cask, for we wanted about that quantity for the rest, and to have them filled and put on board.[6]

4 TNA, ADM 51/407; *Tangier Papers*, p. 273.

5 TNA, CO 279/32, fols 137–8, 164–5, 271; ADM 51/407; *Tangier Papers*, pp. 264–5, 285.

6 HMC, *Eleventh Report, App. V*, III, p. 47; SRO, D742/0/6/51. Account of water-casks delivered by the victualler of Tangier garrison, February 1684; SRO, D742/0/6/59. State of the fleet, 29 February 1684.

The Names of the Comission Officers Belonging to the Govern:r Regim:t being att Tanger on ye arinall of the Ld Dartmouth Sep ye 17th 1683 -

Coll	Capt Lt Berry	Ens Hillton
Lt Coll	Lt Westcomb	Ens Atkins
Major	Lt Withers	Ens Elliott
Capt Giles	Lt Thomas	Ens Mortimer
Capt St John	Lt Webster	Ens Fairborne
Capt Eley	Lt Wingfeild	Ens Roch
Capt Rowe	Lt Gerard	Ens Penotier
Capt Geo Wingfeild	Lt Addams	Ens Fitzgarell
Capt Barbour	Lt Lewis	Ens Duff
Capt Mathews	Lt Billing	Ens Kirke
Capt Charl Wingfeild	Lt Houghton	Ens Barbour
Capt Talbott	Lt Burke	Ens Senous
Capt Bazilrell	Lt Norwood	Ens Jeson
Capt Tate	Lt Wilson in slavery	Ens Farrell
Capt Gay	Lt Pinkney	Ens Parker
Capt Burgis	Lt Maber	Ens Lester

Names of the commissioned officers belonging to the Governor's Regiment, 17 September 1683. (SRO, D742/0/4/10) (Courtesy of Staffordshire Archives)

The Mole, intended to provide a safe harbour and provisioning station for shipping, remained unfinished, and since the Moors retained control of the quarries at Whitby, there was little prospect of its completion. Without a good harbour and an effective seaward line of military defences Tangier was practically useless. Charles II could ill-afford the injury to his prestige occasioned by the loss of a colony through military defeat. Over the course of the 22 years of its occupation, Tangier represented immense expenditure for the English Crown. Tangier had proved a disappointing experiment and there was nothing to suggest that further outlay was worthwhile. During the Parliamentary debate on the matter on 17 November 1680, Sir William Jones remarked, 'Tangier is no part of England, and for us to provide for it, as things stand now, is to weaken our own security'. Another, MP said 'Tangier is not only a seminary for Popish priests, but for soldiers too', whilst

Sir William Temple concluded, 'I should be glad, either that we never had it, or if it was by an earthquake blown up'.[7]

The failure of Mohamed ben Haddū's embassy in 1681–82 marked the end of realistic prospects for Tangier's survival. If a renewal of peace on better terms could have been obtained from the Moors, the King might have maintained the Tangier garrison for longer. The Duke of York, and other close advisers of Charles II, urged him to recall the veteran troops from Tangier, so that they would bolster the standing army in England and do much to improve the King's security. Besides, significant funds would be saved by withdrawing the garrison. Childs suggests the possibility that the decision to evacuate Tangier was taken in October or early November 1682, when Kirke sold his captaincy in the Royal Horse Guards, and 'would not have done so, effectively selling himself out of the standing army, unless sure that his 1st Tangier Regiment was going to be entered on to the permanent establishment on return to England'.[8] By early 1683 the King reluctantly decided to abandon Tangier. Having decided to part with 'the brightest jewel of his Crown', Charles was keen to push ahead. He accepted all responsibility for the project, allowing it to be known that he was 'the fondest man in the world of it', and 'discoursed publicly of the folly of keeping Tangier any longer'.[9]

On 2 July 1683, clandestine orders were issued to the young admiral, George Legge, Baron Dartmouth, to command an expedition to Tangier, which would bring about the evacuation of the garrison and port. The details of the enterprise were arranged with considerable secrecy, and not a word of its true purpose was made public. Dartmouth's commission and instructions as Admiral of the Fleet, and Captain-General in Tangier, for greater precaution, were written personally by the King's Secretary of State, Sir Leoline Jenkins. Moreover, the Admiralty was kept wholly in the dark until the Admiral's flag was hoisted.[10] Even Pepys, who was commanded to join the expedition as special advisor to Lord Dartmouth, knew nothing of his business till he had been five days on board, when he reported, 'my Lord in discourse in his cabin, broke to me the truth of our voyage, for disarming and destroying Tangier, the first moment he ever spoke or I ever thought of that, as the intent of our going'.[11] Dartmouth was instructed 'to demolish and utterly to destroy the said city and the Mole erected in the port belonging to it, so as they may be altogether useless, and no pirate or enemy of the Christian faith may at any time hereafter make their abode or retreat there'.[12]

A paper endorsed 'The first proposals for Tangier', was issued sometime in August 1683, and read:

7 Anchitell Grey (ed.), *House of Commons, Grey's Debates* (London: T. Becket and P. A. De Hondt, 1769), VIII, p. 3.

8 Childs, 'General Percy Kirke', p. 200, note 72.

9 *Tangier Papers*, p. 60.

10 SRO, D(W)1778/V/1397. Minute Book of the expedition of Lord Dartmouth to Tangier, 2 July 1683–27 June 1684; HMC, *Eleventh Report, App. V*, I, p. 93; *Tangier Papers*, pp. 58–66.

11 *Tangier Papers*, p. 12.

12 SRO, D(W)1778/V/1397; HMC, *Eleventh Report, App. V*, I, pp. 83–5; *Tangier Papers*, pp. 58–66.

> An order to be sent by Sir John Berry [appointed second in command to Dartmouth] to Colonel Kirke to banish the Jews. Major Beckman and Nelson to go away as soon as may be or with one of the Turkey convoys, to mine the walls of the town and place furnoes, with some small cuttings off as if the town were to be so defended if a close siege should be laid to it hereafter. To repair Middleton's line from the Castle to York Fort, to carry with them a convenient quantity of sulphur and mealed powder, &c., with fifty of the largest unused grenadoe shells and twenty sets of miners' tools.
>
> Sir John Berry immediately to return with the battalion of the Guards. Sir John Wyborne and the other ships to carry the Scotch Regiment for Ireland, and return back victualled well from thence to Tangier by the latter end of May, which is proposed to be the time for the rendezvous of all his Majesty's ships that can conveniently be there. The inhabitants are not above 100 families at most exclusive of the garrison and about 500 in number. These consist of Portuguese, French, some few Italians, Spaniards, Irish, and English.
>
> The forces drawn of May be thus provided for:
>
> The Scotch Regiment in Ireland and likewise the four independent companies that were drawn from thence.
>
> The battalion of the Guards in the Guards here.
>
> The four independent companies to be broken into the other forces here in the room of such as shall be found defective or married men upon a strict muster.
>
> The two Tangier Regiments may be reduced to twenty or twenty-four companies, by which means his Majesty's necessary garrisons may be reasonably supplied, and the two regiments of Guards be entire to attend his Majesty's person.
>
> The four troops of horse may be continued here as troops of dragoons, they will be very useful and less chargeable than now they are at Tangier.
>
> All the rest of the charge of Tangier may be wholly saved and such storekeepers, gunners, miners, and others that belong to the train (and have proved good men) may be provided for in the Office of the Ordnance here.[13]

Almost at the last minute, the Portuguese Ambassador in London got wind of the operation and (probably encouraged by Queen Catherine) hastily offered to buy back his nation's former possession, pressing that the huge increase of piracy that would surely follow the withdrawal of the English from the Mediterranean would damage both Portuguese and English trade. It was further suggested that the seasoned Portuguese army might regarrison

13 SRO, D(W)1778/V/1397; HMC, *Eleventh Report, App. V*, I, pp. 81–2.

John Seller, *The Royall City of Tangier in Africa*, engraved by John Oliver (1677). (Creative Commons Public Domain)

Tangier.[14] The Portuguese proposals had some effect on Charles II, and Dartmouth was hurriedly summoned to Windsor, just before he embarked for the colony. The King was persuaded, however, that Portugal could not long hold Tangier, and the likelihood that it would fall into the possession of the French. Dartmouth urged that no advantage to England could be gained by offering the place to a lesser power and was subsequently instructed to continue with his orders.[15] On 7 August 1683 he informed Jenkins:

> I cannot but think of the project I was sent for to Windsor, and how unsettled such variations of counsels would have seemed, the delivery of it to Portugal would have raised jealousies of a trick with France in most men's minds. I cannot but think it best for his Majesty to save the lives and estates of his subjects before any necessity or dishonourable misfortune happen to the place. By the help of God I will so order it that it shall be no reproach to his Majesty, nor any future annoyance to Christendom, at least in our age.[16]

Dartmouth's expedition was delayed for several days by strong winds and 'thick dirty weather', while he complained 'how unserviceably the ships were shuffled out of the river'.[17] Though he raised his standard on the *Grafton* on 8 August, it was not until 15 days later that the taskforce embarked from Plymouth Sound.

The men charged with the destruction of Tangier had all been sent home earlier, to settle details with the King, and were now returning. As much care and skill went into arrangements for the devastation as had gone into construction. Aboard were Pepys, who was tasked with evaluating compensation claims from property owners in the colony; Beckman, who had directed the fortifications in 1664–5, and the 1680 defence against the Moors; and Sheres who was to be given the heart-breaking job of destroying the 'stupendous Mole' he had worked so hard to construct. None of these men knew the purpose of their voyage when they set sail that August, although they may have had their suspicions. Dartmouth put a strict interpretation on his instructions, which urged him to take 'all imaginable care how to prevent strangers and our own subjects' from relaying the scheme to the Moors. Once at sea, Beckman was asked to produce a strategy for carrying out the demolition, a lengthy and complicated job involving engineers, fire-masters, miners, and drillers. Most were to be supplied by the garrison, but a team of expert miners was taken aboard when the fleet called in at Plymouth. Beckman submitted his plan on 28 August, recommending that they begin preparatory work on mining the fortifications without waiting until the civilian population had been evacuated. He informed Dartmouth, 'I do not doubt, but the news (though it be but guessing) of demolishing of the place will arrive before we shall arrive there'.[18]

14 TNA, CO 279/32, fol. 274. Dartmouth's report from Tangier, 19 October 1683.
15 HMC, *Eleventh Report, App. V*, I, pp. 88–9.
16 TNA, CO 279/32, fol. 79. Dartmouth to Jenkins, 7 August 1683.
17 *Ibid.*, fols 79, 87. Dartmouth's letters, 9 and 19 August 1683.
18 HMC, *Eleventh Report, V*, I, p. 89.

On 14 September 1683, 21 ships of Lord Dartmouth's expedition arrived at Tangier and berthed alongside the Great Mole. Ten vessels were men-of-war, but the rest were empty transports, while 10 more merchant ships currently held station there. The following evening, Kirke received his written orders from Dartmouth during dinner on board the *Grafton*. Although Pepys commonly referred to Kirke as 'the governor', he now came under the orders of his superior officer. The latter reported that his fellow officer 'very readily embraced the proposition, and I am confident will heartily assist me in all things for his Majesty's service. We agreed together to endeavour to allay the noise of blowing it up what possibly we could for the present'.[19] On 17 September Pepys tersely recorded:

> The ship weighing anchor, up by break of day (entering the mouth of the straits) to see the shore on both sides, to my great pleasure; the Levanter [an easterly wind] still very strong … Kirke, the Governor, saluted us with all the guns of the town, near which we found the Alcade [an envoy of the Sultan] encamped. But, Lord! how could anybody ever think a place fit to be kept at this charge, that, overlooked by so many hills, can never be secured against an enemy … Amazed to think how the King hath lain out all this money upon it. Good grapes and pomegranates from Spain. Tonight, infinitely bit with chinches [mosquitoes].[20]

The next day Pepys had his first direct experience of conditions in Tangier. He reported:

19 *Tangier Papers*, pp. 67–71.

20 *Ibid.*, pp. 17–18.

Wenceslaus Hollar, *Prospect of Tangier from the Sea* (*c.* 1669). (University of Toronto, The Wenceslaus Hollar Collection, Creative Commons Public Domain)

> After dinner rode out with my Lord [Dartmouth] and Kirke to see the town without and did it with no pleasure, but great danger, I thought, and so did William Hewer, and wondered all the way at the folly of the King's being at all this charge upon this town. No water in our command about this town. Tonight, I used several ways to preserve myself against the chinches, as the lime, candles, removing my bed, but still bit. At our coming back into the town tonight we saw the Moors' exercise hour upon our shore.

Kirke had met the commander of the Moorish forces on neutral ground a month earlier but found him evasive and making complaints about the absence of gifts, which he claimed to have been promised. He also opposed the sale of cattle to the garrison, the grazing for the horses beyond the city walls and activities such as quarrying.[21] On arrival in Tangier Dartmouth discovered that his secret mission, which had been the focus of much speculation in England, was already known, or at least suspected there. On 16 September he reported to Secretary Jenkins:

> My coming hither seems to have been long expected and the errand I come upon, the inhabitants ready to be packing up at my first appearance … thus the great secret hath been kept … much of this may come from the flying reports that were in London, yet I am sure the Governor hath had full information of all, and that a good while since … the Moors have likewise had the same intelligence.[22]

21 HMC, *Eleventh Report, V*, I, p. 90.

22 TNA, CO 279/32, fols 137–9; SRO, D(W)1778/V/1379; HMC, *Eleventh Report, V*, III, p. 33.

There was much to accomplish before the destruction of Tangier's defences and Mole could be begun. Dartmouth ordered an immediate assessment of the strength of the military garrison, which mustered on the morning of 17 September 1683. Muster rolls of this date, combined with abstracts of musters, dated 1 October 1863, record that the 1st Tangier Regiment of 16 companies had 48 commissioned officers, 128 NCOs and 820 soldiers; the King's Battalion of five companies consisted of 14 officers, 60 NCOs and 277 men; Trelawny's Regiment of 16 companies mustered 48 officers, 112 NCOs and 723 men; Dumbarton's Regiment of 12 companies (combined with four independent companies attached) possessed 47 officers, 152 NCOs and 917 men; the four troops of Horse amounted to 16 officers, 20 NCOs, 79 mounted men and 100 unmounted men; there were 32 gunners, as well as a company of miners commanded by Captain Richard Basset, comprising four NCOs and 48 men. The overall strength of the Tangier garrison amounted to 3,898, inclusive of officers and NCOs, the largest it had been for some time.[23] Further abstracts of musters, drawn up for the purpose of issuing beef and other provisions to private soldiers in the garrison, record 2,520 on 4 November 1683; 2,592 on 12 November 1683; 2,508 on 28 January 1684; and 2,366 on 4 February 1684.[24] This gradual, yet apparent reduction in troop numbers reflects the withdrawal of sick soldiers and minor units, along with their families and officials of the colony in the months leading up to the final evacuation of Tangier.

In late September 1683 Governor Kirke had issued orders to the gunners of the garrison, 'to attend daily in their turns at the several posts'. The document recording this provides important information, not only about the names and ranks of the gunners, but on the positioning of artillery at the garrison's various batteries and outposts.[25] During the next few months, surveys of the military stores and victuals in the garrison and fleet were made, which exposed once again, various logistical problems and quantities of wasted rations.[26] A survey of naval provisions, taken on 25 September, found that 15,580 pieces of salt-pork, 'mentioned to be defective, do so stink and are rotten, and not fit for men to eat', while 'the 35 bushels [and] 3 gallons of peas are musty and stink'.[27] On 6 November 1683, Dartmouth issued the following warrant to 'the officer employed in the victualling his Majesty's Navy at Tangier':[28]

> Whereas as well for the lengthening out of the sea provisions which is on board his Majesty's fleet now under my command, as for the benefit of the seamen's health under their present labours on the works here ashore, I have thought fit to direct that the several ships now here be victualled for some time with fresh beef. These are to will and require you to send on board his Majesty's respective

23 SRO, D742/0/4/2; D742/0/4/6–10.
24 SRO, D742/0/3/50–1; SRO, D742/0/3/68–9.
25 SRO, D742/0/4/12A; D742/0/4/14; *Tangier Papers*, pp. 71–4.
26 SRO, D(W)1778/I/i/836; D742/0/3/28; D742/0/5/54.
27 SRO, D742/O/3/29; HMC, *Eleventh Report, V*, III, p. 40.
28 SRO, D742/0/6/19.

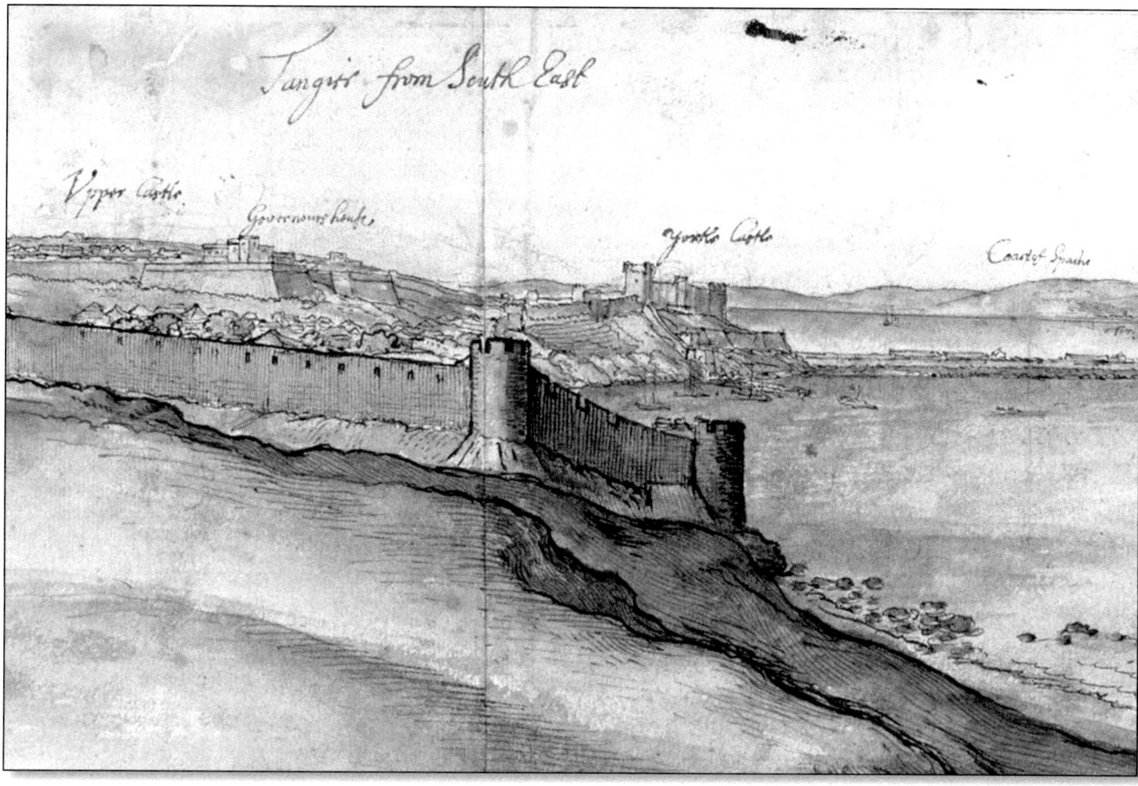

Wenceslaus Hollar, Sketch, *Tangier from the South East* (*c.* 1669). (University of Toronto, The Wenceslaus Hollar Collection, Creative Commons Public Domain)

ships herein mentioned, the number of oxen (which are to be reckoned 2,000 lbs weight one with another) against their names expressed, which is to serve them for six days, at the rate of 8 lbs for each man, being the proportion of flesh allowed by his Majesty to the seamen serving in his ships, and take the several pursers' receipts for the same. For which this shall be your warrant, dated at Tangier, 6 November 1683.

The number of oxen to be delivered to the evacuation fleet, to serve for six days, at the rate of 8 lb per man was as follows: the *Grafton* 330 men, 13 oxen and 40 lb of meat; the *Montague* 215 men, 8½ oxen and 20 lb; the *Oxford* 185 men, seven oxen and 80 lb; the *Happy Return* 185 men, seven oxen and 80 lb; the *Woolwich* 185 men, seven oxen and 80 lb; the *James Galley* 200 men, eight oxen; the *Dover* 200 men, eight oxen; the *Bonadventure* 150 men, six oxen; the *Tyger* 150 men, six oxen; the *Tyger Prize* 150 men, six oxen; the *Sapphire* 90 men, 3½ oxen 20 lb; the *Greyhound* 75 men, three oxen; the *Drake* 75 men, three oxen; the *Deptford Ketch* 30 men, one ox and 40 lb; the *Ann Yacht* 50 men, two oxen; the *Pearl* 100 men, four oxen and 80 lb; total 2,380 men, 95 oxen and 40 lb

Dartmouth's special instructions were to conceal from the Moors, for as long as possible, his purpose of withdrawing the garrison from Tangier. However, their spies quickly discovered the design, and according to Kirke's report, they 'knew all our affairs, even the deliberations of the Council at home'.[29] Anxious that their suspicions might induce them to attack the city, and to avoid the complication of war before his task should be accomplished, Dartmouth entered into sociable negotiations with Qā'id Omar, sending him presents, including cloth, lances and 12 barrels of fine powder. The English commander was also keen to discover how large a force the Moors had in the field. To maintain the peace, and to disguise the noise and smoke of the demolition parties, it was decided that the Tangier garrison would make a show of force in the form of a review of all the military units (supported by 800 sailors). According to Dartmouth's own report, on 28 September 1683:

> Seamen ordered ashore from ships in the roads. Lord Dartmouth clothing a good part of them in the red coats we brought over with us for the Scotch and Trelawny's Regiments … About eleven o'clock, his Excellency drew out, in order, upwards of 4,000 men, besides strong guards and the burghers left in the town. His Excellency kept Pole Fort on his right hand, and the whole body stood under cover of that; Brown George, the Irish Battery, and the Seamans' lodgements, where seven small pieces were planted towards the sandhills, and a battalion of Trelawny's regiment, and the guns, were posted with them. The left of the garrison reaching to Fountain Fort, and then the seamen, to upwards of a thousand, were drawn from thence all along the sands by the seaside, and the guard-boats, and the rest of the boats of the fleet, commanded by Captain George Aylmer, flanked beyond the seamen, close in with the shore. At the utmost extent of the seamen, across the sand, his Excellency stood, attended by several gentlemen, the volunteers of the fleet, commanded by my Lord Berkeley, and most of the horse, where the Alcaide met him, drawn up very orderly and to the best advantage of ground, according to their way of discipline. They made as much show as they could, though their foot was not judged to be about 2,500 and about 500 horse. After many compliments from the Alcaide, and civilities passed on both sides, at his Excellency's desire. Colonel Kirke and the Alcaide shook hands; which done, the Alcaide, and his horse, exercised, a full hour and a half, before his Excellency. After this, the Alcaide and Lord Dartmouth took leave of each other, the Alcaide ordering all his small shot to be fired, which his Excellency commanded to be answered by ours, and all the artillery of the town and castle, and from the ships. Which ceremony being over, the Alcaide drew off his people, and his Excellency commanded our forces to march into the town again, but by that time, the Alcaide drew off, and sent Almocadem Abdala, with a party of horse, upon the sandhills. Colonel Kirke's two battalions were marched as far as the Spur at Peterborough Tower, and the whole body being in motion, begirt the whole town round with soldiers, towards them, that we seemed more than we really were. The small frigates were, all the time of our drawing out, in motion as near the shore as they could.[30]

As part of the deployment of the seamen, Dartmouth's own battalion of 200 men – from the ship's company of the flagship *Grafton*, commanded by

29 HMC, *Eleventh Report, App. V*, I, pp. 90–2.

30 TNA, CO 279/32, fol. 273; SRO, D(W)1778/V/1397; HMC, *Eleventh Report, Appendix V*, III, pp. 51–2.

Lower parade ground and eastern gate of York Castle. (Author's photo)

Sir William Booth – were clad in white and blue striped linen, and armed with muskets, pikes and poleaxes, with four Union flags. Sir James Berry's battalion was clothed 'with the clothes Mr Hewer shall give', with four Irish colours. The other two, each consisting of 200 sailors, were dressed in the red soldiers' coats that had been brought for Dumbarton's and Trelawny's regiments; they also carried the eight new colours brought for the latter. This force was drawn up 'on the sands to the best advantage as Colonel Kirke shall direct'.[31] Pepys remarked, 'they and their officers did make as good an appearance and gave with the small shot as good a volley or better, than the soldiers'.[32] He further described how, 'About eleven my Lord and we, and his family, went out on horseback without the town. We had a sight of our army, finely disposed above the hills, and wholly down to the sea, just without the town-walls'. For added security, all the boats in the fleet were manned and commanded by a captain, and armed with blunderbusses and hand grenades, and positioned 'for the well flanking of the sands'.

With the entire military garrison of Tangier assembled, the Moorish commander advanced to meet the English officers. Pepys reported, 'His army was drawn up not so thick as ours, but very artificially, two deep, and that in but few places to make a greater show, though we believe they had not above 2,500 in the field, but we few horse and they a great many'.[33] Compliments were exchanged – through interpreters – between Dartmouth and Qā'id Omar, which lasted for half an hour. Favourably impressed with the Moors,

31 HMC, *Eleventh Report, App. V*, I, p. 94.

32 *Tangier Papers*, pp. 27–9. The captain of the *Grafton* recorded in the ship's log on 7, 8 and 11 October 1683 that his crew had 'exercised in small arms' (TNA, ADM 51/407; *Tangier Papers*, pp. 271–2).

33 *Ibid.*, p. 31.

Pepys observed, 'Their style is extremely fine and most for compliment, the Alcade and his company appeared like very grave and sober men. His discourse and manner was very good, and I thought, with more presence of mind than our master's, though he also did extremely well. Their appearance and habits I liked very well. The Alcade's son, a pretty youth, in particular exercised by and by, very neatly'. Following a handshake between Governor Kirke and Qā'id Omar and promises of peace, the Moorish horsemen made their customary display for state occasions, 'showing great dexterity in horsemanship and handling their lances, but very confused in their order. Their halloo is an odd sort of noise, nothing so mellow nor cheerful, nor strong and full as ours'. There was then, 'great shooting with small shot on both sides', and all the English guns fired salutes as the Moors withdrew. The Tangier Regiment then marched to Peterborough Tower, and 'the whole body being in motion, begirt the whole town round with soldiers towards them, so that we seemed more than we really were'.[34]

The encounter between the Tangier garrison and the Moors had the desired effect. Dartmouth later reported, that although Qā'id Omar left with all expressions of goodwill, 'the truth was the Alcade was willing enough to be friends, for with all the kind words that passed he did not at all like our countenances, for I believe he never saw so formidable a force together since his Majesty had Tangier … they have lived extremely well with us ever since'.[35] On 4 October, the English commander read the official proclamation of his mission in the Market Place. He acquainted the 'Mayor Corporation and inhabitants of Tangier', with Charles II's commands, 'to draw off and bring back all his subjects, both soldiers and inhabitants, and then forthwith demolish and utterly destroy the place, Mole and harbour'. In a long speech Dartmouth brought forward all the 'arguments for destroying Tangier', which had been judiciously prepared by Pepys during their voyage. He insisted:

> the King has gone to great expense and trouble to make it a secure habitation, a commodious harbour, and a place for trade to flourish in, yet the results have been encouraging, and so many brave men's lives have been post in the defence of the town, which is now in so ruinous a state as to make it dangerous to live in owing to the hospitality of the Moors … the perpetual alarms and interruptions to be expected from the Moors, now much more knowing in the Art of War, skilful, better armed, and supplied with cannon and ammunition, and more insolent, troublesome and dangerous than could be foreseen, when his Majesty accepted Tangier.[36]

Dartmouth also emphasised the difficulties of provisioning the colony, and the inherent risk of starvation to the inhabitants, in addition to the increasing futility of the Mole, which made it impossible to retain naval stores there. He stated that the King's tender care for his subjects had resolved him no longer to expose them to such great perils from 'potent and ambitious

34 SRO, D(W)1778/V/1397; HMC, *Eleventh Report, Appendix V*, III, p. 52.
35 TNA, CO 279/32, fol. 273.
36 SRO, D(W)1778/I/i/885; TNA, CO 279/32, fols. 96–7, 191.

neighbours or merciless Muhammadans'. The announcement was generally received with professed approval, and two addresses to the King were drawn up, one from the city of Tangier, and another from the governor, officers and soldiers. They commended his Majesty's decision and thanked him for his gracious care of his subjects, whilst Kirke and his officers loyally declared that they would be content to quit Tangier, and would be better employed in his Majesty's service at home 'amidst the present just apprehensions occasioned by the late horrid conspiracy [the Rye House plot] which still threatens your Royal person and the disturbance of your Government'.[37] Following the breaking of the news of the evacuation by Dartmouth resulted in a festive mood descending on the colony. According to one pamphlet, the inhabitants were delighted to receive formal assurances of fair compensation for their properties. The writer declared:

> I cannot tell you whether our cannon the day before or our shouts today made the greater noise. Everyone was pleased with the change, but more with the reprisals, being gladder to have the liberty of a subject, and a free estate in England than an old musty prison or hospital in Tangier … It is impossible to express our joys, which continued all that night with bumpers and bonfires, the cannons playing in the air like rockets, and the foot soldiers with their muskets were our squibs and serpents. The bells rung themselves out of the steeples, you could not hear above two in all the town.[38]

The commissioners tasked with assessing Tangier's walls and fortifications – Henry Sheres, surveyor-general of the Mole and fortifications; Colonel Trelawny; Lieutenant Colonel Boynton; Major Beckman, Captain John Giles, Mr Edward Tessin and Mr Thomas Phillips – drew up an extensive report and estimate of the repairs and buildings that would be necessary to place the colony in a strong state of defence, and of the forces required to maintain it during the 12 years that the works would be in progress. Essential works would cost £1,297,201 16s. 6d., while the cost of a military force would add a further £3,501,561.[39] On 13 October Sir John Berry and his assistants examined the Mole, and declared it 'altogether unuseful to his Majesty for receiving, careening or preserving his Majesty's ships, so in our opinions grounded on the foregoing considerations, it is not a place to be rendered so to answer in any degree the time and expense of doing it, if it can be done'.[40] During this period the removal of surplus ordnance and ammunition from the garrison began in earnest. On 4 October 1683 two boats of shot were taken aboard the *Grafton*, two brass cannons followed five days later, whilst 12 guns and 224 mortar shells were loaded onto the same

37 TNA, CO 279/32, fols 208, 245; HMC, *Eleventh Report, App. V*, I, pp. 96–8. Address to Charles II, 8 and 14 October 1683.

38 *A Letter to a Friend in London, Describing the Causes, Manner and Time of this Demolishing of Tangier, November the Fifth in the Year 1683* (London: J. Smith, 1683).

39 TNA, CO 279/32, fols 137–164.

40 SRO, D(W)1778/V/1397; HMC, *Eleventh Report, App. V*, III, p. 43.

Renovated section of Upper Castle opposite the seaport. (Author's photo)

vessel on 5 November.[41] Moreover, on 18 October the victuallers of Tangier had requested permission from Dartmouth to ship surplus stores back to England, 'now the garrison is closing'.[42]

Before commencing the destruction of the city, Dartmouth shipped off as many civilians as possible, leaving only the soldiers and some of the Molemen to undertake the work. The private residents of Tangier were estimated at around 500, with perhaps over 400 children in the colony. Owing to the dearth of provisions, Dartmouth experienced considerable difficulty in carrying out his instructions to take off the inhabitants. On 22 October he complained to the Admiralty:

> so little care has been taken at home to provide sufficient quantities of victuals for this fleet or garrison to enable them to perform the service, his Majesty has been pleased to send us hither for, that I dread the fatal consequences that neglect may prove of to his Majesty's service without a speedy and good supply reach us here. To perform my duty in this matter, in the prevention of those inconveniences all that may be, I have and am making all the provision this country will afford, which is but very inconsiderable, the late great droughts having made corn not only very dear, but to be had in great scarcity … Our victuals are the thing most wanting to carry on this service as it ought to be, the victuallers ought to answer it to his Majesty how they come to let the garrison and fleet be so ill-provided for and yet dare give his Majesty so contrary an account to the truth … it has been the chief want for carrying on always his Majesty's services in these parts, therefore pray sir, let the victuallers send what they are able with all possible speed.[43]

The garrison stores in September 1683 held food for barely eight weeks. Likewise, much of the naval stores were unfit for consumption and had to disposed of, while several vessels were already out of provisions.[44] Dartmouth's directives from Charles II included specific orders for him to ensure that the sick and wounded soldiers of the garrison, with their families, were safely evacuated aboard hospital ships – the first recorded use by an English force. If men were too sick to make the journey, they were to be carried to Spain, where the English Consul would provide for them until their recovery. Initially, Dartmouth was told that only one ship (the *Welcome*) would be made available to him, but he estimated that this would be insufficient for the task. Whilst sailing to Tangier, Dartmouth wrote to Jenkins, 'pray move that a hospital ship be sent after me, for consider how ill it will be to mix the sick with the well, and I may chance to send the people away in several parcels, the one ship cannot serve all … there are many families and their

41 TNA, ADM 51/407; *Tangier Papers*, pp. 274–5, 277.

42 SRO, D(W)1778/I/i/874.

43 HMC, *Eleventh Report, App. V*, III, p. 45.

44 SRO, D742/0/6/12. Observations on victualling of fleet at Tangier sent out under Lord Dartmouth, and also of victualling of soldiers of Tangier garrison, November 1683.

Interior of Upper Castle. (Author's photo)

effects to be brought off … here is but one hospital ship, the other which is pretended is ordered upon two services at once'.[45]

Having obtained no official agreement to his request for a second vessel, Dartmouth decided when he arrived in Tangier to requisition the *Unity*, a merchantman originally chartered by the Ordnance Department. He ordered its conversion into a hospital ship by local craftsmen, explaining that a second vessel of this type was completely necessary as the sick were increasing each day. On 28 September 1683, 28 days' provisions for 200 men were loaded onto the *Unity* hospital ship, and on 18 October she slipped her moorings with 114 invalid soldiers (87 from the 1st Battalion of Kirke's Regiment, and 27 belonging to Dumbarton's), 34 civilian males, 104 women and children aboard. John Eccles, gunner, usher and writing master to the school, was placed in charge of these soldiers' families. They were to be provided with 'lodging and other necessary accommodations' in Pendennis Castle and the local area, with an allowance of 3d. a day to each soldier's wife, until the arrival of the bulk of their respective regiments.[46] Accompanying *Unity* on her voyage were the *Virtue* (carrying several orphans of soldiers killed in service in Tangier, who had been in receipt of the colony's poor relief), and the *Diamond*, with the wives, families and servants of the garrison's senior officers (including Kirke's wife and daughters, numbering some 19 males and 20 females – there were 20 official governor's servants, 11 for Kirke and

45 TNA, CO 279/25, fols 260–1; CO 279/32, fols 87–8. Dartmouth to Jenkins, 19 August 1683. See also SRO, D(W)1778/I/i/816. Secretary Brisbane to Dartmouth, 14 August 1683, regarding hospital vessels for wounded soldiers from Tangier.

46 SRO, D742/0/2/4; TNA, CO 279/32, fol. 100. Lists and orders relating to evacuation of Tangier garrison, 16 October 1683; CO 279/32, fol. 269. Dartmouth to Eccles, 18 October 1683; SP44/69, fol. 71; *CSPD 1683–84*, p. 87. Royal warrant to Lord Arundel, Governor of Pendennis, 11 November 1683.

nine for his wife, including five Black children).[47] The *Diamond* arrived in England on 14 December 1683.

On 12 November, the day before *Unity* berthed at Gravesend, Dartmouth was informed that a surgeon had been ordered to take care of all her passengers. The 'infirm' soldiers, 'probably invalids employed on the strength of the garrison on light duties in much the same way as invalid battalions were utilised to undertake sedentary duties in England in lieu of pension provision', were eventually settled in the Royal Hospital at Chelsea.[48] Even so, 24 soldiers from Dumbarton's Regiment complained that no provision had been made for them. In a classic case of military oversight, Mr Flowers, the agent appointed to process the returning troops, had been advised to expect men from Kirke's, and so in the absence of instructions for him to administer to anyone else, he ignored those from another unit. By 20 November Secretary Jenkins was in a position to assure Dartmouth that 'an officer appointed by his lordship was gone down to take care of them, and that he was furnished with a sum of money to answer their necessities', and hence Dumbarton's men were duly cared for.[49] More inhabitants and officials of Tangier followed in a second batch of ships. On 22 October, the *Centurion* started for Lisbon with Portuguese inhabitants aboard, whilst on 27 October the *St David* and the *Swallow* left (the former with the mayor, aldermen, and their families and servants aboard).[50]

During the succeeding week the *Dartmouth* got under way with several inhabitants, while the *Swan* frigate, commanded by Captain Hobson, sailed for Marseilles and Livorno, with 30 French and Italian passengers.[51] In all, eight transports were at sea, conveying 262 men, and 349 women and children. On 12 December 1683 a royal warrant, containing a list for quartering of troops from Tangier on their return to England, instructed that the King's Battalion, the troops of Horse, and the company of miners, were to go to London; Colonel Kirke's Regiment to Pendennis Castle and Plymouth; Colonel Trelawny's Regiment, Plymouth; and Dumbarton's Regiment of 16 companies, eight were assigned to Rochester, six to Winchester, and two to Southampton.[52] In England, the question of placing the returning troops greatly disturbed the Whig Party, who viewed the coming of the garrison as a further blow by the King's increasingly authoritarian regime against Parliamentary government. Dartmouth wrote, 'It is easily to be apprehended that these troops upon their arrival, will be great eyesores, not only to those that own themselves Whigs, but to all that are not thoroughly affected to his Majesty and his Government'.[53]

Dismantling an entire community was a complicated matter. Pepys compiled a list of 180 freeholders and leaseholders (civilians, army officers,

47 TNA, CO 279/32, fols 110, 368; SRO, D742/0/7/6.

48 Gruber von Arni, *Hospital Care*, p. 24.

49 HMC, *Eleventh Report, App. V*, I, p. 101.

50 SRO, D742/0/2/14; D742/0/7/4; HMC, *Eleventh Report, App. I*, p. 101.

51 TNA, ADM 51/407; SRO, D742/0/7/8; *Tangier Papers*, p. 284.

52 SRO, D(W)1778/I/i/925; HMC, *Eleventh Report, V*, I, p. 103.

53 TNA, CO 279/33, fol. 58. Dartmouth to Jenkins, 5 January 1684.

and absentee landlords) who needed to be compensated. There was some wrangling over values, but affairs were settled within weeks, at a cost to the Crown of around £11,300. By now the work of destruction at the Mole had begun in earnest, but as it had been so strongly constructed, various attempts to blow it up with demolition charges and mines proved most difficult. The most optimistic estimates forecast a timescale of about two weeks, but by 21 September 1683, Sheres was openly pronouncing that more than three months would be required to destroy the Mole alone.[54] Pepys, as well as Dartmouth, expressed serious doubts about the effectiveness of the gunpowder charges that were being set. In cold and stormy conditions, during which soldiers, workers and sailors often found themselves confined to their quarters, it would take upwards of 2,000 men working round-the-clock for three months to finally destroy the fortifications and Mole. Tons of debris were cast into the sea to choke up the harbour. Hurried and ill-coordinated measures were taken to finish blowing up the walls and other fortifications of the city and Castle – one firemaster, Jacob Woolferman, spent five weeks in undermining York Castle, whilst another, Isaac Neilson, toiled on the town defences for nine.[55] Initial attempts to blow the foundations of the Mole were unsuccessful, but this was a Herculean task. Notwithstanding, Pepys remarked:

> I hear from our land soldiers here upon discourse concerning powder, that we Englishmen are to this day reckoned the best gunners and that even in foreign service by land, Trelawny saying that in the French army they had several men taken out of their regiment to be gunners in others, and I find they agree in the reason of it. Not that every Englishman has skill more than others, but that they do handle powder with more readiness and boldness [than] any people in the world. It seems very plain how ignorant our master-gunner of England is in the business of mines, by his attempt to blow up a piece of the Mole with a bomb, and of the master of the ordnance, himself in his two trials of doing the like with a culverin overcharged with powder and a shot which did no good at all, but shot the shot two foot into the ground. And both he and the master-gunner in their method of mining the outmost chest, which they took into their charge to do, to show Sheres how easily they could do what he discoursed of as so hard, and they find it so; while he on the other hand has made twice the despatch in the next chest, and flings up pieces of the Mole in other places to a wonder, in other places of the Mole. And he has foretold them always beforehand the effects of what they have tried in blowing up with their guns and bombs, and all proves true. And God knows what their skill will do when it comes to its most considerable occasions of showing itself in the great mines of the town and Castle, both as to Phillips and Beckman.[56]

The destruction of the Mole was the most formidable part of the demolition of Tangier. Even as the *Unity* was leaving the Bay of Tangier,

54 *Tangier Papers*, p. 19.
55 SRO, D742/0/3/68.
56 *Tangier Papers*, pp. 149–50.

Renovated north-west corner of Peterborough Tower. (Author's photo)

Dartmouth's engineers were excavating a series of explosive mines. In his work on siege warfare (published in 1740), Sébastien Le Prestre de Vauban, the French military engineer who served under Louis XIV, codified principles of military mining that remained valid well into the 19th century.[57] Tunnel mines, usually employed under enemy fortifications, but also for the demolition of other structures, were time consuming to set. They were worked by miners and labourers, by the depth and size of the charge. The surprise and effectiveness of tunnel mines was significantly increased by exploding large charges of black powder at the end of galleries driven under fortifications. Their work demanded courage and special caution – lack of

57 Sébastien Le Prestre de Vauban, George A. Rothrock (trans.), *A Manual of Siegecraft and Fortification* (Ann Arbor: University of Michigan Press, 1968); Jamel Ostwald, *Vauban Under Siege: Engineering Efficiency and Martial Vigor in the War of the Spanish Succession* (Brill: Leiden, 2007).

oxygen, possible flooding, and injury or death from premature demolitions were particularly hazardous. To ignite the mine, the engineer fed an ignition fuse or 'sausage' out of the mine chamber. Made of linen, and filled with black powder, the device led back to the point of ignition, and was normally laid in a wooden duct or box, and covered with a board to protect it from moisture or other damage.

The explosives prepared by the engineers and firemasters for the demolition of the Mole, mines and fortifications in the Laboratory at Tangier on 4 January 1684 were as follows: 12 cwt of quick match for the mine; 500 grenades for the hand mortars; 1,000 hand grenades; 100 train boxes fixed for the mines; 60 fire wreaths; 30 wooden petards with strong powder; 15 great grenades for the mines; 2,000 puddings of canvas for the mines; 600 fuses for the grenades; 12 stinkpots; 21 great wall grenades; 200 grenades for the mortars; three brass petards; 3,000 fire fuses for the mines; 75 great grenades to shoot out of the ground.[58]

On 19 October 1683, Dartmouth's master-gunner, Captain Richard Leake, fired two explosive devices under the arches at the landward end of the Mole, but the earth was so loosely packed that no damage was done. The next day, Sheres drilled out a cavity, packed it with powder, and detonated it to more effect. On the last day of October 1683, the Mole finally succumbed, the explosion hurling great lumps of rock and timber skywards and setting fire to a nearby house. Work continued apace, causing one eyewitness to testify:

> Then we fell to work with the houses on the upper end of the town, next the town wall, having removed the people, with their goods and movables, on shipboard. When this part of the town was blown up, there was a party of the Moors, about 10,000, within two miles of the walls, which were totally routed by the strangeness of the surprise. They run seven miles forward as if Hell had burst open and the Devil himself had been at their heels, before they looked about, either horse or man; for either some of the stones or timber fell amongst them, or the greatness of the noise scared them away; there has not been one of them since appeared within view of the garrison. We have had by this means time to select and gather all the best of our stone and timber or anything that is worth preserving, which we have sold to the Spaniards on the other side of the Straits. We are now undermining the outward walls, the castle and citadel, which the governor has ordered to be blown up all together, on 5 November, for one solemn bonfire.[59]

It was on 6 December, that Sheres submitted his final draft of his technical report on the state of the Mole and recommendations for its demolition to Dartmouth:

> First, casting the solid quantity of the Mole into cubic feet, I consider it under these dimensions, viz., the length of the Mole is 1,436 feet, the mean breadth about 110 feet, the mean height from the top to low water mark about 18 feet, amounting in

58 SRO, D742/0/3/68.
59 *Letter from Tangier to a Friend in London.*

all by cubical computation to 2,843,280 solid feet, which being cast into tons are 167,251 tons. Of this mass 25,000 tons at least is *tarrass* work so bound in chests, with timber and iron, and so well performed, that it is by all people agreed (and indeed is found) more difficult to demolish than so much solid rock.[60]

Thus, the engineer recommended:

To the work might be assigned daily about 1,000 men of all sorts, of which number 400 should be constantly employed in carrying away stone and rubbish, the rest in cutting of stone, tending, filling and the like. Which 400 men will carry away about 800 tons daily; so that the whole 167,251 should be removed in about 209 days ; but the additional difficulty of demolishing the tarras work (estimated as above at 25,000 tons) by great mines and at least 1,500 small mines, by drills and other more troublesome methods would add at least 25 days to the time above noted. Foul and rainy weather, incident to this season of the year, wherein men cannot work as they ought and for many days together perhaps not at all, is another contingency to be taken into the calculation.

Twelve days later Lord Dartmouth ordered his senior officers and engineers to bring about the final destruction of Tangier:

To Colonel Percy Kirke, Colonel Charles Trelawny, Lieutenant Colonel Boynton, Sir James Leslie, Major Zachary Tiffin, Captain George Bowes, Captain Robert Douglas, and Captain Andrew Munroe, and to Henry Sheres, Esquire, surveyor-general of the fortification at Tangier. Warrant to the respective field officers [of the] garrison and Mr Sheres to survey the several mines prepared for the blowing up and demolishing the town and castles, etc., and to make report thereof.

It being very necessary in the execution of his Majesty's pleasure and command touching this place, that all ways and means be considered of, and used for the total destruction of the walls of the town, the castle, forts and fortifications within and without it, so as to leave it uninhabitable, and without any sort of succour or defence for the Moors, or any other that shall attempt to possess themselves of it. There are to desire and direct you with the assistance of Major Beckman, Mr Thomas Phillips (the rest of the engineers here now present) and any of the officers of the garrison whom you shall think qualified, to give you any, forthwith to take a view and consider of the several mines and other things prepared for the blowing up and demolishing the said walls, castle and forts, and to give use your opinions in writing under your hands, whether you think the same will be sufficient (if they answer the reasonable success expected from them) to complete the aforesaid ends of destroying this place; and that if anything further to be done, or in any other manner seem reasonable and fit in your judgement towards it, you do offer the same to me, in order to it's being further considered of, and put in execution, and therein to use all the care and exactness to the best of your abilities, required in a work of this nature and consequence, for which this shall be to you and every of you a sufficient warrant.[61]

60 HMC, *Eleventh Report, App. V*, I, p. 102; III, pp. 40–3.
61 SRO, D(W)1778/V/1397.

George Legge, 1st Baron Darmouth (*c.* 1647–1691). (Creative Commons Public Domain)

In accordance with Sir Hugh Cholmeley's original design for the Mole, a stone rubble mound or bank had been cast into the sea and elevated to low water level. Onto this he fabricated a superstructure of masonry-work, many of the stones being attached together with lead and iron rods, and then bound with mortar. As the Mole proceeded outwards and thus became exposed to the winter storms, it had become essential to modify the design by adding for large wooden crates or chests (designed by Sheres) that were towed out and sunk on the rubble mound. These were filled partly with large loose rocks, and partly with solid blocks, fastened to the chests by iron straps. The general concurrence during the demolition operations of 1683–4 was that the destruction of the Mole's chest-work would be especially problematical, although the foundations, would be much easier to obliterate. Dartmouth wrote that Sheres' structures were as tough and resilient as rock, 'though the former part is but rubbish and will easily be dispersed when the water-breaks made by him to secure it are gone'.[62] It was soon discovered, however, that Cholmeley's foundations were far more resilient than expected, causing Dartmouth to appeal to Jenkins a month later:

> The Mole is a very heavy piece of work and though most of the tarras work is already destroyed by powder, yet that can take no effect of the rubbish and body of Sir Hugh Cholmeley's part, which is very great and must be removed into the harbour by hands and labour, but this good will follow that the harbour will be fully choked up by it … for God's sake, Sir, I implore his Majesty not to think the time long, for I protest I do all that is possible to be done … the work is much greater than was imagined.[63]

Thus, all available labour was directed towards the Mole, until finally, in January, it was so reduced that the sea had free passage over it, and only for an hour or so at low water could its ruins be observed. During the final few weeks, under seemingly endless rain, the last stages of the demolition of the outer defences occurred. At 4:00 a.m. on 15 January 1684, 200 seamen belonging to the *Grafton*, armed with muskets and poleaxes, with parties from each of the other vessels in the harbour, were put ashore. Joined by the soldiers of the garrison, they passed through Catherina Port into the open field, where some men took up the 300-yard-long stockade leading from

62 TNA, CO 279/32, fol. 274. Dartmouth's report, 19 October 1683.

63 TNA, CO 279/32, fols 275–6; HMC, *Eleventh Report, App. V*, III, p. 34. Dartmouth to Jenkins, 16 November 1683.

the city to Pole Fort, as well all other defences around the fortification. That being completed, a mine was set under the fort, in readiness for the last of the Tangier defences to be rendered useless.[64] On 20 January the field officers and engineers of the garrison reported to Dartmouth that all the mines were ready. The same day, the naval captains, led by Sir John Berry, second-in-command to Dartmouth, produced their official report, which concluded:

> As for the Mole itself, it is so entirely ruined and destroyed, and the harbour so filled with stones and rubbish, and made so unfit to receive, harbour, or protect in any manner from the weather, or from an enemy, any ships or vessels, and that in very many degrees worse than the bay itself naturally would have done, before the building the Mole, that when you shall think fit to order the little hillock of sand, lying at the hither end of the beach, and that of stones on the other, to be made level with the other parts of it, we do unanimously, in our best judgments, not only think what has been done does fully and completely answer all the ends of making one and the other in no capacity to give any kind of refuge or protection to the ships or vessels of any pirates, robbers, or any enemies of the Christian faith, or any others.[65]

The Moors were now close at hand, watching from the nearby hillsides. Thus, a carefully planned withdrawal was to be executed by the garrison. At 4:00 a.m. the following day, the soldiers mustered fully armed at the alarm posts without beat of drum, all soldiers being equipped with serviceable weapons and ammunition. The carpenters, artificers and Molemen came under the command of military officers, and the carpenters carried their tools with them. Having been issued two days' rations (3 lb of bread and ½ lb of butter per man) the 2,366-strong military garrison, led by the King's Battalion of Foot Guards, departed in good order to the waterside, where the soldiers were rowed company by company to the awaiting transports. The Mole guard mustered under Whitby Gate, whilst the water guard, galley guard, Salley-port guard and governor's guard gathered at Johnson's Battery, before making their way to the ships.[66] All the fortifications and walls were mined for last-minute destruction, and on 20 January 1684 Martin Beckman and his assistant engineer Thomas Phillips, blew up all the outlying forts and the city walls on the landward side. Only York Castle and Peterborough Tower remained defensible. By 4 February, the houses in the city were reported to be 'all down to the ground'. A good deal of demolition work inside the walls was done by physical work with picks and crowbars. Some 6–700 men were detailed to dismantle the roofs, floors, and walls of structures.

Only buildings requiring too much time to pull down by hand were to be blown up, given the shortage of explosives and the magnitude of the task. Part of York Castle, near the shoreline, was severely damaged by an explosion, the spectacular blast almost levelling most of the structure. As the Moors pressed

64 TNA, ADM 51/407; *Tangier Papers*, p. 283.

65 SRO, D(W)1778/I/i/979; *Eleventh Report, App. V*, III, p. 42. Answers to questions on the state of the Mole, 20 January 1684.

66 SRO, D742/0/4/30.

closer, Dartmouth felt obliged to warn them, via the hoisting of a white flag on the beach, not to advance into the ruins until all the demolition charges had ignited, although some of their more eager soldiers entered and eight of them were killed in various explosions. Finally, the next day (5 February 1684) the last mines were detonated, the most spectacular bringing down Peterborough Tower. Dartmouth then fired the final charge, beneath Whitehall Fort, before withdrawing to his flagship. According to Berry:

> This morning at 4 o'clock I went ashore with all the boats in the fleet having a lieutenant out of each ship. My Lord employed us all the day in carrying off whatever continued on shore (of stores or other things) on board the small frigates which were ordered to come in very near, to that purpose; and in carrying off soldiers, who were also put on board the small frigates. My lord employed his men that he had ashore with him, in blowing up the walls and other fortifications of the town and castle, the houses being all down to the ground. About 12 at night, my Lord (having seen every man that was ashore put into boats with which I lay ready for that purpose) came into his own boat and so quitted Tangier. Upon his coming off he gave fire to the last mine himself, which about an hour after blew up. We had but 2 men killed and 5 or 6 wounded, in quitting the place, although we had perpetual showers of stones flying as the mines were sprung. It blew fresh and rainy weather the whole day.[67]

Hence, Tangier was officially abandoned by the English Crown, leaving devastation and a lost opportunity, although as some writers and the *in situ* structures visible today confirm, the destruction was less complete than official propaganda and Phillips' carefully dramatic vistas of 1683 and 1684 imply.[68]

That evening, the merchantman *Charles*, with the cavalry troops aboard, sailed for Cadiz, *en route* for England.[69] The day before, Dartmouth had contracted with Robert Lurting, the ship's captain, to transport the garrison horses homewards. It has been suggested, based on a petition of the officers of the Tangier Horse to Dartmouth, requesting transportation of their horses to England, that the garrison's mounts were unloaded at Cadiz and sold in exchange for rations, but evidence for this is lacking.[70] The remaining English fleet weighed anchor on 5 March 1684 and sailed away. On 23 February 1684 the captain of the flagship *Grafton*, recorded 'the *Charles* merchantman that had the troopers and horses on board, came likewise out [of Cadiz] and anchored here [the Bay of Bulls]'.[71] In Tangier the troopers had been supplied with Iberian-type horses, called the Andalusian in both Portugal and Spain, strongly built, compact and intelligent. Officers had to purchase their own at between £30 and £80 apiece – an inflated figure, given that during the 1640s Parliamentarian armies obtained saddle mounts in London for £10

67 TNA, ADM 51/407; *Tangier Papers*, pp. 67–71, 285–6.
68 Routh, *Tangier*, pp. 262–5; Elbl, *Portuguese Tangier*, p. 14.
69 SRO, D742/0/2/20; D742/0/7/9; TNA, ADM 51/407; *Tangier Papers*, p. 285.
70 TNA, ADM 106/371/1; SRO, D(W)1778/I/i/868.
71 TNA, ADM 51/407; *Tangier Papers*, pp. 288–9.

or £12, although for bulk purchases £6 to £8 was normal.[72] A decision had previously been taken to reorganise the four troops into dragoons, to be the core of a new regiment under the command of Lord Churchill. Following their arrival in England the troops rode to London, where they handed in their corselets and helmets, before being equipped as dragoons. They were subsequently quartered in various garrisons in Hertfordshire and Hampstead. Two new troops were raised in England, and by May 1684 the new unit, called 'Our Own Royal Regiment of Dragoons', was formally taken onto the establishment of Charles II's army, with six troops of 50 men each.

Seven companies from the eldest Battalion of Colonel Percy Kirke's (First Tangier) Regiment boarded the *Montague*, whilst the remaining company under Captain John Giles embarked in the *Ann* yacht.[73] The 'list of soldiers and other passengers to be transported from Tangier to England by his Majesty's ship the *Montague*', dated 7 February 1684, included the following:

> Colonel Percy Kirke's company, consisting of Colonel Kirke; Captain William Berry; James Whaley, surgeon; William Pountney, marshal; three sergeants, three corporals, two drummers, and 54 men.
>
> Captain Thomas St John's company, consisting of Captain St John; Lieutenant Jenkin Thomas; Ensign Stafford Fairburn; three sergeants, two corporals, two drummers, and 46 men.
>
> Sir James Leslie's company, consisting of Major Sir James Dartmouth; Lieutenant Henry Withers; Ensign Roger Elliott; three sergeants, three corporals, two drummers, and 35 men.
>
> Captain Barbour's company, consisting of Captain Thomas Barbour; Lieutenant Richard Lawes; Ensign Simon Duff; three sergeants, three corporals, two drummers, and 37 men.
>
> Captain George Wingfield's company, consisting of Captain George Wingfield; Lieutenant James Adams; Ensigns Garret and Fitzgerald; three sergeants, three corporals, two drummers, and 27 men.
>
> Captain John Burgess' company, consisting of Captain Burgess; Lieutenant Phillip Maher; Ensign Martin Lester; three sergeants, three corporals, two drummers, and 39 men.
>
> Captain Charles Wingfield's company, consisting of Captain Charles Wingfield; Lieutenant William Storton; Ensign Nathaniel Barber; three sergeants, three corporals, two drummers, and 27 men.

72 Peter Edwards, *The Horse Trade of Tudor and Stuart England* (Cambridge: Cambridge University Press, 1988), pp. 45–6; 'The Supply of Horses to the Parliamentarian and Royalist Armies in the English Civil War', *HR*, 68 (1995), pp. 49–66.

73 SRO, D742/0/2/16; D742/0/7/12; TNA, ADM 51/407; *Tangier Papers*, p. 287.

Thomas Roberts, apothecary; Thomas Pate, victualling agent; and William Scott, surgeon; Elizabeth Gardner, a sergeant's wife, with her daughters Parthenia and Sabra; and Elizabeth Scott, wife of Captain Scott were also passengers.

Soldiers: 340
Male passengers: 3
Female passengers: 4
Total: 347[74]

Departing with the *Montague*, the *Henrietta* carried four companies of the King's Battalion (Sackville's, Bowe's, Tollemache's and Kirke's). The fifth, commanded by Captain James Fortrey, was transferred from the *Tyger* to the *Foresight* in the Bay of Bulls before heading for England.[75] Nine wives and six children travelled with the battalion. Dartmouth planned that following the unit's arrival from Tangier in April 1684, he would personally lead the Guards, 'extraordinary men', to London, together with the elite grenadier companies of all the Tangier regiments. Here, they would form the garrison of the Tower under his command as Master-General of the Ordnance.[76] Dartmouth's connection with the Tower was an important one. In 1682 he was appointed Constable of the Tower, after the post had been allowed to lapse for over a century, and by royal warrant dated 11 June 1685 he raised the 7th Foot, The Royal Regiment of Fusiliers, in response to the threat of the Monmouth Rebellion and as one the steps taken by James II to enlarge the standing army. As it happened, when the King's Battalion reached England, it was reduced to 235 effectives, and having marched to the capital, the companies simply re-joined their parent regiments. Six companies of the second battalion of Kirke's Regiment, led by Lieutenant Colonel Marmaduke Boynton, sailed in *Centurion* (which had returned from shipping the Portuguese priests to Lisbon).

Of the remaining companies, Captain James Guy's men were put into the *Dragon*; Captain Francis Chantrell's command was put aboard the ten-gun ketch, *Deptford*; and the regiment's grenadier company, under Captain William Matthews, embarked on the *Grafton*. In all there were 751 officers and men, plus 30 wives and children.[77] After reaching England the regiment was placed on the English Establishment on 1 May 1684. The strength of the unit was reduced from 16 to 11 companies in June, the companies of Chantrell, Talbot, Guy and Burgess being transferred to the army in Ireland, while Tate's Company was disbanded. A few months previously, Mary, wife of Captain George Talbot, 'now under the command of Colonel Percy Kirke, Governor of Tangier', petitioned the King, stating that she understood:

> that six of the youngest companies of that regiment are to be disbanded, that her said husband having served faithfully for nineteen years in the said garrison

74 SRO, D742/0/7/10; HMC, *Eleventh Report, App. V*, I, pp. 108–9.
75 SRO, D742/0/2/5; D742/0/7/11.
76 TNA, CO 279/33, fols 273–4. Dartmouth to Jenkins, 19 October 1683.
77 SRO, D742/0/2/1; D742/0/7/5; D742/0/7/13; D742/0/7/18; D742/0/7/24; D742/0/7/28.

> had continued as sixth captain, had he not been put by through some pique between Lord Inchiquin and Sir Palmes Fairborne, but was afterwards about the time Charles Fort was lost restored to the command of the fifth company of which he is now captain, and that he has laid out his estate in building in Tangier, and in consideration of the deplorable condition of her husband, herself and children imploring a grant to him of a command of the grenadiers to be made out of the said regiment.[78]

Samuel Pepys, Secretary to Lord Dartmouth (1633–1703). (Creative Commons Public Domain)

Kirke's Regiment became known as the Queen's Regiment of Foot (later, the Queen Dowager's), and in mid 1684 its establishment was one colonel, one lieutenant colonel, surgeon and mate, adjutant, quartermaster, 10 captains, 10 lieutenants, 20 sergeants, 30 corporals, 10 drums, 500 soldiers, and one company of grenadiers consisting of one captain, two lieutenants, three sergeants, three corporals, two drummers and 50 soldiers.[79]

Colonel Trelawny's (Second Tangier) Regiment departed Tangier on 13 or 14 February for Plymouth with 48 officers, 112 NCOs and 541 men, and 33 women and 23 children. Trelawny himself left with eight companies aboard the *Woolwich*, whilst the remaining eight boarded the *Happy Return*.[80] The regiment garrisoned Charles II's new citadel in Plymouth upon its arrival in England, whereupon its strength was reduced from 16 to 11 companies. During the autumn of 1684 Trelawny's was termed the Duchess of York and Albany's Regiment of Foot. Its new Establishment was one colonel, one lieutenant colonel, surgeon and mate, adjutant, quartermaster, 10 captains, 10 lieutenants, 20 sergeants, 30 corporals, 10 drums, 500 soldiers, and one company of grenadiers consisting of one captain, two lieutenants, three sergeants, three corporals, two drummers and 50 privates.[81] Dartmouth proposed to convey part of Dumbarton's Regiment from Tangier to Portsmouth, the strategic hub of the coastal garrisons along the English Channel. He testified, 'I will not tell you, how old a corps, and how serviceable men and officers these are, and therefore I choose them for Portsmouth, where they are not far out of his Majesty's call, if ever he shall have occasion in earnest for them'.[82]

Though Captain Hume's Company had gone ahead with the first flotilla of ships the previous October, 10 companies sailed aboard Dartmouth's

78 *CSPD 1683–84*, p. 352.
79 *CTB*, II, p. 1xvii; Davis, *Second Queen's*, II, p. 2.
80 SRO, D742/0/2/19; D742/0/7/14; D742/0/7/19; TNA, ADM 51/407; *Tangier Papers*, p. 205.
81 *CTB*, II, pp. 1xvii-lxviii.
82 HMC, *Eleventh Report, App. V*, I, p. 112.

flagship, while the remaining five joined the *Oxford*, a 4th-rate vessel, on 24 February 1684.

Captain Monroe's Company, consisting of Captain Andrew Monroe; Lieutenants Robert Gordon and Andrew Rutherford; Ensign Rory Mackenzie; three sergeants; three corporals; two drummers; and 33 men.

Captain Rollo's Company, himself absent; Lieutenant Matthew Smelt; three sergeants; three corporals; two drummers; and 30 men.

Sir James Murray's Company, consisting of Captain James Murray; Lieutenant Andrew Scott; three sergeants; three corporals; three drummers; and 33 men.

Captain Berkeley's Company, himself absent; Lieutenants George Stewart and William White; Ensign Andrew Berkeley; three sergeants; three corporals; two drummers; and 29 men.

Captain Home's Company, himself absent; Lieutenant John Mowatt; Ensign John Bannerman; three sergeants; three corporals; two drummers; and 28 men.

Alexander Mackenzie, captain of Horse; his sons John and James, Madam Lewis Mackenzie, his wife, Mary; Martha and Penelope, daughters; Edward Wroth, late alderman; Captain St Michell, agent-general for the navy; Samuel Barker and Alexander Oldys, his instruments; Robert Tarres, late inhabitant; sergeants' wives and children.

Total soldiers: 205
Male inhabitants: 11
Females: 17
Total: 233[83]

Prior to the regiment's embarkation, Charles II wrote to Dartmouth, signifying his pleasure that:

> notwithstanding any former directions to the contrary, he takes care that the Scotch foot regiment coming from the late garrison of Tangier be brought immediately on shipboard into the Downs, where he shall receive further orders for the disposition thereof, the King having thought fit to alter the quarters intended for them. With memorandum that the above was twice written and signed and one directed to Lord Dartmouth at Portsmouth and one at Plymouth.[84]

Three days later, Dartmouth received a warrant 'to cause the Scotch Foot Regiment coming from Tangier to be conveyed on shipboard direct to Rochester and landed there, he having been lately directed to take care that the said regiment be brought into the Downs, where he was to receive further orders'.[85] On the regiment's arrival in England, the companies

83 SRO, D742/0/7/22; HMC, *Eleventh Report, App. V*, I, p. 110.

84 TNA, SP44/164, fol. 104; SRO, D(W)1778/I/i/928. Royal warrant for quartering the Scotch companies, 12 December 1683; D(W)1778/I/i/999. Royal warrant altering the quarters of the Scotch Regiment, 12 February 1684.

85 TNA, SP44/69, fol. 95; *CSPD 1683–84*, p. 276.

commanded by Halkett, Monroe, Rollo, Moncrieff, Lundy, Carr, White and Hodges (grenadiers) were quartered in Rochester and Chatham; Lauder and Barclay's were at Southampton; whilst Douglas', Melville's, Murray's, Forbes' and Urquhart's companies were at Winchester.[86] The whereabouts of Hume's command, which had previously arrived at Gravesend, at this juncture are uncertain. The regiment was reunited with the five companies that had been left in Ireland, and from 1 May 1684 it was designated as His Majesty's Royal Regiment of Foot. The distribution of the veterans of the Tangier garrison following their evacuation to England was to a large extent motivated by political and strategic necessity on the part of Charles II. The plan was to land these troops at critical coastal garrisons. Colonel Kirk's first battalion was ordered to oversee the construction of the citadel at Pendennis, a fastness constructed by Henry VIII on the Falmouth peninsular, which was in disrepair and its accommodation inadequate.

Kirke himself would govern the garrison, thus displacing the local commander and militia. His regiment's second battalion was meant to relieve the companies of Foot Guards from the forts along the Thames, tightening Crown control of the capital's lifeline, and increasing the size and prestige of the Household infantry as the King's personal bodyguard. Similarly, the first battalion of Trelawny's Regiment was to land at Plymouth, where it would garrison the fortress. The unit was local to the west of England and its presence would assist in recruiting for the army. The second battalion, commanded by Lieutenant Colonel Charles Churchill, would be deployed to the border stronghold of Berwick, while some companies were to be placed at Tynemouth.[87] In the event, the first battalion replaced Dumbarton's veterans on the south coast. Charles II's army was transformed by the Tangier garrison in 1684. The addition of four troops of Horse and seven battalions of foot – highly experienced, battle-hardened veterans – doubled the size of the forces in England.

One of the final tasks confronting Dartmouth was the liberation of English captives from the Moors. Since 1681 promises for the release of slaves had been made and broken, yet the persistent Kirke managed to negotiate the emancipation of 54 of the 130 men remaining in captivity, some of whom had been held for over a decade. On 12 February 1684 the captain of the *Grafton* recorded taking eight English captives from the shore, 'which my Lord redeemed, these were five seamen and two volunteers belonging to the *Greyhound*, who had been taken four months earlier, and Lieutenant Wilson, captured four years previously in Henrietta Fort.[88] Dartmouth later reported to the King, 'The greatest difficulty was to get off Lieutenant Wilson, but I thought it not for your Majesty's honour to leave a commissioned officer behind that had behaved himself so very well in your service, and I believe will do again upon a little encouragement, though at present his misfortunes and long captivity seem too much to have dejected

86 TNA, WO 5/1, fols 21–2.

87 TNA, CO 279/32, fol. 275; Cowper, *King's Own*, pp. 33–4.

88 TNA, ADM 51/407; *Tangier Papers*, pp. 287–8

him'.[89] According to a petition of John Palmer, he had served 15 months in Tangier as a private soldier under Captain Francis Trelawny, before being taken prisoner on 13 May 1680 defending Charles Fort (where Trelawny was killed). He remained in slavery until being redeemed in 1684.[90] At 6:00 p.m. on 19 February the *Greyhound*, commanded by Captain McDonell sailed for England with 43 captives aboard (the release of 11 of them had been delayed by the Sultan of Morocco), and other passengers. Captains Langstone and Neville also went with the ship, carrying dispatches from Dartmouth.[91]

The final vessel to depart from Tangier was hospital ship *Welcome*. Her captain waited until all the troops were embarked to pick up the remaining invalids and did not sail until 26 February 1684.[92] Dartmouth commended to Jenkins that the cause of the 'widows, fatherless, sick, lame and almost all manner of ways necessitous that can need the help of a good man'. In reply, Sir Leoline recommended that the widows and children, whose husbands and parents had been related to the sea, might be cared for taken care of by Trinity House and other London hospitals, and that 'the soldiers may find relief from the Deputy Lieutenants in the several counties if they are earnestly pressed to it'. Jenkins further assured Dartmouth that Charles II had given special orders for their reception, and discovered even Lord Rochester, the notorious libertine, 'resolved to do all that is possible for these poor people, and for those that are coming, with that speed and method as to prevent clamour, it being far better to do that with charity and expedition, and with a good grace, since we must sooner or later be forced to do it'.[93] On 8 April 1684, after a rough passage lasting 41 days, the *Welcome* arrived opposite Sandown Castle, and the next day she continued to London.[94]

Eventually, in late March 1684, following 'a very tedious and stormy' passage to England – the worst weather and sea conditions in a generation – Dartmouth wrote to the King from Plymouth:

> The forces are brought entire off from the garrison, and are men generally well-qualified for any service your Majesty can have for them; but being to come to the liberty of English soldiers, I thought it my duty to give very strict orders for the officers to stay with their men and have provided for them with ready money for a month's subsistence, for which time at least I am confident your Majesty will hear of no disorders, being all upon their good behaviours and expecting your Majesty's favour and commands.[95]

During the final days of the English project in Tangier a cordial, but frank letter was sent by Sultan Mawaly Ismā'īl to Charles II, which is given below in full:

89 TNA, CO 279/33, fols 74–6, 98; HMC, *Eleventh Report, App. V*, I, p. 105.
90 TNA, SP44/18, fol. 159; *CTB*, VII, p. 1445.
91 SRO, D742/0/7/21; D742/0/7/28.
92 SRO, D742/0/2/12–13; D742/0/2/22. Names of soldiers and seamen on board the *Welcome* hospital ship, April 1684.
93 HMC, *Eleventh Report, App. V*, I, pp. 99–101. Jenkins to Dartmouth, 12, 19, 26 November 1683.
94 TNA, ADM 51/407; *Tangier Papers*, p. 297.
95 SRO, D(W)1778/V/1397; HMC, *Eleventh Report, App. V*, I, p. 105.

To the great one of the Europeans, Charles the Second of the English.

Peace be upon him who follows the right way.

Be it known to you that you were pleased with our companions and servants who came to you, since you asked them to come. We are thankful to you for your pleasure at them and your welcome to them, for you welcomed them in a way in which the nations of the Christians do not welcome Muslims. We are pleased at your doing this, for it emanated from you to our side made impregnable by God. We resolved to grant you a truce of four years over Tanja during which none would cause you fear even though only a single Christian woman remained there, as we have mentioned. And today is the completion of your goodwill and the establishment of your good relations with us, since you have lightened our shame and left the land of the Muslims. So now, if you desire good relations, they shall take place between us. There shall be good relations between us and nothing will damage them, for you have alleviated [our disgrace] and made amends for the shame you have caused us and your coming. We shall not do for you anything but what you desire, if God wills it, in everything that you want today from us and desire in the ports of the Muslims, and we shall receive you only with that. As to what has happened heretofore, anyone who has told you that I would make a treaty of peace with respect to Muslim land while you are covering it with your cannon has lied to you and spoken to you with a hidden purpose, and said what is not true, for I cannot make a treaty with you over Muslim land while you are occupying it by force. The Turks would revile me for that if I did it and deride me because of it, for the Turks, if they make peace with the Christians, do not do so until they have them under a treaty of *dhimma*, not like you, who had your watchtowers and cannon while desiring that I should make peace with you. God will not consent to our doing that. As for your good relations with us and good intentions towards us, we are certain of this and acquainted with it. By God, if you had written to me secretly and sent a letter to say you desired to depart from Tanja, and go out from it and had informed us of that so that we might make what you desire easy for you till you depart as you intend without inconvenience, you would not have encountered any tent or expeditionary force, or contingent, and that would have been between you and me. But when the Muslims saw you companions beginning to demolish and uproot, and they were told that the French had asked you to sell Tanja so that the Muslims would be at the mercy of the French, on this account the *mahalla* has remained there these six months; but there was never anything else besides this. By God, the Muslims asked me [to allow them] to do you harm on the day when they saw your companions beginning to uproot and I prevented them from doing that and forbade it and said to them: 'During the four years' truce which I have granted them they will not see us do any harm to Tanja as long as a single day of its full reckoning remains'. By this I persuaded them to desist from harming you and turned them back from you. By God, if you wish to remain there nobody will contradict what we have said to you nor harm you with respect to it. Since you have relieved our shame and handed over our country to us, this is the perfection of good relations, and your mind may be at rest as far as we are concerned. Even that Mole which you have wrecked – if you had left it how it was, we would have given you the price of it, and it would have been useful to you, because your ships often journey to India and other countries and might have relaxed there. They might even take on fresh water and find it on their outward passage, and on the return, because you have shown goodwill towards the Muslims and countered them with their due.

The coming of our servant Muhammad ben Haddū was against his will. When you asked that one of our servants should come to you we sent him to you; but since he reached you and you rejoiced at him, and welcomed him he says to you: 'We shall fulfil for you with Our Lord your aims, and he will be kind towards you'. When he reached us and mentioned this to us here – now you have heard what happened to him. Anybody who said anything to you before this has lied to you. Now, if you desire any benefit and there is no harm in it to what we hold most dear, we will do it for you, and you will have good relations with us. Everything you desire in the ports of the Muslims shall be nothing but what you purpose, if God wills.

Peace.

On the sixth of blessed Rabīᶜ the First of the Prophet, One thousand and ninety-five years [26 February 1684].[96]

96 TNA, SP102/2, fol. 128; J. F. P. Hopkins (trans. and ann.), *Letters from Barbary, 1576–1774: Arabic documents in the Public Record Office* (London & New York: Oxford University Press, 1982), pp. 30–2; Bejjit, *English Colonial Texts*, Letter XIII.

Conclusion

The English colony of Tangier, maintained by its military garrison and English naval operations, had been established in 1661 in great optimism, yet the survival of both was ultimately dependent on the political interests and ambition of the English Crown. With notable, and sometimes calamitous exceptions, its governors were uncertain in their policies, and disadvantaged by financial and material constraints imposed from London. Indeed, in late Stuart England, the fortunes of precarious overseas settlements would be dictated by the cut and thrust of politics within the equally fragile centre. The imperial ambitions of the Crown and government were proclaimed against a background of internal and international hostilities. Opportunities to consolidate Tangier as an international trading the colony, and possible springboard for future ambitions in the Mediterranean and beyond, were missed through unrealistic expectations, complacency, incompetence, poor fortune and the reticence of both the Tangier Committee and certain governors. The timorousness of the latter meant that the colony failed to assert itself sufficiently to command the respect of Morocco's Sultan or its local chieftains. The lack of territorial expansion meant that Tangier never developed as a burgeoning base for English settlers and merchants.

But despite assertions that the somewhat hybrid garrison of Tangier 'left minor footnotes in English history', the regiments – largely consisting of experienced veterans of various wars – fought against an unfamiliar foe, often in extremely demanding circumstances, with great skill and resolve. These soldiers pioneered the use of new weapons, such as hand grenades and the plug bayonet, during a period of great change within Charles II's army, of which they constituted a sizeable, if remote element. This they undertook, devoid of regular pay, provisions, clothing, and drafts of recruits, during a period of anti-Catholic sentiments at home. Besides, although some of the commissioned officers leading the rank and file were experienced men of energy, valour, skill and imagination on the battlefield, others were amongst the lowest quality, and least attentive towards the privations suffered by their men. Colley has situated the collapse of the Tangier colony and garrison in a pattern of encounters that revealed the weakness of colonial settlements in the face of dynamic local rulers. The revival of Alouite Morocco as a regional power, as well as the increasing maritime supremacy of North African Corsairs, underlined 'the scale of the disparity between Britain's massive imperial pretensions on the one hand and its modest domestic size and resources on the other'.[1]

Correspondingly, Tristan Stein credited the decline of Tangier to opposing trends in the English political economy, the effect of which was to leave the colony trapped between 'competing models for the organisation of overseas trade and empire'.[2] Hence, the loss of Tangier was not widely grieved in England, yet the commercial and military benefits of a naval station at the entrance to the Mediterranean were not forgotten. Forty years after its acquisition, Bishop Burnet would recall Tangier as a place 'then spoken of in the court in the highest strains of flattery', adding that 'such mighty things were said of it, as if it had been reserved for the King's reign, to make it as glorious abroad, as it was happy at home'.[3] It was true that remarkable levels of expectation and money had been invested in such an overseas colony, never before part of the English strategic imagination. The English possession of Tangier in 1661–2 capitalised on the optimism created by the Restoration of Charles II, when the basis for expanding trade and establishing new territories included Crown related endeavours in Morocco and other overseas locations. As one pamphleteer declared, 'His Majesty hath an Imperial name, it was Charles that brought the Empire into France. Charles that brought it first into Spain. Why should not Great Britain have his turn?'.[4]

1 Colley, *Captives*, pp. 5–6.

2 Tristan Stein, 'Tangier in the Restoration Empire', *HJ*, 54 (2011), pp. 985–1011 (p. 987).

3 Burnet, *History of His Own Time*, I, p. 173.

4 William de Britaine, *The Interest of England in the Present War with Holland by the author of The Dutch Usurpation* (London: Jonathan Edwin, 1672), pp. 20–1.

Appendix I

Commission of Henry Mordaunt, Earl of Peterborough, as Commander-in-Chief of the King's Forces in Tangier, 6 September 1661[1]

Charles, by the Grace of God, King of England, Scotland, France and Ireland, Defender of the Faith, etc.

To Our right trusty and right well-beloved Henry Mordaunt, Earl of Peterborough, greeting. Know ye, that we, reposing special trust and confidence in your approved wisdom, fidelity, valour, and great abilities, have assigned, made, constituted, and ordained, and by these our letters-patent do assign, make, constitute, and ordain you to be our Captain-General, Chief Governor, and Vice-Admiral of our City of Tangier, and of the ports and coasts adjacent, and any of our dominions and territories, castles and forts, in or near the kingdom of Tangier, Fès, and Morocco, in Africa, which are or shall be in our possession, or reduced to our obedience.

We intend forthwith to settle and secure Our city of Tangier, and the territories and dominions in or near the coasts of Barbary or the kingdoms of Sus, Fès, and Morocco, some or one of them in the continent of Africa. And for that purpose have resolved by and with the advice of our Privy Council forthwith to raise, draw forth, and transport thither such forces of horse and foot as we shall judge necessary for our service in the defence of the said city of Tangier, and our dominions or territories in or near the said kingdoms … we do further by these presents give full power and authority to you, our said Captain-General, from time to time to muster, exercise and train our

1 TNA, CO 279/1, fol. 29; BL, MS Harley 1595, fols 10–11; MS Sloane 1956, fols 68–9.

said forces, and all other our armies and forces which you shall there raise or entertain into our service or which shall be sent to you from hence or any other place, and to arm, train, conduct, and lead out, or otherwise employ the natives or other inhabitants if need shall require, and with them to defend our said city of Tangier and any other our dominions which already are or which shall be hereafter be in our power or possession, and to lead them forth against any enemies, rebels or traitors, and them to fight, kill, or slay and subdue to our obedience, and to invade, surprise and reduce such towns, forts, castles, or countries as shall declare or maintain any hostility against us. We do further appoint you Vice-Admiral, with authority to give orders to all naval forces and commanders commissioned to attend on Tangier and on the coast of Africa, and to require them to prosecute any design which you shall judge to be for the service of the king. You are empowered to constitute a Court of Admiralty for the hearing and determining all maritime causes, and to make laws and ordinances as near as may be conformable to the laws of England for the better carrying on of the civil government of our city of Tangier. Our main design in putting Ourself to this great charge for making this addition to our dominions being to gain our subjects the trade of Barbary and to enlarge our dominions in that sea … we are graciously pleased that no duties or customs or other taxes whatsoever shall be laid by us upon any goods imported to or exported from our city of Tangier, and that it shall be and remain a free port.

Letter from Charles II to Peterborough, 21 October 1661[2]

My Lord Peterborough, I am very well satisfied of your care and diligence in the employment you are in, for which I thank you very heartily and assure yourself I have so just a sense of this and all your other services as you shall find upon all occasions how much I esteem and value those who serve me faithfully. I have no more to add at present only to desire you to let those honest men know who go along with you that they shall always be in my particular care and protection, as persons that venture themselves in my service, and so wishing you a good voyage, I remain, your very affectionate friend, Charles R.

2 BL, MS Harley 6844, fol. 115r.; Routh, *Tangier*, p. 13.

Appendix II

Proclamation by Charles II Declaring his Majesties Pleasure to Settle and Establish a Free Port at his City of Tangier in Africa, 16 November 1662[1]

As We cannot but know that the welfare and prosperity of Our good Subjects depends very much upon the safety and improvement of trade, and have therefore made it a great part of Our Princely care and study to find out ways and means for the advancement and security of their general traffic and commerce. So We cannot but hope that these Our just ends and purposes (which We had chiefly in Our prospect) will be very much promoted by gaining the city of Tangier in Africa as an accession unto Our dominions.

It being not unreasonable to believe, that by means of this Our city of Tangier a way may be opened to trades not yet used, and such as could not heretofore with any safety be at tempted: wherein if the success should not answer Our desires, yet certainly many of those trades which are now frequented, will hereafter be carried on with much more ease and security to Our merchants, when they shall have a good port in the entry of the Mediterranean to befriend them. To the end therefore that all fit encouragement may be given to make use of the advantages of this port. We have thought fit to declare, and do hereby declare and publish Our Royal Will and Pleasure, that Our city of Tangier is and shall be port free to all merchants, as well foreigners as others, with their ships and vessels, except such ships and vessels which shall

1 London: John Bill and Christopher Barker, printers to the King's most Excellent Majesty, 1662; Bejjit, *English Colonial Texts*, pp. 58–9.

come from beyond the Cape of Good Hope, commonly called *Capo de bon esperanza;* and except ships coming from any of Our English plantations, for and during such time, and upon such terms, articles, and conditions as are herein after expressed (that is to say)

I. First it shall lawful for all Our good subjects, and the subjects of any other nation in amity with us (except before excepted) to come freely into Our port at Tangier, with their ships, vessels, and merchandizes, and to land the same, or any part thereof, and lay them up in such warehouses or other places as they shall think fit.

II. All persons coming into Our said port with any ships, or merchandizes, shall enter, or cause to be entered in the registry there to be kept for that purpose, all the goods, wares, merchandizes and commodities by them landed, and shall pay, or cause to be paid for every hundred pounds' worth of goods so landed, according to the rates and values of merchandizes set down in the book of rates established in England, five shillings for the entry thereof, and no other duty or payment whatsoever.

III. If any person shall refuse or neglect to make entry of his goods so imported and landed, or shall not make entry without fraud or deceit; the person so refusing or neglecting to make entry, or making short entry, shall lose and forfeit the ship or vessel, together with all the goods so imported, and be utterly incapable of any of the privileges or benefits herein before or after mentioned.

IV. It shall be lawful for all persons to export or sell upon the place, the goods so imported, at his and their will and pleasure, without paying any further or other imposition or duty whatsoever.

V. All persons exporting any goods from Our said port and city of Tangier, into any part of Our kingdoms of England or Ireland, shall be obliged to export the same in English shipping, and with English mariners.

VI. This liberty and freedom of Our port at Tangier shall continue from the nine and twentieth day of September 1662, for and during the full time and term of five years from thenceforth next coming; in all which time there shall be no further or greater improvement of Our customs within Our said port. And We do also declare, that when those five years shall be elapsed, We shall not make any new or greater imposition upon the trade of that port, without first giving public notice thereof after the expiration of five years, by the space of two years before any such new or greater imposition shall take effect.

Appendix III

Instructions for Colonel John Fitzgerald, Going to Tangier as Lieutenant-Governor, 7 June 1664[1]

I. You are to take with you copies of the late Earl of Teviot's commission and instructions of 27 April and 21 December 1663, for the government of Tangier and command of the forces there till we dispose of the government otherwise and direct yourself thereby except as varied by these instructions.

II. You shall embark with the men, arms, etc., now ready at Portsmouth for the recruit of that place in the ship appointed by the Duke of York.

III. On arrival you are to take a perfect survey and review of the men, provisions and arms and all other things relating to the garrison with the assistance of Colonel Bullen Reymes and by him give us an account thereof.

IV. You are to take particular notice of the 4th, 5th and 6th articles of the said instructions of 27 April, viz., concerning the proclamation declaring Tangier a free port, the administration of justice and the worship of God.

V5. As for what relates to exportation and importation of goods, restraint of trade with Tétuan and Sale, making peace or war with Gayland or anything of the like nature, we cannot well prescribe rules at present for want of necessary information and therefore leave you full power to act according to the best of your understanding what shall be most for our service and the benefit of the place, keeping correspondence with the Saint and other potentates there, and on any offer for the surrender of the castle of Sale you shall govern yourself according to the instructions already or hereafter given you.

1 TNA, SP71/174B, fol. 34; *CSPD: Charles II, Addenda 1660–1685*, pp. 103–7.

VI. You shall be very careful in seeing the peace with Algiers, Tunis and Tripoli maintained but be wary of doing or suffering anything to be done in favour of the Turkish government to the offence and scandal of our Christian allies and confederates, remembering always that the said peace is to be observed so far only as you shall understand they have given Sir John Lawson satisfaction in the present dispute with them.

VII. As to the directions we gave for making an estimate and valuation of the houses in Tangier, you shall direct yourself by the instruction and commission we shall give, remembering that the garrison is first to be provided for and that the houses bought by the Earl of Sandwich and some officers of his fleet and likewise the house of Simon Lopez de Mendoza granted to the Earl of Peterborough be reserved to them and that no more strangers be suffered to inhabit there than will consist with the security of the place; especially you must have a watchful eye over the Jews, if you suffer any. As for the Portuguese, no cause being given by them to make you jealous of their fidelity, you are to give them a more avowed encouragement, preserving those that are of any religious order in all the privileges and immunities promised them by the first articles but not suffering new ones to be admitted in the place of those dying nor making any scruple of ejecting those yet living if you find them tampering or guilty of any dangerous correspondence nor allowing them nor the Roman Catholics there the use of any of the churches more than what shall be requisite to the proportion of their number.

VIII. Having mustered and reviewed the remaining soldiers, you shall as before put them into two foot regiments to be commanded by yourself and Colonel Norwood, allotting nine companies to your regiment and eight to his, each of 100 men, besides officers. The two companies of horse to be commanded by Sir Tobias Bridges, from whom you are to receive a more express account of the condition of the garrison, delivering him our letter and thanking him in our name for his care on the Earl of Teviot's loss and availing yourself of his advice and assistance, we having a very particular esteem for him. We think it needless to repeat the same of Colonel Norwood. You shall generally confirm the officers appointed by Sir Tobias Bridges, if you find them fit, keeping entire the two companies from Portsmouth with their own officers and disposing of the rest of the recruits into the companies now at Tangier as you shall see cause, abolishing as much as you can that national distinction of English, Irish and Scotch.

IX. In making the review of the men, stores and provisions of all kinds you are to call to your assistance Colonel Bullen Reymes, with whose assistance, joining therein Colonel Norwood, Sir Tobias Bridges, Hugh Cholmeley and Captain Simon Hewer, or any three of them you are likewise to examine all the Earl of Teviot's papers relating to the garrison.

X. You shall dispose of the £14,000 as you have been directed by the Committee for Tangier, passing the piece of eight at 4s. 9d., not suffering any to be issued but by your orders, the like to be observed in the disposing of all stores, the profit of dead places to be added to the fund for contingencies.

XI. We warn you by the unhappy example of what has lately happened there not to affect making inroads into the country nor extending the limits of the garrison further than you are secure of maintaining them, endeavouring only for the present to preserve the redoubts. You shall with special care promote all things conducing to the advance of the trade and commerce, intending principally the progress of the mole by encouraging those laborious therein and punishing those remiss and disobedient to their officers. You are to thank in our name all our officers and soldiers for their good behaviour in the actions with the Moors and their sober comportment after this last misfortune.

XII. In any occasion of more than ordinary importance while the city shall want a governor and remain under your command you are to consult with Colonel Norwood and Sir Tobias Bridges and also with Colonel Bullen Reymes as long as he shall continue there.

Appendix IV

Lord Dartmouth's Commission as Admiral of the Fleet and Captain-General in Tangier, 2 July 1683[1]

Charles by the grace of God King of England, Scotland, France and Ireland, Defender of the Faith etc. to our right trusty and well-beloved counsellor George, Baron of Dartmouth, Master-General of our Ordnance and Armouries, greeting.

We having judged it necessary for our service forthwith to draw off all our loving subjects, inhabitants of our city of Tangier, together with their goods and effects, as also all our officers and soldiers there in garrison, with the arms, ammunition, provisions and stores thereto belonging, and immediately thereupon to demolish and utterly to destroy the said city and the Mole erected in the port belonging to it, so as they may be altogether useless, and no pirate or enemy of the Christian faith may at any time hereafter make their abode or retreat there, to the annoying of the seas and the coasts in those parts. And we having for the effecting of the premises designed an expedition to be presently made, and having also, as much as in us lies, put in readiness all things necessary to accomplish those ends, know ye that we reposing special trust and confidence in your fidelity, courage and ability, have made, constituted and appointed, and by these presents do make, constitute and appoint you, George Baron of Dartmouth, Admiral and Commander-in-chief of our fleet to be employed in this expedition, and also Captain-general, Governor and Commander-in-chief of our said city of Tangier and the territory thereto belonging, and of all our forces, both horse and foot, that now are, or at the time of your arrival there, shall be under the command of any person or persons whatsoever, in our said city and in the port, harbour and territory thereto belonging. To have, hold and enjoy the said place and

1 SRO, D(W)1778/V/1397; HMC, *Eleventh Report, App. V*, I, p. 93; *Tangier Papers*, pp. 58–66.

places of Admiral, Captain-general, Governor and Commander-in-chief to you the said George, lord Dartmouth, during the time and term hereafter limited, with all the powers, privileges, immunities and advantages which any of our admirals, captains-general, governors and commanders-in-chief at any time had or ought to have had and enjoyed, and to that end, you may act and proceed with full and unquestionable authority in the execution of this our Commission. We do hereby determine and revoke all commissions by us granted to any person or persons whatsoever, whereby they, or any one of them, have been or are constituted and appointed captains-general, governors lieutenant-governors or commanders-in-chief of our said city of Tangier, and of our garrison and forces there, and particularly we do by these presents determine and revoke our Commission lately issued out under our Great Seal of England to our trusty and well-beloved Percy Kirke Esquire, the present governor of our said city of Tangier, with all the powers and authorities thereby granted to him, or to any other under him, and we do hereby give and grant you full power and authority to suspend, displace or cashier any officer or soldier belonging to our said garrison, as also any officer or mariner serving in our said fleet as you shall [think] him or them to deserve respectively, and also to pardon offences and misdemeanours as you in your discretion shall think fit. Likewise to nominate and appoint new officers in the room and stead of those that shall be so displaced and cashiered, or whose place shall be vacant by death, until we shall by our royal commission otherwise dispose of the same. And for the better government and discipline of the forces under your command both by sea and land, we do hereby give you full power and authority to put in due execution, certain articles and rules by us heretofore made for the better government of our forces by land, printed and published by our command in the year 1673, a copy of which articles and rules will be delivered you together with certain Instructions under our royal signet and sign-manual, bearing the same date with these presents, that we have thought fit to prepare for you relating to this expedition, which articles and rules you are to observe and execute in all cases of discipline and punishment to be inflicted upon our officers and soldiers at land, and for crimes and offences committed upon the sea by any person whatsoever, being in our service and pay, you are to proceed in all things according to a certain Act of Parliament made in the thirteenth year of our reign, and intituled An Act for establishing Articles and Orders for the regulating and better Government of His Majesty's Navy, Ships of War, and Forces by Sea, and by no other rules, constitutions or customs whatsoever. And we do hereby give and grant you full power and authority to employ all and every the officers and soldiers of our said garrison and all the mariners and soldiers that can be spared from on board our fleet, not only in and for the defence of our said city and good subjects there until you have demolished the place and made good your retreat, but also in and for the demolishing and utterly destroying of the city and Mole aforesaid. And we do further give and grant you full power and authority by these presents to draw off, embark and transport all our loving subjects that you shall find upon the place, as well the magistrates, officers and inhabitants of our said city, with their families, goods, merchandise and effects, as also all our officers and soldiers of the garrison, together with the artillery, arms, ammunition, provisions and stores thereto belonging, and them and all of [worth] to carry away and land in such ports and places as they shall desire, provided it be consistent with the Instructions above mentioned, where to you are referred in that behalf. And we do further give and grant you full power and authority by these presents to make and cause to be made such mines, fourneaus and works of all sorts in and about the said city, and in the said Mole, as may be with most effect made use of to blow up in the Instructions aforesaid, the showing or exhibiting of these our Letters Patent and the showing of the said Instructions respectively, shall be in all and every of our Courts of Justice and elsewhere, to you and them respectively, a sufficient warrant, discharge and acquittance. And we do hereby declare this our Commission and all the powers and authorities therein given you, to be in full force from the day of the date hereof, during the whole expedition and until such time as we do by warrant or other signification of our pleasure under our sign-manual or privy signet, determine and revoke this our Commission.

Instructions to our right trusty and well-beloved counsellor George Baron of Dartmouth, Master-General of our Ordnance and Armouries, for an expedition to be forthwith made to Tangier, and for services to be performed there, 2 July 1683[2]

Whereas we have by our Commission bearing date the 2nd day of this present month of July, constituted and appointed you our Admiral, Captain-general, Governor and Commander-in-chief for and during an expedition that we have thought necessary to be made at this present to the Straits of Gibraltar, in order to draw off and bring back from our city of Tangier all our subjects, inhabitants of the place, and also all our officers and soldiers there in garrison, and then forthwith to demolish and utterly to destroy the place and also the Mole that has been begun by us in that port, you are therefore to repair with all the convenient speed you can on board our man-of-war called the Grafton, or on board any other ship that we shall appoint, and to take upon you the command of our fleet now lying in the Downs, or otherwhere upon the coast attending and appointed for this present expedition. You are to wear the Union flag at the main top masthead of the ship you shall be on board of, and with our said fleet to sail away for the port of Tangier, with all the speed the wind and weather will permit.

2. Being arrived at Tangier, you are to take upon you the execution of the place and trust of Captain-general, Commander-in-chief and Governor of our said city of Tangier, and of all our forces there, and in order thereto you are, at such time as you shall think convenient for our service, to communicate our said Commission to the present Governor and the officers in the garrison,

2 SRO, D(W)1778/V/1397; HMC, *Eleventh Report, App. V*, I, pp. 83–5; *Tangier Papers*, pp. 58–66.

and likewise to the Mayor and aldermen in that our city, in their assembly. And you are, when you do it, to make appear to them the necessity there is for us at this time to abandon and demolish the place, and you are to exhort them that everyone in his station, and according to his power, do endeavour that this service be well performed, assuring them of our protection and of the gracious care we have of them upon this occasion.

3. This being done, you are, soon as you can conveniently, to cause a general muster to be made of our garrison, and you are to see that both officers and soldiers do duly receive their shares in such pay as the Lords Commissioners of our Treasury shall be able to send them by your conveyance.

4. You are likewise to apply yourself to the taking a true estimate and valuation of the estates and interests that the proprietors and inhabitants have in their houses and tenements respectively, and to reduce the same into the form of a general certificate to be laid before us, to the end we may not be without the light requisite, when we shall apply ourselves to make some reasonable compensation (as in our princely compassion we mean to do) to our good subjects for those rights and interests they shall have given up and quitted upon this occasion, always provided that our said subjects do acquiesce in a moderate estimate of their said interests and declare themselves so to do within such a time as you shall prefix.

5. But in regard it would be a work too tedious for you (that will have so many other things upon your hands) to audit and state every man's particular case and interest that shall pretend to a compensation in this kind, we do hereby give you power to depute two or three discreet persons who may and shall in your room treat and agree with the parties interested, about the particular values to be certified to us. And where they shall not be able to bring the parties to agree to and acquiesce in a moderate value, then and in that case the matter in difference to be brought before you, to hear and determine what is reason able and fit to be certified as touching the value that shall be controverted.

6. Among those that are to be considered for such rights and interests, our will and pleasure is that you have a first regard to the Portuguese and other strangers, whose indemnity is provided for by the treaty that we made with the Crown of Portugal, when the right and possession of the city of Tangier was passed over to us, and that they be either paid or secured the value of their interests before they depart the place.

7. You are also, as much as in you lies, to help the said Portuguese and all merchant strangers to recover and get in their just debts from such of our natural born subjects as are solvent, or otherwise have money due to them from us, paying or securing the value to the said Portuguese and strangers, and stopping it for our reimbursement when we come to reckon with our said subjects.

8. You are to take care that the said Portuguese and strangers, with their families, goods and effects be shipped off in the first place and that they be accommodated as much as conveniently may be, according to their several conditions and needs, and transported to their native countries, or to such ports as they shall reasonably desire, if it be not a prejudice to our service.

9. You are to take care, before you draw off any of our garrison, that all our natural born subjects, inhabitants of the said city, their families, effects and goods (excepting lumber of little value to the owners, and of great en cumbrance to the rest of the passengers) be carefully shipped off and as well as may be, accommodated according to their respective qualities and conditions. And to that end you are to require and give order that the captains and commanders of our men-of-war, as well as of other ships attending this expedition, do receive on board them, such provisions and accommodations as may be suitable to the number and quality of the persons distributed to each ship.

10. You are to take order that such of our subjects as being inhabitants of Tangier, and not soldiers, are natives of our Kingdoms of England, Scotland and Ireland, be so disposed of for their transportation, that those of each nation respectively may be carried to their native country, or to such ports as shall be nearest to it. And in case any of them shall desire to be transported to any of our plantations or any place of our dominions that is not their native soil, you are, if they be in any considerable number, to comply with them as far as it can be done without too great an expense or prejudice to our service.

11. You are to take notice that we allow those who have been born in Tangier to be transported to any of our kingdoms, dominions or plantations, as they shall reason ably desire and choose to go, along with their friends.

12. After that the magistrates, officers and inhabitants of the city are embarked and disposed of, your next care is to be about the transporting and accommodating the soldiers, and herein it is our will and meaning that the Scottish regiment and also the Irish forces be transported directly into our Kingdom of Ireland, there to receive our further orders. And you are to take special care that the aged, the maimed, the sick and weak officers and soldiers of the garrison be put on board the hospital ships that we have ordered to be provided for that purpose, with such provisions and attendants as is suitable to their needs, and if there be any among them, or the townsmen, so sick and weak as not to be able to endure a voyage by sea for any of our ports of England or Ireland, then you are to cause them to be transported and set down on the opposite Spanish shore and by our consuls in Spain, or some such means, to order some subsistence for them there, and some provision for their passage homewards when they do recover.

13. While you are thus preparing and disposing things for the drawing and transporting of our said subjects from Tangier, it is our will and meaning that your main care and application be from your first arrival there, to bring all

things to a readiness to blow up, demolish and destroy the said city and Mole. You are therefore to employ all the hands you can get, by such numbers, in such places and at such hours as you shall think convenient, to make such mines, fourneaus and works as may be most proper and effectual for the utter demolishing of the said city and for destroying the said Mole. And when you have put all things in a readiness, and have shipped off all our liege people there, as well foreigners as natural born subjects, and secured your own retreat and the retreat of our whole garrison, you are to blow up and destroy the whole place and the Mole, as much as is possible for you to do.

15. When you have blown up and destroyed the town and the Mole, you are together with our fleet under your command to make the best of your way homeward to give us an account of what you shall have done in the execution of our Commission. In the interim, you are to correspond punctually with one of our principal secretaries, to the end we may, with every convenience that offers, be informed of your proceedings.

16. And because in the execution of so great a work many difficulties will arise which cannot be foreseen, and by reason of the distance, no timely supply can be made to these Instructions, in case they should prove defective, our further pleasure is, and you are to take notice that we leave it to you and give you full power notwithstanding these Instructions to do all things at such times and in such order, as you shall judge most convenient, and to do all such further things as you shall think necessary for the carrying on of this service, or to omit the doing anything which you shall upon the place find to be inconvenient for the same.

Additional Articles of Instruction to our right trusty and well-beloved counsellor George Baron of Dartmouth for this present expedition to Tangier, 27 July 1683

Whereas in the twelfth article of our Instructions to you, bearing date the 2nd day of this month of July, it is signified to you that it was then our will and meaning that the Scotch regiment among other our forces now in Tangier should be transported directly into Ireland, there to receive our further orders, we now finding that our present service do require it, do hereby alter that Instruction and order and appoint that the said Scotch regiment and each company in it be directly transported into England and landed at any port in the West that wind and weather will permit, to the end they may be so much nearer hand to receive our orders as our service shall require.

2. And whereas it is fit that the horses now in our garrison of Tangier be removed and disposed of before that place be demolished, you are to use all the endeavour you can to have all the said horses transported to the opposite shore of Spain, there to be sold to the best advantage and the proceeds to be returned to the true owners in order to remount them here in England.

Appendix V

Major Martin Beckman's Proposals for the Demolition of the Fortifications at Tangier, 28 August 1683 Aboard the *Grafton*[1]

Memorandum of what is necessary to go in hand with soon as please God my lord shall arrive at Tangier, in order for the demolishing the same if his Lordship shall think fit for his Majesty's service.

1. To draw from the fleet and the garrison 60 carpenters with two masters and four mates; 30 of these carpenters with a master carpenter that belongs to the garrison and two mates to attend the mines about the town and castles, to do what they shall be directed by the chief engineer. Fifteen carpenters with a master carpenter and one mate to attend the works of the Mole. Fifteen carpenters and one mate or foreman to take down and lay by of the houses when they shall be pulled down, such timber, joists, planks and boards for the support chests etc. of the mines and for the stopping up of the same, and for making of sheds on the Parade for the officers, soldiers etc. to lie in when their quarters shall be pulled down. The parade may be kept on the marketplace. The carpenters that shall be drawn out of the garrison will expect payment 8d. per day. For those that belong to the regiment and the commanded battalions as the guards etc. and any carpenters of the corporation, 18d. per day. work at the mines and the Mole, these men to be duty free and not relieved; those that work in the mines as labourers to have 8d. per diem, those that work with the drills deserve 15 to 18d. per day.

2. The above-mentioned officers commanded with these 200 fixed soldiers

1 HMC, *Eleventh Report, App. V*, I, p. 89; *Tangier Papers*, pp. 67–71.

for labourers, a lieutenant cannot well have less than 3s. per day, an ensign 2s. and a sergeant 12d. or 15d. per day, but these officers and soldiers must be choice men, and the soldiers for the drills strong fellows, the payment to be every Saturday night. To these men must be a clerk or prick master, whose accounts ought to be vouched by the officers above mentioned, who must be present always when the clerks call their parties over, and the engineers to vouch for such men that do work at their stations or posts, this clerk deserves 3s. per day, finding himself paper, books, ink and pens.

3. That your lordship would be pleased to grant a warrant to the storekeeper on the place to deliver anything that the chief engineer shall send his note for, signed with his hand and specified for what service such materials or ammunition be for, for to run always for a new warrant from your lordship will bring the work in confusion, and his Majesty's service in a great measure neglected.

4. That the chief engineer may have authority by your lordship's order, which the town major must deliver to the sergeants when he gives the word, to demand, when any occasion shall serve, a certain number of men from the next guard or guards, to help to carry a piece of timber or anything else, not to take above the guard, and that only for one time or two, which shall not exceed one hour or thereabouts.

5. That the guard, when occasion serves, that every morning goes to relieve, leave their colours and arms on the Parade, under a guard of one file and a sergeant of old men that cannot carry anything, and march with their officers with drums beating, as is usually beaten upon works, to such place or places as the chief engineer shall have acquainted the town major, who is to ride at the head of them, show them to carry a turn or two of deals, timber etc., where the chief engineer shall appoint, and then to return to their arms and march to their respective posts.

6. That six or seven hundred men be commanded every day with sufficient officers to command them, to pull down the roofs and floors and most part of the houses that is built with lime.

7. That Captain Giles and under him the boatswain of the Mole be overseers of the drillers. Captain Giles deserves 8s. per day and the boatswain 3s.

8. Mr Phillips to have his post and overseeing of the miners and mines from [blank] battery, that is beginning with the one whole and two half bastions of the Upper Castle and so from Stayner's Battery up to the great bastion near the sally port, that the works or mines be done according to the direction from the chief engineer.

9. Captain Moncrieffe is to have his post from the place where Mr Phillips begins to the place where the said Mr Phillips' post ends, meeting one another.

10. The old engineer, Mr Tessine, to have his post from the Devil's Tower round the water side up to Stayner's Battery.

11. Young Mr Tessine to have his post from the Devil's Tower all around the town up to the Upper Castle, where Mr Phillips takes his beginning.

12. Captain Leake with his gunners from the Tower, those in the garrison and 20 or 30 gunners from the fleet, be employed to blow up such houses that shall require much time in pulling down.

13. That the miners from Plymouth be nowhere employed but at the Upper Castle, where all the mines will be in rock, where they shall be placed as the chief engineer shall think fit.

14. That the engineers and fire-masters may be allowed for their travelling charges what his lordship shall think fit per day, and that they may be paid every Saturday with the rest that receive payment, all things being very dear and no credit but for ready money.

15. That the fire-masters may have a shed built them on the Parade near York Castle for their laboratory, where to work according to the direction of the chief engineer.

16. That the engineers, fire-masters, miners and drillers be not disturbed or bound to take notice of anybody's directions, but what they receive from [the] chief engineer, and that the chief director be not tied to receive any order or direction, but from your lordship, who is to give your lordship an account every morning and night of the proceedings of the several works.

17. That no man but the engineers and miners that are in their respective posts be suffered to enter into the mines, lest the workmen and miners must at the time stand still.

18. When the mine or mines be finished and the train laid, that no man upon pain of death, the chief engineer excepted, who must every day go and visit them, offer to go near the head of the mines, nearer than 10 yards, upon which the sentries must well look after, and that no sentry upon the same penalty take any mattocks near the mines, nor to have any other arms but firelocks, or rather a pike.

19. That one of the public houses near the water side may be allowed for a suttling house, one for all those that belong to the train or Ordnance, which house may be undermined and blown up with the rest.

20. That the retreat of the whole garrison be on board one hour before the mines begin to play.

21. That a wooden bridge to be made for the landing of the boats.

22. That a guard house be made without the Watergate, where the coals use to lie and another at Johnston's battery, and one without the sally port in the Castle, these three places being much convenient for surprise.

23. I am in opinion we may freely go to work after your lordship shall first have surveyed or examined the place or situation or resolved upon a demolishing, for to stay till the corporation be removed with their goods and families, near half of the time will be perfectly lost, and I do not doubt but the news (though it be but guessing) of demolishing of the place [will arrive] before we shall arrive there.

24. That we work in the mines the nights as well as days, and therefore necessary that a horse guard be ordered every night without Catherina Gate, to keep a perpetual round or patrolling all along the ditch, that the enemy may not discover the miners, and so hinder us from our design. All this I most humbly submit to your lordship's wise correction.

Report by Sir John Berry and other naval officers about the Mole and harbour at Tangier, 20 January 1684[2]

We find that vast mass of stone and earth, of which the Mole consisted, which upon our former survey at your first arrival here, was measured 479 yards in length, to be levelled and carried into the harbour so low that the sea has free passage over it the whole tide, till within an hour and a half of low water, and that thereby that part of the harbour which was esteemed the best, and had the deepest water, is now, for the whole length of that which was the Mole, made solid earth, 170 feet together from the altar of the Mole into the port, and several piers of stone run out besides, of 310, 220, 180, 170, 368, 160, and 275 feet in length, and that in the rest of the harbour vast quantities of stones and rubbish are thrown in and sunk all over it, in boats and other vessels fitted for that purpose, upon which we have considered whether they are reduced to such a state, as that the one may not be rebuilt and the other cleansed, and made useful by any Christian prince, or by the people of this country, if they should attempt it, and are of opinion that for a Christian prince, besides the necessity of being master of this country, and fortifying all the high ground overlooking and commanding the harbour, there is not any one of the motives which always give encouragement to the doing works of that kind, to be found in this, to make it reasonable, if it be possible, for any such to endeavour it. And in relation to the Moors of this country, we conceive it a work very impracticable and impossible. And whereas a very great and essential benefit and advantage to any harbour or port is a good and secure road for ships to ride safely without. We have some of us formerly,

2 SRO, D(W)1778/I/i/979; *Eleventh Report, App. V*, III, p. 42. Answers to questions on the state of the Mole, 20 January 1684.

and all of us very lately, bad such experience of this, that we cannot on this occasion, but observe to you that the foulness of the ground were in the great depth of water and very dangerous seas which come without, render it so bad and insecure for ships to ride, especially considering they are sometimes to ride without their guns, ballast, and in other circumstances which your Excellency very well knows is required to prepare them for the benefit of the harbour or port within, in their cleaning and fitting, that it can no way incite or encourage any people to attempt the doing such a work, were it in other respects reasonable. As for the Mole itself, it is so entirely ruined and destroyed, and the harbour so filled with stones and rubbish, and made so unfit to receive, harbour, or protect in any manner from the weather, or from an enemy, any ships or vessels, and that in very many degrees worse than the bay itself naturally would have done, before the building the Mole, that when you shall think fit to order the little hillock of sand, lying at the hither end of the beach, and that of stones on the other, to be made level with the other parts of it, we do unanimously, in our best judgments, not only think what has been done does fully and completely answer all the ends of making one and the other in no capacity to give any kind of refuge or protection to the ships or vessels of any pirates, robbers, or any enemies of the Christian faith, or any others.

Appendix VI

Lists of Stores and Equipment at Tangier

Table 43. Ammunition and other habiliments of war remaining in his Majesty's stores, as appears by a survey taken 14 April 1664.[1]

Barrels of powder, whereof 56 came from onboard the Ormond	1,125½	Beds whereof 28 decrepit	370
		Sheets pairs	854
Great gunshot of all sorts	2,092	Rugs whereof 28 decrepit	280
Tuns of small shot	13½	Blankets	2
Hand-grenade shells	10,500	Hammocks	287
Caps for hand-grenade barrels	6	Iron poles	189
Tuns of match	49	Swine feathers	1,000
Old pikes	138	Bullet-mould pairs	
Matchlock muskets most unfixed	1,296		84
Long fouling piece whole and broken	11	Delivered by order from his Excellency the Earl of Teviot 3 May, the particulars following:	
Ramrods	940		
Collars of bandoliers	502	Barrels of powder	12
Pairs of pistols with holsters	85	Barrels of small shot	11½
Pairs of empty holsters	24	Collars of bandoliers	40
Bridles with bitts	325	Bundles of match skeins	107
Barrels of flints	2½		
Rammer heads for great guns	12	Delivered by order from Sir Tobias Bridge from 3 May 1664 to 27th the same:	
Rammer heads	26		
Linstocks	57	Barrels of powder	11
Cartridge cases	49	Barrels of small shot	14
Formers	4		
Reams of paper royal	5	Bundles of match	24
		Collars of bandoliers	176
		Flints ready cut	600

1 SRO, D742/0/3/4.

Table 44. Stores wanting in Tangier, July 1664.[2]

Collars of bandoliers	800
Lanceheads for horsemen	100
Good ash lance staves for horsemen, 20 feet long	150
Long carbines for the Horse	100

Table 45. Stores wanting in Tangier, 13 August 1666.[3]

Flints barrels	6
Fuses for the smallest size of hand grenades	3,000
Union flags for the town	4
Powder horns for the ordnance	50
Paper royal for cartridges reams	20
Paper royal for fireworks reams	10

Table 46. A particular, dated Ordnance Office, 9 January 1675, and signed by Edward Sherburne, Jonas Moore, Sam Fortrey and Edward Conyers, of what guns, shot, powder, match and other stores and habiliments of war is shipped on board the *Chichley* frigate, William Rickets commander, being for his Majesty's service at Tangier.

Iron cannon:	
Demi-culverins	20
Round shot for culverins	1,000
Round shot for demi-culverins	3,000
Round shot for sakers	1,500
Round shot for falcons	2,000
Round shot for 12-pounders	3,000
Round shot for 3-pounders	2,000
Nails of sorts:	
Spikes	500
Weight nails, lbs	5,000
6d. nails	10,000
4d. nails	10,000
2d. nails	10,000

2 SRO, D742/0/3/1.
3 SRO, D742/0/3/3.

Flock beds, furnished	350
Sheets, pairs	500
Deals	2,000
Snaphance muskets, packed in mats	1,500
Flints, ready cut in 4 barrels	60,000
Iron bars	471
Muscovia lights	12
Stocklocks	100
Padlocks	100
Linseed oil, caskets of 133 gall.	2
Corn powder, barrels	800
Match, packed in mats	6 tons
Paper royal, fine, reams	5
Paper royal for cartridges, reams	20
Pitch, barrels	20
Rubstones for scythes	12 doz
Sackcloth, yards	2,050
Musket shot	5 tons
Tar, barrels	20
Twine	75 lb
Iron wire	50 lb
Great iron pots	200
Pulleys great, pairs	60
Fir baulks	600
Bags for powder	30
Drumheads of vellum	4 doz
Pistols with holsters, pairs	50
Heads and rammers, great, pairs	50
Heads and rammers, small, pairs	50
Iron crowbars	60
Long pikes	600
Shovels	400
Ladle staves	200
Sheepskins	5 doz
Scythes, with all appurtenances	40
Thread	50 lb
Drums, furnished, in cases	24
Lanterns, ordinary	40

Table 47. An account of the remaining state of the stores of war at Tangier, taken 20 August last, with a particular of all the stores of war since sent thither, making together the present state, compared with the proportion for the remaining stock, showing the differences thereupon, 22 June 1680.[4]

	Remained 20 August 1679	Supplies sent Since	The state as at present	Proportion of stock
Cannon	1		1	1
Demi-cannon	7		7	7
Culverin	28		28	28
12 pounder	25		25	25
Demi-culverin	65 with 3 split		65	65
6 pounder	2		2	2
Brass and iron sakers	10		10	10
Ordnance mounted 3-pounder	2		2	2
Falcon	5		5	5
Falconet	6		6	6
Standard standing carriages				
Cannon	1		1	2
Demi-cannon	1		1	2
Culverin	0		0	6
12-pounder	7		7	5
Demi-culverin	9		9	10
6-pounder	0		0	0
Saker	3		3	2
3-pounder	0		0	2
Falcon	1		1	1
Falconet	4		4	0
Block carriage				2
Round shot				
Cannon	106		106	100
Demi-cannon	654		654	770
Culverin	5,156		5,156	3,220
Saker	3,220		3,220	1,200

4 SRO, D742/0/3/6.

Minion	2,534			
12-pounder	9,066			
Demi-culverin	13,696			
6-pounder	5,02			
Falcon	1,350			
Falconet	9,279			
8-pounder	1,043			
3-pounder	4,765			
Double-headed shot (hammered)				
Cannon	131		131	70
Culverin	570		570	420
Demi-culverin	892		892	
Saker	18		18	975
24-pounder	485		485	200
12-pounder	645		645	
Double-headed shot (cast)				
Demi-culverin	20			20
Saker	40			40
12-pounder	220			220
8-pounder	220			220
Tin cases filled with musket shot				
12-pounder	17	100	117	375
Demi-culverin	554	200	754	975
Saker	570	100	670	200
Mortar pieces				
11ins		1	1	1
10ins	1		1	1
9ins				1
Brass petard	3		3	
Grenado-shells				
10 ins		10		
12 ins		40		

9¾ ins		200		
8¾ ins		200	200	300
10¾ ins				300
9½ ins		60		60
6¾ ins			50	50
Barrels of iron	300			
Hand-grenades	11,744 + 1,074 fixed	15,000	26,744 + 1074 fixed	18,000
Fuses for				
Grenades great	400	276	676	120
Hand-grenades	9,908	20,600	30,508	21,000
Ladles and sponges				
Cannon	1 ladle, 1 sponge		1 ladle, 1 sponge	1 ladle, 1 sponge
Demi-cannon	1 ladle, 1 sponge		1 ladle, 1 sponge	4 ladles, 7 sponges
Culverin	30 ladles, 65 sponges		30 ladles, 65 sponges	14 ladles, 18 sponges
12-pounder	22 ladles, 38 sponges		22 ladles, 38 sponges	20 ladles, 35 sponges
Demi-culverin	42 ladles, 62 sponges		42 ladles, 62 sponges	30 ladles, 65 sponges
6-pounder	7 ladles, 17 sponges		7 ladles, 17 sponges	1 ladle, 2 sponge
Saker	19 ladles, 46 sponges		19 ladles, 46 sponges	6 ladles, 10 sponges
3-pounder	7 ladles, 18 sponges		7 ladles, 18 sponges	1 ladle, 2 sponges
Falcon	1 ladle, 4 sponges		1 ladle, 4 sponges	3 ladles, 5 sponges
Falconet				4 ladles, 6 sponges
24-pounder	16 ladles, 32 sponges		16 ladles, 32 sponges	
8-pounder	5 ladles, 4 sponges		5 ladles, 4 sponges	
Minion	10 ladles, 25 sponges		10 ladles, 25 sponges	
Ladle staves	304		304	200
Powder bags (tanned calf skin)	12	30	42	80
Fuse bags	71			110

Iron bars	137½ cwt		137½ cwt	80 cwt
Powder barrels	41		41	100
Wheelbarrows	149	100	249	300
Handbarrows	189	200	389	220
Bedding				
Flock beds	21	200 + 830 quilts	221 + 830 quilts	300
Bolsters	20	300	320	300
Rugs	39	630	669	300
Blankets	42	400	442	300
Pillows		860	860	
Cords		308	308	
Carbine belts				30
Belts for hangers				1,900
Shoulder belts	149		149	120
Waist belts	47	442	476	40
Cartridge boxes	52		52	50
Harquebus bullets	795		795	50
Calthrops		20,000	20,000	20,000
Drums furnished	2	40	40	30
Drum cases	16	38	54	20
Snares for drums		24	24	30
Drumheads		4 doz.	4 doz.	60
Drum cords	16	24	24	60
Swedish feathers	353		353	300
Corn powder	1,831½ bls	265 bls	20,96½ bls	3,228 bls 33lbs
Match	8,133 cwt 11lbs	6 cwt	14,133 cwt 11lbs	12 cwt
Halberds	17	40	57	60
Long pikes	224	1,532	1,756	300
Three-quarter pikes	543		543	200
Short pikes	452		452	300
Bills	146	200	346	160
Hatchets	118		200	
Swords	280	432	712	600
Hangers	179		179	1,900
Snaphaunce muskets	608	1,248	1,856	2,500
Musketoons	48	24	72	60
Musket rods	1,326		1,326	3,000

Bandoliers	568 collars	2,768 collars	3,336 collars	2,500 collars
Blunderbusses	17	50	67	60
Pistols	38 prs	20 prs	58 prs	100 prs
Holsters				100 prs
Carbines	4	150	151	30
Carbine bullets		6 cwt	6 cwt	2 cwt
Musket bullets	155 bls	8 cwt	15 cwt 15lbs	18 cwt
Matchlock muskets	201	1,460	374	18
Union flags	1	2	3	6
Flints for				
Blunderbusses and musketoons	290		290	500
Muskets and pistols		40,000	40,000	30,000

Table 48. Stores and ammunition to be kept at the alarm posts, Tangier, 27 January 1684.[5]

Ammunition at the alarm posts:		**Stores to be shipped:**	5
Peterborough Tower		Headpieces	149
Powder	2 bls	Backs	151
Hand-grenades	450	Breasts	115
Match	1½ cwt	Pikes	4,000
Musket shot	3 cwt	Bandoliers	30
		Fire pikes	4
Lawson's Battery		Harquebuses	5
Match	½ cwt	Matchlock muskets	15
Musket shot	1 cwt	Snaphaunces	50
		Musket barrels	139
Johnson's Battery		Three-quarter pikes	260
Hand-grenades	950	Double-headed shot	
		3-pounders	26
Irish Battery		Musket shot	21 cwt
Powder	½ bl	Horseshoes	1300
Match	½ cwt	Pistols	3 doz.
		Holsters	10 prs
Catherina Gate [Port]		Tents	10
Hand-grenades	750	Musket rods	100

5 SRO, D742/0/3/13.

Powder	1½ cwt	Half-pikes	42
Match	½ cwt	Heads and rammers	70 prs
Musket shot	1 cwt	Hand-grenade shells	700
		Partisans	70
Colonel Trelawny's Parade			
Hand-grenades	200	Spur without the castle	150
Match	½ cwt	Hand-grenades	½ cwt
Musket shot	2 cwt	Match	1½ cwt
Powder	½ cwt	Powder	

Table 49. List of the Gunners belonging to the Tangier Garrison, late 1683.[6]

	Home station	Position/where employed
James Hunter		Master-Gunner, Irish Battery
Ralph Thomas	Pendennis	Irish Battery
Thomas Sessions		Irish Battery
William Hart		Irish Battery
Henry Weedon	Pendennis	Irish Battery
Edward Coates		Irish Battery
David Williams		Irish Battery
Edmund Pipes		Irish Battery
Peter Riddings	Pendennis	Irish Battery
Mr Edward Pickering	Pendennis	Lawson's Battery
John Thornton		Lawson's Battery
Thomas Williams	Pendennis	Lawson's Battery
Robert Jackett		Lawson's Battery
James Harwood		Hyde's Battery
Thomas Walker	Pendennis	Hyde's Battery
Richard Jeatur		Johnson's Battery
John Clements		Johnson's Battery, also carpenter employed at the Mole by Mr Sheres
William Walker	Pendennis	Johnson's Battery
John Bishop		Johnson's Battery
John Platt		Johnson's Battery
John Watts		Johnson's Battery, also carpenter in the town
Thomas Wheeler	Pendennis	Stayner's Battery

6 Composite table taken from SRO, D742/0/4/13 ('List of Gunners of the Garrison', 1 November 1683); D742/0/4/19 ('Account of the Train of Gunners', 3 December 1683); D742/0/4/20 ('Names of Gunners, their posts, etc.', 24 December 1683); RMG, DAR/26 ('Miscellaneous book, Tangier, petitions and reports, journals and letters, list of army officers, gunners and guns, minutes of council-of-war 5 October 1683 and others, court-martial, some accounts').

Mr [Thomas] Silver		Commanding gunners in Peterborough Tower
James Hutt senior	Pendennis	Peterborough Tower
Ralph Roe	Pendennis	Peterborough Tower
Thomas Holman		Peterborough Tower
John Mollidge		Peterborough Tower
John Dyson		Peterborough Tower
Thomas Groome		Peterborough Tower
James Lambert		Peterborough Tower
Thomas Rumsby		Old Parade
Thomas Kimber		Old Parade, and carpenter employed at the Mole by Mr Sheres
Roger Pinkerman	Pendennis	Sally-Port
James Hutt junior	Pendennis	Bastion next to the Governor's House
Christopher Berry		Bastion next to the Governor's House
Thomas Wilmott	Pendennis	Smith, employed by Major Beckman on bastion next to the Governor's House
Miles Maxfield		Carpenter employed at Mole Forts by Major Beckman
Gilbert Christopher		Carpenter employed at the Mole by Mr Sheres
Thomas Rumley	Tower	Several posts around the garrison
William Theobalds		Sick
William King	Pendennis	Sick
William Good		Governor's Barge
Edward Weedon		Governor's Brigandine
John Moseley	Pendennis	Groom attending Lord Dartmouth's horses
Thomas Wood		Shipped off and sent away for England
William Weedon		Shipped off and sent away for England
John Eccles		Shipped off and sent away for England
Henry Masters		Shipped off and sent away for England

Table 50. Account of men belonging to the Mole which receive their provisions from Captain Gregory Fryer, 31 October 1683.[7]

David Price	John Redhead	Thomas Hopkins	Isaac Eids	Francis Meacham
William Woodfield	William Asher	John Barrett	George Goss	William Austin jr
John Clement	John Pitcher	Nicholas Juniper	John Cotton	Luis Canary
Thomas Kember	Henry Smith	William Whiting	Gabriel Pickering	Richard Nickson
Thomas Westwood	and his wife	John Martino	Edward Cutts	Richard Jetur
Gilbert Christopher	William Gibson	John Dodsham	William Austin sr	Bernardo Surneedo

7 SRO, D742/0/4/22.

Matthew Whitfield	Martin Gardner	Thomas Barnsfield	John Humphries	John Shelley
and his wife	Robert Ord	James Walton	John Brown	Henry Parr
Charles Wooten	John Mason	Robert Rowland	James Clark	John Maple

Table 51. Survey of artillery pieces in service, October 1683.[8]

Battery	Cul.	Drake	D-Cul.	3-pdr	6-pdr	12-pdr	Saker	Mortar	Falc.
Hyde's Bty		1	4		1				
Old Parade		1	4						
Ordnance Rabonnett								3	
Mole			2		1	2	3		2
Governor's Bastion	2		2		2	3			
Stayner's Bty			1			1			
Johnson's Bty		12							
Irish Bty		15	1						
Sally-Port		2		1					
Peterborough Tower	12	5				2			
Lawson's Bty		2			2	3			
Boling Bar		5			2	3		10	
Curtain [wall]			2			4			

Table 52. Abstract of the guards drawn up five deep, 17 September 1683.

Posts of guards	Capts	Lts	Ens	Sgts	Drms	Files shot	Odd men	Files pikes	Files grens
Pole Fort	1	2	2	8	1	22			5
Fountain Fort with detachments; Brown George, Seamen's Battery		1		3	1	8			
Catharina Fort with detachments; Johnson's Battery, Irish Battery		1		4	1	8	1	3	
Castle Guard with detachments; Peterborough Tower, Spur, Redoubt		1	1	5	2	12		4	
Main Guard	1		1	2	1	5	5	2	
Mole Guard with detachments; Mole End, Bell Guard		1		3	1	8			

8 SRO, D742/0/4/20.

The Galley Guards			1	2	1	4			
Sandwich Port with detachments; Old Parade, Eastern Tower		1		3	1	4	2	2	
Total of the guards	2	7	5	30	9	71	8	11	5

Numbers of men that daily mount guard		
The King's Battalion	**Files**	**Odd men**
Musketeers	7	0
Pikes	2	2
Total	9	2
Dumbarton's Regiment	**Files**	**Odd men**
Musketeers	25	1
Pikes	4	0
Grenadiers	1	1
Total	30	2
Old Tangier Regiment	**Files**	**Odd men**
Musketeers	23	0
Pikes	2	2
Grenadiers	1	4
Total	26	6
Second Tangier Regiment	**Files**	**Odd men**
Musketeers	17	1
Pikes	3	1
Grenadiers	2	4
Total	22	6
Total files and odd men	**Files**	**Odd men**
Musketeers	72	1
Pikes	11	1
Grenadiers	4	6
Total	87	14
Total sentinels 449		

Table 53. The several alarm posts for the foot and horse as hath been observed in his Majesty's garrison of Tangier, whilst under the command of Colonel Percy Kirke, undated.[9]

The King's Battalion	Market Place
Dumbarton's Regiment	Old Parade
Kirke's Regiment (eldest battalion)	Under Peterborough Tower
Kirke's Regiment (second battalion)	By Shire Hall
Trelawny's Regiment	Hyde's Battery
Lord Dumbarton's reformadoes	Catherina Port, 5 deep in 1 bank, the right of them not exceeding Colonel Boynton's door, the left extending towards the Market Place
The governor's grenadiers	On the right of their alarm post, under Peterborough Tower
Colonel Trelawney's grenadiers	Catherina Port, opposite the Scotch (Dumbarton's) grenadiers, to be drawn up 4 deep
Captains McKenzie's and Langston's Troops	On the Parade before their casemates
Captain Neatby's Troop	At Catherina in the rear of Trelawney's grenadiers
Captain Coy's Troop	In the castle against the foraging port
The troopers of each troop that want horses to be drawn up in one rank in opposition to them to be commanded by a quartermaster	Against the foraging port
All gunners that are not on the guard	Stayner's Battery

9 SRO, D742/0/4/28.

Appendix VII

Petitions to the Crown for Arrears in Pay by Officers, Soldiers, Craftsmen, Widows and Dependents of the Tangier Garrison, and Gratuities Paid, 1680–86

4 December 1680
Petition of Widow Ennis as referred to the Treasury Lords from the King, 27 November last, petitioner showing that her late husband, Robert Ennis, served as 'Aid Major' and Lieutenant under the Earl of Dumbarton in France many years, and when called home was sent into Ireland, and thence to Tangier, where he was wounded in fight against the Moors and died. She therefore prays charity, being wholly destitute.[1]

4 December 1680
Petition of Francis Morris for payment of his arrear of £9 02s. 00d. having served 20 years and upwards as a private sentinel at Tangier and received many wounds and now disabled.

Petition of Jane Abram, widow of Richard Abram, late a private sentinel at Tangier, who served 20 years at Tangier and died there, leaving her and two children very poor. She prays payment of an arrear of £3 10s. 00d. owing to him.

Petition of Mary Heather, widow of Edward Heather, for payment of an

1 TNA, SP44/18, fol. 145; *CTB*, VII, p. 1427.

arrear of £6 03s. 03d. due to her husband, who served 12 years at Tangier, petitioner being left with a sister and young children all in great want.[2]

13 December 1680
Petition of Thomas Pownall, cornet in the late garrison at Tangier, praying some recompense, having been wounded in the wars against the Moors.[3]

15 December 1680
Petition of John Monck, who served for three years and upwards to 5 May 1684, as sergeant and sentinel in Captain Griffith's Company in Colonel Trelawney's Regiment of Foot at Tangier and was discharged on said 5 May last, being then in arrear 447 days on his sergeant's pay and 273 on his pay as sentinel, or £25 15s. 3d. in all, out of which £1 16s. 0d. is to be abated. He therefore prays payment of the £23 19s. 3d. balance of arrears due.[4]

15 December 1680
Petition of Thomas Roberts, apothecary to the garrison of Tangier, praying payment of the £1,038 16s. 10d. due to him from the private soldiers and non-commissioned officers for physic according to the agreement of 6d. per week from 1 April 1682 to 1 April 1684.[5]

18 December 1680
Petition of Robert Singleton and Richard Seaden, showing that they served at Tangier in Captain Tollemache's Company in the King's Battalion of Foot Guards for several years and praying to be paid their arrears of pay for the period 1 April 1682 to 30 April 1684.

Petition of John Anker, showing that he served for four years as sergeant in Captain Bridgeman's Company in the King's Regiment of Foot Guards under the Earl of Craven, and until 9 December 1684, at which time he was discharged, and praying payment of his arrears from 1 April 1682 to 1 May 1684, as sergeant in the late company of Captain Thomas Tollemache in the King's Battalion of Foot Guards, commanded for the service of Tangier. Petitioner being in great want.

Petition of Susan Williams, Ann Luck and Katherine Smallwood showing that their son and husbands served in said Captain Tollemache's Company and praying for the arrears, unstated, due to the said persons at the time of their decease.[6]

2 TNA, SP44/18, fol. 148; *CTB*, VII, p. 1428.
3 TNA, SP44/18, fol. 154; *CTB*, VII, p. 1446.
4 TNA, SP44/18, fol. 157; *CTB*, VII, p. 1447.
5 TNA, SP44/18, fol. 160; *CTB*, VII, p. 1451.
6 TNA, SP44/18, fols 160–1.

18 December 1680

Petition of Jane Urquhart, widow of Thomas Urquhart, showing that her said late husband served 18 years at Tangier as Sergeant in Captain Forbes' Company and lost his life there in the battle against the Moors, 27 October 1680, leaving petitioner in a poor condition with three children: therefore prays relief for her maintenance and for the education of her children.[7]

19 December 1680

Petition of Thomas McBourney for payment of £11 9s. 4d. due to him at the time of his disbanding as drummer in Captain Rodney's Company at Tangier. Petitioner being in great want.[8]

20 December 1680

Petition of Captain Toby Caulfield, showing that in 1680 he bought of Captain Chidley Coote his command of a company in the army in Ireland, which company was one of the four commanded for Tangier before said purchase; that the petitioner served four years in Tangier and being at last two years in arrear for himself and company, and provisions being very scarce there he was forced to contract over £400 of debts in order to supply the wants of himself and officers; that for £100 thereof petitioner stands engaged for his present lieutenant, and £50 for his first lieutenant who was slain there and most of the remainder [of said debt] for several other of the officers and soldiers slain also in said service: that being visited with much sickness petitioner was forced, a month before the arrival of Lord Dartmouth, to go to England for his health and in his absence an account of the debts of the whole garrison being taken and returned to the Treasury Lords petitioner has not been in the least satisfied therein, though the officers and soldiers have since received their arrears; that petitioner's pay has been stopped from the same above six months past and will be so yet these three years until the same be fully satisfied; that he cannot expect to receive from his lieutenant the £100 he so stands engaged for, his pay being also stopped for other debts contracted by him amounting to above £400 which will not be satisfied in four years' time, nor [can petitioner expect] one farthing from any other person for whom he stands engaged, so that he is destitute of a maintenance to support himself until said debts be fully paid: therefore prays some sum out of the royal bounty money of Ireland for his support during his stop of pay.[9]

1 July 1684

Petition of Captain Alexander McKenzie and the rest of the officers belonging to the troop of horse late in Tangier under his command. Petitioners show that not being entered on the rolls at Tangier they are kept back in their pay about eleven months from the date of their commissions and that upon petitioning for pay from the dates of their respective commissions, the Lords Commissioners for Tangier did [on] 7 June 1683, refer their petition to the

7 TNA, SP44/18, fol. 161.

8 TNA, SP44/18, fol. 165.

9 TNA, SP44/18, fols 163–4.

governor of Tangier to certify what has been the general usage at Tangier as to the commencement of pay whether from the date of the commissions or from the first entry of them at Tangier upon the rolls or from the first muster there. Thereupon Colonel Kirke, the last governor there, certified that it was the custom of the said garrison before his time for all officers to be paid from the date of their commission. This is also certified by the Earl of Inchiquin and Colonel Sackville for the time of their commanding there.[10]

2 July 1684

Treasury warrant to William Hewer to pay to the following persons: Tangier widows and orphans lately come from Tangier, the yearly sums as below by quarterly payments until further order from the Treasury Lords to the contrary; the first quarter to commence the 1st inst. and to be paid Oct. 1 next: the Treasury Lords having represented to the King the condition of the said poor persons whereon the King has directed the allowance of the said yearly sums to them.

Appended:

List, certified by William Smyth, late Mayor of Tangiers, and by Mr Hughes and Mr Morgan, late ministers there, of the names of widows and children belonging to officers and soldiers slain or dead in the service at Tangier who were relieved there out of the royal bounty of £200 per ann. and are by age or other infirmities unable to maintain themselves here in England, having since their arrival been weekly supplied by the late Mayor and Mr Hewer. Wherefore it is prayed that they be allowed the following sums as an act of charity to prevent them perishing:

Widows

Elizabeth Swaine, very lame, aged 65; had two husbands, both killed: £8 per annum.

Elizabeth Cole, 21 years at Tangier, aged 64; her [late] husband, a private sentinel in the Governor's Company: £8 per annum.

Dorothy Dowty, aged 64; had two husbands, one killed with the Earl of Teviot, the other died in the service of the Mole: £6 per annum.

Ann Trigg, almost blind, aged 61; her husband, a serjeant, killed: £8l. per annum.

Mary Helme, a little crazed; her husbands, four troopers, all killed and their horses: £4 per annum.

Elizabeth Bean, aged 60; two husbands, one killed with the Earl of Teviot, the other taken out of Henrietta Fort and died in captivity: £6 per annum.

Elizabeth Holmes, aged 60; her son John, aged 7, and daughter Sarah, aged

10 TNA, SP44/18, fol. 132.

12; one husband, a gunner, killed: £6 per annum.

Katherine Griffes, aged 60; one husband, an ensign since 1660 and killed: £8 per annum.

Joan Abraham, 20 years in Tangier, aged 57; one husband, a sentinel, died in the service: £4 per annum.

Ann Fowle, aged 55; three husbands, two killed, the other died: £4 per annum.

Ellen Cubbidge, aged 50; two husbands, both died in the service: £4 per annum.

Elizabeth Mottershead, lame with the palsey [and her daughter] Sarah; two husbands, both killed: £8 per anum.

Elizabeth Ashroft, aged 50, and her daughter Martha, aged 10; her husband, a private sentinel, died after 16 years' service: £4 per annum.

Bridgett Katnes, aged 45; two husbands, one an ensign and killed: £6 per annum.

Mary Stephens, aged 40; her husband, a private sentinel in the Earl of Dumbarton's Regiment, killed: £4 per anum.

Mary O'Connor, aged 40, and her boy aged 4; her husband, a private sentinel, dead: £4 per annum.

Francis Jones, aged 38, and three children; her husband, a trooper, who was condemned and run away; eight years' service: £6 per annum.

Hannah Keys, aged 38, and two boys, aged nine and five; two husbands, one a serjeant killed in Charles Fort, the other a carpenter, dead: £6 per annum.

Susan Baker, aged 37; three husbands, all died in the service: £2 per annum.

Barbara Hughes, aged 29, and her sons Peter and James, aged six and four; two husbands, one killed, the other dead: £4 per annum.

Sarah Carr, aged 28; her husband, a private sentinel, killed: £8 per annum.

Ann Brennon, aged 19, and her boy aged two; her husband, a private sentinel, died: £2 per annum.

Widow Laney, aged 60; two husbands killed: £6 per annum.

Louise Fryer, aged 60; one husband, died in the service of the Mole: £6 per annum.

Orphans
Elizabeth Marrow, aged four; at present kept by Elizabeth Holmes: £6 per annum.

Francis Fife, aged five; at present kept by said Elizabeth Holmes: £6 per annum.

Richard Jelly; aged eight; at present kept by John Norton: £6 per annum.

Thomas Crewes, aged seven; at present kept by Elizabeth Cole: £6 per annum.

Elizabeth Williams, aged eight; at present kept by Mistress Story: £6 per annum.

Christopher Pinder, aged nine; at present kept by Elizabeth Holmes: £6 per annum.

Alexander Brown, aged nine; at present kept by Robert Cuthbertson: £6 per annum.

Frederick Fleetwood, aged nine.

Elizabeth Marsh, aged nine.

Total orphans: £54 per annum.; widows: £128 per annum; in all: £182 per annum.[11]

8 July 1684
Petitions of Thomas Gresham, Thomas Hearne, Richard Wise, John Baxter and Richard Stanwell [returned Tangier soldiers] who pray relief in their distressed conditions.

Ann Brennon, widow of Hugh Brennon, a soldier for many years under Captain Giles at Tangier, and died coming over for England, leaving her and one child; she therefore prays a pension among the other widows.

The 33 poor disabled Tangier soldiers who came over in 1680, and who pray payment of their quarterly pensions.

Elizabeth Cooke, widow, showing that she was [formerly] wife of Sir Anthony Haviland, kt., who was a very great sufferer for the King and died in his journey from Scotland to England in 1660; that she subsequently married Henry Prendergast, gent., a very loyal person, and killed in his Majesty's service at Tangier; that [Cooke] her [last] husband left her [with] a small

11 TNA, SP44/4, fols 437–9; *CTB*, VII, pp. 1202–5.

child and she is in a very low and miserable condition.[12]

23 July 1684
Treasury warrant to William Hewer, Treasurer for the affairs of the late Garrison of Tangier, to pay £50 to John Earlsman, late Controller of the revenue of Tangier, on his salary of £200 per annum, to be for the quarter from 24 October 1683 last, when he was last paid to 26 January 1684, when he embarked for England.[13]

23 July 1684
Same to same to pay to said Earlsman such money as the Treasury Lords shall put in said Hewer's hands of the sum of £80 due to said Earlsman for his propriety in a house at Tangier according to the adjustment and report of the commissioners appointed by Lord Dartmouth to adjust and settle the same, which report is lately delivered to the Treasury Lords by said Lord Dartmouth. The Treasury Lords are content to advance said sum to Earlsman to enable him to proceed on his voyage, being appointed Consul at Algiers whither he is hastening to go by his Majesty's ship *Centurion*. In his receipt for the money Earlsman is to indemnify the King from any further claims or demands from any other person whatsoever on account of the said house.

Treasury warrant to William Hewer, Treasurer for the affairs of the late garrison of Tangier, to pay to the abovesaid Earlsman £39 4s. 11d. for the several debts as follow due to him from the military officers lately serving the King at Tangier: taking from him the several notes of the said debt and charging them upon the arrears of pay due to the said respective persons.

Appending:
Note of said debts, viz. the date of the note, from whom due and to whom due.

Colonel Kirke's Regiment
£150, 23 December 1683, from Colonel Boynton due to Mr Tobin and assigned [to Earlsman].

£6 6s. 0d., 27 September 1683, from ditto, due to same.

£6 6s. 0d., 27 September 1683, from Captain Rowe, due to same.

£4 10s. 0d., 24 September 1683, from Ensign Mortimer, due to same.

£6 12s. 0d., 8 October 1681, from Ensign Parker, due to Mistress Fisher and assigned to same.

12 TNA, SP44/18, fols 41–3; *CTB*, VII, p. 1214.
13 TNA, SP44/5, fol. 19; *CTB*, VII, p. 1243.

Colonel Trelawney's Regiment
£2 18s. 5d., 14 May 1681, from Ensign Malham, due to same.

£7 10s. 6d., 22 June 1681, from Ensign Le Bruce, due to same.

£1 12s. 0d., 21 January 1683, from Ensign Hobbs, due to same.

£1 10s. 0d., 26 January 1683, from Ensign Culliford, due to same.

Dumbarton's Regiment
£1 14s. 0d., 10 December 1683, from Lieutenant Gordon, due to Richard Connelly [and assigned to same].

£1 13s. 0d., 10 December 1683, from Ensign Entash, due to same.

£15 10s. 0d., 29 September 1683, from Lieutenant Alexander Pierson, due to same.

The following five notes being all dated March 1683, following officers of Dumbarton's Regiment owing for quartering: Lieutenant Murray £10, Lieutenant Smelt £8 10s. 0d., Lieutenant William White £6, Lieutenant Clarke £4 17s. 0d., Lieutenant Stuart £3 16s. 0d.[14]

23 July 1684
Report to the king from the Treasury Lords on the petition of Captain John Graham [Dumbarton's], as by the order of reference from the king of 2 May last. We referred said petition on the 17th last, to Mr Hewer, late treasurer of Tangier, and agree with his report as follows:

By a commission dated 26 June 1660, from the Duke of Albemarle, said Graham was made a lieutenant to Colonel Roger Alsop's Company and afterwards served at Tangier as quartermaster of horse and captain of a foot company. It is certified by Captain Giles, Captain McKenzie and others that he behaved well, was a brave officer, was wounded with a lance under the right breast when he took the standard from the Moors in the Earl of Teviot's time. There is no certificate as to his allegations relating to the gold chain and medal which the king sent him for his good service in taking the said standard, but from information from some of the Tangier officers I believe it to be true. He is about 60 and disabled by fits from further service and is in great want. Until provision can be made for him in Chelsea College or otherwise, I think he should be allowed £30 per annum, which is less than half pay for a lieutenant.[15]

14 TNA, SP44/5, fols 20–1; *CTB*, VII, p. 1244.
15 TNA, SP44/9, fols 399–400; *CTB*, VII, p. 1245.

23 July 1684

Report to the king from the Treasury Lords on the petition of several carpenters, smiths, drill men and other artificers employed in building the Mole at Tangier, praying payment of their wages: said petition having been referred to the Treasury Lords from the king the 14th inst. We have referred same to William Hewer, Treasurer for the affairs of Tangier and he certifies the debt due to petitioners to be £3,298 17s. 0d. to 63 men, of which some few are dragoons in your Majesty's service so that there will not be need to pay anything to them at present. As for the rest the speediest way to stop the growing charge and of supplying their present necessities is to pay [in full] all debts under £10, and the clerks and accountants who have assisted in making up the present accounts and to pay a third of all debts above £10 The sum required for this will be £1,210 6s. 2d.

Hewer's report dated 23 July 1684: There are 63 persons reckoned to be in pay and their wages to 1 June last amounted to £3,298 17s. 0¼d. after deduction of what has been paid them by Mr Sheres on account and [after deduction of] what their debt to the inhabitants of Tangier comes to. As to what works the said men have been employed on or how advantageously for his Majesty's service I must refer you to Colonel Kirke, the late governor of that place. Since the arrival of Lord Dartmouth, the said men have been employed in destroying and demolishing the mole and garrison there.[16]

24 July 1684

Henry Guy to Lord Dartmouth, to inform the Treasury Lords if Edmund Pipe, late fire-master at Tangier, be not employed as a gunner at Hull and when his pay begins.[17]

25 July 1684

Petition of Daniel Vansurer, John Forgean, James Waring, and Richard Bonner, showing that they supplied the King's hospital at Tangier formerly with bread, meat, wine and oil to the value of £992 13s. 6d. (£235 15s. 0d. by Waring; £549 18s. 6d. by Forgean; £38 by Vansurer; £169 by Bonner), as appears by the certificate of the principal overseer: that further, one William Smith has supplied the hospital with some necessaries since petitioners [did] and has received £700 as an overseer of the hospital money and has made no dividend among petitioners of the same. Therefore pray for their money or that Mr Hewer be ordered to detain in his hands Mr Smith's money for his houses till petitioners are satisfied their proportion of the £700 be received and that he may not keep it all to himself, his being the last debt accrued.[18]

29 July 1684

Petition of Hannah Ridings, widow of Peter Ridings, gunner, praying, in her miserable condition, for the arrears of her husband's pay of 12d. a day

16 TNA, SP44/9, fols 404–7; *CTB*, VII, pp. 1245–6.
17 TNA, SP44/7, fol. 395; *CTB*, VII, p. 1246.
18 TNA, SP44/18, fols 60–1; *CTB*, VII, p. 1248.

from 1 April 1682 to 28 April 1684, he having been drawn out for Tangier and there received many wounds, languished and died.[19]

30 July 1684

Warrant to Mr Fox [paymaster of the forces] to pay Thomas Best £773 14s. 9d. towards furnishing clothes for Colonel Kirke's Regiment; said sum to be deducted out of the off-reckonings of said regiment.[20]

31 July 1684

Same to Fox to pay to Hewer, £51l. 2s. 6d., whereof £20 is intended for John Eccles, gunner and conductor of the women and children [belonging to Kirke's Regiment] transported from Tangier to Pendennis (which sum is to be placed to the account of Pendennis [garrison]) and the remaining £31 2s. 6d. is for discharging Richard Stanning, Thomas Gresham, John Baxter and Richard Wise, four soldiers come from Tangier.[21]

TNA, SP44/5, fols 29–30; *CTB*, VII, p. 1272.

6 August 1684

Warrant to Hewer to pay the arrears as follows to four soldiers lately come from Tangier. Care is to be taken to deduct payments already made to them by Treasury orders and moneys which they owe to their captains, and these men are to be put out of the muster rolls of their several companies to prevent double payment when the rest of the company comes to receive their arrears. The said soldiers are: Thomas Gresham (of Colonel Kirke's Company) 16s. due on the 7th pay, £9 18s. 0d. due for 792 days to 31 May 1684, at 3d. a day; deductions, 19s. 10d.; total arrears due, £9 14s. 2d. Richard Stanning (same company), arrears for 792 days as above, £9 18s. 0d.; deductions, £1 9s. 10d.; total arrears, £8 8s. 2d. Richard Wise (Captain Webster's Company), arrears for 603 days at 3d., £7 10s. 9d.; ditto for 189 days at 6d., £4 14s. 6d.; deductions, £4 11s. 0d.; total arrears, £7 15s. 4d. John Baxter (Webster's), arrears as above; deductions, £4 2s. 5d.; total arrears, £8 2s. 10d.

6 August 1684

Petition of Job Atkins, having been 22 years in that [the Tangier] service: prays payment of the £22 19s. 00d. due to his son as late master-gunner of Tangier; and prays grant of a pension, he being aged.[22]

12 August 1684

Petition of Elizabeth Price, widow of Jonathan Price, who served the King many years in the troops of the garrison of Tangier, shewing that she is a poor

19 TNA, SP44/18, fol. 62; *CTB*, VII, p. 1256.
20 TNA, SP44/7, fol. 401; *CTB*, VII, p. 1257.
21 TNA, SP44/5, fol. 32; SP44/7, fol. 402; *CTB*, VII, p. 1257.
22 TNA, SP44/18, fol. 68; *CTB*, VII, p. 1272.

sickly woman unfit to procure a livelihood for herself and child.[23]

19 August 1684

Warrant to pay £30 1s. 8d. to Patrick Farrell as one moiety of what is due to him for his services at Tangier as an ensign in Captain Zouch Tate's Company, the said company being broke and he put out of pay and deprived of employ. It appearing that after deducting a nineteenth part as is customary on the Tangier establishment and also the debts due from him to the inhabitants there, there is due to him £78 3s. 5d. for his pay as ensign in Captain Mathew's Company, 1 April 1682 to 1 February 1683; and in Captain Tate's Company, from 1 February 1683 to 30 April 1684, in all 731 days at 3s. a day.

Same to same to similarly pay £71 18s. 6d. to John Wilson, late a lieutenant in Captain Zouch Tate's Company. His arrears after deductions as above being £143 17s. 1d. for 731 days (1 April 1682 to 30 April 1684) at 4s. a day.[24]

1 November 1684

Petition of Susanna Baker for 21 months' pay due to her late husband as Sergeant in Captain Guy's Company at Tangier, she being in great want.[25]

6 November 1684

Petition of Major Harsenett shewing that Samuel Dunn, gent., and cornet of horse in the garrison of Tangier, and his servant dieted with petitioner, but never paid for same, though often promised: therefore prays that the £96 12s. 0d. due to him may be deducted from the pay due to said Dunn.[26]

9 November 1685

Report to the King by Treasurer Rochester on the petition presented to the late king by Captain Alexander McKenzie and the rest of the officers of the troop of horse late under him in Tangier. I find that the late treasury lords referred same 1 July 1684 to William Hewer, who reported 6 August following that the 30 horse formerly borne on the establishment of Tangier with one officer only at lieutenant's pay, were about April 1682 formed into a troop under their then commander, Captain McKenzie, and Francis Delarne was appointed lieutenant by commission dated 25 April 1682, John Chappell as cornet by commission dated 26 April, and John Dennis as quartermaster by commission dated 27 April. That from the muster rolls it appears they were mustered only from April 1683, the time of their appearance at Tangier, but that it appeared from certificates of the Earl of Inchiquin, Colonel Sackville and Colonel Kirke, late governors of Tangier, that the custom and practice of that garrison has always been to pay officers from the dates of their commissions. Their pay from the dates of their commission to 1 April 1683, if allowed will be £136 to McKenzie at 8s. a day to make up his 6s. on

23 TNA, SP44/18, fol. 71; *CTB*, VII, p. 1283.

24 TNA, SP44/5, fols 56–7; *CTB*, VII, p. 1296.

25 TNA, SP44/18, fol. 101; *CTB*, VII, p. 1378.

26 TNA, SP44/2, fol. 108; *CTB*, VII, pp. 1384–5.

the establishment into 14s. a day; £170 to Delarne on 10s. a day; £152 11s. 0d. to Chappell on 9s. a day; £101 8s. 0d. to Dennis on 6s. a day. Total: £559 19s. 0d.[27]

11 November 1684
Petition of the inhabitants of Tangier who are creditors to the officers and workmen belonging to the mole and fortifications, most [of them] having Mr Sheres' obligation for their debts, who they are unwilling to molest.

Petition of the Tangier officers belonging to the Mole and fortifications, praying payment [of their salaries] they being four years in arrear and the only persons come from Tangier who have not received some sort of relief since their arrival.[28]

12 November 1684
Petition of Margaret Jarvis, widow of George Jarvis, late a private sentinel in Tangier garrison, who after 20 years' service in Portugal and Tangier, died of wounds after the last fight leaving petitioner with three children; and being absent through lameness, petitioner was not included in the general list of widows.[29]

14 November 1684
Petition of Edward Hughes, late Muster-master at Tangier … praying to be continued in his employment which is discontinued since his return from Tangier; he having served the late and present King since 1642.[30]

20 November 1684
Petition of Jane Emerson, widow, showing that her husband, a private sentinel in the horse and foot at Tangier, died there shortly before the dissolution of the place, by reason whereof she is put out of her habitation and livelihood, being 60 years old.[31]

20 November 1684
Warrant to William Hewer to pay £20 per annum to Job Atkins, late master-gunner of the garrison of Tangier, as royal bounty for his support during his life in consideration of his 22 years' faithful service in said garrison, being now rendered incapable of earning a livelihood by age and other infirmities.[32]

20 November 1684
Treasury warrant to William Hewer to pay sums to the persons following, in accordance with his report and answer to several petitions relating to Tangier:

27 TNA, SP44/11, fols 134–5.
28 TNA, SP44/18, fol. 119; *CTB*, VII, p. 1393.
29 TNA, SP44/18, fol. 121; *CTB*, VII, p. 1395.
30 TNA, SP44/18, fol. 127; *CTB*, VII, p. 1396.
31 TNA, SP44/18, fol. 128; *CTB*, VII, p. 1398.
32 TNA, SP44/5, fol. 102; *CTB*, VII, p. 1399.

Ann Page, widow, for her husband's arrears as a trooper to Captain Neatby. £10 11s. 11d.

Henry Old for his arrears as a sergeant to Captain Rodney. £19 18s. 09d.

Thomas Cleves for his arrears as a sergeant to Captain Ely. £32 04s. 11d.

Elizabeth Phillips for her husband's arrears as a trooper to Captain Neatby. £26 17s. 10d.

Simon Beauchamp for his arrears as a sergeant to Captain Rodney. £32 09s. 06d.

Hannah Riding, widow, for her husband's arrears as a gunner. £35 09s. 00d.

Elizabeth Price, Elizabeth Cook, Margaret Collins, Sarah Whittaker and Jane Hollinghurst, poor Tangier widows, £5 each as royal bounty and as in full of all future pretenses. £25 00s. 00d.

Richard Senhouse, late *pratique* master at Tangier, for his salary to 23 February 1683, viz. £29 7s. 3d. and for two boats bought of him for the service of Tangier, viz. £32. £61 07s. 03d.

Joshua Foxley, messenger to the late commissioners for the affairs of Tangier, for 1½ years' salary to 24 June [being] then discharged £45 00s. 00d.

Barbara Hughes, widow, in full satisfaction of the pension of £4l per annum settled on her by treasury warrant, being to defray her charges in going over to her own country of Lorraine in France. £10 00s. 00d.[33]

22 November 1684
Petition of Elizabeth Franklyn for payment of £39 due to her for maintenance of the child of Thomas Wilmott, late a gunner in Tangier, from September 1672 to 17 August 1684, at 2s. 6d. a week.[34]

22 November 1684
To Treasurer Hewer to stop out of Lieutenant Dunn's pay the £96 12s. 0d. due to Henry Hordesnel, his Majesty's late Recorder at Tangier, for the diet of said Dunn and his servant in Tangier for two years and seven weeks.[35]

33 TNA, SP44/5, fols 103–4; *CTB*, VII, p. 1399. See also Hughes' petition, dated 15 December 1684, for speedy payment of the two years' arrears due to her late husband, Peter Hughes, a private soldier under Sir James Leslie at Tangier: petitioner being about to go into France, her native country (SP44/18, fol. 159).

34 TNA, SP44/18, fol. 132; *CTB*, VII, p. 1406.

35 TNA, SP44/7, fols 451–2; *CTB*, VII, p. 1408.

24 November 1684

Petition of Lieutenant Francis Gorman, formerly deputy town mayor in Tangier, praying payment of £237 8s. 9d. arrears due to him during the time of Lord Middleton's government.[36]

27 November 1684

Henry Guy to Mr Hewer. The King has directed Lord Dartmouth to demand an account from each captain of the effective men of the respective forces that he should find upon his arrival at Tangier. This account is taken [accordingly] and returned to his Majesty. The Treasury Lords direct that instead of the muster taken 1 October 1683 by the muster-master you are to state the pay account of said garrison from the number of soldiers so given in by each officer to Lord Dartmouth upon 16 October, which is to commence from the first. You are to take care that the King have right done him likewise as to the victuals when the account for same shall come before you.[37]

20 December 1684

Petition of Captain Toby Caulfield, showing that in the year 1680 your petitioner bought off Captain Chidley Coote his command of a company in your Majesty's Army in Ireland, which company was one of the four commanded for Tangier before your petitioner purchased the said employ of captain. That your petitioner did serve your Majesty four years in Tangier, and being at last two years in arrear for himself and company, and necessaries very scarce there, he, to supply the wants of himself and officers, was forced to contract many debts amounting to above £400, for part of which, the sum of £100, your petitioner stands engaged for his present lieutenant, £50 more for his first lieutenant, who was there slain, and most of the remainder for several other of the officers and soldiers slain also in the said service. That your petitioner, being visited with much sickness, a month before the arrival of the Lord Dartmouth, was forced to come to England to gain his health, in whose absence, an account of the debts of the whole garrison being taken and returned to the Lords Commissioners of your Majesty's Treasury, the officers and soldiers have since received their arrears, and your petitioner by reason of his absence hath not been in the least satisfied, or discharged from any of the aforesaid debts. But your petitioner's pay hath been stopped for the same above six months past, and will be so yet these three years until the same be fully satisfied. That your petitioner cannot expect to receive from his lieutenant the £100 he stands so engaged for, his pay being also stopped for other debts by him contracted amounting also to above £400, which will not be satisfied in four years' time, nor one farthing from any other person for whom he stands engaged as aforesaid, so that he is destitute of a maintenance to support him until the said debts be fully paid.[38]

36 TNA, SP44/18, fol. 137; *CTB*, VII, p. 1410.

37 TNA, SP44/7, fol. 452; *CTB*, VII, p. 1415.

38 HMC, *Ormonde*, VII, p. 299.

26 December 1684

Treasury to Colonel Percy Kirke. Several petitions and certificates have been lately presented to the Treasury Lords for arrears of pay due to soldiers discharged, viz. for their service at Tangier, which [cases] my Lords apprehend to be contrary to what the king formerly directed, and fearing if the like practice should be continued it would prove very inconvenient and prejudicial to his service, they direct that you forthwith signify to the captains of the respective companies under you that they do not from henceforth without special order for their so doing discharge any soldier or give certificate for the arrear of pay due to any of them that came from Tangier and now belong to any of their companies, it being neither for the honour of his Majesty's service nor the satisfaction of their Lordships to have any of the said persons discharged out of his service until their lordships shall be in a condition to pay and provide for them.

[Like letters of same date to Colonel Trelawny, Captain Alexander McKenzie, Captain John Coy, Captain Thomas Langston, and Captain Charles Neatby, relating to the discharge of troopers. Also similar letter, dated 30 December 1684, to Lord Churchill to give like notice to the captains of troops under his command, which came from Tangier.][39]

17 August 1685

Treasurer Rochester to the Earl of Dumbarton. Several of the inhabitants of the late city of Tangier have applied to me concerning the debt of £8,519 14s. 2d. owing to them from the officers of your regiment for their subsistence during their serving at Tangier, towards which debt (so adjusted and stated by the commissioners appointed by Lord Dartmouth) only £3,958 14s. 10d. appears to be paid, although several of your officers allege to the said inhabitants that the whole of their debts are stopped out of their pay. Likewise, Mr Hewer has laid before me a memorial of money advanced by him upon account of clothes supplied to the said regiment whilst at Tangier and also of money advanced by order of Lord Dartmouth to your officers, there which was to be repaid to Lord Dartmouth or to Hewer out of their first pay after their arrival in England: viz. £530 paid 30 November 1680 for clothes supplied to the 200 recruits sent to Tangier by order of the Commissioners for the affairs of Tangier; £400 paid 5 December 1683 to Captain Douglas and Captain Monroe; £49 10s. 0d. paid 20 January 1684 at Tangier by order of Lord Dartmouth and £480 similarly paid 8 February 1684, or in all £1,459 10s. 0d. Hewer is to attend you as to both these matters. I recommend it to you that his Majesty may receive no further trouble herein and that I may not be obliged to put a stop to the pay due to the regiment.[40]

39 TNA, SP44/8, fols 15–18.

40 TNA, SP31/10, fol. 168; *CTB*, VIII, pp. 307–8.

13 December 1686
Warrant by Treasurer Rochester to William Hewer, Treasurer for the affairs of the late garrison of Tangier, to forthwith proceed to the adjusting and paying the nineteen months' or 578 days' arrears due from 1 October 1682 to 1 May 1684, to the several officers, regiments, troops and others as follows, the King being graciously disposed to pay off the said arrears to the several officers, soldiers, field and staff officers, troops, train gunners, carpenters and others belonging to the late garrison of Tangier. The payment to be according to the following seven muster rolls: 1 October, 1 December 1682; 1 February 1683; 1 April, 1 June, 1 August and 1 October 1683; [all to the following]: (1) the staff officers and train borne on the old establishment [of Tangier]; (2) the commissioned officers of the regiment commanded by Colonel Percy Kirke and the four companies formerly belonging to the late Duke of Monmouth added to the said regiment; (3) the commissioned officers of the regiment commanded by Colonel Charles Trelawney; (4) the commissioned officers of the four troops of horse; (5) the ordinary and extraordinary gunners, carpenters and gunsmiths; (6) the non-commissioned officers, soldiers and troopers only of each regiment and troop who shall personally appear with certificates under their captain's hands or to the relations and administrators of such as be dead. Care is to be taken herein to make the due deductions for clothes, forage, physic and money advanced, and also for what has been paid by the king to the late inhabitants of Tangier as impressed and upon account of debts entered against them at Tangier by said inhabitants. And forasmuch as there appears to be due and owing from several of the said officers and soldiers (over and above the debts which were entered against them at Tangier as aforesaid) several sums of money according to notes and obligations under their hands, and the entries made thereof here in England by my [treasurer's] directions. The same are hereby to be stopped out of such pay as herein and are to be paid to the persons to whom they are so due.[41]

21 December 1686
Petition of James Waley, surgeon, for an allowance for his service in taking care of eight troops of horse at Tangier, as is usually allowed to surgeons of horse.[42]

41 TNA, SP44/6, fols 477–8.
42 TNA, SP44/2, fol. 423.

Appendix VIII

Sir Hugh Cholmeley, A Short Account of the Progress of the Mole at Tangier, from the First Beginning of that Work[1]

His Majesty having declared the earl of Teviot governor of Tangier and constituted certain Commissioners for the care of that place, about the year 1662. The business of building a Mole there was discussed in the presence of engineers sent from Genoa, and others that could be found versed in such sort of work, and because Tangier was at that time only an open bay, and that chests could not be framed but in a secure harbour, it was found of absolute necessity to begin the work with great loose rocks, after the manner that all other Moles are built, excepting the New Mole at Genoa. Many of the Tangier lords declaring such a work could never be carried well on, but by way of contract, they gave encouragement to the said earl of Teviot, Sir John Lawson, and Mr Cholmeley, to enter into Articles for building the same by the Cubical Yard. Thirteen shillings for every such yard was the price asked, and as readily consented to, in so unusual a work there was no other measures to go by than such as the contractors themselves laid down, who wanted not private assurance to secure them from the danger of such accidents as might render the bargain over-hard on their side, nor were they indeed otherwise mistaken in their measures, than from such contingent causes as could not be foreseen at first, viz. the softness of the stone, which upon opening the quarries wrought to half loss, the uncertainty of the weather, and the very bad and dilatory payments by tallies. This contract for building the Mole was signed in February 1663, and the first payment began the tenth of April following.

It was no easy matter at this time to get workmen to go to Tangier, because of the ill-reputation the place had, from the mortality of our countrymen, and the great sufferings they at first met with. Mr Cholmeley by the interest he had

1 [Sir Hugh Cholmeley], *A Short Account of the Progress of the Mole at Tangier, from the First Beginning of that Work* (London: 1679); Bejjit, *English Colonial Texts*, pp. 153–60.

in the North, and by going himself, prevailed with about 40 masons, miners, and other proper artists and workmen to undertake the service, with whom he arrived at Tangier about the beginning of June 1663. The place being destitute of all conveniences; much of that summer was spent in providing quarters for men and stores, and in putting together engines prepared for the weighing stones, so that it was the end of August when the first foundation of the Mole was laid, soon after which the earl of Teviot went for England, and at his return, about the end of December, found the Mole advanced beyond his expectation, but Mr Cholmeley being obliged to go for England in February, because of the death of his elder Brother, who left a son in infancy, had not been long there, when news came of the loss of the earl of Teviot, chief of the contractors, which occasioned Mr Cholmeley to return for Tangier so soon as he could settle affairs, provide himself of officers and stores necessary, which delayed his arrival there until January 1665. And then he found little work had been done in his absence, chiefly because the workmen at the Mole, by reason of the loss the garrison had with the earl of Teviot, were forced to the duty of soldiers, and because the water engines were found to be of little use, by reason of the frequent Levant winds; this made Mr Cholmeley soon alter the method from water to land-carriages drawn by horses, and to build at the quarries a little town called Whitby, which contained stables for a hundred horses, large magazines for all sorts of stores, and quarters for the workmen and their wives. He also advised Sir John Lawson of the many impediments which made it impossible to carry on the work at the rate of the contract, which procured an Order of Council of 31 March 1665 by which His Majesty was pleased to explain the intentions of the contract, so as to leave the contractors free from danger of loss, and to reduce the work to an account, if the same were insisted upon.

Tangier was at this time under the government of the Lord Bellasyse, and the Mole advanced so well, that there was a battery built upon it which did secure the trade of the place from the attempts of the Dutch, but Sir John Lawson also dying in that war, the burden of the Mole was left to Mr Cholmeley the only surviving contractor, whose nephew dying about the same time, left unto him the business and the estate of his family, and this occasioned him to pass into England the end of this year, having put the affairs of the Mole into an excellent method, and left the care under knowing and intelligent officers.

The plague and the war did occasion that want of money, it was impossible to get any other payment than tallies anticipated from 24 to 30 months, so that money could not be had but by additional security, which forced stores to be bought at the worst hand, and the business to be carried on in the way of trade, and much time to be spent barely in keeping account of the money and the interest, and in the continual negotiating the same by yallies, which received no amendment, notwithstanding Sir Hugh Cholmeley his daily complaints.

The Earl of Sandwich being called from Madrid in the year 1668 had instructions to call at Tangier, and take a survey of the Mole, which he did in the month of August by the help of one Mr Sheres, and at his return to Court towards the end of that year reported the same to be 380 yards in length, carried on by the conduct of excellent officers, and under such a good economy as could not well be mended: but the work of the Mole being now carried into so deep water that there was a possibility of building with chests, and some necessity appearing to proceed in the future work in a more solid way than the contract seemed to oblige, the carrying on of the work was reduced into an office by order of the king in council, dated 27 August 1669. under the care of Sir Hugh Cholmeley as surveyor-general, who framed the method for governing the work, and issuing the money under such checks, and so well to the liking of the Tangier lords, and the lords of the treasury, that upon the greatest disquisition it hath not since met with one single amendment.

Sometime before this settlement there was noise of breaches at Tangier, which occasioned discourses of the necessity of building with chests, and obliged Sir Hugh Cholmeley to frame two chests for a trial under the survey of Mr Sheres a gentleman, Sir Hugh had lately entertained, who was experienced in such works, and under whose care they were sent to Tangier, from whence Mr Sheres embarks for Genoa, to take exact observations of their proceedings, at his return to Tangier gives his advice for building an inner Mole with chests, and for protection of this an outward work in dimensions much greater than that which was contracted for, and in the same way advised Sir Hugh at his arrival at Tangier, April following, to proceed upon the repair of the work. The work with chests seemed to Sir Hugh superfluous, because it required an outward one for protection of it, and this was proposed to be made of stones from 25 to 30 tons each, which by reason of the continual agitations of the seas was at Tangier wholly unpracticable: He therefore immediately applied himself to the repair of the work by artificial pillars of about 100 tons in bigness, which suddenly secured about 50 yard of the side that was most exposed, and the end of the work he secured by one of the great chests he had sent from England.

About the month of July, this year, Sir Hugh received a letter from the Lords Commissioners for the affairs of Tangier, taking notice of the ill reports they heard of the Mole, and commanding the matter to be discussed in the presence of the chief on the place, and be proceeded in the way [it] should be generally approved. The chief officers of the garrison, the best of the citizens and commanders of ships being summoned, the whole matter was discussed in the presence of his Excellency my Lord Howard, now duke of Norfolk, the Earl of Middleton and the mayor of the place, Mr Sheres being also present, who all unanimously concluded the present practice with pillars was the most probable expedient for the repair, and that if the same resisted the storms of the approaching winter, the work ought to be carried on in the same way for the future, and to this purpose signed a letter to the lords commissioners under all their hands. The work continued to resist the sea, not only the following, but many winters, so that the present practice gave satisfaction almost to every man, excepting Sir Hugh himself, who did then declare that the work was such as he was able to carry on under the exceeding bad payments with which it laboured, but such as could not be of lasting continuance. And having for above two years managed the work almost wholly without money upon his own credit, was forced to return to England the beginning of the year 1672 where the wars made arrears impossible to get, beside that the trouble in soliciting for money, and accounting for the same, caused such an attendance as was incompatible with the service at Tangier.

The winter ending, the year 1674 brought news of some breaches at Tangier, which Sir Hugh being much troubled to hear, and assured within himself he knew to cure the evil, so as would take off all future complaints, if the want of money, and perplexities of an exchequer account could give him leave to go to Tangier, offered unto the lords in the year 1674 certain proposals whereby he undertook both to repair the present work, and to carry it 100 yards farther into the sea, by which means there would be a harbour for ships to ride safely in four fathoms at low-water, and all this to be done in six years, for the annual establishment, and though he could not give security for the whole sum, he offered to give, from year to year, security for the money he should receive, and to be punished or rewarded according to his yearly performance. Mr Sheres taking advantage of these proposals, framed others, by which he undertook the work at £10,000 less in the whole, and with great upright chests, maintaining that figure best against the reflux sea; whereas by Sir Hugh's offers the same was to be done in solid work, and with chests too, yet so placed that the force of the sea should be wholly dissipated by a slope and gradual interception of the waters, after the imitation of nature, that from this position doth in many places guard the coast merely by a bank of sand.

At the same time the Lord Privy Seal gave in other propositions from certain artists who offered to do the work at a much cheaper rate than that proposed by Mr Sheres, and to give £60,000 security for their performance, but Mr Sheres had the preference, and without security is trusted with the issuing and paying of the money with a [yearly] reward of £2,000 if he performs and nothing if he fails in the same. Sir Hugh was happy in the greatest exigency of the work, and upon the most severe enquiries to hit upon such expedients for the repair and advance as gave satisfaction to Mr Sheres, and all upon the place without one dissenting man, and this after Mr Sheres had been at Genoa, and considered the way of their practice, it had been no unusual thing for one that had been so many years trained in the work under Sir Hugh to profit himself upon such defects as he might have observed. Let us then take a view of the present state of the work, by which we shall see how far Mr Sheres hath exceeded or come short of Sir Hugh his proposals, or how near he hath hitherto complied with his own undertakings.

Sir Hugh having carried the Mole 500 yards into the sea, within which there was about eighteen feet depth at low-water, was very desirous to leave the same complete and finished, that so it might have had comparison with any future work. He offered for one year's establishment to complete the repair, and to finish the same, as well on the inside as outward, and to carry it farther 15 yards into the sea, and to give security to do all this in so substantial a way, as upon view and trial should be judged and found durable; and in case of failure, to pay back the whole money, or as much as should be judged the deficiency might amount unto. But it was concluded that this repair should also be undertaken by Mr Sheres, who having now received £60,000 and spent three years last midsummer about the same, we hear hath repaired the old work, but there was not at midsummer one foot advanced into the sea, nor will the expense of another year, at his rate of work, scarce finish that which Sir Hugh offered to give security to do for one year's allowance; yet Mr Sheres computes he hath every year performed his complement of work, which was 30 yards yearly in length, until the whole were finished, and possibly he may have done so according to the numerical quantity of cubical yards contained in the chests placed; but certainly there is much more work to secure the foundations of his chests, and that according to his own proposals, than barely the placing and filling the same.

And what Mr Sheres hath done in the years past will be best understood by the progress of his future work, if in other three years be can completely finish ninety yards in length, which is his undertaking, then may it be concluded, the past work, though it comes much short of what Sir Hugh offered security to perform, is yet in proportion to his own agreements. And now that the work done by Sir Hugh is completely finished and made durable by Mr Sheres himself. Sir Hugh will allow he was mistaken in his measures, if the future work be done in proportion anything cheaper; but if it shall happen to cost the king much more than the past work now repaired hath done, Sir Hugh humbly conceives the way of building is nothing improved, and that it had been better to have continued the work in the old way, and afterwards to have secured it as Mr Sheres hath done the past work, than to prosecute it in a way much more costly, and by confession of himself no less durable; Sir Hugh was for building with chests as well as Mr Sheres, he differed only in the way of placing these chests, which Sir Hugh proposed by several rows, one set within the other, gradually breaking and intercepting the sea, Mr Sheres maintained, and undertakes to do the work by one solid body, and an upright side, which from its own strength should secure the work without any other outward work or defence whatever; to this Sir Hugh's objections were, the difficulty of placing these chests close one to the other, as at Genoa, and the danger of the works falling when the worm had consumed the wood of the chest.

By what hath been practised it is plain the chests cannot be close joined scarce nearer than four foot one to the other, which occasions the supplying the vacancy with a small chest, which hath little substance, and therefore must occasion many fears, and for the great chests, they are made of such strong plank, and so bound with timber, that it is not possible for the worm suddenly to destroy them, and it is plainly demonstrable, that if the chests were filled with sand, they cannot possibly give way whilst the woodwork continues unperished, and therefore no trial of the work can be suddenly expected; but if Mr Sheres be obliged to secure his great chests by other lower chests set outwards towards the sea, then whatever he may pretend, his proceeding is directly according to Sir Hugh's proposal, only in the way of a far greater and needless expense by all the cost of the great chest, which is plainly demonstrable from the solidity of the old work, built without chests, and made durable by means of such an outward work as in the foresaid case is presumed necessary to secure the present work with great chests.

It is not the intention of this paper to diminish ought from Mr Sheres, whose diligence Sir Hugh heartily wishes may have all encouragement in so public a work; but not being conscious by the progress since he left the work, or by the future advance, that it will appear he hath any ways misemployed the king's money, he thought it not unreasonable, in order to his own justification, to set down this short narrative of the whole affair. Written in the Year 1669.

Appendix IX

English Report of the Evacuation of the Tangier Mole and Garrison[1]

11 January 1684. The Alcaide complains to Mr Cuthbert that our people wrought in the fields, contrary to the treaty; the Alcaide riding about the lines said this going on near Pole Fort, and elsewhere. It was explained to the Alcayde that what our people were doing in the fields was in order to prevent the damage his men might receive at our quitting this place, by reason of several mines which were formerly made by Sir Palmes Fairborne. The Alcaide said he could not stand still and see the Christians possibly laying into the ground for new fortifications, and collected an attacking force at Pie Corner. Lord Dartmouth remonstrated and the Alcaide promised the offence should not be repeated.

15 January 1684. Part of the fleet being come together in the road, and the weather being more moderate, and the Mole and harbour quite destroyed. Lord Dartmouth, with the advice of a council of war held on the 13th, resolved on demolishing and quitting our posts. Taking in all the palisadoes and stores he began at Pole Fort, the situation of the place being such that it was not judged convenient to part with it before we were in good readiness to quit the town. The whole garrison was drawn out with a battalion of seamen. The small boats from the fleet were in continual motion from Fountain Fort to Tangier River, and the small frigates, under sail, standing towards the shore. The colours of the regiments, that were not carried out, were posted on such eminent places on the walls, as were thought most convenient. All the artificers with the burghers and some seamen, were employed in taking in the palisadoes and other stores, and, in the interim, the mines were preparing to be blown. About 2 o'clock, orders were given for marching in the several battalions … the horse bringing up the rear of the field. All the passes, where there was any probability of the Moors' horse approaching us, being strewed with crow's feet. When the men were all in safety, the mines

1 SRO, D(W)1778/V/1397; HMC, *Eleventh Report, App. V*, I, pp. 51–4.

were fired. Lord Dartmouth sent to warn the Alcaide of the danger which would attend any of his people remaining near the lines. The ground being as aforesaid covered with crows' feet, after the forces returned into the town, our guards perceiving some Moors coming to pick them up, fired upon them and Lord Dartmouth desired the Alcaide to warn his people not to come within our lines for, … if they did, it should be upon their peril.

29 January 1684. Several guns and horses taken on board ship.

31 January 1684. General preparations made for the retreat.

1 February 1684. Withdrawal before Peterborough Tower.

3 February 1684. The three companies of grenadiers marched out of the Salley-port to Seamens' Battery, at the head of the King's Battalion. All the town guards, consisting of Colonel Trelawny's Regiment, besides those at Catherina and the Spur, marched out at the Salley-port, then manned the line of the Old Spur at Seamens' Battery. Before the drawbridge, Colonel Kirke's, having the guard of the Catherina and Mole, those of the Castle were drawn up at that regiment's parade nigh Peterborough Tower, the Mole guards being secured under the arch at Whitby Gate, and all the small vessels commanded off, lest damage should happen; all the men being thus secured, the mines of that part of York Castle, with the square tower next to the Mole were blown up. At this time was also fired one mine in Stainer's Battery and another in the Governor's bastion, which was left standing to secure conversation betwixt the town and the castle. Cambridge Fort was blown up and destroyed; and in the evening, Colonel Kirke's regiment took the guard of the castle, and Colonel Trelawny's those of the town. When the aforesaid mines were so happily blown up, a form of prayer, prepared by Dr Ken, relating to the present conjuncture, was read at the Town House – the church being no longer fit to be made use of – where his Excellency, attended by the principal officers of the garrison, returned God thanks for his infinite mercies to us hitherto.

4 February1684. Weather very bad, but the garrison forces, were employed in pulling down all the remaining quarters, guardhouses, churches, etc., and in shipping the remaining sick and stores. The remains of the buildings were thrown into the common sewer. None but serviceable men were now left on shore, and there supplied with ammunition and victuals for two days, so that all things being in a readiness for the blowing up and demolishing the town and castle, [on] the 5th, in the evening, orders were given that the guards should be at their arms by break of day. About 9 in the morning the garrison was commanded to draw to the port. The first mines to be blown were those at Stainer's Battery, and from the Water Gate to the Devil's Tower. The other mines were successfully fired, neither the garrison nor the fleet sustaining any injury. The mine from the Devil's Tower up to the Bowling Bear, were next ordered to be blown; after this, the mine of Peterborough was sprung with the same good success, the tower falling flat, on which many of the Moors

appeared, giving a great shout. After firing the mines at Lawson's Battery, and elsewhere, the signal was given for the small embarkations to stand in, for the putting our men on board. Colonel Trelawny's men advanced in good order to the galley and were put into the boats, company by company, the same order was followed by Colonel Kirke's and the other regiments. But it was noticed that as our men left, greater numbers of Moors appeared on the sandhills, and drew near the town and castle; three companies of grenadiers were therefore to be drawn up in grand parade. Sir William Booth was ordered to inspect the ships and see they were not crowded. About midnight the wooden fort and the galley were set on fire, and more of the remainder of the men sent to the ships. The unfired mines in York Castle were then fired, those that did it being received into boats to go to the ships. The last mine under Whitby Fort was fired by his Excellency himself, and this, with the rest of the town and forts, utterly destroyed. The small boats rowed off to the fleet early in the morning, and Lord Dartmouth saw all the men put on board, and then went in his barge towards the shore to look upon the mines. The Moors, 3,000 horse and foot, on seeing [them] Lord Dartmouth put up a flag of truce by the seaside. He sent to them to warn them from coming within the ruins, advising them for their own safety to withdraw at once; but the Moors, with their usual stubbornness, did not mind it, which they heartily repented a little after, for whilst they were swarming among the ruins, an unfired mine blew up and killed above 40 of them. In this whole transaction there was only one gunner slightly wounded, one Spaniard and one Englishman killed, and three other stragglers hurt by their own negligence. Many complimentary expressions were conveyed to Lord Dartmouth by the Alcaide on his Excellency's leaving.

Appendix X

Table 54: Order taken from Lord Dartmouth's minute book relating to the destruction of the garrison of Tangier, 18 December 1683.[1]

Warrant to the respective field officers [of the] garrison and Mr Sheres to survey the several mines prepared for the blowing up and demolishing the town and castles etc., and to make report thereof.	George Lord Baron of Dartmouth Captain General Governor and Commander in Chief of his Majesty's Royal City and Garrison of Tangier, etc. It being very necessary in the execution of his Majesty's pleasure and command touching this place, that all ways and means be considered of, and used for the total destruction of the walls of the town, the castle, forts and fortifications within and without it, so as to leave it uninhabitable, and without any sort of succour or defence for the Moors, or any other that shall attempt to possess themselves of it. There are to desire and direct you with the assistance of Major Beckman, Mr Thomas Phillips (the rest of the engineers here now present) and any of the officers of the garrison whom you shall think qualified, to give you any, forthwith to take a view and consider of the several mines and other things prepared for the blowing up and demolishing the said walls, castle and forts, and to give use your opinions in writing under your hands, whether you think the same will be sufficient (if they answer the reasonable success expected from them) to complete the aforesaid ends of destroying this place; and that if anything further to be done, or in any other manner seem reasonable and fit in your judgement towards it, you do offer the same to me, in order to it's being further considered of, and put in execution, and therein to use all the care and exactness to the best of your abilities, required in a work of this nature and consequence, for which this shall be to you and every of you a sufficient warrant. Given under my hand and seal Tangier this 18th day of December 1683.
To Colonel Percy Kirke, Colonel Charles Trelawny, Lieutenant Colonel Boynton, Sir James Leslie, Major Zachary Tiffin, Captain George Bowes, Captain Robert Douglas, and Captain Andrew Munroe, and to Henry Sheres, Esq., surveyor-general of the fortification at Tangier	Dartmouth By his Excellency's Command Samuel de Par

1 SRO, D(W)1778/V/139/217.

Bibliography

Manuscript Sources

Greenwich, National Maritime Museum

JOD/4 (Journal of Edward Barlow, 1659–1703); P43 (Bernard de Gomme, plans of Tangier, 1664)

Chippenham, Wiltshire and Swindon History Centre

865/8/1/434–5 (Bullen Reymes' Journal and letter)

Leeds, Royal Armouries' Collection

XXVIA.104; XXVIA.137; XXVIA.170

London, Royal Collection Trust

RCIN 402578

London, The British Library

MSS Add. 16370, 17021, 19872, 23119, 27277, 28928, 28938; MSS Harley 1595, 6844; MS Lansdowne 192; MSS Sloane 1952, 1956–7, 1959–60, 3299, 3498, 3509–14

London, The National Archives

ADM 51, 106; AO 1/51/28; CO 279/1–33 (Colonial Office Papers); MPH 1 (Maps and Plans of Tangier, 1661–1684); SP9/209/136; SP28/89/9; SP29/52; SP29/83; SP31/10; SP44/1–3; SP44/5; SP44/7–8; SP44/14; SP44/18; SP44/29–30; SP44/41; SP44/48; SP44/58–9; SP44/62; SP44/64–5; SP44/69; SP44/104; SP44/164; SP44/187; SP71/13; SP71/174B; SP72/1; SP89/6; WO 4/1; WO 5/1; WO 24/1; WO 24/3; WO 25/11; WO 26/5; WO 55/1082; WO 93/1082; WO 93/1786

Longleat, Longleat House

CO 70 (Coventry Papers)

Madrid, Biblioteca Nacional de España

Res/285

Munich, Bayerische Staatsbibliothek

BSB Cod.icon. 361

New Haven, University of Yale Library

MS 2572 (Letter Book of Colonel Percy Kirke)

Northallerton, North Yorkshire Record Office
ZCG 5/1/1/2

Nottingham, University of Nottingham Library
Me C 10/4; Pw A/2028/14/C

Oxford, Bodleian Library
MS Bodl. 972; MSS Clarendon 81, 85; MSS Carte 73, 75, 179; 222; MSS Rawlinson A185, A323, A341, C423, D491, D916; MS Tanner 47

Preston, Lancashire Record Office
DDKE/HMC/426 (Letter from King of Morocco to Charles II, 1681)

San Marino, Huntington Library
8471; 8473 (Correspondence of Sir Palmes Fairborne)

Stafford, Staffordshire Record Office
D742; D(W)1778/I/i; D(W)1778/V/1397 (Papers of the Legge family, Earls of Dartmouth)

Stockholm, Arquivo Militar de Estocolmo, Krigsarkivet
Atlas de Leonardo de Ferrari, 1655

Worcester, Worcestershire Archive and Archaeology Service
L6/1625–5, 28–9; 1/1/123/29

Printed Primary Sources

Contemporary Newsbook
Domestick Intelligence
London Gazette
Mercurius Publicus

Contemporary Tracts and Pamphlets

Addison, Lancelot, *The Moors Baffled, being a discourse concerning Tangier, especially when it was under the Earl of Teviot* (London: William Crooke, 1681)

Addison, Lancelot, *West Barbary, or, A short narrative of the revolutions of the kingdoms of Fez and Morocco with an account of the present customs, sacred, civil, and domestick* (Oxford: John Wilmot, 1671)

A Brief Relation of the Present State of Tangier and of the Advantages with which his Excellency the Earl of Teviot has Obtained against Gayland (London: T. Mabb, 1664)

A Description of Tangier, the Country and People Adjoining with An Account of the Person and Government of Gayland the present Usurper of the Kingdom of Fez; And a short Narrative of the Proceedings of the English in those Parts (London: Samuel Speed, 1664)

A Letter to a Friend in London, Describing the Causes, Manner and Time of this Demolishing of Tangier, November the Fifth in the Year 1683 (London: J. Smith, 1683)

A Particular Narrative of a Great Engagement between the Garrison of Tangier and the Moors (London: Thomas Newcomb, 1680)

A Particular Relation of the Late Success of His Majesty's Forces at Tangier against the Moors (London: Thomas Newcomb, 1680)

A True and Exact Relation of the Great Victories Obtained by the Earl of Manchester and the Lord Fairfax Against the Earl of Newcastle's Army in the North (London: 1643)

An Exact Journal of the Siege of Tangier, from the first sitting down of the Moors before it on March 25, 1680 to the Late Truce, May following In Three Letters, written by Three Eye-Witnesses on the whole Transaction (London: Joseph Hindmarsh, 1680)

Britaine, William de, *The Interest of England in the Present War with Holland by the author of The Dutch Usurpation* (London: Jonathan Edwin, 1672)

By the King A Proclamation Declaring His Majesty's Pleasure to Settle and Establish a Free Port at His City of Tangier in Africa (London: John Bill and Christopher Barker, 1662)

[Cholmeley, Sir Hugh], *A Short Account of the Mole at Tangier, from the First Beginning of that Work* (London: 1679)

E. M., *The Present Danger of Tangier or An Account of its being Attempted By a great Army of the Moors by Land, And under some Apprehensions of the French at Sea In a Letter from Cadiz, dated 29th of July 1679 (old style) To a Friend in England* (London? 1680?)

Philips, George, *The Present State of Tangier in a Letter to His Grace, the Lord Chancellor of Ireland* (London: H. Herringman, 1676)

Rich, Jeremiah, *Death's Envious Triumph: In a Brief Memorial of the Losse of the Late Incomparable and Excellent Andrew Lord Rutherford Earle of Teveot, &c. Killed by an Ambuscadoe of Moores, May the 3rd, 1664* (London: 1644)

Ross, John, *Tangers Rescue, or a Relation of the Late Memorable Passages at Tanger ... and Particularly of that Bloody Engagement* (London: Henry Hills, 1681)

Sheres, Sir Henry, *A Discourse Touching Tangier in a letter to a person of quality* (London: 1680)

The Present Interest of Tangier (London: 1680)

Books and Edited Collections

Ackerman, John (ed.), *Moneys Received and Paid for Secret Services of Charles II and James II* (London: Camden Society, 1851)

An Abridgement of the English Military Discipline (London: John Bill and Christopher Barker, 1676, 1678 and 1686 edns)

Anderson, R. C. (ed.), *The Journal of the 1st Earl of Sandwich, 1659–1665* (Navy Records Society, 64, 1928)

Arlington, Henry B., *The Right Honourable the Earl of Arlington's Letters*, 2 vols (London: Thomas Bennet, 1701)

Birch, Thomas (ed.), *A Collection of State Papers of John Thurloe, Esq; Secretary to the Council of State*, 7 vols (London: 1742)

Boyle, Roger, Earl of Orrery, *A Treatise of the Art of War dedicated to the King's Most Excellent Majesty* (1677)

Bray, William (ed.), John Evelyn, *The Diary of John Evelyn*, 2 vols (Washington and London: M. Walter Dunne, 1901)

Brooks, Nathan, *A General and Complete List Military of Every Commission Officer of Horse and Foot now commanding His Majesty's Land Forces of England* (London: J. Gain, 1684).

Buren, Hendrick van, *Drilkonst* (1672)

Burnet, Gilbert, *History of His Own Time*, 4 vols (Oxford: Oxford University Press, 1823)

Calendar of State Papers Relating to English Affairs in the Archives of Venice, 1661–64 (London: HMSO, 1932)

Cannon, Richard, *Historical Records of the Life Guards* (London: 1835)

Chapel, Edwin (trans. & ed.), *The Tangier Papers of Samuel Pepys* (Navy Records Society, 73, 1935)

Cholmeley, Sir Hugh, *An Account of Tangier with some Account of Himself and his Journey through France and Spain to that Place, where he was engaged in building the Mole in the Time of King Charles the Second; and a Journal of the Work carrying on* (London: 1787)

Christie, W. D. (ed.), *Letters Addressed from London to Sir Joseph Williamson*, 2 vols (London: Camden Society, 1874)

Clarendon, Edward Hyde, Earl of, *The Life of Edward, Earl of Clarendon, in which is included a continuation of his History of the Grand Rebellion*, 3 vols (Oxford: Clarendon, 1827)

Dalton, Charles (ed.), *English Army Lists and Commission Registers, 1661–1714*, 2 vols (London: Eyre & Spottiswoode, 1892)

Elton, Richard, *The Complete Body of the Art Military* (London: Robert Leybourn, 1668 edn)

Firth, C. H. (ed.), *The Memoirs of Edmund Ludlow, Lieutenant-General of the Horse in the army of the Commonwealth of England, 1625–1672*, 2 vols (Oxford: Clarendon Press, 1894)

Hopkins, J. F. P. (trans. and ann.), *Letters from Barbary, 1576–1774: Arabic documents in the Public Record Office* (London & New York: Oxford University Press, 1982)

Iria, A lberto, *Cartas dos governadores do Algarve (1638–1663)* (Lisboa: Academia Portuguesa de História, 1978)

Kane, Richard, *Campaigns of King William and Queen Anne, from 1689 to 1712. Also, A New System of Military Discipline for Foot on Action* (London: J. Millan, 1745)

Kaufman, H. A. and Kaufman, P. (eds), *Tangier at High Tide: The Journal of John Luke, 1670–1673* (Geneva: Librairie E. Droz, 1958)

Latham, Robert and Matthews, William (eds), Samuel Pepys, *The Diary of Samuel Pepys*, 11 vols (London: Bell and Hyman, 1970)

Lubbock, Basil (ed.), *Barlow's Journal of His Life at Sea in King's Ships, East and West Indiamen and other Merchantmen from 1659 to 1703*, 2 vols (London: Hurst & Blackett, 1934)

Lytton Sells, A. (ed.) *The Memoirs of James II: his campaigns as Duke of York, 1652–1660* (Bloomington: Indiana University Press, 1962)

Macray, W. D. (ed.), Hyde, Edward, Earl of Clarendon, *The History of the Rebellion and Civil Wars in England*, 6 vols (Oxford: Clarendon Press, 1888)

Magolotti, Count Lorenzo, *The Travels of Cosimo the Third, Duke of Tuscany, through England during the Reign of King Charles the Second, 1669* (London: J. Mawman, 1821)

Markham, Francis, *Five Decades of Epistles of Warre* (London: Augustine Matthew, 1622)

McCance, H. M. (ed.), Halkett, Sir James, 'Tangier–1680: The Diary of Sir James Halkett', *Journal of the Society for Army Historical Research*, 1, Special No. (1922), pp. 1–24

Morgan, Sir Thomas, *A True and Just Relation of Maj. Gen. Sir Thomas Morgan's Progress in France and Flanders* (London: J. Nutt, 1699)

Oldys, William and Malham, John (eds.), *The Harleian Miscellany: A Collection of Scarce, Curious, and Entertaining Pamphlets and Tracts* (London, 1810)

Roper, A. (ed.), *Original letters of His Excellency Sir Richard Fanshaw, during his embassies in Spain and Portugal* (London: 1702)

Scoble, Andrew R. (trans.), Guizot, François, *Monk: Or the Fall of the Republic and the Restoration of the Monarchy in England in 1660* (London: Henry G. Bohn, 1851)

Smith. J., *The Life, Journals, and Correspondence of Samuel Pepys … including a narrative of his voyage to Tangier*, 2 vols (London: R. Bentley, 1841)

Smythe, Sir John, *Instructions, Observations and Orders Mylitare* (London: 1595)
Turner, Sir James, *Pallas Armata: Military essayes of the ancient Grecian, Roman, and modern art of war written in the years 1670 and 1671* (London: Richard Chiswell, 1683)
Vauban, Sébastien Le Prestre de, Rothrock, George A. (trans.), *A Manual of Siegecraft and Fortification* (Ann Arbor: University of Michigan Press, 1968)
Venn, Thomas, *Military Observations, or the Tacticks Put into Practice* (London, 1672)
Vernon, John, *The Young Horseman, or, The honest plain-dealing cavalier* (London, 1644)
Walker, Sir Edward, *A Circumstantial Account of the Preparations for the Coronation of His Highness, Charles the Second* (London: Baker, 1820)
Webster, William (ed.), Thomas Skinner, *The Life of General Monk, Duke of Albemarle* (London: J. Graves, 1724)

Reports of the Historical Manuscripts Commission

Calendar of the Manuscripts of the Marquess of Ormonde (1902–20)
Eleventh Report, Appendix I (1887)
Eleventh Report, Appendix V (1887)
Fifteenth Report, Appendix II (1896)
Report on the Manuscripts of Allen George Finch (1913)
The Manuscripts of J. M. Heathcote, Esq. (1899)

Secondary Sources

Books and Reports

Abbey, W. B. T., *Tangier under British Rule 1661–1684* (Channel Islands: J. T. Bigwood, 1940)
Abun-Nasr, Jamil M., *A History of the Maghrib in the Islamic Period* (Cambridge: Cambridge University Press, 1987)
Bakker, Johan de, *Slaves, Arms and Holy War: Moroccan Policy vis-à-vis the Dutch Republic during the Establishment of the 'Alawī Dynasty, 1660–1727* (Amsterdam: s.n. 1991)
Barnett, Correlli, *Britain and Her Army: A Military, Political and Social History of the British Army, 1509–1970* (London: Allen Lane, 1970)
Barratt, John, *'Better Begging than Fighting': The Royalist Army in Exile in the War against Cromwell 1656–1660* (Solihull: Helion & Co., 2016)
Barthorp, Michael, *British Cavalry Uniforms Since 1660* (Poole: Blandford Press, 1984)
Barthorp, Michael, *British Infantry Uniforms Since 1660* (Poole: Blandford Press, 1982)
Barthorp, Michael, *The Armies of Britain 1485–1980* (London: National Army Museum, 1981)
Bejjit, Karim, *English Colonial Texts on Tangier, 1661–1684: Imperialism and the Politics of Resistance* (Farnham: Ashgate, 2015)
Bennison, Amira K., *Jihad and its Interpretations in Pre-Colonial Morocco: State-Society Relations during the French Conquest of Algeria* (London and New York: Routledge, 2002)
Blackmore, David, *Destructive and Formidable: British Infantry Firepower, 1642–1765* (Frontline Books: London, 2014)
Bruce, A. P. C., *The Purchase System in the British Army, 1660–1871* (London: Royal Historical Society, 1980)
Cannon, Richard, *Historical Record of the First, or the Royal Regiment of Dragoons* (London: Longman, Orme & Co., 1840)

Cannon, Richard, *Historical Record of the First, or Royal Regiment of Foot* (London: Parker, Furnivall & Parker, 1847; reprint Outlook Verlag, 2018)

Cannon, Richard, *Historical Record of the Fourth, or the King's Own, Regiment of Foot Dragoons* (London: Longman, Orme & Co., 1839)

Cannon, Richard, *Historical Records of the Life Guards* (London: Longman, Orme & Co., 1835)

Childs, John, *General Percy Kirke and the Later Stuart Army* (London: Bloomsbury, 2014)

Childs, John, *The Army of Charles II* (London: Routledge & Kegan Paul, 1976)

Colley, Linda, *Captives: Britain, Empire, and the World, 1600–1850* (New York: Anchor Books, 2004)

Corbett, Julian S., *England in the Mediterranean: a study in the rise and influence of British power within the Straits, 1600–1703*, 2 vols (London: Longmans, 2nd edn, 1917)

Cowper, Julia M., *The King's Own: The Story of a Royal Regiment*, 3 vols (Oxford: Oxford University Press, 1939)

Davies, Godfrey, *The Early History of the Coldstream Guards* (Oxford: Clarendon, 1924)

Davies, Godfrey, *The Restoration of Charles II* (Oxford: Oxford University Press, 1955)

Davis, John, *The History of the Second Queen's Royal Regiment: now The Queen's (Royal West Surrey) Regiment*, 7 vols (London: Richard Bentley, 1887)

Drenth, Wienand and Riley, Jonathon, *The First Colonial Soldiers: A Survey of British Colonies and Their Garrisons, 1650–1714. Vol. 1: the British Isles, Europe, Asia and Africa* (Eindhoven: Drenth Publishing, 2014)

Duffy, Christopher, *Siege Warfare: The Fortress in the Early Modern World 1494–1660* (London & New York: Routledge, 1997)

Ede-Borrett, Stephen, *The Army of James II: The Birth of the British Army* (Solihull: Helion & Co., 2017)

Elbl, M. M., *Portuguese Tangier (1471–1662): Colonial Urban Fabric as Cross-Cultural Skeleton* (Peterborough, Ontario: Baywolf Press, 2013)

Firth, Charles and Davies, Godfrey, *The Regimental History of Cromwell's Army, 2 vols* (Oxford: Clarendon Press, 1991 edn)

Fisher, Sir Godfrey, *Barbary Legend: War, Trade, and Piracy in North Africa, 1415–1830* (Oxford: Oxford University Press, 1957)

Foard, Glenn, *Naseby: The Decisive Campaign* (Barnsley: Pen & Sword, 2004 edn)

Fraser, Antonia, *King Charles II* (London: Phoenix, 1979)

Glozier, Matthew, *Scottish Soldiers in France in the Reign of the Sun King* (Leiden: Brill, 2004)

Godfrey, Richard T., *Wenceslaus Hollar: A Bohemian Artist in England* (New Haven: Yale University Press, 1994)

Greene, Molly, *A Shared World: Christians and Muslims in the Early Modern Mediterranean* (Princeton NJ: Princeton University Press, 2000)

Gruber von Arni, Eric, *Hospital Care and the British Standing Army, 1660–1714* (London: Routledge, 2017)

Hajji, Mohamed, *Al-Zawiyah al-Dilaiyah wa-dawruha al-dini wa-al-ilmi wa-siyasi* (Rabat: Matbat An-Najjah Al-Jadida, 1988)

Hamel, Chouki El, *Black Morocco: A History of Slavery, Race, and Islam* (Cambridge: Cambridge University Press, 2013)

Hamilton, Sir Frederick William, *The Origin and History of the First or Grenadier Guards*, 3 vols (London: John Murray, 1874)

Harris, Frank R., *The Life of Edward Montagu, First Earl of Sandwich, 1625–1672*, 2 vols (London: J. Murray, 1912)

Harris, Tim, *Restoration: Charles II and his Kingdoms* (London: Penguin, 2006)

Hornstein, Sari, *The Restoration Navy and English Foreign Trade, 1674–1688: A Study in the Peacetime use of Sea Power* (Aldershot: Scolar Press, 1991)
Kaufman, Helen A., *Conscientious Cavalier* (London: Jonathan Cape, 1962)
Lawson, Cecil C. P., *A History of The Uniforms of The British Army*, 5 vols (London: Kaye & Ward, 1940)
Lord, Walter Frewen, *The Lost Possessions of England: Essays in Imperial History* (London: Richard Bentley and Son, 1896)
MacKinnon, Daniel, *Origin and Services of the Coldstream Guards*, 2 vols (London: R. Bentley, 1833)
Marshall, Alan, *Intelligence and Espionage in the Reign of Charles II, 1660–1685* (Cambridge: Cambridge University Press, 1994)
Matar, Nabil, *Britain and Barbary, 1589–1689* (Gainesville: University Press of Florida, 2005)
Meakin, Budgett, *The Moorish Empire* (London: Swan Sonnenschein & Co., 1899)
Miller, John, *Popery and Politics in England 1660–1688* (Cambridge: Cambridge University Press, 1973)
Nicolle, David, *The Moors: The Islamic West 7th–15th Centuries AD* (Oxford: Osprey, 2001).
Ostwald, Jamel, *Vauban Under Siege: Engineering Efficiency and Martial Vigor in the War of the Spanish Succession* (Brill: Leiden, 2007)
Pipes, Daniel, *Slave Soldiers and Islam: The Genesis of a Military System* (New Haven & London: Yale University Press, 1981)
Reece, Henry, *The Army in Cromwellian England 1649–1660* (Oxford: Oxford University Press, 2013)
Reese, Peter, *The Life of General George Monck: For King and Cromwell* (Barnsley: Pen & Sword, 2008)
Riley, Jonathan, *The Last Ironsides: The English Expedition to Portugal 1662–1668* (Solihull: Helion & Co., 2014)
Rommelse, Gijs, *The Second Anglo-Dutch War (1665–1667): raison d'état, mercantilism and maritime strife* (Hilversum: Uitgeverij Verloren, 2006)
Routh, Enid, *Tangier: England's Lost Atlantic Outpost 1661–1684* (London: John Murray, 1912).
Saunders, Andrew, *Fortress Builder: Bernard de Gomme, Charles II's Military Engineer* (Liverpool: Liverpool University Press, 2004)
Smithers, A. J., *The Tangier Campaign* (Stroud: Tempus, 2003)
Tincey, John, *Sedgemoor: Mar lborough's First Victory* (Barnsley: Pen & Sword, 2005)
Tincey, John and Embleton, Gerry, *The British Army 1660–1704* (London: Osprey, 1994)
Walton, Clifford, *History of the British Standing Army AD 1660 to 1700* (London: Harrison & Sons, 1894)
Williams, Noel T. St John, *Redcoats and Courtesans: The Birth of the British Army (1660–1690)* (London: Brassey's, 1994)

Articles and Chapters

Appleby, David J., 'Veteran Politics in Restoration England, 1660–1670', *TSC*, 28 (2013), pp. 323–42
Aylmer, G. E., 'Slavery under Charles II: The Mediterranean and Tangier', *EHR*, 114 (1999), pp. 378–88
Barbano, Matteo, '"Most thought the City in no security but under Lock and Key": Tangeri, gli inglesi e la frontiera nordafricana (1662–1684)', Gallia, A., Pinzarrone, L., Scaglione, G. (eds), *Isole e frontiere nel Mediterraneo moderno e contemporaneo* (Palermo, 2017), pp. 35–47

Barbano, Matteo, 'Una guerra discreta: la minaccia ispano-moresca a Tangeri del 1663', *Mrs*, 32 (2014), pp. 511–24

Beach, Adam R., 'Baffled Colonial Discourse: Representing the First Decade of English Tangier', *Restoration: Studies in English Literary Culture, 1660–1700*, 31 (2007), pp. 21–41

Beckmann, Paul E., 'Martin Beckman and the English Occupation of Tangier 1662–1684. Part 1', *FM*, 41 (2013), pp. 146–56; 'Part 2', *Fort Magazine*, 42 (2014), pp. 182–90

Belcher, G. L., 'Spain and the Anglo-Portuguese Alliance of 1661: A Reassessment of Charles II's Foreign Policy at the Restoration', *JBS*, 15 (1975), pp. 67–88

Bookin-Weiner, Jerome, 'Anglo-Moroccan Relations in the First Decade of the Occupation of Tangier (1662–1672)', *HespT*, 18 (1978–79), pp. 63–75

Boxer, C. A., '"Three Sights to Be Seen': Bombay, Tangier, and a Barren Queen, 1661–1684', *PS*, 3 (1987), pp. 77–83

Boxhall, Peter, 'Tangier: An English Military Outpost', *AQDJ*, 119:3 (1989), pp. 327–35; 119:4 (1989), pp. 442–52

Buchanan, Brenda J., 'The Birth of British Gunpowder Engineering Overseas: the case of the Mole at Tangier, 1661–1684', Buchanan, Robert A. (ed.), *Landscape with technology: essays in honour of L. T. C. Rolt* (Bath: Millstream, 2011), pp. 22–42

Childs, John, 'The British Brigade in France, 1672–1678', *History*, 69 (1984), pp. 384–97

Chtatou, Mohamed, 'Tangier as Seen Through Foreign Eyes', *JNAS*, 1 (1996), pp. 266–78

Clark, G. N., 'The Barbary Corsairs in the Seventeenth Century', *CHJ*, 8 (1944), pp. 22–35

Collins, Stephen, 'Longford Musketeers: The Farrells of Annaly and the Sieges of St Ghislain and Tangier', *HI*, 11 (2003), pp. 17–21

Collyer, P., 'The British Occupation of Tangier, 1662–1674', *MJSMS*, 1 (1996), pp. 52–61

Collyer, P., 'The British Occupation of Tangier, 1674–1680', *MJSMS*, 2 (1997), pp. 77–87

Cutter, Nat, 'Turks, Moors, Deys and Kingdoms: North African Diversity in English News before 1700', *MHJ*, 46 (2018), pp. 61–84

Dale, Donald, 'Samuel Pepys and Tangier', *N&Q*, 180 (1941), pp. 146–49

Davis, R., 'England in the Mediterranean, 1570–1670', Fisher, F. J. (ed.), *Essays in the economic and social history of Tudor and Stuart England, in Honour of R. H. Tawney* (Cambridge: Cambridge University Press, 1961), pp. 117–37

Elbl, M. M., '(Re)claiming Walls: The Fortified Médina of Tangier under Portuguese Rule (1471–1662) and as a Modern Heritage Artefact', *PSR*, 15 (2007), pp. 103–92

Field, C., 'Service Uniforms of Officers at Tangier, 1661–1684', *JSAHR*, 6 (1927), pp. 51–3

Fielding, Xan, 'A 17th century Atlantic outpost: the British occupation of Tangier', *HT*, 5 (1955) pp. 463–72

Firth, C. H., 'Royalist and Cromwellian Armies in Flanders, 1657–1662', *TRHS*, New Sers, 17 (1903), pp. 67–119

Fletcher, Ian, 'Teviot's Last Stand', *MMM* (January 1986), pp. 44–47

Glickman, Gabriel, 'Empire, "Popery", and the Fall of English Tangier, 1662–1684', *JMH*, 87 (2015), pp. 247–80

Hardacre, P. H., 'The Further Adventures of Henry Norwood', *VMHB*, 67 (1959), pp. 271–83

Lincoln, Margarette, 'Samuel Pepys and Tangier, 1662–1684', *HLQ*, 77 (2014), pp. 417–34

Malcolm, Alistair, 'Serving the King at Home and Abroad: The Tangier Garrison under Charles II, 1662–1684', McElligott, Anthony, et al. (eds), *Power in history: from the medieval to the post-modern world* (Dublin: Irish Academic Press, 2011), pp. 109–24

Malcolm, Joyce Lee, 'Charles II and the Reconstruction of Royal Power', *HJ*, 35 (1992), pp. 307–30)

McCully, Bruce T., 'From the North Riding to Morocco: The Early Years of Governor Francis Nicholson, 1655–1686', *WMQ*, 19:4 (1962), pp. 534–56

Meyer, Alan R., 'Class, Ethnicity, and Slavery: The Origins of the Moroccan 'Abid', *IJAHS*, 10 (1977), pp. 427–42

Meyer, Alan R., 'Slave Soldiers and State Politics in Early Alawi Morocco, 1668–1727', *IJAHS*, 16 (1983), pp. 39–48

Miller, John, 'Catholic Officers in the Later Stuart Army', *EHR*, 88 (1973), pp. 35–53

Mojuetan, B. A., 'Legitimacy in a Power State: Moroccan Politics in the Seventeenth Century', *IJMES*, 13 (1981), pp. 347–57

Mungeam, Gerald I., 'Contracts of the Supply of Equipment to the 'New Model Army' in 1645, *JAAS*, 6 (1968–70), pp. 53–114

Murtagh, Harman, 'Irish soldiers abroad, 1600–1800', Bartlett, T. (ed.), *A Military History of Ireland* (Cambridge: Cambridge University Press, 1996), pp. 294–314

Routh, Enid, 'The English Occupation of Tangier (1661–1683)', *TRHS*, New Sers, 19 (1905), pp. 61–78

Ruiz, Jose, 'De Tanger a Gibraltar: el estrecho en la praxis commercial imperial Britanica (1661–1776)', *HREH*, 65 (2005), pp. 1043–62

Rumbold, Horace, 'Notes on the History of the Family of Rumbold in the Seventeenth Century', *TRHS*, 6 (1892), pp. 145–65

Saunders, Andrew, 'Tangier and fortified British bases in the Mediterranean', *AP*, 19 (2015), pp. 49–60

Scouller, R. E., 'Purchase of Commissions and Promotions', *JSAHR*, 62 (1984), pp. 217–226

Shirley, Evelyn Philip, Dinely, Thomas and Graves, James, 'Extracts from the Journal of Thomas Dineley, Esquire, Giving Some Account of His Visit to Ireland in the Reign of Charles II (Continued)', *JKSIAS*, New Sers, 4 (1862), pp. 38–52, 103–109

Springell, F. C., 'Unpublished Drawings of Tangier by Wenceslaus Hollar', *BM*, 106 (1964), pp. 68–74

Stein, Tristan, 'Tangier in the Restoration Empire', *HJ*, 54 (2011), pp. 985–1011

Williams, Gillian, 'Wenceslaus Hollar in Tangier', *HT*, 33 (1983), pp. 36–81

Williams, Neville, 'The Tribulations of John Bland, Merchant: London, Seville, Jamestown, Tangier, 16431680', *VMHB*, 72 (1964), pp. 19–41

Wreglesworth, John, 'Tangier, England's Forgotten Colony (1661–1684)', *RHM* (2002), 215–31.

Zaky, A. Rahman, 'Introduction to the Study of Islamic Arms and Armour', *Gladius* I (1961), pp. 17–29

Unpublished Theses

Lette, Rickie, 'Confronting Barbary: Reappraising the Responses of Britons to Engagement with Moroccans, and their Influence on Anglo-Moroccan Relations, 1625–1684', PhD thesis (University of Tasmania, 2018)